A Baseball Dynasty
Charlie Finley's Swingin' A's

Bruce Markusen

St. Johann Press
Haworth, NJ

Originally published as *Baseball's Last Dynasty: Charlie Finley's Oakland A's* in 1988 by Masters Press, this is an enlarged and expanded edition.

ST. JOHANN PRESS

Published in the United States of America
by St. Johann Press
P.O. Box 241
Haworth, NJ 07641

Copyright ©2002 by Bruce Markusen

Cover illustrations courtesy of The Topps Company, Inc.

Library of Congress Cataloging-in-Publication Data

Markusen, Bruce
   A baseball dynasty: Charlie Finley's swingin' A's/Bruce Markusen.
     p. cm.
   Expanded ed. of: Baseball's last dynasty. 1998.
   ISBN 1-878282-23-9 (alk. paper)
     1. Oakland Athletics (Baseball team)--History. 2. Finley, Charles Oscar, 1918- I. Markusen, Bruce. Baseball's last dynasty. II. Title.

   GV875.O24 M364 2002
   796.357'64'0979466--dc21   2002036898

The paper used in this publication meets the minimum requirements of American National Standard for Information Sciences—Permanence of Paper for Printed Library Materials, ANSI/NISO 239.48-1992

Manufactured in the United States of America

Dedication

This book is dedicated to the memory of Curt Blefary, Bobby Brooks, Jim "Catfish" Hunter, Deron Johnson, Gonzalo Marquez, and Cesar Tovar.

Contents

Dedication	iii
Acknowledgments	vii
Introduction	ix
A Cross Between Branch Rickey and VinceLombardi	1
Spring Training Follies	11
Low Expectations	17
A New Sheriff in Town	23
The Runaway	31
He's Human After All	47
Facing the Defending Champs	63
Offseason Shuffle	73
Holdouts, Mustaches, and McLain	79
Revolving Doors	97
A Catcher Plays Second, and a Shortstop Blows His Stack	131
The 1972 World Series	141
Game Seven	165
World Series Fallout	177
The Encore	193
Second-Half Soap Opera	219
Same Series, Different Team	239
Finley vs. Andrews	245
Oh by the Way, the A's Do It Again	255
No More Dick Williams to Push Around	263
Great Players, No Manager	267
The Return of the Dark Age	279
Gunning for the Three-Peat	289
The Fight	297
A Rematch with the Birds	317
The Freeway Series	321
The Kingdom Begins to Crumble	341
The Perils of Arbitration	347
Still Good, But Not Great	353

A Flop at Fenway	375
The Last Hurrah	381
A Baseball Dynasty	397
Appendix A: 1971 Oakland A's Regular Season Stats	408
Appendix B: 1972 Oakland A's Regular Season Stats	410
Appendix C: 1973 Oakland A's Regular Season Stats	412
Appendix D: 1974 Oakland A's Regular Season Stats	414
Appendix E: 1975 Oakland A's Regular Season Stats	416
Index	419

Acknowledgments

I would like to thank Kristen Aiken and Tamara Holmes for their diligent help in creating and organizing the index. I'd also like to thank David Biesel for his enthusiasm in willingly embracing this project.

Introduction

I was seven years old when the Oakland A's won their first World Championship in 1972. I had been a fan of the New York Yankees (and still am today), dating back to the final playing days of Mickey Mantle in 1968. Yet, the green and gold uniforms of Charlie Finley's A's caught my eye. At the time, most major league teams wore boring white uniforms at home and drab grays on the road, but I found the A's' on-field clothing refreshingly different. I even tried to dye my white undershirts green in tribute to Oakland's vividly unique baseball colors.

When the A's won the World Series in the fall of '72, I became even more intrigued beyond the colorful uniforms. Given my youth, I couldn't fully appreciate how efficiently the A's won ballgames, but I had an inkling. Those 1970s A's teams, solid at most every position, had no major weaknesses. They made all the plays defensively, ran the bases with aggression and wisdom, hit well in the clutch, and pitched with precision and power. In the years that have passed since watching the A's of the seventies, my appreciation of their ability has only grown. Only one team, the Yankees of the late 1990s and the new millennium, has been able to match the level of play achieved by the A's of 1972 to 1974. (In fact, the performance of the Yankees has necessitated the re-titling of the second edition of this book.) Yet, the performance of those Yankees of more recent vintage doesn't diminish the regard that I have for those "Swingin' A's." In fact, I'm glad that younger generations of baseball fans have been able to watch these Yankees so that they might have a better understanding of how much the A's achieved. In many ways, the accomplishments and on-field styles (emphasizing excellent pitching, good baserunning, and an ability to execute fundamental plays) of those two baseball dynasties mirror each other—even though they represent different eras in the game's history.

Off the field, the A's and Yankees operated far differently—in clubhouses that were as distinct as the colors of their uniforms. Indeed, baseball observers have marveled at Oakland's ability to win in spite of constant in-fighting, persistent meddling by owner Charlie Finley, and a never-ending streak of controversies. Some experts have claimed that championship teams require cohesion and harmony to win pennants, not arguments and controversies. The Yankees featured such compatibility; the A's certainly did not. Clearly, there is no single, clear-cut formula for successful team chemistry.

Perhaps teams like the A's—a team filled with conflict and tension—have such feelings because their players care more about achievement than players on some losing teams, where mediocrity is too easily accepted. On certain losing teams, players tend to be far too forgiving of their teammates' mistakes. They create the perception of harmony, at the expense of complacency. Perhaps they simply don't care enough about winning to bruise other players' feelings. Everyone "gets along," but no one improves and the team comes no closer to reaching a championship level.

The A's of the seventies had a passion for the game—and for winning. Players with passion tend to strive for perfection and become upset when they don't achieve it. When John "Blue Moon" Odom crumbled under the pressure of a fifth and decisive playoff game in 1972, Vida Blue took him to task for it. Blue maintained that he was only kidding, but his words toward Odom seemed tinged with sincere disappointment in his friend's performance. On another occasion, when Billy North didn't hustle in the eyes of Reggie Jackson, the A's' slugger berated him for it. The ensuing confrontations created an uncomfortable tension in the Oakland clubhouse, which served as fodder for both the local and national media. Yet, it also served as a reminder that A's players considered winning far more important than hurt feelings.

Another intriguing aspect of those A's teams involved the maneuverings of Charlie Finley, who served as his own general manager. Finley never felt satisfied with the composition of his teams, regardless of the current won-loss record. He continually traded for veteran "name" players, especially hitters of accomplished reputation whom he felt could help the team down the stretch. I was fascinated by Finley's ability to acquire a Matty Alou, an Orlando Cepeda, a Vic Davalillo, or a Rico Carty, to help his bench during the second half of a season. When he needed a relief pitcher to assist a youthful Rollie Fingers, he acquired a capable veteran like Jim "Mudcat" Grant. When Blue held out in 1972, Finley swung a deal for Denny McLain. Some of the trades worked out and others didn't—like the ones for McLain and Cepeda—but it was always fun to watch these newly acquired notables put on the green and gold uniforms for the first time. It was also intriguing to see how they would react to playing in the unique world of Charlie Finley's Oakland.

Gaudy uniforms, newsmaking controversies, a revolving door of baseball stars, and boatloads of winning. We find all of these story lines by exploring the Oakland A's of 1971 to 1975, a true baseball dynasty.

Chapter One

A Cross Between Branch Rickey and Vince Lombardi

Dateline: October 1970

During his controversial reign as owner of the Kansas City and Oakland A's, Charlie Finley had tinkered far too often with the managerial office. In 10 full seasons as owner, Finley had plowed through a flock of managers. Joe Gordon, Hank Bauer (twice), Eddie Lopat, Mel McGaha, Haywood Sullivan, Alvin Dark, Hall of Famer Luke Appling, Bob Kennedy, and John McNamara had all experienced the feeling of being hired and fired by Finley. But on October 2, 1970, one day after the A's' season had come to an end, Finley made perhaps the best move he had ever engineered as chieftain of the franchise. Finley named Montreal Expos coach Dick Williams as manager, replacing McNamara. Yet, the reasoning behind the sacking of McNamara was neither logical nor fair.

Under McNamara's guiding hand, the A's had won 89 games, the most for the franchise in 38 years. The A's had finished a respectable second place, nine games behind a very good Minnesota Twins team. Most of the Oakland players liked playing for McNamara, including power-hitting first baseman Don Mincher. "John McNamara was probably the most striking gentleman I ever played for," recalls Mincher, the owner and operator of the Huntsville Stars of the Double-A Southern League in his post-playing days. "He was a guy that really insisted that you stay in shape and play hard, but he really didn't have the hard intensity you see of a lot of managers today and a few back in those days."

That lack of intensity may have played a part in Finley's decision to lay the ax on McNamara. Yet, Finley claimed he had other reasons for making the change. At a lengthy press conference announcing the firing, Finley spent the first half-hour ranting and raving about one of the team's three catchers, Dave Duncan. Finley blamed Duncan for the firing of McNamara. Come again? Why would Finley fire McNamara because of the team's second-string catcher? The veteran receiver had batted a respectable .259 with 10 home runs, but had seen a decline in playing time under McNamara the second half of the season. After the season's final game, Duncan fired away—not at McNamara—but at Finley. "There's only one man who manages this club—Charlie Finley," Duncan told Ron Bergman, the A's' correspondent for *The Sporting News* and the team's beat writer for the *Oakland Tribune*. "And we'll never win so long as he manages it."

"We had the team to win it [the American League West]," Duncan continued. "But because of the atmosphere he [Finley] creates, there's no spirit, no feeling of harmony. We should be close like a family, but it's not here." When Finley learned of Duncan's remarks, he decided to use the opportunity to fire McNamara. "He didn't lose his job," Finley claimed in an interview with the Associated Press. "His players took it away from him." Finley reasoned that a manager who could not prevent his players—Duncan and right fielder Reggie Jackson, in particular—from making critical remarks about their owner had lost control of his own clubhouse. Therefore, Finley felt justified in firing McNamara.

Duncan's comments most likely infuriated Finley on two fronts. Finley resented Duncan's portrayal of him as a meddler, as someone who tried to undermine his manager. That was bad enough. When Duncan took his criticism a step further, by portraying Finley as an *incompetent* meddler, one who prevented his team from winning, Finley felt motivated to take action. The Oakland owner did not take well to being called a loser—even indirectly.

Many players on the A's agreed with Duncan's remarks. Reggie Jackson had publicly criticized Finley for interfering with the ballclub during the 1970 season. Jackson had also accused Finley of ordering McNamara to bench him on several occasions. Jackson's displeasure with Finley ran so deep, that on one occasion, he gestured obscenely toward the owner's box after clubbing a long home run. Such gestures and angry words typified the strange relationship that Jackson had with Finley. "Let's face it, Reggie would say outrageous things about Charlie at various times," says Rick Monday, Oakland's starting center fielder in 1970. "Then he'd run to the clubhouse and call Charlie."

While no other players had made their feelings known *on the record*, several had complained privately to the team's beat writers about Finley's constant meddling. In fact, some players had even used the unfortunate situation to their advantage by calling Finley directly and moaning about a lack of playing time in the hope that the owner would force McNamara into making lineup changes. On several occasions, a player contacting Finley found himself in the lineup within the next few days. Finley's interference had created an impossible situation for a well-liked baseball man like McNamara, whose integrity was now under interrogation. A more experienced, proven manager might have been able to ignore Finley's "advice," but McNamara had no choice but to follow along, or lose his job *during* the season.

In essence, Finley decided to use Dave Duncan's scathing words as an excuse for firing the manager. *After all*, Finley might have wondered aloud, *if McNamara's own players questioned his authority, then he must not be performing his role of leading the team.* Finley also seized the opportunity to make a scapegoat of his backup catcher, while shielding himself from a critical media that was bound to roast him for firing yet another manager.

Most of the Oakland media did not accept Finley's reasoning. Two beat writers following the A's had predicted—well before Duncan's remarks—that McNamara would be fired. Reports in the *Oakland Tribune* and the *San Jose Mercury News* had indicated that McNamara would not return for the 1971 season. Those published accounts had stated that either Finley would fire McNamara, or that McNamara would reject a new contract offer from the overbearing Finley.

Both McNamara and Duncan denied that the catcher's comments about Finley had rendered any significant impact on the manager's job security. "It's ridiculous to believe that the reason McNamara was fired was because of me," Duncan insisted in an interview with Ron Bergman, reporting for *The Sporting News*. "It was obvious to everyone a long time ago that Finley was going to fire him." McNamara supported Duncan's contention. "I've been fired since last May when the club started out under .500," McNamara said. Furthermore, another recently fired manager Billy Martin, late of the Minnesota Twins, claimed that Finley had offered him the Oakland job in mid-July, and then again in late August, before he had decided to accept an offer from the Detroit Tigers.

After dismissing McNamara during a one-hour meeting, Finley immediately held a press conference announcing the change. Finley spent most of the press conference criticizing Duncan for a variety of reasons, in particular his living situation. "One day I found out that Duncan was sleeping with [batting] coach Charley Lau," Finley exclaimed to *The Sporting News*, in an extremely poor selection of words. "By that I mean they were rooming together, sharing expenses. When I found out about this, I...asked them to break it up immediately, because as we all know, in the Army, troops don't fraternize with officers."

Duncan and Lau, whose firing was also announced at the press conference, had refused to comply with Finley's order. Both men had recently separated from their wives, and had decided to cut costs by sharing an apartment. Now, Finley had tried to aggravate Duncan by intimating that he was "sleeping" with one of the team's coaches. It was as if Finley had intentionally used the phrase "sleeping with" as a way of falsely suggesting some romantic involvement between the player and coach. Later, after finishing his winter ball season in the Dominican Republic, Duncan would request a meeting with Finley before eventually reaching a temporary truce with the owner.

With McNamara and most of his coaching staff out of the picture, the leadership of the A's now rested on the vast abilities of Dick Williams, who would officially sign a two-year contract at the World Series. The hiring of the 41-year-old Williams represented the 10th managerial change Finley had made, covering a total of nine different managers (including two terms for Hank Bauer), since purchasing the franchise in December of 1960. Once a top prospect in the Brooklyn Dodgers' organization, Williams' hitting and throwing abilities had been undermined by a severe shoulder injury he had sustained while making a diving catch in left field. The three-way shoulder separation left Williams a pedestrian player, one who would make stops in Baltimore, Cleveland, Kansas City, and Boston. Williams actually enjoyed two productive seasons for the Kansas City Athletics in 1959 and '60, but a trade to the Baltimore Orioles during the spring of '61 prevented him from playing for Finley, who had just bought the club in the aftermath of the death of A's owner Arnold Johnson.

As a minor league player, Williams had been strongly influenced by his manager in the Texas League, Bobby Bragan. Williams had noticed Bragan's strengths as a manager: the ability to teach and instill discipline. These attributes would become essential parts of the Williams dossier. Williams' manager in Baltimore, the successful and innovative Paul Richards, noticed the journeyman outfielder's knowledge of the game and encouraged him to pursue a managerial calling. Williams decided to abandon a mediocre playing career for what he hoped would be a higher standard of achievement as a manager.

A fiery, militaristic kind of leader, Williams had patterned his "tough-guy" managerial style after that of men like Branch Rickey and Vince Lombardi. Williams stressed the importance of fundamentals and basic execution, demanded absolute hustle from his players at all times, and challenged them to play for more than themselves and the lure of a contract. "A player should have something other than the name of his city on the front of his uniform," Williams explained to Oakland sportswriter Ron Bergman. "He should have P-R-I-D-E written there."

In his first managerial tenure in the major leagues, Williams had molded a soft group of ninth-place Boston Red Sox into a hardened, gritty American League pennant winner—the authors of the "Impossible Dream." The transition had taken just one season. Prior to his arrival in 1967, the Red Sox had been regarded as baseball's "country club," where team owner Tom Yawkey consistently spoiled his players. Two years later, the Red Sox had deemed Williams as too tough, overly militaristic and dangerously unyielding in the ways that he dealt with his players. Williams also clashed with Yawkey, who repeatedly undermined his manager by pampering Red Sox players after Williams had tried to discipline them. Williams believed that Yawkey regarded the Red Sox as a toy, a philosophy that conflicted with Williams' more businesslike approach. On one occasion, Yawkey belittled his manager in a Boston newspaper, giving him a rating of 2 on a scale of 1 to 4. The lack of confidence understandably angered Williams.

During the 1969 season, Yawkey fired Dick Williams, who took a job as a coach under Gene Mauch in Montreal. Williams credited Mauch with equipping him to become a better manager the second time around. "The best manager in the business," Williams said of Mauch in an interview with Al Hirshberg of *Sport* Magazine. "You watch him and you learn. If I ever had a seminar on managing, I'd want Gene to run it for me. He's a baseball genius—a marvelous organizer and the greatest handler of men I ever saw." While with the Expos, Mauch also taught Williams to be more compromising and conciliatory when dealing with his team's owner. Williams would need to follow this advice with the A's. Although Finley was a far different kind of owner than Yawkey, he found his own ways to circumvent the power of his managers.

At least one Oakland player agreed with Finley's choice of Williams as the A's' new manager.

"If his reputation is what's it's supposed to be, he will be an asset," predicted team captain Sal Bando in an interview with *The Sporting News*.

"We need a guy to kick us in the rear now and then. Mac [McNamara] said he just wasn't the type to jump all over guys and we liked that. We knew that if we made a mistake, it wouldn't be too bad. But we didn't learn from our mistakes. We didn't take them seriously. I think that hurt us as the season wore on."

Bando added that he liked McNamara and would miss him as a friend, but maintained that the A's needed a tougher, more demanding manager to reach their potential as a pennant contender.

"It was a different personality," Bando says in retrospect, in discussing the differences between Williams and his predecessor. "John McNamara, in most cases, we all grew up with John because we played for him in the minor leagues. So, in some ways, the familiarity was not an asset because we got too close to John. Whereas Dick had that distance between you and him, and you just zeroed in on baseball."

Williams owned a personality not only unique from McNamara's, but also different from the parade of other managers that Finley had employed. "You've got to realize that also listed in there was Alvin Dark, Luke Appling, Bob Kennedy, and Hank Bauer," says Rick Monday, who played for all of the above during his tenure with the A's. "So we really ran the gamut as far as the number of different managers that we had at that particular time." Williams' direct, no-frills approach most similarly resembled one of his predecessors. "Hank Bauer, also no-nonsense," Monday says, "but a little bit differently." While Bauer had alienated some of the A's with his militaristic style, Williams' gruffness only annoyed his players, but without turning them off completely. "Dick Williams had a job to do," Monday says. "And he wanted to get through all the clutter to get down to the task at hand—and that was to try and move his ballclub from day one in spring training... and get to the end of the season, where you have a chance to have a post-season."

As Monday puts it, Williams cared most about the end result of winning, to the extent that he occasionally bruised feelings. "He didn't care about the laundry list that it took to get from point A to point B," explains Monday, a broadcaster with the San Diego Padres and Los Angeles Dodgers after his playing days. "He didn't care if he ruffled your feathers or not. If you played well, you would be in the lineup. If you did not play well, well, he had other ideas and ways to approach it."

In contrast to Williams, John McNamara's gentlemanly demeanor may have interfered with his managerial ability, even though it made him so likable. "He was just such a nice person," Don Mincher says of McNamara, "that you wanted to go out and kill for him. He remains one of my best friends; I see him frequently even today. He was, maybe, to a fault, too nice. I mean, our ballclub at that time was just beginning to formulate and there were some pretty tough characters there, like Reggie [Jackson] and Sal [Bando], and some of those guys were sometimes quite individual-like... It was a time when we were just entering that stage of being a dominating team, and it was tough on John to handle that. Consequently, he didn't make it through."

When Mincher heard that Williams would replace McNamara, he knew that the atmosphere on the ballclub would change drastically. "Well, I knew one thing right away; there would be some confrontations. I knew that," says Mincher. "I knew Dick Williams from playing against him, his reputation and what-have-you. And I knew there would be some confrontations that would take place, and I knew that Dick Williams would win 'em all."

Mincher believed that turmoil would result from the heated interaction between the feisty Williams and some of the egocentric players on the A's. "You could just feel it coming, and sure enough there was." More importantly, Mincher sensed that with the hiring of Williams, the A's were about to start winning a lot of games—and perhaps some championships. "That was really the beginning of a great ballclub," Mincher says, "when Dick Williams was signed to that contract."

Although Finley had hired Williams immediately after the conclusion of the 1970 season, his new manager did not meet the media until January 26, 1971. At his opening press conference, Williams spoke confidently of Oakland's potential to reach the post-season. "I don't see any reason why we can't win this division," Williams bellowed. "I don't see anyone running away from the rest of the division, unless it's us." Williams viewed his A's as the most talented team in the American League West, and far better than the Red Sox' team he had led to the American League pennant only four years earlier. "This club is head and shoulders above the Boston club I had in '67," Williams said bluntly, surprising some of the reporters in attendance. Williams felt the A's had a stronger and deeper pitching staff, as well as more team speed than the Red Sox of the "Impossible Dream."

Williams realized that he was joining the A's at just the right time. He recognized the work that Oakland scouts like Clyde Kluttz and Don Pries had done in assembling talent throughout the mid-to-late 1960s. The nucleus of young players, which featured Bert "Campy" Campaneris, Sal Bando, Joe Rudi, Rick Monday, and Reggie Jackson among the position players, and Jim "Catfish" Hunter, Vida Blue, and John "Blue Moon" Odom on the pitching staff, had just begun to flourish at the major league level.

Williams viewed the Minnesota Twins as Oakland's biggest obstacle in trying to win the American League West. The two-time defending divisional champs had dominated the A's during regular season play over the previous two seasons. In both 1969 and '70, the Twins had forged identical records of 13–5 against Oakland. Still, Williams realized that the Twins, while still very talented, were an aging team. Harmon Killebrew, the Twins' top slugger, was now 34 years old. Tony Oliva, though only 30 years of age based on his birth certificate, hobbled around on the knees of a 40-year-old. Thirty-five-year-old Jim Perry and 32-year-old Jim Kaat headlined Minnesota's pitching staff.

Although the A's had finished nine games back of the Twins each of the past two seasons, veteran baseball observers realized that a changing of the guard was about to occur. Twins beat writer Bob Fowler, who covered the team in the sixties and seventies, recognized two clubs proceeding in opposite directions. "Oh, I think you could see it," says Fowler. "We had a veteran team, with Harmon Killebrew,

Tony Oliva, Bob Allison, and Jim Perry, guys of that nature. Oakland had a young team, with Catfish Hunter, Sal Bando, and Rick Monday. They were nine games out, [but] they had great talent. And then in 1971, the Minnesota team—we suddenly got old."

The astute Dick Williams soon recognized the identities of the A's' three primary leaders: Sal Bando, Reggie Jackson, and Catfish Hunter. He moved quickly to bolster the confidence of the two position players in the group, both of whom figured to play regularly for Oakland. In one of Williams' first publicly announced decisions, he showed strong regard for the leadership abilities of Bando, his starting third baseman. Williams announced that he would retain Bando as team captain, even though he had seen fit to strip Carl Yastrzemski of his captaincy in Boston.

With one pronouncement, Williams had succeeded in gaining the confidence of one of the most respected players on the Oakland club. "They were very good," Bando says of his first impressions of Williams. "I had the opportunity to get together with Dick prior to spring training [at the A's' winter caravan]. I got to talk to him a little bit there. I think the one thing Dick had going for him was his reputation, because he didn't have to live up to it, as being a tough disciplinarian. It was already in place."

After confirming Bando's captaincy, Williams made an even more significant announcement in discussing the important role that his new everyday right fielder would play in 1971. "I expect Reggie Jackson to play everyday. I have no thoughts of benching him against left-handers," Williams insisted in an interview with sportswriter Ron Bergman. During the 1970 season, Jackson had held out for five weeks and had become embroiled in several verbal battles with Finley. The Oakland owner allegedly ordered John McNamara not to play the controversial young outfielder. At times, McNamara platooned Reggie; at other times, he flat-out benched the potential superstar. Most people around the A's believed that McNamara did whatever Finley told him to do when it came to playing or sitting Jackson. At one point, Finley even threatened to demote Jackson to the minor leagues. As a result of the holdout, the benchings, and the irregular playing time, Jackson finished the season with only 23 home runs.

Although Williams quickly recognized the talents of Jackson, the feeling did not appear to be mutual. Jackson, when first asked about Williams, expressed skepticism about his new manager. "I've heard a lot of bad things about him from other players, unfavorable comments, " Jackson admitted to *The Sporting News*. "I heard that when things get tough, he wouldn't stick up for you." Jackson initially asked Williams to trade him. Reporters circulated rumors that the A's might trade Jackson to the Pittsburgh Pirates for slugging outfielder Willie Stargell, or to the Baltimore Orioles for outfielder Paul Blair and pitcher Tom Phoebus.

Jackson later retreated from his trade request. "I saw Reggie down in Puerto Rico," Williams told *The Sporting News* after watching his slugger play for the Santurce Crabbers in the Puerto Rican Winter League. "His attitude was so good it was scary."

Williams clearly realized the potential of Jackson, who had been drafted by the Kansas City A's in 1966 after a terrific sophomore season at Arizona State University. After making Jackson the A's' first pick in the draft, Finley personally recruited Jackson's signature on a contract. The owner offered the college star an $85,000 bonus and a new car, in the hopes that he would give up his football scholarship with the Sun Devils. "He came driving up in a big Cadillac," Jackson told Glenn Dickey of *Sport* Magazine in describing his first meeting with Finley. He "kept talking about what a big star I was going to be and how we were going to be champions. He really overwhelmed me."

Finley wanted to start Jackson at Double-A, but Kansas City scouts Bob Zuk and Ray Swallow begged the owner to start him at a lower level. Finley gave in to the advice of his scouts. Jackson debuted professionally that summer, making two pitstops for Class-A teams in Lewiston and Modesto. Reggie then moved up to Double-A Birmingham in 1967 and so dominated Southern League pitching that he earned a promotion to the major leagues midway through the season. When Jackson batted only .178 in 35 games, the A's targeted him for additional work in the Instructional League. Kansas City coaches tutored Jackson on hitting inside pitches and cutting down on his frequent strikeouts.

In 1968, with the A's now entrenched in Oakland, Jackson spent his first full season in the majors and worked daily with batting coach Joe DiMaggio, the former New York Yankees' legend. For over an hour each day, DiMaggio schooled Jackson on the art of making better contact. "Reggie is still green as grass," DiMaggio admitted to sportswriter Ed Rumill. "We've just got to bring his talents to the surface. They're all there, no question."

Jackson terrorized American League pitchers during the first half of the 1969 season, setting a record with 37 home runs before the All-Star break. Jackson seemed destined to break Roger Maris' single-season record for home runs, but encountered a second-half power drought brought upon by nerves and excessive media scrutiny.

In addition to his obvious power, Jackson possessed all the other requisite skills to become a star: a burst of speed that reminded some of Willie Mays in his prime, and a thunderous throwing arm that reminded others of a young Al Kaline or even an older Roberto Clemente. When he was playing well, Jackson was merely the best player on the Oakland roster.

During the winter following the 1970 campaign, Jackson started to make some important changes in his approach to the game. While playing for Santurce in winter ball, Jackson tinkered with his batting stance by crouching at the plate. "I've torn down my batting style and I'm reconstructing it," Jackson told Ron Bergman. "I've forgotten about hitting the home run ball and I'm just hitting the ball somewhere." The crouch helped Jackson improve his ability to make contact with the ball. "This way, as long as I stay down in the crouch and swing, I don't lose contact with my eyes and overswing and hit the ball all over."

By accident, Jackson also discovered that he needed to wear eyeglasses. During a visit to an eyewear store in search of some new sunglasses, he met with an eye doctor. The doctor performed an examination of Jackson's eyes and discovered the slugger to be nearsighted. After donning his new eyeglasses, Reggie raised his batting average 70 points in winter league play. "I've hit five home runs in the six games I played after I began wearing them," Reggie exclaimed to *The Sporting News.* "It's amazing."

Unfortunately, Dick Williams could do little to help the third leader of his team—Catfish Hunter—as he battled Charlie Finley on the contract front. Hunter was upset by the offer of a $5,000 raise, which he considered inadequate in light of his career-high 18 wins in 1970. Finley preferred emphasizing Hunter's 14 losses and his earned run average (ERA) of 3.81, the highest of Catfish's career since 1966. Critics of Hunter also cited his supposedly extreme reliance on relief ace Jim "Mudcat" Grant, who had rescued eight of Catfish's wins with tightrope bullpen work in the late innings. One Bay Area sportswriter had come to call the duo the "Cat People," in reference to the similarities of their nicknames and the frequency with which they teamed up to post wins for the A's.

Hunter didn't appreciate the implication that he had depended so heavily on Grant to enjoy a successful season. "Mudcat was a good relief pitcher last year," Catfish said diplomatically in an interview with Ron Bergman, "one of the best I've ever seen. But I didn't like it when some sportswriters suggested that he get half my salary this year. He did his job and I did mine." One week before the start of spring training, Hunter and Finley would finally agree on a 1971 contract.

Hunter, Jackson, and Bando formed the nucleus of the A's, with each player providing leadership in different manners. "Catfish was quiet," says Bando, "but he was ace of the staff. Catfish was a jokester, one of the guys, and very unassuming. He was liked by everybody. Reggie was outgoing, but Reggie did his leading by what he did on the field. And I was probably the guy in between. I was outgoing, but not the Reggie Jackson-type of player. I was more outgoing than Catfish, but I was out there every day at third base, so I kind of helped bridge that gap."

With Bando, Hunter, and Jackson firmly in place, Oakland's prospects for a good season looked favorable. With the proper additions of veteran players to their young talent base, the A's would be ready to contend—and win—in the American League West. Finley and Williams set out to acquire, or in this case, re-acquire one of those veteran players, first baseman-outfielder Tommy Davis. In September, the A's had traded Davis to the Chicago Cubs for minor league catcher-first baseman Johnny Hairston and cash. In another deal, Charlie Finley had sent his best relief pitcher, Mudcat Grant, to the Pittsburgh Pirates. Since the A's had fallen completely from the race, Finley had decided to trade Davis and Grant to two contending National League East teams. At the time, Oakland players had criticized Finley for the deals, but the owner had defended himself, saying that he needed those players only to finish first, not second.

After the season, the Cubs released Davis, an aging, but still skilled right-handed hitter. Davis had long battled an unfair reputation as a clubhouse lawyer, a label that may have been created out of racism. Like other outspoken black players of the time, Davis was termed a troublemaker by some critics. One prominent baseball publication mysteriously described Davis as a "problem" player without further explanation, but Finley and Williams thought otherwise of the veteran who was highly respected in some circles. In 1970, Davis had batted a solid .290 in 200 at-bats for Oakland. The A's' high command viewed Davis as just the kind of steadying hand needed to supplement a team whose nucleus consisted mostly of younger players who had never experienced the rigors of a pennant race.

While the A's gained Davis, they had apparently lost the services of another important veteran, second baseman Dick Green. In 1970, Green had hit a career-worst .190, a performance that had prompted him to consider retirement. Saying he didn't like to travel, Green announced that he would probably devote himself to operating his family's moving business in Rapid City, South Dakota. Given the tone of Green's statements, the A's felt that they would be without their starting second baseman by the time spring training began.

Aside from the hiring of Williams and the return of Davis, the A's made one other significant offseason change, though this move had nothing to do with the personnel on the field or in the dugout. Shortly after the firing of John McNamara, the A's had announced the departure of controversial broadcaster Harry Caray. The former St. Louis Cardinals' announcer had worked only one season in Oakland, where his work had drawn mixed reviews. Caray impressed some listeners with his candid, insightful pre-game interviews and his willingness to discuss controversial issues. Caray's frequent criticisms of A's players ruffled others, including the since-fired batting coach, Charley Lau, who nearly exchanged punches with Caray on a team flight. Some writers speculated that Charlie Finley had pushed for Caray's removal. (Could it have been because Caray refused Finley's request to switch his signature phrase from "Holy Cow" to "Holy Mule," in reference to the owner's animal mascot?) Other writers indicated that the veteran broadcaster merely wanted to retreat to the Midwest, where he had forged a popular following with the Redbirds. Caray would not return to St. Louis, but would sign on to broadcast Chicago White Sox games.

Caray had also clashed with the A's' other broadcaster, veteran play-by-play man Monte Moore, a favorite of Finley's. When Caray first showed up in the Oakland booth, he allegedly told Moore to refrain from interjecting during any of his humorous monologues, which became Caray classics. Caray made it clear that *he* wanted to be the lead broadcaster with the A's, not Moore. Whatever the reasons for his short tenure in the A's' booth, the marriage of Caray and Finley, two headstrong personalities, had come to an expected and abrupt ending.

The flurry of offseason maneuverings—the departure of Caray, the sacking of McNamara, and the hiring of Williams—apparently did not please fans in the Bay Area, who had become disgusted with Finley's style of ownership. A group of fans manufactured and distributed bumper stickers, which had obviously not been endorsed by Finley. "FREE THE A'S," read the stickers, summarizing the feelings of some of the angrier fans toward the meddlesome owner.

Chapter Two

Spring Training Follies

Newsmakers in 1971

Nearly 10,000 marchers converge on Washington, D.C. to protest the Unites States' continuing involvement in the Vietnamese War... A major earthquake strikes the Los Angeles area, killing 51 people and injuring nearly a thousand others... A total of 10 hostages and 32 prisoners lose their lives in the riot at Attica—the largest prison riot in American history.

After a 121-day trial, a jury finds Charles Manson and three women guilty of murdering actress Sharon Tate and six other people... President Richard Nixon orders a freeze on wages and prices in the effort to fight inflation... A federal survey indicates that 31 per cent of college students have tried marijuana and that 14 per cent are regular users of the illegal drug.

Jim Morrison, the lead singer of The Doors, dies in Paris from a drug overdose... Muhammad Ali loses for the first time in his professional boxing career, falling to Joe Frazier in a 15-round decision for the heavyweight championship... The Soviet Union defeats Sweden to win the world hockey championship for the ninth consecutive time.

In February, the A's reported to Mesa, Arizona for their first spring training under the supervision of Dick Williams. The new manager immediately defended the way in which he had run his former team, the Boston Red Sox. "I had to be tough with the Red Sox," Williams insisted in an interview with Ron Bergman. "They'd finished ninth the year before. I had to change an I-don't-give-a-damn-attitude to a winning attitude." Williams once again proclaimed his A's superior to the team he skippered in Boston, but felt some adjustments needed to be made. "This club here is a contending ballclub—they've finished second for the past two years. Basically, what I've got to do here is have the A's eliminate mistakes [and] mental errors, play good, sound fundamental baseball, and win head-to-head against the Twins."

Williams immediately tried to create a new mindset among Oakland players. "What he set out to do first was establish a winning attitude," observed Charlie

Finley in an interview with sportswriter Ed Rumill. "I liked that tremendously. He didn't talk much about batting eyes or pitching arms. He talked attitude, attitude. He drummed it into their head at his very first clubhouse meeting."

Williams raved about the talent available to him among his pitchers. "I've got a hell of a pitching staff here," Williams bragged to *The Sporting News*. "They're 100 per cent better than the pitching staff I had in Boston." Williams announced that he would deploy a five-man rotation, which would almost certainly include Jim "Catfish" Hunter, Vida Blue, and, if healthy, Chuck Dobson. The other two starters would come from a group that featured John "Blue Moon" Odom and two relievers, Roland "Rollie" Fingers and Diego Segui.

Williams did have some concerns about his pitching staff, however. In 1970, Odom had spent 44 days on the disabled list with elbow pain. Doctors had diagnosed the problem as floating bone chips, which needed to be removed from below his elbow in order to save his career. The surgery posed a risk; with the bone chips located so close to vital nerves and tissue, an operation could just as easily end Odom's career. With the prognosis of recovery listed at 50/50, Dr. William Bickel of the Mayo Clinic cut open Odom's elbow on December 14 and removed several bone chips, including a large one that was the size of a fingernail. Although Dr. Bickel declared the operation successful, he could not guarantee Odom's availability for the start of the new season.

Chuck Dobson, who had pitched five shutouts and won eight straight games before experiencing elbow problems, had finished the 1970 season with a sore arm. The question marks surrounding Odom and Dobson left Catfish Hunter and Vida Blue as the only certainties in the starting rotation. Under a worst-case scenario, Williams might have to pluck a pitcher from his bullpen, further depleting an area of the staff that had been foolishly weakened by the late-season trade of relief ace Mudcat Grant to the Pirates.

One of the aforementioned contenders for a spot in the rotation caused a stir during spring training when he admitted to the use of "greenies," or legal pep pills. Dobson, who had gained a favorable reputation for being talkative, humorous, and frank with the local media, admitted to reporters that he had used greenies several times during his career. The use of greenies by major league players had first been disclosed in Jim Bouton's controversial book, *Ball Four*, which had been released after the 1969 season. Such pep pills enabled players to overcome fatigue and muster more energy to play in games. "I don't see anything wrong in it," Dobson told Ron Bergman, while claiming that he had pitched a shutout in 1970 after taking a greenie. "A lot of guys use them, and I've used them."

Commissioner Bowie Kuhn, who had tried to censor Bouton's book, did not agree with Dobson's opinion. Prior to spring training, Kuhn had warned players to comply with federal and state drug laws. Although greenies were not considered illegal drugs in and of themselves, they were supposed to be available through prescription only and were often obtained through illegal means. "If the commissioner says we can't use them anymore, then the next time someone asks me whether I use them, I'll say no, go around the corner, and pop," Dobson told *The*

Sporting News. Dobson had just stepped over the line from brutal honesty into sheer foolishness.

In the April, 1971 issue of *Baseball Digest*, two team doctors expressed concern over the use of pep pills. Dr. Joseph Finegold of the Pittsburgh Pirates and Dr. Jacob Suker of the Chicago Cubs suggested the possibility of a player suffering a heart attack on the playing field after ingesting pep pills. The article indicated that pep pills posed a special danger to older, overweight players who did not play on a regular basis. "Amphetamines and speed—there is no place for them," Dr. Suker told William Jauss of *Baseball Digest*. "They won't make a Billy Williams out of a 'Billy Nobody.' And they can be very dangerous and habit-forming."

On March 9, Dobson revised his statements regarding the use of greenies. Dobson issued a press release that read as follows:

> My recent statement in regard to taking a greenie was misunderstood and completely blown out of proportion. These are the facts: Yes, I did take a greenie last year prior to pitching a game after I'd had a bout with the flu. At that time, I was of the opinion it had been of help to me. Since it has been brought to my attention by medical authorities the harmful effects that greenies or any other drugs can have on an athlete, I want it known that I am strongly against anyone using drugs in any form.

After Dobson released his revisionist statement, Commissioner Kuhn held a private conversation with the right-hander to discuss his use of greenies. Kuhn apparently accepted Dobson's new story, in which he claimed to have used greenies only one time during his major league career.

With that controversy averted, the A's suffered their first major setback of spring training when they learned that Blue Moon Odom would not be able to pitch until after the mid-July All-Star break. After making the All-Star team in 1968 and '69, the talented right-hander had encountered a series of elbow problems. As a result, Odom had won only 10 games since the All-Star break in 1969. Now healthy after offseason surgery, Odom had opened up spring training with a pain-free right elbow and had routinely pitched batting practice. Then, one day, without warning, Dick Williams approached Odom and told the right-hander that he would no longer be allowed to throw batting practice and would not pitch in an actual game until mid-season, at the earliest. Dr. William Bickel, the surgeon who had removed bone chips from Odom's elbow, had ordered the shutdown of Odom's arm, in order to allow scar tissue around the elbow to heal. With batting practice deemed off limits, Odom could do no more than field grounders on the mound and feign throws to second base.

In the past, the temperamental Odom might have reacted angrily to the doctor's orders. As one of the most fiercely competitive players in the major leagues, Odom hated the idea of going through the motions in spring training. Yet, Odom seemed to understand the long-term wisdom of Dr. Bickel's decision. "I'm not happy about this because I felt pretty good throwing in batting practice," Odom said in an interview with *The Sporting News*. "But one breaking pitch could ruin my whole career."

The A's received some good news in the spring when Dick Green changed his mind about retirement. "I've had a change of heart and I'm more anxious than ever to play in 1971," Green stated through a press release. "My lousy season last year bothered me and I wasn't in the right frame of mind to play. I used to cringe just thinking about seeing my name in the lineup, but I feel entirely different now." Prior to Green's turnabout, Charlie Finley had contemplated drastic measures in trying to goad his second baseman into returning. "I told him that I was going to put on some snowshoes and go up to see him in Rapid City, South Dakota, to try to get him to change his mind," said Finley. "Dick told me that I was getting too old for that, so I said I would hire a helicopter that would drop me into his front yard." Considering that it was Finley making such a statement, it was not unfathomable for the owner to attempt such a stunt. Prior to Green's turnabout, Finley had been trying to make trades for veteran infielders Ted Kubiak of Milwaukee and Larry Brown of Cleveland. Yet, neither of those players possessed the range or fielding skills of a healthy Dick Green.

The veteran second baseman's initial threat to retire had also prompted the A's to invite a 26-year-old minor league second baseman named Tony LaRussa to camp and give him Green's locker. LaRussa had sipped cups of coffee with the A's in 1963, '68, '69, and '70, but had never been able to establish himself at the major league level because of a questionable bat. A stunning series of injuries had also curtailed LaRussa's progress. From 1964 to 1967, LaRussa had suffered torn ligaments in his arm, a pulled muscle in his back, and two shoulder dislocations.

The A's apparently thought so little of LaRussa's potential that they had left him off their 40-man roster since 1968. Yet, the hard-nosed LaRussa had played well enough at Triple-A stops Vancouver and Iowa to earn himself two brief promotions to Oakland in the interim. Now, with Green back in the fold, LaRussa would have to battle to make the A's' roster as a utilityman instead of having any chance of becoming the starting second baseman.

As the exhibition season began, Reggie Jackson began to offer evidence that his winter league improvement might carry over to the regular season. In the first 10 exhibition games, Jackson ripped seven home runs—including homers in four straight games—and drove home 17 runs. In an interview with sportswriter Bill Libby, Reggie credited the influence of his winter league manager, Frank Robinson, who had skippered Jackson's Santurce team in Puerto Rico. Jackson roomed with Robinson, the Baltimore Orioles' right fielder, for seven weeks. "He's very inspiring," Jackson said of Robinson. "He has a great record so I have to respect his knowledge... And he battled back from bad years, so when he tells me I can do it, I feel he knows what he's talking about. He's been there." In one of his most important lessons, Robinson emphasized to Jackson the importance of keeping his anger under control.

Jackson took full advantage of his day-to-day contact with Robinson. "Every time after I had a turn at bat, I'd go to Frank and ask him how I did," Jackson explained. "I was looking for his criticism and suggestions, and he helped." Armed with a new philosophy and an improved attitude, Jackson seemed ready to embrace his new roles under Dick Williams—as the team's No. 3 hitter and everyday right fielder. As Hall of Famer Ted Williams had said about Jackson after watching him play for the first time, "He's the most natural hitter I've ever seen."

During the 1971 exhibition season, the A's began experimenting with one of Charlie Finley's many inventions: the three-ball walk. Finley had petitioned other teams to adopt the rule as a way of speeding up the pace of games and introducing more offense into the major leagues. Finley also figured that since baseball could not bring violence to its game the way that football did, the three-ball walk would at least provide the game with more action. Yet, of all the teams the A's were scheduled to play in spring training, only the Milwaukee Brewers agreed to experiment with the rule. On March 6, in the first of four scheduled Cactus League games between the two teams, the A's and Brewers played a nine-inning game using Finley's brainchild. After many fans booed the pre-game public address announcement of the three-ball walk, the in-game results proved predictable. The teams' pitching staffs combined to allow 19 walks and six home runs, as the A's won, 13–9.

Having seen the effects of the rule on their pitchers, the Brewers no longer liked the three-ball walk. Cleveland Indians manager Alvin Dark expressed a little bit of interest, but most other teams looked upon Finley's new rule with disdain. The California Angels traveled to Mesa to play the A's one day, only to learn that Finley wanted to play the game using the three-ball walk. Angels manager Harold "Lefty" Phillips and general manager Dick Walsh refused, saying that they had not been given any advance warning of the rule, one that they had not liked from its inception. Finley tried to convince the umpiring crew that he did not need the approval of the visiting team to use the three-ball walk. When Commissioner Bowie Kuhn expressed his discontent with the rule, which created too many bases on balls and appeared to swing the balance of power too far to the side of the hitters, Finley's three-ball walk died quickly.

Rollie Fingers, like most of Oakland's pitchers, probably breathed a sigh of relief when he learned that Kuhn had ordered the discontinuation of the three-ball walk. As an unproven 24-year-old, Fingers had already overcome one of his problems—that of a protruding waistline. In 1970, an overweight Fingers had won just seven games and lost nine, while switching between the bullpen and the starting rotation. Critics had often suggested that Fingers' poor eating habits contributed directly to his mediocre pitching results.

Ironically, the six-foot, four-inch Fingers had been anything but heavy as a teen-ager growing up in Steubenville, Ohio. In 1964, the beanpole right-hander had won the American Legion Player of the Year Award before signing a professional contract with the Kansas City A's. After debating whether to make Fingers a pitcher or a position player, the organization assigned him to moundwork with Leesburg of the Florida State League. Fingers ascended the A's organizational ladder slowly, making it to Class-AA Birmingham in 1967. On opening night, Fingers threw a change-up to a minor league hitter named Fred Kovner. A line drive soon returned in Fingers' direction. "I saw it," Fingers told Ron Bergman, "about three feet from my face." Fingers tried to block the ball with his glove, but reacted too late, the drive striking him in the jaw. Fingers fell to the dirt, face first. When manager John McNamara rolled him over, he fixated on a stream of blood flowing from Rollie's right eye. Doctors repaired the eye, which had caused blurred vision, and also wired his jaw shut. When a nurse gave Fingers a drug that created an allergic reaction, he had to vomit repeatedly—through his teeth. Fingers spent three days in the hospital, losing several pounds during his stay.

After the 1970 season, Fingers located another unconventional answer to what had become a tangible weight problem. The solution arrived in an undesirable way; Fingers experienced a severe bout with intestinal flu and lost 25 pounds in the process. The illness proved to be a blessing, though, as Fingers reported to spring training lighter, quicker, and more durable. In just over 36 spring training innings, Fingers compiled a record of 4–0, with an ERA of 2.23. On March 27, Fingers pitched the most masterful exhibition game of any Oakland starter to date. Despite struggling with his control, Fingers shut down the San Diego Padres, 9–2, with a complete game, five-hit effort. The performance marked the first complete game for an A's starter in spring training.

The A's had originally projected Fingers as no higher than their third best starter, after Catfish Hunter and Vida Blue. Finger's unforeseen spring training success convinced Dick Williams to name him the A's' No. 2 starter. Hunter, a notoriously poor spring training pitcher, fell to the No. 3 slot, despite leading the staff with 18 wins in 1970. As for Chuck Dobson, Williams deemed him healthy enough to merit the status of fourth starter, despite being slowed by a spring training back strain.

The improvement of Fingers strengthened the rotation, but weakened a thinning bullpen core. The A's harbored concerns about the readiness of Diego Segui, the American League's ERA champion in 1970, who had reported late to spring training because of a contract dispute. Another veteran right-hander, Bob Locker, appeared unusually nervous and fidgety during his spring training appearances and experienced difficulty throwing his sinkerball for strikes. From the left side, Jim Roland allowed only three runs in 19 innings, but appeared best suited for the unglamorous role of long relief. The other southpaw, Paul Lindblad, pitched solidly in the spring, but like most of the other relievers, lacked the intimidating fastball preferred from a late-inning, game-saving reliever. With Mudcat Grant now in Pittsburgh, the A's lacked a dominating "fireman" (1970s parlance for a "closer") who could handle opposing batting orders in the seventh, eighth, and ninth innings. The A's would have to find relief from a completely unexpected source later in the season.

Chapter Three

Low Expectations

Opening Day Lineup, 1971

Bert "Campy" Campaneris, ss
Felipe Alou, lf
Reggie Jackson, rf
Don Mincher, 1b
Sal Bando, 3b
Rick Monday, cf
Dave Duncan, c
Dick Green, 2b
Vida Blue, p

The play of longtime minor league journeyman Tony LaRussa provided the A's with one of their most intriguing story lines of spring training. Once veteran second baseman Dick Green had foregone retirement and reported to camp, LaRussa seemed destined to return to the minor leagues for a 10th consecutive season. The A's, however, did need a utilityman, someone who could back up Green, Campy Campaneris, and Sal Bando. In the past, LaRussa had played almost exclusively at second baseman, but an offseason stint in the Dominican Republic had afforded him a chance to play the other infield positions. LaRussa successfully carried that experience over to spring training, where he impressed the A's with nearly flawless defensive play at second base, shortstop, and third base.

The motivation of qualifying for a major league pension had spurred LaRussa. "I'm 26 now. My oldest daughter is three," LaRussa explained to Ron Bergman, corresponding for *The Sporting News*. "I've still got a year and a third to get my pension and I'd like to get that if I can."

Although LaRussa didn't hit much during the pre-season, his fielding and versatility so impressed the A's that he made the team's 25-man roster over two other players: the more experienced John Donaldson and the more highly touted Dwain Anderson. For the first time in his sporadic major league career, LaRussa had made an Opening Day roster on merit. In 1963, LaRussa had spent the entire season with the Kansas City A's, but only because his status as a "bonus baby" had mandated, according to baseball rules, that he remain on the major league roster.

The good feelings provided by LaRussa's assault on the utilityman role notwithstanding, the A's opened the 1971 season as only the third-place choice in the American League West. Respected baseball writers like Joe Durso and Murray Chass of the *New York Times* made the upstart Angels the fashionable choice in the Western Division, leaving the A's and the Twins to battle for second place. In general, most baseball writers seemed captivated by the Angels' offseason acquisition of Red Sox slugger Tony Conigliaro, who had hit 36 home runs and driven in 116 runs in 1970. The scribes felt Conigliaro would join left fielder Alex Johnson (the defending league batting champion) and Gold Glove center fielder Ken Berry in forming one of the best outfield combinations in the American League. Angels pitching seemed strong, too, with 22-game winner Clyde "Skeeter" Wright buttressed by 16-game victor Tom Murphy and a talented 24-year-old change-up artist named Andy Messersmith.

The writers considered the Twins too much on the dark side of thirty, with key players like Harmon Killebrew, Leo Cardenas, Jim Kaat, and Jim Perry creeping up in age. In contrast, the experts regarded the A's as too young, and too lacking in pitching depth to win the division outright. Oakland's 11–17 spring record left further doubt in the minds of the writers, who also noticed the unusual, poorly balanced structure to the season-opening team. Oakland's 25-man roster included only nine healthy pitchers, and featured seven outfielders, an abnormally high number. The A's had discussed the possibility of trading left fielder Felipe Alou to the Milwaukee Brewers, perhaps in exchange for utility infielder Ted Kubiak, but the veteran outfielder remained in Oakland. (The failure to trade for Kubiak had also ensured that Tony LaRussa would remain with the team.) With Alou stationed in left, Rick Monday positioned in center, and Reggie Jackson entrenched in right (and no designated hitter rule in effect), quality players like Joe Rudi and Tommy Davis seemed destined for minimal playing time. The bevy of veteran outfielders left talented youngsters like Angel Mangual and Steve Hovley buried further on the depth chart, with little opportunity to develop their skills at the major league level.

The installation of Dave Duncan as the starting catcher indicated that Dick Williams might be more in charge of lineup decisions than his predecessor, John McNamara. After all, Charlie Finley had battled verbally with Duncan during the offseason. Given his past track record, Finley might have dictated that either the hard-hitting Gene Tenace or the strong-armed Frank Fernandez perform most of the catching duties, with Duncan restricted to "clipboard" status. Williams seemed assured of solid offensive production no matter whom he selected as his starting catcher. In 1970, Duncan, Tenace, and Fernandez had combined for 32 home runs and 93 RBIs.

Williams surprised most of the Oakland media by naming Vida Blue as his Opening Day starter in Washington, where the A's would play the Senators in the traditional Presidential opener. At the start of the season, Williams had considered Blue as no better than his No. 2 starter. The 21-year-old left-hander had made only a handful of major league starts prior to the season, while Catfish Hunter was coming off an impressive 18-win campaign in which he had logged 262 and one-third innings. Blue, however, had been dominant in two late-season starts in September. In what was just his fourth start of 1970, Blue hurled a no-hitter. Throwing 90 per cent fastballs, Blue shackled the Twins, the eventual Western Division champions. Two starts earlier, Blue had nearly equaled that effort when he one-hit the Kansas City Royals, allowing only an eighth inning single to Pat Kelly.

Twins beat writer Bob Fowler, who saw Blue's no-hitter in person, says Minnesota hitters recognized Blue's ability well before his masterful performance. "Obviously, he pitched a no-hitter," Fowler says, "but that was in September. Before that, he was admired by our team. Yes, he was a good left-handed pitcher, a great left-handed pitcher. But I think that our players [in Minnesota] recognized him, admired him for his athletic ability. I mean, he was a great fielder; he was a good athlete. You know, a good hitter; this was before the DH. He was just somebody that they really admired as an athlete."

The sleek left-hander had made a profound first impression, even on a Hall of Fame pitcher from an earlier generation, Whitey Ford. "The first time you see him—if you think like a pitcher—you have to say, 'This one can throw the ball.' " Ford remarked to Jerry Izenberg of *Sport* Magazine. "He has a loose, easy windup. He coils himself up and that way, he gets the most spring out of his body. He's smooth and he comes right over the top."

Blue prepared to face the Senators, who had lost eight consecutive Opening Day games. Washington had also dropped its last 14 games of the 1970 season to finish a dismal last in the American League East, an unsightly 70–92. Yet, the Senators still had reason for optimism heading into the new season. Senators owner Bob Short had signed former All-Star outfielder Curt Flood, who was still in the midst of battling baseball's reserve clause, and had acquired onetime 31-game winner Denny McLain in a trade with the Detroit Tigers. The Senators also liked the prospects of 22-year-old shortstop Toby Harrah, who had made veteran infielder Eddie Brinkman expendable in the deal for McLain.

The United States President usually attended Washington's home opener and threw out the ceremonial first pitch, but Commander-in-Chief Richard Nixon, a noted baseball fan, could not attend the game at RFK Stadium due to other commitments. In his place, Vietnam veteran Daniel Pitzer tossed out the first ball before the capacity crowd of 45,061, prior to the more determined throwing to be done by Blue and Washington's Dick Bosman.

Blue started the game throwing hard but a bit wildly, surrendering three walks in the second inning. An error by Campy Campaneris at shortstop allowed two unearned runs to score, putting the A's in an early hole. An unsettled Blue ended up surrendering four runs in a jittery start. "He didn't know where he was," observed third baseman Sal Bando in an interview with famed sportswriter Dick Young. "Anything you said to him, he shook his head and said, 'Yes.' You could have said you're full of bull, and he would have said, 'Yes.' " The Oakland bullpen did not help matters, either, allowing four runs over the final six and one-third innings. On offense, the A's managed only six hits and no runs against Bosman, a competent, but hardly overpowering veteran starter. Lumbering left fielder Frank "Hondo" Howard, considered one of the worst defensive outfielders in the American League, also made two terrific catches on the run, preserving Bosman's six-hit, 8–0 shutout.

Two days later, the A's played their home opener at the Oakland Alameda County Coliseum. At the behest of Charlie Finley, the A's had scheduled something unusual for the home opener: a doubleheader. A sparse crowd of just over 23,000 fans showed up to watch Catfish Hunter and Rollie Fingers pitch miserably in both ends of the twinbill. The A's lost 6–5 and 12–4 to the Chicago White Sox, who had somehow managed to lose more games—106—than any other team in 1970. Oakland pitching, which Dick Williams had raved about during spring training, appeared on the verge of an early-season collapse.

With his team's record sitting ugly at 0–3, Williams called his entire pitching staff into his office for a meeting. Having noticed his pitchers' unwillingness to challenge hitters, Williams encouraged them to stop nibbling at the corners. He urged them to concentrate on the most important task at hand: *throwing strikes*. The Oakland manager also recognized the organization's mistake in trying to open the season with only nine pitchers: Blue, Fingers, Hunter, Chuck Dobson, Diego Segui, Jim Panther, Bob Locker, Jim Roland, and Paul Lindblad. Dobson, the team's scheduled fourth starter, was clearly not healthy enough to pitch. He had performed poorly in his final exhibition start, and seemed to be favoring his arm during his delivery to the plate. "You know we can't get by with eight pitchers," Williams told Ron Bergman after announcing that Dobson would be placed on the disabled list. "Heck, you know we couldn't even get by with nine."

Armed with a surplus of outfielders, Charlie Finley decided to pull the trigger, or some might say the panic button, on an early-season trade. On April 9, just four days after the start of the season, the A's dealt Felipe Alou, the team's Opening Day left fielder. Instead of sending Alou to the Brewers for infield help, as had been rumored during the spring, Finley traded Alou to the New York Yankees for pitchers Rob Gardner and Ron Klimkowski. While Yankee management was thrilled to have acquired a professional hitter and veteran leader like Alou, some Oakland writers criticized Finley for not receiving equal value in return. Klimkowski had pitched well in 1970, with an ERA of 2.66, but had done so in the relatively low-pressure role of long and middle relief. Gardner, a 16-game winner for the Syracuse Chiefs of the International League, had failed to make the Yankees' pitching staff in the spring.

Oakland players knew that they would miss Alou, one of the most well-liked and respected players throughout the major leagues. Captain Sal Bando had previously offered Alou the ultimate praise. "He's one of the greatest men I've ever met in baseball," Bando once told Ron Bergman. "You think a man who's been around as long as he has would pace himself a little. But he embarrasses you the way he hustles."

Dick Williams attempted to defend the deal, which he felt was mandated by the team's lack of pitching depth. "The name of the game is pitching," Williams declared to *The Sporting News*, "and we haven't had it yet. In fact, we've been bombed." In their first three games, A's pitching had surrendered 26 total runs, or an average of nearly nine runs per outing.

The timing of the trade—just a handful of days into the regular season—caught Alou by surprise. Although Alou maintained a permanent home in Atlanta, he had just moved his wife and children into an Oakland apartment, where they were scheduled to stay for the entire 1971 season. Those plans would have to be scrapped, but the Yankees graciously gave Alou the necessary time to move his family out of the Oakland apartment and make new accommodations in the New York metropolitan region. When Alou finally reported to the Yankees a few days later, he found a positive spin to the trade in the strangest of places—the simplicity of his new uniform. "At least I know this is the uniform I'm going to be wearing every day," Felipe told Murray Chass of the *New York Times* in referring to the traditional home Yankee pinstripes. "Out there [in Oakland], I didn't know which uniform to wear when. We had one uniform for the first game of a doubleheader and another for the second. Once I put on the wrong uniform." Indeed, the A's led both leagues in the number of uniform combinations, which featured Charlie Finley's favorite colors: wedding gown white, Fort Knox gold, and Kelly green. (Or as Bay Area sportswriter Wells Twombly once wrote, "*Finley* gold and *currency* green.") On some days, the A's wore green uniforms with gold undershirts; on other days they donned white jerseys and pants with green sleeves; and on still other days they wore gold uniforms with green undershirts. When the A's played home doubleheaders, they wore white jerseys in the first game and gold ones in the second game. The arrangement proved confusing to the players, but entertaining to Finley.

On Friday night, April 9, the same day that Finley announced the trade of Alou, the A's finally displayed some of the championship potential that Dick Williams had beamed about during the offseason and spring training. Oakland scored five runs against Kansas City in the second inning, thanks to four walks, an error, a two-run single by Joe Rudi, and a sacrifice fly by Reggie Jackson. The offensive fireworks proved to be more than sufficient for Vida Blue, making his second start of the season. In stark contrast to his unsettled performance in the opener against Washington, Blue proved overpowering against the Royals, striking out 13 batters in a 5–0 six-inning, rain-shortened win. For the first time in his brief managerial tenure with the team, Williams sat back and enjoyed a dominating pitching showcase by one of the American League's most dazzling young pitchers.

The next day, Diego Segui made his first start of the new season. The forkballing—and some claimed *spitballing*—right-hander struggled, giving up four runs in five innings. As a result, the A's trailed, 4–3, heading to the bottom of the ninth inning. With one out, No. 8 hitter Dick Green singled and moved up to second on a walk to backup outfielder Steve Hovley. Royals reliever Jim York then retired leadoff man Campy Campaneris for the inning's second out. Since Williams had pulled a double-switch earlier in the game, the pitcher's spot, featuring relief pitcher Bob Locker, was now scheduled to bat. In Locker's place, Williams called upon his most experienced pinch-hitter, Tommy Davis. With two on and two outs, and the A's facing their third loss in four games to start the season, Davis belted a hard-hit ball into the left-center field gap. Green scored easily from second to tie the game, and Hovley raced all the way home from first base to give the A's a dramatic come-from-behind victory. Tommy Davis, who had been acquired from the baseball scrap heap known as the waiver wire, had paid his first major dividend as the leader of Oakland's bench brigade.

In the early 1960s, Tommy Davis had been arguably the National League's best all-around hitter. In 1962, he had led the league with a robust .346 batting average and a Hack Wilson-esque 153 RBIs. In 1963, Davis' numbers fell, but he still led the league in hitting with a .326 mark. Two years later, Davis caught his spike on the second-base bag while executing a take-out slide, shattering his right ankle. The fracture robbed Davis of much of his speed and power-hitting capacity. Davis learned to hit off his front foot, but the injury rendered him a journeyman player, as he floated from Los Angeles to New York (Mets) to Chicago (White Sox) to Seattle (Pilots) to Oakland to Chicago (Cubs). In total, Davis had been traded three times, sold twice, made available in the expansion draft, and even released—on Christmas Eve, no less. Now, Davis had found a home in the Bay Area, as arguably the best backup player on the A's' roster and perhaps the best pinch-hitter in the American League. As Dick Williams would later tell sportswriter Phil Pepe of his skilled batsman, "Tommy Davis can hit at midnight with the lights out." By the time he ended his 18-year major league career in 1976, Tommy Davis would rank first on the all-time pinch-hitting list with a batting average of .320.

Chapter Four

A New Sheriff in Town

In spite of the win over the Royals, the A's were not playing the kind of crisp baseball that Dick Williams had envisioned. After losing the next game to the Royals, 10–5, the A's fell to 2–4 on the season, further wearing the patience of their demanding skipper. While on the team bus at the Milwaukee airport, one of the Oakland players decided to play a practical joke by stealing a battery-operated megaphone from the team airplane. Williams was not amused. He angrily lectured his players about the incident, demanding the device be returned immediately.

"Gentlemen," Williams addressed his players, "some of you think you can be *bleeps*. Well, I can be the biggest *bleep* of them all. I've been mild up to now." Williams then delivered his first major pronouncement. "The serving of booze on planes is terminated for the rest of the seasons." Ouch. Williams continued his diatribe. "The plane can't leave without the megaphone, and we won't leave until the plane does." As Williams continued his lecture, one of the players dropped the megaphone from the bus window onto the sidewalk. Williams saw the megaphone fall, but continued talking. "I suggest that you stay in your rooms the entire trip." And one more thing. "If any of you want to telephone Charlie Finley to complain," Williams said, "I have three phone numbers where he can be reached." In other words, Williams was challenging his players to go over his head and complain to the owner. Oakland players had never seen the mild-mannered John McNamara react in such a way. The reign of Dick Williams had officially begun.

And exactly who stole the megaphone in the first place, setting off Williams on his first tirade as Oakland manager? In the years after the incident, several Oakland players identified Catfish Hunter, perhaps the team's most cunning practical joker, as the main culprit, with a possible assist given to relief pitcher Paul Lindblad. As Gene Tenace recalls, Hunter enjoyed making lighthearted "trouble," either through practical jokes or by needling teammates during the club's travels. " 'Cat' was a great person, but 'Cat' was a little bit of an instigator, too," says Tenace, a major and minor league coach in his post-playing days. "Our bus rides were great. Catfish would get it rolling [by needling someone]. He'd get two people going at each other and then back out of it and watch."

Hunter's hijinks aside, the A's responded to Williams' disciplinary measures by winning their next five games, including two-game sweeps of Milwaukee and Minnesota. After losing a single game to the White Sox, the A's strung together seven more victories, making it 12 wins in 13 tries. The A's moved into first place on April 16, slipped back to second briefly, and recaptured the top spot on April 20. The A's would finish April with a record of 17–8, a ledger that became even more impressive in light of the club's three-game losing streak at the start of the season.

The key man in Dick Williams' plan, Reggie Jackson, contributed game-winning hits in three consecutive games, and powered two long home runs in a victory against the Twins. One of the home runs traveled an estimated 437 feet, while the other managed a distance of 422 lengths. Jackson continued to credit his winter league manager—and American League rival—Frank Robinson for his improved play. "Being around Robinson matured me as a person and as a player," explained Jackson to the *New York Times*. "When I got down there, I was rock-bottom in morale and confidence...From then on, we talked almost continuously about baseball, and I did most of the listening."

"We talked about temper and then I learned things by watching him control his. We talked about being a black man in baseball, and he helped me put myself in perspective."

Robinson's life lessons had seemingly taken hold on Jackson. "I feel I'm a different person because of Frank Robinson," Jackson told the *New York Times*.

Although Jackson was delivering timely power to the Oakland cause, he was struggling to make contact. In his first 51 at-bats, Jackson had struck out 20 times, or nearly 40 per cent of the time. Another Oakland slugger, third baseman Sal Bando, helped compensate for Jackson's early-season penchant for swinging and missing. Bando homered five times in his first 16 games, and enjoyed a remarkable stretch of 12 plate appearances, which included four long balls, two singles, a double, and three walks.

The Oakland captain also expressed extreme confidence in his team's ability to contend in the American League West. With less than a month of the regular season completed, Bando seemed to be looking ahead to a post-season matchup with the defending World Champion Baltimore Orioles. "Definitely, we're going to win our division," Bando boldly told *The Sporting News*. "We haven't the depth Baltimore has, and of course, not the pitching, but in a short series, you never can tell."

The play of second baseman Dick Green also bolstered the A's. Green had endured a miserable season in 1970, batting under .200 with four home runs and 29 RBIs. Green admitted that he had allowed his poor hitting to affect his usually reliable fielding. In general, he had grown disenchanted with the lifestyle of a baseball player. He didn't like to fly and didn't like spending long stretches away from his family. All of the signs pointed toward his retirement. At the end of the season, Green returned his contract offer unsigned and later mailed back a check he had received for upcoming spring training expenses.

Faced with the loss of one of his key starting middle infielders, Dick Williams had tried to pry away his former second baseman, Mike Andrews, from the Red Sox. The Sox eventually dealt Andrews to the White Sox in a trade that brought future Hall of Fame shortstop Luis Aparicio to Beantown. The A's later tried to acquire middle infielder Larry Brown from the Cleveland Indians, but Charlie Finley considered the asking price too steep.

When the trades for Andrews and Brown fell through, Finley went to work. He telephoned Green, put on his best salesmen's pitch, and offered the infield veteran some improved financial considerations. Green eventually agreed to return to the A's and once again teamed with his double-play partner, shortstop Campy Campaneris.

In his first 24 games in 1971, Green batted only .205, but totaled four home runs and 15 RBIs. Those power numbers ranked behind only Sal Bando on the Oakland roster. More importantly, the slick-fielding Green committed only one error, which had occurred on an errant throw and not because of his mishandling of the ball. One of Green's American League counterparts, Orioles second baseman Dave Johnson, praised his rival's defensive ability, especially his courage in turning the double play. "Greenie's the least scared of the opposing baserunners of all the second baseman in the league," Johnson informed Ron Bergman. "He shows the most guts. He sacrifices something, trying for that double play."

Even with Green in tow, the A's decided to pull the trigger on a deal for Larry Brown. On April 24, Finley acquired Brown from the Indians—at the cost of $100,000. Finley clearly overpaid for Brown, who had entered the 1971 season with a lifetime batting average of .239 and only 45 home runs in eight seasons. Now, with Green "un-retired" and playing well, the A's viewed Brown as a pricey backup, not as their starting second baseman.

The day before the acquisition of Brown (which gave Oakland three players named after colors of the spectrum, Dick Green and Vida Blue being the others), the A's finished off a three-game sweep of the pre-season darlings, the Angels. Blue picked up the victory, becoming the first four-game winner among American League pitchers.

Although Dick Williams had managed the club for only a month, he had already succeeded in gaining more authority than his predecessor, John McNamara. Williams had quickly and firmly dealt with the megaphone incident and had banned alcohol from team flights as punishment for the childish prank. Most importantly, Williams had accomplished his most important task as manager—helping his players to perform better. "He instills confidence in you," Dave Duncan told William Leggett of *Sports Illustrated*. "I think we are 75 per cent better than last year. It's a great feeling."

Fortunately for Williams, Charlie Finley had not yet chosen to attend a game in Oakland, which removed an ominous shadow that might otherwise have lurked over the shoulders of the new A's' skipper. The Oakland media, however, had taken note of Finley's absence, and had decided to criticize the owner for his lack of interest. "The fans do not care whether Charles O. Finley comes out to the games," Finley told *Sports Illustrated*, referring to himself in the third person as he attempted to fend off the latest criticism.

In early May, the A's' record stood at 19–11, good enough for first place in the American League West. Still, Finley felt he could improve his team by tinkering with his roster. On May 8, the A's made a major five-player trade, dealing veteran first baseman Don Mincher, backup catcher Frank Fernandez, reliever Paul Lindblad, and cash to the Washington Senators for power-hitting first baseman Mike Epstein and reliever Darold Knowles. Reports differed as to the amount of cash the A's included in the deal. Estimates ranged from $75,000 to $300,000, the latter a massive amount of money to be included in such transactions at the time.

Prior to his tenure in Oakland, Mincher had played stints with the Washington Senators, Minnesota Twins, California Angels, and Seattle Pilots. Minnesota beat writer Bob Fowler remembers Mincher well from his days in the Twin Cities. "Don Mincher was a very big guy, six-four, maybe 220 or so," says Fowler. "Excellent power hitter, pretty good fielder. A real quiet, gentlemanly type of guy." The veteran first baseman's polite, easygoing demeanor made him popular with the other Oakland players, while offering a soothing balance to a team filled with more volatile personalities like Reggie Jackson and Vida Blue. Mincher's leadership, professionalism, and hustle also made him a favorite of managers like John McNamara and Dick Williams.

On the surface, the deal seemed questionable for the A's. Mincher and Mike Epstein were similar players: left-handed power hitters with limited range at first base. Yet, Mincher had paced Oakland with a career-high 27 home runs in 1970, and had proven to be a clutch hitter, driving in the tying or go-ahead run 23 times. Mincher had also forged a reputation for being a solid clubhouse force, while Epstein had created periodic friction in Washington with his brash, outspoken complaints about managers and playing time.

The loss of "Broadway" Frank Fernandez—so dubbed because of his Staten Island heritage and his acquired dislike of playing for the Yankees—seemed the most inconsequential part of the deal. Fernandez, the third-string catcher behind Gene Tenace and Dave Duncan, had come to bat only four times all season. One Oakland reporter had suggested that Fernandez join a local softball league in order to stay in shape. At least the A's didn't punish Broadway Frank by returning him to the team in the Bronx.

From the A's' perspective, the key to the trade appeared to be the exchange of relievers. Paul Lindblad and Darold Knowles were both 29-year-old left-handers, each suited to pitching in middle relief. Lindblad, however, had lost the confidence of Dick Williams. His ERA had risen to nearly 4.00, and he had struck out only four batters in 16 innings. Meanwhile, Knowles had displayed a livelier arm with Washington, striking out 16 batters in 15 innings. Knowles had also earned 27 saves while pitching for a last-place Senators team in 1970.

Yet, Senators owner Bob Short had criticized Knowles' more recent performance, suggesting that the left-hander had lost several miles off his fastball. Short hinted that Knowles' value was declining with each passing day. "I didn't realize I was so horsemeat," Knowles said sarcastically in an interview with Ron Bergman. "From the way [Short] talked, I don't know how I've stayed in the big leagues for five years."

The trade, though surprising to some, did not catch all of the participants off guard. "I had heard rumors," says Don Mincher. "I knew that Darold Knowles...was what the club was really after. And Mike Epstein, who became a great player for them, really worked out well, too. I had heard rumors, and I could remember very vividly that I was called to Dick Williams' room that night along with Paul Lindblad." The prospect of joining a last-place ballclub in Washington did not appeal to a veteran like Mincher, who realized that his career might be coming to an end within the next few seasons. "I was not very happy with that," Mincher says of the trade to a non-contending team, "and I told Dick so. Although there was nothing you could do about it back in those days. I mean, you went where they told you; you had no options whatsoever, except to get packed and get going. Washington, we knew they were not going to be anywhere close to contending. . .Washington was a place back in those days that if you had a competitive spirit, you really didn't want to be there."

In the back of his mind, Mincher knew what he was leaving behind. "We also knew that Oakland was going to be a club that was really gonna be there," Mincher says. "I hated to leave Oakland because I could tell—and most people could tell—what was coming with that ballclub." Yet, Mincher did *not* know that he would eventually be making a return to Oakland, thanks to the handiwork of Charlie Finley.

Although both Epstein and Mincher had endured poor starts to the 1971 season, and questions continued to linger about Epstein's attitude, the A's felt they enjoyed an advantage in trading for the more youthful player. After all, the 28-year-old Epstein was nearly five years younger than Mincher. For his part, Epstein reacted with near ecstasy to the trade that brought him closer to family and friends who lived throughout California. When Bob Short informed Epstein that he had traded him to Oakland, the strapping first baseman offered the owner a kind response. "Thanks for trading me to a first-class ballclub," Epstein told Arnold Hano of *Sport* Magazine.

A reporter soon asked Epstein how he would react to platooning with the A's. In the past, Epstein had battled with Senators manager Ted Williams, who liked Epstein but didn't feel he could hit left-handed pitching well enough to fill an everyday role. "Even in 1969, when I had my best year, I didn't face left-handers," Epstein gasped. "In 1970, the same story. I'd get hot and then they'd throw a left-hander against us, and I'd sit on the bench and cool off. I sat on the bench more and more. It was discouraging." While Ted Williams had made up his mind to platoon him in Washington, Epstein held out hope that Dick Williams might eventually change his status in Oakland. "Dick told me that Tommy Davis is playing against left-handers," Epstein acknowledged in an interview with *The Sporting News*. "But I can get real hot with the bat and maybe not platoon." Epstein was in for a rude awakening.

During spring training, the A's had envisioned Davis exclusively as a bench player and pinch-hitter deluxe, but the veteran batsman had a different plan in mind. When Don Mincher started the season in an 0-for-17 slump and went hitless in 12 at-bats against southpaws, Williams decided to increase Davis' playing time against left-handers. Mincher, for his part, had little complaint with Williams' decision. "I've always been very cognizant of the fact that I had my ups and downs against left-handers, and [even] right-handers," Mincher admits, "Dick Williams and I had some problems with that, but I really didn't mind because I *did* have trouble with left-handers at times in my career. There were times when it was better for the ballclub if a Tommy Davis—who was a great right-handed hitter; he wasn't just a right-handed hitter, he was a great right-handed hitter—played instead of me. It was better for the club."

On April 28, in a game against the Orioles, Mincher had struggled badly in three hitless at-bats against veteran left-hander Mike Cuellar. In the seventh inning, Baltimore manager Earl Weaver brought in another southpaw, Grant Jackson, to face Mincher. Having seen enough of Mincher's futile swings against left-handers, Williams summoned Davis to pinch-hit. Davis worked a deep count against Jackson, eventually drawing a walk. Then, in the ninth inning, Davis stayed in the game to face right-handed reliever Dick Hall, who featured a deceptive delivery and impeccable control. With one out and the winning run in scoring position, Davis battled Hall, fouling off several two-strike deliveries before lacing a game-winning single.

From that game on, Williams decided to employ Davis as his first baseman against all southpaw starters. "The next time a left-hander pitches against us," Williams told reporters after the game against Baltimore, "Tommy will be in there. I told him so... Tommy was upset tonight because he didn't start and I can't blame him. He wants to play. Now he's convinced me."

Although the season was less than two months old, Davis had twice won games with ninth-inning base hits. He had also served as a batting mentor to several of Oakland's younger players, including superstar-in-waiting Reggie Jackson. The A's' right fielder had struggled to make contact at the start of the season, striking out 11 times in his first 23 at-bats. During an early-season season game against the Twins, Davis had noticed a flaw in Jackson's technique as he began his swing and strode toward the pitcher. Davis escorted Jackson to the clubhouse, showed him that he was making an improper movement with his back leg, and quickly corrected the bad habit. Jackson returned to the dugout and eventually blasted two home runs against Minnesota pitching. Without the benefit of film or videotape, Davis had helped Jackson make a critical in-game adjustment.

Although Davis' success against left-handers had reduced Don Mincher's playing time, the man known as "The Mule" harbored no resentment toward his partner at first base. While veteran platoon players around the major leagues often encountered strained relationships with each other, Mincher and Davis enjoyed an excellent kinship. "Tommy Davis was, still is, and always will be one of my closest friends," Mincher says. "Oddly enough, the guys that I did alternate with, Tommy Davis, and for awhile with the Angels—Moose Skowron—and with the Twins—Harmon Killebrew played over there some, Bob Allison some—they all were terrific people, and we got along great. There was no real competition-type thing that we ever talked about. When you go on the field, you want to win the fulltime job, but there was never any point of confrontation with any of the guys that I ever platooned with. As a matter of fact, oddly enough, we were all great friends and remain so today."

Unfortunately for Mincher, the popular first baseman would have to leave his friends in Oakland behind and make some new ones in Washington, where the perennially last-place Senators resided. Mincher would have to wait until the following season to experience the new atmosphere of winning that was beginning to develop in the Bay Area.

Chapter Five

The Runaway

After losing the Presidential Opener to the Senators, Vida Blue had forged a run of seven straight complete-game victories. The solidly built left-hander mastered American League hitters with a devastating fastball and an occasional curveball, also an overpowering pitch in his repertoire. Yet, Blue seemed surprised by his early run of success. "I was always confident I would win in the majors," Vida mused in an interview with Roy Blount of *Sports Illustrated*, "but 7–1?"

Some sportswriters began calling Blue the "black Sandy Koufax," in reference to the former Brooklyn and Los Angeles Dodgers' left-hander, who was now broadcasting for NBC-TV. As the most dominant pitcher of the mid-1960s, Koufax had claimed three Cy Young awards and authored four no-hitters. "Sandy Koufax came to me just before he was to interview Vida Blue," Dick Williams told *New York Times* columnist Arthur Daley. Koufax wanted to know a little bit more about Blue. "Whom does he remind you of?" Koufax asked Williams, a teammate of the future Hall of Famer during the 1956 season. "The guy I'm talking to," responded Williams.

Koufax reportedly blushed when informed of his similarity to the A's' pitching sensation. "I don't know if he's faster than I was," Koufax responded when asked for a comparison by Bay Area sportswriter Wells Twombly, "because I never saw me pitch. I always thought Jim Maloney [of the Cincinnati Reds] threw harder than I did, anyway." Koufax said Blue did surpass him in at least one facet of pitching. "I do know that I couldn't get the ball over the way he does at age 22. He's not only ahead of me, he's ahead of the world."

Dick Williams agreed with Koufax's assessment of Blue. "This kid has a five-year advantage over Sandy," Williams told the *New York Times*. "He has the control and the poise." Koufax, a remarkable pitcher from 1962 to 1966, had struggled with command and control during his initial major league trials. The early part of his career—1955 to 1960—had included ERAs as high as 4.91, 4.48, and 4.05 and won-loss records such as 2–4 and 8–13. "I'd say [Vida's] already ahead of Sandy," said Tommy Davis, who had played with both shades of Koufax—covering a span from 1959 to 1966—and now shared an apartment with Blue. "There's no limit to [Blue's] future."

When one New York reporter told Blue he looked like Koufax, the African-American left-hander responded deftly: "You mean I look Jewish?" In general,

Blue reacted humbly to the continuing streams of Koufax comparisons, a man he knew little about. "I never saw Koufax pitch," Blue admitted to Joe Durso of the *New York Times*. "Not in person or on TV. The only guy I used to try to imitate was Willie Mays—hitting." American League teams couldn't *hit* Blue, who proceeded to win three more starts—including a three-hit shutout against the Brewers and a five-hitter against the Twins—to extend his winning streak to double figures. In 12 starts overall, Blue had amassed 10 wins, all before the calendar had turned from May to June. Except for his Opening Day loss and a no-decision on May 14 against the Royals, Blue had notched a complete-game victory every time he had taken to the mound.

Blue's double-digit win total included a pair of dominating performances against the defending World Champion Orioles. In 18 innings against Baltimore's stacked lineup, Blue had allowed only one run, a mere eight hits, and had struck out 18 batters. "That's the best stuff I've seen in a long, long time," future Hall of Famer Frank Robinson informed Ron Bergman after the second loss to Blue. "It's not fair to compare talents but this kid takes a back seat to no one. He's as good right now as Denny McLain was three years ago," Robinson told *Sport* Magazine in referring to McLain's outstanding 31-win season for the Tigers in 1968. "You know what he's going to throw and you still can't catch up to it."

In another game, Blue had struck out 11 batters, while tossing a four-hit shutout. That performance came against the powerful Tigers, whose lineup included another future Hall of Famer in Al Kaline, along with sluggers Bill Freehan, Norm Cash, and Willie Horton. Blue's performance impressed Kaline, who felt that Blue appeared more confident and relaxed than he had during his debut in 1970. "What impressed me was that when he got in a jam," Kaline told *The Sporting News*, "he could strike somebody out. That's important."

A third future Hall of Famer marveled at Blue's ability to pinpoint his pitches on all four corners of the plate. "In the games I've faced him," Twins slugger Harmon Killebrew recounted for *Sport* Magazine, "I figure he's thrown about 30 pitches. Not one damned one has been down the chute. He's in, out, up, down—with something on every pitch."

Dave Duncan had caught most of Blue's 12 starts, playing an important role in the young left-hander's fast development. Duncan had beaten out the hard-hitting Gene Tenace for the A's' No. 1 catching job in the spring. Dick Williams had indicated early in spring training that he considered a catcher's defensive ability the most important facet of his game. "Catching is a defensive position," Williams had said to *The Sporting News*. "To me, the biggest thing is handling the pitchers, calling the pitches, and defensive work."

An excellent receiver, Duncan played the position with surprising mobility for a large man. Adept at using a thinking man's approach to catching, he also established a fluid game-day rapport with the team's pitchers, especially Blue. Duncan offered a variety of reasons for Blue's sudden success. "Vida has three things going for him," Duncan explained to Ron Bergman. "First he's overpowering. Second, his ball moves. Third, he's sneaky. He has that nice, easy motion, so you think you can hit him. But you can't pick up the ball until it's too late."

Although overshadowed by the powerful pitching of Blue, right-hander Catfish Hunter had quietly won eight consecutive starts after an 0–2 beginning. In the absence of an intimidating repertoire such as the one owned by Blue, Hunter relied on the less inspiring principles of control and movement. After one particular defeat of Milwaukee, Brewers manager Dave Bristol admonished his hitters. "If you can't hit Catfish," said a scolding Bristol, "you can't hit anybody." Hunter, unshaken by the critique, would win two more decisions against Milwaukee in 1971, improving his season record to 3–0 against Bristol's Brewers.

Hunter made up for his lack of arm strength with a discernible tenacity, a characteristic noted by both teammates and opponents. "When I was with Washington, Catfish was never afraid to challenge me," observed recently acquired Athletic Mike Epstein in an interview with sportswriter Pat Jordan, "when lots of guys with better stuff were. He's a helluva competitor." As a result of his aggressiveness, Hunter often yielded home runs—but usually *solo* home runs because of his ability to avoid bases on balls.

In their last 19 combined starts, Blue and Hunter had teamed up to win 18 games (with 17 complete games), while holding opponents to an average of 1.91 runs per nine innings. The devastating left-right combination provided by the Oakland aces made the A's the envy of the American League. Spearheaded by Blue and Hunter, the A's raced out to a record of 30–15. Oakland starters as a whole piled up complete games in 23 of the 45 games. The A's, who had been picked by most to finish third in the Western Division, had emerged as the best team in the division, and perhaps the class of the American League.

Yet, Charlie Finley wanted more. The A's' owner frothed at the possibility of adding another hammer to Oakland's intimidating staff of starting pitchers. Finley initially talked to the White Sox about the availability of left-hander Tommy John. But the A's' leader desired a bigger name, one who would make headlines in the Oakland newspapers. Finley approached the Indians about the status of their ace, hard-throwing left-hander Sam McDowell. Finley offered a package of players that included injury-plagued right-hander Chuck Dobson, who had been activated in May after starting the season on the disabled list. The rumors intensified after Dobson made his second start of the season on May 12. Dobson handcuffed the Indians, 8–1, with a complete-game, seven-hit effort. Ironically, Dobson outperformed McDowell himself, who fell to 1–5 after giving up 12 hits in five and two-thirds innings.

During the game, reporters overhead Finley talking to Indians owner Vern Stouffer. Finley reportedly told Stouffer that he didn't care how many runs McDowell gave up against Oakland in that game; he still wanted the veteran left-hander for his rotation. In spite of the rumors, the deal involving McDowell never did take place. In June, Finley claimed that he no longer had any interest in acquiring "Sudden Sam." More likely, Finley found Cleveland's asking price for McDowell too high.

The A's might have regretted adding McDowell to their club, given his struggles with alcoholism, which he would later reveal. McDowell had also experienced a recent feud with one of Oakland's pitchers, Blue Moon Odom. In 1969, Odom had disparaged the Cleveland lineup, predicting he could shut out the Indians any time he faced them. The boast prompted some harsh words from Indians slugger Ken "Hawk" Harrelson, Odom's former teammate with the Kansas City A's. Odom then ridiculed Harrelson, who was hitting just .177 at the time. McDowell came to Harrelson's defense and challenged Odom. "You tell Blue Moon that I want a piece of his action when we get to Oakland," McDowell told Cleveland reporter and intermediary Russell Schneider. "I want his game." When a writer relayed the remarks to the Oakland clubhouse, Odom belittled McDowell's intelligence. "Sam's dumb," said Odom bluntly. "If I had his stuff, I'd win 25 games a year. He don't have no kind of brain. Why? He's just dumb. He don't know how to pitch."

Such harsh words typified Odom, especially in the early stages of his career. "Blue Moon Odom came up as a very brash young fellow with a great arm," says Jack Aker, a reliever with the A's from 1964 to '68. "He's a fellow that went right to the major league mound, not a bit afraid, not a bit nervous. I can remember one incident especially, the first year that he was with us. We came into New York to play the Yankees, and it was a day game—a Saturday game—and we were gonna play a Sunday game, which he was gonna pitch. At the end of batting practice that Saturday, I was walking off the field with Blue Moon. Whitey Ford was nearby on the other sideline. And Blue Moon stopped and asked me who it was. I said, 'That's Whitey Ford, he's gonna pitch against you tomorrow.' Blue Moon, at that point, turned around and yelled at Whitey, 'Hey tomorrow, Whitey, it's gonna be you and me dealin' in the sun!' Well, needless to say, Whitey just gave him a look like, 'Who is this guy?' The next day, *Whitey* was dealin' in the sun, but by the second inning, Blue Moon was in the clubhouse. He'd been knocked out of the game."

In May of 1971, the A's activated Odom from the disabled list—well ahead of his scheduled arrival in July. Odom pitched well in his first start, allowing two runs in six innings against the Royals. "I feel great," Odom told the Associated Press after the game. "I feel better now than I've felt in two years. I'm beginning a new life—pitching without that pain."

To make room for Odom and Chuck Dobson in the starting rotation, Williams shifted Rollie Fingers to the bullpen in early May. Fingers, who had struggled as a starter, had been heavily sought after by the Senators in trade talks. Washington wanted to acquire him in the recent deal involving Mike Epstein and Don Mincher, but the A's refused to part with the talented young right-hander.

Williams had previously hoped that Fingers would prosper as a starter. In his first major league start in 1969, Fingers had pitched a complete game shutout against the Twins, whose lineup included Rod Carew, Tony Oliva, and Harmon Killebrew. With a hard, sinking fastball that moved in two different directions and a knee-buckling slider, Fingers owned the physical requirements needed to become an excellent starting pitcher. Yet, Fingers' personality and make-up posed a problem, working against him in that role. "They were trying to use him as a starter,

He was one of those kids that was just so nervous," recalls former A's outfielder Joe Rudi. "If he knew he was going to start, by the time the game started, he had worked himself into such a frenzy that he would almost throw up." An onslaught of anxiety and anticipation plagued Fingers' mind and body. "I just couldn't handle a starting job," Fingers conceded in later years. "If Dick Williams hadn't moved me to the bullpen in 1971, I would have been out of baseball a long time ago."

Fingers initially resisted the move to pitching in relief, considered an unglamorous residential area in 1971. "Rollie thought it was banishment to begin with, to go to the bullpen," says Rick Monday. "Bill Posedel was the pitching coach and did a wonderful job, and constantly stayed on top of Rollie." The move to the bullpen also put Fingers' mind at ease. "If he didn't know he was going to pitch," says Rudi, "and you brought him in out of the blue, he'd do well."

At the time, the decision to move Fingers to the bullpen created few headlines. No one around the A's realized the significance of what was to become a critical career change. "Rollie Fingers was just becoming Rollie Fingers in 1971," recalls Don Mincher. "He had been a starter—a lousy starter before—and all of a sudden somebody realized the guy can get somebody out for two innings. So, he becomes a Hall of Famer." Fingers would establish himself as arguably the game's most consistent reliever over the next 13 seasons, a span that included stints with the A's, San Diego Padres, and Milwaukee Brewers. Fingers' 341 saves and 2.90 ERA would earn him election to the Hall of Fame—following Hoyt Wilhelm as only the second reliever to receive baseball's highest honor. If not for the foresight of Dick Williams—and the work of Bill Posedel—Fingers might have settled for a pedestrian career as a middling starting pitcher.

Later in May, the A's made a deal to further shore up their bullpen by acquiring right-hander Darryl Patterson from the Tigers for minor league second baseman John Donaldson. The addition of Patterson, which occurred on May 22, put the A's one player over the 25-man roster limit. As a result, the Oakland brass decided to outright spring training sensation Tony LaRussa to Triple-A Iowa. The timing of the move must have struck LaRussa as eerie, considering that he had been recalled by the A's exactly one year ago to the day.

LaRussa had played in only seven of Oakland's 43 games and had come to bat only twice. The durability of infield starters Dick Green, Campy Campaneris, and Sal Bando, coupled with the in-season acquisition of utilityman Larry Brown, had doomed LaRussa to afterthought status with the A's. Although LaRussa would earn another promotion to Oakland, his A's career had essentially come to a crossroads. On August 14, the A's would sell LaRussa's contract to the Atlanta Braves.

The intelligent, well-spoken LaRussa would not return to Oakland until 15 years later. On July 7, 1986, he would debut as the Oakland's new manager and begin a terrific 10-year run as the leader of the A's, prompting some to call him the game's best manager of the late 1980s and early 1990s. Yet, no one residing in Oakland in 1971 had any idea of the successes to come for Tony LaRussa.

On May 26, the strange saga of journeyman pitcher Rob Gardner continued. The A's traded Gardner to the Yankees—the same team that had dealt the southpaw to the A's four days after the start of the season. Gardner had previously been optioned to Triple-A Iowa after seeing little action with the A's, primarily because of all the complete games being thrown by Vida Blue and Catfish Hunter.

In exchange for the human yo-yo and another minor league pitcher, the A's acquired the $40,000 contract of versatile backup Curt Blefary, who could catch, man first base, or play the outfield. Blefary initially considered the possibility of *not* reporting to Oakland, but quickly changed his mind when he realized the A's might make the playoffs. As a result of his change-of-thought, the bulky Blefary would shed baseball's most traditional uniform for the game's most radical attire. "Hey, we play you guys next week, don't we?" Blefary said to his soon-to-be former Yankee roommate Bobby Murcer. "I wonder how I'll look in white shoes?" After a short pause, Murcer replied, "Like a white whale."

After a poor April, Reggie Jackson began to deliver on the promise that he had shown during his winter league play in Puerto Rico. During the month of May, Jackson batted .337, crushed seven home runs, and collected 17 RBIs. Reggie attributed the resurgence to the shortening of his swing, coupled with his improved ability to hit with two strikes. "Why do people want me to hit 75 homers?" Jackson asked of Ron Bergman during an interview. "I'll hit my 30 with that .300 average and be satisfied." With 10 home runs by the start of June, Jackson was on a pace to reach 30 by season's end, but his batting average still lingered in the .270s.

Jackson had also improved his fielding in right field, which had been an inconsistent part of his game during his first three major league seasons. Jackson had begun to take advantage of his best defensive trait—a cannon-like throwing arm. Over the first two months of the season, Reggie had thrown out nine runners, including five at the plate.

While Jackson, Vida Blue, and Catfish Hunter captured most of the media attention in April and May, another player had quietly assumed two important roles on the team, as the starting left fielder and No. 2 hitter in the lineup. Prior to the season, Joe Rudi figured to be a little-used backup, buried behind Jackson in right field and veteran Felipe Alou in left field. The trade of Alou to the Yankees during the first week of the season created regular duty for Rudi—except for those weekends when he had to fulfill his military requirements in the Marine Reserves. "I was driving to my Marine Reserve meeting when I heard Felipe was traded," Rudi told *The Sporting News*. "I was so high, I could have jumped off the roof."

Rudi had overcome considerable odds just to make the major leagues. As a high school star in Modesto, California, Rudi impressed a horde of professional scouts until he suffered a badly broken hand on a pitched ball. Only one scout—the A's' Don Pries—continued to show interest in him, even setting up medical treatment for Rudi's injured hand. Rudi rewarded Pries' loyalty by signing a 1964 contract with the Kansas City A's.

The A's originally signed the six-foot, two-inch Rudi as a shortstop but quickly realized that he was too tall and awkward for the position. A move to third base proved equally treacherous, as evidenced by Rudi's 37 errors, the most in the Midwest League in 1965. The A's finally settled on Rudi as an outfielder, but after watching him hit .223 and .254 in his first two minor league seasons, the organization placed him on waivers. The Cleveland Indians claimed Rudi, only to return him to the A's in a subsequent minor league deal. The A's assigned him to Modesto, his hometown, where he rejuvenated his hitting while playing for one of the greatest teams in minor league history. In 1966, Rudi batted .297 with 24 home runs and 95 RBIs for the California League champions. The Modesto club featured 14 future major leaguers, including Rudi, Reggie Jackson, and Dave Duncan.

Yet, Rudi struggled badly in major league trials in 1967 and '68, failing to hit as much as .200 each time. Rudi realized that his use of a sweeping, uppercut swing and his insistence on trying to hit home runs hurt his development at the major league level. In 1970, Rudi reported to spring training and encountered a new hitting coach in Charley Lau, who convinced him to change his approach at the plate. Rudi responded to the newfound tutelage by hitting .309 in 350 at-bats.

In 1971, some writers questioned the decision to trade an established outfielder like Felipe Alou for two uncertain pitchers, while making room for an unproven player like Rudi. Yet, captain Sal Bando defended Rudi's ability to step in and play left field. "I liked Felipe, but he can't do any more than what Joe can do," Bando insisted in an interview with Ron Bergman. "Joe can play every day, hit the ball, and play good defense." In early June, Rudi's batting average resided at a mediocre .260, but his productivity had impressed Dick Williams. In his first 52 games, Rudi totaled 27 RBIs and scored 31 runs. As the second-place hitter behind Campy Campaneris, Rudi led the A's in sacrifice bunts and consistently deployed his most effective offensive weapon—driving the ball to right field. Rudi's ability to execute the hit-and-run regularly created first-and-third situations for the A's.

Furthermore, Rudi had greatly improved his defensive play. "He was very below average, I'd say, with his fielding," reveals former A's relief pitcher Jack Aker, who played with Rudi during his first two major league seasons. Rudi had shagged fly balls daily under the direction of manager Bob Kennedy, who supplied the young outfielder with an assortment of line drives and bloopers. Rudi had also received assistance from Hall of Famer Joe DiMaggio, a coach with the A's in 1968 and '69. After frequently butchering balls hit to him in 1970, Rudi evolved into an above-average flychaser in 1971. Rudi also lengthened a below-average throwing arm by embarking on a series of weight training exercises designed to strengthen his shoulder and arm.

In the meantime, Vida Blue had become the American League's new pop sensation. In his first 16 starts of the season, Blue had pitched before crowds that averaged over 21,000 per game. Although that number might not sound impressive in the context of baseball attendance in the 1990s and 2000s, a team drawing 20,000 or more fans per game in the early seventies was considered a good drawing card. (Crowds of 20,000 or more at the Oakland Coliseum, where the A's often struggled to attract fans, were especially good.) At times, Charlie Finley ordered Dick Williams to alter his rotation, so as to give Blue extra starts at home. On one occasion, Williams switched Blue and Catfish Hunter, so that Blue would not pitch on "Bat Day" in Oakland. "He's enough of a promotion by himself," said Williams in an interview with *The Sporting News*.

Blue's Koufax-like pitching in the season's first half helped Oakland's opponents at the gate, as well. In a series in early June at Yankee Stadium, Blue drew a crowd of 30,052. The Yankees sold approximately 20,000 tickets in their day-of-the-game gate sale, or about four times the usual rate. New York fans watched Blue retire 17 batters in a row on the way to a 5–2 win over their Yankees.

Blue displayed little nervousness in setting down the Yankees in front of the Bronx crowd, but expressed little desire for pitching in the big city. "I can't stand New York; it's too fast for me," Blue complained to the *New York Times*. The more laid-back atmosphere of Oakland proved more attractive for Blue, who had thus far dealt well with the increasing media and fan attention. Even at home, Blue tried to accommodate the press within reason—with an assist from one of his teammates. Blue kept his home phone number unlisted, but writers and potential girlfriends still called. "No, he's sleeping," said roommate Tommy Davis to an inquiring reporter from the *New York Times*. "He pitched last night. Certainly he'll talk to you. Vida's good about that. Can he call you back—say in about three hours? That should still give you plenty of time to talk, right?"

Although Davis screened most of Blue's calls and supplied him with some advice, he admired his young teammate's ability to handle fame on his own. "What I do know from living with him is that everything that's happening to him is not getting to him," Davis told sportswriter Milton Gross. "He knows how to relax. He knows what's going on. He's 22, but he acts like a man of 30."

Blue reminded himself to remain levelheaded as the media continued to shower him with attention. "I think I'm for real," Blue said of his early-season pitching in an interview with the *Newark Star Ledger*, "but I keep telling myself: 'Don't get cocky... Talk to the press... Be nice to the kids... Throw a baseball into the stands once in a while.' " Blue wanted no part of becoming a prima donna, an affliction that had fallen on many players who had suddenly found stardom at the major league level.

Unlike Blue, Reggie Jackson did not handle himself well during a mid-season series at Yankee Stadium. As a reporter interviewed Blue in the Oakland clubhouse, Jackson watched from his neighboring locker. Jackson suddenly interrupted the conversation, which had been cordial in tone. "Don't talk to him, Vida," Jackson warned Blue sternly. "They're all the same. You don't need the press. Just wait until you ask for a raise next year. You'll see that they'll take the side of management. You'll see." Jackson remembered his difficult contract negotiations after his breakthrough season of 1969 and the way that some of the media had sided with Charlie Finley during the dispute. The entire episode had convinced Jackson that the media at-large served as a mouthpiece for baseball ownership.

Left uncomfortable by Jackson's unprovoked diatribe, Blue politely wrapped up the interview with the reporter. Jackson remained ill-tempered. When a clubhouse attendant asked Jackson what kind of soft drink he wanted, the right fielder erupted again. "Get me the kind niggers drink," Jackson shouted. "I'm a nigger. You know I'm a nigger and we all drink the same thing."

In contrast to Jackson, Blue handled the barrage of media and fan requests diplomatically. "He has to put up with a lot," Tommy Davis explained to a reporter for the *New York Times*. "He's a bachelor, and mothers are always taking their daughters to meet him." Blue, however, showed little interest in being set up on dates, or in involving himself with women that might be classified as baseball groupies. "They might be impressed with me, but I'm not impressed with them." Blue preferred a quieter, simpler, stay-at-home lifestyle. "I don't usually go out more than three or four times during a two-week road trip," Blue told *Sport* Magazine. "I do OK with women. But most of the time, I'd just rather get me a bottle of soda and a paper, watch some TV, and go to bed."

Blue seemed most at ease when relating to younger baseball fans. "He's great with kids," Davis told the *New York Times*. "We live in a middle-income to low-income project [in the Oakland area] and the kids are always knocking on the door. He has a lot of patience with them and he spends a lot of time talking to them."

As well as Blue had pitched for the A's, Charlie Finley still found a way to involve him in several controversies. The owner had offered Blue a $2,000 bonus to officially adopt the middle name "True," giving him the rhythmical appellation of "Vida True Blue," already one of the many nicknames previously administered by minor league sportswriters. Blue refused to accept what he considered such an undignified moniker. "I couldn't believe he was serious," Blue told sportswriter Wells Twombly. "Vida was my father's name. I loved my father. He was a good, good man. Vida means life in Spanish…Now that my father is dead, I honor him every time the name 'Vida' appears in a headline. Why would I want to be called 'True Blue?' "

Blue also felt insulted by Finley's attempt at bribing him to change his name. Finley defended himself by claiming that he was only offering Blue the money to defray the legal expenses of changing one's name in court. It was not until many years later that Blue comprehended Finley's motivation. "That was his attempt at marketing," Blue said in a 1996 interview with *Sports Collectors Digest*, "and now I understand it."

During one of Blue's 1971 starts, Finley ordered the scoreboard operator to flash the name "True Blue" on the message board at the Oakland Coliseum. Upon seeing the unwanted nickname in lights, Blue relayed a message to public relations director Michael Haggerty. "Tell Mr. Finley I don't like it and I wish he would have it stopped." Yet, Finley remained persistent. On several occasions, Finley told broadcasters Monte Moore, Bob Elson, and Red Rush to refer to his star pitcher as "True Blue." During a broadcast at Yankee Stadium, Elson repeatedly called Vida "Charlie Finley's Blue Boy." Outraged by the racial implications of such a label, a San Francisco television announcer publicly criticized the Oakland broadcasting crew for using the word "boy" in association with an African-American player.

Another controversy occurred when Finley decided to reward Blue's standout pitching by giving him a new powder blue Cadillac, with the letters V-B-L-U-E adorning the license plate. Finley formally presented his prized left-hander with the $8,000 car during a game at the Oakland Coliseum. Although Finley claimed the Cadillac was a gift, an Oakland newspaper reported that Finley continued to hold the title to the car. Finley called a press conference to deny the accusation. Later, Blue resolved the controversy by saying that he himself held title to the car. Blue then said that he couldn't afford paying the insurance on the car, not to mention the gas and oil expenses created by a Cadillac. Finley initially balked at helping Blue out, before agreeing to pay the expenditures.

In 1970, the A's had drawn only 778,355 fans to the Oakland Coliseum, or about 200,000 fewer than their mark on the road. While the A's' on-field performance in 1971—spearheaded by Blue—had reached a level higher than any of the previous Oakland teams and had drawn the attention of opponents and the national media, it had barely created a ripple with the Bay Area fans. Through their first 29 games of the new season, the A's had drawn a measly total of 310,640 fans—or an average of fewer than 11,000 per game. Even that figure was deceivingly high, considering that the A's had attracted two unusually large throngs for "Cap Day" and "Helmet Day," which served to inflate the attendance totals at the Oakland Coliseum.

Most of the A's players had taken note of the paucity of fan support. When a New York reporter asked Reggie Jackson if the Oakland community had much interest in the A's, he responded, not with words, but with an all-knowing laugh. The lack of rabid fan involvement represented one of the few negatives of a player's baseball existence in Oakland, where many of the A's liked the pace of life, the climate, and the people. "It's great here," first baseman Mike Epstein informed sportswriter Leonard Koppett, "even if you are playing before 2,000 people." Ironically, Oakland fans supported the A's as if they were playing as badly as Epstein's former team, the doormat Senators.

In spite of the sagging attendance, Charlie Finley ventured into his wallet to procure a veteran player. On June 14, Finley made a quiet pickup, but one that would greatly strengthen the Oakland bench in the second half of the season. The A's purchased first baseman Mike Hegan from Milwaukee, the last-place team in the American League West. Although Hegan's batting average seemed unimpressive at .221, his penchant for drawing walks raised his on-base percentage to a respectable .358. Furthermore, Hegan's nifty glove work made him one of the best defensive first basemen in the American League, and a perfect backup to Epstein, who had far more limited fielding skills.

Although the trade afforded Hegan the opportunity to leave a bad team and play for an improving one, he had some reservations about switching cities. "It was kind of a mixed emotion because my wife and I had just purchased a home in Milwaukee," recalls Hegan. "We had come to the Brewers as part of the Seattle Pilots, and at the time we had come to Milwaukee, we were looking at planting some roots and living someplace year-round for a change, something we hadn't done [before]. I think at first it was kind of a shock, although I knew the Brewers at that point really didn't have plans for me to be playing every day. So, if I wasn't going to play every day in Milwaukee with a team that was struggling, I think the best alternative at that time was to go to a winning team, and have a chance to go to the playoffs and World Series. After the deal set in and once I got to Oakland and I became comfortable with the surroundings, it turned out to be probably the best thing that happened in my career."

Like many other players who had joined the A's as mid-season acquisitions, Hegan appreciated the fact that Dick Williams sat down with him to explain specifically his role with the new ballclub. "I think Dick for a lot of reasons was probably the best man for that job at that time," Hegan says. "There are a lot of people who have negative impressions about Dick Williams; I'm not one of them. He sat me down, told me exactly what his plans were for me in certain roles. You know, that's all a player really wants is to know what kind of a role he's going to be used in, whether it be a starter, or a defensive player, or a pinch-hitter. That was the first thing that Dick did, and very frankly, he stuck to it. That's the other thing. I've played for some managers who will tell you one thing, and another thing happens. That wasn't the case with Dick, and I appreciated the fact that he was very up front."

Hegan had never before played for Williams, but he had encountered Charlie Finley during his days as an amateur player. "I've got lots of recollections of Mr. Finley," Hegan says. "Back in 1960 or '61, after my freshman year at Holy Cross, I was playing summer league in Boston. Lenny Merullo and I were playing summer league and getting ready to head down to the Cape to play. And Len's dad was a scout with the Cubs. We had started to hear rumors that no longer was there going to be free agency [for amateur players being pursued by major league teams], that a draft was gonna come in and it would restrict some of the ability for bonuses. In about early or mid-June of that year, we kind of passed the word around that instead of going back to Holy Cross for our sophomore years, that we were probably gonna sign [a pro contract].

"Mr. Finley came in himself to scout one ballgame and came back to my grandmother and grandfather's house. My father [former major league player and coach Jim Hegan] was still coaching at the time and I was living with my grandparents during the summer. He [Finley] came right to my grandparents' house, sat at the kitchen table, and wrote out a blank check and asked me to fill in the numbers that I wanted. I was stunned, you know. After our meeting, I talked to my father, who was coaching with the Yankees. And the only thing he said about Mr. Finley was that he was a maverick and an eccentric, and you make up your mind, but if you want to go with a "quality" organization, give some thought to signing with the Yankees. That's what I eventually did."

When Hegan found out that he had been traded to the A's, he thought about what it would be like to meet Finley for the second time. "You talked about that day I arrived in an Oakland uniform," Hegan says. "I saw Mr. Finley, he shook hands and said, 'I finally got you.' So Charlie waited 11 years, but I finally joined his ballclub."

Perhaps inspired—or angered—by the acquisition of another first baseman, Mike Epstein experienced a memorable two-game stretch on June 15 and 16. After struggling in April and May, Epstein's hitting had prospered in recent days. Playing against his former team, the Senators, Epstein tied a major league record by homering in four consecutive at-bats over a two-day span. Epstein's overlapping power surge helped Chuck Dobson and Vida Blue coast to easy complete-game wins over Washington. In the meantime, former Athletic Don Mincher went 0-for-7 in the two games against *his* former mates.

Nine days after netting Mike Hegan, the A's continued to display an infatuation with husky backup catcher "Broadway" Frank Fernandez. In early May, the third-string receiver had been dispatched to Washington as part of the five-player deal that brought Epstein and Darold Knowles to the Bay Area. Now the A's had decided to re-acquire Fernandez, purchasing him from the Senators for cash, and assigning him to their Triple-A affiliate at Iowa.

Why did the A's want Fernandez back? On the surface, the answer was hard to fathom since Oakland seemed well-stocked in major league catchers. Starting catcher Dave Duncan had successfully assumed command of the pitching staff, while Gene Tenace and the recently acquired Curt Blefary provided excellent depth. But the A's knew that Duncan would be required to serve two weeks in the military reserves in August. Since Blefary lacked the defensive skills to catch on a regular basis, the A's desired a more reliable receiver like Fernandez, who had been Oakland's first-string catcher at the start of the 1970 season.

On June 25, Vida Blue won his 16th game of the year when he five-hit the Royals. The victory put Blue three games ahead of Denny McLain's pace in 1968, when the former Tiger right-hander had won 31 games. Thus, the Oakland and national media began to regularly compare Blue's victory pace to that of McLain's. Aside from the pure numbers, the manner in which Blue won games left a stark impression on teammates and opponents. "I think overpowering," says Rick Monday, when asked to provide his own recollections of Blue during the summer of '71. "I mean to the point where you would see ballclubs come in and say, 'We're gonna get him tonight, we're gonna get him tonight.' And then they would leave town and say, 'Well, we'll get him next time.' He would just very, very quietly slice through a lineup."

Opposing hitters knew that Blue would throw his fastball the vast majority of the time, but still couldn't catch up to his particular brand of power pitching. A's pitching coach Bill Posedel explained the key to the late explosion of Blue's fastball. "He has this extra flick of the wrist," Posedel pointed out to sportswriter Wells Twombly. "You get the idea that his motion is all through, then he gets this extra snap on the pitch... Vida has that something else. It's the difference."

Red Sox star Carl Yastrzemski observed the last-second movement of Blue's fastball. "Maybe it's an optical illusion, maybe it isn't," offered Yaz in an interview with *New York Times Magazine*. "Maybe we all get fascinated by that wrist flick, like a mongoose watching a snake." Senators manager Ted Williams—the last man to hit .400 in a season—also focused his keen batting eyes on Blue. "This Blue throws a heavy fastball," explained the Hall of Fame outfielder. "It doesn't soar by you...It does most of its damage when it gets in close to you...When he comes into the plate, it either swoops away or sinks rapidly on you. When a batter makes contact, he's hitting something dead."

The power and pulse of Blue provided a contrast to the trickery and precision of the A's' No. 2 starter in 1971. "It was a pretty good one-two punch," says Rick Monday, "when you had Vida Blue, who would basically gas hitters and did surgery with the fastball and the hard breaking stuff, and then you'd turn around the next night and get Catfish Hunter, who just defied guys, and they'd shake their heads and couldn't wait to get up and make an out the next time and they'd go back scratching their heads. In between, there was a lot of power pitchers that we had—[Chuck] Dobson and [Blue Moon] Odom, who was constantly moving the ball back and forth."

Blue's pitching had created a nationwide stir, as did one of Charlie Finley's patented promotions. On June 27, the A's hosted the Royals in a doubleheader at the Oakland Coliseum. Finley offered free admission to all women who wore "hot pants" to the game. Expecting about 1,000 not-so-shy women to accept the invitation and take part in the between-games fashion show, the Coliseum staff found itself overwhelmed when 6,000 ladies showed up for the festivities. The lengthy parade of hot pants caused a one-hour delay in between games, compared to the usual 20-minute break. "Hot Pants Day" nonetheless represented a huge financial success for Finley, as the promotion resulted in an overall attendance of 45,302, with a paid crowd of 33,477. By comparison, the next game—a Monday night tilt with the Twins—drew only 4,654 fans to the Coliseum.

By the end of June, the A's had compiled the best record in all of baseball. On June 28, the A's became the first major league team to reach the 50-win plateau. At 50-26, the A's owned a double-digit lead on the surprising Royals, who trailed the division leaders by a full 11 games in the American League West. How did the A's manage to win 17 of 25 games in June, as they had done in April? Primarily because of a pitching staff that continued to dominate opposing lineups. Aside from Blue and Hunter, the A's received major contributions from a comebacking Chuck Dobson, who had won all six of his decisions while featuring an ERA of 3.14. After a shaky start, Blue Moon Odom had won three straight games. Odom sported an ERA even lower than that of 11-game winner Hunter.

Prior to Odom's three-game winning streak, several teammates had complained privately that Blue Moon's presence was hurting the team's chances of winning. "Every time he pitches," one teammate had said snidely to Samuel J. Skinner of *Black Sports* Magazine, "we know we've got to come from behind." Other players had maintained that Odom, at less than full strength, was taking up a space on the roster that belonged to a healthier, more deserving pitcher. Several fans had even written letters to Dick Williams, asking him to cease his use of Odom as one of the four regular starters. The criticism had placed Odom in an awkward position. "I felt like a rookie," Odom told *Black Sports*. "Everyone was watching my every move and pitch, just to see if I would falter…Fans expected too much of me."

In a related development, Charlie Finley pushed for a new rule that would allow players who had undergone offseason operations to start the season in the minor leagues on a rehabilitation assignment. Under the existing rule, the A's could have tried sending Odom to one of their affiliates, but would have risked losing him on waivers to another team. Although the major leagues initially resisted adopting Finley's suggestion, they would eventually institute the rule during the 1980s. As the frequency of placing players on the disabled list increased dramatically during the eighties and nineties, the ability to assign rehabilitating players to the minor leagues for extended stretches would prove extremely valuable to all major league clubs. Once again, Finley's thinking proved to be well ahead of his contemporaries.

While Blue Moon Odom's reemergence had strengthened the rotation, an unexpected source had lifted the bullpen. Converted starter Rollie Fingers, pitching brilliantly in his new role, had surpassed veteran right-hander Bob Locker as the club's best reliever. In six relief stints during the month of June, Fingers did not allow a single run. The string extended his consecutive scoreless innings streak to 29 and two-thirds innings, covering 11 appearances. On July 9, Fingers pitched seven shutout innings of relief during a marathon 20-inning, 1–0 win over the Angels. Fingers had emerged as a capable bullpen successor to Mudcat Grant, who had been the club's best reliever in 1970 prior to the trade that sent him to the Pirates for outfield prospect Angel Mangual. "He's to us now in the bullpen what Vida Blue and Catfish Hunter are to us as starters," gushed an enthusiastic Dick Williams to a reporter.

Although the Oakland brass loved the natural movement of Fingers' pitches, Williams and his coaches had become concerned over his tendency to daydream and become distracted. During a game early in his career, Fingers had tried to hold a potential base stealer close to first base. Fingers spun and pretended to throw to first base, a clear violation of the balk rule. While the rules permitted pitchers to fake pickoff throws to second or third base, Fingers had completely forgotten the most obvious aspect of the balk rule—no fake throws to first base while still in contact with the pitching rubber.

Both on and off the field, Fingers' penchant for daydreaming had become legendary. "He has a rubber arm and a rubber head," one of the A's said good-naturedly to Ron Bergman. Several teammates recalled the time when Fingers was scheduled to take an at-bat during an exhibition game in Salt Lake City. Fingers left the dugout and grabbed his helmet, but forgot one important item—his bat—on his way to home plate. During another game, Fingers and the other pitchers stood for the playing of the National Anthem at the Oakland Coliseum. When the anthem ended, all of his teammates placed their caps back on their heads and sat back down, except for one. Fingers continued to stand, holding his cap over his heart. "I realized [something was wrong] when I heard everybody clapping," Fingers explained to Bergman. "I asked myself, 'Why is everyone clapping?' Then I figured out that the National Anthem had ended. I was just thinking about the ballgame."

On another occasion, Fingers' mind-wandering actually avoided a tragic accident that might have claimed the life of one of the A's' best players. Playing in the California League in 1966, Fingers drove one of his teammates, Steve Kokor, to the minor league stadium in Modesto. Fingers and Kokor became so riveted in conversation that Rollie forgot to pick up two other teammates, a pitcher named Stan Jones and an outfielder named Reggie Jackson, on the way to the ballpark. As they neared the stadium, Fingers drove his car through an intersection. Another vehicle ran through a red light and smashed into Fingers' car, severely damaging the left rear end. The impact crushed and rolled over the back seat, where Jackson and Jones would have been sitting if Fingers had not forgotten to pick them up. "Our roof came right down to the seats," Fingers explained. "If Reggie had been in the back seat, it probably would have been all over for him." Fingers escaped with a bruised ribcage, while Jackson safely made his way to the ballpark in a taxicab.

Fingers' forgetfulness aside, the young right-hander needed to make some on-field adjustments to achieve consistency in the major leagues. The A's had discovered that Fingers' tendency to drop down and throw sidearm harmed his most effective pitch—a sinking fastball. Catcher Dave Duncan and third baseman Sal Bando constantly harped on Fingers to throw over the top, in order to allow the natural "sink" in his fastball to take effect. "Sal is yelling on every pitch, 'Stay on top, stay on top!'" Fingers disclosed to Ron Bergman. "I'm getting to the point where I can figure it out for myself. I'm not dumb."

While the pitching of Fingers and Blue Moon Odom had supplemented the pitching, the A's' hitting had also contributed to the first-half surge. Among the offensive contributors was the newly acquired Mike Epstein, who had overshadowed the other headline player that Oakland had acquired from Washington, Darold Knowles. While Knowles struggled out of Oakland's bullpen, Epstein batted over .300 with 10 home runs in his first 37 games with the A's. "Mike's always been a bear-down son of a gun," Dick Williams informed *The Sporting News*, while praising Epstein for making better contact and expanding his one-dimensional power game. "He's hitting singles and doubles now to drive in runs and he's playing great defensive ball at first base, too." Epstein had so impressed the A's that Williams temporarily abandoned his first-base platoon arrangement with Tommy Davis. Then, Epstein went 0-for-13 against left-handers, prompting Williams to re-institute the platoon with Davis. The decision so upset Epstein that he requested a face-to-face meeting with Williams to discuss the situation. After all, this was Oakland, where peace and serenity never resided for too long without interruption.

Chapter Six

He's Human After All

The A's continued to win games in July despite injuries to two starters, shortstop Campy Campaneris and right fielder Reggie Jackson. Campy missed several weeks with a severely sprained left ankle, while Jackson spent a few games on the sidelines with a pulled hamstring muscle. In their place, Dick Williams called upon his quality supply of reserves, including recently acquired shortstop Larry Brown and young outfielders Angel Mangual and George Hendrick. Dubbed the "Little Clemente" because of his facial and physical resemblance to Pirates right fielder Roberto Clemente, Mangual especially impressed Williams. Through his first 152 at-bats, Mangual batted .322, while playing center and right. Mangual played so well that he had taken away playing time from starting center fielder Rick Monday, who had been slumping.

Jackson, the team's regular right fielder, and third baseman Sal Bando gained election to the American League All-Star team, as did Vida Blue, who had won 17 of 20 decisions, posted a 1.42 ERA, and established himself as baseball's best pitcher over the first half of the season. On July 13, Blue started the Midsummer Classic at Detroit's Tiger Stadium against Dock Ellis of the Pirates. The occasion marked the first All-Star Game in history that pitted two black starting pitchers against each other. Moments before the game, Blue admitted to an extreme case of nerves. "I'm scared stiff," Blue revealed in an interview with *The Sporting News*. "I'm shaking." Yet, Blue's first-inning performance showed no effects of tension, as he retired the side on seven pitches.

The next two innings proved troublesome. Blue permitted a two-run homer to Johnny Bench of the Reds in the second inning and a solo home run to Hank Aaron of the Braves in the third. "When they say the guy throws harder than [Sandy] Koufax," a skeptical Aaron told Dick Young of the *New York Daily News*, "then I gotta say they're a damn liar." Aaron and National League teammate Joe Torre, an infielder with the Cardinals, claimed that five pitchers in their league threw harder than Blue, including the Mets' Tom Seaver and Nolan Ryan, Philadelphia's Steve Carlton, and Houston's Don Wilson.

Still, other observers, such as Astros superscout John Mullen, offered a defense of Blue. "You didn't see the real Vida Blue tonight," Mullen told Dick Young. "His fastball was straight. I've seen him when his fastball moved three ways, in or out or up. He was [just] nervous tonight."

In the bottom of the third, American League manager Earl Weaver sent up Reggie Jackson, a last-minute roster substitute for the injured Tony Oliva, to pinch-hit for Blue. As Jackson left the clubhouse to prepare for his pinch-hitting appearance, Sal Bando jokingly advised him not to strike out. When Dock Ellis reached two strikes on Jackson, Reggie remembered Bando's words. On the next pitch, Jackson assaulted an Ellis fastball, driving it to the deepest lengths of right field. Still seemingly on the rise hundreds of feet from home plate, the ball carried over both decks and caromed off a Tiger Stadium light tower. If the ball had not struck the tower in right-center field, it would have easily cleared the outer dimensions of the ballpark. Some witnesses estimated the home run at 520 feet. "Hardest ball I ever saw hit," observed Detroit's Al Kaline in an interview with Dick Young, while noting he had previously seen teammate Norm Cash hit several titanic shots into the right-field deck at Tiger Stadium. When a reporter asked Jackson for his opinion of the blast, Reggie offered one of his typically blunt responses. "I didn't travel 2,000 miles to strike out," Jackson told Dave Nightingale of the *Chicago Daily News*. Yes, he had managed to heed the advice of Sal Bando.

After the All-Star Game, the A's continued their attack on the rest of the American League. One of Oakland's non-All-Stars, Chuck Dobson, won his ninth consecutive decision before finally losing a game. On July 31, Dobson's record stood at an incredible 10–1. Prior to the season, Dick Williams had examined the veteran right-hander's career record. The ledger of 57 wins and 58 losses did not impress the demanding skipper, who summoned Dobson into his office for a pre-season chat. "So I called him in," Williams related to Ron Bergman, "and said, 'What the hell is this? You're 57 and 58 lifetime? With that arm? On this club?'" Williams continued his line of rhetorical interrogation. "'I'd be embarrassed if I were you. You're pitching on a pennant contender and you're 57 and 58. You know what that means? That means you haven't contributed. Your contributions have been nil.'"

A more sensitive player might have been crushed by Williams' biting commentary. Dobson, an intense competitor on the mound, took a different approach, taking Williams' remarks as a challenge. "Before this year, everybody told me how to pitch, but not how to win," Dobson explained to *The Sporting News*. "I'd go out and lose, 3–2, on an eighth-inning homer and everybody would shake my hand, tell me it was a nice game, tough luck. But it wasn't a nice game. It was a loss."

Dobson was also involved in one of the most interesting off-the-field situations on the A's. Beginning in 1968, Dobson, a white man, had started rooming with Reggie Jackson, an African American, on A's road trips. Earlier in the '68 season, Dobson had roomed with reserve outfielder Jim Gosger. When Dobson slept late and missed three Oakland bus trips, he complained that he needed a roommate who could wake him up. Jackson volunteered for the duty. "You know Reggie," Dobson said in a 1969 interview with Ron Bergman. "He kind of swaggered up to me and said, 'I'll get you up in the morning.'"

In breaking one of baseball's long-standing traditions, Dobson and Jackson became the first regularly paired interracial roommates in major league history.

Jackson and Dobson tried to downplay the significance of the living situation, claiming they were not trying to make a civil rights statement. "I don't want to be known for rooming with a white guy and I don't think Chuck wants to be known for rooming with a Negro guy," Jackson informed *The Sporting News*. Jackson explained that he and Dobson simply enjoyed each other's company.

While such an interracial arrangement would become fairly commonplace in later years, (before teams generally adopted a policy of assigning one player to each hotel room) it was still highly unusual in 1971. Most major league teams continued to assign players of the same skin color to live with each other on the road. Furthermore, most white players preferred to room with each other and most black players elected to do the same.

As well as the A's had played through the first four months of the new season, attendance continued to lag at the Oakland Coliseum. For some reason, the Bay Area did not seem infatuated with a team that featured two dynamic young superstars (Vida Blue and Reggie Jackson) and an array of exciting support players (Campy Campaneris, Sal Bando, Joe Rudi, Catfish Hunter, and Rollie Fingers). During the offseason, Charlie Finley had spent half a million dollars with an advertising firm, which suggested a makeover for the team. As a result, Finley had changed the team's official name from "Athletics" to "A's," and had adopted the slogan, "The Swingin' A's," to lead the advertising campaign. Neither the formal name change nor the quantum leap in the quality of play had succeeded in attracting significantly more fans to the ballpark.

Critics of the Oakland owner pointed to the lack of radio affiliates featuring the A's' broadcasts, which minimized the team's exposure throughout northern California. Others claimed that Finley did not spend enough money in staging promotions. The promotions that Finley did organize usually involved little cash outlay on his part, such as "Hot Pants Day." Some of his other gimmicks, while amusing, did little to attract more fans. Prior to some games, players rode in on his pet mule, appropriately named "Charlie O" in tribute to the owner. "Many of the promotions he draws up are hick-town promotions that don't go over here," explained Bay Area columnist Glenn Dickey, a frequent critic of the owner. "The town is a lot more sophisticated than he is."

During the A's' years in Kansas City, Finley had taken great pride in maintaining a sheep pasture beyond the outfield and in holding an annual "Farmers' Night" at Municipal Stadium. The promotion included a haywagon, a cow-milking contest, a hog-calling demonstration, and a squealing, greased-pig competition. On "Farmers' Night" in 1966, A's catcher Ken Suarez won the hog-calling event, but Catfish Hunter lost the cow-milking to Joe Adcock of the Angels. The team's most promising pitcher, Hunter almost lost the use of his hand when the cow kicked his milking pail three times, denting it in the process. Although "Farmers' Night" in 1966 drew a crowd of over 24,000 in Kansas City, Missouri, such a promotion held little appeal in Oakland, California.

Promotions aside, many fans in the Bay Area seemed turned off by Finley's brash, outlandish style of running the team. "People resent him," said Glenn

Dickey, "because he overshadows the team and because he doesn't live here." Finley, who lived in Chicago almost all-year round, generally attended Opening Day at the Oakland Coliseum, but rarely watched his A's play in person during the regular season.

The Oakland Coliseum represented another problem for Finley. Dubbed the "Oakland Mausoleum," writers described the Coliseum as drab and cavernous, lacking the character of some of the American League's more charming ballyards, like Fenway Park, Tiger Stadium, and Yankee Stadium. Finley also faced direct competition across the Bay, in the form of his National League rivals. Some skeptics questioned the wisdom of having two major league teams in the Bay Area, where the population base indicated a better chance of survival for a single franchise. In 1970, the A's and the San Francisco Giants had basically split a total attendance figure of about 1.5 million fans, with the A's drawing slightly more than half that figure. A team that drew 1.5 million fans in the early seventies was doing well; a team that was drawing half that number was probably losing money.

But not the A's of Charlie Finley. "He was a very shrewd businessman," says Dave Duncan, a pitching coach with the A's, Chicago White Sox, and St. Louis Cardinals in his post-playing days. "He made a statement one time that he had never lost money on his baseball team, and there were a lot of years when there weren't very many fans coming to the ballpark." Only twice during Finley's reign in Oakland—1973 and '75—would the A's draw as many as one million fans in a season. Yet, by keeping player salaries and front office expenses to a minimum, Finley was able to keep his club profitable, at least until the latter stages of the seventies.

On August 7, Vida Blue won his 20th game of the season when he shut out the White Sox on five hits. Blue became the first pitcher in franchise history to reach 20 wins since 1952, when left-hander Bobby Shantz had accomplished the feat for the *Philadelphia* Athletics. Blue managed to win the game, 1–0, despite a bout with nerves and an upset stomach. "I started shaking in the ninth inning because I wanted to win so bad," Blue explained to *The Sporting News*. "I took three Alka Seltzers during the game. That's how shaky I was."

The milestone should have been a pleasant achievement for Blue, but the swarm of media pressure and fan expectation aggravated the young left-hander. Blue had failed to win his 20th game in two previous starts, and had begun to show a dislike for the constant barrage of questions from newspaper reporters and television and radio broadcasters. According to A's beat writer Ron Bergman, Blue had resorted to compiling a list of his 10 most hated questions from reporters.

Earlier in the season, Blue had disclosed to reporters that he carried two dimes in his pocket, to signify his quest for 20 wins. When Blue won his 20th, a reporter asked him if he would carry a *third* dime as a symbol of an effort to win 30 games. Some athletes might have reacted to the question with humor, but Blue responded angrily. "There you go again," Blue snapped, while slamming his fist on a nearby table. "There's that damn pressure."

After Blue won his 22nd game—a difficult 6–4 win over the Yankees that he called his "longest, hardest game"—Blue admitted to having difficulties with his emotional stability. "I feel the tension every day," Blue told a reporter for the Associated Press. "Physically, I'm all right... but I sometimes feel like I'm going to crack up mentally." In an interview with Robert Vare of *Sport* Magazine, Blue described how awkward he felt in the presence of so many media members and their questions. "It's a weird scene," Blue explained to Vare. "You win a few baseball games and all of a sudden you're surrounded by reporters and TV men with cameras, asking you about Vietnam and race relations, and stuff about yourself. Man, I'm only a kid. I don't know exactly who I am. I don't have a whole philosophy of life set down."

Although Blue was still pitching well, he had ceased being the dominant pitcher the A's had become accustomed to watching during the first half of the season. Blue's heavy reliance on his fastball may have contributed to his August falloff. "He threw 95 per cent fastballs in 1971," Dick Williams would say two years later in an interview with Larry Eldridge of the *Christian Science Monitor*. "He just blew it by them. But he did tire some in the second half of the season." By August, American League hitters had started to familiarize themselves with Blue's simplistic pitching pattern.

Other factors caused Blue's performance to level off. Aside from the media pressure, Charlie Finley's insistence on using Blue on short rest, in order to maximize the number of starts that he made at the Oakland Coliseum, had taken a toll on Vida's left arm. Extra starts on three days rest and a pileup of midsummer innings had removed some of the life from Blue's fastball. The unnecessary juggling of the rotation had also affected the timing and rhythm of Catfish Hunter, who was usually pushed back a day or two in order to accommodate the added starts for Blue.

In August, the A's faced two weeks of play without the availability of starting catcher Dave Duncan, who had performed admirably in his role of quarterbacking the pitching staff, Blue in particular. Duncan wasn't hurt; like many other major league players during the Vietnam War, he had to serve two weeks of duty in the Marine Reserves. The absence of Duncan forced Williams to use little-known backup Gene Tenace in a starting role.

In 1965, the A's had drafted Tenace out of high school in Lucasville, Ohio, where he starred as an all-state *shortstop* and played on the same American Legion team as future major leaguers Al Oliver and Larry Hisle. The A's quickly switched Tenace to the outfield, where he appeared clumsy and unsure. In one minor league game for Peninsula of the Carolina League, Tenace showed his versatility by playing all nine positions, as a promotional means of drawing more fans to the ballpark. In 1968, with the A's owning a bevy of young outfielders—including Joe Rudi, Rick Monday and Reggie Jackson—Tenace thought about quitting. The organization responded to the overload by converting Tenace to catcher. The A's felt confident that Tenace, an excellent hitter with power, could make the adjustment to a radically different position, which happened to be one of the thinnest throughout the Oakland system. Tenace proceeded to work with former major league catcher Gus Niarhos, the manager of the A's' affiliate in Birmingham, Alabama.

Niarhos compared Tenace to his former teammate with the Yankees, Yogi Berra, also a catcher converted from the outfield. Tenace impressed Niarhos with his strong throwing arm, but struggled in other phases of defensive play. By 1970, largely on the strength of his bat, Tenace reached the major leagues to stay. He batted .305 in his rookie season and succeeded in wresting the No. 1 catching job away from Frank Fernandez and Dave Duncan during the final month of the regular season.

When Dick Williams became the A's' manager, he had announced his preference for a defensive-minded catcher who could handle pitchers. Prior to the 1971 season, Williams declared an open competition on the catching position. Duncan, a far superior defensive receiver to either Tenace or Fernandez, won the three-way battle during spring training.

Now Williams was entrusting his pitching staff to the defensively challenged Tenace. Hitting, though, did not present a similar concern. During a 13-game road trip, Tenace batted a robust .500 with 11 RBIs, raising his season batting average to .322. That came as no surprise; the A's had always recognized Tenace's ample ability with the bat. On the same road trip, Tenace also displayed an improved knack for handling Oakland's pitching staff. None of the A's' pitchers, privately or publicly, complained about Tenace's pitch-calling or general defensive skills behind the plate.

Tenace's surprising all-around performance on the long road trip helped the A's increase their lead in the American League West from 10 to 14 and a half games. It also left Williams with a dilemma. What would happen when Duncan returned from his short tour of duty in the Marines? Williams tried to sidestep the question, saying that he would give Duncan some extra time off to get back into playing shape. As if the Marines would allow Duncan to get out of shape in the first place!

Oakland beat writers asked Tenace about the possibility of remaining in the starting lineup after Duncan's return. Tenace answered the question with a combination of diplomacy and chutzpah. "It's not up to me to decide who'll play. That's No. 23's [Williams'] decision," Tenace said politely to Ron Bergman. "But if I do my job and he takes me out, then I think he'll be making a mistake. But it's his decision." Williams was clearly facing his first major controversy in regard to playing time for his catchers.

Despite Oakland's commanding lead in the West, Charlie Finley continued to tinker with his roster. During spring training, Pirates general manager Joe Brown had promised Finley that if and when he decided to unload veteran reliever Mudcat Grant, he would give the Oakland owner the first chance at trading for him. On August 10, Brown, living up to his promise, sold the soon-to-be 36-year-old Grant to the A's for the waiver price of $25,000. After pitching brilliantly for the Pirates the first two months of the season, the aging Grant had fallen into an extended pitching slump. The Pirate brass worried that Grant's days of effective pitching had come to an end.

In September of 1970, the A's had traded Grant to the Pirates for a player to be named later, which turned out to be young outfielder Angel Mangual. In an embarrassing mistake, the A's had misspelled the outfielder's name, referring to him as Mangu*e*l five times in an introductory press release. In the meantime, Oakland writers and fans roasted Finley for making the deal. Oakland players privately questioned Finley's sanity. In 72 games with the A's, Grant had saved 24 games, forged an ERA of 1.83, and emerged as one of the American League's most effective firemen. Without Grant, the A's lacked an established closer.

If not for Grant's return to Oakland's bullpen in 1971, Rollie Fingers might not have developed into the game's most consistently effective reliever of the 1970s. "I learned how to become a reliever from Grant," Fingers told a reporter for *Baseball Magazine* many years later. Fingers watched Mudcat attack opposing hitters by mixing his pitches, rather than trying to rely on one dominant pitch. Fingers also observed the different ways that Grant warmed up in the bullpen. "If a pitcher in the game gets out of a jam, I stop warming up and sit down," Fingers explained to *Baseball Magazine*. "If he gets in another jam, I don't go at it hard in the bullpen. A lot of relievers burn themselves out in the bullpen." Grant did not, and as a result, Fingers didn't, either

Grant also supplied the A's with a positive clubhouse force, as he had done earlier in his career with the Indians and Twins. As an African American, Grant became one of the few black stars to populate the Twin Cities area in the 1960s. "He was really the catalyst of that [Minnesota] team," says former Twins beat writer Bob Fowler. "First of all, he was black. I think that was very significant to the Minnesota franchise. He wasn't Cuban. He was [an American] *black*. And the Minnesota area is basically Scandinavian. Sandy Stevens was a quarterback at the University of Minnesota in '61, when they went to the Rose Bowl. And Bill Muncie was a running back then. They had a couple of good [black] college basketball players…But we didn't have one [African-American star] in baseball."

Upon his arrival in Minnesota in 1964, Grant quickly made an impact on his Twins' teammates. "Mudcat came in and he was a loosy-goosy guy," Fowler explains. "But the Minnesota team basically was a white team, outside of the Latins we had. It was basically a white team. And he came into that clubhouse, and he was the synergy of that ballclub. Harmon [Killebrew] was a quiet guy. Bob Allison was a quiet guy. We had a clubhouse of quiet guys. And Mudcat was sort of the spark, really."

Grant served as a role model for his black teammates, while helping to unite players from different racial backgrounds. "Oh, I think so," says Fowler. "Yes, I would definitely say that. He was a guy that players, whether they were black or white, looked up to. So, consequentially, if you were black, you may have looked up to him more so. Here was a guy who was admired by everybody. Liked by everybody. Didn't have an enemy." Favored by both teammates and the Oakland media, the smiling Grant always seemed upbeat, supplying a counterbalance to the moodiness of stars like Reggie Jackson and Vida Blue.

By re-acquiring Grant, Charlie Finley also saw a chance to reverse his original trade, a deal that had brought him criticism from the players, media, and fans. Furthermore, Finley loved to bring back players he had previously traded or released. The list of re-acquisitions already featured Tommy Davis, "Broadway" Frank Fernandez, and Diego Segui. Finley especially enjoyed bringing back such players in exchange for less compensation than he had originally surrendered. For example, Finley had originally traded Grant to the Pirates for Angel Mangual, considered a top-flight prospect in the Pittsburgh organization. Now, Finley had reacquired Grant for a small sum of cash, without having to yield any players in return.

Upon completing the deal, Finley phoned Grant in Pittsburgh almost immediately. According to an interview with Grant in *The Sporting News*, Finley delivered the following plea: " 'We need you. Join the team in Boston as quick as you can.' " Grant explained that he first needed to take care of some business in Pittsburgh over the next couple of days. Finley would have none of it. "Charlie screamed into the phone, 'Oh no you don't,' " said Grant. " 'You've got to be with the club tomorrow.' " The telephone exchange, blending anger with a tinge of humor, typified the association between Finley and Grant. "Every now and then it was a little bit fiery," Mudcat recalls, "but it was generally a good relationship."

Grant followed Finley's orders about reporting to the A's immediately and arrived the following day, just in time to pitch in the second game of an August 10th day-night doubleheader in Boston. In the nightcap, Williams summoned Grant to relieve Blue Moon Odom with two outs in the sixth inning. Sporting his trademark mutton chop sideburns, Grant proceeded to pitch three and a third innings of one-run baseball. Grant saved a 7–5 win for Odom and the A's, giving Oakland a sweep of its doubleheader against the Red Sox. A classic Finley trade had delivered an immediate reward for the A's.

Within days, Grant noticed a distinct change in the A's from the time he had spent with the club in 1970. "I've seen more guys give themselves up," Grant informed Ron Bergman, "like hit behind the runner, in one week than I did all of last year. You've got to give Williams credit. He's done a tremendous job to orchestrate things." The re-acquisition of Grant also gave the A's of 1971 another distinct advantage over the team of 1970. Now, the A's had two quality firemen in Grant and Fingers, as opposed to just one.

Much to the delight of Charlie Finley, Grant also added a dash of color. The veteran pitcher had the A's' clubhouse man stitch the letters, "MUDCAT," on the back of his uniform jersey, in lieu of the traditional use of the letters of his last name, "GRANT." The fashion statement was reminiscent of something that several of Finley's players had done during the franchise's years in Kansas City. In the early 1960s, catcher Doc Edwards wore his nickname above his number on the back of his vest jersey. Shortstop Wayne Causey, the predecessor to Campy

Campaneris, wore "KOOZ" on his uniform shirt. And popular outfielder Rocky Colavito joined in the trend by sporting "ROCK" on the back side of his jersey.

Finley liked the uniform innovation so much that he encouraged other players to wear their nicknames, or their first names, on the backs of their shirts. In 1973, Vida Blue would wear the name, "VIDA," on the back of his jersey and Billy Conigliaro would feature the letters, "BILLY C." Future Athletic Dick Allen would use the word, "WAMPUM," on the back of his jersey, signifying the name of his hometown in Pennsylvania.

Finley's willingness to tinker with the traditional baseball uniform typified his efforts toward innovation. "He was a good promotional person," says Mudcat Grant. "Charlie advocated some things that baseball was against but found out a little bit later on that they were actually good ideas. For example, the uniforms. Finley came up with the idea of having the A's wear two or three uniforms [instead of the standard white at home and gray on the road]. And little things like the mechanical 'rabbit' [located behind home plate], delivering the ball to the umpires." As for the latter innovation, Finley had introduced the rabbit during the team's days in Kansas City, but eventually abandoned it during the team's tenure in Oakland.

Finley enjoyed making other alterations to the traditional ballpark setting, as part of his scheme to bring color and dash to the sport. Bored with the traditional white-colored bases used throughout the major leagues, Finley once instructed his grounds crew to paint the bases at the Oakland Coliseum a bright gold. The innovation lasted briefly—until major league officials instructed Finley that gold bases did not conform to the game's official rules. On another occasion, Finley suggested a multi-colored approach, indicating that each base be painted a different color: one red, another yellow, and the third blue. Not surprisingly, that innovation never came to pass, again falling by the wayside because of baseball's stringent set of rules.

The rulesmakers, however, could not prevent Finley from successfully introducing another newfangled ballpark feature. Disdaining the tradition of ballboys, Finley employed attractive ballgirls, who wore tight-fitting outfits and carried cookies and water to the umpires in the middle of each game. One of the ballgirls, a young lady named Debbi Sivyer, eventually reached her own level of fame when he she became the founder and owner of *Mrs. Fields Cookies*.

Without the benefit of cookies—and without actually playing in the game that day—one of the A's' bench players contributed to a tough road win over the Yankees on August 14. Backup catcher Curt Blefary lent his bat to Sal Bando, who drove in the game's lone run with a ninth-inning single. Bando had been slumping while using his regular bat, so he decided to try Blefary's bat, a slightly lighter model. Aided by the fractional increase in wrist quickness and bat speed, Bando lined a game-deciding single against Yankee right-hander Steve Kline, accounting for the 1–0 win.

The following day, the New Yorkers staged an unusual promotion at Yankee Stadium. Instead of giving away a traditional freebie or honoring one of the great players from their rich and storied past, the Yankees paid tribute to the *opposition's* starting pitcher. "Vida Blue Day" attracted over 45,000 fans to Yankee Stadium. The Yankees granted free admission to all customers named Blue—126 people showed up with identification proving their monikers—and printed special game-day programs that featured a blue tint. Blue, who battled fatigue but seemed undisturbed by the Yankees' offbeat recognition of his celebrity, pitched the A's to a 6–4 victory. "I've been sharper, but I've never been more tired," Blue revealed to Joe Durso of the *New York Times* after the game.

On August 17, as the A's prepared to face Washington in the start of a two-game road series, Oakland players received an audience with United States President Richard M. Nixon. President Nixon chatted with manager Dick Williams, who then introduced each of his players and coaches to the nation's highest-ranking official. Nixon, a die-hard baseball fan, exchanged several words with each player. Blue offered the President a modern "soul" handshake, saying, "That's the way we do." Later, Nixon posed with the Oakland players for a group photo, and then held up an A's cap, given to him by Blue. "You must be the most underpaid player in the game," the President told the 22-game winner, who was making only $13,000 in 1971. "I would hate to negotiate your contract next year." Blue appreciated the President's endorsement, which didn't figure to hurt Vida's bargaining power. Blue's best friend on the A's, Tommy Davis, also commended the President on his ability to talk baseball. "I was very impressed with his knowledge of the game," Davis told a reporter for the Associated Press.

The A's' contingent at the White House included backup first baseman Mike Hegan, who says the meeting with the President revealed a side to Finley not often acknowledged or seen by the general public. "Shortly after I joined the ballclub—of course Vida was having his big year and was the talk of the country—we were going into D.C.," says Hegan, "and President Nixon wanted to meet Vida Blue. Charlie wouldn't have anything to do with it; he said, 'Either he meets the whole ballclub or he doesn't meet anybody.' So, they set up a reception for the entire ballclub with the President in the Oval Office." With little publicity, Finley had shown even the President that the concept of "team" mattered more than any individual celebrity.

Perhaps distracted by their visit to the White House, the A's lost two straight games in Washington. The defeats, however, did little to dampen what had been a productive stretch for the team. Prior to the visit to RFK Stadium, the A's had won seven straight games. They had also captured 12 consecutive decisions on the road. The A's would go on to win nine of their last 12 games in August to finish the month with 23 wins and a mere eight losses. As well as the A's had played from April to July, they had exhibited their best ball-playing ability during the month of August.

In spite of their high level of play, Oakland fans continued to show a lack of interest in the A's. In late August, the A's hosted the Yankees in a three-game set at the Oakland Coliseum. While the Yankees usually drew better on the road than any other team in the American League, the series in Oakland managed to lure a total of only 29,110 fans. Even that figure was deceptively high, considering that over 18,000 of those fans had shown up for the middle game of the series, a 1–0 game lost by drawing card Vida Blue.

At the end of August, the frequent journeys of backup catcher Frank Fernandez continued. Now that Dave Duncan had returned from his stint in the Marine Reserves, the A's were back to full strength behind the plate and traded Fernandez—yet again! On August 31, Oakland sent Fernandez and minor leaguer infield prospect Bill McNulty to the Chicago Cubs for minor league outfielder Adrian Garrett. By the end of the season, Fernandez' 1971 itinerary would read as follows:

— Oakland to Washington
— Washington to Iowa
— Iowa to Oakland
— Oakland to Iowa
— Iowa to Chicago

As the A's began play in September, their record stood at 87–47, a phenomenal 40 games above the .500 mark. With a 16-game lead on the Royals, the American League West had long since been decided. Only a few questions remained. Would Vida Blue reach the elusive 30-victory plateau? Would Catfish Hunter win 20 games for the first time in his career? And which Oakland player would win the American League MVP Award, the heralded Blue or underrated third baseman Sal Bando?

Some baseball writers opposed the idea of selecting a starting pitcher for the Most Valuable Player Award. They reasoned that since a typical starter pitched only once every four or five days, he could not possess the same value as an everyday position player. Other writers felt that the MVP should be reserved solely for catchers, infielders, and outfielders, even though MVP guidelines specifically indicated that pitchers *should* be given consideration. Those writers surmised that pitchers had their own award—the Cy Young. A's manager Dick Williams shared that opinion in an interview with *The Sporting News*. "That's why they made that special award, the Cy Young Award. That's why it was invented, in my opinion."

According to Sal Bando, Williams' philosophy regarding MVP voting has plenty of merit. "I agree with him," Bando says. "I don't think a starting pitcher should qualify for the Most Valuable Player. That player is only out there every fourth or fifth day. I would change that in terms of a relief pitcher. A relief pitcher would qualify as an MVP because he's out there a lot more when the game's on the line. So I do think it's an unfair criteria that a starting pitcher qualifies as the Most Valuable Player."

Yet, recent history dictated otherwise. In 1968, Denny McLain had won 31 games for the pennant-winning Tigers. After the season, the Baseball Writers' Association of American rewarded McLain with both the MVP and Cy Young awards. If Blue could approach the 30-win level for the division-winning A's, precedent might dictate that Blue win both of the prestigious awards.

Risking the wrath of Blue, Dick Williams cast his unofficial, but public MVP vote for Sal Bando. After an early-season slump, Bando had cashed in on a tip from batting coach Irv Noren, who had suggested that he stop dropping his elbow during his swing. Through games of September 2, the A's' captain was batting .278 with 19 homers and 84 RBIs, had played exceptional defense at third base, and had provided the team with its largest dose of day-to-day leadership. "You can see what Sal means to us when he's in there," Williams explained to *The Sporting News.* "Whether he bats in a run or not. It's just his presence." Williams also credited several other players, including Reggie Jackson, Dave Duncan, and the underrated second baseman, Dick Green. "But if I had to get down to one," Williams said, "it would be Sal."

While some Bay Area writers expected a close vote between Bando and Blue, the Baseball Writers' Association of America would issue a convincing mandate in favor of one of the two stars. The media coverage given Blue throughout the season helped his cause; he appeared on the covers of *Sports Illustrated* and *Sport* Magazine, and even made the cover page of the highly respected non-sports weekly magazine, *Time*. Blue also made guest appearances on two nationwide television programs, the *Dick Cavett Show* and NBC's *Today* Show. "He had such a dominant year," says Bando in retrospect, "that you couldn't help but write about him and talk about him. I've never seen anyone—maybe [Bob] Gibson's year in St. Louis [in 1968] would be comparable—but Vida just had a phenomenal year."

In voting announced after the World Series, the writers would name Blue on all 24 ballots, giving him 14 first-place votes. One week earlier, those same writers made him the youngest winner in the history of the Cy Young Award. Blue thus became only the fifth pitcher to win both the Cy Young and the MVP in the same season, joining Denny McLain, Bob Gibson, Don Newcombe, and Sandy Koufax—the man he had been compared to so often—on the list of double winners. As for Bando, he received four first-place votes and trailed Blue in the final MVP balloting, 268 points to 182.

Was Bando disappointed that he finished second in the MVP balloting? "As it turns out," responds Bando, "I was the most valuable *position player* that year, being beaten out by a pitcher. Yeah, I was disappointed because that's something that comes once in a lifetime. I had a good year at an inopportune time and it didn't happen." Although Bando would enjoy a fine career with both the A's and Brewers, he would never win a Most Valuable Player Award. Bando would place as high as third in 1974, when he finished behind MVP Jeff Burroughs of the Rangers and his own A's teammate, Joe Rudi.

On September 13, Catfish Hunter attempted to join Vida Blue as fellow 20-game winners. Hunter faced the Royals, the surprising second-place residents of the Western Division. Pitching masterfully, Hunter edged the Royals, 2–1, to post his 20th win. In the process, Catfish rapped out two hits to raise his season batting average to an incredible .357. Hunter may have been the second-best pitcher on Oakland's staff behind Blue, but he ranked as the best *hitting* pitcher in all of baseball.

For the first time in his major league career, Hunter had reached the 20-win plateau for a single season. In appreciation of the achievement, Charlie Finley promised to reward his ace right-hander with a Cadillac, much like he had done with Blue earlier in the season. Hunter initially told Finley that he preferred the car to be royal blue, with a white vinyl top, but later on asked the owner to take the money he would have spent on the Cadillac and invest it in some stocks. Cadillacs and blue chips aside, the milestone represented the high point of Hunter's young career. "This 20th win," Catfish told *The Sporting News*, "[means] more to me than the perfect game [I threw] in 1968."

On May 8 of that 1968 season, Hunter had faced the minimum 27 batters in achieving a piece of baseball immortality. Hunter struck out 11 batters in carving a 4–0 shutout against the hard-hitting Twins. With two outs in the ninth inning, Hunter struck out pinch-hitter Rich Reese on a three-and-two count to finish off what A's coach Joe DiMaggio termed "a masterpiece." Normally relying on control and finesse, Hunter possessed an unusually strong repertoire of pitches that night. "Jimmy was always a very strong control pitcher," says Jim Pagliaroni, who caught Hunter's perfect game. "But that night, not only did he have a hopping fastball moving around quite a bit, but he could throw his curveball [for strikes] at will. His slider was breaking exceptionally well. Plus, he also had a great change-up. It's quite unusual when a pitcher keeps all of his pitches throughout the game—you usually have to work around one [ineffective] pitch—but Jimmy literally hit the spot. He was exceptional that night."

And much like he did in winning his 20th game of 1971, Hunter ably supported his own cause at the plate, driving in three runs in the perfect game against Minnesota. Hunter also exhibited his typical modesty, refusing his teammates' attempt to lift him onto their shoulders in appreciation of his perfect game. "I just wanted to get out of there as quickly as possible," Hunter explained to Pat Jordan of *Sport* Magazine. "I was too embarrassed."

In 1970, Hunter won 18 games, but struggled through a typically torturous August, when he failed to win a game. Hunter's August swoon had been caused, at least in part, by a loan given to him by Charlie Finley. Prior to the 1970 season, Finley had loaned Hunter $150,000, which Catfish planned to use to purchase some property. Hunter had agreed to pay back $20,000 at the end of each season in addition to six per cent interest. Finley, however, couldn't wait. He began pestering Hunter regularly to pay back the loan. "It seemed like he never called me about it except on days when I was going to pitch," Hunter revealed later in an interview with Paul Hemphill of *Sport* Magazine. "I started eight games that August and didn't have a single win the whole month." Hunter asked Finley why he insisted on calling on those days on which he was scheduled to start. "He said he didn't know who was going to pitch when," Hunter related to Hemphill. "That's bull. Charlie Finley knows more about the ballclub than the manager." Exasperated by Finley's stubborn attempts to secure the loan money, Hunter decided to sell off several acres of the land he had purchased and pay the owner the money.

August of 1971 proved far more fruitful for Hunter, who went a career-best 5–1, putting him on track for the 20-victory mark. Hunter also displayed the ability to pitch deeper into games. He had already thrown 16 complete games in 1971, compared to only nine the previous season. Hunter credited much of his improvement to a change that pitching coach Bill Posedel had made in his pitching motion. Instead of raising his hands above his head at the start of his windup, Hunter kept his hands closer to his waist. The adjustment allowed Hunter to hide the baseball behind his left knee, thereby preventing opposing hitters from seeing the ball as quickly as they had in the past. Hunter gave full credit to his pitching coach for the prosperous change in motion.

Hunter's ability to pinpoint his pitches, his inclination to pitch quickly, and his accommodating nature made him a welcome partner for his catchers, especially No. 1 receiver Dave Duncan. "Catfish adjusts easily," Duncan told writer Pat Jordan. "If I call a curveball and he's thinking fastball, he just reprograms himself for my pitch. He never shakes me off. He just reprograms his mind and then my pitch really becomes his pitch. This makes him an easy man to catch."

Two days after Hunter claimed his 20th victory, the A's officially laid claim to a team milestone. After the A's won the first game of a doubleheader with the White Sox, the second-place Royals then fell to the Angels, officially clinching Oakland's first American League West title. Fittingly, the team's most valuable everyday player, Sal Bando, hit a two-run home run in the top of the eighth inning to give the A's a come-from-behind, 3–2 win. The recently acquired Mudcat Grant also hurled three shutout innings of relief to pick up his first win for the A's since his trade from Pittsburgh.

Bando's home run and Grant's relief work had helped the A's to their first title of any kind in Oakland or Kansas City franchise history. (The franchise had won numerous championships during its tenure in Philadelphia.) Oakland players held a subdued celebration in the visitors' clubhouse at Comiskey Park. The A's decided not to revel *too* loudly for two reasons. First of all, they had lost the second game of the doubleheader to the White Sox, 7–3. Secondly, the clinching had come as a mere formality. The A's had held possession of first place since April 20. By the end of June, Oakland had constructed a 10-game lead. By the completion of August, the gap had grown to a season-high 17 games. After building up such a sizable lead on the Royals, the team had known for weeks that it would win the division. The A's were now setting sights on beating the defending World Champion Baltimore Orioles, who would provide the opposition in the American League Championship Series.

After the clinching, Dick Williams elected to limit his starting pitchers to five innings per outing, unless their pitch counts were remarkably low. Williams wanted to ensure that his top three starters—Vida Blue, Catfish Hunter, and Chuck Dobson—would be fully rested for the playoff series against the favored Orioles. Blue and Hunter had already amassed a large total of innings, while Dobson required constant monitoring due to his troublesome elbow.

The A's played out the string over the final two weeks of the season, and finished September with 14 wins and 13 losses. Although the record represented the A's' worst for any single month, they had still managed to post winning ledgers in April, May, June, July, August, September, and October—in other words, every month of the regular season. Along the way to a record of 101 wins and 60 losses, the A's dominated their Western Division rivals. The A's won 10 of 18 games against the Twins, who had dominated Oakland the previous two seasons. The A's performed even better against the Royals and Angels, winning 13 and 11 games, respectively.

In the area of team pitching, the A's finished second only to the Orioles. A fatigued Vida Blue tailed off in August and September, settling for 24 wins, second most in the American League to Tigers ace Mickey Lolich. Blue did capture the league's ERA title, allowing a mere 1.82 runs per nine innings. Catfish Hunter finished with 21 victories, 16 complete games, and an ERA of 2.96. Chuck Dobson and Blue Moon Odom, both huge question marks at the start of the season due to physical ailments, combined to win 25 games. Right-handers Rollie Fingers, Bob Locker, Diego Segui, and mid-season pickup Mudcat Grant all pitched effectively in relief, giving the A's one of the major leagues' deepest bullpens. Fingers saved a staff-high 17 games despite opening the season in the starting rotation. One of the few pitching disappointments was left-hander Darold Knowles, who saved seven games after being acquired in mid-season, but failed to re-capture the form that he had displayed with the Senators in 1970.

On the hitting side, the A's scored 691 runs, putting them in a third-place tie with the Red Sox in the American League rankings. Although Reggie Jackson did not experience the breakout season that many had anticipated, the slugging right fielder still led all A's regulars with a .277 average, 32 home runs, and 19 game-winning hits. Hustling at all times, Jackson swiped 16 stolen bases and greatly improved his defensive play. "My attitude is better," Reggie explained to Ron Fimrite of *Sports Illustrated* during the season. "Last year I was thinking in my own little circle." Team captain Sal Bando finished with 24 home runs and a team-leading 94 RBIs. Mike Epstein ripped 18 home runs and delivered 11 game-winning hits after joining the team from Washington. Epstein's platoon partner at first base, Tommy Davis, batted a team-high .324 with 42 RBIs in only 219 at-bats. Dave Duncan, Dick Green, Joe Rudi, and Rick Monday all contributed power hitting and capable defense.

Campy Campaneris, the team's everyday shortstop, represented one of the few offensive disappointments for the A's. In 1970, Campaneris had slugged a career-high 22 home runs. "He hit some home runs leading off one year," Rollie Fingers says, recalling Campy's unusual power output in 1970. "Right out of the shoot, you were up 1–0, and that certainly helped."

Campaneris failed to find a similar power stroke in 1971. He didn't hit for a high average either, struggling through an up-and-down season at the plate. Much to the chagrin of Dick Williams, Campaneris tried to hit home runs the way he had in 1970, rather than concentrate on putting the ball in play and getting on base. "We called him 'Baby Hondo,' " Fingers says with a chuckle, "because everybody thought he swung the bat like Frank Howard [of the Washington Senators]." The six-foot, seven-inch Howard weighed well over 250 pounds, while Campaneris measured five feet, 10 inches tall and weighed barely 155 pounds. Using a long, overextended swing, Campaneris hit only five home runs and saw his batting average, runs scored, and stolen base totals fall off from his career-best season of 1970. On the plus side, Campy did rebound from a poor start defensively—which had seen him make 10 errors in his first 24 games, including errors in four consecutive games—and began to emerge as a reliable, sure-handed shortstop who still had excellent range to either side of the ball. That was just the kind of play the A's hoped to receive from Campaneris—and all of their defenders—in their first-ever appearance in the American League Championship Series.

Chapter Seven

Facing the Defending Champs

The A's had known since August that their playoff opposition would be provided by the Baltimore Orioles, the 1970 World Champions. The usually penurious Finley spared no expense in preparing to face major league baseball's elite team. Finley hired former Tiger manager Mayo Smith specifically for the purpose of tracking and scouting the Orioles in September. Thanks to the work of Smith and other Oakland advance scouts like Al "Boots" Hollingsworth and Sherm Lollar, Finley presented Dick Williams with a thickly-bound scouting report, replete with a green and gold cover. The document provided Williams and his coaches with infinite details on the strengths, weaknesses, and tendencies of the defending American League champs.

While he was adding employees in the area of scouting, Finley was losing employees in other departments. As the A's were making Championship Series—and potentially World Series arrangements—public relations director Mike Haggerty announced his resignation. Haggerty's secretary, Mary Brubaker, also left the front office. The untimely departures left the A's without a public relations department, at a time of the season when they needed such a staff more than ever. Finley would not replace Haggerty until after the season, when he made play-by-play man Monte Moore the interim public relations director. In the spring of 1972, just before the start of the new season, Finley would finally get around to hiring a full-time person for the job when he transferred Art Popham from the team's promotions department. In hiring Popham, Finley had saved himself from adding another salary to his skeleton front office staff.

Finley learned to save money in other ways, too. He sometimes hired relatives, like his nephew, Carl Finley. The owner also employed young staff members, whose lack of experience allowed him to pay them smaller wages. For example, Finley once hired a teen-aged boy named Stanley Burrell, whom he discovered breakdancing one day in front of the Oakland Coliseum. Initially hired as a batboy, Burrell was later given the title of "executive vice president," but actually served as a glorified "gofer." The young Burrell would eventually find much more legitimate success when he changed careers, switching from baseball to the music industry. As a professional rap star, the resourceful and talented Burrell became known as "M.C. Hammer." (Burrell would owe part of his new identity to A's players, who remarked that he bore a physical resemblance to Atlanta Braves star Hank Aaron, also known by the nickname, "Hammer.")

Prior to the playoff series against the Orioles, Dick Williams raised the possibility of benching his regular first baseman, Mike Epstein, and replacing him with Tommy Davis or mid-season pickup Mike Hegan. Although Epstein had initially hit well after joining the team from Washington, he had slumped in the second half. During one failed stretch, Epstein had gone 45 days without hitting a home run. "I'd stopped swinging," Epstein explained to Arnold Hano of *Sport Magazine*. "I was just *feeling* for the ball." Epstein's sullen nature had also annoyed Williams. "He's too big to mope," the A's' manager said of Epstein in an interview with Ron Bergman. "We've got to play the men who're doing the job. I don't know who'll start in the playoffs."

Epstein presented a strange defense of his second-half performance. "You can't expect superstar statistics from someone not making superstar money," Epstein reasoned in an interview with *The Sporting News*. "I'm just an average ballplayer trying to do his job. Why do people expect me to hit 40 or even 30 home runs a year? I'll hit 20." Then, in a lighter mood, Epstein joked about his abilities. "You can't polish a turd," the wisecracking first baseman told Arnold Hano of *Sport Magazine*. While most players tended to have overinflated opinions of their own value, Epstein seemed willing to belittle his own talents. Or, perhaps Epstein was making a ploy for a sizable pay increase after the season. *If the A's pay me more money*, Epstein seemed to be saying, *then I will produce better offensive numbers.*

After considering his options, Dick Williams ultimately retained Epstein's services against Baltimore's right-handers in the playoffs. Epstein would platoon with the righty-hitting Tommy Davis, who paid the Orioles the utmost compliment prior to the series. "The toughest [post-season] series will be with Baltimore, not the National League winner," said Davis in an interview with Ron Fimrite of *Sports Illustrated*. In other words, Davis and some of the other Oakland players regarded their series with the O's as the *true* World Series. As such, confident Baltimore fans had already dubbed their city "Flagtown USA."

On another front, the A's learned that Blue Moon Odom would be unavailable for the Championship Series against the Orioles. Odom had experienced a dead arm, having accumulated a workload of 141 post-surgical innings. The A's deactivated Odom for the post-season, replacing him with journeyman Ron Klimkowski. The right-handed reliever, acquired in the Felipe Alou deal, had pitched effectively for the A's in between trips to the minor leagues.

The loss of Odom didn't appear to hurt the A's too significantly since Dick Williams figured to go with only three starters in the playoffs: Vida Blue, Catfish Hunter, and Chuck Dobson. Yet, there remained a question: who would start in Game One, Blue or Hunter? Some players, including captain Sal Bando, suggested the possibility of using Hunter, who had been Oakland's best starter over the last six weeks. Williams chose Blue instead. On paper, the first game matchup of Vida Blue against any one of the Orioles' fine pitchers seemed to favor the A's; after all,

Blue and Detroit's Mickey Lolich had outclassed all other American League starters in 1971.

A closer look at Blue's season, however, revealed some reasons for worry. Blue had ceased being a dominant pitcher over the final two months of the regular season. He had won only four games since August 7, perhaps the result of pitching too heavy a workload. With his second-half struggles a concern, one reporter asked Orioles slugger Frank Robinson if he expected to see a "different" Blue in the playoffs. "Why?" Robinson responded sarcastically to the question from Murray Chass of the *New York Times*. "Is he pitching right-handed?"

An even greater concern for the A's involved the mindset of Blue, who continued to display a high level of irritation with the media. Blue arrived late as the A's worked out prior to the first game against Baltimore. Blue did not dress with the other players and brushed off several attempts at interviews. "I can't talk to you," Blue said to one reporter. When the writer asked why, Blue responded, "Because I don't want to." Any reporter looking for cogent analysis or insight would have to look elsewhere.

Blue walked off to the sanctuary of the trainer's room—deemed off limits to reporters—putting a quick end to the media's attempts at interrogation. "Don't ask questions because I'm going back to the hotel and going to sleep," Blue declared to the *New York Times*. "Sorry this is just one of my moods." Blue shortness with the media was apparently prompted by a recent gossip column item. The article, written by a non-baseball writer, speculated as to the skin color of Blue's girlfriend. The invasion of privacy did not sit well with Blue. "I don't know whether that's what has him put out," said roommate and friend Tommy Davis in an interview with *The Sporting News*, "but if that's what it is, I don't blame him one bit." The gossip column's intrusive theme, coupled with its racial implications, clearly angered Davis. "What business is it of anyone?" Davis asked rhetorically. "He goes out with a number of girls. Maybe his girlfriend is chartreuse, who knows? Who keeps track?"

Although Blue had justification to be upset with the gossip column, his outward personality had undergone an alteration since the first half of the season. "I think he's changed," a vigilant Sal Bando told the Associated Press. "The fame has changed him some. He's been more of a loner. He doesn't talk to many people... He's not as carefree as when he first started."

Perhaps out of consideration for the recent spate of lackluster pitching by Blue, or perhaps out of respect for Baltimore's previous post-season experience, the oddsmakers installed the Orioles as favorites to win the playoff series. Negative prognostications aside, Dick Williams expressed confidence over his team's ability to challenge the defending American League titlists. "I don't think they'll beat us three straight," Williams proclaimed to Murray Chass of the *New York Times*, "but I think *we* can beat them three straight."

The best-of-five playoff series opened at Baltimore's Memorial Stadium. Playing the first two games on the road didn't figure to faze the A's, who had won an American League record 55 games away from home. The A's also expressed relief that Earl Weaver had chosen Dave McNally, one of Baltimore's four 20-game winners but not the staff ace, to start Game One. "I'm surprised they are going to go with McNally in the first game," backup catcher Curt Blefary, a former Oriole, told a reporter for United Press International. "I think they should go with Jim Palmer. Palmer's fastball, maybe the best in the league, explodes...Once he gets his rhythm, it's all over. He'll take you every time."

Although Oakland hitters had examined Mayo Smith's scouting reports on the Orioles, they also relied heavily on Blefary's input in developing strategies against the Baltimore pitchers. "I've caught everyone of their pitchers," Blefary told UPI, "and I've also batted against them, so I think I know what I'm talking about." Dick Williams certainly seemed to think so. "I'm depending on Blefary to help out with the more personal touches about the individual players," the A's' manager informed UPI, "things such as habits, what a player can be expected to do in a certain situation."

Against the advice of Blefary, Earl Weaver started 21-game winner McNally against Vida Blue. The series opened a day later than scheduled because of a day of rain in Baltimore. The rainout marked the first postponement in the short history of the Championship Series. Although the rains ceased the next day, they had been replaced by small swarms of bees that had infiltrated the humid air above the playing field. Amidst the stings, the A's touched McNally for two runs in the second inning to take the lead. With Dave Duncan on second base and still no one out, Williams ordered No. 8 hitter Dick Green to lay down a sacrifice bunt, which he did successfully. With Blue the next scheduled batter, Williams predictably called for the squeeze play. The Orioles anticipated the strategy, pitched out, and nailed Duncan in a rundown between third and home.

The A's scored a run in the top half of the fourth to extend the lead to 3–0, but the Orioles answered with a run of their own in the bottom half of the inning. Blue held the Orioles scoreless in the fifth and sixth innings, before running into trouble in the seventh. Frank Robinson drew a leadoff walk, followed by a Boog Powell strikeout. Brooks Robinson singled, before Andy Etchebarren's fly ball pushed Frank Robinson to third. With runners on first and third and two outs, Blue prepared to face the light-hitting Mark Belanger. On paper, Belanger seemed like an easy target for Blue, but the reed-thin shortstop responded with a line single to center, scoring Frank Robinson.

By now, Blue had thrown 120 pitches. Belanger's ability to turn on Blue's fading fastball should have sent a red flag to Dick Williams, but he chose to ignore the signs of fatigue. Another non-threatening batter, the .189-hitting Curt Motton, pinch-hit for McNally and pounded a double into the left field corner, scoring Brooks Robinson with the tying run. Leadoff man Paul Blair, who had hit only .196 vs. Oakland during the regular season, followed with another ringing double to left, scoring Belanger with the go-ahead run and Motton with an insurance tally. Blue finally retired Dave Johnson to end the rally, but not before a two-run lead had turned into a two-run deficit.

Baltimore's top reliever, the side-arming Eddie Watt, blanked the A's over the final two innings to preserve a 4–3 victory. Afterwards, reporters questioned Vida Blue about his schizophrenic game; he was great for six innings, then awful in the seventh. Why? Blue answered the questions in whispers, sighing often during his pauses in speech. "I blew my lead; that's the big thing," Blue commented quietly to Murray Chass of the *New York Times*.

During the seventh inning, home-plate umpire Hank Soar had called a few borderline pitches balls, pitches that might have been strikes. "The umpiring was tough," Blue said diplomatically in his interview with Chass, refusing to blame Soar directly. "There were a lot of close calls, but I guess they were just calling them the way they saw them."

For one of the few times all season, reporters and fans roasted Dick Williams for what they considered major strategic gaffes. Several writers criticized Williams for several of his choices in Game One, principally his questionable decision to bunt with his eighth-place hitter in the second inning. Sal Bando had started the inning with a double, Angel Mangual had followed with a triple, and Dave Duncan had completed the extra-base hit parade with a double. With Duncan on second and still no one out, Williams asked Dick Green to lay down a bunt, rather than play for a large rally against a struggling McNally.

The second-guessers also wondered about Williams' failure to lift a tiring Blue during the Orioles' seventh-inning rally. According to Orioles manager Earl Weaver, Blue's mounting pitch count through the first six innings may have sapped his fastball of necessary life by the seventh inning. "He was throwing a lot of pitches," Weaver noted to the *New York Times*, "and we felt that had to have an effect on him. We figured maybe he'd slow down a bit or his fastball would straighten out." Both effects had taken place, making Blue an easier mark for mediocre-to-poor hitters like Curt Motton and Mark Belanger.

Down one game to none, Williams called upon his other 20-game winner, Catfish Hunter, to pitch Game Two. Hunter faced left-handed craftsman Mike Cuellar, who had won an even 20 games during the regular season. Even though the A's would return home for Game Three, and possibly a fourth and fifth game, they needed to win Game Two to have any realistic chance of winning the series.

Early home runs gave the Orioles a 2–1 lead. In the top of the sixth inning, Reggie Jackson led off with a double. That brought up first baseman Tommy Davis, the cleanup hitter against left-handed pitching. To everyone's surprise, including Dick Williams, Davis bunted, pushing Jackson to third. Cuellar then retired Sal Bando and rookie Angel Mangual, stranding Reggie at third.

The A's had lost out on their last remaining scoring opportunity. Oakland would fail to score a run over the final three innings, while Baltimore would tack on a single run in the seventh. In the eighth, the Orioles put the game away despite a lapse in fundamental play. Boog Powell, playing with a painfully sore wrist, tried twice to sacrifice a runner over to second base, failing each time. Powell then pulled a Hunter delivery into the right field bleachers for his second home run of the game.

Powell's blast capped off the scoring, as the Orioles won the game, 5–1, on Cuellar's six-hitter.

Much like they had done after Game One, reporters questioned Williams about the decision to have Davis bunt in the sixth inning. "I did not have the bunt sign on," Williams revealed to the Associated Press. "I would have preferred it if he took the shot." Although Williams made it clear that he had not ordered the bunt, he deflected some of the blame from Davis by admitting that he, as manager, had put too much recent emphasis on advancing runners from second to third with no one out.

Catfish Hunter blamed *himself* for the loss, especially for the two home runs to the injured Powell, whose wrist injury should have sapped much of his power-hitting ability. Powell had originally injured his hand two and a half weeks earlier when Tigers relief pitcher Tom Timmerman hit him with a pitch. Powell then re-aggravated the injury in Game Two, when he slid awkwardly into second base on a double-play takeout. "Even though his hand hurt, [Powell] still looks like 900 pounds up there," Hunter said to Murray Chass. "With a hurt hand, a broken leg, or anything, he's tough."

An ultra-conservative offensive approach, coupled with the failures of Blue and Hunter, had put the A's in a two-game hole, facing elimination. The A's would host Game Three at the Oakland Coliseum, where they figured to play with a more relaxed sense of security. The home fans, however, did not seem to believe that the A's could come back, at least based on the attendance figures for Game Three. Only 33,176 fans bothered to show up, leaving over 17,000 empty seats at the Coliseum.

Charlie Finley hoped to change Oakland fortunes by resorting to several superstitions. The Oakland owner wore his patented Blue blazer, or as he called it, his "Vida Blue" blazer. Finley brought out his pet mule, aptly named "Charlie O," for a pre-game stroll at the Coliseum. Lastly, Finley made arrangements for one of his own players, the multi-talented Mudcat Grant, to sing the National Anthem. In 1970, Grant had become the first active major leaguer to sing the anthem on Opening Day.

Good-luck charms and superstitions aside, the more pertinent issue centered on the game's pitching matchup, which did not favor the A's. As if the playoffs hadn't gone badly enough, Dick Williams learned that Chuck Dobson would not be available to start Game Three. The fragile 15-game winner informed Williams that he could not pitch because of a sore elbow. With Blue Moon Odom already sidelined, Williams turned to veteran Diego Segui, who had pitched primarily as a reliever during the regular season. Segui would have to do his best to match the performance of Baltimore right-hander Jim Palmer, the Orioles' leader in ERA (among starters) and simply their best pitcher.

Dick Williams made several lineup changes in an effort to counteract Palmer. The manager benched catcher Dave Duncan, first baseman Tommy Davis, and left fielder Joe Rudi, all right-handed hitters. In their place, Williams inserted Gene Tenace behind the plate, the lefty-hitting Mike Epstein at first base, and hard-hitting rookie Angel Mangual in left field. The strategy would not work, however, as the trio would manage a combined 1-for-11 against the future Hall of Famer.

At his best, Diego Segui baffled hitters with his sharp-breaking forkball—or spitter, as some charged him with throwing. At his worst, Segui's inability to hold runners close and his deliberate pitching style undermined the Oakland defense. Over the first four innings, the *former* Segui prevailed, allowing only one run. Then, in the top of the fifth inning, with the score tied at 1–1, the Orioles put runners on second and third with two outs. Dick Williams ordered Segui to walk the lefty-swinging Elrod Hendricks in favor of Brooks Robinson. Segui had mastered Robinson in recent head-to-head matchups, holding Brooks to a mere .154 average over the last three seasons. Segui fired his first pitch, which Robinson promptly lined up the middle. The two-out safety scored two runs, giving Baltimore a 3–1 lead. Williams summoned Rollie Fingers to finish out the inning.

Williams' strategy in the fifth inning raised questions. Hendricks had managed only two hits in 16 regular season at-bats against Oakland pitching. Robinson, in contrast, had collected nine RBIs in 11 games vs. the A's in 1971. Robinson was a future Hall of Famer; Hendricks was a platoon player. "Walking Hendricks was a percentage move," Williams would explain after the game. "Hendricks hurt us more, and by putting him on, we have a force play at any base." Robinson had foiled the strategy by lining a hard-hit ball over second base, out of the reach of Dick Green and Campy Campaneris.

In the bottom of the sixth inning, Sal Bando slammed a solo home run to draw the A's within one. Unfortunately for Oakland, Fingers and Darold Knowles could not keep the A's close. In the seventh, a Frank Robinson double and a wild pitch by Knowles enabled the Orioles to stretch the lead to three runs. Jim Palmer gave up a harmless run to the A's in the eighth inning, but returned to the mound in the ninth. Palmer ended the game and the series by striking out former Oriole Curt Blefary, who had made several outspoken comments about Baltimore prior to the playoffs. One reporter had quoted Blefary as predicting an easy victory for the A's. "Curt gave Oakland 24 positions over us," crowed Game One star Curt Motton in an interview with Phil Jackman of *The Sporting News*. For his part, Blefary claimed he had been misquoted.

As the Orioles celebrated their return to the World Series, photographers captured telling shots of a heartbroken Reggie Jackson, who was slumped on the steps of the A's' dugout, his shoulders hunched over, his eyes moistened by tears. Unlike many professional athletes who had been taught to hide, or at least lessen their outward displays of emotion, Reggie was crying—openly.

Another star player, Vida Blue, reacted differently to the defeat in Game Three. Blue expressed a desire to put the long, pressurized season behind him and begin a stage of offseason relaxation. "I'm going home, if they want me [there]," Blue told Joe Durso of the *New York Times*. "I'm going to get a job standing on the corner—just resting."

Oakland problems did not end with the loss in Game Three. "In fact," says Rick Monday, "when we came back from Baltimore to Oakland, we went to the plane we had chartered...and there were fire trucks all around the airplane—because there had been threats coming in. And people had to offload their luggage."

For the A's, a 101-win regular season had translated into nothing more than a three-game sweep in the playoffs at the hands of the defending World Champions. The playoff losses left the A's stunned. Granted, the Orioles had won more games than any major league team in 1971, but were they *this* much better than the A's? How could a team that had played so efficiently during the regular season—and run away with its division—lose three straight games in the playoffs? How could a club featuring two Cy Young candidates in Vida Blue and Catfish Hunter fall so quickly in the post-season? "I think we were surprised, certainly," says Rick Monday, who played in only one of the three games against the Orioles," Surprised from the standpoint that we felt we had a pretty good ballclub...We had a remarkable road record...Going into that series, we thought that we had a very good chance to at least prolong that series, and all of a sudden, we turn around and we're not only having trouble in the series, that series is over and we're sending it home."

Mike Hegan says the lack of post-season experience damaged Oakland's chances of advancing to the World Series. "I think there was probably more pressure in the playoffs back then than maybe there is now," explains Hegan, in referring to the best-of-five Championship Series format used at the time. "Baltimore was a very experienced ballclub, and although we won the 100 games, I think when we went into the playoffs, the Orioles' experience paid off for them."

Sal Bando agrees with Hegan in regards to the differences in the teams' post-season histories. "I think there were two things that stood out in my mind," Bando says, trying to explain the three-game sweep. "One, their experience was greater than ours, and that was a big, deciding factor. And we also at that point did not have a solid [or deep] rotation. We had Vida and Catfish. And after that it was Diego Segui, Chuck Dobson." While Segui and Dobson were respected veteran starters, the pair was no match for the likes of Jim Palmer, Mike Cuellar, and Dave McNally.

The rainout in Game One of the playoffs had succeeded in further shortening the paper-thin Oakland rotation, by eliminating the scheduled off day between the second and third games of the playoff series. "[That's] right," Bando says. "That rain[out] would not allow you to come back with Vida right away. We ended up having to have four starters, and in reality, we only had two."

The realization that the season had come to an end especially frustrated the veterans on the club who had played together since the mid-1960s. "Disappointing, I think certainly," says Rick Monday, "because this is a ballclub that had really battled at the minor league level. Almost everybody that had signed had been under the magnifying glass of all the experts: what were they going to do, how could you draft that guy first, why was he a No. 2 pick? All of a sudden, boom, here we are collectively and we turn [it] around and it was the same guys that had been on that bus and the same guys that had been on that field for a number of years. It was a good ballclub. Of course, we happened to be matched against a terrific [Baltimore] ballclub and some outstanding pitching of their own."

As frustrated as the Oakland players felt, they were able to learn from the losing experience in the playoffs, as part of the process of bettering themselves for 1972. "Absolutely," says Mike Hegan, "When I arrived in Oakland and you've got the Bandos and Campanerises and Reggie Jackson and Vida Blue and Joe Rudi and Catfish Hunter, the interesting part about that is that this is a club that kind of started together back in '67, '68; some of those guys played in Kansas City. But it was a growing experience for them, watching those young players, and they were at that time still very young, kind of maturing and then [we] win 100 ballgames. There is a stepping stone, if you will, and you win a hundred games, but then it comes down to pressure time of the playoffs, and at that juncture, nobody made big money, so to get to the World Series and get a World Series share that was a big accomplishment. Back at that time, some guys could make twice as much money from World Series shares as they were making in salary."

Rick Monday says the A's eventually succeeded in turning an emotional low into a motivating force. "Devastated?" Monday asks himself. "I don't know if we were devastated. I think, if anything else, that [playoff loss] may have driven a ballclub that had a taste of post-season play, and the initial stages of it, to come back and play even better."

Several writers also criticized Dick Williams for being too conservative throughout the series, perhaps overemphasizing the bunt and various one-run strategies. Mike Hegan says that the second-guessers failed to understand the true nature of the Oakland offense, which was not capable of producing many big innings. "That ballclub was a club which won on pitching, defense, and execution. Dick Williams did not play like Earl Weaver did for the three-run inning, the home run, the big hit. We always tried to execute to manufacture runs. Maybe in a short series and against a club like Baltimore, where you know that you're not gonna score many runs because of their pitching, there are certain [little] things that you have to do more of. If that was a criticism from the press, it certainly wasn't a criticism from the players."

Some players, like Sal Bando, don't remember such critical attacks being directed at Williams. "No, I don't," says Bando. "In fact, I don't remember reading about him being second-guessed because we were just outplayed by a superior team; there wasn't anything he could have done."

Nonetheless, Williams heard rumors that he would be fired. Charlie Finley had questioned him throughout the playoffs, especially his decision to start Diego Segui in Game Three. But who else could have started? Vida Blue had pitched only two days earlier and Chuck Dobson was hurt. That Finley would even consider a firing seemed ridiculous, given the widespread feelings of respect toward Williams. Termed a "giant in this clubhouse" by pitching coach Bill Posedel, Williams had taken a perennial also-ran to a 100-win season and its first playoff berth. He had been responsible for placing Rollie Fingers in the bullpen and had integrated mid-season pickups like Mike Epstein and Mudcat Grant into the Oakland equation. Williams had also succeeded in establishing his managerial rules. "I only ask two things," Williams had said in an interview with sportswriter Melvin Durslag. "I want a player to give 100 per cent on the day he plays, and I don't want him to make mental mistakes...We have the same sign in our clubhouse that the old Yankees used to have. It says, 'Don't mess with my money.' " Playoff money, that is.

Unlike rumors about previous Oakland managers, the rumblings about a Williams firing proved to be false. Williams would return to the A's in 1972, a just reward for the man who was named the *Associated Press* Manager of the Year. "He was very demanding," Rick Monday says of Williams, "from the standpoint that once the season was over, there were no shortcomings that you did not allow yourself the opportunity to go ahead and take care of as a club, individually or collectively." Williams and Charlie Finley would soon address those shortcomings. Unfortunately for Monday, the solutions to those shortcomings would result in his own departure from baseball's developing dynasty.

Chapter Eight

Offseason Shuffle

Both Charlie Finley and Dick Williams realized that changes needed to be made to improve the A's. With both Chuck Dobson and Blue Moon Odom ailing, Oakland needed to acquire another starting pitcher. Perhaps the A's could use their surplus of quality outfielders and first baseman as part of a package for a third starter behind staff aces Vida Blue and Catfish Hunter. One player the A's considered dangling as trade bait was backup first baseman Mike Hegan. After being acquired from the Brewers on June 14, Hegan had delivered six hits in 16 pinch-hit at-bats for Oakland. An excellent defensive first baseman, Hegan had also served the A's as a caddie to Mike Epstein. In one stretch of 16 games, Dick Williams had employed Hegan as a defensive substitute on 15 occasions. Hegan's ability to play the outfield made him even more valuable, especially to a pennant-contending team.

Aside from Hegan, two other quality bench players figured to prove attractive in potential trades. One was first baseman-outfielder Tommy Davis, who batted a league-leading .464 as a pinch-hitter. The other was part-time catcher Gene Tenace, who batted .308 in 13 pinch-hitting appearances.

In late November, major league executives and general managers convened at the annual winter meetings in Phoenix, Arizona. The meetings had traditionally become a mid-winter trade fest, where major league general managers discussed and engineered blockbuster deals. On November 29, the first day of the meetings, the San Francisco Giants and Houston Astros traded away future Hall of Famers Gaylord Perry and Joe Morgan, respectively, in separate deals they would come to regret. On the same day, the A's announced a deal of their own, one they would *not* regret. As expected, Oakland traded an outfielder for a starting pitcher. Yet, the deal involved neither Mike Hegan nor Tommy Davis. The A's instead sent starting center fielder Rick Monday to the Chicago Cubs for left-handed pitcher Ken Holtzman.

The A's parted with Monday reluctantly. In 1965, the A's had selected Monday with the initial pick of the first-ever free agent draft of amateur talent. Charlie Finley had given Monday a $100,000 signing bonus and a new car, in the anticipation that the former University of Arizona outfielder would blossom into major league stardom. Monday exhibited flashes of potential with his considerable power, speed, throwing arm, and defensive skills. He also impressed the A's with his constant hustle and strong character. Unfortunately, a series of frustrating injuries hindered Monday's progress: a broken wrist in 1967, torn tendons in his leg in 1968, another broken wrist in 1969, and a fractured rib and bruised kidney in 1970. Monday also showed little improvement in mastering his biggest weakness: left-handed pitchers. Monday struck out too often, failed to make consistent contact, and tried to pull almost every pitch.

As much as the A's liked Monday's potential and personality, they deemed him expendable because of the emergence of Angel Mangual. The 26-year-old Monday, an everyday player in the past, had not felt comfortable in a platoon role. "I figured that something was going to happen," says Monday. "You never know [for sure] that you're going to be traded, but I figured that certainly from a platoon situation, that's what Dick Williams had decided to do. He was going to go with Angel Mangual against left-handed pitching and go with me against right-handers. I would also go in and play defense in later stages of the ballgame. That's a situation for a young player that you're not particularly pleased with, because that's the first time it had ever taken place."

The A's reasoned that they had a greater need for a starting pitcher than for a platoon center fielder. Yet, critics of the deal wondered why the A's settled for Ken Holtzman. The veteran southpaw had suffered through a miserable season in 1971, winning only nine of 24 decisions while posting a bloated ERA of 4.48. "I just had a bad year," the left-hander explained to a reporter for *The Sporting News*. "There were no physical problems. I just couldn't get started. I couldn't get straightened out." On several occasions, Holtzman had found his season interrupted by stints in the Marine Reserves. Holtzman had also experienced difficulties in his relationship with Cubs manager Leo Durocher.

Holtzman and Durocher had hardly spoken during the second half of the season. Durocher had previously criticized Holtzman for not using his fastball often enough and relying too much on what he called a "lollipop" curve. Durocher also questioned Holtzman's effort. "I wasn't happy when Leo Durocher was quoted in the paper saying I wasn't trying," Holtzman said later in an interview with Bay Area sportswriter Glenn Dickey. After Durocher publicly criticized Holtzman, the left-hander asked Cubs general manager John Holland to trade him.

Holtzman claimed that Durocher's handling of the team, rather than his own relationship with the manager, prompted his trade request. "I didn't have any real trouble with Leo," Holtzman explained to Dickey. "I got along all right with him. But I didn't like the way he'd criticize players sometimes in the papers, instead of confronting a player directly." Other Cubs players, good and bad, struggled to get along with "The Lip," whose interpersonal skills had always been lacking. In recent years, the aging Durocher cultivated increasingly strained relationships with the new wave of "mod" players. "Baseball has changed a lot since Leo was a player," Holtzman reasoned. "You're not getting a lot of players from small towns in the South anymore. The players are very intelligent now. You've got players in the game with college degrees, sometimes even Masters degrees. I don't think Leo understood that."

Given his problems in 1971, Charlie Finley welcomed Holtzman by cutting his salary by 10 percent. Still, the A's liked Holtzman for many reasons. Despite his off performance in 1971, Holtzman was still only 26 years old—and healthy. "I've never had arm trouble in my life," Holtzman told *The Sporting News*. "I've worked between 275 and 280 innings a season for the last five years and that's a lot of pitching." Once likened to his pitching hero—another Jewish left-hander by the name of Sandy Koufax—Holtzman had enjoyed back-to-back seasons of 17 wins in 1969 and '70, and had forged a lifetime record of 65–54. Holtzman had twice pitched no-hitters, a sign of his powerful repertoire of pitches. His most recent no-hitter occurred during the 1971 season, when he shut down a Cincinnati Reds lineup that featured dangerous right-handed hitters like Hal McRae, Lee May, Johnny Bench, Tony Perez, and George Foster. Furthermore, Holtzman managed to no-hit the Reds despite his inability to spot his most effective pitch—the curveball—for strikes. Over the last five innings of his June 7th no-hitter against Cincinnati, Holtzman threw only two curveballs. Using his fastball almost exclusively—much to the delight of Leo Durocher—Holtzman dominated one of the National League's most feared lineups.

Holtzman's new manager, Dick Williams, hoped that the stylish left-hander would dominate American League batters and balance the A's' starting rotation. Oakland already had three fine right-handed starters in Catfish Hunter, and when healthy, Blue Moon Odom and Chuck Dobson. Yet, the A's had only one capable left-hander in Vida Blue. Williams figured that Holtzman would prove effective against some of the American League's best left-handed hitters, like the Twins' Tony Oliva and Rod Carew, the Orioles' Boog Powell, Boston's Carl Yastrzemski, Detroit's Norm Cash, and the Yankees' Bobby Murcer.

The trade of Monday represented the initial breakup of a nucleus of players that had come up together with the Kansas City Athletics in the mid-sixties. Dick Green, who had been with the A's longer than any other player, remembered all too well the misfortunes of the Kansas City teams of 1963 and '64. "Those A's were the worst," Green told sportswriter Joe Gergen. "I don't know how bad the Mets were then but I don't see how they could have been any worse than we were."

Although those early Finley teams had struggled, Monday remembers the Kansas City days as important in laying the groundwork for future success in Oakland. "They selectively rushed some guys because, quite frankly, we didn't have a real strong ballclub at Kansas City," Monday says. "We were really a very close group because we had to band together as a young club that went out and basically continued to get beat upon by other clubs. We were trying to gain that experience, trying to learn fundamentals.

"I mean this was a ballclub that really kind of stretched its wings under fire at the big league level. Most of us that were with the ballclub [in 1971], myself—I signed in '65 out of Arizona State University. I played in 1966, not quite the full season, under John McNamara at Mobile, Alabama. I was called up at the end of the year, and Sal Bando and I drove all night to get to Kansas City. We arrived at seven o'clock in the morning, we're at the ballpark at 10:30 working out, and then came [back] that night at seven-something to play the ballgame. And that was *really* under fire."

By 1971, the seeds of struggle had given way to a cash crop—a team filled with leaders, not dependent on any player. "It finally came together," Monday says. "And then finally, collectively, we got together. When you [try to] single out any one person, I don't think you can single out one person. Everybody played an integral role depending upon what they were gonna be called upon to do.

"If you look around major league baseball [today], those guys are still sprinkled around, in and around the game in one way or another."

A scan of post-playing career resumes bears out Monday's contention. Since finishing a productive major league career with the A's, Cubs and Los Angeles Dodgers, Monday himself has worked as a broadcaster for the Dodgers and San Diego Padres, while Mike Hegan has performed similar duties for the Milwaukee Brewers and Cleveland Indians. Felipe Alou, who played briefly for the A's at the start of the '71 season, became one of the game's finest managers with the Montreal Expos before being fired during the 2001 season. Sal Bando worked in the front office for the Brewers, eventually becoming the team's general manager. Reggie Jackson served George Steinbrenner as an executive with the Yankees. Dave Duncan became one of the most successful pitching coaches in the major leagues, working under Tony LaRussa with the A's, Chicago White Sox, and St. Louis Cardinals. Gene Tenace worked as a coach for the Houston Astros and Toronto Blue Jays, before becoming a minor league instructor with the Boston Red Sox. George Hendrick, a backup on the '71 A's, became a hitting instructor for the Cardinals and Anaheim Angels. Joe Rudi, Tommy Davis, and Darold Knowles coached briefly for the A's, Seattle Mariners, and Cardinals, respectively.

In perhaps the most intriguing story of success after a playing career, former A's slugger Don Mincher has become one of the few ex-major leaguers to own and operate a minor league franchise, while also serving as president of a minor league. As the Twins' beat writer throughout the sixties, Bob Fowler grew to know Mincher well during his playing days in Minnesota. Fowler isn't surprised that Mincher has become successful in baseball management. "He's doing a great job today," Fowler says of Mincher's involvement with the Huntsville Stars of the Double-A Southern League. (In 2000, Mincher also became the interim president of the Southern League.) "He's the Huntsville general manager, has done a terrific job with that. I think that's another aspect of that era that you see nowadays. Here's Don Mincher, I mean, here's a guy that could so something other than play first base. He could do something other than play professional baseball; he had other talents. And now they're coming out. Quality guy."

The day after making the Rick Monday-for-Ken Holtzman trade, Charlie Finley made a puzzling move when he announced the unconditional release of 36-year-old right-hander Mudcat Grant. The A's cited concerns over Grant's age, but the veteran reliever had pitched brilliantly for Oakland since being reacquired from the Pirates in August. Grant had picked up a win and four saves, to the tune of a 2.00 ERA. "It looks awful strange when Finley could buy me back from Pittsburgh just to release me," a bewildered Grant told Ron Bergman, while expressing skepticism over Oakland's emphasis on age as the reason for his release. "They keep telling me I'm an old man and that I'm through," Grant told reporters, "but I look around and see guys as old as me not doing as well." In reality, Finley had been motivated by financial concerns; in 1971, Grant earned $60,000, a figure that Finley considered too lofty for a relief pitcher.

Rather than attempt to re-sign with the A's at a reduced salary, Grant would receive a spring training invitation from the Indians, one of his former teams. Mudcat would fail to make the major league roster, instead signing a contract with the A's' Class-AAA affiliate at Iowa. Incredibly, Grant would never again pitch in the American or National leagues. Given the constant need for pitching at baseball's highest level, the exclusion of Grant from the major league scene ranked as near criminal.

With Chuck Dobson set to undergo surgery to remove a piece of bone from his right elbow, Finley set out to acquire another starting pitcher. The A's offered first baseman Mike Epstein to the Yankees for one of their starting pitchers, believed to be right-hander Mel Stottlemyre. Epstein, a left-handed pull hitter with tremendous power potential, would have provided a natural fit for Yankee Stadium. The Yankees, however, did not want to part with Stottlemyre and turned down the deal.

Epstein himself contemplated retirement during the offseason. As Epstein and his family celebrated the Thanksgiving holiday, the emotional first baseman considered quitting the game. His second-half slump and Dick Williams' decision to bench him for the playoff series against Baltimore had preyed on his mind. "I'd let a lot of people down," Epstein explained later in an interview with Arnold Hano of *Sport* Magazine. "Things had snowballed." Having decided that mental fatigue had caused his late-season problems, the 235-pound first baseman embarked on a strict weight-reducing program. After losing 30 pounds during the winter, Epstein would report to spring training weighing 205 pounds, the lightest weight of his professional career.

With Dobson's health a major question mark, the A's nearly lost another one of their pitchers—for good. On January 6, 1972, Blue Moon Odom attempted to prevent a burglary near his mother's home in Macon, Georgia. Odom's wife, Perrie, had noticed three young men trying to enter one of the neighboring houses. She phoned both the police and her husband, who was working at a liquor store only four blocks away. Odom grabbed a gun that he kept in his car and made his way to the neighbor's home. Odom actually passed the youths on the street when his wife signaled to him that *they* were, in fact, the perpetrators.

"Hey, I want to talk to you," Odom called out to the young men as he followed them. One of the robbers turned around to face Odom, asking him, "What for?" Almost simultaneously, the youth pulled out a .38 caliber pistol and fired three shots. Two bullets struck Odom, one in the neck and another in the side of the chest. Odom returned fire with his own gun, but missed hitting any of the young men. Over the span of a few seconds, Odom first thought his baseball career, and then his life, had come to an end. "I was thinking I never would pitch again after that first shot," Odom told the Associated Press afterwards. "After the second shot, I thought it was all over."

Medics rushed Odom to the Medical Center of Georgia Hospital, where he received treatment for three days. "I didn't bleed enough to cover a small wash rag," Odom joked in an interview with *Black Sports* Magazine, while trying to minimize the severity of his injuries. Fortunately, each gunshot had passed through Odom's body while causing only minimal, non life-threatening damage. Odom's doctor predicted that the gunshot wounds would not affect his pitching career, and believed that the veteran right-hander would be able to resume throwing in about a month. Considering that he had almost lost his life just a few days earlier, the doctor's words had to sound very good to the man known as Blue Moon.

Chapter Nine

Holdouts, Mustaches, and McLain

Newsmakers in 1972

Authorities arrest five men and charge them with breaking into Democratic headquarters at the Watergate complex in Washington D.C.... President Nixon, making the first official visit to Moscow by an American president, conducts historic talks with Communist Party leader Leonid Brezhnev...The U.S. Supreme Court rules the death penalty unconstitutional, sparing the lives of 600 criminals on death row.

J. Edgar Hoover, the director of the FBI for nearly 50 years, dies at the age of 77...In testimony to the Knapp Commission, New York City detective Frank Serpico alleges widespread corruption in the police department... "The Godfather," starring Marlon Brando, is released in theaters nationwide.

Arab terrorists massacre 11 members of the Israeli team at the Olympic Games in Munich, Germany... John Wooden's UCLA Bruins win their sixth consecutive NCAA men's basketball crown... In golf, Jack Nicklaus ties Bobby Jones' record by winning his 13th major title.

With spring training only two weeks away, half of the A's' 40-man roster remained unsigned. In one case, the A's braced for what seemed to have all the makings of an ugly contract showdown, one that reminded team observers of the 1970 salary battle between Reggie Jackson and Charlie Finley. Pitching superstar Vida Blue had earned under $15,000 in 1971, despite winning 24 games, the Cy Young Award, and the Most Valuable Player. Blue's agent, Bob Gerst, wanted a contract that would make Blue one of the 10 highest-paid pitchers in all of baseball, somewhere in the range of $100,000. In stark contrast, Finley had offered a raise to about $50,000.

On January 8, Gerst met with Finley for five hours to discuss a new contract. The meeting left Finley outraged. Gerst had informed Finley of his initial asking price—$115,000. After a few months of heated self-deliberation, Finley asked Gerst if he knew what floor of the building they were standing on. When Gerst replied that they were standing on the 27th floor, the owner, according to a story by sportswriter Dick Young, shot back: "Mr. Gerst, you have as much chance of getting $115,000 as I have of going out that window and landing on my feet." As Finley was well aware, the fine art of bungie-jumping had not yet been invented.

Finley also reminded Gerst that while Blue had pitched brilliantly during the regular season, he had struggled in his one post-season start against the Orioles. "Some of the players believe from the way they talk about salaries this year that we won the World Series last year," Finley told *The Sporting News*. "We didn't even get in the World Series. We didn't win the American League pennant. All we did was win our division."

After making an initial demand of six figures, Gerst and Blue lowered their sights to an asking price of $92,500. Finley continued to balk at Blue's demands, refusing to move from his $50,000 figure and insisting that he would not raise ticket prices to meet the salary request. Not surprisingly, contract negotiations became bitter. Gerst accused Finley of blackmail, lying, and attempting to end Blue's career. "I won't trade him and I won't sell him," Finley told Red Smith of the *New York Times*. "Either he accepts what we have offered or he is through in baseball."

In explaining his negotiating stance, Gerst attempted to justify the figure of $92,500. "He is at a minimum one of the 10 best pitchers in baseball and should be paid accordingly," Gerst told the Associated Press, while pointing out the salaries of star pitchers like Bob Gibson ($150,000), Ferguson Jenkins ($125,000), Tom Seaver ($120,000), and Gaylord and Jim Perry ($90,000 each). "In addition," continued Gerst, "[Blue's] proven his importance to the financial well-being of his club and to the league." Nearly one million fans had watched Blue pitch in 41 games, including the All-Star Game and the American League Championship Series.

Every American League team had profited from Blue's command performances of 1971. Many of Oakland's opponents had held special promotions coinciding with the games that Blue was scheduled to pitch at their ballparks. For example, the Twins presented special buttons to any fans wearing blue-colored clothing and apparel to Metropolitan Stadium on September 3. The buttons contained the following inscription:

"Roses are red
My clothes were blue
When I was there
To see Vida Blue!"

The Twins drew over 22,000 fans for Blue's start, after drawing fewer than 9,000 fans for their previous game.

Yet, Finley felt lack of service time weighed heavily against Blue's case. "I don't mind paying a player that has proved himself, but a player can't prove himself in just one year," countered Finley. The owner explained that if he conceded to Gerst and gave Blue a contract for $92,000 and the pitcher responded with a poor season, he could cut his salary by only 20 per cent in 1973. "Nope, I have to be firm on paying him $50,000 for 1972," insisted Finley in an interview with the Associated Press. "Based on the fact that Vida has had only one full year in the majors...I think it is a fair offer."

The A's opened up spring training in Mesa, without the presence of Blue. As negotiations continued, Gerst explored the avenue of making Blue a free agent. Gerst raised the possibility that Blue had signed an illegal contract with the A's in the first place. "When he signed the contract [back in 1967]," Gerst explained to *The Sporting News*, "he was a minor. When a minor signs a contract with a movie studio, it has to be approved by the courts. We're checking to see if this applies in this case." It didn't. On another front, Gerst hinted that Finley might not have made a payment of $2,500 due to his client on his original contract. "There is a clause in the contract," Gerst said, "that says the contract will be rescinded if the club does not live up to any part of the agreement." Gerst was clearly grasping at loopholes, but to no avail.

Two weeks into spring training, with Blue still unsigned, and with the status of the fragile Chuck Dobson and Blue Moon Odom uncertain, the A's took major action. No, Finley did not give in and pay his star left-hander what he wanted. Instead, Finley announced the acquisition of another Cy Young Award winner— 27-year-old Denny McLain.

The A's picked up McLain from the Texas Rangers (formerly the Washington Senators) for two pitching prospects, Jim Panther and Don Stanhouse, the latter a 21-year-old reliever who had drawn rave reviews. At first, the A's had offered either Blue Moon Odom or Chuck Dobson, but Rangers owner Bob Short had rejected the oft-injured veterans. Showing a preference for younger players, Short called Stanhouse and Panther the two best pitching prospects in Oakland's organization. At 27 years old, Panther was the same age as McLain, but had yet to win a single major league game.

In 1968 and '69, McLain had won a combined 55 games, captured an MVP award, and earned two Cy Young awards as the American League's most dominant pitcher. Only a few years removed from his peak and still three years short of his 30th birthday, the talented McLain now belonged to the A's. Unfortunately, McLain had experienced one of the most precipitous declines in major league history. In 1970, Commissioner Bowie Kuhn suspended McLain for half of the season because of his involvement with illegal bookmakers and unsavory ties with the gambling world. McLain also received suspensions for carrying a gun and for maliciously treating members of the Detroit press. After the season, the Tigers traded McLain to the Senators, where he feuded with manager Ted Williams and struggled with increasing weight and a decreasing fastball. In 1971, McLain won only 10 games while losing a league-leading 22 decisions.

Plain and simple, McLain had pitched badly for a bad team in Washington. Yet, the controversial right-hander blamed his struggles on the way that his manager used him in the starting rotation. "I threw the ball up until July as well as I ever have for both velocity and strikes," McLain insisted in an interview with Ron Bergman. "Then Ted Williams said after he had seen me for two months, that it would be better for me to pitch every fifth or sixth day. I thought I was better every fourth day. He had two months of statistics. I had six years of statistics."

While McLain had fallen into disfavor with the Rangers, he filled a specific need for the A's. Dick Williams explained that the trade for McLain had occurred as a direct result of the failed negotiations with Vida Blue. "We started talking on and off with other clubs when it looked like we would have trouble signing Vida," Williams told *The Sporting News*. "When you don't have your big starter in camp, and it's been open for two weeks, you've got to take action." Although McLain had struggled over the past two seasons, he had generally been impressive in games against the A's. Over his career, McLain had posted a lifetime record of 15–5 against Oakland. Considering his relatively youthful age and overall history of success, the A's considered the acquisition of McLain a reasonable gamble. Furthermore, the Rangers had agreed to swallow $25,000 of McLain's $75,000 salary. In other words, the A's would pay him $50,000—the same amount of money offered to Vida Blue.

McLain reported to the A's, joining the club in Arizona. McLain arrived in Phoenix, where the team's spring training hotel was located. As McLain relaxed by the hotel pool on his first day with the team, a reporter from ABC television approached him in an effort to record his reaction to the trade. The volatile right-hander, who had once dumped a bucket of water on two sportswriters, yelled at the reporter and made indirect threats against ABC sportscaster Howard Cosell, who had previously criticized McLain. While McLain had changed teams, he had unfortunately retained the same nasty streak he had displayed in both Detroit and Washington.

McLain's disposition matched his dreadful spring training performance. In his first exhibition start for the A's, a shell-shocked McLain allowed 10 runs on 10 hits and six walks. McLain defended himself by explaining that he had thrown only curveballs and change-ups in his A's debut and had refrained from unleashing his best fastball early in the spring. Yet, his second start produced another series of ghastly numbers: seven runs on a collection of 14 hits. Although McLain had not pitched well for Washington the previous summer, he hadn't pitched *this* badly, either.

Meanwhile, the A's enjoyed no progress on the Vida Blue front. The acquisition of McLain served to annoy Gerst, who couldn't understand Finley's willingness to assume a $50,000 salary for a pitcher who lost 22 games. "Finley is not acting the part of a man who wants to be fair," Gerst told Red Smith of the *New York Times*, "but that of a man who wants to be in command." Nonetheless, Finley refused to budge on what he called his first, last, and only offer to Blue—$50,000. On March 2, Finley invoked baseball's reserve clause, which allowed an owner to automatically renew an unsigned player's contract. If Finley had invoked the clause earlier, he could have given Blue a 20 percent pay cut from his 1971 salary of $14,500. Because Finley had already offered Blue $50,000, he had to agree to pay his star left-hander at least that much money in 1972. "I think Vida is entitled to [the] 300 percent pay increase because he accomplished quite a bit," Finley acknowledged in an interview with sportswriter Bill Verigan before suddenly launching an attack on Bob Gerst. "Vida has been brainwashed and browbeaten by his attorney. I do not like the image his attorney is creating for him."

Blue refused to sign the renewed contract or report to spring training. Surprisingly, most of Blue's teammates expressed their agreement with the stance taken by Finley—and not by Vida. Curt Blefary and Mike Epstein, in particular, voiced remarks critical of Blue and his agent, Gerst. "He's foolish for giving up $50,000," Blefary told the Associated Press. "He could have made it $100,000 with endorsements." Epstein placed most of the blame on Gerst. "I'm sorry for Vida," Epstein claimed in the interview with the AP. "He obviously hooked up with the wrong guy." Another player, team captain Sal Bando, also sided with Finley. "I'm for a guy getting all he can, but Charlie has offered Vida a fair contract," Bando reasoned to the Associated Press. "We can win without Vida Blue. It would be harder, but we can."

Only one Oakland teammate publicly showed support for Blue. Tommy Davis, also a Gerst client, offered Blue some sympathy. "I'd like to see him in uniform, but I respect his decision."

Blue and Gerst offered Finley several proposals. Under one scenario, they would agree to Finley's offer of $50,000 if Blue could become a free agent after the 1972 season. Finley called the request absurd. Gerst then asked to submit the contract negotiation to Commissioner Bowie Kuhn, who would be asked to arbitrate a settlement. Finley, a bitter enemy of the commissioner, turned thumbs down on Kuhn's involvement. Gerst then suggested that he might take his client to the Japanese Leagues. There existed an obstacle to such a plan, however. By international agreement between the major leagues and the Japanese teams, no player could jump from one continent to the other without receiving his owner's permission. Given the agreement, Finley laughed off the possibility of Blue suiting up in Japan.

The player and his agent decided to explore their options. Even though he had no professional acting experience, Blue reportedly signed a deal with MGM to star in the second of a series of planned sequels to the movie studio's successful venture, *Shaft*. Blue attended a press conference with actor Richard Roundtree, the star of the original *Shaft*, to promote the new venture, but would never appear in such a film. Blue and his agent called another press conference in Oakland. Reading from a prepared statement, Blue told the gathered reporters that he had accepted a position as vice-president of public relations for Dura Steel Products, a company that specialized in making bathroom and toilet fixtures. "It is with deep regret and sadness I announce my leaving baseball," Blue said, making his retirement official. "I had hoped my career could have been longer. While it was short, it was packed with excitement." At the urging of Gerst, Blue did not answer any questions at the press conference.

None of the reporters took Blue seriously, especially when he smiled and giggled repeatedly while reading from the press release. Finley reacted to Blue's announcement with a dose of sarcasm. "I'm happy to hear that he is entering the steel industry and starting as a vice-president," Finley chortled to a reporter for the Associated Press before dramatically detailing his own career in steel. "I too was associated with the steel industry, as a worker with U.S. Steel Corporation in Gary, Indiana. I worked there for five years, the first four of which I served my machine shop apprenticeship."

The following night, Finley and Blue met at the Edgewater Hyatt Motel in Oakland. Blue made it clear that he was interested in playing baseball, rather than with toilet fixtures, but Finley refused to budge from his initial offer.

According to some players, Finley could be at his worst during long contract negotiations, often forcing his players into bad moods. "I remember once Charlie called me up during the offseason," recalls Rick Monday. "We were talking contract. And he basically just—he really irritated me. And then there was name-calling. I went to a hockey game that night and I said, 'I hope there's the biggest fight I've ever seen in my life.' By God there was and somebody had to be carried off the ice on a stretcher. I said, 'Oh, I didn't want that big of a fight.' But Charlie was constantly there [calling players over the phone] and Charlie was in a constant mood swing because physically his clock ran 24 hours. There was no such thing as a 12-hour workday or an 18-hour workday; it was 24 hours."

Monday says he tried to use an agent during one offseason negotiating session, but the strategy did not please Finley.

"I did [have an agent] one year, and Charlie and I did not leave on the best of terms. He made some promises that he came considerably short of, and some of those were in writing. There was a lawsuit that was going to be instituted, and finally, at the last second, he made amends for it. There was a financial arrangement that was taken care of. He called my attorney once; he said, 'Get that bird off my back, or I'll squash him.' Charlie was different."

Indeed.

After repeatedly failing in efforts to lure Blue into signing a new contract, Finley adopted a bizarre strategy, while revealing a strange chain of command in the Oakland organization. On the advice of equipment manager Frank Ciensczyk, the A's' self-proclaimed "sock and jock man," Finley ordered several of his players to fly up to Oakland to talk to Blue. At first, Finley dispatched catcher Gene Tenace, with orders to bring Blue to Arizona, where the A's trained throughout the spring. Tenace returned without the ace left-hander. Finley then assigned utilityman Curt Blefary the duty of baseball bounty hunter. The third-string catcher dined with Blue one night, then met with him for two hours the next day. Still, Blefary returned to Arizona empty-handed, except for $60.00 in taxicab receipts. Finley referred to Blefary as the "last of the goodwill ambassadors." Alas, the plan of the "sock and jock man" had gone for naught.

As the start of the season neared, Dick Williams resigned himself to the fact that Blue would not be with the team come Opening Day. Several other pitchers, however, impressed Williams in the spring. The newly acquired Ken Holtzman pitched brilliantly in exhibition games, making the Rick Monday trade look like a potential coup for the A's. Blue Moon Odom, now recovered from his offseason gunshot wounds, threw the ball harder than he had in the last two seasons. The liveliness of Odom's pitches gave the A's hope that the veteran right-hander had fully overcome his chronic elbow troubles. Catfish Hunter also pitched well in his last two spring starts, giving every indication that he could repeat his 1971 performance.

Out of the bullpen, both Rollie Fingers and Bob Locker looked impressive. To the surprise of some observers, Fingers expressed a preference for working as a starting pitcher, in spite of his successful conversion to the bullpen the previous summer. "Starting is where the money is," Fingers said bluntly to William Leggett of *Sports Illustrated*. Rollie's pursuit of big money would have to wait until after the 1976 season, when he would leave Finley's clutches and sign a lucrative, multi-year contract with the San Diego Padres.

The holdout of Vida Blue and the trade for Denny McLain overshadowed another building Oakland controversy. Reggie Jackson had reported to spring training replete with a fully-grown mustache, the origins of which had begun to sprout during the 1971 American League Championship Series. To the surprise of his teammates, Jackson had used part of his off-season to allow the mustache to reach a fuller bloom. In addition, Jackson bragged to teammates that he would not only wear the mustache, but possibly a beard, come Opening Day.

Such pronouncements would have hardly created a ripple in later years, when players would freely make bold fashion statements with mustaches and goatees, and routinely wear previously disdained accessories like earrings. But this was 1972, still a conservative time within the sport, in stark contrast to the rebellious attitudes of younger generations throughout the country. Given that no major league player had been documented wearing a mustache in the regular season since Wally Schang of the Philadelphia A's in 1914, Jackson's pronouncements made major news in 1972.

In the post-Schang era, several players had donned mustaches during spring training, including Stanley "Frenchy" Bordagaray of the Brooklyn Dodgers in the mid-1930s and, more recently, Richie Allen of the St. Louis Cardinals in 1970. Yet, in each case, the player had shaved off the mustache by Opening Day, either by his own volition or because of a mandate from the team. After all, there existed an *unwritten* rule within the conservative sport, one that strongly frowned upon facial hair. In addition, several individual teams had more recently instituted their own formal policies (most notably the Cincinnati Reds in the 1960s), policies that forbade their players from sporting facial hair.

Baseball's conservative grooming standards, which had been in place for over 50 years, were now being threatened by one of the game's most visible players. Not surprisingly, Jackson's mustachioed look quickly cornered the attention of Charlie Finley and Dick Williams. "The story as I remember it," says Mike Hegan, "was that Reggie came into spring training...with a mustache, and Charlie didn't like it. So he told Dick to tell Reggie to shave it off. And Dick told Reggie to shave it off, and Reggie told Dick what to do. This got to be a real sticking point, and so I guess Charlie and Dick had a meeting, and they said well, 'Reggie's an *individual* so maybe we can try some reverse psychology here.' Charlie told a couple of other guys, I don't know whether it was [Dave] Duncan, or Sal [Bando], or a few other guys to start growing a mustache. Then, [Finley figured that if] a couple of other guys did it, Reggie would shave his off, and you know, everything would be OK."

According to Sal Bando, Finley wanted to avoid having a direct confrontation with Jackson over the mustache. For one of the few times in his tenure as the A's owner, Finley showed a preference for a subtle, more indirect approach. "Finley, to my knowledge," says Bando, "did not want to go tell Reggie to shave it. So he thought it would be better to have all of us grow mustaches. That way, Reggie wouldn't be an 'individual' [anymore]."

Rollie Fingers, Catfish Hunter, Darold Knowles, and Bob Locker followed Reggie's lead, each sprouting his own mustache. Instead of making Jackson fell less individualistic, thus prompting him to adopt his previously clean-shaven look, the strategy had a reverse and unexpected effect on Charlie Finley.

"Well, as it turned out, guys started growing 'em, and Charlie began to like it," says Mike Hegan in recalling the origins of baseball's "Mustache Gang." Finley offered a cash incentive to any player who had successfully grown a mustache by Father's Day. "So then we all had to grow mustaches," says Hegan, "and that's how all that started. By the time we got to the [regular] season, almost everybody had mustaches." Even the manager, Dick Williams, known for his military brush-cut and clean-shaven look during his days in Boston, would join the facial brigade by growing a patchy, scraggly mustache of his own. Baseball's longstanding hairless trend had officially come to an end.

The mustache-growing represented only part of the grooming and fashion changes that had begun to take root among the Oakland players. Sal Bando, previously the owner of a short, close-cropped haircut and one of the most conservative dressers on the team, showed up at spring training looking like one of the feature characters on the television show, *The Mod Squad*. "My hair is growing over my collar," Bando whispered to Ron Bergman prior to spring training. "It's going to cover my ears." As an accessory to his longer hair, Bando also parted ways with the traditional line of clothing that he had worn throughout the 1960s. His wardrobe now included bell-bottom trousers, large lapel shirts, sportscoats with vents and wrap-up around belts in the back, and new-style ties. "I like wide ties," Bando said enthusiastically in an interview with Bergman. "I really like those wide ties."

As late as 1969, most major league players still wore their hair short and preferred conservative-looking clothes. Any player daring to wear high-heeled shoes, plaid bell-bottoms, gaudy multi-colored shirts, and wide-lapeled suits with vests would have become the immediate target of public ridicule. Over the next few years, such fashions started to become accepted among professional athletes. Some managers, even the supposedly militaristic Dick Williams, loosened the requirements of the team's dress code on road trips. Starting in 1971, Williams allowed his players to travel on buses and plains without ties. Such a practice had previously been considered taboo by the major league establishment. Fashions and dress codes were changing around baseball, and the A's were at the center of the revolution.

The A's also created a stir in 1972 when they unveiled a major change in their on-the-field appearance. Oakland players sported baseball's newest uniforms, which Charlie Finley hoped would stimulate marketing and fan interest. Finley retained his favored color scheme of green and gold, but eliminated the effect of a sleeveless jersey over a contrasting colored undershirt. The new double-knit uniforms now featured bright, pullover V-neck tops with sleeves, elastic waistlines instead of the traditional buckle belts, and shimmering white pants with green and gold racing stripes. Finley also announced that the A's would alternate jerseys, wearing a bright "Kelly green" one day, followed by a gaudy "California gold" the next. The shirts featured "A's" in white lettering on the left side of the chest, the player's uniform number in smaller white lettering to the right, and three bright stripes—either green or gold—on the edge of the sleeves.

The A's had first adopted the green and gold pattern in 1963, while still in Kansas City. In breaking with the tradition of wearing white, gray, and one-color trim—a color scheme that Finley abhorred, referring to it as "eggshell white and prison gray"—the A's became the first major league team to employ multicolored uniforms, along with white shoes. "We were embarrassed the first time we went on the field," says Jack Aker of the radical new uniforms that Finley instituted in the early sixties. "We saw the uniforms, we wore them on the field, we were embarrassed. I think almost everybody on the ballclub was. We did feel clownish. This was not baseball as we knew it. The white shoes especially grated on a lot of players. We'd never had white shoes; everybody wore black in those days."

Former sportswriter Bob Fowler remembers the first time he encountered Charlie Finley's splash of green and gold. "First met Charlie Finley in 1963, I believe it was," Fowler says. "The Kansas City A's came to Tiger Stadium and I was a freshman baseball writer. They came in their green and gold uniforms. Opened the season and Jim Schraff was the public relations guy. He passed out green bats in the press box, with gold 'Charles O. Finley' signatures on the green bats."

Schraff passed out the green bats to a disbelieving group of media members. "After the game," Fowler says, "the media didn't want the bats, wouldn't take the bats home. So I had like six of them." Unlike most of his media brethren, Fowler found the bats somewhat appealing. "I thought, why not? So now, I take them home, I move to Minnesota, I get married, I have kids. Now my kids get these green bats out of the garage and they're playing baseball in the backyard and in the street. Now, I'm a collector of memorabilia and people say, you know, 'Gee, those bats could have been, could be worth something.' So I went home and said, 'Where are those green bats? I got some money here, you know.' Well, my wife says the kids ruined them all. I said, 'No, they can't do that!'" All that remained for Fowler were a half-dozen broken green bats.

Fowler also has distinct memories of observing a Hall of Famer who looked hopelessly out of place in the A's' unusual uniforms, which Finley retained after the move from Kansas City to Oakland. "I'll never forget," Fowler says, "Joe DiMaggio was the hitting coach. People were teasing DiMaggio about being in this green and gold and wedding gown white, whatever the colors were. Gold, green, and they had gray on them; white was used at home. Anyway, they were teasing DiMaggio, saying, 'Gee, you know, we're used to see you in Yankee pinstripes and now you got on this clown outfit.' It was going on around the batting cage before the game; it was quite humorous. That was the institution of color into baseball, you know."

The revolutionary new uniforms of the A's brought howls of amusement from some observers in the baseball community, especially those who considered green and gold inappropriate colors. Fans in the stands taunted the players on the A's. "They would call us clowns," recalls Jack Aker. "They would start the music that goes with Ringling Brothers, Barnum and Bailey, they'd start singing this." A's players eventually became more comfortable with their new outfits and other teams started to follow suit. In 1971, the Baltimore Orioles adopted an alternate uniform consisting of bright red—red shirts *and* pants. In 1972, the San Diego Padres began using brown and yellow as their signature colors. The Chicago White Sox, Milwaukee Brewers, Montreal Expos, Philadelphia Phillies, and St. Louis Cardinals started to wear powder blue road uniforms as a substitute for the traditional gray appearance. By 1975, the Houston Astros would institute rainbow-striped shirts and the Cleveland Indians would adopt a blood red uniform featuring matching jerseys and pants.

Whether they cared to admit it or not, several owners had followed Finley's lead in creating colorful new uniforms for their own teams. This was not the first time that Finley's influence had fueled change, nor would it be the last. During the 1960s, Finley had called for the playing of World Series games at night. By 1971, the first night game in Series history would take place—Game Four at Three Rivers Stadium in Pittsburgh. Finley had also pushed for the adoption of a designated hitter rule, a radical concept that American League owners would eventually ratify in 1973. "He was a great innovator," says Reggie Jackson. "Night All-Star games, night World Series games for the working man to be able to enjoy. He wanted to do things that added color to the game and created excitement for the game that the fan could enjoy."

"He was very creative," says Dave Duncan. "He was always trying to attract more interest in the game of baseball from the fan's standpoint. He was always trying to entertain. You have to give him credit for that." Yet, few owners wanted to give Finley credit for anything, given his abrasive style, pushiness, and stubborn demeanor. They refused to heed his warnings about the systems of free agency and arbitration and grudgingly listened to his reasons for supporting the DH, night World Series games, and interleague play. "Charlie was different," says Rick Monday, "but at the same time he certainly left his footprint on baseball. A lot of things that he said about baseball way back in the seventies, if they had listened to him a little bit closer, maybe things would not have gotten out of hand like they have."

Aside from the changes in fashions and uniforms, the spring of 1972 produced several baseball-related surprises for the A's. Angel Mangual, expected to be the starting center fielder now that Monday had been traded, reported to spring training with a torn leg muscle. The A's optioned Mangual to Triple-A, instead of having him start the season on the disabled list. Mangual's injury opened up center field for an obscure seven-year minor leaguer named Bobby Brooks, who had started the spring as a non-roster player. Nicknamed the "Hammer," the hard-hitting, well-built Brooks batted .344 with three home runs and 11 RBIs in 61 pre-season at-bats. As the end of spring training neared, Dick Williams announced to the media that Brooks would be his Opening Day center fielder.

In an even more stunning development, the A's waived veteran first baseman-outfielder Tommy Davis. "I knew I was in trouble when I got my contract," Davis said of the pact that Charlie Finley had mailed him during the winter. I hit .324 for him and he offered me [only] a $3,000 raise," Davis told Phil Pepe of the *New York Daily News*. In 1971, the 33-year-old Davis had performed exceedingly well as the A's' best bench player. He had led all American League pinch-hitters in batting average and had responded brilliantly in clutch situations, collecting 13 RBIs with his 12 pinch-hits. Davis had also continued to hit well in the spring exhibition games, assaulting pitchers at a .563 clip prior to his release. So why did the A's essentially throw away such a valuable bench player while receiving nothing in return? The A's claimed that the condition of Davis' oft-injured legs prevented him from playing a position in the field. "He could no longer do the job defensively," Dick Williams explained to Murray Chass of the *New York Times*.

In reality, Davis' defensive limitations had little to do with his sudden unemployment. The real reason could be found in the name of Davis' agent—Bob Gerst—the same man representing celebrated holdout Vida Blue. Davis had first introduced Blue to Gerst, an act that Finley now considered unconscionable. "If that's the reason they cut me," Davis reasoned to the *New York Times*, "there's nothing I can do about it. If it is [the reason], it's very childish."

Davis later explained that he had brought Blue and Gerst together during the first half of the 1971 season, when the left-hander's assault of American League batters had attracted commercial suitors. "I didn't introduce Gerst to help Blue with his contract," Davis explained to Bob Cottrol of *Black Sports* Magazine. "I introduced him to help him with endorsements and personal appearances—and that was early in the season." Regardless of Davis' intentions, Finley had sought retribution for the current crumbled state of salary negotiations with his star pitcher."He wanted a scapegoat," Davis said. "He didn't want to get rid of Blue, but he wanted to show how strong he could be."

With teams looking to reduce their rosters to the 25-man limit late in spring training, the timing of the release did not help Davis. "I figure I had a job, hitting for Oakland and maybe playing sparingly...the next thing I'm out of baseball," Davis told *Black Sports*. Davis would eventually find work with the Cubs and in later years would make Finley regret his foolish decision to release him.

After the strike by the Players' Association, which delayed the start of the season, the A's announced their Opening Day roster. The list of newcomers included the following: pitchers Denny McLain and recently signed reliever Joel Horlen, whom the White Sox had surprisingly released; third-string catcher Larry Haney; and a trio of outfielders, youngsters Bobby Brooks and George Hendrick, and veteran Brant Alyea. The A's also placed Chuck Dobson, still recovering from offseason elbow surgery, on the disabled list. That left the A's with a roster decision to make on Vida Blue. Since Blue was not injured, he could not be put on the disabled list. Charlie Finley thus placed Blue on the rarely used restricted list, which allowed Dick Williams to replace him with another pitcher. In spite of the absence of Blue and the delicate status of both Dobson and Blue Moon Odom, Williams expressed satisfaction with his Opening Day roster.

On the eve of the opening game, Curt Blefary expressed his *dissatisfaction* by issuing a play-me-or-trade-me order. The veteran utilityman had become famous for making such proclamations during his journeyman career with the Orioles, Astros, Yankees, and A's. Blefary had begun spring training as the team's third-string catcher behind Dave Duncan and Gene Tenace. After hitting .360 during the spring, Blefary had managed to fall to *fourth*-string catcher behind Duncan, Tenace, and Larry Haney. He also found himself as the third-string first baseman behind Mike Epstein and Mike Hegan, as well as the team's sixth outfiielder.

Blefary's clumsy play behind the plate made him too much of a liability to play except on an occasional basis. "Sometimes my mouth went into gear before my brain was engaged," Blefary told the *Baltimore Sun* in explaining his frequent criticisms of managers who did not play him regularly. "I had to play every day or I was mad." The next day, Blefary apologized to Dick Williams for making such a public outburst and putting his manager on the spot right before Opening Day.

Both Tenace and Duncan had been involved in trade talk during the spring, though neither had asked to be dealt. With the A's possessing two catchers of starting caliber, in addition to a fine defensive receiver in Haney, and a solid bat in Blefary, Charlie Finley shopped both Duncan and Tenace in a potential deal for a starting second baseman. The A's would have loved either of the Pirates' young second basemen, Dave Cash or Rennie Stennett, but knew that the Bucs already had a fine No. 1 catcher in Manny Sanguillen. As for other options, the Orioles' Dave Johnson and the Cubs' Glenn Beckert represented two of the better veteran second basemen that might be available in a trade for a catcher.

Sporting their new Charlie Finley-mandated uniforms, the A's opened the 1972 regular season on a Saturday, an oddity created by the duration of the players strike. Most likely upset by the Players' Association walkout, the fans didn't seem too curious about the new look in pullover polyester, as only 9,912 showed up for the April 15th lidlifter at the Oakland Coliseum. With Vida Blue unsigned, Dick Williams handed the Opening Day ball to former Cub Ken Holtzman, who had worked out, by his own estimation, for the grand total of five minutes during the players strike. The rest of the Oakland lineup looked much the same as it had in 1971:

Campy Campaneris, ss
Joe Rudi, lf
Reggie Jackson, rf
Sal Bando, 3b
Mike Epstein, 1b
Bobby Brooks, cf
Dave Duncan, c
Dick Green, 2b
Ken Holtzman, p

Aside from the installation of the unknown Bobby Brooks in center field, the biggest surprise involved the catching position. At the start of spring training, Williams had declared an open competition between Dave Duncan and Gene Tenace. In Cactus League play, Duncan batted only .138, while Tenace sizzled at .316. Tenace believed that his superior spring hitting had earned him the first-string position, but on Opening Day, Duncan found himself behind the plate. Duncan's shotgun throwing arm and agility behind the plate gave him a stronger defensive presence than the offensive-minded Tenace. Williams diplomatically told Tenace that he wanted Duncan to catch Holtzman in the opener since the two had worked together more frequently during the spring. In actuality, *Tenace* had caught Holtzman more often in exhibition games. Once again, Williams had decided to reward the better defensive catcher with the honor of opening the season as the starting receiver.

Williams respected Duncan's ability to read other teams' hitters and help his own pitchers make in-game adjustments. After his playing career, Duncan would become one of the game's most respected pitching coaches. As part of his coaching duties, Duncan would maintain records on every opposing batter. Duncan's files would indicate the type of pitch each batter hit, the location of the pitch, and a description of where the batter hit the ball. Every game, every batter.

Former National Leaguer Ken Holtzman pitched well in his A's debut, giving up just two runs in eight innings. The A's defeated the Twins in the 11th inning, when Joe Rudi raced home from third on a one-out grounder to third base. Eric Soderholm's throw easily beat Rudi to the plate, but catcher George Mitterwald dropped the ball when the Oakland left fielder crashed into him. The results of the fierce collision gave the A's a dramatic 4–3 win.

After losing to the Twins on Sunday afternoon, Denny McLain made a memorable debut for the A's on Tuesday night against the Royals. McLain scattered eight hits over seven-plus innings, giving up a pair of unearned runs. With relief help from Darold Knowles and Rollie Fingers, and the long-ball support of Dave Duncan and Mike Epstein, McLain earned a 3–2 win.

Although McLain had dressed in the green and gold of the A's for fewer than two months, he had already determined Oakland to be baseball nirvana. "It's great to be back in the big leagues," McLain exclaimed to the *New York Times*, while taking a shot at his former team, the Washington Senators-turned Texas Rangers.

"Fundamentally, [Oakland] is the best ballclub I've been on in my life...The execution here is almost flawless. They hit the cut-off man, they make the double play, they do just about everything they're supposed to do." McLain's comments struck some as particularly intriguing, considering that he had previously played for the 1968 World Champion Tigers.

The day after McLain's A's debut, Ken Holtzman topped his Opening Day performance by blanking the Royals, 4–0, on five hits. Through his first two games, Holtzman had pitched 17 nearly impeccable innings, without having surrendered a single walk. Although the season was less than a week old, Holtzman had made a dynamic first impression on his new team and had lessened the A's' worries about the continuing absence of their *other* left-handed starter.

On May 2, two weeks after the start of the strike-delayed season, the Vida Blue saga finally came to an end. Charlie Finley, having agreed to raise the ante on his initial offer of $50,000, reached agreement on a one-year deal with his unhappy pitcher. Finley consented to give Blue a contract for $63,000, which would be prorated back to April 27, but only after Commissioner Bowie Kuhn had interceded in the talks. In the days leading up to the agreement, even President Richard Nixon had put pressure on Finley by raving about the talent of Blue. "Maybe Finley ought to pay," the President mused in an interview with United Press International. "It would be a great tragedy if a young player with all that talent stayed out too long."

With all of spring training and the start of the regular season having already elapsed, Blue expressed little optimism over his ability to pitch well. "I'll be lucky if I win 10 games," Blue informed a reporter for UPI. Indeed, Blue would need three to four weeks of conditioning before returning to game action. Blue's words certainly could not be pleasing to Finley, given his willingness to prorate the contract. In other words, Finley had agreed to give Blue back pay even though he would not be able to pitch for another month. Now Blue was hinting that he might not be able to regain his dominant form once he actually returned to the mound.

Blue had actually come to terms with the A's in Chicago on April 27, when Finley agreed to pay him a base salary of $50,000, give him a $5,000 bonus for his 1971 performance, and set aside another $8,000 that would be put toward the pitcher's continuing college education. The package, totaling $63,000, appeared to satisfy Blue, but he refused to sign the deal when Finley insisted that all terms of the contract be publicly revealed. At the time, most major league teams did not announce the specific stipulations of contracts signed by their players.

After the disagreement over "public revelation" led to a collapse in the talks between the two sides, Commissioner Kuhn had stepped into the negotiations, much to the chagrin of Finley. At first, Kuhn told reporters that Finley had made a fair offer, and felt Blue should agree to the $63,000 contract. Kuhn then ordered Finley to keep the offer on the table until May 2. Finley resented the notion of the commissioner *ordering* him to do anything when it came to offering contracts. An angry Finley tried to remove the offer from the table, but Kuhn insisted otherwise. "I am ruling that the offer has been made and will remain in effect," Kuhn succinctly told the Associated Press.

"The commissioner has no business being in this," Finley fumed to Ron Bergman, corresponding for *The Sporting News*. "I don't believe he had the authority to do so. I didn't like it one damn bit." The commissioner later fined and reprimanded Finley for criticizing him through the media. Finley and Kuhn didn't see eye-to-eye on most matters; the handling of the Blue case just added to the list of angry disagreements between the two men.

The holdout of Blue had not only created hard feelings between Finley and the commissioner, but also between the owner and his star pitcher. Blue had not appreciated Finley's condescending tone throughout their protracted contract negotiations. As he prepared himself to resume playing baseball, Blue criticized the owner for his handling of the contract stalemate. "Charlie Finley has soured my stomach for baseball." Blue also introduced racial overtones to the recently concluded dispute. "Finley treated me like a damned colored boy," the pitcher claimed in an interview with the Associated Press. Blue's assertion represented the first time—but certainly not the last time—that he would charge Finley with racism.

As he looked back on his 1972 holdout in later years, Blue expressed some regrets over a few of the negotiating tactics that he and his representatives employed throughout the ordeal. "I was doing what I thought was in the best interests of Vida Blue," the former major league pitcher said in a 1996 interview with *Sports Collectors Digest*. "The unfortunate part of it, at that time, was I still thought of baseball as a game, but the people I had assisting me in contract negotiations knew it was a business and approached it that way. If I had to do it all over again, I would probably change many of those things." Yet, Blue maintained that he deserved to be paid commensurate with his 1971 performance and not based on his lack of major league longevity at the time. "You're getting paid for what you did last year in this business," Blue explained to *Sports Collectors Digest*, "especially back then [in the early seventies]. Thus, that gives you a legitimate negotiating right to say your value is this amount in dollars and cents."

Now that the A's had signed Blue, they had to face another controversy, one that involved the all-important catching position. Although Dick Williams had given Dave Duncan the honor of starting on Opening Day, he had subsequently decided to employ Gene Tenace in a time-sharing program behind the plate. Williams alternated the two backstops, playing each man every other day. The plan didn't sit particularly well with Duncan, the team's No. 1 catcher in 1971. Despite his unhappiness, Duncan enjoyed one of the hottest hitting streaks of his career, blasting four home runs in his first seven games. Duncan hadn't shown such power-hitting capacity since his spectacular minor league season of 1966, when he had clubbed 46 home runs for Modesto of the California League. Williams would now have to consider playing Duncan on an everyday basis.

During the strike-shortened month of April, the A's won seven and lost four, before reeling off four consecutive wins. After 16 games, Oakland's record stood at 12–4. Even reserve players like Mike Hegan had contributed significantly to the quick start. On April 25, Dick Williams had installed Hegan as a pinch-hitter in the top of the 12th inning of a 3–3 tie. With a runner on second base, the lefty-swinging veteran faced right-hander reliever Lindy McDaniel, one of the Yankees' best relief pitchers. Hegan laced a McDaniel fastball into right-center field, just a few feet in front of his father, Jim, the Yankees' bullpen coach. As the elder Hegan watched from the Yankee bullpen beyond the right-field fence, Mike chugged into second base, the owner of a game-winning hit.

Hegan's clutch pinch-hit may have won the game, but he was still thinking about his father, who would have preferred to see him draw an intentional walk rather than beat the Yankees with a hit. "I kind of took a look toward the bullpen when I got to second," the younger Hegan revealed to the Associated Press, "but I didn't see him." Mike remembered that he had scheduled a post-game dinner date with his father. While the dinner with Jim was still on, Mike realized that his hit would cost him a few dollars. "I bought lunch," Jim pointed out to the AP, "so he better buy dinner."

The A's had managed their fine start with no contribution from Vida Blue, who hadn't signed until May 2, and wouldn't pitch his first game until three weeks later. Without Blue, Dick Williams had smartly used a three-man starting rotation—Ken Holtzman, Catfish Hunter, and Denny McLain—which had been facilitated by several open dates and rainouts. The bullpen had also picked up the slack for the absence of the reigning Cy Young Award winner. Through the first 17 games of the season, Oakland relievers had allowed only one run in 33 and a third innings. The bullpen troupe of Rollie Fingers, Bob Locker, Diego Segui, Joel Horlen, and Darold Knowles had played a direct hand in winning or saving nine of Oakland's first 12 victories.

"Without a doubt, the best bullpen in baseball," Dick Williams assessed of his relievers in an interview with *The Sporting News*. "They throw hard and have good control. My three stoppers, Fingers and Locker from the right side and Knowles from the left, can get either right-handers or left-handers out... My two long and middle men, Segui and Horlen, are just outstanding."

During the 1960s, the side-arming Locker had used his hard, moving sinker to become the relief ace of the White Sox and one of the best firemen in the American League. As a 27-year-old rookie in 1965, the offbeat Locker had drawn snickers from his veteran teammates by wearing a 10-pound weighted canvas vest that looked like a bullet-proof jacket used by members of a SWAT team. When Chicago reporters asked him about wearing the vest during spring training drills, Locker offered some unconventional logic. "You see," Locker told Edgar Munzel of *The Sporting News*, "most of the players come to camp about 10 pounds overweight, while I never gain an ounce [during the offseason]. The fellows with the extra weight are strengthening their legs just carrying it around during these workouts before they finally take it off. Since I never am overweight, I saddle myself with those extra pounds to put me even with them." At least Locker didn't wear the vest while pitching.

Away from the field, Locker loved to hunt and fish, to the extent that he often woke up at 2:30 in the morning to embark on various expeditions. An expert fisherman, Locker once caught 100 fish in a lake—in one day. He had other interests, too. Locker avidly followed the philosophies professed in the book, *Jonathan Livingston Seagull,* which he encouraged his A's teammates to read as a way of life.

The success of the bullpen enabled the A's to overcome a series of adversities. A bad back sidelined starting second baseman Dick Green. Joe Rudi missed several games with the flu. Chuck Dobson, still recovering from elbow surgery, started his season pitching in Double-A. Denny McLain, after pitching well in his Oakland debut, struggled in his next three starts.

On May 9, the A's swept a doubleheader from the Brewers, while showcasing all aspects of their multi-faceted game. In the opening game, the A's scored all 10 of their runs in the fourth inning to support Ken Holtzman, who improved to 4–1 with a complete-game effort. Curt Blefary, filling in for Rudi in left field, contributed a single, a double, and a run scored. Angel Mangual drove in three runs, clearing the bases with a double. In the nightcap, Blue Moon Odom and Rollie Fingers combined on a six-hit, 3–0 shutout. Fingers pitched four scoreless innings to extend the current domination of the Oakland bullpen. With the doubleheader sweep, the A's stretched their winning streak to five games.

After winning his first start, Denny McLain had pitched poorly virtually every time he took to the mound. In his second start, McLain had lasted only four innings against the Yankees, giving up five hits and three runs. In his next outing, McLain pitched creditably against the Brewers, but took the loss after pitching six and one-third innings of three-run baseball. On May 7, McLain failed to reach the fourth inning, giving up eight hits and five runs to the Yankees. Five days later, McLain lasted only two innings when the Red Sox pounded him for four runs. The latest start left McLain with an ERA of 6.05.

Most alarmingly, in all five of his starts, McLain had exhibited extremely poor velocity. One rival player was asked to compare the difference between McLain's fastball in 1972 and the heater he threw in 1968, when he won 31 games for the Tigers. "About 20 miles an hour," Red Sox catcher Duane Josephson told *Sports Illustrated.* "McLain's ball comes up to the plate as straight as a string."

With his fastball lacking both speed and movement, Dick Williams exiled McLain to the bullpen. Rumors circulated that Charlie Finley would offer McLain a $25,000 settlement if he would retire and forego the balance of the $50,000 that the A's owed him. Another report said that Finley would release McLain. The right-hander reacted philosophically to such speculation. "If the game ends tonight," McLain told the Associated Press after his last appearance as a starter, "I've had thrills other people never dreamed of having...They'll have to rip the uniform off me." A few days later, the A's did the next best thing. Instead of releasing him and paying off his guaranteed contract in full, the A's demoted McLain to their Double-A affiliate at Birmingham in the Southern League.

As a veteran player, McLain had the choice of refusing the demotion, but that option would have meant sacrificing the balance of his 1972 salary. McLain delayed reporting to the minor leagues for three days, causing some writers to speculate that he was pondering retirement. Others claimed that McLain was intentionally stalling, so as to continue drawing paychecks at the rate of his annual salary for an extra few days. That theory didn't make sense, however, since the A's would have to pay McLain his major league salary regardless of whether he pitched for them or in the minor leagues. Finally, McLain agreed to report to Birmingham—as a matter of survival. "There were a lot of reasons for my decision [to report to the minor leagues]," McLain explained to *The Sporting News*. "But when you come right down to it, it's a matter of eating."

Eating may have been the root of McLain's problems in the first place. During his days with the Senators, McLain had gained too much weight, which had affected his pitching. Prior to the trade to Oakland, he had begun taking diuretic pills, a medication that results in weight loss. The pills helped McLain lose weight, but also resulted in a loss of fluids and a reduction in potassium, which had caused a general weakening of the muscles. Although observers in Washington insisted McLain had already lost his good fastball by 1970, the loss of strength may have been responsible for robbing him of further velocity. "He can't throw that high, hard one anymore," Dick Williams told Arthur Daley of the *New York Times*. A reporter asked Williams if McLain could still pitch at the major league level. "From the way he's throwing, and the statistics show it," Williams candidly told the Associated Press, "I don't think he could help anybody right now."

Based upon McLain's poor performance, Williams had sufficient reason to demote him to the minor leagues. But there was more. Although Williams, in an interview with the *New York Daily News*, said McLain was a "good fellow and didn't cause us any problems," he knew of the pitcher's past, which included a burdensome gambling habit and associations with illegal bookmakers. The A's' manager, a strict believer in self-responsibility and discipline, felt McLain's habits presented a *potential* threat to the winning atmosphere that he had successfully established in the Oakland clubhouse.

Other factors may have contributed to McLain's decline. He had been stricken with the flu almost immediately after joining the A's in the spring. The players' strike had limited his ability to work out and improve his conditioning. Furthermore, his wife, Sharon, had undergone a difficult pregnancy that had forced her into an unexpected stay in the hospital.

McLain made his first start for Birmingham on May 20. Even though he was facing hitters two classes below the caliber of major leaguers, McLain continued to struggle—embarrassingly. In five innings against Montgomery, McLain gave up nine hits, including three home runs, and suffered a 9–3 loss. Somehow, McLain had managed to pitch worse in Double-A ball than he had in the major leagues.

Chapter 10

Revolving Doors

The A's played well throughout most of April and May, but Charlie Finley continued to tinker with his roster. On April 28, the A's made a curious move, selling quietly effective reliever Jim Roland to the Yankees. The departure of Roland left the A's with Darold Knowles as the sole left-hander in the bullpen.

Ten days later, the A's replaced Roland with a pitcher of lesser ability in Mike Kilkenny. The curveballing left-hander came over from the Tigers for minor league outfielder Reggie Sanders, whom the A's regarded as a very good Triple-A player, but not a major league prospect. On May 15, Finley added another lefty reliever when he acquired Don Shaw from the Cardinals for promising infielder Dwain Anderson. Two days later, the A's made their most puzzling move of the month, trading valuable backup Curt Blefary, a player to be named later, and the recently acquired Kilkenny to the Padres for veteran outfielder "Downtown" Ollie Brown, whom Finley had been seeking off and on since 1969. The trade left the A's with only one reliable left-hander in the bullpen [Darold Knowles], deprived them of Blefary—one of their best left-handed bats off the bench—and gave them a slumping right fielder in Brown, who was hitting just .171 with no home runs and three RBIs and happened to play the same position as Reggie Jackson. The next day, Finley made another move when he dealt backup outfielder Brant Alyea to the Cardinals for utility infielder Marty Martinez. Finley then sold Opening Day center fielder Bobby Brooks to the Tigers' organization. In the span of three weeks, Finley had completed six transactions involving 12 players.

The trade of the versatile Blefary appeared mystifying, at least on the surface. Although Blefary had requested a trade moments before the start of the season, he had served the A's well in a backup role, rapping out five hits in 11 at-bats. "I got off to a good start there," Blefary said later in an interview with the *Palm Beach Times*, "but I've stopped trying to figure things out. I do what I'm told now and keep my mouth shut. [Dick] Williams told me it wasn't his idea to trade me."

So why did *Finley* decide to trade him for Ollie Brown, who figured to be a backup right fielder? Blefary's constant complaints over playing time may have sealed his fate with an annoyed Finley, but former teammate Mike Hegan offers another theory. "When you did look at the other people that were there," recalls Hegan, "I think that Dick [Williams] felt and maybe Charlie [Finley] felt that we had enough left-handed hitting coming off the bench, and that we needed some right-handed hitting coming off the bench. Very frankly, Curt—and I love him, Curt and I [were] great friends—but very frankly, he was kind of a one-dimensional player, if you will, and that [one dimension] was offense."

Blefary had long since earned the nickname "Clank," which represented the imaginary sound the ball made when it caromed off any of his less-than-reliable gloves. Blefary carried around *eight* different gloves, in the eventuality that he might catch, play first, second or third base, or patrol the outfield. Although Blefary brought enthusiasm and versatility to the utility role, he represented a defensive liability *everywhere.*

Most scouts considered first base Blefary's best position, and even there he had struggled, committing a National League-leading 17 errors for the Astros in 1969. "There wasn't any place you could put him in the field," explains Hegan, "and he knew that. So you might have gotten the one shot from him as a pinch-hitter, but again, he was the guy who was probably more valuable to a ballclub given four shots to play, rather than one shot." After the announcement of the trade, Blefary threatened to retire and become a policeman if the Padres did not renegotiate his contract, but soon changed his mind. "Clank" played sparingly with the Padres, who released him after the season. The move ended Blefary's major league career at the age of 29, only one season before the American League adopted the designated hitter rule—a rule that would have perfectly suited the man known as "Clank."

Ollie Brown, despite playing the same outfield position as Reggie Jackson, did bring some strengths to Oakland. "I think that we needed some right-handed power and some defensive help," says Hegan, "and Ollie Brown provided both." Reds superscout Ray Shore had once called Brown's throwing arm the best he'd ever seen from an outfielder. Other scouts rated Brown's arm on a par with Pittsburgh's Roberto Clemente, often referred to by fans and writers as the owner of the game's greatest throwing arm among outfielders. Brown had also shown some hitting prowess earlier in his career. In 1970, Brown had enjoyed his most productive season, reaching career highs with 23 home runs and 89 RBIs.

The series of player moves reflected Charlie Finley's general concerns about the Oakland ballclub. After winning five straight games to open up the month of May, the A's had lost three games in a row. For the first time all season, the bullpen played the part of culprits. In a 7–6 loss to Boston, the Red Sox tagged both Bob Locker and Rollie Fingers for late-inning runs, including a game-winning home run in the 12th inning. The next day, Joel Horlen allowed a three-run homer in relief of Ken Holtzman, who suffered a hard-luck loss.

Injuries also played a role in depleting the A's. A week after the Horlen blowup, starting second baseman Dick Green underwent surgery to remove a herniated disc in his back. Green had initially suffered the injury on April 25 after bending over to lay down a sacrifice bunt. At first, the A's worried that Green would miss the entire season, but doctors encouraged him by predicting that he could return by the first of September.

On May 19, the A's suffered their most one-sided loss since Charlie Finley had moved the franchise from Kansas City to Oakland in 1968. A's pitchers gave up 20 hits in a 16–1 loss to the Royals. Blue Moon Odom lasted only three and a third innings. Rollie Fingers allowed three runs without retiring a batter. The newly acquired Don Shaw, exhibiting why the Cardinals had given up on him, surrendered nine runs in a torturous three-inning stint.

"It was a circus," Sal Bando told *Sports Illustrated* in assessing the embarrassing loss to the Royals. "[The game] should have been played in a tent." The performance did not amuse Dick Williams, who watched his pitchers toil miserably, witnessed physical errors by Reggie Jackson and Bob Locker, and observed numerous mental lapses by his fielders and baserunners.

After the game, Williams called a team meeting to let the players know of his displeasure. As the A's had often reacted to previous Williams diatribes, they responded by winning their next four games. After a loss to the Angels on May 24, the A's won five more games in a row, and six of their next seven. The stretch gave the A's 18 wins in 26 games during the month of May, and an overall record of 25–12 heading into June.

The A's had started to solve some of their nagging personnel problems. Vida Blue had rejoined the starting rotation after his lengthy holdout and delayed conditioning program, while Blue Moon Odom had returned to health, giving Williams two more viable starters after Catfish Hunter and Ken Holtzman. Utility infielder Larry Brown, though hitting only .168, had successfully replaced Dick Green at second base, giving the A's a reliable double-play partner for Campy Campaneris. In addition, top prospect George Hendrick had been summoned from the minor leagues to fill the center-field gap created by the offseason trade of Rick Monday to the Cubs and the subsequent struggles of Bobby Brooks and Angel Mangual. Hendrick responded by hitting game-winning home runs in two consecutive games against the White Sox.

The A's' offense ranked as the best in the American League, thanks largely to the play of Joe Rudi. The anonymous left fielder, who hadn't even been listed on the American League's All-Star ballot, had emerged as an early MVP candidate. On June 1, Rudi's .324 batting average ranked him second in the American League. Rudi rated in the top five in runs scored, hits, doubles, and triples, all while batting out of the demanding No. 2 slot in the batting order. Rudi would later put together a 17-game hitting streak, the longest in the short history of the Oakland franchise. "If I had been scouting him, I'd have been completely wrong," says Jack Aker, a teammate of Rudi during his first two major league seasons. "I really didn't feel he was gonna be a major league *everyday* player; I thought possibly a fourth outfielder and extra man, but he just kept improving, made himself into a star, really."

Rudi claimed that previous stints in the U.S. Marine Reserves, which caused him to miss 35 to 40 games a year, had affected his timing and rhythm at the plate. As an example, Rudi had fallen off to a mediocre .267 in 1971, the last season in which he periodically reported to the reserves. Now that Rudi's military obligations had ended, he was free to pursue the art of hitting to the fullest. A pull-hitting power hitter in the minor leagues, Rudi had transformed himself into a successful gap-hitting opposite field hitter. "Joe has the ideal temperament for a professional athlete," an admiring Dick Williams told *Sport* Magazine. "He's *always* working to improve." Under former Oakland batting coach Charley Lau's tutelage in 1970, Rudi had worked hard to radically change his batting approach. Rudi began choking up on the bat while adopting a severely closed stance with a deep crouch at the plate. Using an unusual diagonal stance, Rudi placed his left foot close to the front corner of the plate, while nearly planting his right foot outside of the batter's box. In the meantime, Rudi rested his bat flatly on his right shoulder, making it parallel to the ground. Although an awkward-looking Rudi hardly seemed ready to handle incoming pitches, the new stance actually made his swing quicker and more compact. "Charley Lau changed my whole theory on hitting and what I was trying to do with the ball," said Rudi, making sure to credit his former batting instructor. "He taught me about hitting behind the runner, thinking about what I wanted to do with the ball... All of a sudden, it was there. It was like being in the boonies all your life and walking into a big city and finding a metropolitan library. I just milked that guy every second I could about hitting."

Rudi had obviously not been consulted by Charlie Finley at the time that the owner fired Lau for "sleeping with" catcher Dave Duncan. "It was," Rudi told *Sport* Magazine in the recounting the first time he met Lau, "the turning point of my career. Charlie got me to shorten up on my swing and to forget about hitting home runs. He also taught me how to hit to right field." Rudi pointed out that the since-departed Lau had also helped Duncan, who tended to overswing and chase too many bad pitches, making his hitting throughout the sixties a chronic struggle. Now aided by a shortened swing, Duncan hit 10 early-season home runs in 1971, putting him in a tie with Reggie Jackson for the team lead.

While Rudi garnered a few headlines with his surprising hitting, Jackson enjoyed a quietly productive season at the plate, providing the team with both a decent batting average and his usual measure of long ball. In June, Jackson described his philosophy of power at the plate, and his love of "taters," a nickname that Red Sox slugger George Scott had originated to describe his own home runs. "The home run is very important to me," Reggie Jackson explained to *Sports Illustrated*. "Sure, I like to keep a respectable average, like .280 or .290, but average is like the wind; it can disappear overnight. Those taters, them they can't ever take away from you."

The team's two most productive hitters, Jackson and Rudi enjoyed a special long-term relationship, even though their personalities differed as much as the color of their skin. In 1966, Jackson and Rudi had played for Modesto, the Class-A affiliate of the A's. The next season, both players moved up to Double-A Birmingham, where segregation in the South prevented Jackson from enjoying the same experiences as his white teammates. Jackson found Rudi the most accepting among his fellow players. "Joe was the first player ever to have me over to his house for dinner," Reggie said of his days in Birmingham. "There were a lot of places in Birmingham I couldn't eat. I couldn't even live where the Rudis were staying."

Rudi himself found the racial attitudes of some of his neighbors distasteful. "Our landlady kept coming around asking why that *black guy* was coming over all the time," Rudi told *The Sporting News*. "For the [rent] money we were paying her, we figured we could have anyone over we wanted."

In addition to his terrific on-the-field play, Jackson continued to have an effect on the A's in more peripheral matters. In May, Charlie Finley called a press conference to announce that the A's would hold a special promotion on Father's Day; major league baseball's first-ever "Mustache Day" would take place at the Oakland Coliseum. In a continuation of a story that had begun with Jackson's full-grown sprouting of a mustache in spring training, Finley promised to pay $300 bonuses to each player who featured a mustache on Father's Day. In addition, all mustache-bearing fans would receive free admission to the Coliseum.

Finley had gone full circle—from an initial dislike of Reggie Jackson's mustache to a desire to have every player on his 25-man roster wear facial hair below his nose. "Guys that didn't have mustaches, and I was one of them, were required to grow a mustache so that Charlie could put on a 'Mustache Day' at the Coliseum," Mike Hegan recalls. Some players, like Rollie Fingers, willingly fulfilled Finley's request for mustaches. "For $300," Fingers admitted to Phil Pepe of the *New York Daily News*, "I'd grow one on my rear end."

A small group of players felt differently. "There were three guys that didn't want to do it," says Sal Bando. "Larry Brown, Mike Hegan, and myself. [Finley] had to call us in and convince us—not twist our arm or anything—but just reiterate he wanted us to do it." After initial misgivings, Hegan eventually caved in to the owner's wishes. "I finally grew a mustache, did it for about six weeks until 'Mustache Day,' and then shaved it off." In ridding himself of the mustache, Hegan gave in to a higher authority than Finley. "My wife didn't like it."

All 25 players on the active roster—Bando, Brown, and Hegan included—sported mustaches by Father's Day. In return, Finley fulfilled his promise of cash considerations. "Yeah, at the end of the game," confirms Hegan, "there was a couple of hundred bucks in everybody's valuable box. [There was also] a little thank-you note for growing the mustaches." At the cost of $7,500, Finley had put together a successful promotion.

By July, most of the other A's would shave their mustaches, only to bring them back later in the season. Why did so many of the Oakland players revert back to the hairy-lipped look? "Well, we had success as a team," explains Bando, "so everybody stayed with it." As a team, the A's' mustachioed, longhaired, and even bearded look would stamp them with an identity starkly different from the rest of the teams throughout the major leagues.

Rollie Fingers profited most from the facial hair episode, eventually growing a stylish handlebar mustache that became his trademark and helped him become the "best-looking guy in all of baseball," according to Joe Falls of *The Sporting News*. Fingers even made sure to negotiate Finley's $300 bonus into his 1973 contract with the A's. In a comically written press release, Finley discussed his contract talks with Fingers. "Rollie not only got a substantial increase in salary," Finley expounded, "but his 1973 contract also includes a year's supply of the very best mustache wax available. In fact, this is what held up the final signing. I wanted to give Rollie $75 for the mustache wax and he wanted $125 for it." The two parties settled at $100, allowing Fingers to wax the tips of his mustache two times a day.

More than any other player, catcher Dave Duncan embodied the image of the A's as hippies. Not only did Duncan grow a mustache; he also sported a scraggly, unkempt beard that made him suitable to appear at a *Grateful Dead* concert. Duncan also allowed his blonde hair to flow past his shoulders, far longer than any of his teammates. Duncan's appearance proved disconcerting, and perhaps even intimidating, to some observers, especially those who didn't know him. "With that long hair, he kind of looked goofy as a player," Tigers shortstop Eddie Brinkman told the *Chicago Sun-Times*. A few years later, Brinkman would work with Duncan as coaches on the staff of the White Sox. "But once you get to know him," Brinkman said, "you realize he's one of the kindest, smartest men you'll ever meet."

In the meantime, Denny McLain continued his stay of execution in Class-AA Birmingham. The former Cy Young winner aggravated some of his minor league teammates by continuing to live a major league lifestyle. McLain lived in an expensive suite at the Savannah Inn and Country Club, where he roomed with another former Athletic right-hander, Chuck Dobson. McLain spent most of his days playing golf and sun-tanning before riding to games in a luxurious El Dorado Cadillac driven by another former Athletic, Ken "Hawk" Harrelson, a resident of Savannah. "How you like my 'team bus,' boys?" McLain said to his teammates, many of whom made minimum minor league salaries.

McLain also failed to make any friends with his on-field performance. After bombing in his first start, McLain fared no better in his next, giving up three more home runs. In his first 11 innings at Double-A, McLain had given up six home runs, 19 hits, and 16 runs. In his third start, McLain appeared on the verge of extinction, giving up two walks and a single in the first inning. The sore-armed right-hander told manager Phil Cavarretta that his shoulder was "killing him," but insisted that he be left in to pitch. Somehow, McLain recovered to throw seven innings of one-run baseball, while striking out eight. The positive performance soon gave way to harsh reality, as McLain gave up four homers and 12 runs in his next start. "My report will be exactly what I saw," Cavarretta said candidly to a reporter for the Associated Press. "A man pitching with no real velocity, no real control, and a man who must be hurting inside." Out of shape, overweight, and his shoulder causing him pain, McLain appeared light years away from a return to the major leagues.

After losing their first game of June, the A's racked up a season-high eight-game winning streak, which also represented the best stretch in the history of the Oakland franchise. Ken Holtzman, Catfish Hunter, and rookie left-hander Dave Hamilton pitched three consecutive shutouts against the Orioles. Hunter's game was particularly impressive: a 91-pitch, two-hit masterpiece. Catfish faced only 28 batters, one above the minimum, and retired the last 20 Orioles that he faced. In the next series, Blue Moon Odom threw only 76 pitches in beating the Indians, 3–2, in 10 innings.

Despite the win over the Indians, Dick Williams laced into his players for a series of baserunning mistakes. The tongue-lashing, even in the wake of a victory, impressed some players. "I liked that," Gene Tenace told *Sports Illustrated* in assessing Williams' reaction. "It showed he cares. Some managers will let you get away with a mistake. Not Dick." Not satisfied with playing badly in a win, Williams demanded near perfection from his players. The A's responded well to the Williams tirade, pounding out 20 runs in back-to-back wins over the Indians and Tigers. The A's put together two more winning streaks in June, one of five games and another of four games. The streaks gave Oakland another winning month—18 wins against 11 defeats.

Even high-profile players like Reggie Jackson respected the demanding nature of Williams. "If you don't win," Reggie said to a writer for *Sports Illustrated*, "he's ready to fight. I'm loyal to him. He's the best baseball man I've ever known. He keeps you scared enough so you've gotta do your job." Jackson's assessment of his manager had evolved considerably since his initial negative description of Williams in 1971.

Despite their winning ways on the field, Charlie Finley continued to maneuver his players in the transaction column. Encouraged by the fine pitching of Dave Hamilton and Joel Horlen, Finley deemed one of his veteran pitchers expendable. On June 7, Finley sold former American League ERA champion Diego Segui to the Cardinals. The sale of the utility pitcher marked the third time he had been traded or let go by the A's. Segui's gentlemanly demeanor and refusal to complain about his many pitching roles had made him a likable figure in the clubhouse. Teammates also respected the physical strength of Segui, regarded by some as the strongest man pound-for-pound in all of baseball. Some players wondered how the move might affect Campy Campaneris, who felt closer to Segui than any of the other A's. In 1969, the two Cubans had spent so much time together that fans regularly mistook one for the other. Curiously, Campaneris and Segui had simultaneously enjoyed career seasons in 1970.

Another veteran, Mike Epstein, remained an Athletic, despite his rollercoaster status with Dick Williams. In early June, Epstein had embarked on a home run tear, cementing his favor with the manager. Then, on June 17, Epstein hit a weak pop fly in a game against the Indians. Frustrated by his poor swing at the ball, Epstein failed to run out the pop-up. Furious over Epstein's lack of hustle, Williams pulled him from the game immediately. The next day, Williams returned Epstein to the lineup and watched the left-handed slugger collect two hits in four at-bats and drive in four runs.

The day after Epstein returned to Williams' good graces, Vida Blue finally won his first game of the season. During his spring holdout, Blue had spent much of his time making public appearances for Dura Steel Products and Jantzen Sportswear and had neglected to work out on a regular basis. The lack of conditioning, coupled with his absence from spring training, seemed to cost Blue, who had lost three consecutive starts before pitching a 9–0 shutout vs. the Indians. In contrast, Blue had already won eight games by the same date in 1971.

Blue would struggle throughout much of the 1972 season, paying the price for the spell of inactivity created by his contract battle with Charlie Finley. Although the holdout unquestionably hurt Blue, some observers have wondered whether he might not have held the upper moral ground during his lengthy contract dispute with a penurious owner. "At this point," counters Sal Bando, "I'm not sure it matters who was right or wrong, but the bottom line was Vida Blue was never the same dominant pitcher he was in '71. He still had a good career, but coming off that '71 season he was unhittable. I think he became hittable after that. He just never had the same fastball, the consistency with it. So, if anybody suffered, I think Vida did for missing that time."

Blue also began his use of illegal drugs during the 1972 season. His involvement with drugs, including cocaine, would lead to his arrest in 1984. Blue would spend 81 days in a federal institution in Fort Worth, Texas, for attempting to purchase cocaine. After his release from prison, Blue began serving another drug-related punishment—a yearlong suspension from Major League Baseball. Commissioner Bowie Kuhn banned Blue, by now with the Kansas City Royals, and three of his teammates, Willie Mays Aikens, Jerry Martin, and Willie Wilson.

The end of June would bring another flurry of trades for the A's, including the exit of another veteran right-handed pitcher. On June 28, the A's acquired first baseman-outfielder Art Shamsky from the Cubs in a cash deal. Shamsky, a member of the 1969 "Miracle Mets," figured to replace Curt Blefary in the role of left-handed pinch-hitter. Finley announced two more deals the next day. The A's dispatched outfielder Ollie Brown, the former backup right fielder who had most recently moved into the starting lineup when Dick Williams decided to move Reggie Jackson to center field. Not satisfied with Brown's hitting, the A's sent him to Milwaukee for what was announced as cash considerations. In actuality, Finley secretly acquired the rights to negotiate with recently retired outfielder Billy Conigliaro. On the same day, Finley finally resolved the Denny McLain dilemma.

McLain had pitched much better after his first two disastrous starts with Double-A Birmingham. With his minor league record now a respectable 3–3, McLain telephoned Dick Williams, asking him to be placed on Oakland's 25-man roster. "I've done everything they've asked," McLain told the *New York Daily News*. "My instructions were to get myself in shape and get my arm in shape. I've done that." Even though the A's possessed only nine healthy pitchers at the time, Williams told McLain that he had no current need for a starting pitcher. "We're not recalling him," Williams told the *Daily News*, while noting that McLain had given up 10 home runs in his five earlier major league starts. "We have five starting pitchers and they are all doing a good job. What we need is a left-handed reliever and the last time I looked, McLain didn't fit that bill."

Since McLain had no plans to become a left-handed pitcher, it appeared that his future rested with another major league organization. McLain said that two major league teams—the Braves and Expos—expressed interest in him. The right-hander asked Charlie Finley to work out a deal. Finley said he would do his best to trade him, which would alleviate the A's' responsibility of having to pay the balance of

McLain's overall salary. Finley certainly didn't want to release McLain outright. Under baseball's new collective bargaining agreement, McLain's salary was 100 percent guaranteed. If the A's released McLain, they would still have to pay the balance in full.

Faced with having an unwanted player at an exorbitant salary, Finley made an unusual transaction on June 29. The Oakland owner sold his Double-A albatross to the Braves, who had earlier turned down a deal with the A's. "I'm as happy as hell," McLain responded to *New York Newsday*. As someone who hated pitching in the minor leagues, McLain realized he would have an opportunity to return to the major league level. While McLain headed to Atlanta, Finley simultaneously purchased 1967 National League MVP Orlando Cepeda, who had managed four home runs and a .298 batting average for the Braves, but had been limited to 84 at-bats by knee troubles. Although the A's and Braves announced the transactions as separate sales, the two teams had essentially traded onetime league MVPs for another, the first time in history that such a deal had taken place.

If this trade had been made five years earlier, it might have been hailed as the deal of the century. At his peak in 1967, Cepeda had batted .325 with 25 home runs and 111 RBIs for the World Champion Cardinals. In 1968, McLain had forged an eye-popping record of 31–6 with an ERA of 1.96, which earned him American League MVP honors.

By 1972, both players had fallen on hard times, McLain victimized by his weight and gambling problems and the 34-year-old Cepeda undermined by his chronically bad knees. Because each player had to clear waivers before the trade could be officially consummated, any of the other 22 major league teams could have claimed McLain or Cepeda for $25,000. Five years earlier, any team would have jumped at the chance to pick up Cepeda or McLain at such a price, but by 1972, both were considered damaged goods. *New York Times* columnist Arthur Daley aptly summarized the trade of onetime MVPs with the following sentence: "It is a trade that is a lot more historic than it is momentous."

Like McLain, Cepeda was pleased to hear the trade news. "I am always happy," Cepeda told the Associated Press. "Only when I do not play am I unhappy." With the Braves, Cepeda had lost his starting job when manager Luman Harris decided to move Hank Aaron from the outfield to first base. Harris questioned whether Cepeda could play every day because of his wavering physical condition. Cepeda balked at his demotion by walking out on the team and the Braves responded by suspending him—albeit for only two days.

Now that Cepeda had arrived in Oakland, how would the A's use him? Perhaps Dick Williams envisioned a platoon of Cepeda and Mike Epstein at first base, with Orlando playing against left-handed pitchers. Although Epstein had managed a respectable .250 average against portsiders, he had hit only one home run against lefties. According to Cepeda, Williams made a point of explaining his role with a new team. "Yes, he told me," Cepeda says, "because they didn't know I had a bad knee. They didn't know that. But [Williams] told me that Mike was the first baseman, but when they have a tough left-handed pitcher, to be ready because you're gonna be playing many games with this ballclub."

Predictably, the arrival of Cepeda angered Epstein, who had been enjoying his status as an everyday first baseman. Epstein wondered aloud why Williams didn't approach him to explain how his role might be affected. "What hurt me is that Dick Williams hasn't called me into the office and told me what they're going to do with Cepeda," a frustrated Epstein complained to the Associated Press. "I busted my tail for this team and then I read in the paper where we got another player to platoon with me." Williams countered by saying it wasn't the responsibility of the manager to explain every one of his lineup decisions. "All a player has to do is check the lineup card every day and see if his name is on it," Williams angrily told *The Sporting News*. "If it is, he goes out and busts his rear." When a reporter pointed out Epstein's reputation as a moody player, Williams shot back, "Well, I'm a moody manager."

Epstein had become associated with moodiness dating back to his days in Washington. Although his critics considered his temperamental nature a flaw in his personality, Epstein disagreed. "Moodiness is an outgrowth of pride in a person," Epstein explained to *Sports Illustrated*. "My so-called moodiness stems only from desire. Now, at 29, I feel I've matured enough to handle problems."

But could he handle the presence of Cepeda? When Orlando learned of Epstein's concerns over his arrival in Oakland, he sought out the big, left-handed hitting first baseman and offered him some reassurance. "Yes, I told him, 'I didn't come here to take your position away. I just came here to try to help win some games and see what happens.'" Cepeda's chat evidently eased Epstein's mind. The incumbent first baseman proceeded to pick up 13 hits in his next 20 at-bats, including seven safeties against left-handed pitchers. As it would turn out, Epstein and Williams would have little to worry about with regards to a first base controversy.

The trade of the unhappy McLain ended one of the shortest chapters in his baseball life. In the spring, Charlie Finley and Dick Williams had quietly hoped that McLain could recapture his former pitching dominance, or at least some percentage of it. By mid-season, those hopes had been transformed into the realities of a lost fastball and an expanding waistline. Although McLain lasted less than half a season in Oakland, he succeeded in leaving an impression on his teammates. "Yes, I got to know Dennis," says captain Sal Bando. "He was still kind of recovering from being on the downward cycle of his career. Even at that point, he was a gambler; he liked to go play golf for money, bowl for money, whatever it was. He was a character."

As the team's manager, Williams might have been concerned about McLain's history of gambling and the threat it created to the discipline that he had worked hard to establish in the Oakland clubhouse. Bando, however, saw no evidence of McLain's gambling habits interfering with his preparation for the game. "We really didn't see that because he wasn't there that long," Bando says. "It really was during the strike so there was a lot of free time. People were looking to do different things. So, he'd go out with Ken Holtzman and Rollie Fingers, and they'd play golf for money or go bowling for money. You could see that gambling was a major part of [McLain's] focus."

According to Bando, McLain posed no problem for his teammates, despite his reputation as an annoying egotist who had antagonized teammates in Detroit and Washington. "In the clubhouse he was fine," Bando insists. "He was a kibitzer. He was a guy who'd like to have a good time and yet he worked. He did his baseball work."

McLain's quick departure from the A's was sad for several reasons. Still only 28 years old, McLain seemed to be wasting his talents, which earlier in his career had him pointed in the direction of Cooperstown. Furthermore, his flamboyant, somewhat abrasive personality would have been a natural fit for the A's, given their colorfully controversial tendencies throughout the early 1970s. "He would have fit in very well," agrees Bando. "Now that we can look back, you can see obviously that there were some problems in his life." McLain's problems would continue after his retirement from the game. After allowing his weight to balloon to 300 pounds, McLain, looking unrecognizable to those who remembered him as a player, suffered a heart attack. He later served 29 months in prison on racketeering, drug, and gambling convictions. McLain's daughter, Kristen, died in a 1992 car accident. In 1997, McLain returned to federal prison after a jury convicted him of stealing millions of dollars from a union pension plan.

While journeyman players like Denny McLain and Downtown Ollie Brown had now departed from the fast-changing Oakland scene, other veterans like Art Shamsky and Orlando Cepeda were now entering the revolving door. The latest influx of players left the minds of players and writers spinning. With more than half the season to go, Charlie Finley had already orchestrated 34 personnel moves. "He was probably one of the only guys who told you that he treated the game as a business," Vida Blue would tell sportswriter Bill Ballew in 1996. "He was real cut and dried with trading or cutting or releasing or swapping a player. He was quoted as saying he would trade his mother if he could get the right player he felt he needed."

The addition of Shamsky provided an unusual footnote to the composition of the Oakland roster. With Shamsky aboard, the A's now had three players of Jewish descent—along with Mike Epstein and Ken Holtzman—on their 25-man roster. Bay Area writer Ron Bergman pointed out the oddity to Holtzman, who responded tongue-in-cheek, "I hear we're going to have Golda Meir as a shortstop."

While Holtzman was willing to joke about the religious makeup of the team and Epstein reveled in calling himself "Super Jew," both players took pride in their heritage. Later in the year, when terrorists murdered several Israeli athletes during the Olympic Games, Holtzman, Epstein, and Reggie Jackson wore black armbands in tribute to those who had been slain. "It hit us like a ton of bricks," Epstein told the *New York Times* in explaining the players' reaction to hearing of the tragedy. "Of course, Ken and I are Jewish, but we'd feel the same way if it was any other team. The Olympics are supposed to foster international brotherhood."

In the meantime, the constant changes in player personnel might have affected a less talented, or weaker-willed team, but seemed to do little harm to Oakland. The A's continued to pile up wins, while separating themselves further from the second-place White Sox and the third-place Twins, who had paced the West the first month of the season. While Finley had tried desperately to upgrade his bench and his bullpen, he had wisely not tinkered with the core of his team: Hunter, Holtzman, and Blue in the starting rotation; Fingers and Knowles in the bullpen; Duncan behind the plate; Green, Campaneris, and Bando on the infield; and Rudi and Jackson in the outfield. Those 11 players represented the most important segment of the 1972 A's; if Finley had traded any of them, he might have done irreparable harm to the team's chances of making the World Series.

No Oakland player had been more indispensable than Holtzman, who had filled the void created by the long holdout of Blue. Though not a power pitcher in the mold of Blue, Holtzman had won 11 of his first 17 starts, compiled 11 complete games, and given up slightly over two runs per nine innings. Holtzman credited his catching partner with his improvement. "Dave Duncan and I think a lot alike," Holtzman told *The Sporting News*. "I'd say Duncan and I try to challenge the hitters 99 per cent of the time." By attacking opposing hitters with fastballs early in the count, Holtzman had cut down on his walk total, while also reducing his pitch count. In 135 innings, Holtzman had walked only 19 batters, or just over one per start.

Such numbers represented major improvement over Holtzman's final season in Chicago, where he had pitched in a ballpark—Wrigley Field—that was much friendlier to hitters than the Oakland Coliseum. Holtzman had also struggled under the management style of Leo Durocher, whose antiquated style of dealing with players had affected the thoughtful left-hander's performance. (According to at least one writer, Durocher had repeatedly made anti-Semitic slurs toward Holtzman, even calling him a "kike.") In contrast, Holtzman liked his relationship with his new manager, Dick Williams. "Williams is just super," Holtzman gushed in an interview with Ron Bergman. "He's a great fundamentalist. I think he's as fair as a manager can be in the major leagues."

Holtzman's businesslike professionalism on the mound impressed his teammates and the media, but his aloof personality bothered others around the team. Holtzman refrained from socializing with most of his teammates, showing little interest in visiting bars or restaurants after games. "I'm not really outgoing," Holtzman explained to Glenn Dickey in an article for *Sport* Magazine. "When we go on the road, I like to buy four or five paperbacks in the terminal so I'll have something to read in my hotel room."

On the field, Holtzman had pitched far better than expected. So had comebacking right-hander Blue Moon Odom, who regained his arm strength after persistent elbow problems the past two seasons. Although Odom didn't make his first start until early May, he quickly emerged as one of the American League's most effective right-handed pitchers. Odom successfully regained the good, moving fastball that he had featured prior to his elbow problems. "He's one of the few guys I've ever seen in baseball that could not throw a ball straight, which was great," says Jack Aker. "He would have had a little trouble at another position." In a 1968 game against the Senators, Odom had tried to pick off speedster Ed Stroud three times. With the three throws, Odom hit Stroud, first baseman Danny Cater, and umpire Larry Napp in succession.

In a sense, Odom had benefited from his 1970 elbow surgery, which forced him to improvise and add other pitches to his repertoire. In 1971, when he could not throw his fastball with its same level of pre-surgical pop, he worked diligently at developing a change-up and improving his breaking ball. Now adept at the art of pitching and equipped with a more deceptive motion, Odom won six straight games.

Odom also made strides in curbing his temper, which he had often vented at teammates when they made fielding errors behind him. "I know they're not perfect," said Odom in 1972, "and there's no reason to get mad. I just tell them to get them next time or try to make it up with the bat. I guess I'm more grown up this year. I used to have a quick temper. I know how to control it now."

The pitching of Odom helped carry the A's while Blue scuffled to regain his 1971 form. The lack of spring training had left Blue physically ill prepared for the new season; the ugly contract negotiations with Charlie Finley had left him emotionally tainted. "Yes, I'm bitter," Blue said in July. "It all seemed unnecessary to me, all that trouble." Blue claimed he no longer wanted to play for Finley and asked for a trade to one of three teams: the Cardinals, Mets, or Yankees.

In addition to concerns over the fragile psyche of the talented left-hander, a series of injuries threatened to undermine the A's. Second baseman Larry Brown encountered back pains, which forced him into traction for 10 days. With starting infielder Dick Green already on the shelf after back surgery, the A's were now down to their third-string second baseman—former Senator Tim Cullen, who had been picked up on waivers prior to the start of the season. Smaller injuries nagged the A's, as well. Blue missed a turn because of a severe bruise on his leg. Joe Rudi, vying for the American League batting lead, found his swing hampered by a sore left hand, which had been hit by a pitch.

As the A's prepared to face the White Sox in Chicago for a weekend three-game set, Dick Williams learned about another setback to his personnel. One of his recent acquisitions was in no condition to play. Orlando Cepeda, who had recently undergone knee surgery, could not run well enough to play the field or move along the base paths. In a way, Cepeda's injury delayed a difficult decision for Williams. "Even if Orlando could play," the manager informed *The Sporting News*, "I don't know where I'd put him. The guy we have at first base now [Mike Epstein] is doing the job. He's got the hot bat."

On June 30, another one of the new acquisitions made his Oakland debut. With the Cubs, Art Shamsky had come to bat only 16 times, mostly as a pinch-hitter, and had collected only two hits. Worn down by rust, the veteran outfielder pinch-hit unsuccessfully for the light-hitting Tim Cullen. The next day, Williams asked Shamsky to do the near impossible: pinch-hit against Angels ace Nolan Ryan, the most intimidating right-hander in the American League. "He was really throwing the ball," Shamsky told the *New York Times* in assessing Ryan, who regularly approached the 100-mile-per-hour barrier on the radar gun. "I figured I'd go up swinging, and I did—I fouled out." At least Shamsky made contact with the ball, something that most of the Oakland batters failed to do that night at Anaheim Stadium. Ryan struck out 16 A's in earning a 5–3 win for the Angels.

On July 3, Orlando Cepeda finally made his Oakland debut when he pinch-hit for Cullen in a game against the Angels. Three days later, Williams called upon Cepeda to pinch-hit for reliever Joel Horlen against the Yankees. The next day, Cepeda appeared as a pinch-hitter for Bob Locker during a 9–4 loss to the Brewers. Cepeda failed to register a hit in any of the three at-bats. More alarmingly, Cepeda looked bad in each of his plate appearances. "The Baby Bull" could hardly run. His knees ached severely. Cepeda and the A's came to a logical conclusion; he would need another surgery to be performed on his knees.

Doctors performed the operation, and the A's hoped that Cepeda might become useful to them by early September, but the big first baseman didn't seem confident that he would be able to return before the end of the season. Either way, Finley was furious. While he had traded away Denny McLain and his $50,000 commitment to him, he had picked up an even larger tab—the balance on Cepeda's $90,000 contract. Finley had gone from a pitcher who had no fastball to a first baseman who couldn't even walk. Neither was of much use to a baseball team.

Although the sorry condition of Cepeda's knees prevented him from enjoying a longer stay in Oakland, "Cha Cha" traveled with the team on a few occasions and relished the opportunity to witness a terrific team first-hand. "Yes, I made a couple of trips with the team," Cepeda recalls. "In Oakland, I had the opportunity to play with Reggie and Bando and Vida and some of the great ballplayers...They had a great ballclub. I mean, what a baseball team."

Even though Cepeda's season ended quickly, it didn't take long for him to notice the swirl of conflict surrounding the A's, and how it emanated from the team's controversial epicenter. "You know Reggie," says Cepeda. "You know how Reggie is."

Reporters, whether they be local or national, print or electronic, swarmed around Jackson If a writer needed a quote to spice up a bland story, he ran to Reggie. Some reporters interviewed Jackson reluctantly, turned off by his ego and mood swings. Others, like Twins beat writer Bob Fowler, found Jackson an engaging personality. "Well, the best guy, the best guy on the A's, the guy I really enjoyed the most—and I don't mean that we became buddy-buddy—I liked Reggie Jackson," Fowler says.

" I mean, Reggie Jackson was a real businessman. Reggie Jackson knew what you wanted. I don't know that he had ever been schooled at Arizona State in media relations, but he could sense what was a good story, what was a good quote. And he was willing to give it. Other writers said, 'Oh, he's an egotist.' I don't feel that way at all. He knew his role; he knew your role. He was happy to give you his part of the mutual relationship, the working agreement that you had. And then that was it. He would go his way and you'd go your way." Some writers felt intimidated around Jackson, but not Fowler. "Oh no," Fowler says, "not at all. Not a twit."

Yet, When Jackson first joined the Kansas City A's in 1967, he irritated most of his veteran teammates. "Personally, Reggie was very hard to like," says Jack Aker. "Reggie was so brash; he actually was a braggart. It started right from his first day in a major league clubhouse. He came in and told us how good he was, what he expected to do, that he expected to be a regular player. That he was gonna lead our team. Of course, all the players who had been around for awhile sat back and said, 'Well, let's see what you can do.'"

Jackson gained acceptance by backing up his words. "The thing about Reggie," says Aker, "is he could do everything he said he could do. He turned out to be a magnificent player. As soon as we saw him in spring training throw the ball from right field—a rifle arm. He could run like a deer. When he made contact, he hit balls farther than anybody on the club. Really, looking at him as a young player, I was thinking to myself, 'This is as close to Mickey Mantle as I'm gonna see; this guy can actually do everything he said.'"

Gene Tenace observed a similar tendency with Jackson. "Reggie wanted to be the center of any discussion, which was fine," Tenace says. "[Because] he could back it up between the lines. This guy was an unbelievable talent. He'd come into that clubhouse and tell you what he was going to do that particular day. Reggie would come in and say he was going to drive in two runs—*at least*. And if anyone could get on ahead of him, he's gonna drive in more. And he'd go out and do it."

Tenace recalls an episode in later years when Jackson predicted that he would go deep against a particular pitcher. "Reggie came into the clubhouse," Tenace recalls, "and he said, 'I'm gonna get one home run. And if that guy makes a mistake, I'm gonna take him out of the yard *twice*.'"

As evidenced by such incidents, Jackson didn't back off on his bragging, even *after* establishing himself as a star. "No, he continued [to boast]," Jack Aker says with a laugh. "Reggie, as I say, is hard to like off the field. For me, he throws in a lot of 'I's' and 'Me's' in his conversation, but I have to admire him as a ballplayer. I really do."

Jackson's brashness sometimes made him a target of ridicule in the Oakland clubhouse. Reliever Darold Knowles resented Jackson's arrogance more than most. In one of baseball's most famous quotations, Knowles offered a memorable characterization of Jackson during the 1974 season. "There isn't enough mustard in the whole world," Knowles said in describing his most celebrated teammate, "to cover that hot dog."

Yet, some of the A's enjoyed Jackson's presence in the clubhouse. One of the team's most colorful pitchers appreciated the unpredictability that Jackson brought to the team, while also respecting the outfielder's extraordinary talent. "It was great playing with him," says Blue Moon Odom, who sometimes made controversial statements himself, ala Jackson. "You never knew what he was going to do from this day to the next. It was great playing with that guy."

"Reggie and I have always gotten along," says Rollie Fingers, like Jackson a member of the Hall of Fame. "We kind of came up together through the minor leagues. I played with him in Birmingham, Alabama, played with him in Modesto,

California. We had a lot of fun in the minor leagues together. Reggie came up the year before I did. Reggie and I always got along. I never had any problems with Reggie. You know, I'd get on him a lot; of course, I got on everybody. But he knew it was in jest. We always had a good time."

Tony LaRussa, who played with the A's over parts of four seasons (1968 to 1971), respected Jackson as a teammate committed to winning. "I had a chance to watch Reggie from the beginning and watch him develop," LaRussa says. "Just a very competitive player with great talent. He really knew the value of winning and was a really good teammate. It was just a thrill to say that you were in the same lockerroom as people like that."

In early July, Jackson and another Oakland star found themselves in the midst of a mid-season slump. On July 6, Jackson took a seat on the bench, the result of a 4-for-46 tailspin and a drought of 14 games without a home run. With the A's facing Yankee left-hander Mike Kekich, Dick Williams made an unusual move, placing catcher-first baseman Gene Tenace in the unfamiliar environment of right field, where Jackson usually played. Tenace handled the unaccustomed position (which he had played years ago in the minor leagues) without incident and went 1-for-4 with a run scored against Kekich and Sparky Lyle, but couldn't stave off a 6–2 loss to the Yankees.

The next day, Vida Blue endured his worst start as a major league pitcher—and a small fallout with some of the Oakland fans. Blue allowed eight runs in six innings against the light-hitting Brewers, who saddled the left-hander with an embarrassing 9–4 loss. In the fifth inning, Blue ran slowly to first base on a routine grounder to shortstop, prompting a few boos from the fans at the Oakland Coliseum. Those fans, believing that Blue was failing to hustle, didn't realize that the left-hander had twisted his knee one inning earlier. "I hope better days are coming," Blue told *The Sporting News* after the debacle, which dropped his season record to an unsightly 2–5. At the same time a year ago, Blue's record stood at 17–3.

Blue's inconsistency proved especially frustrating to the A's. In his previous start, he had shackled the Angels, striking out eight batters in an impressive 3–1, complete-game victory. Incredibly, the win represented only his second of the season. "It would be nice to see the season start over," moaned Blue in an interview with Gerald Eskenazi of the *New York Times*, "so I could have some spring training." Of course, Blue had no one to blame but himself for missing all of spring training and failing to keep himself in proper pitching condition during his holdout.

Much like the quick disappearance of Orlando Cepeda, the A's didn't have much success, or patience, with another one of their June 29 acquisitions. On July 19, Finley released Art Shamsky, after the former "Miracle Met" hero went hitless in seven pinch-hit appearances. The Oakland owner replaced Shamsky the next day, when he announced his 40th transaction of the season. Finley reacquired two former A's—first baseman Don Mincher and utility infielder Ted Kubiak—from the Rangers for infielders Marty Martinez and Vic Harris, who had been recalled from the minor leagues only a few days earlier, but had not appeared in a single game for the A's. On the surface, the deal seemed to heavily favor the A's, but

Oakland sources indicated that the A's would also surrender a promising young pitcher to the Rangers once waivers could be cleared. Six days later, the A's sent Triple-A prospect Steve Lawson to Texas to complete the deal for Mincher.

Like many of Finley's acquisitions, the trade caused some controversy. Since the deal occurred after the traditional June 15th trading deadline, each player had to wait to clear the waiver wire. As a result, Kubiak, Mincher, and Martinez actually knew about the trade two days before it was announced. In his last game with the A's, Martinez started and collected three hits against Milwaukee. The Brewers, who had gotten wind of the deal with Texas, protested the game, claiming that the A's had announced the trade of Martinez before the game. They reasoned that a player who already been traded should not be allowed to play for his old team. As with most protests, the American League turned down the appeal.

"I do remember some odd things [about the trade]," Mincher recalls years later. "I knew of the trade early because we had some friends from Huntsville staying with us; they had just come by on vacation. And I remember having to stay quiet for a couple of days, even while they were there…And I even played, I think I dressed out [with Texas], and was still in [a Ranger] uniform, knowing that I was traded already." Such was the cloak-and-dagger life of a baseball player who had been involved in a trade orchestrated by Charlie Finley.

The acquisition of Mincher gave Dick Williams a quantity he desperately wanted—a left-handed power hitter to bring off the bench. The A's had tried, and given up, on both Art Shamsky and Curt Blefary in that role. Although Mincher had struggled to a .236 average in 61 games, he had been hitting the ball well of late. Mincher had lifted his batting average 70 points in the last three weeks, and continued to lead the Rangers in RBIs, despite his status as a platoon player. With six home runs, Mincher figured to provide the A's with a decent long-ball threat in the late innings.

Mincher would have to make the difficult adjustment from playing regularly to being used in spots. At first, Mincher objected to the trade. "I'm just not ready to sit on the bench," said Mincher, a semi-regular for the Rangers, in an interview with *The Sporting News*. "Although I don't want to get into a lot of name-calling, and I won't, but I'm really disappointed…This trade knocked me off my feet."

Charlie Finley did not approach Mincher to explain his new role with the A's, but Dick Williams quickly stepped in to soothe the disappointed slugger. "Finley, of course, didn't," Mincher replies. "Charlie and I never really talked about baseball; we talked about a lot of other things. We were good friends. But Mr. Williams sure did [talk to him about playing time] and I appreciated it so much. It's what made him a great manager. He told me right away that I was going to play occasionally, that I was gonna be the No. 1 pinch-hitter. When I got there, Dick sat me down and we had a long talk, and he told me exactly what was gonna go on and I appreciated that."

Williams also realized that the announcement of a trade for a first baseman might have a damaging effect on the psyche of incumbent Mike Epstein. After all, Epstein had expressed frustration when he heard about the acquisition of Orlando Cepeda.

Williams quickly sought out Epstein, telling him that the A's had acquired Mincher to improve the bench, not to play first base everyday. "You're my first baseman as long as you can do the job," Williams assured Epstein, according to an article that appeared in *Sport* Magazine.

The trade provided renewed life for Mincher and Kubiak, who went from a rebuilding mode in Texas to World Series hope in Oakland. In contrast, the deal cost Martinez a chance at playing post-season ball for the first time in his career. After his three-hit game, Martinez boarded the Oakland bus, soon to be joined by reliever Bob Locker. The well-traveled Locker, who had pitched for the White Sox, Seattle Pilots, Brewers, and A's, tried desperately to supply some philosophical psychology from his own experiences. "I don't know what I can say to make it easier for you," Locker told Martinez, according to an article in *Sports Illustrated*. "These things happen."

The A's arrived at the All-Star break with a comfortable six-and-a-half-game lead in the Western Division. The margin, however, seemed less substantial when compared to Oakland's 11-game lead prior to the break in 1971. Nonetheless, a fine first half translated into ample All-Star rewards. American League fans chose Reggie Jackson to start the '72 classic; in fact, Jackson led all league outfielders in votes. Orioles manager Earl Weaver selected five other A's players as reserves for the All-Star Game: infielders Campy Campaneris and Sal Bando, outfielder Joe Rudi, and pitchers Catfish Hunter and Ken Holtzman.

Several other Oakland players felt they should have been selected to the All-Star team, as well. The most deserving of the group appeared to be overlooked catcher Dave Duncan, whose 14 home runs and 48 RBIs highlighted his power hitting. In addition, his all-around defensive play placed him among the elite of the league's receivers. The snub by Weaver greatly upset Duncan, who had yet to play in an All-Star Game during his career. "I'm the best defensive catcher in the league," argued Duncan, "and I'm doing the best with the bat." Instead of Duncan, Weaver chose Red Sox catcher Carlton Fisk and Brewers journeyman Ellie Rodriguez as backups to the Tigers' Bill Freehan. Weaver also ignored A's first baseman Mike Epstein, who ranked in the league's top five in both home runs and RBIs. "I guess statistics don't mean anything," Epstein said with resignation to Ron Bergman. Weaver also bypassed the surprising Blue Moon Odom, who felt the Oriole manager had played favorites by choosing his own pitcher, Pat Dobson. Odom said Weaver should have picked either himself or Angels left-hander Clyde Wright.

On the same day that he learned of his All-Star Game rejection, Duncan relieved his frustrations in a game against the Brewers. After being struck three times by the backswings of Brewer batters, Duncan felt the impact of a breaking ball thrown by Milwaukee right-hander Jim Colborn. Duncan charged the mound, only to be intercepted by several of the bench-clearing Brewers. Players and coaches from both dugouts piled onto the field, followed by residents of the bullpens. Even 50-year-old bullpen coach Vern Hoscheit tried to catapult himself over the bullpen wall, only to break his arm while tumbling to the ground.

Of the four Oakland position players selected for the All-Star Game, three received a chance to play against the National League. Earl Weaver chose not to play Campy Campaneris, upsetting the veteran shortstop. Campy vowed to himself that he would exact revenge on Weaver, by playing as well as he possibly could in head-to-head matchups against Earl's Orioles.

Typically, a player like Campaneris tended to be overshadowed by the A's' other, more recognizable stars. "I mean, you've got those superstars, Sal and Reggie, and the pitching staff, Vida and Rollie Fingers," says former baseball writer Bob Fowler. "They had 10 really Hall of Fame quality guys. And so those other guys seemed to get lost in the shuffle. A guy like Bert Campaneris was really significant and instrumental to them. And another thing about him that people miss nowadays—and I say this with all due respect to Cal Ripken—Campaneris played every day. I mean, he was out there every inning of every day and every game. You don't see that much nowadays in the modern player. They rest against [certain] pitchers, with the exception obviously of Cal, but Bert was out there and gave his all, and was really a big, big part of the success of that team."

Orlando Cepeda, who played with Campaneris briefly in 1972, raves about the subtle, understated importance of the scrappy shortstop to the Oakland teams of the seventies, offensively, defensively, and in the clubhouse. "Campy Campaneris, it's too bad he don't get the recognition he deserved," laments Cepeda. "Boy, he was the guy. I remember that Dick Williams told me that year, 'This is my MVP. If we don't have this guy on this ballclub, no way we're gonna win no pennant.' Campy was a guy who play every day; he's a great teammate, a great human being. I'd like for him to be in the Hall of Fame someday."

Although Campaneris batted only .259 for his career and never drew as many walks as desired from a leadoff man, he did spark the A's' offense with speed and aggressive baserunning for 12 full seasons. Perhaps more importantly, Campaneris also cemented a middle infield that found itself in a state of flux due to a constant jumble of second basemen. Campaneris' range—which was supplied by his quick, scampering feet—and his swiftness in turning the double play made him one of the American League's best defensive shortstops of the era.

While Campaneris wanted to play in the All-Star Game, but couldn't because of a managerial decision, another A's regular couldn't play at all—because of an unusual ailment. Felled by an eye infection, Mike Epstein missed nine consecutive games sandwiched around the All-Star Game. Epstein had damaged his eye in a July 17th game against the Brewers, when he had slid headfirst into the third base bag. Dirt had lodged in his right eye, behind his contact lens. Later that day, Epstein repeatedly rubbed his eye, causing an abrasion, and ultimately an infection. With Epstein's eye shut and covered by a patch, Dick Williams called upon mid-season pickup Don Mincher to play first base. The A's expected Mincher to supply power off the bench, but he struggled as Oakland's cleanup hitter. Mincher went only 2-for-21 in Epstein's absence and failed to drive in a single run. The veteran first baseman, who had been productive in 1971, suddenly seemed like an old hitter with a slowed swing.

Mincher realized, perhaps sooner than anyone else, that he was losing some of his abilities as a hitter. "Yeah, I knew it then," Mincher recalls. "I really had been struggling a little bit beforehand, before the All-Star break. I knew that I was having problems getting to the inside fastball. The first indication was that the guys I used to hit very well, I was not hitting anymore because I just couldn't get in there to get to that pitch. I remember having a bad start [with Oakland]; I was really, really struggling."

With Epstein sidelined by his closed and covered eye, great pitching kept the A's in front in the Western Division. On July 31, Vida Blue shut out the Rangers, 2–0, on a pair of hits. The next day, Ken Holtzman spun a three-hit shutout against the Royals. Catfish Hunter then made it three consecutive blankings with a five-hitter against Kansas City. Oakland managed to win repeatedly despite scoring only 11 runs combined in the three games.

The series against the Royals, however, proved costly to Oakland's manpower. In the August 2nd game won by Hunter, Royals pitcher Dick Drago fired a fastball that clipped Sal Bando in the ankle. Bando stepped toward the mound, only to be intercepted by Kansas City's burly catcher, Ed Kirkpatrick. Bando and Kirkpatrick tangled, leading to an eruption of players from both benches onto the playing field. Dave Duncan tackled Kirkpatrick, preventing him from doing any further bodily harm to Bando. During the melee, Reggie Jackson pulled a muscle in his ribcage, aggravating an injury that already existed.

Just as Mike Epstein had returned to the lineup from his eye injury, the brawl with the Royals forced Jackson to miss a series of games with what doctors diagnosed as bruised ribcage cartilage. Later, the doctors discovered that the cartilage had actually torn away from the ribcage, forcing Jackson onto the 15-day disabled list. Jackson would miss three weeks of playing time.

When healthy and in the lineup, Epstein and Jackson provided the A's with a needed lethal combination of left-handed hitting power. Ironically, the two sluggers had experienced difficulties relating to each other off the field. Jackson had started referring to himself as "Mr. B and B," an abbreviation for "bread and butter," as if to say that he drove in all of the important runs for the A's. Epstein didn't appreciate the arrogance of the self-appointed nickname and let Jackson know about it. Prior to another game, Epstein approached Jackson, the team's player representative, about obtaining some complimentary tickets for an upcoming A's game. Jackson asked Epstein whom he intended to give the tickets to, reminding the first baseman that he could only provide passes for relatives, not friends. "It is none of your business," Epstein snapped at Jackson, prompting a conversation filled with curses and shouts. Angry words soon gave way to the throwing of fists by the two strongest men on the A's' roster.

Jackson, a taut, muscle-bound man, proved no match for the hulking Epstein. According to witnesses in the Oakland clubhouse, Epstein floored Jackson with his first punch. Although not as well-known as Jackson for power hitting on the field, Epstein's show of strength in the lockerroom should not have surprised any of his Oakland teammates. After growing up in the Bronx, where he had experienced frequent neighborhood fights, Epstein had starred in football at the University of California at Berkeley. A ramming fullback during the season, Epstein built himself up during the summers by engaging in the most physical of jobs: lugging carcasses around a meatpacking factory, toting bags of sand for an oil rig, and running a jackhammer on a construction crew.

After the back-to-back shutouts against the Royals, the A's headed to Minnesota and Kansas City for a seven-game road trip. The A's, who had enjoyed 17 consecutive winning road trips, suddenly lost six of seven on their journey to the Midwest. After struggling to a record of 16–15 during July, the A's had followed up by losing six of their first nine games in August. In the midst of their worst stretch of the season, the A's prepared for a critical four-game home series against the White Sox, who had managed to climb within a half-game of first place and featured the league's most dangerous hitter in Dick Allen.

In the meantime, a Chicago radio station circulated a surprising report. According to the radio rumor, Charlie Finley was ready to fire Dick Williams, whose contract was scheduled to run out at the end of the season. During a White Sox game broadcast, former A's announcer Harry Caray talked about Williams' imminent firing. Reports out of Chicago and California indicated that the Cubs and Angels would pursue Williams—either immediately, if Finley were to fire him, or after the season, when Williams' contract would expire.

Well, not so fast. Prior to the first game against the White Sox, Finley telephoned Williams. The two men verbally agreed to a two-year contract extension that would keep Williams in the green and gold of the A's through the 1974 season. Williams then summoned Sal Bando to his office, putting the captain on the phone with Finley. Upon hearing of Williams' contract extension, Bando told the other Oakland players the news. Almost to a man, the A's greeted Finley's decision with approval. "It's good," Campy Campaneris told *The Sporting News*. "Some people [the players] had pressure [on them]. They thought maybe he wasn't coming back. Everybody started to say he wasn't coming back. Everybody started to say he might be fired. But now he can be more loose. He's a good manager. I think we can get to the World Series with him."

Joe Rudi also offered his full support of Williams. "We all had been worried about him," Rudi told Ron Bergman in offering his reaction to Williams' extension. "We knew he had other offers. It eased my mind a lot. I love that man."

While many baseball historians have classified Williams as abrasive and dictatorial in his managerial style, players like Sal Bando say such descriptions are inaccurate. "I think a lot of things are mislabeled on Dick," Bando says. "I mean, he was a strong disciplinarian, in terms of fundamental baseball and what he expected. [But] as far as being a disciplinarian in terms of your curfew, your dress, your hair, Dick was very flexible there." In 1972, Williams chose not to stand in the way of his players growing mustaches and beards and wearing their hair long, in direct contrast to almost every other management type of that era. Williams himself sprouted a mustache and let his hair grow past his collar, a fashion style that was quite unlike the conservative crewcut he had worn with the Red Sox only five years earlier.

"He's very fair," utility infielder Ted Kubiak told *Sport* Magazine during the 1972 season. "Once he chewed me out when I missed a hit-and-run sign in Kansas City," said Kubiak, "but when Jerry Adair, the first-base coach, told Dick he had missed the sign, too, Dick apologized." Bando says Williams' orderly, militaristic style of managing in Boston created a false notion about his personality. "He was really a very friendly and outgoing guy," Bando says, "but everyone knew his reputation, so everyone kind of stayed in line." Bando says many sportswriters and broadcasters have helped created the myth of Williams as a mean-spirited, inflexible tyrant. "I think a lot of it has to do with the media buildup," Bando says, " because he wasn't the ogre that everybody thought him to be."

Many sportswriters considered Williams an ogre, at least on the surface. On one occasion, *Sport* Magazine writer Al Hirshberg approached Williams and asked him what he had done to improve Mike Epstein as a hitter. "Nothing," Williams fired back angrily while giving Hirshberg a glaring stare. Former sportswriter Bob Fowler contends that Williams' gruff exterior often proved misleading. Fowler enjoyed interviewing Williams, in spite of his outward appearances. "Oh, Dick Williams was outstanding," Fowler says without hesitation. "He was, how can I say? You had to accept the gruffness. And I don't mean to sound like an old-timer. But you had to accept if you asked [Williams] a dumb question, and Dick Williams said, 'Gee, that's a dumb question.' You wouldn't retreat with your tail between your legs. You would say, 'Well, OK, give me a dumb answer.' And then you would go on."

With Williams and Finley having verbally settled on a contract, Catfish Hunter bested Stan Bahnsen, 5–3, in the opener of the series against Chicago. In the second game, the White Sox edged the A's, 1–0, on the shutout pitching of youthful left-hander Dave Lemonds. Chicago then took the third game, 3–1, in 11 innings, when knuckleballing veteran Wilbur Wood baffled the Oakland lineup. At their peak, the A's had enjoyed an eight-game lead in the American League West. Now, with the calendar reading August 12, the A's had lost eight of their last 10 and actually found themselves trailing MVP candidate Dick Allen and his revitalized White Sox by .001 percentage points—and one-half game in the standings. For the first time in 46 days, the A's were no longer in first place.

After the Saturday loss to the White Sox, Finley made his new contract offer to Williams official. Under terms of the two-year deal, the manager would earn $60,000 a year. Williams accepted the contract, which meant that he could continue to cash paychecks from Finley through the end of the 1974 season. With Williams' new contract in hand, the A's prepared to play the final game of their series against the White Sox.

While the A's' players were happy to see Williams retained, they needed to start winning games again—and quickly. If the A's lost the finale of their series in Chicago, they would fall a game and a half back of the surging Sox. Vida Blue took the ball against Stan Bahnsen, who was pitching on only two days' rest after working in relief in the series opener. The A's pounded out 11 hits, including home runs by Campy Campaneris and Dave Duncan, and knocked Bahnsen from the box after six innings. Pitching on three days rest, Blue shut down the White Sox on four hits. A 3–0 victory put the A's back in first place by one-half game. "We won that one for Dick Williams," injured second baseman Dick Green told *The Sporting News*. "Everyone played a lot looser. It [the contract extension] helped a lot."

Spurred by the win over the White Sox and the knowledge that Williams would remain in place for the foreseeable future, the A's proceeded to win their next three games. The White Sox, however, won their next four games to remain virtually even with Oakland in the standings. The A's then lost five of their next seven to fall out of first place. During the stretch, even the normally astute Williams made a mistake when he sent up lefty-swinging outfielder Bill Voss (recently acquired from Milwaukee) as a pinch-hitter against an Oriole southpaw. An embarrassed Williams fined himself $100 for the oversight.

By August 27, the A's faced a crisis. Although Reggie Jackson had just returned from the disabled list, the team was still not hitting. Angel Mangual remained mired in a season-long slump. Voss, a veteran of seven major league seasons who had never hit more than 10 home runs or batted higher than .261 in a single year, did not appear to be the answer to the center field problem. With players like Felipe Alou, Tommy Davis, and Art Shamsky long gone, the A's had virtually no depth in the outfield. Still, Charlie Finley had one more trading card to play.

In June, Finley had practically given pitcher Diego Segui to the Cardinals—or so it seemed. At the time, the Cardinals fancied themselves contenders in the National League East. Segui proceeded to pitch brilliantly as the Cardinals' No. 1 reliever, but by late August, St. Louis had faded from the pennant race. Cardinals general manager Bing Devine, looking to shed salary and rebuild with younger players, realized that now was the right time to repay Finley for the favor of giving him Segui earlier in the season. Devine agreed to send veteran outfielder Matty Alou and his $110,000 salary to the A's for minor league pitcher Steve Easton and Voss, the journeyman outfielder.

Although the Cardinals felt that the aging Alou was no longer capable of playing the outfield on an everyday basis, he was still a competent major league hitter. At the time of the trade, Alou led the Cardinals with a .314 batting average, a better mark than that of hard-hitting teammates like Joe Torre, Lou Brock, and Ted Simmons. More impressively, Alou's hitting placed him fifth in the National League, behind only Cesar Cedeno, Billy Williams, Ralph Garr, and Dusty Baker. The 33-year-old Alou had also retained enough footspeed to steal 11 bases.

Dick Williams immediately installed Alou as his everyday right fielder, with Reggie Jackson moving over to center field. In his first game in an Oakland uniform, Alou batted in the No. 3 slot of the batting order against Indians right-hander Steve Dunning. Throughout his young career, "Stunning" Dunning had impressed Cleveland's management with a hard fastball and a repertoire of power pitches. Yet, the straightness of Dunning's pitches and the lack of deception in his motion usually led to trouble by the middle to late innings.

The hard-throwing right-hander shackled the Oakland lineup over the first six innings. With the A's trailing 2–0 in the bottom of the seventh inning, Alou began to figure out Dunning. Alou led off with a single, igniting a five-run rally against Dunning. The sudden offensive outburst helped the A's to a 5–4 come-from-behind win.

After helping the A's to victory in his Oakland debut, Alou struggled in his next few games, as Oakland's team-wide batting slump continued. During one stretch, Sal Bando had collected only six hits in 66 at-bats. Joe Rudi, bothered by the flu, went only 4-for-24. Dave Duncan managed only two hits in 26 at-bats and went to the bench in favor of backup catcher Gene Tenace.

Thanks to the bullpen, however, the A's won five consecutive games to recapture first place from the White Sox. Dick Williams called upon his relievers in each of the five wins, and with good reason, given their recent run of success. Middle reliever Bob Locker extended his scoreless games streak to 11. Short man Darold Knowles went nine games without allowing a safety. Rollie Fingers pitched scoreless relief in nine of his last 10 outings.

The timely winning streak did not prevent Charlie Finley from engaging in controversy. In September, Finley issued an edict barring talented beat writer Ron Bergman from traveling with the team. Bergman had upset Finley with an item he had included in the September 16th edition of *The Sporting News*. "Listening to the A's' play-by-play announcers," Bergman wrote about broadcasters Monte Moore, Jimmy Piersall, and Jim Woods, "you get the impression they're in some sort of contest to see which one can make the most complimentary remarks about owner Charlie Finley." In response, Finley claimed that Bergman made "my announcers look like prostitutes." Finley told A's traveling secretary Tom Corwin to physically remove Bergman from any charter flights he tried to board. Finley also ordered Corwin not to speak to Bergman, and not to make any of the writer's hotel reservations, as had been the customary practice of the ballclub.

Finley's treatment of Bergman typified his stormy relationship with the Oakland media. When local reporters wrote negatively of the A's and especially Finley, the owner responded vindictively. If a reporter described Finley in a positive light, he became an instant friend. "Such an irascible individual, almost difficult to describe in a pattern of words," said John Steadman, the longtime *Baltimore Sun* sportswriter who encountered Finley as far back as his days in Kansas City. "I remember once when he was going to build his [pennant] porch in right field to emulate what they had at Yankee Stadium. I wrote that he had every right in the world to do that. Charlie reacted in a very positive manner, and I guess he thought I was kind of a bright sportswriter. So he called me to thank me. And he talked and talked and talked. Someone in the office put the clock on it, and it was two hours and 45 minutes with one conversation." And how much did Steadman get to speak during the marathon talk? "I was able to do a lot of listening," said Steadman, "I can tell you that."

Steadman recalled an incident during Finley's tenure in Kansas City, when a local sportswriter named Ernie Mehl implied that A's manager Joe Gordon was acting as the owner's puppet. Mehl wrote that Gordon had once filled out a lineup card with the words, "Approved by C.O.F.," scrawled across the bottom. The letters "C.O.F." represented the initials of one Charles Oscar Finley. Although Mehl's sentiments did not reflect any unusual or uncommon view, Finley felt a need for retribution. "He ridiculed Ernie Mehl, the sports editor of the *Kansas City Star*," said Steadman. "Ernie Mehl was one of the most delightful men that the newspaper business has produced." Finley had decided to exact some revenge on Mehl—and in a very public way. "He had a 'Poison Pen Day' [at Municipal Stadium] to denigrate a lovely man like Ernie Mehl," Steadman recalled. "I'd say in the newspaper business, you could go to the end of the world and not find a nicer, more compassionate or equitable man [than Mehl]. But that was Charlie."

Steadman felt special sympathy for the local writers in Kansas City and Oakland who periodically came under Finley's fire. "I know that Charlie had to be a tough man to live with if you were a sportswriter and you were working and covering his games. It had to be a test–a terrible test–to your patience"

While the Bergman controversy did not involve any of the A's themselves, the 1972 season marked the beginning of an era of ill feelings between certain Oakland players. "It was beginning in those days," remarks Don Mincher, one of the few players who never seemed to be involved in conflict. "I can remember a lot of animosity in that clubhouse between individual guys, and it became a little bit cliquish to some degree at that time. Not very much, but I remember it forming. It was amazing the guys that had trouble with each other just forgot about it when they went out on the field, and then picked it up after the game. It was amazing to do that."

Mincher says the manager deserved most of the credit for keeping the players unified in their goal of playing winning baseball, despite the periodic squabbles. "I still attribute a lot of that to Dick Williams, who really controlled that clubhouse," says Mincher. "He had good rapport with everybody, and everybody really respected him. A guy like that who was real intense, but once you know [that] he knows what he's talking about, then you follow him. He managed to keep that [team] together for awhile until he couldn't keep his own job, reluctantly and sadly."

Mincher would be long retired by the time player and owner controversies had fully overtaken the team in 1973 and '74, including Williams' eventual departure from the organization. Yet, Mincher had observed the seeds of controversy grow in their earliest moments. "Yeah, I can remember it beginning in '72. Of course, I wasn't there when it really got hectic, but I can imagine what happened, and I can imagine who was in the middle of it. It wasn't any fistfights or brawls or anything like that [in '72], but I remember the bickering, sure."

Fights and arguments might have made some of the Oakland sportswriters hesitate briefly before entering the A's' clubhouse. According to Mincher, the media coverage of one player, in particular, served as a stimulator to controversy. "Reggie [Jackson], who is probably the most intelligent individual I ever played with, was always the center of the media attention, either good or bad. And he seemed to always be there. I can remember some bickering with other players and him. You know, Dave Duncan, who was Reggie's good friend—they had some problems. But David was a very stern individual himself, just like he is now, really demanding a lot of the pitching staff and himself. When an outfielder caused a pitcher to get in trouble with an overthrow or an error or something like that, there could be some things said and some words exchanged in those situations. And I can remember some of those. Of course, my old roomy, Sal Bando, he wasn't very shy about stepping up to the plate either as far as telling people exactly what he thought. And there would be some words back and forth."

At times, the wars of words forced a likable, even-keeled player like Mincher to assume the role of peacemaker. "I did," Mincher says, adding that he usually preferred to stay in the background. "Of course, when you're not playing regularly and you're just doing your thing, you try to get along with the players, and just sit down and be quiet...I tried to do my part and console everybody. But really, with those kinds of mentalities, egos, and talent, they worked themselves out."

Mincher says the uncomfortable feelings created by such verbal outbursts never seemed to interfere with the team's on-field playing ability. "These guys were great, great players, and they learned from most things, and while I was there we never had any fistfights or anything like that. And all of the confrontations [actually] led to good things, and they just played better, it seemed like, as they went along."

On August 30, just before the deadline for freezing a team's potential post-season roster, Charlie Finley made one last move to improve his team for the stretch run. Finley once again turned toward the rebuilding Cardinals, who surrendered longtime shortstop Dal Maxvill for minor league catcher Joe Lindsey and a player to be named later. Although the A's already possessed a fine shortstop in Campy Campaneris, they viewed Maxvill as another option at the troublesome second base position, which had seen its share of attrition. Dick Green and Larry Brown had already been sidelined by serious back problems, and Marty Martinez had been sent away as part of the Mincher deal. Although never a threatening hitter, Maxvill still possessed reliable defensive skills as a middle infielder and also brought championship experience from his days with the Cardinals in 1967 and '68.

Shortly after the acquisitions of Maxvill and Matty Alou from St. Louis, rumors sprang up that the A's would release both players after the season due to their salaries. At $110,000 per season, Alou ranked as one of the highest paid players in the game. Maxvill made a comparatively smaller total of $40,000, but even that figure was considered high for a 33-year-old infielder past his prime. Another rumor indicated that the A's still owed the Cardinals another player as part of the Alou transaction. One newspaper report claimed that player would be starting pitcher Ken Holtzman, Oakland's best hurler during the first half of the season. Dick Williams emphatically denied the preposterous rumor. After the season, the A's would send minor league catcher Gene Dusan, a far less valuable commodity than Holtzman, to the Cardinals to complete the trade for Alou.

Second Basemen Used By the A's In 1972

Tim Cullen—65 games
Ted Kubiak—49 games
Larry Brown—46 games
Dick Green—26 games
Dal Maxvill—24 games
Marty Martinez—17 games
Ron Clark—11 games
Gene Tenace—2 games
Dwain Anderson—1 game
Sal Bando—1 game
Curt Blefary—1 game
Larry Haney—1 game

With the addition of Maxvill to the team's muddled middle infield picture, Dick Williams had yet another option to consider for his second base derby. At the behest of Charlie Finley, Williams devised an intriguing, but strange plan to use Maxvill and the other second basemen on the team. "It was always a circus atmosphere with that ballclub," Don Mincher says. "Charlie had decided that the second basemen on our ballclub should never hit. Therefore, we had four pinch-hitters ready. Every time the second base position come up, we'd pinch-hit." Williams installed Maxvill as his starting second baseman, but pinch-hit for him during his first or second at-bat each game. Williams then installed utilityman Ted Kubiak at second base, before pinch-hitting for him. Williams followed with Tim Cullen, before replacing him with *another* pinch-hitter. Once Maxvill, Kubiak, and Cullen had been exhausted, Williams employed catcher Gene Tenace at second base, despite the fact that he had never before played the position during his professional career.

With Dick Green and Larry Brown on the disabled list, Finley felt it best that Williams give his second basemen as few at-bats as possible in order to mask their offensive deficiencies. In his first 14 games with the A's, Maxvill came to bat only 23 times, and totaled only five singles. In the meantime, Cullen was batting .250 with no power or speed. Kubiak was faring even worse, with an average of .196. "Well, I don't think any of us really liked it," says Kubiak, now a minor league manager in the Cleveland Indians' organization. "The way I looked at it after awhile—since I was a utilityman—I just said, 'Well, this is my job. I have to do it.' It was nerve-wracking…I mean you were under pressure to perform there."

While Maxvill's lack of hitting came as no surprise, given his .219 lifetime batting average heading into the season, the struggles of Matty Alou concerned the A's. Alou batted a mediocre .266 in his first 17 games with Oakland. Given his lack of power and unwillingness to draw many walks, the A's needed a higher average from Alou, their No. 3 hitter against most pitchers. Some writers reasoned that Alou, a line-drive, ground-ball hitter, missed playing on the artificial turf of St. Louis' Busch Memorial Stadium. For his part, Alou disagreed with such an assessment. "When you've got more than 1,500 hits in your career, you've got to have all sorts of hits," Alou explained to Ron Bergman, "line-drive hits, high-bouncing hits, bunts. There are 300 players over there in the National League, and they don't have that many guys hitting .300, do they?" Furthermore, Alou had once won a batting title while playing the majority of his games on natural grass. More than likely, Alou had simply suffered in his transition to the American League because of his lack of knowledge of opposition pitchers.

Although Alou's hitting disappointed the A's, his defensive play in the outfield came as a *pleasant* surprise. Prior to the trade, the Cardinals had already decided to move Alou to first base. National League scouts and beat writers roundly criticized Matty's range in center field. After making the trade, the A's wisely moved Alou to right field, where he handled all of his fielding chances without incident and made a fine running catch to save a game against the Tigers. "I'm a good defensive outfielder," Alou insisted in an interview with *The Sporting News*. "Reading that I'm not doesn't bother me because I know a lot more about baseball than they [sportswriters] do. I read these things and I laugh."

By September 11, the A's had opened up a three-and-a half-game lead on the White Sox, who had lost a key doubleheader to the Twins and had begun to fade from the race. The A's then lost a doubleheader of their own to the Twins, allowing the White Sox to move to within two games of first. On September 12, Alou enjoyed his best game to date, driving in four runs with two singles and a sacrifice fly. Alou's timely hitting sent Oakland to an important 7–4 victory over Minnesota. The following day, Alou collected two more hits to help the A's to an 8–0 win, while expanding their lead over the White Sox to three games. In Oakland's next game, Alou drove in four more runs with a sac fly and a bases-loaded double, spearheading a 12–3 win over the Rangers. Meanwhile, the White Sox lost a 1–0 heartbreaker in 11 innings to fall four games back of the A's. In three straight games, when the A's needed his timely hitting the most, Alou had rapped out five hits in 10 at-bats, collected nine RBIs, and scored three runs.

After his initial struggles with the A's, Alou had vindicated his supporters. The unorthodox batting approach of the five-foot, nine-inch Alou—his swinging at pitches out of the strike zone and hitting off of his front foot while using a remarkably heavy bat—had drawn criticism for several years. Alou strode with his right foot first, kept his bat back as long as possible, and then flicked his wrists. The result? Alou often blooped balls into short left field for base hits. Former Cardinal ace Steve Carlton had previously called Alou "the worst .300 hitter I've seen" and Ted Williams had once offered the following critique of Alou to *The Sporting News*: "He violates every hitting principle I ever taught." Yet, by bunting, chopping down on the ball, and spraying line drives to all fields, Alou won the National League batting title with a .342 average in 1966, and bettered the .330 mark each of the next three seasons. At the time of his trade to Oakland, Alou ranked fifth in career batting average among established major league regulars, behind only Hall of Famers Hank Aaron and Roberto Clemente, and stars Rico Carty and Tony Oliva.

On Sunday, September 17, the A's expanded their Western Division lead to five games when Catfish Hunter registered his 20th win, a 4–1 knockdown of the Rangers. Hunter became the first pitcher in franchise history since Hall of Famer Lefty Grove—of Philadelphia A's fame—to win 20 games in consecutive seasons. Considering his pedestrian repertoire of pitches and his struggles with mediocrity in the late 1960s, Hunter's emergence as a two-time 20-game winner ranked as an unexpected development.

In 1964, the year before baseball established its amateur draft, a horde of scouts had launched an all-out assault on Hertford, North Carolina, and its population of 2,012 residents. That's where Jim Hunter, one of the best high school pitchers in the country, resided. Charlie Finley successfully shooed away scouts from other major league teams when he arranged for a police escort and a black limousine to bring him to the modest Hunter home. "Mr. Finley started passing out green warm-up jackets and green bats and orange baseballs," Hunter told Pat Jordan of *Sport* Magazine, "and it sort of scared off all the other scouts. They figured Mr. Finley had me all sewed up." Finley and the Kansas City A's didn't—at least not yet. The owner refused to give Hunter the new Thunderbird automobile that he wanted, but relented on a $75,000 bonus and a major league contract. For the hard-working farming community of Perquimans County, a $75,000 check represented an unheard-of windfall.

Shortly after he signed Hunter to his first professional contract in June, Finley discovered that the youngster's right foot contained 30 shotgun pellets. During a high school rabbit-hunting expedition, Hunter's brother had tripped and accidentally shot him in the foot, resulting in the loss of his small toe. "My folks worried I would get hurt playing football," Hunter told the *New York Daily News*. "So, instead, my brother shot my toe off accidentally." His brother fainted, forcing Hunter to slap him in the face in an effort to bring him back to consciousness. The two boys then walked off together to a local hospital.

Taking a passive approach, a local doctor decided to leave the buckshot pellets in Hunter's foot. Once he learned about Hunter's condition, Finley wanted to tear up his major league contract with the injured teen-ager and replace it with a minor league deal—for far less money. The Commissioner's Office ruled that the original contract remained valid. Having failed to void the contract, Finley decided to make every effort to repair Hunter's foot. Finley instructed Clyde Kluttz, the scout who had signed Hunter, to take the teen-ager to the famed Mayo Clinic in Rochester, Minnesota. Doctors there removed half of the pellets and some bone fragments from Hunter's four remaining toes, but the surgery pushed him to the disabled list for all of the 1964 season.

Baseball's bonus rule mandated the A's keep the 19-year-old on the major league roster in 1965, even though he had displayed only an average repertoire in spring training. The following spring, the A's planned to send Hunter to the minor leagues, but his surprising maturity, along with injuries to a few veteran pitchers, enabled him to stay with Kansas City.

"It just so happened that he was my roommate," says Jack Aker, who had first joined the A's in 1964. "They decided he could stay with me, that I was safe and wouldn't lead him astray. Catfish was so impressive, not because of what he did pitching, but here's a kid right out of high school who goes on the major league mound and pitches as if he were a veteran. Catfish never showed a bit of fear or nervousness, anything that most rookies would show in that situation. He just picked up on major league baseball like it was another day back at his high school in Hertford, North Carolina." Hunter remained with the A's on a full-time basis, never spending a single day in the minors.

Hunter quickly impressed the veteran A's' players with his demeanor, both on the pitching mound and in the clubhouse. "Very calm, cool customer on the field," says Aker. "Very personable off the field. Very shy when he was young. But a guy that, even though it took awhile to get to know him, everybody liked."

Although Hunter insisted that he pushed off the mound with his right foot as hard as ever, the high school hunting misadventure appeared to have robbed his fastball of some its velocity. Still, some baseball scouts liked Hunter's control, ball movement, and pitching instincts so much that they predicted he would become a right-handed version of the Yankees' ace, Whitey Ford. The A's liked Hunter enough to reject an enticing trade proposal from the Orioles, who had offered onetime American League Rookie of the Year Mike Epstein and two pitchers in a deal for Hunter.

From 1966 to 1970, Hunter pitched creditably, earning selection to a pair of American League All-Star teams. Yet, he fell short of the level of stardom predicted by Charlie Finley, who hoped that Hunter would become a 20-game winner in 1968. That didn't happen until 1971, when Hunter finally became a bonafide star, aided by the development of a slider, continued improvement of his control, and the addition of deception to his pitching motion.

On the same day that Hunter reached the 20-win milestone for the second straight year, Chicago ace Wilbur Wood lost his bid for his 25th win when the Angels turned back the White Sox. Two days later, the A's and White Sox opened up a brief, but critical two-game series at the Oakland Coliseum. The Sox needed to sweep in order to have a realistic chance of catching the A's with fewer than two weeks remaining in the regular season. The A's needed to win just one of the games to maintain a five-game lead and put themselves in comfortable position to win the division.

Blue Moon Odom and Tom Bradley started the opener of the series. Four hours and fifty one minutes later, the White Sox remained hopeful of catching the A's when they emerged with an 8–7 victory thanks to Jorge Orta's 15th-inning home run. The two teams combined to use 51 players (which was possible given the expansion of rosters to 40 men in September), establishing a new major league record. The White Sox employed 21 players to snare the win, while the A's set a single-team record by using 30 players on the night. Dick Williams called on so many players that he found himself forced to utilize veteran minor leaguer Allan Lewis, who almost never played a defensive position, in right field. Dal Maxvill,

Ted Kubiak, Dick Green, Tim Cullen, and catchers Gene Tenace and Larry Haney all made appearances at second base, setting a record for most players used at that position in one game. Only Tenace and Haney came to bat, as the others saw themselves lifted for pinch-hitters under Charlie Finley's revolving-door plan at second base.

The A's now needed a victory in the second game of the series to keep the White Sox five games back. Reggie Jackson and Sal Bando, who had struggled all season after his near MVP performance in 1971, hit second-inning home runs against Wilbur Wood, giving Ken Holtzman a 3–0 lead. The White Sox scored twice in the fourth inning to draw close, but the A's rallied for two runs in the fifth and one more in the sixth. Rollie Fingers pitched three and two-thirds innings of brilliant relief to maintain a 6–3 win and return the A's to a five-game lead in the West. With only 12 games remaining, the A's had effectively closed out the pennant hopes of the upstart White Sox.

With a week to go in the regular season, the A's lost one of their most valuable pitchers to a freak injury. Darold Knowles, Oakland's best left-handed reliever, broke his pitching thumb after flying out to left field. Knowles hadn't suffered the break during the actual swing; he had tripped while running out the ball, falling awkwardly on his left thumb. The injury ended Knowles' season, forcing the A's to find another southpaw reliever. Charlie Finley summoned Don Shaw, who had pitched miserably with the A's during a brief early-season stint. Finley reached Shaw at the Palace Car Club in St. Louis, where the veteran pitcher was working as a bartender.

On September 27, a White Sox loss to the Royals, coupled with Oakland's doubleheader sweep of Minnesota, reduced the A's' magic number for clinching the division to one game. The next day, the A's hosted the Twins, who raced out to a 7–0 lead against starter Blue Moon Odom and reliever Bob Locker. The A's pecked away, scoring single runs in the fifth and sixth, three runs in the seventh, and two more in the eighth, to tie the game. In the bottom of the ninth, Twins relief ace Dave LaRoche hit Sal Bando with a pitch to lead off the inning. Dal Maxvill, the fourth second baseman of the game for the A's, came to bat in the cleanup spot of Dick Williams' jumbled lineup. Williams instructed Maxvill to bunt, but LaRoche threw three straight balls before finally finding the strike zone. With the count now three-and-one, Williams flashed the hit sign to Maxvill, who surprised the Twins—and probably the A's—by ripping a double. The extra-base hit scored Bando from first with the winning run, clinching Oakland's second consecutive American League West title.

Bando retains strong recollections of the moments prior to his scoring the division-clinching run. "I'll tell you what I remember most," Bando says. "I was having a good day offensively—I felt very good. I was leading off the inning, and in the on-deck circle, I said to Maxie, 'I'm gonna get hit with a pitch,' and he said, 'Just get a base hit.' Sure enough, I got hit with a pitch, and Maxie couldn't believe it."

In the recent and critical win over the White Sox, Maxvill had made two exceptional defensive plays. Now, with Dick Williams having run out of legitimate pinch-hitters, Maxvill had turned one of his rare Oakland at-bats into a pennant-winning double. Much like Matty Alou earlier in the month, one of Charlie Finley's late-season pickups had played an important role in the A's' defense of the West against the White Sox.

The acquisitions of Alou and Maxvill had capped off a summer that saw eight to 10 of Oakland's roster spots in a constant state of flux. "[It] was like a revolving door," says Joe Rudi. "We never knew who was going to be in the clubhouse when we walked in. You look at the players that came through—Don Mincher, [Orlando] Cepeda came in there...[Matty] Alou—I can't even remember all the guys. Finley had a great knack for picking up guys at the end of their careers that came in and helped us to win."

By adding such veteran role players as Maxvill and Alou to the mix, the A's had continued the transition from being a divisional contender to a team that was now capable of winning a pennant, or even a World Championship. "When they added to their ballclub through trades," says former Twins beat writer Bob Fowler, who covered the A's' division-clinching game at the Oakland Coliseum, "they were really destined for great things. You look down the line, their bench was good. They had role players. They were a complete 25-man unit versus some of these other teams you see even today, where they've got 10 or 15 top-of-the-line players, but they've got 10 guys sitting on the bench who don't know their roles or who aren't content sitting there; they're too young, they want to be playing, they're itchy. So you need that type of player, a Dal Maxvill. That's a good example of the Oakland team. They didn't clinch it by Reggie hitting a home run. They didn't clinch it by...Vida Blue pitching a shutout. They won it with a Dal Maxvill hit."

After the game, the A's celebrated their second Western Division championship with a variety of beverages. Backup first baseman Don Mincher, who had missed out on the 1971 division title because of a mid-season trade to Washington, dumped water on the head and shoulders of manager Dick Williams. In another corner of the clubhouse, veteran reliever Joel Horlen poured a bottle of wine on star pitcher Catfish Hunter.

The A's would finish the season with a record of 93–62, far inferior to their 101-win season of 1971. Yet, the 1972 A's had overcome much more adversity: the holdout and subsequent mediocre pitching of Vida Blue; the season-long slump of Sal Bando; mid-season injuries to Reggie Jackson and Mike Epstein; and a constant upheaval of personnel that dramatically altered the composition of the starting outfield and the bench. Several players stepped up for the A's in their pursuit of the pennant. Left fielder Joe Rudi enjoyed a breakthrough season, batting a team-high .305 with 19 home runs and 75 RBIs. Epstein and Jackson, despite their physical woes, combined for 51 home runs. Catcher Dave Duncan banged out a career-high 19 home runs before slumping in September. On the pitching staff, Catfish Hunter led the way with 21 victories, matching his 1971 total. Ken Holtzman added 19 wins as the rotation's top left-hander, helping to make up for

Blue's interrupted season. Blue Moon Odom earned votes for Comeback Player of the Year honors by winning 15 games, losing six, and spinning an ERA of 2.50. And in relief, Rollie Fingers, Bob Locker, Darold Knowles, and Joel Horlen comprised the best bullpen in the American League—bar none.

Chapter 11

A Catcher Plays Second, and a Shortstop Blows His Stack

The A's prepared to play the American League Championship Series against the Tigers, who had unseated the Orioles as Eastern Division champions despite sporting a roster of players that averaged 32 years of age. Considered too old to contend prior to the season, the Tigers had reacted well to the fiery personality of new manager Billy Martin. Tiger pitching helped carry an offense that was harmed by injuries to Al Kaline and Willie Horton. Mickey Lolich won 22 games, while Joe Coleman missed the 20-win plateau by just one decision. Mid-season acquisition Woodie Fryman won 10 of his 16 starts, while Tom Timmerman and the comebacking John Hiller, returning from a 1971 heart attack, fortified the bullpen. In addition, veteran players like Bill Freehan, Norm Cash, Dick McAuliffe, and Mickey Stanley brought loads of post-season experience to the Championship Series.

The matchup of the A's and Tigers brought another intriguing story line to the playoffs: these two teams, though members of different divisions, did not like each other. The A's and Tigers had already engaged in one full-scale brawl during the course of the regular season. Furthermore, Martin and Charlie Finley had carried a grudge against each other ever since the ex-Twins skipper had rejected Finley's managerial overtures in 1970. Prior to the playoffs, in an article that appeared in the *Chicago Daily News,* Martin called Finley a "chicken-bleep owner." Finley responded by labeling Martin with three insults, terming him "a liar, a phony, and a 24-karat kook."

Finley faced a more significant concern heading to the post-season, one that ranked slightly higher on the priority list than Martin's mental condition. Who would replace Darold Knowles on the 25-man roster? The A's had already moved rookie starter Dave Hamilton to the bullpen, giving them one competent left-handed reliever. If Williams desired another left-handed reliever, he would have to choose part-time bartender Don Shaw, whose ERA of 18.00 testified to his ineffectiveness.

Even though Williams loved the idea of having two left-handers available in the bullpen, the Oakland brass did not have enough confidence in Shaw to include him on the 25-man roster. Instead, the A's decided to carry a little-known first baseman named Gonzalo Marquez. The 26-year-old Venezuelan had been summoned in August from Triple-A Iowa, where he had batted .309. Due to his lack of power, the A's did not consider him a long-term prospect. Yet, the singles-hitting Marquez responded with seven hits in 16 pinch-hit at-bats for Oakland, including a game-winning RBI during the final week of the season. Marquez's ability to handle the bat so impressed team broadcaster Monte Moore that he dubbed the Venezuelan "Mandrake the Magician." With Finley still insisting that Williams pinch-hit for his second basemen whenever possible, the A's recognized the value of keeping an extra left-handed hitter like Marquez on the post-season roster.

In terms of pitching decisions, Williams selected Catfish Hunter, the A's' best second-half starter, to work the first game of the series at the Oakland Coliseum. Tiger manager Billy Martin countered with his own ace, left-hander Mickey Lolich. Hunter and Lolich each surrendered an early run, before pitching shutout baseball over their remaining innings. Hunter lasted eight frames, before giving way to Vida Blue and Rollie Fingers. Lolich kept the A's off the scoreboard through 10 innings. In the top of the 11th, the Tigers' future Hall of Famer, Al Kaline, managed to break the tie, connecting on a solo home run against Fingers.

Now leading the game, 1–0, Martin elected to stay with Lolich in the bottom half of the inning. Lolich allowed the first two batters, Mike Epstein and Gene Tenace, to reach base safely. Martin reacted by calling on right-hander Chuck Seelbach to relieve his best starting pitcher. Seelbach faced Gonzalo Marquez, Oakland's 11th-hour addition to the post-season roster. Marquez continued his Mandrake-like hitting by roping a single that dropped in front of Kaline in right field. Mike Hegan, pinch-running for Epstein, scored easily to tie the game, as Tenace raced from first to third base. Possessing a strong right fielder's arm, Kaline attempted to gun down Tenace for the inning's second out. Unfortunately for the Tigers, Kaline's throw bounced in front of surehanded third baseman Aurelio Rodriguez, who could not block the ball as it caromed past him into foul territory. Tenace scurried home with the game-winning run, giving the favored A's a dramatic win at home to start the series.

The A's carried the emotion of the extra-inning victory into the second game, as they pounded out seven hits in the first five innings, scoring a single run in the first inning and four more in the fifth against Woodie Fryman. The offensive outburst sent Fryman to the showers, forcing Martin to dip into his weak-link bullpen. Meanwhile, Blue Moon Odom dominated the Tiger lineup, holding Detroit to three singles, in a 5–0 shutout. The second game, however, would be most remembered most for an ugly incident that took place in the bottom of the seventh inning.

A's leadoff man Campy Campaneris faced Tiger reliever Lerrin LaGrow, who had entered the game in the sixth inning. Campaneris had done considerable damage in his first three at-bats: three hits, two runs scored, and a pair of stolen bases. Throughout the game, Tiger pitchers had thrown fastballs in the general direction of Campy's legs, in an attempt to brush him back off the plate, or perhaps even injure the Oakland catalyst. Predictably, LaGrow threw his first pitch—a fastball—down and in on Campaneris, hitting the Oakland shortstop in the ankle.

Most of the Oakland players knew that one of the A's' batters, given the Tiger struggles in the early part of the series, would eventually become the victim of a deliberate brushback pitch. "I was in the on-deck circle," said Joe Rudi in an interview that appeared in the *Binghamton Press*, "and I feel the Detroit pitcher threw at him. Campy had run the Tigers ragged in the first two games, and when [Billy] Martin gets his ears pinned down, he's going to do something about it."

Other members of the A's agreed with Rudi's analysis, including Mike Hegan, who observed the fateful pitch from the Oakland dugout. "There's no question in anybody's mind," says Hegan, "and I think if the truth be known, I think we saw something was gonna happen, but didn't know exactly what it was gonna be. Those orders to Lerrin LaGrow came right from Billy Martin—to start something, to do something. We had won the first game, and I think Billy Martin wanted to light a fire under his ballclub, and Campy was the guy that they were going after because he was the guy that set the table for us. There's no question that Billy Martin instructed Lerrin LaGrow to throw at Campaneris."

There had also been recent history of ill feeling between the Tigers and A's. Earlier in the season, Tiger relief pitcher Bill Slayback had thrown at Campaneris and Angel Mangual back-to-back, prompting Mangual to charge the mound. During the ensuing melee, Mangual punched Slayback, Billy Martin ran after Mangual, Willie Horton decked Mike Epstein, and Duke Sims and Oakland coach Jerry Adair brawled. Another Oakland coach, Irv Noren, found himself injured by Tiger relief pitcher Tom Timmerman. The 15-minute incident, which included fights and pileups, left simmering feelings of hatred between the two teams.

When LaGrow's fastball struck the bone of Campaneris' ankle, the A's' shortstop staggered for a moment, glared at the Tiger pitcher, and then, in an unusually violent reaction, flung the bat toward LaGrow. Spiraling about six feet off the ground, the bat helicoptered toward the pitching mound. The six-foot, five-inch LaGrow ducked down, barely avoiding contact with the bat, which ended up a few feet behind the mound.

Billy Martin led the charge of Tiger players and coaches from the dugout. Martin ran directly toward home plate, but three of the umpires managed to hold back the Tiger manager, preventing him from completing his assault on Campaneris. Nestor Chylak, the home-plate umpire and crew chief, ejected both Campaneris and LaGrow, while attempting to calm an infuriated Martin. "You bet I was after him," Martin told United Press International after trying to fight Campaneris in a 60-foot area located between the teams' clubhouses. "There's no place for that kind of gutless stuff in baseball," seethed Martin. "That's the worst thing I've ever seen in all my years of baseball...I would respect him if he went out to throw a punch, but what he did was the most gutless [thing] of any man to put on a uniform. It was a disgrace to baseball."

The volatile reaction of a quiet and respected player like Campaneris surprised his Oakland teammates. "Absolutely," says Mike Hegan. "And I've talked to

Campy many times [about it] since. He just snapped. He, at that point, got so frustrated that LaGrow kept backing him off and throwing at his feet. It was something that was well out of character for Campy. But he just said that he snapped, and that was the first thing that he could think about, and that's what he did—unfortunately."

Why did Campaneris resort to throwing the bat, rather than the standard charging of the mound? "I don't know why I threw the bat," Campaneris said later in an interview with Bob Hertzel of the *Cincinnati Enquirer*. "My ankle hurt so bad. I knew he was going to throw at me, but people now tell me it's better to go and fight. I don't know. I just lost my temper." Campaneris' unusual reaction left him confused and apologetic. "I'm sure he was regretful about it," Hegan says. "You know, sometimes in the heat of a battle like that you do things that you don't think about, [you don't] contemplate the consequences. Unfortunately, Campy did it, and had to live with it for the rest of the playoffs and the Series." In fact, the incident left Campaneris stigmatized for the balance of his career.

After the game, American League President Joe Cronin suspended Campaneris for the balance of the playoff series against the Tigers, and added a $500 fine to the punishment. On the matter of Campy's availability for the World Series, Cronin chose to defer to Commissioner Bowie Kuhn. To the disappointment of Charlie Finley, Cronin elected not to suspend either Billy Martin or Lerrin LaGrow. "Nestor Chylak said he didn't think LaGrow was throwing at Campy," Cronin told the *New York Daily News*, "so he isn't being punished." And what about Martin? "Martin didn't hit anybody," Cronin continued, "because the umpires subdued him quickly and so there will be no action against him." The A's had lost on all counts.

Several days later, Commissioner Bowie Kuhn announced that Campaneris would have to sit out the first week of the 1973 season without pay, but would be deemed eligible for any potential World Series games involving the A's. The A's were now 1-for-4 on the matter. All things considered, Mike Hegan says that Cronin and Kuhn handed down appropriate and fair punishments. "I think that was the right thing to do," says Hegan. "The incident happened within our league, and against the Tigers, so he got the suspension for the rest of that series, which took him out of those games, and that was punishment enough for him for that period of time. Then you're going to a World Series, kind of a neutral set of ballgames [against a different league], if you will, and then you go back to league play [in 1973], where you punish him and the ballclub the following year. I just think that was the right thing to do."

According to Dick Young of the *New York Daily News*, Bowie Kuhn had initially planned on a much longer regular season suspension—one lasting 30 days. Yet, negotiations with Charlie Finley and the Players' Association resulted in a more lenient punishment, a suspension of 10 days, which Kuhn later whittled down to one week. Young estimated that the suspension would cost Campaneris about $3,000 in salary, but speculated that Finley would make it up to his favorite shortstop by paying him a larger salary in 1973.

A Catcher Plays Second, and a Shortstop Blows His Stack

Although Blue Moon Odom held the Tigers scoreless over the final three innings to maintain a 5–0 win, Campaneris' bat-throwing escapade served as motivating anger for the Tigers. Campy's indiscretion also removed one of the hottest bats from the Oakland lineup, while depriving Dick Williams the services of his regular leadoff man.

Trailing two games to none in the series, the Tigers could take some comfort in the loss of Campaneris and the switch in venues, from the Oakland Coliseum to Tiger Stadium. Detroit rallied to win Game Three, 3–0, behind the pitching of Joe Coleman. The veteran right-hander pitched a seven-hit shutout, striking out a playoff-record 14 Oakland batters along the way. Coleman's surprising exhibition of power pitching eclipsed the previous American League playoff record of 12 strikeouts, set by Baltimore's Jim Palmer in the 1970 Championship Series against Minnesota.

The low-scoring theme of the series continued in the next game, as the A's and Tigers each scored only one run through nine innings. With the score still tied, hard-luck Mickey Lolich left for a pinch-hitter in the bottom of the ninth. The Tigers failed to score, forcing extra innings for the second time in the series. The A's then scored two runs against an ineffective Chuck Seelbach in the top of the 10th, closing in on what appeared certain to be the franchise's first American League pennant since the Philadelphia A's of 1931.

Unfortunately for the A's, Dick Williams had already burned his best reliever, Rollie Fingers, who had bailed out Catfish Hunter in the bottom of the eighth. Williams had followed with Vida Blue, who pitched a scoreless ninth, but then left the game for pinch-hitter Gonzalo Marquez. Those moves left Williams with a choice of three middle relievers to work the 10th: right-handers Bob Locker and Joel Horlen, or left-hander Dave Hamilton. Although left-handed hitter Dick McAuliffe was scheduled to lead off the inning, Williams opted for the more experienced Locker instead of the rookie, Hamilton.

McAuliffe and Al Kaline started the inning with singles, sending Locker to the dugout in favor of Horlen. Showing a lack of control, Horlen unfurled a wild pitch, moving the tying and winning runs into scoring position. Facing the lefty-swinging Gates Brown with no one out, Horlen walked the veteran pinch-hitter, loading the bases. With the A's playing the infield back, Bill Freehan followed with a grounder to Sal Bando at third base. Conceding the Tigers' second run of the game, the A's opted for what seemed like a sure third-to-second-to-first double play. The A's, however, were playing with a second-string infield. With Campy Campaneris suspended, Dal Maxvill had started the game at shortstop, before giving way to a pinch-hitter and two utility infielders, Tim Cullen and Ted Kubiak. Starting second baseman Dick Green had also been lifted for a pinch-hitter, but with Kubiak now committed to playing shortstop, Dick Williams chose to use his starting catcher—Gene Tenace—at second base in the late innings.

Tenace ran to cover second base, readying himself to receive the throw that would give the A's a force out, and perhaps the start of a twin killing. The novice infielder bobbled the toss from Bando, allowing Gates Brown to reach second base safely. "I think [Tenace] heard my footsteps," offered the 230-pound Brown in an interview with sportswriter Dave Nightingale, "because he got out of there before he had the ball." McAuliffe scored from third, to make it a 3–2 game, while the bases remained loaded. Instead of recording at least one, and possible two outs, the makeshift Oakland infield had come up empty. Reliever Dave Hamilton, the heavily sideburned rookie, now prepared to face two left-handed hitters, Norm Cash and Jim Northrup. Perhaps rattled by Tenace's error, Hamilton walked Cash to tie the game. Hamilton then watched helplessly as Northrup lashed a game-ending single to right field, in front of Matty Alou.

For one of the few times all season, the A's' strange second-base shuffle had cost the team a game—and a critical one at that. Williams had never really liked the constant lifting of his second basemen for pinch-hitters, but for the first and only time during his Oakland tenure, he had agreed to follow one of Charlie Finley's *in-game* orders. Finley had often made pre-game lineup suggestions, which the manager felt compelled to follow, but once the game started, Williams usually did what he wanted, not what Finley demanded. In this case, Williams' decision to go along with Finley's rotation of second basemen had led directly to an important playoff loss. Williams vowed to himself never to use the second base shuffle again.

The Tigers had managed to tie the series at two wins apiece, and now enjoyed the benefits of momentum and home field advantage as they headed to Game Five. In the meantime, Charlie Finley seemed obsessed with finding a way to restore the suspended Campy Campaneris to the lineup. At midnight, Finley held a press conference in his hotel room, pleading desperately for Campy's reinstatement. With Campaneris in attendance, Finley claimed his starting shortstop was legitimately sorry for the act he had perpetrated against Lerrin LaGrow. Standing off to the side of Finley, Campaneris nodded in agreement—perfectly on cue. Campaneris said only two words during the press conference: "I'm sorry." Dick Williams looked on disgustedly, wondering why he couldn't be securing some much-needed sleep in his own hotel room.

After presenting his defense of Campaneris to the media, Finley proceeded to attack the character of Billy Martin, whom he blamed for starting the bat-throwing incident. "I say with all sincerity that Mr. Martin instructed—no, demanded—that his pitcher throw at this young great star," said Finley in his best prosecuting-attorney voice. Finley then brought up some old news that had little to do with the Campaneris incident. He claimed that he had tried to hire Martin in 1970, only to be talked out of the move by one of Martin's former employers. "Cal Griffith, owner of the Twins, told me I would be taking a chance with Martin's past record," Finley explained to the Associated Press, before detailing Martin's rap sheet. *A fight with Twins pitcher Dave Boswell. A scuffle with Twins vice president Howard Fox. A knockdown of Cubs pitcher Jim Brewer, which broke the left-hander's jaw.* "That's Billy Martin," Finley told the AP. "He suckered Brewer, he beat up a club executive, and he took advantage of one of his own players who was intoxicated."

"He's a liar about the managing job," Martin retaliated in his own interview with the Associated Press. "We shook on the job and I was all set to go with them.

Then the A's started winning and he couldn't very well fire Johnny McNamara with the team moving towards first place." According to Martin, Finley agreed to send him scouting reports and films on the Oakland players, but never followed through. Martin then wrote the owner a letter, telling him that he was no longer interested in managing the A's.

Without Campaneris in the lineup and with Martin fully inflamed, the decisive matchup pitted a nerve-wracked Blue Moon Odom against a calm Woodie Fryman. The two starters had met in the series' second game, when Odom spun a shutout. That performance didn't seem to give Blue Moon any extra confidence prior to Game Five. Odom hardly slept before the final game, perhaps two hours, if that much.

The game started ominously for Odom and Oakland, when the Tigers reached the right-hander for a run in the first inning and the A's lost their most dynamic position player in the second inning. With Mike Epstein at first base and Reggie Jackson at third base, Dick Williams called for a delayed double steal. As Tiger catcher Bill Freehan delivered a weak throw to second base, Jackson raced home. Crashing feet-first into Bill Freehan, Jackson beat the return throw home and scored the tying run. Unfortunately for the A's, the run came at a high cost. On the play, Jackson injured his hamstring muscle severely, forcing him to leave the game. The A's now faced the undesirable situation of having to play the final seven and a half innings without both Jackson and the previously suspended Campy Campaneris.

At six feet, 200 pounds, Jackson possessed the build of an Adonis. His impressive musculature, strong wrists, and whipping bat speed made him one of the game's most feared power hitters, but his 27-inch thighs and 17-inch biceps made him susceptible to frequent muscle pulls and strains, such as the one he incurred while running home on the double steal. After Dick Williams and several Oakland players helped a teary-eyed Jackson leave the field for treatment in the trainer's room, Mike Hegan and Darold Knowles moved Reggie to a spot in the clubhouse where he could observe the remainder of the game on television.

Jackson watched his center-field replacement, rookie George Hendrick, reach base in the fourth inning against Woodie Fryman. With Hendrick on second base and two men out, the slumping Gene Tenace stepped to the plate. Tenace, who was 0-for-15 in the series and one of the principal goats in the fourth game, delivered a sharp single. Hendrick rounded third, fast approaching home plate. The lanky, fleet-footed center fielder slid feet first, away from Bill Freehan's sweeping glove. As Freehan tried to apply the tag, he bobbled the ball, allowing Hendrick to score the go-ahead run.

Battling his nerves, Blue Moon Odom continued to shackle the Tigers, holding them to just one unearned run through the first five innings. Although Odom appeared fine on the mound, he complained to Dick Williams that he was having difficulty breathing. Odom then asked to be taken out of the game. Williams complied, turning the ball over to Vida Blue to start the bottom of the sixth. The starter-turned-reliever responded with one of his best efforts of the season: four innings, three hits, no walks, and three strikeouts. As Detroit fans repeatedly hurled debris onto the field, Blue continued to keep the Tigers off the scoreboard. With two outs in the ninth inning and the A's still guarding a one-run lead, reserve infielder Tony Taylor lined a Blue fastball to center field. Perfectly positioned, George Hendrick made the catch with ease. A dramatic 2–1 victory gave the A's a three-games-to-two win in the American League Championship Series. For the first time in 41 years, the A's' franchise had won an American League pennant.

Reggie Jackson watched the final out from the clubhouse. After shouting "We're champions!" to himself, Jackson limped over to his locker to wait for his teammates and cover his belongings from the upcoming onslaught of champagne. The other 24 A's soon arrived. Vida Blue and Blue Moon Odom quickly embraced. Pinch-hitting hero Gonzalo Marquez immediately walked over to Jackson's locker, where the injured outfielder stood by with the help of crutches. Reggie let the crutches fall to the ground, hugged Marquez, and cried. Later on, utility infielder Dal Maxvill shook Jackson's hand and assured him of his importance to the team. "You're the biggest reason this club is here," Maxvill told Jackson, according to an account in the *New York Daily News*.

Yet, the tears of camaraderie in the clubhouse soon gave way to feelings of bitterness. Blue chided Odom, his best friend on the A's, for leaving the game early. According to United Press International, Blue snapped at Odom. "Hey man," said Blue, "Why didn't you go nine?" Odom explained that the tension of the situation had caused him to gag, almost to the point of vomiting. "Oh man, I know why you didn't go nine," Blue said, answering his own question. Blue then held his hand up to his neck and mouthed a few more words. "I know why." The insinuation of "choking" infuriated Odom, who retreated to his locker momentarily before making a move toward Blue's locker. Joe Rudi intercepted Odom, preventing him from completing his charge toward Blue. Moments later, Blue apologized to his ally, explaining that he was only kidding.

Like many other altercations in the Oakland clubhouse, what had begun as good-natured ribbing had turned into near fisticuffs. Yet, Odom says that such fights did not reflect any real animosity between players. "All the stories [about the fights taking place] are true," Odom says. "But we loved one another. We were like one big, happy family. It's like anything—if you're together for a long period of time. You have your fights, like brothers and sisters. We would fight a lot, [but] we took it out on the opposing team. That [tension] gave us motivation to win. We always had that tension."

Backup infielder Ted Kubiak, a frequent observer of clubhouse battles, agrees with Odom's assessment. "I think a lot of that had to do with the intensity of the ballclub and the fact that the players were there to win games," says Kubiak. "Guys would be a little edgy, maybe because they weren't performing that well. Some of the guys would be getting on them in a fun kind of way, and it wasn't taken that way. So things got out of hand. But they were able to stop and turn around and do what they had to do."

The presence of a controversial team owner may have also led to more fights than usual in the Oakland clubhouse. "I think Charlie Finley had something to do with that because he was so outspoken," Kubiak explains. "I don't know whether it was his design or whether it was just his method or just his personality, but he allowed the players to speak out also. There were guys that would be pissed off at him and they'd get angry and they'd say things in the papers."

One such blast game from Vida Blue, who was once again firing in the direction of Finley, a man that he had verbally battled since their vicious spring training contract negotiations. According to an article in the *San Francisco Examiner*, Blue charged Finley with "trying to destroy my career." When Blue asked an attendant to give him a bottle of champagne during the playoff celebration, the clubhouse man refused, telling him that the bottle was reserved for Finley's wife, Shirley. "What did she do?" Blue responded sarcastically, according to an article by sportswriter Dick Young. After wondering out loud about what the owner's wife had contributed to the playoff victory over the Tigers, Blue turned his wrath toward Dick Williams, who had elected not to use him as a starter during the playoffs. Rather than tell Blue directly that he had planned to use him as a reliever during the Championship Series, Williams had instructed pitching coach Bill Posedel to relay the message. "Why didn't he tell me himself I wouldn't start a playoff game?" Blue lamented to Al Hirshberg of *Sport* Magazine.

Jealousies and resentment aside, the Game Five win lifted the Oakland A's to a status never before achieved. Reggie Jackson assembled his words appropriately in discussing the significance of winning the pennant. "It gets us over the hump," Jackson explained to Phil Pepe of the *New York Daily News*. "It makes a lot of us pros. It makes guys on this club leaders. Now we don't have to talk about doing it; we don't have to get ready to do it. Now we've done it. We're the best, man, we're the best."

Chapter 12

The 1972 World Series

Reggie Jackson hoped that he had suffered nothing more than a slight hamstring pull or a severe "charley horse" and might still be able to play in his first World Series. As he sat next to his friend, Dave Duncan, on the team flight, Reggie suspected otherwise. Duncan cried, as did Jackson.

The A's' flight would take them to Cincinnati, home of the National League champion Reds, who had defeated the Pirates in a riveting five-game playoff. The matchup of the A's and Reds offered two sets of clashing physical images: the green and gold uniforms of Oakland against the staid red, white, and gray colors of Cincinnati; and the clean-cut, conservative Reds against the brash, rebellious, hippie-like A's. As an organizational rule, the Reds prohibited all of their players from donning facial hair, either mustaches or beards. A few Reds—Johnny Bench, Pete Rose, and Bobby Tolan—wore their sideburns fairly long, but nowhere near the dimensions of some of the A's. In contrast, nearly 20 of the 25 players on the Oakland roster sported mustaches and/or beards, and some featured sideburns so long and thick that they touched the points of their mustaches in mutton chop fashion. As Arthur Daley of the *New York Times* would surmise, the A's resembled a road company for a theatrical production of *Hair*.

"There's nothing wrong with mustaches or beards," said Reds superstar Pete Rose, who had sported a spring training beard earlier in 1972, during an interview with the *New York Times*. "I wear them in the offseason, in fact." Yet, once the Reds began the regular season, their players had to part with all forms of facial hair. "The boss says no," Rose said, referring to Reds executive vice-president and general manager Bob Howsam. "If he says no mustaches, no mustaches." The more rebellious A's likely would have posed a far different reaction had Charlie Finley tried to implement a similar ban on facial hair.

Ironically, one of Oakland's few clean-cut players returned to the lineup for the World Series. The A's regained the services of starting shortstop Campy Campaneris, who had been suspended for the last two games of the Championship Series. Commissioner Bowie Kuhn, against the wishes of some writers and fans, deemed Campaneris eligible for all World Series games against the Reds.

While Campaneris returned, another A's player officially became unavailable. Dick Williams learned that Reggie Jackson would indeed miss the entire World Series because of a serious leg injury. In the last playoff game against the Tigers,

Jackson had initially pulled his hamstring about 30 feet from home plate. If he had stopped running at that moment, he might have been able to play against the Reds. Instead, Jackson kept running and scored a critical run for the A's, but did massive damage to the leg. "I could feel everything tear loose when I went into Tiger catcher Bill Freehan at the plate," Jackson told sportswriter George Vass of *Baseball Digest*. "I ruptured my hamstring, pulled it away from the bone, stretched the ligaments in my knee." As gory as Jackson's description sounded, the pain felt worse. "Imagine someone reaching inside your leg," Jackson submitted to Dwight Chapin of the *San Francisco Examiner*, "and just pulling everything apart."

Jackson's leg hurt him so badly that he could not sleep the night of the decisive playoff game against the Tigers. Over the next several days, he could not dress himself, instead needing assistance to put on his shoes and socks. Reggie's outfield mate, Joe Rudi, offered tangible support to the injured right fielder. "He's the best friend I have," Jackson told *Baseball Digest* in praising Rudi. "The man came over. He fed me. He helped me put my underwear on, my pants on." Rudi's assistance typified the caring nature of a man whom Oakland pitching coach Bill Posedel, a veteran of 43 baseball seasons, once described to *The Sporting News* as "the nicest guy I've ever met since I've been in baseball."

As part of baseball ritual, the public address announcer at Cincinnati's Riverfront Stadium introduced the starting lineups for both teams prior to Game One of the World Series. As the announcer read off the names of the A's, each Oakland starter ran from the dugout to the third-base line. Reds fans booed Campy Campaneris loudly as he took his place next to Dick Williams. After the starters sprinted onto the field, the announcer made a special introduction of Oakland's injured star. Dressed in a long suede coat and assisted by a pair of crutches, Jackson made his way slowly onto the field. In an impressive show of sportsmanship, the fans at Riverfront Stadium rewarded Jackson with a louder set of cheers than any other A's player. Jackson could also take solace in a ruling by the Commissioner's Office, which agreed to let him sit in the dugout in civilian clothes throughout the Series. Still, it was small consolation for a player who had dreamed of playing in the World Series since debuting with the lowly Kansas City A's in 1967.

The absence of Jackson, who had started in center field throughout the series with the Tigers, forced the A's to make several changes. The A's replaced Jackson on their 25-man roster with Allan Lewis, who was listed as an outfielder, but was actually a pinch-running specialist with limited skills as a hitter or fielder. Even his own manager, Dick Williams, took a shot at the switch-hitting Lewis' ability to swing the bat. "He batted .300 last year," Williams told *The Sporting News*, ".150 left-handed and .150 right-handed."

With Lewis restricted to running situations, the A's would need to call on another player to take Jackson's place in center field. Manager Dick Williams decided to move rookie George Hendrick into Jackson's position. About an hour before Game One, Jackson would spend several minutes instructing Hendrick on the subtleties of playing center field against the Reds.

Even more importantly, the A's would have to find someone to replace Jackson as the No. 4 hitter in the batting order. Williams selected Mike Epstein, his lone remaining home run hitter from the left side, as the cleanup batter against both right-handed and left-handed pitchers. Epstein had power, but lacked Jackson's intimidating presence at the plate and game-breaking ability.

The injury to Jackson only added to the general feeling of Reds superiority. The oddsmakers made Cincinnati the prohibitive favorite to win the Series. Even Reds manager Sparky Anderson, generally a respectful sort when it came to the opposition, boasted of his team's preeminence. During the Championship Series, Anderson had referred to the Pirates and Reds as "the two best baseball teams in the land." Anderson continued to champion the National League refrain on the eve of the World Series. "If I said the American League was as good as the National League," Anderson told Ron Fimrite of *Sports Illustrated*, "I'd be lying. Yes, Oakland could come over and play in our league and maybe Boston [could]. But they're the only ones."

Curiously, Anderson's opinions seemed to find agreement in the opposing dugout. "The National League has more depth, better personnel overall and more good young black players," Jackson informed *Sports Illustrated*. Another Oakland player hinted that players in the American League lacked intensity. "Maybe we're too buddy-buddy in our league," conceded A's captain Sal Bando.

As the Reds' most outspoken player, Pete Rose showed little regard for the talent of the A's. "The real World Series was between the Reds and Pirates," Rose claimed in an interview with the *San Francisco Examiner*, referring to the hard-fought National League Championship Series. "Those are the two best teams in baseball." In contrast to their conciliatory reaction to Anderson's comments, the A's quietly took note of Rose's pre-Series chatter.

On the surface, the outlook for the A's appeared even more dire since Williams could not use staff ace Catfish Hunter in the first game against the Reds. Catfish had pitched in Game Four of the playoffs, making him unavailable to start the opening game of the Series. Williams chose Ken Holtzman as his replacement. Although Holtzman did not carry the same lofty reputation as Hunter, his presence didn't seem likely to please the Reds. In his last start at Riverfront Stadium, occurring during the 1971 season as a member of the Cubs, Holtzman had pitched his second career no-hitter.

Across the field, the Reds' Sparky Anderson considered his own options, gritted his teeth, and selected ailing right-hander Gary Nolan to represent Cincinnati in Game One. Nolan, a 15-game winner and the ace of the Reds' staff, had battled shoulder soreness over the last two months. When healthy, Nolan ranked as one of the half-dozen most effective right-handers in the National League.

According to the Reds' scouting reports, the ability to contain leadoff man Campy Campaneris and also handle middle-of-the-order threats like Joe Rudi, Matty Alou, Mike Epstein, and Sal Bando ranked as the highest priorities for Cincinnati pitchers. Little attention was given to Oakland's No. 7 hitter, Gene Tenace. The Oakland catcher, who had started the season as a backup, had hit only five home runs and batted .225 during the regular season before continuing to struggle in the playoffs, with just one hit (albeit Game Five's pennant-winning RBI) in 17 at-bats. Yet, versus the Tigers, Tenace had swung the bat like a man on a hitting streak. "The ironic thing, going into that World Series, was that against Detroit I started seeing the ball really well," Tenace recalls. "The balls that I was hitting were right on the nose, but right at somebody." Tenace's quality at-bats against the Tigers would foreshadow far more favorable results against the Reds.

In each of his first two at-bats of the World Series, Tenace lofted a Nolan offering deep into the left-field bleachers at Riverfront, thus becoming the first player in major league history to homer in his first two Series at-bats. The two-run blast and solo shot gave the A's a 3–0 lead. "I never hit two home runs in one game before," Tenace revealed to Joe Durso of the *New York Times*. "The first one was on a fastball out over the plate. The second was on a hanging curve." Tenace had taken advantage of a pair of mistake pitches—both thrown in poor locations by Nolan. "No scout in the world could help you on those [pitches]," Sparky Anderson told the *New York Times*, defending the Reds' scouting report and pitch selection against Tenace. Prior to the Series, Anderson had told his pitchers to throw Tenace strikes and not walk him—under any circumstances.

In the meantime, the Reds hit Holtzman well, collecting four hits in the first five innings, while scoring single runs in the second and fourth frames. Holtzman struggled in each inning, but avoided further damage by stranding eight Cincinnati baserunners. In the sixth inning, Dick Williams allowed a teetering Holtzman to face the leadoff batter. When Johnny Bench doubled against the right-field fence, Williams called upon his best reliever. The NBC television graphics still referred to him as *Roland* Fingers—which was his given name—but fans around the country were starting to know the young relief ace as *Rollie* Fingers. Even though Fingers was Oakland's fireman, he had actually begun warming up in the second inning. As was the manager's frequent custom, Williams once again called on Fingers to pitch in the middle innings. "Many, many times," says Joe Rudi, "he would come into the game in the sixth inning, get the last out of the sixth, and then pitch the seventh, eighth, and ninth." Williams was hoping that Fingers could do exactly that in Game One.

The Oakland fireman fanned Tony Perez and Denis Menke and retired Cesar Geronimo on a line drive to Joe Rudi. In the seventh inning, Dave Concepcion grounded a leadoff single to left field. With pinch-hitter Ted Uhlaender at the plate, Concepcion took off for second base. Anticipating the play, the A's called for a pitchout, but Gene Tenace threw high to Campy Campaneris, who arrived late in covering the bag. Campy applied a sweeping tag that appeared to miss the runner. Second base umpire Mel Steiner saw the play differently, calling Concepcion out.

Concepcion briefly protested what seemed like a questionable call. Steiner pointed to Concepcion's head, indicating where Campaneris had placed the tag. But television replays, utilizing a ground-level camera angle, showed that Campaneris had missed Concepcion completely. Since Campy had arrived at the bag late, and had been forced to reach for the high throw, he had been left with only once choice: the sweep tag. Campaneris had come up empty, missing both Concepcion's shoulder and head. The proper call would have allowed Concepcion, the potential tying run, to remain at second base with no one out.

After striking out Uhlaender, Fingers walked Pete Rose on four pitches and gave way to Oakland's newfound relief ace, Vida Blue. The unhappy left-hander, previously offended by Dick Williams' refusal to use him as a starter, hurled shutout ball the rest of the way to preserve the 3–2 win and give the A's the early edge in the Series. "He was told the other day that he'd pitch relief," Williams told the *New York Times*. "He volunteered for it today." Perhaps reluctantly, Blue had indeed offered his services to Williams as a Game One reliever. "Pitching is my job," Blue said tersely. "And when I throw the ball, I'm contributing more than anybody else." As for the immediate future, Williams planned to rest Blue for the next two games and use him as a starter in Game Four.

Prior to Game One, few baseball fans outside of the Bay Area had known much about Fury Gene Tenace (pronounced "tennis"). He had grown up in Lucasville, Ohio, a small Midwestern town. His grandparents had emigrated from Italy and had decided to Americanize their last name, changing it from its original "Tennaci." Tenace's maternal grandfather branded the youngster with the nickname of "Steamboat," in tribute to the unusually clumsy way that he walked—like a steamboat carrying heavy cargo.

Despite his awkward gait, Tenace began playing baseball at a young age, encouraged by his father, a former semipro player. Tenace's father drove him so hard to excel at the game that he developed an ulcer at the age of 13. As a youngster and fan of the game, Tenace idolized the New York Yankees, until an unpleasant encounter with one of their scouts. Having just led his team to Ohio's state baseball finals, Tenace approached a Yankee scout who had attended the game. "He told me there was no way I could play in the big leagues," Tenace informed Bob Hertzel of the *Cincinnati Enquirer*. "That's when I quit liking the Yankees." Tenace also experienced rejection from a Reds scout, Gene Bennett, who informed Tenace that he had no future as a professional baseball player. Undeterred, Tenace eventually signed a bonus contract with the Kansas City A's organization. With the Yankees in the midst of a long post-season drought that would continue until 1976, Tenace was enjoying life as a World Series hero with the A's—against the Reds, no less.

Tenace had served as the A's' second-string catcher, backup first baseman, and pinch-hitter over the first half of the season. In mid-season, when starting catcher Dave Duncan found himself in a lengthening batting slump, Dick Williams encountered one of his first lineup dilemmas. Since Duncan represented the strong defensive catcher that Williams liked, the manager preferred that he remain in the lineup, but knew that he needed better offensive proficiency, as well. Finally, Williams approached Tenace, asking the utilityman if he could catch. At any other time, Tenace would have leapt at the opportunity. Riding a temperature of 104 degrees, Tenace had lost 10 pounds from a case of the summer flu, and as a result, was in no condition to catch. Tenace begged out of the backstopping assignment, but did feel well enough to play first base. Williams gave him a start there, and

Tenace responded with a triple. The next day, Tenace felt well enough to wear the catcher's equipment and toil behind home plate for nine innings. Dick Williams had suddenly found himself another No. 1 catcher.

Given the lack of attention to him prior to Game One, Tenace was able to spend most of his pre-game routine taking batting practice. "There must have been 500 reporters, photographers, and guys with tape recorders cluttering up the field and wanting to talk to Sal Bando and Rudi and Bert Campaneris during batting practice," Tenace said in a 1990 interview with Peter Coutros of the *New York Post*. "No one wanted to interview me, so I stayed in the batting cage, taking my cuts, swinging at one ball after another and looking for Bando, Campy, or some of the other guys coming into the cage to take their licks. But they were all tied up talking to somebody with a pad and pencil or a mike, so I just stayed in there, taking more cuts. That didn't hurt."

No longer an anonymous figure, Tenace received more media attention prior to Game Two, which attracted the largest baseball audience in the history of Cincinnati. A crowd of 53,224 fans, standing room only, watched Hall of Famer Jackie Robinson throw out the ceremonial first pitch—only nine days before his death from a heart attack. In his final public appearance, the 53-year-old Robinson spoke eloquently of his desire to "see a black face managing in baseball." Commissioner Bowie Kuhn then assisted a nearly sightless Robinson to his seat along the first-base line.

At the conclusion of the pre-game ceremonies honoring Robinson, youthful left-hander Ross Grimsley took to the mound and encountered early trouble against an Oakland lineup heavily loaded with capable right-handed bats. In the second inning, Sal Bando, Dick Green, opposing pitcher Catfish Hunter, and leadoff man Campy Campaneris massaged four singles around a pair of outs, to give the A's their first run. One inning later, Joe Rudi reached the seats for the first time in his post-season career, connecting on a solo home run on a "thigh-high" fastball that Grimsley left over the inside third of the plate. "I was surprised how he had developed into a real good hitter," Reds advance scout Ray Shore told the *New York Daily News* in describing Rudi during the Series. "Two years ago I didn't think Joe Rudi would be a good player." A defensive play by Rudi in the ninth inning would provide an even more lasting image than his home run; in fact, it would become the most remembered play of the '72 Series.

Having held the Reds scoreless through the first eight innings with a mix of surprisingly live fastballs and hard sliders, Hunter remained on the mound to start the ninth. He promptly surrendered a leadoff single to Cincinnati's powerful first baseman, Tony Perez. Third baseman Denis Menke followed with a line drive toward left field. The ball carried well, appearing to have a chance to clear the wall for a game-tying home run. As Rudi raced back, he tried to flip his sunglasses into position. Nearing the wall, he peeked over his head toward the flight of the ball. Within a few feet of the unpadded wall, Rudi turned to his right, made a forceful leap, bracing himself against the wall with his right hand. With his back to the infield, Rudi climbed the wall in spider-like fashion. With his left arm fully outstretched and his right hand braced against the wall, Rudi leapt for the Menke drive. His legs hovering several feet above the ground, the six-foot, two-inch Rudi attempted a backhanded snare for the ball. "I jumped as high as I could," says Rudi, "and the ball hit right in the end of my [glove's] web. It was almost like a snow cone." Once his glove grasped the ball, Rudi pulled his glove back as quickly as possible, for fear that the ball might pop loose if the glove made contact with the wall. When Rudi's feet returned to the warning track turf, he held the ball up to the umpires, proving that he had robbed Menke of an extra-base hit.

"It was as great a catch as you'll ever see," gushed Dick Williams in an interview with Bob Stevens of the *San Francisco Chronicle*. But was it really a catch? "There was some discussion that I trapped the ball," Rudi recalls. "Sparky [Anderson] came out later and argued that I had trapped the ball. But I *did* catch it, turned my glove, and came down. I was surprised as anybody when I caught the ball, so I took it out of my glove, held it up in the air for the umpires to see, and then threw the ball in." A stunned Tony Perez, who had already rounded second and was halfway to third, made a hasty retreat for first base. "We came very close to doubling Perez off," says Rudi, "because he was near shortstop when I caught the ball." Regardless, the A's were content to come up with *one* out on the play. If Rudi had not caught the ball, Perez likely would have scored from first and Menke would have coasted into second base. Instead, the disappointed players in the Reds' dugout had to watch Perez, who had already rounded the second base bag, scurry back to first with one man out.

Rudi's defensive heroics should have surprised no one. By 1972, major league scouts considered Rudi among the game's most accomplished defensive left fielders. Yet, only four years earlier, Rudi's play in the outfield had ranked as no better than *atrocious*. Originally signed as an infielder, he didn't know how to throw properly from the outfield—or how to get a good jump on fly balls. Fortunately, the A's had both an astute manager and a famed coach named Joe DiMaggio ready and willing to provide help. "Bob Kennedy was our manager in '68, and between him and Joe D., they started working with me every day beginning in spring training," recalls an appreciative Rudi. "They felt they could make me into an outfielder. Bob Kennedy would stand over by the third-base coaching box and hit me a half-hour to 45 minutes worth of fly balls and ground balls *every day*. Joe D. would come out with me and work with me on how to turn and go back on the ball and run to where you think the ball is coming down—things that a major league outfielder has to do. How to pick the ball up off the bat. A good outfielder should have a step or two before the ball really leaves the bat. Nobody else could have told me that other than somebody who had played for years and had the level of outfield play that he had."

Employing DiMaggio's techniques, Rudi had fashioned a quick start in pursuit of Denis Menke's ninth-inning drive. Still, the play posed a unique problem for Rudi—in the form of the late afternoon glare. "The sun was directly above the hitter. It was right there," says Rudi. "If the ball had been an inch or two to the right, it'd been dead in the sun and I wouldn't have been able to [see] it."

Having avoided one problem, Rudi still wasn't hopeful of making a play. "And when [Menke] hit the ball, I thought it was *out*." Although fearful that the ball would achieve home run distance, Rudi did not give up. "You know how things are sort of like déjà vu. This was the exact play that Joe DiMaggio and I worked on a ton. I just turned and ran back to the wall and flipped my glasses down. I went straight back to the wall, just like [DiMaggio] had taught me to find the wall first, and then the ball. I know the pictures show me with my hand against the wall, because that's how he taught me to go back to the wall, turn back in, and keep your hand against the wall so you knew where you were."

Mike Hegan, playing first base in the ninth inning, saw the play unfold in front of him. "I was pulling for Joe all the way," Hegan says. "I mean when it was hit, you couldn't tell, it was difficult to tell [if the ball would clear the fence]. You're in a ballpark that you're not familiar with. If that ball is hit in Oakland, you probably know that it had a chance to go, or it wasn't gonna go. But there, you're just not sure. Joe Rudi was an excellent hitter, but Joe Rudi, for those of us who saw him play left field every day, may have been one of the best left fielders that I've ever seen. He wasn't very quick, because he was a big country boy, and had heavy legs, but he got a great jump on the ball. Everything that he could get to he caught. Fortunately, he caught that one."

Onlookers at Riverfront Stadium immediately compared Rudi's leaping catch to heroic defensive plays in earlier World Series. "I'd put it ahead of two other World Series catches that have been written about a lot," Dick Williams said definitively to a reporter from the Associated Press. "The one by Al Gionfriddo of the Dodgers against Joe DiMaggio in 1947 and the one Willie Mays made off Vic Wertz in 1954." Several writers mentioned Sandy Amoros' running catch in 1955 and Ron Swoboda's sliding grab in the 1969 Series. While Hegan says there may have been better catches than Rudi's play, few carried more weight within the context of a critical Series game. "I don't know if it rates with the Willie Mays catch," Hegan says, "but in terms of what it meant in a big game at that point in the ballgame, it was as important a catch as any I've seen, or been personally involved [with]."

The next batter, Cesar Geronimo, laced a screeching line drive to the right of Hegan, who had been inserted for defensive measures three innings earlier. Hegan dove to his left to field Geronimo's shot. Hegan caught the ball momentarily, then watched it pop out when his glove smacked the ground. Retrieving the ball with his bare hand, Hegan scrambled on his hands and legs toward first base, tagging the base with the ball for the inning's second out. "At that point in time," remarks Hegan, "what we didn't want to have happen was any doubles down the line, so that that run could score all the way from first, or [possibly] have runners at second and third. So, I was just trying to not get too far off the base line."

Hegan says the late afternoon start time of Game Two made the play even more problematic. "It was very difficult to see because you're in the shadows, and fortunately, when the ball was hit, I just reached out and stabbed; I didn't catch it cleanly, and had to kind of scramble back to the bag. That was another, I guess, game-saving play."

Although Joe Rudi's play against Menke would receive more attention, some in attendance at Riverfront Stadium claimed that Hegan had actually executed a more impressive play. Dick Williams praised Hegan effusively in an interview with the *San Francisco Chronicle*, calling him "the best left-handed fielding first baseman in all of baseball, and that includes Mr. [Wes] Parker." Williams' assessment tweaked the senses of some National League observers, since many considered Parker, the veteran Dodger infielder, the slickest first baseman in either league.

Williams certainly had ample reason to believe in Hegan's credentials. During the regular season, Hegan had set an all-time major league record for first baseman by playing in his 164th consecutive game without making an error. In addition to sure, reliable hands, Hegan possessed cat-like range to either side. Unlike slower first basemen, Hegan felt equally comfortable playing on either grass or artificial turf, where batted balls tended to travel faster and skid more often.

Although the Oakland defense had brought the A's within one out, Catfish Hunter had allowed several hard-hit balls in the ninth. Sal Bando walked to the mound from his position at third base, urging Hunter to finish the game off. "You're not even trying," Bando yelled, according to an interview Hunter did with the *Chicago Daily News*. "He's on me all the time in tough spots, trying to get me mad at myself so I'll pitch out of it," said Hunter, explaining Bando's psychological ploys. As Hunter tried to prepare himself mentally for the next Reds' batter, Sparky Anderson called back his No. 8 hitter, Darrel Chaney, replacing him with pinch-hitter Hal McRae. The backup outfielder grounded a single to left, scoring Perez to make it a 2–1 game.

Recognizing that the last three batters had hit the ball solidly, Dick Williams walked to the mound to remove a tiring Hunter from the game. "I wanted to finish," Hunter told the *Chicago Daily News*. "I begged to finish." Williams refused to listen and called on his relief ace, Rollie Fingers. The Oakland fireman faced pinch-hitter Julian Javier, the former Cardinals' second baseman who had played for the Redbirds' championship teams in 1964, '67, and '68. In his final official major league at-bat, the right-handed hitting Javier weakly popped up a Fingers slider along the first-base line. Mike Hegan ran into foul territory, planted himself squarely in the first-base coaching box, and nestled the ball into his glove for the game's final out.

The pair of excellent defensive plays in the ninth inning typified the way that the A's won games, more so with their gloves than with their bats. "Really, when you look back at it," Hegan says, "We were not a great offensive ballclub. We were a *very good* offensive ballclub and had some explosive people. But Dick Williams, from day one that I remember being in Oakland, talked about pitching, defense, and execution. Those are the things that we tried to do, and what he tried to do was plug the right people in the right spots. Fortunately, Joe [Rudi] made the play, then I made the play, and we win the ballgame."

The acrobatics of Rudi and Hegan overshadowed the clutch pitching brilliance of Catfish Hunter, who had sidestepped several potential Red rallies. In the second inning, the Reds had put runners on second and third with no one out, only to watch Hunter strike out three straight batters. Hunter told a group of reporters that several of the Reds' hitters might have underestimated the speed of his fastball, which featured late movement within the strike zone.

When Pete Rose heard about Hunter's public comments, he erupted. "I don't want to make any excuses, but it's just that we put so much into that series with Pittsburgh," said Rose to the *San Francisco Chronicle*, again referring to the playoffs against the Pirates. "Now he [Hunter] goes and says we were underestimating his fastball." A reporter, sensing Rose's anger at Hunter, asked the Reds' left fielder if he would characterize the Catfish as a "super" pitcher. "No, I wouldn't," Rose responded tersely to the *Chronicle*. "He's a good pitcher, but hell, I'm not gonna make him out to be a super pitcher because he's not." Rose offered an uninspiring comparison of Hunter to two lesser-known National League pitchers. "He reminds me of Rick Wise," Rose informed the writer, referring to the veteran right-handed pitcher with the Cardinals. "That's about how hard he throws, or maybe like Jim McAndrew [of the New York Mets], but he certainly is no Tom Seaver or Bob Gibson." Rose then extended his criticism to the entire Oakland pitching staff. "Don't tell me their pitching is that much better than Pittsburgh's," Rose told the *Chronicle*, in offering a comparison to a Pirates staff regarded by several scouts as only slightly better than average. In the space of a few paragraphs, Rose had supplied the A's with sufficient bulletin board material to last the remainder of the Series.

Although Rose's remarks upset the A's, they remained consistent with the advance reports compiled by the Reds' scouts. In an interview with Phil Pepe of the *New York Daily News*, Reds scout Ray Shore echoed Rose's sentiments. "I wouldn't say they have the best pitching in baseball, but they're good," assessed Shore. "Catfish Hunter is a lot like Rick Wise. Ken Holtzman is like Dave Roberts of Houston... If Vida Blue throws like he threw in Detroit the other day, he's in a category with Steve Carlton."

Sparky Anderson contributed to the Oakland bulletin board by making a bold prediction. "I'm not a betting man," the Reds' manager informed the *Chicago Daily News*, "but even if the Las Vegas people make us 20–1 underdogs now, I still bet we'll win the Series in seven games." Anderson did concede some concern, however. "I'm not going to panic just yet," Anderson told Red Smith of the *New York Times*, "but I'm close to that."

Although Anderson felt confident in his ability to defeat Dick Williams' team, he held a special regard for the Oakland manager. The two men had played together in the Brooklyn Dodgers' farm system. In 1955 and '56, Williams and Anderson played as teammates at Ft. Worth and Montreal, two of the Dodgers' top affiliates. As a result, the two future managers had become good friends. In a World Series marked by hostile statements between opposing players, Anderson and Williams felt no motivation to make any inflammatory comments about one another.

Williams did face some criticism in another corner. Some members of the national media questioned his on-field strategy. Some writers wondered aloud why Williams had seen fit to make so many trips to the mound. Those same scribes criticized him for making too many pitching changes and substitutions during the first two games of the Series. "I've overmanaged two in a row now," Williams said sarcastically in an interview with Dick Young of the *New York Daily News*, "and I'm tickled pink!"

Yet, Williams did second-guess himself over his handling of his pitchers in Game Two. "I left [Catfish] Hunter in two hitters too long," Williams told Al Hirshberg of *Sport* Magazine in assessing his decision to allow Hunter to face Denis Menke and Cesar Geronimo in the ninth inning. "Rudi and Hegan took me off the hook. But they shouldn't have to. I made a mistake." Williams' self-effacing statement indicated his growth as a manager. By his own admission, Williams never would have conceded error during his first managerial reign in Boston. Now a more mature and secure manager, Williams felt comfortable in pointing out his own strategic mistakes.

The victory in Game Two left Williams and 24 of the 25 A's happy. The lone holdout was first baseman Mike Epstein, who was furious with Williams for having removed him from the game for pinch-runner Allan Lewis in the sixth inning. Epstein, known as a below-average defensive player, claimed that he could have pulled off the same kind of play that Mike Hegan had made against Cesar Geronimo.

On the flight to Oakland, Epstein rose from his seat and walked to the front of the plane, where Williams usually sat. Epstein seated himself next to Williams, politely admonishing his manager for taking him out of a World Series game. Williams listened patiently to his frustrated first baseman, who did his best to calmly explain his feelings. "He did not want to come out [of the game]," recalls Mike Hegan. "Apparently, Epstein told Dick [Williams], and I don't know if it was tongue-in-cheek or not, that if *he* was in the ballgame at the time, that would have been a double play," Hegan says, laughing. Anyone who had watched the lumbering Epstein play first base on a regular basis would have held a radically different opinion.

Perhaps Epstein's touch with reality had been skewed by his consumption of alcohol aboard the flight. Epstein and Williams would later admit that they had *both* been drinking. According to Williams, Epstein issued him a kind of warning, instructing the manager to *never* take him out of a game again. "I just feel you don't appreciate the way I've been busting my tail," Epstein told Williams, according to a story by Dwight Chapin in the *San Francisco Examiner*. "I don't want this to happen again." Williams, who moments ago might have been feeling some sympathy for Epstein, was now ready to *strangle* his first baseman. Williams exhibited unusual courage in shouting at Epstein, an oversized man once described by rugged backup catcher Curt Blefary—during an interview with *Sport* Magazine—as being so strong that "he could pinch my head off."

Epstein and Williams exchanged angry words for the next few moments. Yet, Hegan doesn't recall Williams and Epstein physically coming to blows during the argument. "I had heard that something had gone on up front [in the plane] where the coaches and managers were sitting," says Hegan, who was seated in the back. "As far as I know, it was nothing more than verbal." Nonetheless, the exchange left Williams convinced that Epstein was a selfish player, one who was more concerned about the personal issue of playing time than the team's goal of winning the World Series.

While Epstein's complaints had placed him squarely in the manager's doghouse, three other players had earned the monetary affections of an appreciative owner. "I don't know how well-known it is," Hegan says, "but on that plane ride back to Oakland from Cincinnati, he gave Joe Rudi, Gene Tenace, and myself each checks for $5,000 for what we did in games one and two." Commissioner Bowie Kuhn later ruled that the payments were actually illegal bonuses, while Finley insisted they were merely "retroactive" pay raises. "Tenace was getting a minimal salary," Finley pointed out to Red Smith of the *New York Times* in an effort to justify his discussion of pay raises. "He was getting only $20,000." Finley hoped to increase Tenace's salary to $25,000—immediately.

"The commissioner found out about it and tried to void it," Hegan recalls. "Charlie fought it and we ended up able to keep the money. At that point in time, it was interpreted as a bonus, which in contracts, you're not supposed to be able to do. Charlie did it anyway." In an article in *Sport* Magazine, A's captain Sal Bando sided with Finley in voicing his complaint over Kuhn's action. "The ban on cash bonuses for outstanding play is one of the silliest of all concessions to tradition," Bando wrote in the first-person article. "Finley tried to change all that at the World Series. He failed because Commissioner Bowie Kuhn wouldn't let him do it. It transformed something very decent on Charlie's part to something looking underhanded and sordid." Even a generous, kind-hearted act on the part of Finley had prompted a negative reaction from baseball's highest power.

Finley also announced that he had rewarded Dick Williams with a new contract, which also included a pay raise. Media reports speculated that under terms of the new deal, Williams would make between $65,000 and $75,000. If so, Williams would become the highest paid manager in all of baseball. Kuhn could do nothing about *that*.

Kuhn could also do nothing to lessen Finley's thirst for attention. From giving out illegal bonuses, to holding midnight press conferences during the playoffs in protest of Campy Campaneris' suspension, to giving his players well-publicized incentives to sprout mustaches, Finley knew how to manipulate the media. He also knew how to annoy members of the fourth estate, by allowing his celebrated mascot mule to parade aimlessly through the press' hospitality room during the World Series.

Finley also became the subject of some unwanted attention when the Reds and Sparky Anderson saw the Oakland Coliseum for the first time. "It's ugly," a reporter quoted Anderson as saying when the Reds' manager looked out onto the field and into the stands. "I thought Charlie O. had more class than this." Anderson didn't realize he was being quoted when he made the off-hand remark.

The dreary weather in the Bay Area only added to the Coliseum's unsightliness.

After a travel date, the ninth consecutive day of rain in the Bay Area forced postponement of Game Three. Amidst reports that the Series might be shifted to San Francisco's Candlestick Park, which featured artificial turf, Commissioner Kuhn ordered the use of two helicopters to dry the natural grass playing field of the Oakland Coliseum. The strategy enabled the Series to resume the next day. Still, nature would play a factor during the games in Oakland. All three contests at the Coliseum were scheduled start at 5:15 P.M. local time, forcing the A's and Reds to experience the alternating light and shadows created by the Oakland twilight. The unusual start times had been mandated by NBC-TV, which preferred airing the games at 8:15 P.M. on the East Coast.

With the field softened by the continuous rain and puddles dotting the vast expanse of foul territory at the Oakland Coliseum, the Reds sought their first Series victory in front of a hostile crowd. Perhaps angered by Pete Rose's disparaging remarks about Catfish Hunter, a group of fans seated down the left field line pelted the Reds' left fielder with an array of foods and other disposable household goods. "One guy out there must have been a grocer," Rose said to *Gannett News Service*. "They threw everything, including oranges and eggs at me."

Rather than use Gary Nolan on three days rest, Sparky Anderson opted for Jack Billingham, while Dick Williams countered with Blue Moon Odom. Both hurlers pitched brilliantly over the first six innings, maintaining a scoreless tie. Dick Green made two spectacular plays at second base, robbing Joe Morgan and Pete Rose of certain singles. In the seventh, Tony Perez led off with a single and moved to second base on Denis Menke's sacrifice bunt. Cesar Geronimo, better known for his fine defensive skills and cannon-like throwing arm, swatted a line single toward center field. Perez stumbled rounding third, falling to the wet ground face-first, but still managed to score easily when George Hendrick tossed the ball toward Campy Campaneris, who was stationed as the cut-off man between the pitcher's mound and second base. Geronimo's single held up, as Clay Carroll saved the 1–0 game for Billingham with a scoreless ninth inning.

When a reporter questioned Hendrick's decision to throw to second base and Campy Campaneris' failure to throw home, Williams sprang to his players' defense. "Don't make a goat out of Hendrick," Williams said in an interview with Gannett News Service, while scolding the media in general. "He was worrying about Geronimo trying for two bases...As for Campaneris, he couldn't hear our third baseman yelling about Perez because of the crowd noise."

The sinkerballing Billingham, a .500 pitcher during the regular season, struck out seven batters and allowed a mere three hits over an eight-inning stint. "I don't usually strike out that many batters," said Billingham, not known for power-pitching ability, in an interview with the Associated Press. "The twilight no doubt helped me." The tenuous mix of shadows and glare also helped Blue Moon Odom, who struck out 11 Reds in seven innings. During the regular season, Odom had managed a high-water mark of nine K's.

Although the Reds won the game, a piece of unique Dick Williams strategy left a lasting impression on the fans watching the game at the Coliseum and on national television. With Joe Morgan on third and Bobby Tolan on second in the eighth inning, Rollie Fingers faced the Reds' cleanup batter, Johnny Bench. Fingers ran the count to three-and-two, prompting a visit from Williams. The manager pointed to Bench and the on-deck circle, and then aimed his finger in the direction of first base, as if to indicate to Fingers and Gene Tenace that he wanted to intentionally walk Bench. As he went through the motions of calling for the ball-four pitchout, physically pointing at just about everyone in sight, Williams told Fingers to throw a slider over the middle of the plate. After the conference on the mound broke up, Tenace stood straight up behind the plate, signaling for the intentional walk with his right hand. As Fingers began his delivery, Tenace stepped out briefly, then retreated toward his usual position, squatting to receive the pitch. Bench, anticipating the automatic ball four pitchout, watched as Fingers threw a sharp slider that crossed the outside corner of the plate. Bench started to throw his bat away and run to first, before realizing that he had just witnessed "strike three."

Williams had previously tried the unusual trick play, which he learned from famed manager Billy Southworth, during his minor league managing days. "It never worked for me the few times I tried it in the minors," Williams admitted to Al Hirshberg of *Sport* Magazine. "I never tried it in the majors until tonight. I think the only guy in the ballpark who saw it coming was [Joe] Morgan. At the last minute, he yelled to Bench, 'Be alive!' but it was too late." Home-plate umpire Mel Steiner watched Fingers' slider nick the outside corner and signaled strike three, sending an embarrassed Bench back to the Reds' dugout. After an intentional walk to Tony Perez, Fingers retired Denis Menke on a pop-up to keep the Reds from scoring another run.

The 1–0 win for the Reds underscored the domination of pitching in the Series. Through the first three games, the Reds and A's had combined for nine runs, for an average score of 2–1. NBC television opened up its broadcast of Game Four by discussing the extreme low-scoring nature of the Series, which had left some critics pining for more offensive action. Given the absence of Reggie Jackson from the lineup, the A's' lack of offense was somewhat understandable; the Reds' batting order, however, featured Pete Rose, Joe Morgan, Johnny Bench, and Tony Perez in its top five.

In the fourth game pitching matchup, Sparky Anderson chose hard-throwing left-hander Don Gullett to face Ken Holtzman. With the game again scheduled to be played during the twilight hours, Anderson hoped that A's hitters would have difficulty seeing Gullett's quick, rising fastball and hard slider. "The twilight here is hell for hitters," Dick Williams told the *New York Daily News*, in describing one of the most distressing hitting features of the Oakland Coliseum. The twilight had already played a part in determining the nature of Game Three.

Holtzman kept the Reds off balance with an excellent curveball, while Gullett overpowered Oakland batters with his 90-mile-per-hour fastball. The game remained scoreless until the bottom of the fifth, when Gene Tenace measured a Gullett fastball, pounding it over the left field wall. The solo home run by the newly discovered World Series hero gave the A's a 1–0 lead heading into the late innings.

In the eighth inning, Reds shortstop Dave Concepcion bounded a leadoff grounder between short and third. Campy Campaneris made a fine, backhanded pickup, but had no chance to throw out his fleet-footed counterpart. Instead of allowing Don Gullett to attempt a bunt, Sparky Anderson inserted Julian Javier as a pinch-hitter. An experienced handler of the bat, Javier softly bunted toward third baseman Sal Bando, who threw to Mike Hegan at first, as Concepcion moved up to second. Pete Rose followed by smashing a pitch up the middle. The ball deflected off Holtzman's glove toward second baseman Dick Green, who retired Rose at first. The 1-4-3 putout allowed Concepcion to advance to third.

With two left-handed hitters scheduled to bat and Holtzman still pitching well, Dick Williams walked to the mound. The manager surprised several observers on press row by asking for the ball from Holtzman and summoning Vida Blue from the bullpen. Why would he bring in another left-hander when he already had one in the game? The manager explained later that he had asked catcher Gene Tenace how well Holtzman was throwing. "He said he thought Ken had lost a little off his pitches," Williams told the *San Francisco Chronicle*. "I had a fresh arm in the bullpen in Vida Blue."

Blue walked Joe Morgan, the most patient of the Reds' hitters, and one of the National League's fastest and smartest baserunners. Bobby Tolan followed by stroking a clean double down the right-field line. By the time Matty Alou retrieved the ball in the corner and returned it to the infield, both Concepcion and Morgan scored. Williams' unorthodox decision to use Blue over Holtzman had backfired. "The decision was mine," Williams emphasized to reporters. "I'll live and die with it, and believe me, for awhile, I was dying." The Reds now led, 2–1, and would continue to hold the advantage as they entered the bottom of the ninth.

Reliever Pedro Borbon faced backup first baseman Mike Hegan, who had once again replaced Mike Epstein for defensive purposes. Hegan grounded weakly to Denis Menke at third base for the first out. Dick Williams then pinch-hit for George Hendrick, calling upon late-season sensation Gonzalo Marquez. The Reds' scouting report, compiled by Ray Shore, indicated that Marquez usually hit ground balls up the middle. Strangely, shortstop Dave Concepcion, who had played with Marquez in the Venezuelan Winter League, positioned himself several strides to the left of second base. Using a compact swing, Marquez chopped the ball—up the middle. The high-hopper was not hit hard, but managed to elude both Concepcion and Joe Morgan for a one-out single.

Pinch-runner Allan Lewis, the "Panamanian Express" who had been used almost exclusively on the base paths, entered the game for Marquez. Sparky Anderson told Borbon to check Lewis at first base, but not to throw over. Borbon ignored the order, tried to pick Lewis off of first base, and then ran the count to two-and-one on Gene Tenace. Annoyed by Borbon's lack of concentration, Anderson decided to bring in his best reliever Clay Carroll—nicknamed "The Hawk" for his large, protruding nose. Tenace responded with a ground single to left, pushing Lewis to second. With Dick Green representing the next scheduled batter for the A's, Dick Williams instructed his most seasoned pinch-hitter to make his way to the plate.

Don Mincher had struggled after his mid-season acquisition from Texas, batting a mere .148 in an Oakland uniform. When Mike Epstein had been forced to the sidelines, Mincher filled in at first base and failed to drive in a single run. "The Mule" ultimately returned to the bench, where he failed to hit a single home run and managed only five RBIs. Although Mincher finished the season with a career-low .216 batting average, Williams trusted him in the pressurized situations of World Series play. "A lot of times when you're in slumps, like the 2-for-21 [earlier in the season]," Mincher recalls, "I knew in my head—Dick Williams knew in his head—it was nothing pressure-wise that was causing that; it was all physical. My mind-set was right." Williams also realized that Mincher was one of only four Oakland players with previous World Series experience. Matty Alou, Mike Hegan, and Dal Maxvill had played in the World Series for the Giants, Yankees, and Cardinals, respectively.

Playing for the Twins, Mincher had hit poorly in the 1965 Series against an intimidating Dodgers pitching staff, collecting only three hits in 23 at-bats. But Mincher had hit an important home run during that Series, connecting against Don Drysdale in Game One. Mincher says Williams recognized his ability to block out the pressure created by a World Series game. "I was aware of the situation," Mincher says, "but when I stepped in the box, it's just the pitcher and me. That's the only two people on the face of the Earth. And I think Dick knew that my thinking was still that way, even though my bat was sometimes kind of slow. And Clay Carroll was a sinkerball pitcher—he didn't throw hard—and those were the guys that all my career I could hit very well. The fans and the pressure and the TV, all those things did not enter into my mind because I had been there before."

By using Mincher, Williams was taking at least one major gamble. Mincher's ability to hit the ball hard, coupled with his plodding running speed, made him susceptible to grounding into a game-ending double play. Mincher says he never allowed himself to think about that possibility during the at-bat. "I can't think that way," Mincher insists. "I really can't. I know one thing. After my first two or three years in major league baseball, and through my minor league career, with a guy on first base and a ball hit well to second base or shortstop, it's a double play. I'm not gonna outrun a double play. I knew that. So, I learned not to even be concerned about it."

Later in the World Series, when Mincher again came up as a pinch-hitter, Sparky Anderson would counter with one of his left-handed relievers. "All the other appearances that I had had in the World Series, and ended up having," Mincher says, "they always switched to a left-handed pitcher and I was hit for. This was the only official at-bat I had in the World Series. I remember Sparky Anderson saying afterward that he had wished that he had done it again." Anderson resisted the urge to play the percentages in Game Four and chose not to call upon hard-throwing left-hander Tom Hall, who was already warming up in the bullpen. Anderson instead decided to stay with Clay Carroll, who had handled left-handed hitters with regularity throughout the regular season.

Mincher had not swung a bat in a game since the regular season finale. Although he had been used as a pinch-hitter in the playoffs against Detroit, Mincher had taken three pitches—all called strikes. Dick Williams reminded Mincher to be more aggressive in this at-bat against Carroll. "I told him to go up there swinging," Williams said after the game in an interview with sportswriter Dave Nightingale.

The advice not withstanding, Mincher took the first pitch for a ball. With a count of one ball and no strikes, Carroll threw a fastball over the middle of the plate. "I was lucky enough to be able to get a good pitch I could drive, down in the strike zone," Mincher says, in recalling Carroll's second pitch. "I tried to get a ball that you can drive up the middle or pull in the hole to first base. Those were the things I really thought about, and I thought about on that day. The ball went directly over the second baseman's head. If it had been on the ground, it'd been a double play." Mincher's uppercut swing enabled him to lift the ball over the infield. "I remember it just like it was yesterday," says Mincher. "I got it in the right-center field gap, which probably should have been for a double, but I was cold and couldn't run." Mincher's golf shot into the alley scored Lewis with the tying run and sent Tenace, representing the potential game-winning run, to third base.

"It's the last hit I ever got," Mincher says in recalling the key RBI single, "and certainly it's the most vivid in my memory." Mincher left the game for a pinch-runner, while Dick Williams called on his third pinch-hitter of the inning, Angel Mangual, as a replacement for Rollie Fingers at the plate. The youthful outfielder represented an interesting choice for Williams, given the manager's displeasure with Mangual's frequent failures to advance runners during the regular season. With the Cincinnati infield drawn in, Mangual hacked at the first pitch, sending a routine grounder toward the right side of the infield. Playing a shallow second base, Joe Morgan couldn't reach Mangual's dribbler, which squeezed through the infield, giving the A's their most dramatic win of the Series.

"Dick Williams keeps making mistakes, and he lucks out every game," said one National League manager (according to Larry Claflin of the *Boston Herald*), observing from the World Series press room. Several questions might have been asked of the anonymous manager. What *game* was he watching? What *mistakes* by Williams was he referring to? In the ninth inning, Williams had used three pinch-hitters, all of whom delivered, and two pinch-runners, one of whom scored. If Williams had managed any less aggressively, the A's might not have won.

Game Four proved a testament to the depth of the A's' bench, which Charley Finley had tinkered with so often during the regular season. Marquez and Mincher, two players not with the team at the beginning of the season, had delivered key pinch-hit singles. Mangual, who had fallen out of a starting role after an impressive debut in 1971, won the game with the most important hit of his career. Although many of Finley's critics snickered over the incredible number of roster moves he made during the season, the end results of Finley's maneuvering left the A's with the best bench in all of baseball.

In retrospect, the massive number of player transactions executed by Finley—65—surprises even players like Mike Hegan, who managed to play the entire season with Oakland. "You know, that's the first time I've heard that number," Hegan says of the dizzying number of roster moves. "I knew it was a lot; I didn't realize it was that many."

Ted Kubiak, one of the A's' many mid-season pickups that season, says Finley had a knack for acquiring key role players at just the right time. "I guess that's [to] his credit," Kubiak says, "finding guys that he needed to fill in. How about [Gonzalo] Marquez, the pinch-hitter that we had? I mean every time he'd come up, he'd get a base hit."

Another late-season acquisition had also helped the A's to their third win of the World Series. In the fifth inning, right fielder Matty Alou had robbed the Reds of a certain double when he one-handed a Pete Rose drive and crashed into the outfield wall. One inning later, Alou made another fine one-handed catch when he raced in and snared Johnny Bench's sinking line drive. The defensive play of Alou, while generally overlooked, had helped draw the A's within one victory of Oakland's first World Championship.

A's pitching had played an even larger role throughout the first four games, shutting down the front three of the Reds' intimidating lineup. The first three Cincinnati hitters—Pete Rose, Joe Morgan, and Bobby Tolan—had combined to produce four hits in 34 World Series at-bats. As a result of Oakland's concerted pitching efforts against Rose, Morgan, and Tolan, the Reds' fourth and fifth-place hitters enjoyed few run-scoring opportunities. Johnny Bench and Tony Perez teamed up on 12 hits, but without a single RBI between them.

The Series resumed on Friday afternoon at the sold-out Oakland Coliseum, where the A's—regardless of the outcome of the Series—would play their final home game of 1972. Catfish Hunter faced Reds starter Jim McGlothlin in what appeared to be another major pitching mismatch in favor of the A's. Yet, the Reds' offense quickly did its best to remove the advantage. Pete Rose led off the game against Hunter and cracked his first pitch over the 375-foot marker in right-center field.

The A's eclipsed the 1–0 deficit in the bottom of the second inning, scoring three runs on Gene Tenace's record-tying fourth home run of the Series. Tenace, who had hit only five home runs during the regular season, matched the all-time mark for most home runs in one World Series. The scoreboard at the Oakland Coliseum flashed the message that Tenace had equaled a record shared by Hall of Famers Babe Ruth, Lou Gehrig, and Duke Snider, and former Yankee slugger Hank Bauer. "I remember looking up at the scoreboard when they made that announcement and thinking, 'I don't belong with those guys,' " Tenace said 18 years later in an interview with Bill Plaschke of the *Los Angeles Times*. The Reds probably thought the same.

The Reds and A's traded runs in the fourth, before Cincinnati closed to within one run in the fifth. Yet, Hunter failed to last the minimum five innings needed to claim the win for himself. He gave way to the Oakland bullpen, which continued to preserve the lead.

With Rollie Fingers on the mound in the eighth and the A's just six outs away from the title, Joe Morgan walked, stole second, and scored the tying run on Bobby Tolan's single to right. Tolan eventually made it to third base with two outs, but was left stranded when Fingers fanned Denis Menke.

Fingers remained in the game to pitch the ninth, surrendering a leadoff single to Cesar Geronimo. Sparky Anderson decided not to pinch-hit for Ross Grimsley, instead allowing the relief pitcher to attempt a sacrifice bunt on his own. Grimsley popped the ball in the air, a few feet in front of the mound. Instead of catching the ball for a sure out and attempting to double Geronimo off first, Fingers listened to the advice of third baseman Sal Bando and allowed the ball to drop. Fingers hesitated for a moment, then fumbled the ball, realizing he had no chance to retire Geronimo, who had already started running toward second. Fingers then recovered and threw to first, but his toss sailed wide of Ted Kubiak. The throw pulled Kubiak into foul territory, but the acrobatic second baseman managed to tag Grimsley out. At worst, the A's should have recorded one out and held Geronimo at first. At best, they might have turned a critical double play. Unfortunately, they had done neither.

Another mistake soon followed. Dave Concepcion hit a ground ball to third, but Bando bobbled the ball for an error, with Geronimo holding at second base. Pete Rose then laced a single to center field, scoring Geronimo with the go-ahead run.

For the first time on the afternoon, the A's found themselves trailing. Sparky Anderson left Ross Grimsley in to start the ninth, but the erratic left-hander walked leadoff man Gene Tenace. Playing for the tie, Williams elected not to hit for Kubiak. The second baseman squared to bunt, but popped up to Tony Perez at first for an easy out. Williams then decided to insert pitcher Blue Moon Odom as a pinch-runner for Tenace, and sent up to Dave Duncan to pinch-hit for reliever Dave Hamilton. Anderson countered by bringing in sinkerballing right-hander Jack Billingham, usually a starter, to relieve Grimsley. Duncan, the forgotten man of the post-season but an accomplished low-fastball hitter, lined a single down the left field line. By the time Pete Rose retrieved the ball, Odom had reached third base. Billingham now prepared to face the righty-swinging Campy Campaneris, who had gone hitless in four at-bats, but was quite capable of bringing home a run with a squeeze bunt.

Campaneris walked down the line to talk to third base coach Irv Noren, giving further credence to the theory that the bunt might be used. Yet, the strategy session turned out to be nothing more than a decoy; Campaneris was swinging away. Falling behind in the count at 0-and-2, Campy weakly punched a short pop-up down the right field line, not far beyond the first base bag. Joe Morgan, with the best angle toward the ball, drifted into the spacious foul territory of the Oakland Coliseum. About 10 feet past first base, Morgan called off Tony Perez, and with his back to home plate, guided the ball into his glove for the inning's second out.

Even though Morgan made the catch only a few feet behind the bag, third base coach Irv Noren remembered Al Hollingsworth's scouting report on Morgan: *he didn't throw well after making a play on a ball hit to his left.* So, Odom sprung from third base and began an all-out dash for home plate. Stumbling momentarily on the wet grass, Morgan fell to one knee, and then propped himself back onto his feet. Morgan threw a strike to catcher Johnny Bench, who blocked the plate and applied his glove to Odom as he crossed home.

Home-plate umpire Bob Engel, down on one knee, his mask off, and his eyes pointed directly toward the plate, fired his right arm into the air. "Out," Engel bellowed, ending the game. Odom immediately yelled at Engel, enraged by the call. Odom sprung himself from the dirt and bumped into Engel, who had stationed himself in a low crouch near home plate. I wonder what the commissioner will do about that?" pondered Reds general manager Bob Howsam in an interview with Cincinnati sportswriter Earl Lawson. In a controversial decision that would upset the Reds, Bowie Kuhn elected not to suspend Odom for the final two games of the Series, but issued only a $500 fine against the volatile pitcher.

As he sat at his locker, bandaging his bleeding right knee, Odom refused to answer questions from the media. After showering, the angry pitcher finally agreed to talk. "I was safe," Odom insisted an interview with United Press International. "I know I was." Television replays showed otherwise. Johnny Bench, who had blocked Odom from the plate and tagged him before he touched home, questioned the pitcher's decision to run in the first place. "He was dead," Bench said flatly to the Associated Press. "It wouldn't even have been close if the guy [Morgan] hadn't slipped." Dick Williams, who agreed that the umpire had made the right call, contradicted Bench's criticism of Odom. "Anytime you get a ball like that down the foul line," Williams said to the *New York Times*, "even though short, you've got a chance. We had both men tagging up and when Morgan slipped, Odom kept going." Odom, however, hadn't noticed Morgan's brief fall. "I didn't actually see him slip," Blue Moon admitted. "I was going all the way because he had difficult position catching the ball and because he doesn't have the strongest arm." Yet, Morgan had delivered a perfect throw to Bench. A lesser throw would have allowed the A's to tie the game.

Later, when questioned by the media, Dick Williams explained his decision to use one of his pitchers as a pinch-runner, a strategy not favored by many managers. "I hated to do it and usually don't, but we had already used Allan Lewis," Williams reasoned in an interview with *Sport* Magazine. "You have to take the chance. Odom loves to run the bases and knows how. He took a calculated risk and nearly got away with it." Nearly.

Even though the Reds had won the game to draw closer in the Series, they had clearly been upset by the quality of umpiring in Game Five. Both Pete Rose and Clay Carroll had flashed first base umpire Bill Haller the choke sign. Haller ejected Carroll in the ninth inning, one inning after he had already been taken out of the game by Sparky Anderson. Haller allowed Rose to remain in the game, thereby averting a near riot from the Reds. Bowie Kuhn later fined Carroll for using abusive language.

In addition to the argument with the umpires, the A's and Reds had shown anger with each other in Game Five, a continuation of a Series-long theme. With Gene Tenace behind the plate, Rose had come up to bat and taken several close pitches, which Bob Engel called balls. When Tenace questioned Engel's judgment, Rose responded by telling Tenace to cease his complaining, suggesting sarcastically that the catcher umpire the game himself. Rose's interruption infuriated Tenace. "Hush up," Tenace blurted at Rose. "Get in the box and swing."

Other incidents had taken place, as well. In the second inning of Game Four, Hal McRae had toppled Dick Green in an effort to break up a double play at second base. McRae, one of the toughest players in the game, didn't even slide on the play, instead lowering his hip and shoulder into Green, rolling the second baseman about 10 feet behind the bag. McRae felt he executed a clean play; some of the A's thought differently. Two innings later, Johnny Bench viciously knocked Green to the ground. "I don't mind it," Green said of the take-out slides in an interview with the *San Francisco Chronicle*. "I want to be in there playing, that's all. Actually I like it." Some of Green's teammates, however, considered McRae's rolling block unnecessary and dangerous.

Several A's had also grown to dislike Pete Rose, the Reds' brash left fielder, who had belittled Catfish Hunter earlier in the Series. Neither Hunter nor Gene Tenace, in particular, cared for Rose's abrasive and blunt personality. As exemplified by their unpleasant discussion at home plate in Game Five, Rose tried to ride Tenace verbally throughout the Series, repeatedly insulting the Oakland catcher in exchanges at home plate.

The loss in Game Six prevented the A's from clinching the Series on their home field, necessitating a long and uncomfortable plane trip back to Cincinnati. In order to accommodate numerous guests of Charlie Finley, the plane carried a full capacity of 163 passengers. "That was the worst plane ride I ever had," Dick Green complained to the *New York Times*, after the plane had arrived in Cincinnati at 1:30 in the morning. "It was crowded and there was little service," said Green. "The bathrooms were filled with luggage and you couldn't even use them. It was a four-hour flight and I didn't get served dinner until 25 minutes before we landed." Another Oakland player placed the blame squarely on Finley for the unusual airplane conditions. "Finley had his whole damn entourage on the plane," said the player, who preferred to remain anonymous, in an interview with the *New York Times*.

Finley, meanwhile, had experienced his own difficulties on the plane. According to a report in the *New York Daily News*, Finley had invited an unnamed reporter from Chicago to fly the Oakland charter. When the writer boarded the plane, Finley allegedly threw a punch at him, although reports varied as to whether Finley's fist actually connected. It was Finley's attempt to exact revenge for what he considered a negative story the reporter had written the previous week. The reporter, for his part, considered the story a favorable one about the Oakland owner.

More tension awaited the A's in Cincinnati. Prior to Game Six, a woman waited to purchase standing-room tickets at the Riverfront Stadium ticket booth. She overheard a man utter the following words: "If Gene Tenace hits a home run today, he won't walk out of this ballpark." The woman reported the threat to ballpark authorities, who quickly informed the A's of the news.

Dick Williams and Charlie Finley asked Major League Baseball to provide extra security, but elected not to tell Tenace about the menacing threat until after the game. The police also supplied Finley and his wife, Shirley, with extra security. Three officers stood by the owner as he and his wife sat in a front row box near the Oakland dugout.

Finley's mood grew more worried as he watched the A's play miserably in Game Six. Vida Blue, originally scheduled to start Game Four, lasted only five and two-thirds innings in his first start of the post-season. Dave Hamilton allowed four runs in less than an inning. For the Reds, Bobby Tolan and Dave Concepcion teamed up to steal three bases against the ragged tosses of A's catcher Gene Tenace, whose awkward release and throwing motion appeared both strained and painful. In the meantime, Oakland managed only seven hits against a quartet of Reds pitchers. Angel Mangual typified the A's' ineptitude when he beat out a ground ball to third base for an apparent infield single, only to be called out for overstepping the first base bag. The gory details added up to an 8–1 rout for the Reds.

The A's did not take the Game Six drubbing lightly. As Campy Campaneris walked to the plate in the eighth inning of the blowout loss, he sounded a message to Reds catcher Johnny Bench. "We never lose three in a row," Campy told the future Hall of Famer, according to a report by the Associated Press. Bench gave the A's' shortstop a quick reply. "You've never faced the 'Big Red Machine.'"

The "Machine" had handled one of Oakland's best starting pitchers with ease. Prior to the game, Vida Blue had annoyed some of the Reds with what they interpreted as degrading comments. "Vida's a fine pitcher, I'm sure," Joe Morgan told the Associated Press after collecting two hits in the seven-run rout. "But we faced Steve Carlton [a 27-game winner with the Phillies] all through the year, and he's the best left-handed pitcher in baseball." In other words, Morgan felt Blue, who hadn't pitched nearly as well as Carlton in 1972, might be well-advised to keep his mouth shut the next time.

While Blue's statements to the media had upset the Reds, the A's had come away from Game Six burning with resentment toward Cincinnati's players. In the seventh inning, with the Reds already leading by five runs, Bobby Tolan had decided to steal second base. The Reds had stolen at will throughout the Series, partly because of Gene Tenace's subpar throwing arm and partly due to the inability of Oakland pitchers to hold Cincinnati baserunners close to first base. Yet, several A's considered Tolan's stolen base unnecessary and unsportsmanlike, given the one-sided score. Later in the inning, Tolan reached third base. Gene Tenace tried to pick him off by firing quickly to Sal Bando, who drove his leg and arms into Tolan. Bando claimed that he tripped and fell onto Tolan, but the Reds didn't believe him. And the Reds offered no apologies for their aggressive baserunning in the late innings. "We're out to win a World Championship," Joe Morgan told the Associated Press in defending Tolan's late-game stolen base. "You never have enough runs."

The only good news the A's received during the game involved the apprehension of the person who had placed a threat on the life of Gene Tenace. Police arrested a 32-year-old Louisville, Kentucky, man who possessed a loaded gun and a bottle of whiskey. "It's terrible something like that has to happen," a stunned Tenace told the AP. "It's terrible people can't go to a ballgame and enjoy the game without that kind of thing." Although the threat had clearly shaken him, Tenace had no plans to sit out Game Seven. "It scares me, but I'll play tomorrow," Tenace vowed. "I'm a little scared, but what can I do, tell the manager not to play me?"

Even in the face of death threats and arrests, the A's attempted to deflect the situation with morbid humor. As Tenace fielded questions from writers in the clubhouse, Reggie Jackson offered him some twisted encouragement. "If you got to go, Gene," Jackson said, according to the Associated Press, "at least it will be on national television." Another Oakland slugger felt somewhat left out, with Tenace continuing to receive attention as the target of a deranged man. "No one would even bother shooting me," said Mike Epstein, who was hitless in 16 Series at-bats.

Tenace wouldn't hear anything more about the incident until 10 years later, when he was playing in another World Series—as a member of the National League's Cardinals. "I was opening my mail," Tenace told sportswriter Bill Plaschke in 1992, "and there was a letter from this guy saying he was sorry for what he did and that he was glad they caught him." Instead of comforting him, the letter disturbed Tenace, who felt the man might have been following him. Tenace quickly contacted the police and gave them the letter. Fortunately, Tenace never heard from the man again.

Chapter 13

Game Seven

Now that the issue of the death threat had been settled, the A's needed to regroup for Game Seven. "We were overmatched today, but we'll show up tomorrow," a hopeful Dick Williams proclaimed to the *New York Times* after managing only about three hours worth of sleep the previous night. "They got to my secondary pitching today for most of their runs, but we're still confident that we can win."

Williams' confidence aside, the A's had blown a two-game lead, and had forced themselves into having to win a decisive game on the road. The Reds now had momentum, home field advantage, and one of their hottest starters, Jack Billingham, in their favor heading into Game Seven. Williams would have to rely on his third-best starter, Blue Moon Odom, whom many writers felt should have been suspended for his bumping of umpire Bob Engel in Game Five. Oddsmakers liked Cincinnati's chances of winning a third consecutive game, rating the Reds as 3-to-2 favorites to win Game Seven. If the oddsmakers were right, the Reds would become the first team in major league history to capture a World Series after losing the first two games at home.

Williams, who had placed his stamp on the Series with his incessant visits to the pitching mound, prepared several lineup changes for Game Seven. Ever the strategist, Williams wanted to leave nothing to chance in his quest for his first World Championship. Concerned about the Reds' success in stealing six bases over the last two games of the Series, and 11 in 13 attempts over the duration of the Series, Williams inserted Dave Duncan as his catcher and moved the weak-throwing Gene Tenace to first base. Williams also installed Angel Mangual as his center fielder. The flurry of moves resulted in the benching of regular first baseman Mike Epstein, who was hitless in the Series. Consistent with his "hot-hand" managing philosophy, Williams believed in benching slumping, unproductive players and replacing them with others who might be more helpful at the moment.

The news did not please Epstein, who felt he had swung the bat well throughout the Series. "I've been hitting the ball hard," Epstein insisted to Murray Chass of the *New York Times*. "I've hit seven good shots on the nose, but they've been caught." The absence of Reggie Jackson had placed extra pressure on Epstein to produce left-handed power. With Jackson unavailable, the Reds had pitched carefully to Epstein, throwing him off-speed pitches just off the outside corner. For his part, Williams didn't care why Epstein hadn't been hitting; he preferred looking at bottom-line results.

After cloudy skies and light rain threatened Game Seven, the weather cleared moments before gametime. A paid crowd of 56,040 fans—including 5,000 standing-room-only customers—streamed into Riverfront Stadium, eclipsing the Reds' franchise mark set earlier in the Series. The record gathering reluctantly witnessed two small doses of good fortune for the A's in the first inning. With one out, Angel Mangual hit a medium-depth line drive into right-center field. Center fielder Bobby Tolan misjudged the liner, first running in, then trying to retrace his steps backward. Tolan leapt, the ball caroming off of his glove for a critical three-base error. The A's must have felt special satisfaction in watching Tolan falter on the play, considering his late-inning stolen base in the Game Six blowout. After the Series, Tolan would admit that many of the hard feelings between players on both teams had been initiated by the Reds. "We tried to get them upset after we lost the first two," Tolan revealed to Dick Young of the *New York Daily News*. "You're down 2-and-0, you gotta try something."

After the Tolan error, Joe Rudi flied to shallow left field, with Mangual holding at third. Gene Tenace then hit a chopping grounder to third baseman Denis Menke. The veteran infielder readied himself to field the routine grounder on a large carom, then watched the ball bounce high after hitting a seam in the artificial turf. The ball nicked the top of Menke's glove before rolling into short left field. The bad-hop single gave the A's an early 1–0 lead.

In the fourth inning, Dick Williams' seventh-game defensive changes paid a critical dividend. Joe Morgan drew a one-out walk. Having been burned by Reds base stealers throughout the Series, Blue Moon Odom threw over to first base *seven* times. Undeterred by the extra attention, Morgan broke for second two pitches later. Catcher Dave Duncan snapped quickly out of his crouch and hurled a high but strong throw toward second base. For the first time in the Series, the A's had thrown Morgan out on an attempted stolen base.

Odom held the Reds scoreless until the fifth. Tony Perez doubled down the left-field line and moved up to second on a one-out walk. Odom then ran the count to two-and-one on Dave Concepcion. Playing it like the seventh game of the World Series that it was, Williams pulled Odom and replaced him with his best *starting* pitcher, Catfish Hunter. Catfish completed the walk by throwing two more balls to Concepcion. With the bases now loaded, Hunter allowed two long fly balls to Angel Mangual in right-center field, the first one scoring the tying run.

Sparky Anderson paid a price for tying the game in the fifth, however, since he used Hal McRae as a pinch-hitter for an effective Jack Billingham. With Billingham out of the game, Pedro Borbon (who had upset Anderson with his lack of concentration in Game Four) entered and allowed a leadoff single to Campy Campaneris. After a sacrifice bunt by Mangual, Joe Rudi grounded out to second, as Campy advanced to third. With two out and two bases open, Borbon faced Cincinnati nemesis Gene Tenace.

Curiously, Anderson decided not to intentionally walk Tenace, who had already driven in eight runs and collected four long balls in the Series. Tenace promptly lined a Borbon delivery into the left-field corner to score Campaneris with the go-ahead run. Dick Williams then made a curious move of his own by inserting Allan Lewis as a pinch-runner for Tenace at second base, a decision that upset the Oakland World Series hero. Although Lewis had successfully stolen six bases in six late-season tries, Tenace considered *himself* the fifth fastest runner on the team, trailing only Lewis, Campaneris, Reggie Jackson, and Matty Alou. "Look, I'm not a slow runner," Tenace pointed out in an interview with Phil Elderkin of the *Christian Science Monitor*. "I scored plenty of times from second base during the regular season and I could have done it again."

Sal Bando followed Tenace's double with a soaring fly ball toward deep center field. When Bobby Tolan reached the warning track in pursuit of the drive, his left leg collapsed underneath him, the result of pulling a hamstring. The ball landed on the track, bounced off the wall, and into the glove of the injured Tolan, who did his best to return the ball to the infield. Oakland now led 3–1. The A's eventually threatened to put the game away when they loaded the bases with two outs, but reliever Clay Carroll fanned Dick Green to end the threat.

In the sixth inning, the Reds put runners on second and third with two outs before Catfish Hunter retired Denis Menke on a fly ball to short right field. In the seventh, Hunter retired the Reds in order. Hunter's effectiveness that inning convinced Dick Williams to let him start the eighth, with the top of the Reds' order scheduled to bat: Pete Rose, Joe Morgan, and George Foster, who had replaced the hobbled Tolan.

Rose bounced a grounder up the middle past Hunter into center field. With the left-handed Morgan set to bat, Williams replaced Hunter with Ken Holtzman, who had started Game Four. The lefty-lefty strategy did not work. Morgan doubled to right field, advancing Rose to third base. When Morgan's liner bounced off the corner wall away from right fielder Matty Alou, Reds third-base coach Alex Grammas momentarily waved Rose home, then changed his mind. Several Reds players believed that Rose would have scored easily had Grammas *not* told him to retreat.

Sparky Anderson sent up the veteran Julian Javier to pinch-hit for Foster, who had not yet established himself as a feared major league power hitter. Williams countered with his ace reliever, Rollie Fingers, who had already appeared in five of the six Series games. With his trademark toothpick hanging from his mouth, the carefree Fingers casually strode in from the visiting bullpen.

Three days earlier, Fingers wouldn't have believed that he could pitch in Game Seven. "After the fifth game, my arm was completely dead," Fingers would say later in an interview with *New York Post*. "I couldn't comb my hair, wipe my…whatever you want to write." With an off day for travel and no need to pitch in the Game Six rout, Fingers now felt rejuvenated for the Series' decisive matchup.

Sparky Anderson called Javier back to the dugout and sent up the lefty-hitting Joe Hague. The backup first baseman popped up harmlessly to Campy Campaneris, who made the catch in short left field. Williams instructed Fingers to intentionally pass Johnny Bench, in order to set up a double-play opportunity.

The strategy came at the behest of Oakland superscout Al Hollingsworth, who had warned Williams not to pitch to Bench in critical situations, unless he had no other choice. Still, the intentional walk strategy seemed dubious, since it put the go-ahead run on base and brought up Cincinnati's hottest hitter, Tony Perez.

Although Williams wanted to avoid Bench at all costs, some of the Oakland players didn't find much comfort in watching Perez step to the plate with runners on base. "For a time there," says Reggie Jackson, "[Perez] was the No. 1 clutch hitter in the National League, without a doubt. He would hit the ball as hard as anybody—[Willie] McCovey, [Willie] Stargell, Joe Torre—those guys that really creamed the ball into the right-center field and left-center field alleys. Perez hit the ball harder than Bench. He hit the ball harder than [Harmon] Killebrew…The only guy who hit the ball like Tony Perez was Dick Allen, and a guy named Al Oliver. Guys that just creamed the ball so hard that they could hit the ball right next to an infielder and he couldn't move."

Hitting over .400 in the Series, Perez once again hit the ball well, but his long fly ball found Matty Alou in right field. Rose scored on the sacrifice fly, bringing the Reds within one run. After Bench surprisingly stole second, Fingers induced Denis Menke into hitting a routine fly ball to Joe Rudi in left.

The A's had stopped the Reds' rally just in time, preserving an uncomfortable one-run lead. Williams allowed Fingers to bat in the ninth, not wanting to remove his best reliever. In the bottom half of the inning, Fingers retired Cesar Geronimo on a pop-up and Dave Concepcion on a grounder. Having already used up his best pinch-hitting options, Anderson sent up the weak-hitting Darrel Chaney to bat for pitcher Tom Hall.

Much to the displeasure of Dick Williams, Fingers hit Chaney with a pitch. That enabled the Reds to bring Pete Rose to the plate. "Charley Hustle" was batting only .220 in the Series, but had powered a home run while batting left-handed to lead off Game Five. Williams walked to the mound, considering the possibility of bringing in Vida Blue to make Rose hit right-handed—his weaker side. Dave Duncan, huddling with Williams, convinced his manager to keep Fingers in the game.

Batting out of his severe left-handed crouch, Rose intensely eyed Fingers and drove a letter-high fastball to left-center field. The ball was hit well and appeared to have a chance of splitting the gap, though well short of home run distance. Still, if the ball eluded both Joe Rudi and Angel Mangual, Chaney would be able to score the tying run from first base.

The most reliable of the A's defensively, Rudi calmly took several short strides toward left-center, stopped in front of the warning track, and prepared to make a careful two-handed catch. Rudi gleefully clutched the ball in his glove, finalizing the A's' assault on the Bay Area's first World Championship.

Fingers hugged Dave Duncan, his loyal catcher, while Sal Bando jumped on the A's' relief ace from behind. The rest of the A's piled onto the field from the dugout and the bullpen. In the meantime, Dick Williams ran across the third-base line and headed toward first baseman Mike Hegan, who readied himself for an embrace with his manager.

Hegan had played very briefly for the Yankees during their championship year of 1964, but had come to bat only five times during the season and only once during that Series. With the A's, Hegan had played a meaningful role on a World Championship team for the first time in his life. "After having gone through the loss the year before in the playoffs to the Orioles—and really, despite all of the headlines of how much adversity and animosity and hard feelings there were among the [Oakland] players, and very frankly, a lot of that is overrated—I think it was the culmination. I came in on it a year before, and Dick [Williams] was there, and of course, Sal and Dick Green, Dave Duncan, Rudi, and Catfish, John Odom and all those guys had been together from the Kansas City days—for them especially it was something that meant a great deal. For all of us to be a part of accomplishing something, because in that Series, the Reds were favored, and they were 'The Machine,' and they had all the veteran players. Even though we had won the division the year before, we weren't expected to beat them in the Series, and we did.

"The thing about that Series that a lot of people don't remember is that there were six one-run ballgames in that Series. The only game that wasn't a one-run game was when they blew us out in Cincinnati in the sixth game. But every other game was a one-run ballgame. So it was a gut-wrenching Series, to cap a tough playoff with the Tigers. It was a very emotional time."

After Hegan, Williams, Duncan, Bando, Fingers, and the rest of the A's completed their on-field jumping and back-slapping, the A's moved their celebration to the clubhouse. In the clubhouse showers, Campy Campaneris, Dick Green, Joel Horlen, and Don Mincher sang a strange rendition of the National Anthem under the guidance of conductor Vida Blue. Another group of A's—Bando, Duncan, Rudi, and Mike Epstein—poured champagne over their own heads in front of a movie camera. That part of the celebration would later appear on commercial television as part of an advertisement for hair spray. Outside of the clubhouse, several of the Oakland wives chanted, "We're No. 1! We're No. 1!"

Curiously, Mincher doesn't remember singing the National Anthem under the shower stalls. "No, I don't," Mincher laughs, before conceding the strong possibility that he and his teammates had attempted to form an impromptu barbershop quartet. "I remember being in the shower with those guys and doing some crazy stuff," Mincher says, "but I don't remember [the singing]. But I'm sure we did do that. There's no doubt in my mind we did."

While most of the A's sang, laughed, and poured champagne, one player experienced feelings of emptiness and despair. Reggie Jackson, unable to play because of a ruptured hamstring, felt out of place in the clubhouse. "The worst feeling I've ever had, as an athlete and a human being, was the day we won the World Series," Jackson would tell the Associated Press the following summer. "I was so disassociated from it. I couldn't even get out onto the field to shake a hand."

Fortunately for the A's, Gene Tenace had made up for the omission of Jackson's bat from the lineup. Tenace soon received word that he had been named the World Series' Most Valuable Player by *Sport* Magazine, which would reward him with a new car. The previously obscure utilityman represented the lone Oakland hitting star of the Series. "How the hell can you win a car, Gino?" shouted Darold Knowles (according to sportswriter Dick Young), needling Tenace about being removed for a pinch-runner in the sixth inning of Game Seven. "You can't even go nine innings."

What Tenace *had* done was impressive. In a Series criticized for a lack of hitting by both teams, Tenace had tied a Fall Classic record by powering four home runs, and had also driven in nine of Oakland's 16 runs. The little-known catcher-first baseman had also established a new Series record with a .913 slugging percentage, bettering the marks of Hall of Famers Babe Ruth and Lou Gehrig. Tenace modestly discussed his role in beating the Reds. "I don't feel like a hero," Tenace told reporters, while overlooking the fact that he had mauled Cincinnati pitching at a .348 pace. "There was no one hero on this club," Tenace insisted. "There were 25 heroes." The statistics told another story. Other than Tenace, no other Oakland player had driven in more than one run in the Series.

Near the lockers, a West Coast baseball writer poured champagne over the head of Charlie Finley. "This is the greatest day in my life," Finley cried out to a reporter. "None of you can appreciate what this means to me." A reporter asked Finley about the *second* greatest occurrence in his life. "That was when my wife accepted my [marriage] proposal," Finley gushed. "But wait a minute. You better make this my second biggest thrill. My wife might not like it the other way." Two of Finley's children, 17-year-old Martin and 15-year-old Luke, joined their father as he held court with the media. When one of his sons tried to answer a reporter's question, the elder Finley instructed him otherwise. "You nod, I'll answer the questions," the owner said in typically Finley-esque manner.

In another section of the clubhouse, Dick Williams talked to members of the national media, some of whom questioned his moves during the Series. Why, in Game Seven, did Williams pinch-run for Gene Tenace? After all, the A's had led only 2–1 at that point, and Tenace had been their best hitter against the Reds. Why did Williams order Rollie Fingers to intentionally walk Johnny Bench in the eighth inning? The strategy violated the basic baseball rule: *never intentionally put the potential game-winning run on base.*

Other writers felt Williams was more concerned with making appearances on television than actually devising pertinent strategy. At one point in the Series, Williams decided to coach first base. The writers also took note of Williams' frequent visits to the mound. Williams walked to the mound 38 times during the seven-game Series, including 12 trips in the final game. The repeated delays would result in a change in baseball legislation. Commissioner Bowie Kuhn wrote Williams a letter informing him of the new rule. Beginning in 1973, the regular season rules that limited the number of mound appearances by managers and pitching coaches would also apply to the post-season. "I won't need a clean uniform for the playoffs," Williams would tell the *New York Times* in 1973. "The fans won't be seeing me as much this year."

One writer asked Williams to compare the '72 A's to the Boston Red Sox' team he had guided to the pennant in 1967. "This is a much better club than we had in 1967," Williams told *The Sporting News* without hesitation. Williams cited the depth of the A's as far superior to that of the Red Sox. Williams then compared the A's to the Brooklyn Dodgers' teams he had played for two decades earlier. "This club is even better than the Dodgers of the fifties," Williams proclaimed. Those Dodger teams had featured Hall of Famers Roy Campanella, Jackie Robinson, Pee Wee Reese, and Duke Snider, and secondary stars like Gil Hodges, Billy Cox, Carl Furillo, and Don Newcombe.

Although the national media had pegged them as slight underdogs at the start of the Series, the A's had managed to defeat a Reds team laden with Hall of Fame offensive talents. The meticulous scouting work of Sherm Lollar and Al Hollingsworth played an important role in the Series victory. Lollar and Hollingsworth assembled a scouting report so detailed that it advised the A's of even the most obscure tendencies of the Reds. By reading the report, Dick Williams learned that the Reds liked to bunt in situations with runners on third and two out.

In Game One, the Reds had placed the tying run on third base in the ninth inning. With two outs and Pete Rose at the plate, Williams had motioned Sal Bando to move in at third and instructed Vida Blue to throw high fastballs in anticipation of the bunt. Rose fouled off a squeeze bunt attempt before grounding out to Ted Kubiak to end the game.

"We had a meeting the first time we played Cincinnati," Kubiak recalls, "and the scouting report that we got on them was just excellent. We went out to play them and I swear to God it was like we had played them all year. I made the last out of the first game when Pete Rose bounced the ball over the mound—kind of towards second base—but to the right of second base. I made the play, and the next day Rose says in the paper, 'How the hell could he be in that spot?' Well, I played with Pete in the minor leagues, so I now how he hits. I mean, we knew what he would do in certain situations, but that's what that intelligence does. It helps you out."

On a more philosophical front, some media observers regarded the World Series between the A's and Reds as representative of a political battle between contrasting ideologies. Several baseball and political writers contrasted the conservative, old style, straight-laced Reds, whose players were forbidden to wear their hair long or don facial hair, against the liberal A's, a rowdy, unkempt group of players known for rebelliousness. In the *New York Daily News*, baseball writer Joe Trimble referred to the A's as the "bad guys, the ones with the mustaches and beards," and the Reds as the "good guys, the clean-shaven Cincys." Another writer termed the World Series "the Bikers against the Boy Scouts."

"Obviously, that was a focal point of the media," recalls Sal Bando, "simply because you had more of a radical personality in a Charlie Finley, and we had the longer hair and the mustaches. And then you take this very conservative, very inflexible Sparky Anderson and the Cincinnati Reds and their short hair and their high socks and their nice pants. It was a contrast between two different styles."

"Yeah, I guess it was a big deal," says Mike Hegan, laughing loudly. "Of course, the Reds had their rules that they couldn't wear the high stirrups. They couldn't have facial hair, and they had to have their hair cut so that it didn't reach the back of the uniform." In contrast, the A's, under the lead of Dick Williams, had almost no rules when it came to fashion and grooming.

Did players on the A's feel that the majority of the American population was rooting for the Reds, since they seemed to convey the "boy-next-door" image, while the A's represented the anti-establishment? "I think you probably had the youth of the day rooting for the A's," offers Bando, "and the elderly, or the older population, rooting for the Reds. We never even thought anything of it. It was no big deal to us."

Yet, the A's' liberal, hippie image did not necessarily reflect the political beliefs of the Oakland players. "We might have worn our hair longer and had mustaches," Bando admits, "but probably in today's political climate most of us were conservative anyhow." Liberal or conservative, conforming or rebellious, the A's had managed to adapt and change, in some of the same ways that the American culture did in the late sixties and early seventies.

Amidst the vivid imagery created by the Reds and A's, the comments of scruffy-bearded backup catcher Dave Duncan most effectively put the Series in proper perspective. On a team replete with players sporting the flower child look, none looked any more like a hippie than Duncan, whose sandy-colored hair swept well beyond his shoulders. "I think we proved that it's not how a person looks like outside that counts," said Duncan to *The Sporting News*, "but what he's got inside. We had it inside, heart and guts." And thanks to such heart, they had emerged as baseball's best team in 1972.

The Oakland players engaged in a rowdy, but enjoyable plane ride back to the Bay Area. "I remember the plane trip back," Don Mincher says. "It was such a great time. And Finley made sure that we had a good time, don't kid yourself. He had two airplanes chartered. He'd done all the things that let us enjoy ourselves. I don't remember a whole lot of sleep for the next two or three days, but we did celebrate, and it was a great time for me. It's just a cherished memory now. I have that World Series replica trophy displayed for all my friends to see right out in the open. And the ring and what-have-you. I was very, *very* proud."

Once the two planes arrived, the A's received a welcome from about 25,000 fans at Oakland's International Airport. Amidst rumors that the A's might eventually move the franchise to New Orleans, Charlie Finley sang the chorus of his favorite song, "Sugar in the Morning," shouted messages of encouragement, and held up the World Series trophy. Gene Tenace, the World Series MVP, yelled "We're No. 1" repeatedly to the collection of fans and friends.

Some of the onlookers chanted "We want Vida!" but Blue was nowhere to be found. Blue had decided to skip the reception at the airport. "I just can't stand being in crowds like that," Blue explained to a reporter. Blue, who had also missed the airport reception after the A's had won the pennant against the Tigers, would later skip the team's private victory party and the public victory parade in downtown Oakland. Predictably, Blue's string of absences would anger Mr. Finley.

On October 23, the A's officially celebrated the Bay Area's first championship with a 15-block parade through downtown Oakland. A convoy of antique cars escorted Oakland players along the parade rout, as an estimated crowd of 150,000 spectators looked on. Finley accepted the keys to the city—of Oakland that is, not the rumored destination of New Orleans. A number of fans held up signs that read "Tenace the Menace," the new nickname given to their sudden World Series hero.

Having grown up in a small town, Gene Tenace felt uncomfortable in the spotlight afforded to a player who had performed so well in front of an entire country. When he accepted a sports car from *Sport* Magazine as the World Series MVP, Tenace showed little interest or enjoyment in the glamour associated with stardom. "See all this," Tenace told the *New York Times*, pointing to the cameras and television lights surrounding him. "I couldn't care less about it all. I'm the same old me." A quiet reserved man with a dry sense of humor, Tenace preferred spending time with his wife and two young daughters as opposed to traveling the banquet circuit. "Tony Perez called and wanted me to do an act with him, Johnny Bench, Vida Blue, and others at Las Vegas," Tenace told the Associated Press. "But me? I just want to get back to my family."

The unexpected power hitting of Tenace, the clutch pitching of Fingers, Hunter, Holtzman and Odom, the strange but productive strategy of Williams, and yes, the endless maneuverings by Charlie Finley, had translated into a World Series victory. Even though the Reds had outscored the A's in the Series, 21–16, and had forged a lower team ERA, Oakland had managed to overcome a series of obstacles to win. The injuries to Darold Knowles and Reggie Jackson, the playoff suspension of Campy Campaneris, the clubhouse argument between Blue Moon Odom and Vida Blue, the strange rotation of second basemen, and the lack of a proven center fielder in the World Series had not been enough to prevent the A's from completing their evolution from American League also-ran to major league champions.

For a player like Don Mincher, who had already decided to retire after the season, the feeling of winning a World Series represented a special satisfaction. "Yeah, it was," Mincher says. "I knew and I had announced that I was gonna retire. To go out as a winner, and as a World Champion…I had come close to it before, and I had done most of the things that I really wanted to do. My career was somewhat above-average; it wasn't the great-type career. But I had done some good things; I played in the All-Star Game. But I still missed that big ring. When we won that thing, my roommate Sal Bando and the guys that I really got close to, one of them being [Mike] Epstein, we had such a great feeling of, I guess, kid-like joy. Like you were 17 years old and you just beat your high school rival."

While winning the World Series fulfilled the A's' sense of accomplishment, it also forced them to confront the business and financial aspects of baseball. Shortly after the Series, the A's' players voted on how to divide their World Series shares amongst themselves. Such votes have historically proven both difficult and controversial, given the necessity of dividing 25 shares amongst a group of players that usually numbers in the thirties. For the '72 A's, the task proved even more daunting, considering the revolving door theme to the season. Charlie Finley had engineered 65 transactions involving 41 different players. As a result, Finley had employed a total of 47 players (or 49, if you include two players who had been traded to National League teams only to be reacquired later) throughout the tumultuous season.

The A's elected to hand out 27 full shares, with each player receiving a World Series record payment of $20,705. Strangely, the A's voted infielder Larry Brown a full share and Tim Cullen a one-third share, even though Brown had spent far less time on the active roster. In another notable decision, the A's elected to completely shut out onetime pitching star Denny McLain from any World Series money, while giving other short-timers at least a small amount of post-season loot.

Although Finley had made a dizzying number of player moves, he had been smart enough not to interfere with the nucleus of the team. "There was always something going on around there," Don Mincher says in regard to the many player transactions. "But the core, I'm talking about the guys, the Reggie Jacksons and especially the Sal Bandos over at third base, Dick Green and Campy and those guys, never wavered. We had a little wavering at the catching position sometime between Duncan and Tenace, and Tenace played some first base. But the real core of that ballclub never wavered."

In appreciation of what his players had done, Charlie Finley spared no expense in creating a proper reward. Finley placed an order with a jewelry company for a set of beautiful, half-carat diamond rings, which would be distributed to each of the Oakland players. Finley announced that the World Series rings, likely the most expensive to date in major league history, carried an estimated value of $1,500 apiece. Several players, including captain Sal Bando, decided to have the rings appraised for insurance purposes. The appraiser put the value even higher—at $3,500 apiece.

As satisfying as the World Series victory had been, the A's' status as World Champs did not prevent the loss of key players from the ranks. Although media reports indicated that backup first baseman Don Mincher was only *contemplating* retirement, and only if the A's did not meet his contract demands, he had clearly made up his mind. "I was done, quit, I was through. I didn't want to play anymore. My kids were graduating from high school age, you know 10th, 11th grade. And I had never ever had a normal Fourth of July, or anything like that. I was 35, and I wanted to quit.

"It had been a tough season. I knew my bat was slowing down some. And I didn't really enjoy the fact that I was riding the bench so much, even though I understood the situation. So I had announced my retirement, and I was done. I'm telling you, I was absolutely done."

One Oakland writer, Ron Bergman, speculated that Mincher might have been more likely to return had he not achieved a significant milestone during the 1972 season. In July, Mincher had clubbed his 200th career home run, while still playing for the Rangers. Would Mincher have returned had he finished the season one or two home runs short of the milestone? "No," Mincher responds definitively. "No, no, remembering my feelings back in those days, is that I really, in my mind, had had enough. I do remember getting my 200th off of Joe Coleman in Detroit. And it was a big milestone for me. But I don't think that would have kept me from retiring. I think once I had my mind made up, I was done."

For awhile, Mincher considered the possibility of maintaining a baseball career, but in a different capacity. "I had thought about maybe managing in the minor leagues a little bit, but then I soured on that, too. I had some offers to do that. But I went home." Mincher would eventually return to baseball, but not as a manager or coach. "The Mule" would become the general manager and owner of his own minor league franchise, ironically one that had an affiliation with his former team—the Oakland A's.

Although Mincher claims that he had announced his retirement near the end of the season, the A's did not officially publicize the news regarding their popular slugger until December 20. On that day, the A's issued a sloppily written press release informing the fans and media of Mincher's decision to step aside. The media release contained several embarrassing factual errors, including a statement that Mincher had finished his career with *over* 200 home runs when he had hit *exactly* 200. The release also maintained that Mincher had played in *one* All-Star Game, when he had actually played in *two*. The release mentioned that he had played for the Minnesota Twins, California Angels, Seattle Pilots, Texas Rangers, and A's during his career, but omitted his stints with the Washington Senators. Charlie Finley should have been ashamed. A well-respected professional like Mincher deserved a better farewell.

Mincher knew about the erroneous contents of the press release. "I was aware of it," Mincher reveals. "I remember being somewhat upset, but it was one of those things back in those days that was a fleeting moment of being upset, and then I forgot about the whole thing. I never carried it around with me. As a matter of fact, I gotta be honest, I had forgotten all about it, until you just now brought it up. But I do remember *now* about that."

The sloppiness of the press release may have been attributable to Finley's insistence on employing a skeleton crew of employees in his front office, coupled with the frequent departure of beleaguered public relations staff members. "You call *three* people a skeletal staff?" Mincher says while laughing loudly. "Naw, I'm sure he had a couple more than that." Mincher, who says that the frugal Finley once asked the team doctor why he couldn't re-use medical tape, agrees that the poor press release may have been the result of too few people trying to do too much work. "It could have been," Mincher says, "because I remember so many things during those days that we *didn't* have. You know, we didn't have a media relations-type guy. We had to do it ourselves; Dick Williams did it. And Charlie. But I'm sure that probably had something to do with it."

With Mincher gone, writers speculated as to whether the A's would keep expensive veterans like Matty Alou and Dal Maxvill, who were still useful players but were making too much money for Finley's liking. Finley might have been willing to pay them their salaries if they were still in their primes, but Alou could no longer play center field, and Maxvill lacked the hitting ability to play on an everyday basis. With Finley looking to cut payroll, the two former Cardinals wondered whether they, like Mincher, might soon become former A's.

Chapter 14

World Series Fallout

On October 30, Charlie Finley made his first move to bolster the team that he badly wanted to defend its World Championship. The A's reacquired left-handed reliever Paul Lindblad from the Rangers for minor league third baseman Bill McNulty, outfielder Brant Alyea (whom Finley had reacquired from St. Louis in July), and $150,000 in cash. Lindblad had led the major leagues with 66 appearances, and had pitched exceptionally for a bad team. A 2.61 ERA and nine saves convinced Finley and Dick Williams to bring Lindblad back to the Bay Area, perhaps as protection against Darold Knowles' comeback from a broken thumb. The addition of Lindblad gave the A's potentially three left-handed relievers, provided that Dick Williams did not put Dave Hamilton in the starting rotation. With the return of Lindblad, Finley had succeeded in re-acquiring all three players—Don Mincher and Frank Fernandez being the others—he had originally traded to Washington as part of the Mike Epstein deal.

Don Mincher, who played with Lindblad in Washington, Oakland, and Texas, remembers the left-handed reliever as a man of boundless energy, one who always needed to keep busy. "He could not sit still," says Mincher, who recalls Lindblad's trademark habit of searching for money with a metal detector "He'd go to the ballparks and look for pennies and nickels all day long." By Lindblad's own estimation, he collected an average of $11 per city on Oakland road trips and gave the money to his coin-collecting children. When the metal detector beeped, Lindblad used a small screwdriver to dig into the outfield turf and warning track. Yet, Lindblad had to be careful not to dig too deep, for fear of striking a water hose or electrical line. Trips to Cleveland's Municipal Stadium posed a special problem, since groundskeepers Harold and Marshall Bossard took special pride in maintaining the grass field. "If I dig too deep into the Indians' field," Lindblad told the *Cleveland Plain Dealer*, "those two guys would tan my hide."

Although Charlie Finley was happy to have an effective relief pitcher like Lindblad in tow, he would make a far more important transaction on November 21, when he decided to deal one of his other veteran relievers. Finley sent 34-year-old right-hander Bob Locker to the Cubs for minor league outfielder Bill North, who would be given a chance to battle Angel Mangual for the starting center-field position. The switch-hitting speedster had hit only .181 in 66 games for the Cubs before being demoted to Wichita of the American Association. Reports out of Chicago indicated that North had an attitude problem, dating back to his days at Central Washington State College. North had also reacted badly to a lack of playing time with the Cubs. One unsubstantiated report claimed North had threatened to leave the Cubs during the season to become a schoolteacher.

Casual Oakland fans questioned the trade, wondering why the A's would deal an effective reliever like Locker for a virtual unknown with a questionable attitude. Locker had gone 6–1, with a 2.65 ERA and 10 saves during the regular season. Finley, however, paid more attention to Locker's dismal post-season performance. An inconsistent Locker had pitched so poorly in two playoff games against the Tigers that Dick Williams lost all confidence in the sinkerballing reliever. As a result, Locker made only one brief appearance during the World Series.

The A's saw much more in North than his .181 batting average would attest. During spring training, the Cubs had played the A's several times in Cactus League play. North had impressed the A's with his all-around play during those spring matchups. After his demotion from Chicago, North batted .351 with 10 stolen bases in 28 games. Oakland scouts noted North's ability to make contact, aggressively run the bases, and skillfully patrol the outfield. The scouting reports would prove accurate—typically for the A's' scouts.

With North in contention for the troublesome center-field position and Reggie Jackson slated to move back to right field, the A's decided to part ways with Matty Alou, "the man I feel got us into the playoffs," according to an interview Gene Tenace did with the *New York Times*. Three days after the North acquisition, Finley sent Alou and his $110,000 contract to the Yankees for infielder Rich McKinney and (oh no, not him again!) pitcher Rob Gardner. This was the same Gardner that the A's had acquired from the Yankees in 1971 for Felipe Alou, before trading him back to New York later that summer. Thus, Finley's bizarre infatuation with the journeyman left-hander continued.

Players Acquired and then Reacquired by Charlie Finley: (1970–80)

Brant Alyea
Pat Bourque
Rico Carty
Tommy Davis
John Donaldson
Frank Fernandez
Rob Gardner
Mudcat Grant
Dave Hamilton
Larry Haney
Ted Kubiak
Paul Lindblad
Bob Locker

Dal Maxvill
Don Mincher
Diego Segui

The A's' continuing interest in Gardner remained a mystery. Although Gardner had pitched well at the Triple-A level, he possessed neither an overpowering fastball nor a particularly deceptive breaking ball. Most scouts termed Gardner's repertoire as pedestrian.

Several weeks after the trade, Gardner had still not heard directly from Finley, either by telephone or through the mail. Gardner himself questioned why the A's had reacquired him, when they already had two capable lefty relievers in Darold Knowles and Paul Lindblad, a promising swingman in Dave Hamilton, and two fine southpaw starters in Ken Holtzman and Vida Blue. "I've sat down and thought about it many times," Gardner told *The Sporting News* from his home in Binghamton, New York, "and wondered exactly why Oakland made the deal. I'm not too sure whey they did. I'm not even sure they know they did because I haven't heard anything from them. Maybe they don't realize yet they made the trade." Although Dick Williams indicated that he would use Gardner as a long reliever and spot starter, some writers speculated that the journeyman lefty would be traded again before he donned the green and gold of Oakland.

Gardner had now been traded six times during his 10-year professional career. Three of the trades had involved the A's. In two of the transactions, Gardner had been traded for an Alou brother, first Felipe and now Matty. If the pattern continued, Finley would soon trade Gardner to the Astros for Felipe and Matty's younger brother, Jesus. "Where's he, Houston?" Gardner asked a reporter from *The Sporting News*. "Oh well. Two out of three isn't bad."

With the swirl of offseason activity, the 40-man roster took on a strange look. After the addition of North and the subtraction of Alou, the A's now owned only five outfielders, which represented the same bloated number of *first basemen* available to Dick Williams. Mike Epstein, Mike Hegan, and Gene Tenace had all seen playing time at first during the World Series. Don Mincher had not yet made up his mind about retiring—at least according to the A's. Orlando Cepeda, he of the three regular season at-bats, remained on Finley's payroll, collecting his exorbitant $90,000 salary. Clearly, one or more of the first sackers would have to go.

The A's also possessed a glut of second basemen, retaining Dick Green, Dal Maxvill, Ted Kubiak, Larry Brown, and Tim Cullen. Williams didn't need that many middle infield types—or did he? Perhaps Charlie Finley would try to resurrect his plan of revolving second basemen in 1973. In 1972, the A's had used 12 different players at second base, including unlikely candidates like Tenace, Sal Bando, Curt Blefary, and Larry Haney, in addition to utility infielders Marty Martinez and Dwain Anderson.

Finley continued to talk trade with other teams. A blockbuster deal remained a possibility, albeit remote. Finley asked the Phillies about the availability of ace left-hander Steve Carlton, who had won 27 games for the last-place residents of the National League East. In turn, the Yankees and Giants inquired about the availability of Vida Blue, who had annoyed Finley by refusing to partake in any of the post-season celebrations.

On November 30, Finley relieved the logjam at first base. Instead of ridding himself of backups Orlando Cepeda or Mike Hegan, Finley surprised Bay Area writers by dispatching the team's second-best left-handed power hitter, Mike Epstein. Finley traded Epstein to the Rangers for right-handed reliever Horacio Piña, who had gone only 2–7, but had pitched well during the second half of the season and had saved 15 games for Texas. Piña would replace the departed Bob Locker as a veteran set-up reliever.

One of the few people to welcome the deal was Rollie Fingers, who had been overworked during the regular season and had pitched in a record six World Series games. Fingers hoped the acquisition of Piña would lighten his pitching load from 65 games to about 55 appearances.

In contrast, most of the Oakland media criticized the trade, wondering why the A's would deal the productive Epstein for a little-known reliever from a last-place ballclub. Why *did* the A's trade Epstein, who had enjoyed such a productive season in Oakland? Was it his temperamental nature? His battles with Dick Williams over playing time? Perhaps his 0-for-16 in the World Series had sealed his fate? None of the above, Finley answered. Instead, he claimed he had been forced to trade Epstein in order to make room for Gene Tenace at first base. Finley said that Tenace had recently suffered a shoulder injury, which prevented him from catching on a regular basis. Due to the injury, Tenace could not make the throws to second and third base required by the catching position.

The shoulder injury came as a complete surprise to the Oakland beat writers who followed the A's on a regular basis. Although Tenace had struggled to throw out Reds runners, no one had remembered Tenace hurting his shoulder during the World Series. They hadn't heard of Tenace injuring himself during the offseason, either. One writer asked Finley and Williams to describe the injury. Both men said they lacked the "medical knowledge" to give the injury a specific name. One reporter, Glenn Schwarz of the *San Francisco Examiner*, followed up by interviewing the team orthopedist, Dr. Harry Walker. According to Schwarz, Dr. Walker said he knew nothing about an injury to Tenace.

Oakland beat writers arrived at a logical conclusion: Finley had made up the injury to justify trading a malcontent player who had criticized both him and Dick Williams. A's observers wondered why the A's hadn't acquired more than Piña for a left-handed power hitter coming off a 26-home run season. "We didn't get as much for Mike Epstein as we wanted," admitted Finley to reporters, "but we got as much as we could."

Finley expounded on the alleged injury to Tenace. "Tenace came to me at the World Series and told me he had tendonitis," Finley revealed to reporters. "We had to keep him in the lineup, so I made room for him at first base. He can play there, but he can't catch with his present arm problem." In actuality, Tenace's alleged problems had been caused by a bout with bursitis, which had affected his elbow, not his shoulder. Contrary to Finley's claims, the problem didn't seem severe enough to jeopardize his future as a catcher.

Was Tenace *really* injured at the time of the trade? "I don't know if there was any shoulder ailment," Mike Hegan says in retrospect. "The fact is, Dave Duncan was the better defensive catcher and he worked very well with the pitching staff. [Gene] Tenace was on the verge of—especially after winning the MVP in the World Series—you gotta think about playing him every day some place. The natural place was first base...I think Charlie and Dick were looking for a way to get them both in the lineup the following year."

Whatever the condition of Tenace's arm, Epstein had clearly worn the patience of both Finley and Williams. "Mike wanted to play everyday," explains Hegan, who had served as Epstein's backup in 1972. "There was some growing problems between he and Dick simply because he didn't like being taken out in the sixth or seventh inning if we had a lead...With some of the other problems that they had had with Mike and some of his complaining, they felt that was the move to make."

Hegan says he harbored no illusions about playing first base regularly in the aftermath of the Epstein trade. "I pretty much knew during the early offseason that they were gonna try to play Geno [Tenace] at first base," Hegan says. "Dick and Charlie asked me if I would help teach Gene how to play first base in spring training, which I said that I would do, because Gene and I were, and still are, very good friends...Our families were close. I knew I wasn't gonna play every day, but as long as you could help contribute to the ballclub still winning, why not?"

Tenace credited Hegan with unselfishly tutoring him on the art of fielding bunts and how to take throws without getting his feet tangled. The better that Tenace became, the fewer the opportunities for Hegan to play. "All the time Mike was doing this," Tenace pointed out to Phil Elderkin of the *Christian Science Monitor*, "he was pushing himself further and further away from the job. He knew it and I knew it, but he still kept helping me."

The status of another first baseman remained questionable. Orlando Cepeda had undergone knee surgery during the summer and had expressed a desire to play winter ball in Puerto Rico. Finley said that Cepeda should not play at all before being examined by Dr. Harry Walker. Even if Walker proclaimed Cepeda healthy, where would he play in Oakland? The A's seemed committed to the idea of playing Tenace at first base. Platooning was not an option, since Tenace and Cepeda both batted right-handed. Given the balky condition of his knees, Cepeda was not capable of playing another position.

In late December, Finley telephoned Cepeda to update him on his status with the ballclub. Orlando remembers his final conversation with the irascible owner. "After the 1972 season," says Cepeda, "I didn't care about playing baseball because I was in such pain. My knees. And he called me in Puerto Rico and said, 'If you don't call me tomorrow, I gonna release you.' I said, 'Go ahead and do it, because I don't want to call you.' I didn't call him; he released me."

Cepeda's disinterest in playing baseball stemmed only partly from the condition of his knees. Orlando no longer wanted any part of Oakland or the A's. "I didn't like the people," Cepeda said in a 1973 interview with *Black Sports* Magazine. "They were sour on me. I was surprised the A's got me. My knees hurt so much; my mind wasn't on baseball." Mostly, Cepeda didn't want to return to Oakland because of his feelings for Finley. Although Cepeda lasted only a brief time with the A's, he still managed to fully experience the strangeness of the owner. "Yeah, Charlie Finley," Cepeda says, pondering the name for a moment. "He's a weird guy."

Finley's bizarre personality motivated Cepeda *not* to call him back from Puerto Rico, thus expediting his departure from the Bay Area. "I don't want to play for him," Cepeda says. "He was very difficult." In contract negotiations? "On everything."

Finley said good-bye to a total of three veterans the week before Christmas, including Cepeda. The A's also placed infielder Larry Brown and relief pitcher Joel Horlen on waivers, in the hopes that some team would place a claim, take on their salaries, and pay the A's the waiver price. When none of the other 23 major league teams put in a bid, the A's gave the trio their unconditional releases. To his credit, Finley notified the players personally. Finley offered Horlen and Brown minor league contracts with the A's' Triple-A affiliate at Tucson in the Pacific Coast League, but both players declined.

Cepeda, for his part, shed no tears over leaving the A's. "My mother was crying, my friends in Puerto Rico were all excited," Cepeda said several months later in an interview with Ron Bergman. "But I tell them don't worry because this is best for Orlando."

Aside from Finley, Cepeda's largest concern in Oakland had to do with a lack of playing time. In Atlanta, Cepeda had bristled at a pinch-hitting role forced on him by manager Luman Harris. "In Oakland," Cepeda told Ron Bergman, "all Williams and Finley wanted me for was to pinch-hit." Cepeda believed that once he rehabilitated his knees, he would be able to resume a regular playing role—somewhere.

Finley felt otherwise, informing the press that he had been told that Cepeda no longer had cartilage in one of his knees. Finley believed the 35-year-old first baseman would never play baseball again. The A's also doubted whether the 32-year-old Larry Brown would play after electing not to undergo an operation on a herniated disc in his back. The veteran infielder had opted for a non-surgical treatment recommended by White Sox third baseman Bill Melton. Brown hinted that he would either sign a contact with the Tigers, or manage a golf course in Florida. In contrast to the situations involving Brown and Cepeda, the release of Joel Horlen was a bit bewildering. Although Horlen did have a bad knee (which made his status for 1973 questionable), he had pitched well for the A's after being released by the White Sox in spring training.

The timing of Cepeda's release could not have been worse, as Finley would soon learn. Earlier in the month, American League owners had voted unanimously to adopt the controversial new designated hitter (DH) rule for at least the next three years, beginning with the 1973 season. If passed by the Playing Rules Committee of Major League Baseball, American League managers would be allowed to designate a hitter to bat in place of the pitcher throughout each game.

The National League owners bristled at the idea of a designated hitter, voting against such a concept. The senior league also expressed its displeasure with two other American League attempts at innovation: the designated runner and inter-league play. The Playing Rules Committee (which consisted of three National League members, three American League representatives, and three minor league executives) agreed with the National League owners, rejecting the American League's bid for a DH rule and the other innovations. American League President Joe Cronin, who strongly favored the DH, requested a joint hearing with the National League and asked Commissioner Bowie Kuhn to attend the session. Cronin wanted Kuhn to cast the deciding vote on the issues of the DH, the designated runner, and inter-league play.

The National League eventually consented to forming a joint major league committee to study the DH issue further. On January 11, National League owners once again declined the DH for their own teams, but voted to allow the American League to use the DH on an experimental basis, beginning in 1973. The Playing Rules Committee also followed with its approval. "We like the rules the way they are," maintained National League president Chub Feeney in an interview with *The Sporting News*, "but we'll be watching the American League, and who knows, someday we may go along." Charlie Finley, long a champion of the DH, actually voted *against* the rule in the final American League ballot because his fellow owners refused to adopt another one of his favored rules, the designated runner. Finley wanted *both* rules, not just one.

Finley might have had another reason for voting against the DH. He had already released Orlando Cepeda, a productive power hitter who seemed like a natural for the designated hitter slot. Although Cepeda could no longer move well enough to play a position in the field, he likely possessed enough leg strength to sprint four or five times a game, the maximum amount of running that would be required from a designated hitter.

Finley had picked up Cepeda's $90,000 contract in late June, paid off the majority of it, and received a grand total of three at-bats in return. Now, just before Cepeda might become productive again under a new rule, Finley had released the slugger and received no compensation in return. Finley thought he had ridded himself of a sizable headache when he had essentially traded Denny McLain to Atlanta for Cepeda; the short tenure for "The Baby Bull" in Oakland had turned into a much knottier problem.

One week after the designated hitter became reality, the Red Sox announced the signing of Cepeda to a one-year contract. Boston became the first American League team to sign a player specifically for the role of DH. Meanwhile, with Cepeda gone, Don Mincher retired, and Mike Epstein and Matty Alou traded, the A's were left without a logical choice for the DH slot. Ironically, the team whose owner had pushed harder for the designated hitter than any other major league executive was now left holding an empty bag of DH candidates.

The A's' owner tried to save face by insisting that he would not have kept Cepeda even if he had been certain that the DH rule would be adopted. "What bothered me was that our team physician...said that all the cartilage in his knee was gone—that it was almost bone on top of bone," Finley claimed to reporters. "Dr. Walker advised me that it was very, very questionable whether he could hold up. And even if he does hold up, if he gets on base, you have to put in a pinch-runner for him because he can't run. That's two players used right there." The Red Sox obviously thought differently.

In December, Finley had tried to talk one of his former players into making a return specifically to fill the role of designated hitter. Finley had targeted the recently retired Don Mincher. "The real tempting stage came after I had established a business and was working, my wife and I together," recollects Mincher, "and I got a call in December from Charlie Finley." Mincher replays the conversation, mimicking the deep-throated, slow-paced speaking style of Finley.

"I...want...you...to come back...and...play for me," Finley told Mincher.

"Charlie, I don't want to," Mincher responded politely. " You don't want me, either."

"Yeah, I do," Finley insisted without hesitation. "We just passed the rule...called the designated hitter rule...and that's all I want you to do."

"What are you talking about?" replied Mincher, who hadn't even heard of the designated hitter.

"The pitcher hits no more," Finley explained. "And I need a guy to hit in that spot."

"You gotta be kidding me," said a disbelieving Mincher. "Baseball's not like that."

"Well, it is now," Finley snapped back.

After his initial skepticism, Mincher decided to give the DH option some consideration. "So I had to take a couple, three days to think about it," Mincher reveals, "and I was very tempted to go back because that sounded so great. I knew that club was gonna win again and again. But in the end, my wife and I had established a business here [in Huntsville], and the kids were here. I was really enjoying being here, so I said, 'No,' and that took care of it."

Finley and Dick Williams also thought differently on how the DH would affect the composition of the Oakland roster. At a winter banquet, Williams predicted that the A's would reduce the number of pitchers on their roster from 10 to eight, and would also carry more offensive position players. Three days later, Finley painted a different picture. "Dick and I talked for three hours in Oakland," Finley said. "I told him that it would be very difficult to carry only eight pitchers because very few of our pitchers have options left [to be demoted to the minor leagues]." Finley also disagreed with the notion of using the singles-hitting Gonzalo Marquez as a DH. "Marquez, in my opinion, is not the type of designated hitter we're looking for," Finley revealed to Ron Bergman. "This does not eliminate Marquez from being a member of our team, but I don't think he fits our bill for a designated hitter." Finley said he preferred a DH with more power and speed, and listed several other candidates for the role, including newly acquired players like Bill North and Rich McKinney, and holdovers Angel Mangual and Billy Conigliaro. Finley failed to mention that none of the above players possessed an abundance of major league power. Only North had outstanding foot speed. In other words, the A's were in major trouble when it came to finding a qualified DH.

Oakland pitchers weren't necessarily pleased with the news that they would not be allowed to hit during the regular season. Catfish Hunter, Blue Moon Odom, and Ken Holtzman each bemoaned the new rule. Although Odom had batted well under .200 during the regular season, he prided himself on his ability to swing the bat, not to mention his two home runs in 1972. "I may have hit only .121 last year," Odom told *The Sporting News*, "but I was a threat every time up. I'm a better hitter than most pinch-hitters." Hunter echoed the thoughts of Odom. "I don't like the rule," Hunter said flatly to Ron Bergman "I like to hit myself because it makes me feel like I'm more in the game, especially if I come up there to bunt." Hunter had even more reason not to like the DH, given his .350 batting average during the 1971 season.

As they neared spring training, the A's seemed to be receiving very little attention, either through commercial endorsements or from the national media. The defending champions—filled with colorful, well-known stars like Reggie Jackson, Catfish Hunter, and Vida Blue, and a newly discovered World Series hero like Gene Tenace—seemed like perfect fodder for commercial spots and television appearances. Yet, few opportunities arose. "I was not asked to endorse anything," revealed Tenace, the World Series MVP, in an interview with Arthur Daley of the *New York Times*. "I made no commercials. None of the talk shows invited me to be a guest, including Johnny Carson, who's just down the road in Los Angeles. I made no appearances in the Bay Area and only a few elsewhere."

Although Tenace himself preferred exclusion from the spotlight, the lack of attention given to the A's on the whole disappointed him. "It's a strange thing that none of the Oakland Athletics made money by capitalizing on being World Champions," Tenace told Daley. Perhaps Oakland's status as a small market team had discouraged sponsors and corporations from contacting A's players. Or, perhaps the A's had felt the backlash of a general public that was unwilling to embrace a team of rebellious, long-haired, non-traditional baseball players. The general indifference of fans in the Bay Area reinforced the absence of recognition. "It's hard to believe that our ballclub couldn't draw a million in attendance despite winning the championship," moaned Tenace in an interview with *Sports Illustrated*. "Here we are the World Champs and no one pays attention. I don't know, maybe the people in Oakland don't deserve a champion. I know I expected more."

On the field, the A's' chief concern—other than the designated hitter—involved the lack of a proven center fielder. The A's had ended the 1972 regular season with Reggie Jackson in center field and Matty Alou in right field. Given Jackson's running ability, and Alou's sound defensive instincts, that seemed like a workable arrangement. Jackson, however, had asked Williams to return him to right, while Charlie Finley had deemed Alou's contract too extreme at $110,000 per season. Williams agreed to move Reggie back to right but now needed to pick a center fielder from among a platoon of candidates.

How about Angel Mangual? The Roberto Clemente look-alike had qualified for the Topps All-Rookie team in 1971 before flopping both offensively and defensively in 1972. Mangual misjudged several fly balls and batted only .246 with little power. Scouts also wondered whether Mangual possessed enough speed to play center field.

Another prospect, George Hendrick, had played well for a brief stretch before showing that he was not ready to handle major league pitching. Hendrick's wrist-snap batting style had been compared to that of Ernie Banks, but had yet to yield positive results in his brief major league tenure. While Hendrick's supporters lauded his style of play as smooth and effortless, his detractors considered him too nonchalant, perhaps even lazy. Even opposing coaches criticized Hendrick. "He's a real dog," Yankee coach Elston Howard would say in a brutally candid 1973 interview with sportswriter Dick Young. "You could see that the way he played against us. Half-trying. What a shame." Hendrick's reputation as a loner and his unwillingness to speak to the media also concerned some members of the A's' organization. According to one rumor, Oakland considered a winter trade that would have sent Hendrick to the Rangers for right-handed starter Dick Bosman, but the deal never took place.

Perhaps the most intriguing "name" among the center-field candidates was that of Billy Conigliaro, the younger brother of former Red Sox star Tony Conigliaro, who had retired in 1971 due to severe problems with his vision. Billy himself had briefly retired during the season, prompting the Brewers to trade his rights to the A's as part of the Ollie Brown swap.

At the time of the trade, neither the A's nor the Brewers had mentioned the name of Conigliaro. Since the outfielder had been placed on Milwaukee's disqualified list and the trade had taken place after the June 15 deadline, neither team could announce Conigliaro's inclusion. The Brewers simply stated that they had acquired Brown for the waiver price of $20,000.

Conigliaro detested playing in Milwaukee, and was unhappy over his sporadic playing time. In June, Billy left the team to work with his brother at a Boston golf course and nightclub. In December, Finley finally contacted Conigliaro, offering him a contract for the 1973 season. At first, Billy wondered whether he should report to the A's. He remembered that Tony had experienced problems with Dick Williams in Boston. Ultimately, Billy found Finley's offer too good to refuse. Billy accepted a contract, knowing that he would have a chance to play for a World Championship team, one that needed a center fielder. Conigliaro would subsequently report to spring training in Mesa with an improved attitude. In his first five exhibition games with the A's, Conigliaro would hit two home runs while using a new, shortened swing.

Aside from Conigliaro, Hendrick, and Mangual, the A's seemed intrigued by their fourth center-field option. Switch-hitting Bill North, who had been acquired from the Cubs for Bob Locker, featured better speed and defensive instincts than any of the other outfield possibilities. In retrospect, the Cubs had seemingly mishandled North's development. After an impressive spring training, manager Leo Durocher had played North in right field, instead of his accustomed center-field position. When North struggled initially, Durocher damaged his confidence by playing him sporadically and then demoting him to Triple-A.

Center field questions aside, Dick Williams also worried about other positions as spring training began in Arizona. Would former catcher Gene Tenace be able to handle the defensive responsibilities of first base? Tenace had played mostly as a catcher in the major leagues, after coming up in the Oakland system as an outfielder. Tenace expressed his preference for wearing the tools of ignorance. "I worked so hard to become a catcher," Tenace explained to *Sports Illustrated*, "and I never had the chance to prove myself there." In other matters, would 31-year-old Dick Green return from major back surgery and stabilize the troublesome second base position? Otherwise, with Tim Cullen already announcing his retirement, the light-hitting duo of Dal Maxvill and Ted Kubiak would be asked to share time at the pivot. And would Gonzalo Marquez and offseason pickup Rich McKinney effectively man the designated hitter platoon? Charlie Finley had already questioned the qualifications of Marquez, who lacked both speed and power.

As the A's searched high and low for DH contenders, the Bay Area media couldn't help but notice the success of another team's designated hitter. Oakland ex-patriot Orlando Cepeda was batting .346 for the Red Sox in Grapefruit League play, having banged out nine hits in 26 at-bats. While "The Baby Bull" could not be retrieved, the A's seemed to be overlooking an obvious solution to their designated hitter dilemma. Why not make Gene Tenace, an untested defender, the regular DH and play Mike Hegan at first base? In 1972, Hegan had batted a career-high .329 in a reserve role. Furthermore, his everyday presence at first base would have strengthened Oakland's interior defense while lessening the burden on comebacking second baseman Dick Green.

Hegan says the A's wanted more power from the first base position than he could provide. "Other than Reggie, and Sal, who hit some home runs, we were not what you would call an awesome offensive ballclub," Hegan says, refuting the misconception of the A's as a power-packed team. "I think in '72 we only had one .300 hitter [Joe Rudi] and we only had one guy that hit more than 30 home runs [Mike Epstein actually led the team with 26]. And I don't know if anybody drove in a hundred [no one did]... It was a club that [had] to take advantage of that DH spot and put somebody in there who would drive in some runs and hit some home runs."

One player who might have to perform designated hitting duties out of necessity was Reggie Jackson. Reggie had injured his knee in the final game of the American League Championship Series, forcing him to miss the entire World Series. During the offseason, Jackson had favored the knee in workouts, and ended up damaging his other knee. The lingering pain in both knees caused Jackson to struggle at the start of spring training. Jackson gradually worked his knees into better condition, which helped him lead the A's in spring training home runs while pushing his average close to .400. "I still can't go 100 per cent on the knees for an entire game," Jackson told reporters by the end of spring training, "but I can still steal a base, run hard down to first, cover ground in the outfield, and throw." Perhaps he wouldn't have to DH after all.

Jackson seemed determine to have his best season ever in his quest for a $100,000 contract. Jackson felt that if he could avoid injuries and play up to his ability, he would be able to ask Finley for a six-figure deal in 1974. "To get that kind of salary, you have to put a lot of good years together," Reggie explained to Bay Area sportswriter Glenn Dickey, "not just one streak. I'm not taking anything away from Gene Tenace, but he just had one good week and it happened to be in the World Series. It means a lot more when you do it day in and day out, year after year." Jackson felt the key to reaching his salary milestone could be found in his ability to hit for average. "I still need to learn the strike zone," Jackson admitted to Dickey. "I know I've got to be more patient. I'm trying to hit .300 because that's something I've never done. I know I can hit 40 home runs, I know I can knock in 100 runs, because I've done those things. I haven't hit .300."

The A's made news on several fronts early in spring training. George Hendrick requested a trade, after Finley told the second-year outfielder that he wouldn't be considered for the starting center field job. As a result, the A's planned to have Hendrick start the season at Triple-A Tucson. Hendrick, who had experienced the thrill of starting games in the World Series, wanted no part of extended duty in the minor leagues.

Vida Blue refused to sign a contract for 1973, which Charlie Finley had the right to renew automatically at $51,000. Blue's action led some observers to forecast another long holdout by the left-hander. The predictions proved exaggerated, as Blue reported to Mesa in early March, but again kept his signature off Finley's contract renewal. Blue said he would approach the head of the Players' Association, Marvin Miller, to inquire about the possibility of becoming a free agent after the season. "I could be a test case," Blue told United Press International.

Catcher Dave Duncan also decided to hold out at the start of training camp before reporting late. On March 10, Finley automatically renewed the contract of Duncan, who had received an offer of $40,000 in the mail. Three days later, Finley publicly informed both his dissatisfied catcher and pitcher that they were replaceable. "We're going to make every effort to repeat as World Champions," Finley vowed to UPI. "A Vida Blue or a Dave Duncan aren't going to stand in my way. We certainly hope they play, but if they don't, I assure you we'll get along without them very well."

In recalling the contractual tactics of Finley, Duncan has bitter memories. "That's the one area where I might have a little bit of resentment, because negotiating those contracts was always very difficult. The game, the way it was at that particular time, you had no alternative but to sign the contracts that they were offering.[Finley] certainly wasn't going to do you any favors when it came to contracts. He was pretty difficult that way."

In the meantime, Finley executed a major change in contract policy with another player. Finley gave Campy Campaneris a two-year deal—the first multi-year contract he had ever agreed to since buying the A's in 1960. The contract would earn Campaneris an estimated $65,000 over each of the two seasons.

Perhaps the most interesting news item involved the revelation that Gene Tenace might be able to catch after all. The A's had tried to justify the Mike Epstein trade by citing the poor condition of Tenace's shoulder. Most Oakland writers hadn't bought the injury story initially; they became even more justified in their skepticism when Finley said that Tenace's shoulder injury had healed sufficiently over the winter. If that was truly the case, why hadn't the A's waited until spring training to see how Tenace's shoulder had responded before making a hasty trade with the Rangers? More likely, the A's had traded Epstein because of his public arguments with both Finley and Williams during the post-season.

Tenace's role came more into focus on March 24, when the A's made a four-player trade involving one player who had asked to be dealt and another who was playing without a signed contract. Finley sent Dave Duncan, who had refused to sign his renewed pact, and the unhappy George Hendrick to the Indians for former All-Star catcher Ray Fosse and utility infielder Jack Heidemann. On the surface, the deal allowed the A's to rid themselves of two malcontent ballplayers and return Tenace to first base.

Duncan had initially held out of spring training. When he finally reported to Mesa, without the long blonde beard that he had sprouted in 1972, he agreed to work out with the team but declined to sign his renewed contract. The longtime A's' catcher wanted a raise from $30,000 to $50,000. Finley wouldn't budge from $40,000. Duncan hinted that he might not play for the A's come Opening Day. Dick Williams reacted to Duncan's indecision by moving Gene Tenace back to the catching position, and placing Gold Glove left fielder Joe Rudi at first base. Come again? "Even after the great Series I had," Tenace told *The Sporting News*, "they still don't know what they want to do with me." Why would the A's remove the best defensive left fielder in the American League and relocate him to a less demanding position, one that he had played only briefly during his major league career? The moves smacked of Finley.

Finley claimed that Duncan's subtle threat of not playing during the regular season had *not* influenced the trade. "We believe we got the best catcher in baseball," Finley told Ron Bergman in assessing Fosse. The revelation probably came as news to the Reds' Johnny Bench, the Pirates' Manny Sanguillen, and the Yankees' Thurman Munson. Finley also said that Fosse possessed a better arm than Duncan did, most likely an accurate claim.

Duncan felt as if he had been released from a prison operated by a vindictive warden. "I was very happy to be traded," Duncan told the *New York Times* shortly thereafter. "It eliminated a lot of the mental hassles I had." Duncan accused Finley of trying to strip away his dignity and orchestrating his benching during the second half of the 1972 season. The veteran catcher didn't completely absolve Dick Williams of blame, either. "He had been close to the players," Duncan said of his former manager. "Then all of a sudden that changed and he wasn't as close anymore. It's funny it happened around the time he got a new contract and a raise."

As he looks back at his playing career, which included a short stint under Hall of Famer Earl Weaver in Baltimore, Duncan expresses admiration for Williams' managerial skills and his ability to handle a pitching staff. "Dick Williams was probably the best manager that I ever played for," says Duncan. "He didn't have the greatest personality—you weren't always his friend—but day in and day out, he was always ready to handle the game, handle the players. Nobody seemed to ever surprise him with anything they did on the other side of the field."

Although Duncan felt relieved to be leaving the clutches of Charlie Finley, he would realize quickly that the Indians' staff of pitchers—outside of Gaylord Perry—would fall short of the standard achieved by Catfish Hunter, Vida Blue, Ken Holtzman, and Rollie Fingers. "I don't think you really appreciate it at the time," Duncan says in retrospect, "because we all came up through the minor league system. We were all buddies. I don't think you appreciate their talents until you're not catching pitchers of that quality. All of a sudden, you're asking guys to do the things that these guys did so easily, and they're not able to do it."

The trade involving Duncan and the Indians also provided a fresh start for George Hendrick, previously regarded as one of Oakland's top prospects. Not only had Hendrick asked to be traded, he had asked to be traded to the *Indians*. Finley obviously had a warm spot for his young center fielder.

The trade appeased both departing players, but it did not soothe Reggie Jackson, who considered Duncan one of his best friends in baseball. "I don't have many friends, but the ones I have are close ones," Jackson had told sportswriter Phil Pepe during the 1972 World Series. "On this club, my closest friends are Duncan and Joe Rudi and Vida Blue. When I'm looking for somebody to talk to, I go to Dave and Joe. We'll go to dinner together. I usually don't make any plans until I check with them."

While the trade figured to affect the chemistry of the ballclub, the acquisition of Fosse also seemed risky. In 1970, he had played at an All-Star level for the Indians, earning a spot in the Midsummer Classic. Fosse's fortunes changed when Reds All-Star Pete Rose lowered his shoulder and slammed into him while scoring the game-winning run in the ninth inning. Rose collided so brutally with Fosse that he left the muscular catcher with a separated and broken left shoulder.

At first, X-rays showed that Fosse had suffered only a bruised collarbone. Eight months later, a follow-up X-ray revealed the full extent of the injuries, which would continue to cause him pain even after his playing days. The hardened Fosse—nicknamed "The Mule" for his toughness and determination—continued to play after the All-Star break and never went on the disabled list that season, even though he could not lift his left arm above his head. Since the injury was to Fosse's left shoulder, it didn't bother his throwing, but did affect his swing, sapping him of much of his power. Then, in September, Fosse broke his right index finger on a foul tip by Mike Epstein, then with the Senators. The latest injury ended Fosse's season, but didn't prevent him from being selected to *The Sporting News* All-Star team.

Yet, Fosse was no longer the budding star catcher. Although his defensive skills remained well above average, his offensive game fell off severely the next two seasons. Fosse endured his worst full major league season in 1972, batting only .241 with 10 home runs and 41 RBIs. Those numbers represented nine fewer homers and 18 fewer RBIs than Duncan, who had shared time with Gene Tenace behind the plate. Still, Finley's belief in Fosse's superior defensive ability was supported by several Indian players, who criticized Cleveland management for making the trade. Ace pitcher Gaylord Perry was particularly incredulous over the deal. "You've got to be kidding?" Perry told *The Sporting News* in reacting to the trade. "How can they trade our quarterback?" Perry had previously credited Fosse with helping him win the American League's Cy Young Award in 1972.

Finley had included the talented Hendrick in the deal as a mere throw-in, perhaps because he regarded the young center fielder as too lackadaisical to achieve his considerable potential. Finley may have regretted his decision to unload Hendrick after an exhibition game against Cleveland. The Indians had agreed to play the game using orange-colored baseballs that Finley had been pushing heavily on Major League Baseball. Finley believed the orange baseball, which he dubbed the "Orange Alert" ball, would prove more visible for fans and hitters. As Commissioner Bowie Kuhn watched from the stands, Hendrick deposited three of those brightly colored baseballs into the bleachers against his old team. Ironically, several hitters complained that they couldn't see the orange baseballs as well as the traditional white ones. Other players criticized the baseballs because of the similarity in coloring between the red stitching and the dyed-orange horsehide. "As I recall it," Joe Rudi says, "they were regular [Spalding] hardballs that were dyed orange. And that was the problem, because it made it real difficult to pick up the seams on the ball. As a hitter, you look for the seams to pick up the rotation on the ball, to tell you whether it was a slider or some other pitch. With those orange-dyed balls, you couldn't see the seams—they were camouflaged by the dye used on the ball—and that made it tough." Much to Finley's chagrin, the Orange Alert baseballs had failed to receive much favor from the game's participants.

The A's, however, faced more immediate issues of concern than the state of orange baseballs. For example, would the unsigned Vida Blue soon join Hendrick and Duncan on the list of former A's? One intriguing rumor made the rounds at Mesa, indicating that Finley would send his onetime Cy Young and MVP to the lowly Rangers for right-hander Pete Broberg, whom the A's had once drafted with their first-round pick, and former Athletic Mike Epstein. In fact, Finley had been trying to reacquire Epstein practically from the day that he had dealt him to Texas in the first place.

Yet, the prospective trade made little sense for the A's. Broberg, although considered a live-armed prospect, had pitched poorly in 1972, with a record of 5–12 and an ERA of 4.29. Broberg's career record stood at 10–21. As for Epstein, the

A's had only recently traded him away, in part because of his strained relationships with Dick Williams and Reggie Jackson. Why would Finley give up a franchise left-hander, one of baseball's rarest commodities, for an underachieving right-hander like Broberg and a player that his manager and star player didn't like?

On March 18, the *Oakland Tribune* reported that the A's had traded Blue to the Rangers for Broberg, "possibly catcher-outfielder Dick Billings, and one other player plus cash." The story said the trade would be announced "as soon as a check drawn on a Pompano Beach, Florida, bank by Rangers owner Bob Short clears." Curiously, the *Tribune* article also quoted Finley as denying the reported trade. "I can tell you it's not true," the A's' owner told the Associated Press point-blank. "If he has been traded, then my manager did so without my authority." For his part, Dick Williams said he knew nothing of the trade.

Finley had no intention of making such a deal. In fact, he hadn't even talked to the Rangers about a Broberg-for-Blue swap. So what was going on? Finley had floated the false rumor himself, as a way of scaring Blue into thinking that if he didn't sign the owner's contract offer soon, he would end up in the baseball hell known as Texas. The strategy worked. Ten days later, after a three-hour negotiating session, Blue finally signed his contract. Vida received $53,000 dollars, $2,000 more than what Finley had offered but $10,000 less than what he wanted. "Now that we've signed Vida," Finley announced to the AP, "we have the best team in baseball. I predict another World Championship for the Oakland A's."

On April 2, just before the start of the regular season, the orange baseball championed by Finley made its final appearance. Oakland's opponent, the California Angels, committed five errors in losing the exhibition game by the final score of 8–3. Several Angels players grumbled about the difficulty in seeing and gripping the orange-tinted ball. They complained about its slick finish, apparently caused by the method used to apply the orange dye.

Much to the displeasure of the creative owner, the orange baseballs would never see the light of day—or night—in regular season play. Some of the more astute fans at the exhibition game—at least those who sensed the value of souvenirs and the impending demise of Finley's innovation—scurried after foul balls in pursuit of what would become unique collector's items. Unlike the designated hitter, one of Finley's pet inventions had died a quiet spring training death.

The final cuts of spring training brought few surprises, with the exception of pitcher Dave Hamilton. The rookie left-hander, who had pitched so well in 1972, had come to spring training 16 pounds lighter and seemed determined to avoid a sophomore slump. Faced with a surplus of left-handed pitchers, the A's optioned Hamilton to Triple-A Tucson so that they could hold on to Rob Gardner, who was out of options. Gardner, who would serve as the ninth man on a nine-man staff, didn't figure to see much action since the advent of the DH meant the A's wouldn't have to pinch-hit for their pitchers. The effect on their pitchers would rank as just one of several ramifications that baseball's newest rule would have on the defending World Champions.

Chapter 15

The Encore

Newsmakers in 1973

The United States withdraws its troops from the Vietnam War while the North Vietnamese agree to release the last of the American prisoners of war...A group of over 200 members of the American Indian Movement seizes a church and trading post in Wounded Knee, South Dakota, to protest the U.S. government's treatment of Native Americans...Vice President Spiro Agnew resigns in the aftermath of charges of tax evasion.

Four of President Richard Nixon's top aides announce their resignations amidst allegations of a cover-up in the growing Watergate scandal. The departures from Nixon's administration include H.R. "Bob" Haldeman, the chief of staff, and John Ehrlichman, the chief presidential adviser on domestic affairs...A special Senate committee begins its hearings on the Watergate cover-up by questioning one of President Nixon's campaign officials. Senator Sam Ervin, Jr., announces that the committee will "spare no one, whatever his station in life may be"...The Washington Post *earns the Pulitzer Prize for its series of investigative stories, spearheaded by reporters Carl Bernstein and Bob Woodward, on the Watergate affair.*

Women's tennis star Billie Jean King defeats self-proclaimed male chauvinist Bobby Riggs in what is billed as the "Battle of the Sexes" ... Secretariat wins the Belmont Stakes to complete the third leg of thoroughbred horse racing's Triple Crown...Coached by John Wooden, UCLA defeats Memphis State to win its seventh consecutive NCAA basketball title.

The A's looked nothing like their 1972 World Championship team when they opened up the new season against the Minnesota Twins. Billy North became the first designated hitter in the history of the A's and batted leadoff. Dal Maxvill batted second and played shortstop in lieu of Campy Campaneris, who had been suspended for the first five games of the season after his ugly bat-tossing incident during the League Championship Series. Gene Tenace played first base, not catcher. The recently acquired Ray Fosse made his debut behind the plate. Billy

Conigliaro emerged as the Opening Day center fielder, ahead of incumbent Angel Mangual.

While several players from last year's A's had been dispatched to other teams, two members of the '72 A's remained in the organization, only not at the major league level. Pitcher Dave Hamilton and infielder Allan Lewis, both playing at Triple-A Tucson, were flown in to attend Opening Day ceremonies and receive their World Series rings. The Tucson pitching staff, by the way, featured a flock of former A's: Hamilton, Chuck Dobson, Lew Krausse, "Jumbo" Jim Nash, and Tony Pierce.

The new-look A's played nothing like world champs in their first game. Catfish Hunter allowed nine hits in a disappointing three-inning stint. Fosse, Dick Green, and Sal Bando committed costly fielding errors. The Oakland offense managed only a three-spot of runs in the fourth inning against complete game winner Bert Blyleven. The A's played better in their second game, thanks to a complete game start by Blue Moon Odom and a home run by Gene Tenace. The Twins won the game, however, when they scored four of their five runs against Odom in the fifth inning.

The Twins completed the three-game sweep on Sunday, winning an afternoon game, 4–2. Minnesota reached Ken Holtzman for two runs in the first, a run in the third, and another run in the fifth. Errors by Sal Bando and Ted Kubiak made two of the runs unearned. Although the season was only three games old, the A's had managed to look like a complacent team that was already resting on its championship laurels. The suspension of Campy Campaneris for the first five games of the season wasn't helping matters either. "I feel miserable," Campaneris told *Baseball Digest* in describing his exclusion from early season games. "I sit around and can't help. It drive me crazy."

Not so coincidentally, the A's had lost all three games without the services of perhaps their most unappreciated star. When Campaneris played, the A's didn't usually lose three games in a row to any club, much less a rebuilding team like the Twins. "Well, that is a very, very good point," says former Twins beat writer Bob Fowler. "We were talking… about Phil Rizzuto and what he meant to the New York Yankees of the fifties. There is always a catalyst. There is always some guy that you never hear about that does the little things. Again, going back to the Dick Williams mentality, the Billy Martins, the Sparky Andersons, I mean, they admired and appreciated the little things that guys do. And Campy Campaneris was certainly that ilk of a player. He would steal a base, he would get the hit, he would make the play playing the hole at shortstop. When you thought you were gonna get a big rally [against the A's], he would kill it with a great defensive play. He was just that guy. He was always seemingly in the middle of the action. The spotlight wasn't necessarily on him, but he made things happen. He electrified the offense. And he certainly solidified the defense with his spectacular plays."

A native of Cuba, Campaneris had arrived in the major leagues in 1964 with the Kansas City A's, as a replacement for injured shortstop Wayne Causey. After an all-night, sleep-depriving plane ride, Campaneris arrived at the ballpark. The A's' equipment manager, regarding the 155-pound Campaneris as too frail to be a ballplayer, initially refused to give him a uniform. Campaneris surprised the doubting equipment manager by homering in his first major league at-bat—on the very first pitch against Minnesota's Jim Kaat. Campaneris matched his inaugural at-bat by hitting a second home run against Kaat in the seventh inning. The dual home runs tied a modern day record for most home runs in a major league debut. The 22-year-old speedster also contributed a single, a stolen base, and an impressive running catch on a short pop-up into left field.

Separated from his mother, father, and seven brothers and sisters, who still lived in Cuba, the shy Campaneris had few American friends, no girlfriend or wife, and lived by himself in a small apartment near Kansas City's Municipal Stadium. "He was such a loner," says former teammate Jack Aker. "I played with him there for three or four years and never really got to know him." Sensing his reserved nature, several of the A's attempted to incorporate Campaneris into the social atmosphere of the clubhouse. "We tried to get him at least psychologically to be a part of the team," Aker explains, "which we never were able to achieve while I was with the team."

Campaneris' tendency to stay to himself may have been caused by his problems with a new language. At first, Campaneris spoke such little English that teammate Diego Segui, a fellow Cuban who eventually became his best friend on the team, served as his interpreter for interviews with the media. Although A's' coaches had difficulty communicating with him, they quickly came away impressed with his speed and daring base-running style. "He's got guts," Kansas City A's coach Gabby Hartnett told sportswriter Joe McGuff in 1964. "He's got the best pair of wheels I've ever seen. I saw a lot of great base stealers, including [Pittsburgh Pirates great] Max Carey, but I wouldn't rate any of them ahead of this kid." A's third-base coach Luke Appling, also a Hall of Famer like Hartnett, raved about Campy's baseball instincts, calling them "exceptional."

The language barrier forced a determined Campaneris to study pitchers on his own and develop base-stealing techniques by himself. In 1965, Campaneris led all American League base stealers with 51 thefts. Campy topped the 50-stolen base mark three straight seasons, before swiping 62 bases in 1968. At the plate, Campaneris hit consistently in the .260 to .270 range. "We felt he was more of an offensive weapon than a defensive weapon at that time," recalls Aker. One element of his defensive play remained a particular concern, countering his ability to cover lots of ground on the left side of the infield. "An outstanding defensive player as far as his range at the time," says Aker, while pointing out Campy's weakness in handling ground balls. "[But] he wasn't as steady as Dick Green was at second." Although Campaneris' quick, scampering feet allowed him to make spectacular plays, often reaching grounders that other shortstops couldn't touch, he tended to bobble routine grounders because of his unsure hands. Campy made over 30 errors in three of his first four full seasons before settling down defensively in 1969. As with his base stealing, Campy improved his fieldwork through his self-imposed work ethic.

Campaneris wasn't satisfied with improvements on the field. He hoped to learn English to the point where he no longer would need bilingual teammates like Orlando Peña and Diego Segui to help him conduct interviews. He spent one winter with his second cousin, Angels outfielder Jose Cardenal, whose wife gave him lessons in the new language. Thanks in part to his improved skills in speaking English, Campaneris eventually met and married an American woman.

The temporary loss of Campaneris had affected the A's in the season-opening series against the Twins. Writers and scouts had also begun to question offseason deals that had permanently sent away Mike Epstein, Matty Alou, and Dave Duncan. In exchange for three productive regulars, the A's had acquired a middle reliever, a platoon DH, and a catcher in decline. Critics claimed that the A's had too many pitchers and needed a better designated hitter with more power.

After the 0–3 start, the A's boarded a plane to Chicago's O'Hare Airport. On the bus ride to the hotel, Dick Williams noticed loud noises coming from the back of the bus, where Billy North was needling Blue Moon Odom. "Are you guys 3–0, or 0–3?" Williams snapped sarcastically, according to an article that appeared in *Sports Illustrated*.

Odom provided a ready answer. "We're 0–3."

"Well, you better start busting your rears," Williams shot back, not at Odom in particular, but at the entire team of A's.

Williams' outburst was eerily reminiscent of the stern lecture he had given the A's on the team bus three years earlier. In 1971, the A's had responded to Williams' words by winning five straight games and 12 of 13. How would they respond this time?

Oakland routed Chicago, 12–2, knocking White Sox ace Wilbur Wood from the game. Joe Rudi snapped out of a 0-for-13 slump to hit a home run. Although several players tried to downplay the connection between the win and Williams' anger at them, it seemed the manager's temper had once again motivated the team, albeit for the short term. The A's dropped their next game, falling to 1–4. Fortunately, Campy Campaneris would return to the lineup, his five-game suspension having come to a welcome end.

The new designated hitter rule was forcing Wlliams and Finley to make changes with their team. Since Williams no longer had to pinch-hit for his pitchers, he tended to leave his starters in for longer periods. As a result, the A's' relievers became under-worked. Even ace reliever Rollie Fingers found himself spending too much time idle time in the bullpen. "It's a terrible thing for relief pitchers," Fingers told the Associated Press, pointing his finger at the DH rule. "It seems like I'm throwing more on the sidelines this year instead of in games." Fingers also felt the new rule would hurt his chances of earning a pay raise. "We've got four good relievers," Fingers explained to the AP. "Some clubs, like the Yankees, have one guy they use all the time. Sparky Lyle will still probably get about 30 saves this year. I'll have something like 13. That will be *great* when I go in to talk contract with Charlie Finley."

With four quality relievers and the designated hitter in place, Dick Williams realized he didn't need a nine-man staff; four starters and four relievers would be sufficient. The A's dispatched the thoroughly well-traveled Rob Gardner to Tucson. In his place, Charlie Finley substituted Triple-A outfielder Jay Johnstone, fledgling comedian and one of the game's greatest flakes of the late 20th century.

In 1971, Johnstone had hit 16 home runs for the White Sox, but his struggles the following year prompted his release in the spring of '73. Envisioning problems in center field, the A's signed Johnstone to a minor league contract and assigned him to Tucson. Upon his promotion to the major leagues, Johnstone reported to Kansas City, where the A's were scheduled to play a night game against the Royals. At 7:45 P.M., Johnstone received a telephone call in the dugout from none other than Finley. The Oakland owner wanted to wish his newest player good luck, and asked Johnstone if he needed anything prior to his first game. While talking with Johnstone over the phone, Finley heard a loud roar from the fans at Royals Stadium. Thinking that the fans were reacting to an impressive batting practice display, Finley asked Johnstone what had specifically prompted the cheers from the crowd. Johnstone replied matter-of-factly that the fans were reacting to a play *in the game going on between the A's and Royals*. Now at a loss for words, Finley felt a lump in his throat. He had thought that games in Kansas City started at 8:00 P.M., not at 7:30. The embarassed owner hurriedly said good-bye to Johnstone and promptly hung up the phone. Johnstone now realized the strangeness of the new baseball world he had entered.

Johnstone became one of the A's' newest candidates to fill the designated hitter role. The new DH rule, by the way, had met with such media resistance that it caused Dick Williams to lose his patience with at least one television broadcaster. Williams didn't appreciate some of the negative coverage being given to the issue of the designated hitter and expressed his discontent with NBC-TV's "Game of the Week" crew, which had criticized the American League innovation. When Williams saw NBC announcer Tony Kubek patrolling the A's' training room, he asked the former Yankee shortstop to leave. With Major League Baseball rules declaring training rooms as off-limits to the media, Williams found himself technically within his rights to ask for Kubek's removal. Realizing he didn't belong in the trainer's room according to the rules, Kubek responded professionally and apologized to the Oakland skipper. Still, Kubek might have wondered if Williams was seeking some form of retribution for the network's negative coverage of the DH.

DH or no DH, the A's needed a productive one. The absence of a power hitter to fill that role, coupled with the lack of a proven center fielder, left the A's with two major holes in their starting lineup. Plus, with Dick Green struggling in his return from back surgery, second base once again became a problem. The pitching staff, although strong on paper, did not fare well either, failing to pick up the slack for the offense over the first few weeks of the season. Other than starter Ken Holtzman and reliever Horacio Piña, none of the pitchers were performing up to their past resumes.

While Blue Moon Odom was in the midst of an 0–5 start, Horacio Piña represented the other end of the success-failure spectrum, pitching surprisingly well in the first month of the season. The 28-year-old Mexican had faced immediate pressure from the Oakland fans and media, who criticized his acquisition from Texas in the Mike Epstein trade. (Fortunately, Piña didn't hear many of the criticisms, because he understood and spoke virtually no English.) When A's fans took their first look at Piña—with his long, bushy hair and gangly frame—they must have wondered whether he was even an athlete. At six feet, two inches, and 160 pounds, the reed-thin right-hander had earned the nickname "Ichabod Crane" during his early major league days with the Cleveland Indians. An impressive physical specimen he was not.

Initially, Piña had also failed to impress pitching coach Wes Stock, who noted his past inability to handle left-handed batters. Piña, an effective side-arming pitcher against right-handed hitters, seemed unwilling to use that style against lefties. "He was coming over the top to left-handers and his ball always was up," Stock explained to *The Sporting News*. "His natural motion is side-arm, and his ball sinks when he throws it that way."

Stock quickly convinced Pina to rid himself of the overhand delivery and show courage in using his side-winding motion at all times. Piña had been given such advice in the past, but the recommendations never stuck—until now. With his long fingers and large hands, Piña already threw his best pitch, a sinking palmball, more effectively than most pitchers. Piña's palmball now became lethal to left-handed hitters, as well. Piña piled up three wins and a save, which represented the best pitching of anyone on the Oakland staff over the season's first month.

On May 2, the A's finally addressed their troublesome problem at DH. Charlie Finley acquired 34-year-old right-handed slugger Deron Johnson from the Philadelphia Phillies for minor league infielder Jack Bastable and cash. Since the Phillies were retooling with youth, they had decided to trade the aging, slow-footed first baseman. "Deron Johnson is the DH we've been looking for," Dick Williams announced to reporters. The manager emphasized that Johnson would serve as the designated hitter against both left-handed and right-handed pitching. "We changed our thinking on the DH," Williams admitted. "At first we thought we needed someone with speed who made contact." In Johnson, the A's had decided to go with long ball potential and run production.

"Deron Johnson was a prototypical DH," explains Mike Hegan. "Well, he could play first base, too. But I mean he was a professional hitter. That was a pretty good acquisition. He would provide a little more power for the ballclub, as well." Prior to Johnson's arrival, the Oakland lineup featured only three legitimate home run hitters: Gene Tenace and Sal Bando from the right side and Reggie Jackson from the left. Although Williams might have preferred another left-handed power hitter to balance the middle of the order, he now had the services of four players capable of hitting at least 20 home runs.

Johnson delivered immediately as Williams' newfound DH. In his first at-bat with the A's, Johnson plated two runs with a soft line-drive single. Shortly after his arrival in Oakland, the A's reached .500 for the first time in 1973. In surrendering minor leaguer Jack Bastable—a player who would never make the major leagues—for a respected, productive power hitter like Johnson, Charlie Finley had made one of his best trades as Oakland's combination owner-general manager.

On the same day that Johnson debuted as the Oakland DH, Dick Williams unveiled the team's latest second base innovation. Unlike the rotation of second baseman that had been initiated by Finley in 1972, the latest brainstorm seemed to come from the mind of the manager. Williams filled out a lineup card that featured Gonzalo Marquez, a left-handed throwing first baseman, at second base. Yet, Willliams had no intention of playing Marquez at the position. With the A's playing on the road, Williams batted Marquez in the No. 2 slot in the order, after leadoff man Campy Campaneris. Marquez came to bat in the top half of the first inning, and when the A's took the field in the bottom half, gave way to Dick Green at second base. Williams then planned to pinch-hit for Green, and all subsequent second basemen, according to game situations.

"Of course," Williams said, in explaining the strategy to Ron Bergman, "you can only do this on the road." In a home game, Marquez would have had to take the field in the top of the first inning, leaving the A's with a major defensive liability in the middle infield. Williams had first learned of such strategy by observing his minor league manager, Bobby Bragan, in the Texas League during the late 1940s. Williams himself had first used the strategy as a minor league skipper in 1966.

While the A's had filled their designated hitter vacancy by acquiring a player such as Deron Johnson from another organization, they thought they had solved another one of their problems—the center field situation—through internal means. Billy Conigliaro started the season hitting .295 while fielding reasonably well in the outfield. Then, on April 21, Conigliaro damaged interior cartilage in his right knee while sliding into second base. Conigliaro tried playing with the injury for two weeks before agreeing to have the surgery. "I couldn't play in the field with this knee," Conigliaro admitted in an interview with *The Sporting News*. "There was no use limping around out there." Doctors predicted that "Billy C." would miss anywhere from one to two months. Dick Williams hoped he would have the veteran center fielder available as a pinch-hitter by mid-July, and perhaps back in the regular lineup by August. The injury, however, would prove to be a blessing for the A's, who would soon discover their new center fielder.

Billy North had started Opening Day as Oakland's designated hitter, before settling into a sporadic role as a third-string center fielder and intermittent DH, a role that didn't offer much promise of consistent playing time. Despite his status as an occasional starter, North was leading the American League in stolen bases. When Conigliaro went down with a bad knee and Angel Mangual pulled a chest muscle, Williams turned to North—more out of necessity than by choice. Playing in the first game of a doubleheader, the former Cub collected four hits and three RBIs. In spite of the offensive outburst, North sat on the bench in the second game, because Williams had already promised to give Mangual a start. When Mangual committed a two-base error and went 0-for-8 over a two-game span, Williams decided he had seen enough. "Bill North is my center fielder," Williams declared to Ron Bergman. "He stays in there unless he falls flat on his face."

North would not. The 25-year-old switch-hitter raised his batting average with regular playing time, continued to lead the league in stolen bases, and played spectacular defense in center field. "He covers more ground in center than anyone we've ever had," Reggie Jackson boldly told *The Sporting News*. Jackson certainly seemed like a good candidate to make such a strong statement, given that he had played with center field partners like Mangual, Conigliaro, George Hendrick, and Rick Monday since debuting with the Kansas City A's in 1967.

On May 18, North enjoyed a particularly productive game against the Royals, stealing a base, driving home the tying run, and scoring the winning run. Then, in the eighth inning, North faced reliever Doug Bird. North swung and missed, letting the bat fly out of his hands toward shortstop. As North walked out to the infield to retrieve the bat, he mouthed a few words to Bird and then suddenly charged the pitcher's mound.

None of the players on either team, except for Bird, understood why North had reacted so violently. Nothing had happened earlier in the game to forewarn such an incident. After the game, North explained that he had sought retaliation for a minor league incident that had occurred in *1970*, when the two players had faced each other in the Midwest League. Bird, pitching for Quincy, had given up two consecutive home runs to Waterloo batters when North stepped to the plate. In what seemed like an obvious "purpose" pitch, Bird beaned North. Now, in their first head-to-head meeting since the beaning, North successfully fulfilled his quest for revenge.

American League President Joe Cronin handed North a three-game suspension for his actions, prompting an angry reaction from the A's' brass. Dick Williams and Charlie Finley pointed to an incident just 10 days earlier, when two Kansas City reporters quoted Royals outfielder Lou Piniella as saying that he had *intentionally* thrown his bat at Detroit pitcher Jim Perry. Yet, Cronin had elected not to suspend Piniella, despite his admission of guilt. The A's now felt that Cronin had unfairly victimized them by enforcing a different standard of punishment against North.

Williams did not excuse North, however. "If you've got a grudge against a guy," Williams said in an interview with Ron Bergman, "don't take it out [during] my ballgame. The team should come first." Now a full-fledged member of a team with a recent history of winning, North had learned an important lesson from his new manager.

The day before North's attack on Bird, the A's had received an unexpected boost in the American League West pennant race. Dick Green belted a three-run homer against Rudy May at Anaheim Stadium, helping Catfish Hunter to a 4–0 win over the California Angels. On the play, Angels center fielder Bobby Valentine made a leaping attempt at Green's drive. Valentine's spikes caught in the center field wall, and with his momentum pushing his body toward the fence, two bones in his right leg snapped. The multiple fractures ended the season for Valentine, who was hitting

.302 at the time. The Angels considered Valentine one of the league's up-and-coming stars, and a key to their chances of claiming their first Western Division title.

Five weeks later, the A's would once again benefit from the misfortune of one of their rivals. Chicago White Sox first baseman Dick Allen, the American League's MVP in 1972, collided with former Oakland first baseman Mike Epstein, since traded from the Rangers to the Angels. The crash of muscle-bound sluggers resulted in a fracture of Allen's leg. The White Sox' best hitter, Allen was hitting .316 with 16 home runs and 41 RBIs at the time of the injury, and would come to bat only five more times in 1973. With Allen out of the lineup for virtually the rest of the season, the White Sox would lack the offense needed to sustain a serious threat in the Western Division.

Dick Williams had his own reasons to be concerned, however. Both Gene Tenace and Sal Bando were struggling to drive in runs. After a solid April, Williams had promoted Tenace all the way from seventh to third in the batting order, but the 26-year-old first baseman proceeded to go hitless in 18 at-bats. Williams then moved Tenace back to the No. 7 spot. Bando was also having problems getting runners home, and was dropped as low as eighth in the batting order.

After losing his first five decisions, Blue Moon Odom finally won a game, beating the Rangers, 4–2, on May 12. Unfortunately, the victory exacted a price. Odom developed a blister on his right index finger, forcing him to leave the game after five innings. He proceeded to lose his next three decisions, making his record a dismal 1–8. After losing to the Tigers on May 28, Dick Williams removed Odom from the starting rotation and placed him in the role of long relief.

Odom's ineffectiveness, coupled with the enigmatic struggles of Vida Blue, left Williams with two holes in his rotation. Williams began to contemplate the recall of two promising pitchers from Triple-A Tucson: left-handed swingman Dave Hamilton and top right-handed prospect Glenn Abbott. While both pitchers appeared to have solid futures, neither possessed the talent that could come close to matching the ability of Blue.

Even though Blue had signed his 1973 contract fairly quickly, thus avoiding another prolonged salary battle with Charlie Finley, he was clearly grasping to find his old form. His early-season difficulties even prompted Williams to make a change in his rotation of catchers. In five straight games in which Blue started, Williams benched regular catcher Ray Fosse, moved Deron Johnson from DH to first base, and installed Tenace as Vida's personal receiver. The reason? Tenace had caught Blue frequently since the 1969 season, when both were in Oakland's farm system. The two had been paired during Blue's two most significant milestone games: his no-hitter in 1970 and his 20th win in 1971. "A lot of things are still in his head," Tenace told *The Sporting News*, in trying to explain Blue's subpar pitching. "I've known him a long time, so I can make a statement like that. I can tell when something is bothering him. Mentally, he's still not ready to pitch." Tenace believed that Blue was still upset by his 1972 contract negotiations with Finley, and by a demanding fan base that expected him to duplicate his 1971 pitching standards.

"A year like that will never happen again," Blue cautioned his fans through an interview with the *Christian Science Monitor*. "I was new to the league. They didn't know me. I had 150 strikeouts before they realized I wasn't throwing anything but fastballs." Yet, Blue was not throwing his fastball as hard in 1973 as he had in the past. Some observers of the A's pointed to Blue's workload in 1971, when he had pitched a burdensome total of 312 innings. Prior to that season, Blue had never pitched as many as 150 innings in a season, including his years in the minor leagues.

While some observers of the A's have speculated that Blue might have hurt his arm trying to come back too quickly after his 1972 holdout, some players, like Sal Bando, disagree with that theory. "I don't think he hurt his arm; for some reason I don't think he had the total recovery that you need and the buildup of the arm strength," says Bando. "He just, for some reason, was never the same pitcher. Occasionally, he would have a game where it looked like the '71 Vida Blue was there, but again, I can't help but think that the holdout hurt him more than anything else."

On May 25, Campy Campaneris returned to Detroit for the first time since the ugly bat-throwing incident involving Lerrin LaGrow in the 1972 playoffs. For his part, LaGrow claimed that he held no grudge against Campaneris. "Heck, I've forgotten all about it," a forgiving LaGrow told *The Sporting News*. "That's all over."

Surprisingly, Tiger manager Billy Martin—not always the sort to avoid grudges—agreed with the sentiments expressed by LaGrow. "It's all over. It's history," Martin told *The Sporting News*, before acknowledging that his feelings toward Campaneris had been quite different during the controversial playoff game. "If I would have gotten to him at the time," Martin bragged, "I would have kicked the bleep out of him." Still, Martin claimed that recent media reports of him continuing to seek revenge on Campaneris were greatly exaggerated. "I was quoted as saying that if there was another fight, Campaneris would be the first guy I would go after," Martin explained. "That was a little misquote there."

As much as Martin despised Campaneris at the moment he hurled his bat toward LaGrow, the Tiger skipper respected the veteran infielder as a fiery, combative sparkplug who always hustled. Evidence of Martin's regard for Campaneris could be found in 1983, when Campy would conclude his major league career with the Yankees. After a one-year layoff from major league baseball, Campy arrived at the Yankees' spring camp in Ft. Lauderdale, Florida—uninvited. Knowing that the Yankees needed a middle infielder, Campaneris asked New York's manager for a playing job. The manager responded by challenging him to make the team. Campaneris proceeded to earn the final spot on the 25-man roster, and hit .322 as a backup second baseman and third baseman to Willie Randolph and Graig Nettles, respectively. Who was the Yankees manager at the time? It was a forgiving and respectful Billy Martin.

Tiger fans were not as kind as Martin and LaGrow in offering *their* reaction to Campaneris' initial visit to Detroit. Fans at Tiger Stadium lustily booed Campy each time he stepped to the plate. "After I do it," Campaneris told Will Grimsley of the Associated Press in recalling the incident, "I am sorry. In Detroit, they boo me, but others don't. When people bring it up, I no say anything. I want to forget." Some of the Tigers wouldn't let him forget. In the field, Campaneris took a fall when Tiger catcher Bill Freehan knocked him down with a fierce takeout slide at second base. The collision with the rugged Freehan resulted in a pulled right shoulder muscle, which forced Campy to the sidelines for six games. The A's proceeded to lose the first five of those games before salvaging a win, dropping their season record to 2–9 in those games in which Campaneris did not play.

In losing that fifth consecutive game, Vida Blue incurred a no-decision, as the A's dropped a 4–3 decision to the Yankees. Blue didn't pitch badly, giving up only two earned runs in six innings. Yet, the left-hander remained dissatisfied with his performance. "I'm not really worried, but I am concerned," Blue told the *New York Times*, while apparently contradicting himself within the same sentence. "I feel tired. I don't know why. The ball goes, but not the way it should."

The five-game losing streak represented the worst for the franchise since Dick Williams had been named manager after the 1970 season. The frequent losses resulted in roster changes. With left-hander Rob Gardner already on the disabled list, Oakland recalled Dave Hamilton from Tucson. Williams called upon Hamilton to replace the disappointing Blue Moon Odom, who had shuttled between starting and relieving, in the regular rotation.

Upon his promotion, a reporter questioned Hamilton about one of his Tucson teammates, an outfielder named Charlie Chant. The reporter asked Hamilton whether Chant, whose name sounded like that of famed film detective Charlie Chan, was actually of Chinese descent. "No," Hamilton told *The Sporting News* before exhibiting the flakiness of a left-hander. "He's a right fielder." Perhaps Hamilton didn't understand the question. Whatever the case, Hamilton seemed like he would fit in well with the rest of Oakland's menagerie of colorful characters.

The five-game losing skid during Campaneris' absence left the A's with a mediocre record of 23–24, an embarrassing mark for the defending World Champions. Finley decided the time was right to send journeyman Rob Gardner packing. While revealing that the disabled Gardner wasn't hurt very seriously to begin with, the A's sold the oft-traveled southpaw to the Brewers. Oakland fans, however, hadn't seen the last of Finley's favorite pitching yo-yo.

The A's managed to win three of their next four games, salvaging the nine-game eastern road swing with a record of 3–6. In one of the wins, Ken Holtzman retired the first 20 Yankee batters he faced before allowing a seventh-inning single to former Athletic Matty Alou. In the eighth inning, Yankee designated hitter Jim Ray Hart hit a line drive that caromed off Holtzman's leg so forcefully that it landed in the mitt of first baseman Deron Johnson—on the fly. Calling it the "hardest ball ever hit at me," Holtzman limped off the field with a large red welt on the back of his left leg. The A's sent their valuable left-hander to the hospital for precautionary X-rays, which showed no break. In an intriguing twist, Holtzman had been victimized by Hart, a former San Francisco Giant, much earlier in his career. "Jim

Ray Hart hit the first pitch I ever threw in the major leagues for a home run," Holtzman told the Associated Press, in recalling his debut with the Cubs in 1965.

In another victory, a 12–1 rout of the Red Sox, Mike Hegan's errorless games streak finally came to an end. On a routine grounder to first base, Hegan handled the ball cleanly, but then fired an errant toss to Vida Blue, who was covering the first-base bag. The throwing error, though harmless within the context of the game, halted Hegan's lengthy streak, which had lasted 178 games and overlapped four seasons.

After the trip to the East Coast, the green and gold returned to Oakland for a 12-game homestand, only to drop two straight games to the lowly Brewers. The defeats included a frustrating 5–4 loss to the recently traded Rob Gardner. The previous day, the A's had played perhaps their worst game of the season. Although the final score of 2–0 didn't appear unsightly, a review of the game's circumstances showed otherwise. With runners on first and third, Dick Williams signaled for a double steal. Usually an excellent baserunner, Campy Campaneris broke from third, then stopped, and was caught off the bag as he tried to return to the base. Later in the game, Campy foolishly cut off a throw from the outfield, preventing Ray Fosse from making a catch and tag at the plate on what seemed like a certain out. In the outfield, Billy North and Reggie Jackson nearly collided on a fly ball that should have been caught routinely in right field. Jackson caught the ball, but not without a few histrionics. After Jackson scolded North for venturing too far from his post in center field, the right fielder started to run for the dugout, thinking that he had notched the third out. Unfortunately for Jackson, only two outs had been recorded. Later in the game, Fosse failed to make contact on a squeeze bunt attempt, leaving the slow-footed Deron Johnson an easy victim at home plate.

"It's been like this all year," an exasperated Sal Bando told *Sports Illustrated* after the game. "We just haven't been executing." Bando pointed out the following conventional baseball wisdom: teams are generally destined to win one-third of their games and lose one-third of their games, leaving another third up for grabs. According to Bando, Oakland's failure to complete fundamental plays was preventing them from winning their share of those critical "at-large" games.

On June 9, in an historic Finley-esque moment, the A's debuted their distinctive, if not aesthetically pleasing, all-green uniforms. In 1972, the A's had debuted solid green tops, but always wore them with traditional white pants. The new green pants, yet another Finley innovation, gave the A's a surreal, softball-like appearance. In an amusing interview, Bando claimed the matching green tops and bottoms actually provided a helpful, camouflaging effect against Oakland's opponents. "The batters can't see us," Bando explained tongue-in-cheek to *The Sporting News*, "because we blend in with the grass and they hit it right at us."

Ably assisted by their new Irish look, the A's won their next two games against the Tigers. In the June 10th game, Joe Rudi made a catch strikingly similar to his dramatic, spider-like snare against the Reds' Denis Menke in the 1972 World Series. On this occasion, Rudi deprived Willie Horton of extra bases with a sprawling grab, helping to preserve Catfish Hunter's 5–0 shutout win.

The A's finished the homestand with a mediocre record of 7–5, despite a boom period at the plate for Reggie Jackson. Reggie powered six homers and totaled 17 RBIs during the home stretch, putting himself on pace for a 100-RBI season. In one of the games against the Brewers, Jackson drove in five runs, but still heard boos from the Oakland faithful when he misplayed three catchable flyballs in right field. "I had that one bad game [defensively]," Reggie conceded in an interview with *The Sporting News*. "But that's like striking out four times in one game. Those things happen."

Ever since his record-breaking home run streak during the first half of the 1969 season, some members of the national media had been tempted to label Jackson a superstar. While some writers debated that assessment, few players in either league matched his combination of power, raw speed, and rifle-like throwing arm. "His strength is just unbelievable," said former Athletic Dave Duncan in an interview with Bay Area sportswriter Glenn Dickey. "He should be able to hit 30 home runs a year just by accident." Yet, Jackson had reached that single-season milestone only twice in his first five full major league seasons. His home ballpark, the pitcher-friendly Oakland Coliseum, had certainly played a part in hindering his power. There were other reasons, too. Reggie's lack of patience at the plate, coupled with his tendency to overswing, had limited his home run totals while creating too many strikeouts and too few walks. "It's no secret what they get [Jackson] out on," Duncan explained later in the interview. "He strikes out on pitches over his head or in the dirt. When the pitch is in the strike zone, he hits it."

Some observers also felt that Jackson had suffered from an identity crisis. During spring training, some of the A's players and media had whispered about Jackson's tendency to model himself after controversial White Sox slugger Dick Allen, whom he had known from his days growing up in the Philadelphia area. Revered for his immense power and pure hitting ability, Allen had become a kind of guru to a number of black ballplayers throughout the majors. Although as talented as any power hitter in the game, Allen's strained relationships with managers and fans had undermined his reputation, calling into question his desire to win. "I like Allen as a person and admire him as a ballplayer, but I'm not trying to be like him," Jackson insisted in a discussion with Dickey. Still, others in the Oakland clubhouse saw a resemblance. "There's a little of Dick Allen in him. A little of Frank Robinson," said Sal Bando. "He has to learn to be Reggie Jackson."

His strikeouts and insecurities aside, Jackson had played well enough—and shown enough improvement in his game—to merit election to the American League All-Star team. The same could not be said of Jackson's outfield partner, Joe Rudi, who remained mired in a season-long slump. When Rudi's average fell to a season-low .217, Dick Williams placed him on the bench for five straight games. Dubbed "Gentleman Joe" by the Bay Area media, Rudi usually handled such adversity with a calm, even demeanor. On this occasion, however, the benching angered him. "I know what I can do," Rudi lashed out in an interview with *Sports Illustrated*, "but I can't prove anything on the bench."

Jackson wasn't happy with his manager either. Williams had decided to sit his right fielder for a couple of days, saying that Reggie needed to be "rested." Jackson refuted Williams' reasoning. "Why should I need a rest?" Jackson asked a writer from *Sports Illustrated*. "I just had a birthday, but I'm 27, not 37. I'm not tired. What's he thinking of? What did I do wrong? I'm hitting .285 and driving in runs."

On the A's, the voicing of complaints wasn't restricted to stars and near-stars like Jackson and Rudi. Even bench players joined in the discord. One incident involved Angel Mangual, who had moved into Rudi's spot in left field, in what amounted to his last chance to resurrect his career in Oakland. In the late innings of one of the games that Mangual started, Williams sent up the "rested" Jackson to pinch-hit for the light-hitting outfielder. Mangual reacted by throwing his helmet. An observant Williams reacted by fining Mangual $200. While that might not have sounded like a substantial amount, it represented the largest fine that Williams had doled out during his tenure as Oakland's manager.

In a matter of days, Williams had heard and seen signs of disharmony from three of his outfielders. The recurring question of playing time, paired with the team's continuing stumbles on the playing field, irritated the manager. "I can't be concerned whether a guy is unhappy or not," an unsympathetic Williams told *Sports Illustrated*. "I just want them to go out and play."

Mangual said Williams misunderstood his gesture. "I wasn't tossing my helmet because Reggie pinch-hit for me. I did it just to relax," Mangual told *The Sporting News*, employing a rather unconvincing argument. Mangual then allowed his feelings of frustration with the manager to truly show. "If Williams no like me, why doesn't he trade me?" Williams and Charlie Finley faced a basic problem: who would give up anything of substance for Mangual, given his poor 1972 season and continuing struggles at the plate and in the field in 1973?

In addition to the dilemma presented by the enigmatic Mangual, the A's had other concerns with their 25-man roster. During the offseason, Charlie Finley had pushed his fellow owners to adopt a rule allowing a "designated runner," a player who could be substituted at any time for the slowest batter in the lineup. Although American League owners had ratified the rule change, the National League had refused to go along. In a compromise, National League owners had agreed to allow the American League to use the new designated hitter innovation, but had turned their noses against the designated runner and the concept of inter-league play. In protest of the decision, Finley refused to vote in favor of the DH, saying that the designated hitter and designated runner should have been packaged together. Even though the rules wouldn't allow a "designated" runner, Finley still believed in the importance of carrying a player whose *only* value was his ability to pinch-run. Given that roster philosophy, Finley called up Allan Lewis from Double-A Birmingham, while demoting pinch-hitting specialist Gonzalo Marquez to Triple-A Tucson.

Lewis, a Finley favorite who was nicknamed the "Panamanian Express," had been with the A's sporadically since 1967. In 1966, Lewis had set a Florida State League record by stealing 116 bases for Leesburg. Incredibly, opposing catchers had thrown out Lewis only 10 times that season. Yet, in spite of his eye-popping speed, few players had poorer baseball instincts and understanding of the game than Lewis.

Lewis had previously attempted to defend his playing abilities. "When I play regularly, I hit .280," Lewis had told sportswriter Phil Pepe during the 1972 World Series. During his minor league career, Lewis had compiled respectable batting averages of .280 and .288 over full seasons, and averages as high as .319 and .322 during partial seasons. Yet, he had totaled only 13 home runs over 12 minor league seasons and had shown no ability to hit in part-time duty as a major league player. "He's a .300 hitter," Dick Williams had told Pepe tongue-in-cheek. "One-fifty left-handed and .150 right-handed." Lewis had also demonstrated himself to be a major liability in several other areas. Although he ran fast, he often negated that ability with his failure to get good jumps, and played no defensive position particularly well, even though the A's listed him as an outfielder on their roster.

The decision to promote Lewis to the major leagues angered several of the players, foremost Sal Bando, who publicly criticized the 31-year-old pinch-runner's baseball skills. Bando became even more incensed when Lewis made his 1973 debut on June 18, pinch-running for Bando himself in the seventh inning of a 9–5 win over the Royals. The fact that Lewis scored a run did little to soothe Bando, who resented being replaced by an inferior ballplayer during a close game. Bando probably became more infuriated when he watched his replacement at third base, Rich McKinney, commit a late-inning error in the same game.

Other Oakland players publicly expressed their opposition to Lewis' presence on the roster. The resentment grew after a game on June 20, when the A's played the Royals in Kansas City. On this occasion, Dick Williams used Lewis as a pinch-runner for designated hitter Deron Johnson. One inning later, with a chance to break a 4-4 tie in extra innings, the A's loaded the bases with one out. It was now Johnson's turn to bat. Yet, Johnson had already been removed for the pinch-running Lewis, and was now out of the game. Needing a more capable hitter than Lewis, Williams sent McKinney up as a pinch-hitter. McKinney failed to deliver the game-tying run, and the A's went on to lose the game in the bottom of the 12th.

The strategy left Oakland players incredulous. Although Williams had used Lewis as a pinch-runner in two earlier games, the A's had managed to win both times. In this most recent instance, the use of Lewis had cost the A's their best chance to win in extra innings, at least according to most of the players in the clubhouse. *Why did Finley insist on carrying Lewis on the 25-man roster*, the players thought out loud, *and why did Williams insist on playing him?*

As team captain, Sal Bando expressed the most vocal opposition to Lewis' presence. Bando's problem with Lewis had everything to do with baseball—and nothing to do with personality. "At that time, it was kind of new to us to carry a player who would not have made the team based on his baseball skills," Bando explains. "I don't think it was anything personal against Allan as much as it was we were carrying somebody who really, all he could do was pinch-run. It's like putting somebody on the club, that when other guys are competing who have more skills to hit or field, couldn't make the club."

The majority of Lewis' teammates agreed with Bando, feeling that the pinch-running specialist had no business wearing a major league uniform. "It was quite [difficult] for those guys," says Mincher, "to understand that here you have a guy who never had a major league at-bat, as far as I know [Lewis actually came to bat 29 times during parts of six seasons], and he was making the same kind of money as some of the guys on the club, getting the major league treatment, and he never earned it. He [Lewis] never earned the privilege; all the guy's gotta do is run [the bases] one time during a game."

In retrospect, Bando says Finley's decision to include a player like Lewis on the roster made *some* sense. "As you look back, I think there's a lot of merit to having the 25th man on your club being able to do something like that. Especially once you had the DH in place, you really didn't need all 25 players." Like it or not, Dick Williams had received a mandate from his boss to use Lewis in pinch-running situations. "I think Dick Williams probably put up with it [at first]," Bando says, "but then saw some merit to it."

Even though Lewis had been playing professional baseball since the mid-1960s, his baseball instincts had failed to improve by 1973. In fact, Lewis' base-running gaffes had created the stuff of legend in the Bay Area. During one of the A's' "Family Night" games, Lewis strained credibility when he tried to score from second base—without touching third base. Lewis didn't accidentally miss tagging the bag; rather, he attempted to score by running straight from second base, *over the pitcher's mound*, to home plate. For at least the second time in his major league career, Lewis had tried to bypass a base while making his circuit around the bags. Earlier in his career, while serving as a pinch-runner, Lewis had sprinted from first to third on a pop fly. When Lewis reached third base, he realized the high fly ball had been caught. Instead of retracing his steps toward second base, with the idea of trying to get back to first, Lewis decided to employ a shortcut. He raced across the diamond, *over the pitcher's mound*, and made a beeline for first base. Either Lewis didn't realize that *you couldn't do that*, or he was trying to be funny. Or maybe both. Yet, Lewis wasn't alone in committing such a mistake.

"Let me tell you about Bando doing that in Fenway Park," says utility infielder Ted Kubiak. "Yeah, somebody hit a ball out to Yaz [Carl Yastrzemski] in left field, and Yaz faked Sal out. He thought the ball was going to go off the wall, [but] he turned around and caught it. Sal was almost to third base and he tried to cut across the mound. Ask Sal about that one." Bando and Lewis, while at opposite poles of the Oakland clubhouse, now had one embarrassing moment in common.

Several days later, another controversy infiltrated the A's, though this one did not involve the players. Television play-by-play man Monte Moore, who had long been reputed to be a Finley house man, and who allegedly served as a snitch for the owner at the ballpark and in the clubhouse, became involved in a conflict with several longtime sportswriters.

Some players and writers long since believed that if someone made negative comments about Finley in the presence of Moore, those remarks would eventually find their way to the all-knowing owner. Did Moore really betray the confidence of the Oakland clubhouse? "We really felt so," said Jack Aker, a member of the A's from 1964 to '68. "Every meeting that we had—and at this time you have to remember that this was the years that the players' union was getting organized, and we even shut out the manager and the coaches whenever we had a meeting to try to organize this thing—for some reason, Monte Moore seemed to know what went on in the meetings. Either he was close enough by to overhear some of the comments, or in the clubhouse, [where] some of the players would be talking among themselves. So we really felt that this was something that should have been just between the players. I think there was a lot of animosity on the club against Monte Moore."

Others suspected that one of the A's' *players* was serving as a "messenger" to Finley. In Curt Smith's acclaimed book, *Voices of the Game,* former A's broadcaster Jim Woods pointed the finger at shortstop Campy Campaneris. Even after his playing days, Campy maintained a connection with the owner by annually sending Finley a Christmas card, the only former A's player to do so. So was Campaneris acting as an unspoken liasion with Finley? Without any proof, I'd hate to say anything," says Aker. "There were two players that we felt were very close to Mr. Finley. I couldn't say right now for sure if Monte Moore ever said anything to him; I couldn't with the two players, either. It was very obvious to us that *someone* was going up to Mr. Finley. Being player representative, a lot of times the meeting would be over, and someone within five minutes would be summoning me to his office. He could tell me right away what had gone on in the meeting, word for word in some cases."

At the time, most players suspected Moore, rather than Campaneris, of acting as the conduit to Charlie Finley. Moore knew about the allegations and realized that some of the accusations came from baseball writers. On that front, Moore would soon enjoy some payback. In late June, the A's played the White Sox in a weekend series in Chicago. During one of the games, Billy North reached first base on what official scorer and longtime writer Edgar Munzel deemed an infield error. Moore, broadcasting the game back to Oakland, disagreed with Munzel's' decision. Moore felt Munzel should have credited North with a base hit. Moore took his criticism a step further when he accused newspaper reporters, in general, of not paying attention to the action on the field. Several writers resented Moore's accusation. "You newspaper men are so sensitive," Moore told a reporter after the broadcast. "A lot of newspaper men have criticized me, and if they've got a right to criticize me, then I've got a right to criticize them."

While most writers probably didn't want to admit it, Moore had a legitimate point. Although one might have questioned his motives, he did have every right to criticize writers, provided that he could back up his accusations. Moore also proved to be right in his assessment of Munzel's scoring decision, and played a part in having the ruling changed. To his credit, the venerable Munzel asked all of the players involved on the play whether it should be scored a hit or an error. Munzel collected all of the testimony, and two days after making his original decision, changed the scoring of the play. Munzel gave North a hit, drawing the praise of Dick Williams in the process. "Edgar Munzel showed me a lot of class," Williams said afterwards in an interview with *The Sporting News*.

Controversies, slumps, and personnel changes characterized the first half of the 1973 season. Still, the A's remained in contention, and on June 28, the A's moved into sole possession of first place in the American League West for the first time. Vida Blue pitched seven and two-thirds strong innings before giving way to Rollie Fingers, who preserved a 3–2 win. It had taken 75 games, but the A's had finally taken the lead from the Angels, White Sox, Twins, and Royals, who all remained within two games of first place.

After allowing only three hits to Kansas City in his strongest outing of the season, Blue sounded off to those members of the media who had previously proclaimed the demise of his left arm. "All you guys from UPI and AP and *SI* [*Sports Illustrated*] and all the other initials—and anyone else who thinks my arm is dead—come out to the park and get a bat," Blue challenged the assembled reporters. "I'll throw you guys 100 pitches and give any man $500 for each ball he fouls off." Not surprisingly, none of the reporters accepted the offer.

Blue's arm was healthy—and so was one of the team's veteran infielders. Dick Green's recent return from the injured list gave the A's an excess of second basemen. Even though Green and Ted Kubiak were both slumping badly at the plate, Charlie Finley decided to part ways with classy veteran Dal Maxvill, who had helped Oakland clinch the 1972 Western Division crown. Four clubs expressed interest in Maxvill, before Finley settled on accepting a cash return from the Pittsburgh Pirates.

The A's' arrival at the top spot of the Western Division didn't mean that they had completely abandoned controversy. Far from it. In early July, Reggie Jackson committed two errors during a four-game stretch, dropping easy flyballs each time. After a game against the Angels, a reporter asked Jackson how he felt physically, whether he was tired or hurt. Jackson said he felt fine, then quickly—and without warning—changed the subject to Oakland's coaching and managerial staff. "We make a mistake," a frustrated Jackson said to a reporter from the *New York Times*, "and they [the coaches] act as if you did it on purpose. The coaches don't contribute anything. We make their money for them." Jackson added a dose of sarcasm to his diatribe. "The way these guys criticize you, you'd think they were all Babe Ruth when they played," Jackson told sportswriter Murray Olderman.

One of the A's' coaches did not appreciate Jackson's verbal attack. First-base coach Jerry Adair fired back at Reggie. "I'm getting sick and tired of seeing him play half the time," an angry Adair told *The Sporting News*. Jackson then tried to clarify his remarks, indicating that he hadn't intended to include Adair in his critique. Jackson said that he had actually directed his statements at manager Dick Williams and third-base coach Irv Noren, who had criticized Dick Green and Ray Fosse for recent on-the-field mistakes.

The remarks represented the first publicly negative statements Jackson had made about his manager since his hiring in 1970, when Reggie had cited Williams' reputation as a man who did not stand up for his players. Williams didn't appreciate Jackson's most recent sentiments, especially about his underpaid coaching staff. "Everything we do is constructive criticism," Williams told the *New York Times* before borrowing an old cliché. "If you can't stand the heat, get out of the kitchen."

On the team's flight from California to Baltimore, Jackson approached Williams about the issue. A Baltimore newspaper later reported that Jackson had challenged his manager to a fight on the plane. Jackson denied the story. "I never told him to get up and fight," Reggie insisted in an interview with *The Sporting News*. "I told him never to talk to me again, just to write my name in the lineup." And what was Williams' reaction to Jackson's abrupt orders? "He didn't say anything," Jackson replied to *The Sporting News*, "but I could tell he was ticked off." To his credit, Jackson later apologized for the way he had spoken to his manager. "The next day I knew I was wrong and I went up to him and said I wanted it to be forgotten." Williams agreed to do so, hoping to reestablish what had been a solid relationship with his All-Star right fielder.

Still, Oakland beat writers wondered what effect Jackson's recent public comments might have on the future of Williams and his coaches. There had already been speculation that Williams might voluntarily leave the organization at season's end and try to find another managerial job. Perhaps even more importantly, how would Charlie Finley react to his star player's dissatisfaction with the manager? Some writers guessed that Finley might use the opportunity to make public his own criticisms of Williams. Perhaps Finley would reprimand Williams for being overly critical of his players.

Three days after the Jackson firestorm broke out, Finley finally made an announcement. Instead of firing any of his coaches, or Williams himself, Finley surprised almost everyone concerned by announcing that he had *renewed* the contracts of Williams and his entire coaching staff—Adair, Noren, pitching coach Wes Stock, and bullpen coach Vern Hoscheit—for another season.

The A's beat writers tried to discern Finley's motivation in granting the contract extensions at such an unlikely and surprising time. Finley denied that he had been influenced by Jackson's complaints about the "overcritical" managerial and coaching staff. The owner also insisted that the timing of his decision to reward Williams and his coaches with extensions was merely a coincidence and had nothing to do with Jackson. According to Finley, he was simply rewarding his workers for a job well done.

More likely, Finley had decided to send Jackson the following message: *Don't knock your managers and coaches. You work for them, and they work for me. Keep your mouth shut and play.* Finley was making it quite clear that *he* was in charge of the team, not Jackson. In a way, Finley seemed to be punishing Jackson by rewarding Williams and the coaches.

The Jackson controversy overshadowed several positive developments for the A's in July, including a recent boost in attendance at the Oakland Coliseum. Home attendance, which had been awful during the first month of the season, had earlier prompted Dick Williams to make the following remarks to *Sports Illustrated*: "We're World Champions. We've proved ourselves. The area hasn't." In 1972, the A's had drawn a total of 921,323 fans—the worst total for a World Championship team since World War II.

In his continuing frustration over the lack of fan support, Williams had warned fans about the possibility of the A's moving to another city. The A's, however, wouldn't feel any immediate urge to relocate the franchise, since attendance had improved considerably in July. The rise in fan interest led some writers to speculate that the A's might actually break the one million-fan mark for the first time in Oakland's franchise history. Better play and warmer weather had given A's fans stronger incentive to visit the Coliseum.

The middle of the season also brought some pleasant on-the-field developments. Reliever Darold Knowles started to throw his fastball hard again, much like he had during his early major league days in Philadelphia and Washington. According to Knowles, overwork during his last two years with the Senators had robbed life from his fastball. Earlier in the season, Dick Williams had also admonished Knowles for his seeming unwillingness to challenge hitters. Knowles claimed that he never intentionally meant to nibble at the plate; he simply had been unable to throw the ball where he wanted. "I'd hate to have to tell him this," Knowles told *The Sporting News* in assessing Williams' complaints, "but I'm trying to throw the ball right down the middle of the plate." With Knowles throwing his good fastball *and* throwing it for strikes, the A's now possessed another capable reliever who could ease some of the late-inning pressure from fireman Rollie Fingers.

On offense, Ray Fosse started to drive in runs, something he had failed to do over the first half of the season. Fosse hit three home runs during a four-game series against the Brewers, and collected 13 RBIs in Oakland's final 12 games before the All-Star break. Prior to that stretch, Fosse had driven in only 19 runs over the entire first half of the season, having failed miserably with runners in scoring position. The recent hitting surge gave the A's excellent all-around play from their new catcher. Even when he didn't hit, Fosse had played remarkable defense throughout the season, especially in the area of throwing. In his first 98 games, opposing teams attempted only 48 stolen bases against the rocket-armed receiver. Fosse threw out 24 of those runners, or an even 50 per cent. In contrast, former Oakland catcher and current Indian Dave Duncan had encountered season-long struggles in his efforts to stop base stealers. While Indian pitchers did not hold runners as well as Oakland hurlers, Duncan simply did not possess the kind of arm strength featured by Fosse.

On another front, Vida Blue notched back-to-back complete games—something he had not done all season. Blue followed up a four-hit effort against Baltimore with an impressive three-hitter against the Indians. Yet, Vida's newfound success didn't dissuade him from taking a subtle shot at Dick Williams. After the win over the Orioles, Blue hinted that Williams had been too quick in taking his starting pitchers out of games. Blue's observation conflicted with the general media consensus that Williams had been anything but quick in removing his starters; after all, the new designated hitter rule had eliminated the need for pinch-hitting for the pitcher in the late innings and had resulted in an underutilized bullpen.

While the A's had started to play better baseball, Williams' health had taken a turn for the worse. On July 19, the A's skipper suffered an attack of appendicitis, which required an emergency appendectomy that day. The appendectomy would force Williams to miss several regular season games, but did not prevent him from leading the American League in the All-Star Game. Some writers speculated that Finley had ordered his manager to work the Midsummer Classic, even though he didn't feel anywhere close to perfect health. Williams later denied that Finley had made such a demand.

While Williams struggled with his health problem, Catfish Hunter entered the All-Star break at 15–3, having won 10 consecutive decisions. Hunter's pitching earned him a spot on the American League All-Star team, which provided Charlie Finley with an opportunity to unveil his inherent cheapness. The producers of a special All-Star Game portrait asked the A's' publicity office (translation, Finley) to provide them with a photograph of Hunter. The photograph would serve as the model for the painter of the portrait. Instead of providing an updated photo of Hunter, with his longer hair and mustache, Finley sent a five-year-old picture of "The Cat" to be used in creating the portrait. Hunter's appearance had changed considerably in the last half decade, perhaps more so than any Oakland player had. No longer short-haired and clean-cut, Hunter looked unrecognizable to most fans in the outdated photograph and portrait. Another one of Finley's cost-cutting measures ended up embarrassing his star pitcher, and even more so, the organization itself.

Hunter's appearance in the All-Star Game became a regrettable one for more important reasons, as well. In the second inning of the game, Hunter faced Cubs outfielder Billy Williams, who smacked a line drive toward the mound. Instinctively, Hunter tried to field the ball barehanded—an unfortunate decision, as it turned out—and incurred a hairline fracture to his right thumb. Already ailing from his appendectomy, Williams became more pained as he watched helplessly from the American League dugout.

Doctors placed Hunter's thumb in a splint for several days before removing it. A hardy Catfish began throwing six days after sustaining the injury, which led doctors to predict a quick recovery period of only two weeks. If so, the break would force Hunter to miss about four or five starts; that was big news, considering that he had last missed a starting assignment seven years earlier in 1966 due to an appendectomy. An optimistic Hunter mused that the injury might provide a long-term benefit. "Heck, it might help me," Hunter reasoned in an interview with *The Sporting News*. "I need the rest. I'll be strong for August and September."

In the short term, the injury to Hunter left the A's wondering whether to disable their star right-hander. At first, Charlie Finley decided to place Hunter on the injured list and called up nine-year minor league catcher Jose Morales from Tucson. Finley then changed his mind, and told Morales to report back to Tucson after just one day with the major league club. One day later, Finley decided to disable Hunter, and left instructions with Morales to return to Oakland from Tucson. Incredibly, Finley changed his mind a third time and decided to keep Hunter on the active list; yet, instead of demoting Morales, he sent pitcher Dave Hamilton back to Triple-A. Dick Williams finally rewarded Morales with a start as designated hitter in a game at Boston's Fenway Park. Making his long-awaited major league debut, the 28-year-old rookie responded with a double in four at-bats against Luis Tiant—not the easiest pitcher for a right-handed hitter like Morales to face. After nearly a decade of pounding the minor league pavement, and then a series of indecisive moves by the Oakland brass, Morales had finally collected his first big league hit.

With Morales' roster situation settled, the A's hoped to finalize their roster maneuverings with Hunter. The organization initially hoped to place Hunter on the disabled list retroactive to the All-Star Game, but Commissioner Bowie Kuhn refused to allow such a move. Then came more potentially bad news. A New York City doctor informed Hunter that he wouldn't be able to pitch for at least two weeks. The A's physician didn't agree, however. Dr. Harry Walker refuted the New York medical prediction, saying that Catfish could return in less than seven days. Dr. Walker's prognosis pleased Finley but upset Hunter, who claimed his thumb was still very sore. Hunter subsequently tried to throw batting practice, but revealed that his thumb hurt so appreciably that he couldn't cut loose with either his fastball or his most necessary out-pitch—the slider. A few days later, Catfish reported improvement in the hand's condition, lending some credence to the soothsaying skills of the Oakland doctor.

Hand injuries continued to affect the A's when, two days after the All-Star break, Joe Rudi jammed his thumb badly while slipping on a wet patch of outfield grass in Minnesota. Rudi then developed a bad case of strep throat, which forced him into a short hospital stay. Doctors treated Rudi for several sores in his mouth and swollen tonsils before releasing him from the hospital.

Another injured player, outfielder Billy Conigliaro, returned to the lineup on July 27, just in time to face Twins ace Bert Blyleven. The young right-hander possessed one of the biggest-breaking and most deceptive curveballs in the major leagues, in addition to an above-average fastball. Not so surprisingly, the right-handed hitting Conigliaro went 0-for-4 in his start against Blyleven, who struck out nine Oakland batters. One reporter asked Conigliaro why he hadn't delayed his return so as to avoid a date with the sweeping curveball of Blyleven. "You can't wait to come back against some guy you like [to face]," Billy C. responded to *The Sporting News*, while adding that there weren't many pitchers he found easy to hit.

Although the A's improved their level of play considerably in July, their record still lagged behind their won-loss pace of 1972. Charlie Finley believed that one of the reasons for the fallback could be found in the poor play of his once-sturdy bench. Oakland's pinch-hitting statistics revealed plenty about the inability of reserve players to deliver timely hits. Jay Johnstone had gone 0-for-12 as a pinch-hitter since his recall from Tucson. Angel Mangual also went hitless in a dozen pinch-hitting appearances. Rich McKinney, expected to be one of the regular designated hitters at the start of the season, was just 2-for-17 off the bench. Even Mike Hegan, an exceptional pinch-hitter in 1971 and '72, repeatedly failed in pinch-hit situations, with just one hit in 17 at-bats. And the previous year's late-season sensation, Gonzalo Marquez, had long since been demoted to Tucson.

On July 30, the Oakland bats fell completely silent against Rangers starter Jim Bibby. The giant-sized right-hander, who had been acquired in a June trade with the Cardinals, struck out 13 batters in compiling a no-hitter against the A's. Rangers outfielder Jeff Burroughs blasted a grand slam to support Bibby's 6–0 win.

The following day, Charlie Finley reacted to the embarrassment of being no-hit by the last-place Rangers—and the club's continuing pinch-hitting inadequacies—by announcing *three* transactions. Finley signed infielder Mike Andrews as a free agent and purchased two veteran pinch-hitters: the Pirates' Vic Davalillo and the Astros' Jesus Alou. In order to make room for the new players, the A's demoted Johnstone and McKinney to Triple-A, and also optioned rookie pitcher Glenn Abbott, who had thrown the ball poorly in his first major league go-round.

Much like he had in 1972, when he picked up Matty Alou and Dal Maxvill for the stretch run, Finley swiftly and directly addressed the team's greatest need. In 1972, the A's had desperately required help at second base and in the outfield; suddenly, Maxvill and Alou appeared through the sleight-of-hand known as post-deadline waiver trades. Now, with the A's requiring more capable clutch hitting in the late innings, Finley had successfully hand-delivered Matty's brother, Jesus, along with veterans like Andrews and Davalillo.

Unlike Alou and Davalillo, Andrews cost the A's nothing in terms of return talent. Earlier in the summer, Andrews had asked for—and eventually received—his release from the White Sox. The reason for his discontent? He had clashed with Chicago's unpopular general manager, Stu Holcomb, who had publicly criticized Andrews' playing ability, saying he couldn't hit, field, or throw. Holcomb's opinion of Andrews clashed with that of Dick Williams, who had managed Andrews during his first managerial tenure in Boston. Williams had far more pleasant memories of the veteran infielder. In 1967, Andrews had contributed to the Red Sox' "Impossible Dream" by hitting a respectable .263, playing a solid second base, and teaming well with shortstop Rico Petrocelli. More importantly, Andrews had impressed Williams with his professionalism, work ethic, and attitude.

As for Davalillo, he employed one of the strangest batting styles in either league. A left-handed slap hitter, Davalillo bailed out severely on pitches, stepping toward the first-base dugout with his front foot. Although this approach contradicted most fundamentals of good hitting, Davalillo had managed to set a single-season major league record by collecting 25 pinch-hits for the St. Louis Cardinals in 1970. The following year, Davalillo joined the Pirates in an offseason trade, hitting .285 as a part-time player. Davalillo filled in ably at first base and at all three outfield positions, playing a subtle role in helping the Pirates to a World Championship. After another fine season in 1972, in which he hit a career-high .318 in 117 games, Davalillo saw his playing time and hitting effectiveness diminish in 1973. The dwindling role upset the 34-year-old Venezuelan. "I was doing nothing at Pittsburgh except pinch-hitting once every four or five days," Davalillo told Ron Bergman, corresponding for *The Sporting News*. "I don't mind pinch-hitting. It's just hard to do when you do it only once a week. I don't mind it three or four times a week."

Like Davalillo, Jesus Alou featured an unusual hitting style, with his high leg kick and continually twitching neck. Curiously, he also became the third member of the Alou clan to play for the A's. The acquisition of the youngest Alou completed a neat and orderly succession of brothers appearing in Oakland uniforms: oldest brother Felipe had played for Oakland in 1970 and '71; middle brother Matty had arrived late in '72; and now Jesus was joining the green and gold in the midst of '73. Although Felipe, Matty, and Jesus had once played for the rival San Francisco Giants in the same outfield in 1963, their tenures in Oakland failed to overlap, preventing them from becoming teammates as members of the A's.

In reacting to Finley's latest round of trades and signings, Reggie Jackson placed the A's' continuing state of flux in proper—and humorous—perspective. "I want to be a member of the Oakland A's forever," Reggie declared tongue-in-cheek to *The Sporting News*. "That way I get to meet all the famous ballplayers coming and going." As a member of the A's since 1967, Jackson knew of what he spoke. During Reggie's tenure in the Bay Area, Finley had acquired the following list of notable players in mid-season transactions:

1973—Jesus Alou, Mike Andrews, Vic Davalillo, and Deron Johnson (soon to be followed by Rico Carty)

1972—Matty Alou, Orlando Cepeda, Dal Maxvill, Don Mincher, and Art Shamsky

1971—Curt Blefary, Mike Epstein, Mudcat Grant, Mike Hegan, and Darold Knowles

1970—Tommy Davis and Bob Locker

1969—Bob Johnson, Juan Pizarro, and Fred Talbot

1967—Ken "Hawk" Harrelson

Finley's penchant for mid and late-season trades had allowed Jackson to play with several members of one of baseball's most famous families (the Alous); one of the game's greatest stars of the early sixties (Tommy Davis); a future Hall of Famer whose peak years occurred in the late sixties (Orlando Cepeda); two important contributors to the Twins' 1965 American League championship team (Don Mincher and Mudcat Grant); a key member of the lovable Mets championship team of 1969 (Art Shamsky); and one of baseball's most colorful characters, a true symbol of the "mod" generation (Hawk Harrelson). In many ways, Finley had assembled a "Who's Who" of baseball from 1967 to 1973.

Smart man that he was, Jackson expected more well-known names from the recent past to be playing for the A's before the end of the season. "Charlie will probably go over to the National League in September and get someone with 300 to 400 career home runs," Jackson predicted with a grin to *The Sporting News*. "I wouldn't be surprised to see Willie McCovey over here." Although Reggie was most likely being facetious in his comments, he wasn't far off base—just a bit ahead of schedule. The 35-year old McCovey, who was in the midst of a productive 29-home run, 75-RBI season in San Francisco, wouldn't be arriving in Oakland in 1973; his arrival would have to wait three more years, when he would join the A's for 24 late-season at-bats. When it came to star players who were winding down their careers but still had some productivity left in their bats, no one loved them more than Charlie Finley.

Another first baseman, Mike Hegan, had been one of Finley's mid-season pickups during the 101-win season of 1971. Although Hegan had never been a star player along the lines of an Orlando Cepeda or Tommy Davis, he had gained notoriety for two reasons. First, he was the son of former major league catcher Jim Hegan, a fine defensive receiver with the Indians and later a long-time coach with the Yankees. Second, Hegan had played for the 1969 expansion Seattle Pilots, an awful team forever immortalized by Jim Bouton in his famed book, *Ball Four*. Hegan was now making news for another reason. In late July, he announced that he would retire after the current season. Although Hegan was just 31 years old, he had tired of performing as a bench player since his departure from Milwaukee, and longed for an opportunity to play elsewhere as an everyday first baseman or outfielder. With a still youthful Gene Tenace entrenched at first base, and with Joe Rudi, Billy North, and Reggie Jackson established in the outfield, Hegan saw little opportunity to break into Oakland's starting nine. As Hegan says, "I think what happens, and I felt it happening to me, is that the carryover effect of playing every day can only last so long when you're in a utility role. By that, I mean the ability to stay sharp. Once it becomes another year and you only go to bat a hundred times, it's just difficult to compete or be productive over a period of more than a couple of years, I think. It was for me, at least personally. And that's why it's so difficult to come off the bench. That's why maybe a bench player lasts a couple of years [with a team] and then you bring another bench player in. It's just so difficult to go up against a Nolan Ryan in the eighth inning with one shot at him when you really haven't played for two years. Everything is in his favor."

Hegan realized that he had the ability to pursue other careers, having worked as a television sportscaster for WTMJ-TV in Milwaukee during the winters. The A's certainly recognized his broadcasting ability; they had actually asked him to fill in for one of their regular announcers, Jim Woods, earlier in the season. Moments before the July 18th game against the Orioles, Dick Williams had told Hegan to put on dress slacks and a collared shirt and report to the broadcast booth as a replacement for Woods, who had taken ill. Incredibly, the backup first baseman-turned-broadcaster announced the first three innings of the game against Baltimore, then rode the elevator back to the clubhouse to make himself available to play in the later innings. Hegan hurried into his A's uniform and returned to the dugout. As it turned out, Hegan didn't need to rush back, since Dick Williams chose to use Jay Johnstone—and not Hegan—as a pinch-hitter for Dick Green in the late innings. Hegan, by the way, received union scale wages for his three-inning effort in the booth.

Although Hegan did enjoy his part-time broadcasting gigs, a full-time announcing job would have to wait a few years. Deep down, Hegan really wanted to continue his on-field career, assuming he could find another team, one that would provide him with a regular playing role. Just a few days after announcing his retirement plans, the Yankees (in need of some additional left-handed hitting) rescued Hegan, acquiring the backup first baseman for $20,000.

At the time of the transaction, Hegan left one first-place team for another. Within a few days, the Orioles stormed past the Yankees on their way to winning the American League East. Does Hegan, in retrospect, feel any regret over leaving a winning team, one that had just begun to tap its championship ability? "The winning is fine," says Hegan, "but from a personal standpoint, the one reason we all play the game is to *play* the game, if possible. I wanted one more opportunity to play every day again."

Yet, Hegan fully realized he was departing a special team, one that would emerge as a dynasty in the early part of the decade. "I knew that I was leaving probably, what would have been and should have been, the dominating team of the entire seventies. If it hadn't been for free agency, they certainly would have been."

Chapter 16

Second-Half Soap Opera

The A's soon discovered that their new infield acquisition, Mike Andrews, was damaged goods. A solid defensive player in past years, he could not even make a routine throw from his position at second base. Andrews claimed that his arm was fine, but the physical evidence dictated otherwise. After watching him make two bad throws, Dick Williams announced that he would not use Andrews in the field anymore. Williams would restrict his new acquisition to pinch-hitting appearances and occasional use as a designated hitter.

In addition to injuries, illness had become one of the unfortunate themes of the Oakland summer. In July, Dick Williams had been stricken by appendicitis. Charlie Finley had not been feeling well for much of the season, either. On August 7, Finley's health reached a low point when he suffered a heart attack—the probable result of too many long hours spent questioning his manager's decisions and trying to make trades. Unfortunately for Williams and the A's' players, Finley's heart attack would drastically affect his behavior for the duration of the season.

On August 12, the A's played perhaps their wildest game of the season against the Yankees. The A's trailed the Yankees 11–5 after six innings, before scoring six runs in the seventh and two more in the eighth. The incredible late-game rally gave Oakland a 13–12 comeback win on the road. Yet, the A's had played so poorly early in the game that Williams had come close to pulling his regular players in favor of a wave of reserves. "It was so bad," Williams told sportswriter Joe Durso, "that if we didn't score a few runs in the seventh, or at least get within striking distance, I was going to put in all of our other guys. I had six guys on the bench ready to go in the sixth inning." The victory, inspiring enough in and of itself, proved even more meaningful since it allowed the A's to move within one game of first place in the West.

In August, Williams made two important strategic decisions to improve the fortunes of the A's. One involved leadoff man Campy Campaneris, who had been having difficulty getting on base and had failed to steal a single base over a three-week span of time before finally picking up a theft against the Red Sox on August 16. The next day, Williams flip-flopped Campaneris and Billy North in the lineup, putting North in the leadoff spot and pushing Campaneris to the No. 2 slot in the order. Williams recognized that the younger North was hitting for a higher average, drawing more walks, and stealing bases more efficiently than the more experienced—but slumping—Campaneris.

While baseball statisticians might have argued that Wlliams' decision was an obvious one, it still required some degree of courage. Campaneris was one of the A's' most senior veterans, a player who had been with the organization since 1964. Campy and his teammates might have regarded Williams' lineup adjustment as an outright demotion; after all, the leadoff spot carried with it a notion of glamour and excitement, while the No. 2 spot was considered a position for comparatively less capable hitters and baserunners. Yet, Williams understood the following: although the speedy, slap-hitting Campaneris *looked* like a leadoff hitter, he really *wasn't* a leadoff hitter. Campy didn't hit for a high enough batting average or exhibit nearly enough patience at the plate to reach base the requisite 38 to 40 per cent of the time, figures considered acceptable for a table-setting hitter. Although Williams had used Campaneris as a leadoff man in past years, he had done so in large part because of the absence of other players even remotely capable of handling the job. Now, with the off-season addition of North, Williams had been presented with another option. With the more patient North batting leadoff, and Campaneris able to utilize his bunting and hit-and-run skills in the second spot, the top of the A's' lineup took on a far more dynamic ability.

Williams made an even more daring strategic decision with his pitching staff, which presently counted only Vida Blue and Ken Holtzman as certified starters. Faced with a sudden shortage of starting pitchers, a void that was created by the thumb injury to Catfish Hunter and the continuing slide of Blue Moon Odom, Williams turned to his ample bullpen supply for a fill-in starter. He decided to pick his best left-handed relief pitcher, Darold Knowles. It was certainly an interesting choice, given that the nine-year veteran hadn't started a game since 1967, when he had made exactly one start for the Washington Senators.

On August 14, Knowles made his *fourth* start of the season for the A's. Knowles faced the powerful Red Sox at Fenway Park, often noted as a graveyard for left-handed pitchers. Pitching carefully to a lineup that included dangerous right-handed hitters like Tommy Harper, Luis Aparicio, Orlando Cepeda, and Carlton Fisk, Knowles walked five batters on the night and struck out only one. In spite of that unsightly strikeout-to-walk ratio, Knowles scattered only six hits and kept the Red Sox off the scoreboard for nine innings. He also pitched under pressure throughout the night, considering that the A's managed to score just one run against Bill Lee on a sixth-inning squeeze bunt by Dick Green. Knowles' complete-game shutout at Fenway Park represented one of the most amazing—and unlikely—pitching performances of the 1973 season.

Five days after Knowles' masterpiece against the Red Sox, Catfish Hunter returned to the mound. Hunter pitched five innings of three-run baseball, earning a no-decision in the A's' 6–4 win over the Brewers. In that same game, the recently acquired Jesus Alou collected two hits as he continued to fill in ably for the sidelined Joe Rudi. In his last four starts, Alou had managed three two-hit games. Charlie Finley could pat himself on the back for another mid-season deal well done.

The return of Hunter, however, stood out as the big story. "The Cat" had initially been expected to miss only a couple of weeks; he ended up missing nearly a month. During his absence, the A's had seen their two-and-a-half-game lead in the West transform into a two-game deficit, before a late surge enabled them to reclaim a two-game lead by the time Hunter returned. For nearly a month, Dick Williams had scrambled to find starting pitching, plucking Knowles and others for emergency duties.

When healthy, Hunter didn't dazzle onlookers with gasping fastballs or high strikeout games. Even though he lacked the velocity of Vida Blue, he nonetheless challenged hitters. Hunter also displayed the ability to "pitch to the scoreboard," showing a willingness to pitch very aggressively with a big lead. "He isn't afraid of giving up a lot of hits," remarked Reggie Jackson in an interview with Pat Jordan of *Sport* Magazine. "If he's got a big lead in the eighth, he'll just lay it in there and make them hit it. He doesn't care if he beats you, 11–10, as long as he beats you."

Without Hunter, the A's had lacked their most important pitcher, the man most capable of winning big games—both in the regular season and post-season. "There's the most valuable player on our club," shouted Jackson in front of reporters, while pointing directly at Hunter. "[By being injured] he's fouled up a whole pitching staff by himself." A humble Hunter refused to accept Reggie's humorous form of praise. "I don't think I am the club's most valuable player," Hunter told *The Sporting News*. "I would have to say Jackson is with the year he's been having."

In a sense, Catfish was right. During Hunter's layoff, when the A's needed their offense to pick up the requisite slack for a faltering pitching staff more than ever, none of the Oakland hitters had raised their level of hitting as much as the maturing Jackson. On August 18, Jackson simultaneously reached the two seasonal milestones considered most important to accomplished power hitters: 30 home runs and 100 RBIs. Jackson benchmark game included a three-run, first-inning home run against Milwaukee's Jim Slaton, highlighting a 6–3 win over the Brewers. On August 24, Jackson decided to rid himself of one of his season-long features—his beard—but retained his hot hitting stroke with two singles and a pair of RBIs, helping Hunter to his first win since his return from the injured list. "He still looks the same to me," Dick Williams told *Sports Illustrated* in describing his now beardless slugger.

Ray Fosse did notice some differences in *Hunter*, making only his second start since his return from the disabled list. After the game, Fosse told *Sports Illustrated* that Hunter was "not popping, just pushing the ball, maybe afraid to cut loose after his layoff." Since most baseball people considered Fosse an astute observer of pitching, Hunter's right arm would bear watching over his next several starts.

During an East Coast trip that included stopovers in Detroit, New York, and Boston, the A's finally began playing the kind of high-caliber baseball that they had achieved throughout much of the '71 and '72 seasons, but had eluded them for most of the summer of '73. The A's won two straight games against the Yankees, three consecutive vs. the Red Sox, continued the assault at home with three straight wins against the Brewers, and finished the stretch with a single victory over the Tigers. The string of successful games against Eastern Division clubs added up to a season-high nine-game winning streak. The A's lost their next game to Detroit, ending the succession of wins, but the defeat proved to be a minute blip in the day-to-day evolution of the standings. Oakland won the final game of its series with the Tigers, and then swept the Yankees in a three-game set. The new four-game win streak gave the A's 13 victories in their last 14 outings.

In the finale against the Yankees, Ken Holtzman and Vic Davalillo teamed up on a taut, 1–0 win. Unlike another July 31st acquisition, Jesus Alou, Davalillo had struggled badly since trading in his Pittsburgh whites for the green and gold of Oakland. His first hit in 13 days drove home the only run of the game in support of Holtzman, who actually used an injury to *improve* his pitching. Holtzman sprained his ankle slightly while tripping over a loose bat, but the twist in his foot helped prevent him from over-throwing his fastball while also encouraging him to fine-tune his control. Aided by the unfortunate circumstance-turned-benefit, Holtzman set down the final 18 Yankees he faced en route to a complete game shutout.

While the continuing development of Billy North settled Oakland's long-standing search for a center fielder, it made another outfielder extraneous in the playing time plan. Billy Conigliaro, the No. 1 center fielder at the end of spring training, had fallen into a state of disuse. "They're going to retire my uniform," Conigliaro told *Baseball Digest*, "with me still in it." At least Billy had retained his sense of humor, something he had failed to do during his miserable experience in Milwaukee the previous summer.

According to the latest press box rumors, Oakland seemed primed to become the hub of a Conigliaro family reunion. Newspaper reporters discussed the possibility of the A's signing Tony Conigliaro, who had retired from the Angels due to eye problems in 1971. Ironically, "Tony C." had played his final game that year against the A's. In a 20-inning marathon loss that night, Conigliaro suffered through a strikeout-filled 0-for-8, twice engaging in shouting matches with home-plate umpire Merlyn Anthony over balls and strikes. Tony C.'s five strikeouts convinced him he could no longer see well enough to hit a thrown baseball.

If the A's signed Conigliaro, where would they play him? With Reggie Jackson marching toward an MVP Award, right field was out of the question. The designated hitter void had long since been filled by National League castoff Deron Johnson. Perhaps the A's were considering Conigliaro for left field, where Joe Rudi's play had been undermined by prolonged hitting slumps, repeated viral infections, and subsequent losses of weight.

As quickly as the Conigliaro rumor arose in the press box, Dick Williams shot it down. He denied that the A's possessed any interest in the former Red Sox and Angel slugger. Williams' denial seemed plausible, given the strains between him and Conigliaro in Boston several years earlier. After Tony C. had been struck in the head by a Jack Hamilton fastball in 1967, he laid near death in a hospital bed for several days. Conigliaro remained a captive of the hospital for a few more weeks, and bitterly complained when Williams did not visit him even once. Williams reacted to the criticism by insisting that he felt sympathy for Conigliaro, but regarded his obligation to a pennant-contending Red Sox team as his most important job priority. Since it seemed questionable that Conigliaro wanted to attempt a comeback with *any* team two years after his retirement, even observers of the A's (who had come to expect surprises) had to wonder why he would consider a return to a manager whom he felt had abandoned him six years earlier.

The A's did make a roster move, albeit one of less headline-making ability than any signing of Conigliaro. Charlie Finley gave up his World Series pinch-hitting hero, sending Gonzalo Marquez away in a trade, just as he had another 1972 bench stalwart, Mike Hegan, earlier in the summer. Marquez had fallen victim to an unexpected by-product of the newfangled DH rule. With the option of pinch-hitting for the pitcher's spot becoming a moot point, the general importance of a pinch-hitter-deluxe like Marquez had been largely reduced. On the few occasions that Williams had seen fit to use him, Marquez found his batting stroke wanting due to extended stretches of inactivity.

Finley dealt Marquez to one of his favorite trading partners, the Cubs, perhaps hoping that he would strike gold for a third time—after already reeling in Ken Holtzman and Billy North from the Windy City. In exchange for the one-dimensional Marquez, the A's acquired another left-handed first baseman, a little known player named Pat Bourque. Although the Cubs considered Bourque an unremarkable prospect, he did possess two traits foreign to Marquez' game: a competent glove and slightly above-average power. The A's hoped that Bourque would fill the gap created by the dual partings of Marquez and Hegan.

Although Holtzman had pitched well during a major league career that began in 1966, the veteran left-hander had never reached the 20-win plateau in a single season. In 1972, Holtzman had settled for 19 wins, falling short of the milestone due to a run of bad luck and poor run support. On September 4, Holtzman faced the Angels, trying to push his win total from an unglamorous 19 to the magic circle. Holtzman faced hard-throwing right-hander Bill Singer at Anaheim Stadium. Holtzman barely out-dueled his veteran counterpart, winning a 4–3 decision. In his eighth major league season, Holtzman had finally achieved the notoriety that came with winning 20 games.

The next day, reporters asked Holtzman how he felt in the aftermath of win No. 20. "Super," the normally reserved Holtzman replied to *The Sporting News*, before becoming even more candid. "A little hung over, but super." Holtzman seemed relaxed on his off day, in sharp contrast to the way he usually behaved on days in which he was scheduled to pitch. "Ken is always nervous before a game," Dick Williams told *The Sporting News*. "He bites his fingernails and the skin around them. Have you ever seen his nails? Also, he's pretty silent on the days he pitches." Thanks to his 20th win, Holtzman's silence had given way to a momentary outburst of glee.

Both Holtzman's catcher and pitching coach agreed on the reason behind the left-hander's newfound success in the American League. "His control is what makes him so effective," Ray Fosse explained in an interview with Bay Area sportswriter Glenn Dickey. "He has good stuff…but the main thing is, he can get the ball where he wants it." Pitching guru Wes Stock also marveled at Holtzman's ability to throw strikes while maintaining a high velocity. "I've never seen a pitcher who throws as fast as he does who has his control," Stock told Dickey. "He gets the ball exactly where he wants it time after time. You keep waiting for him to miss, but he almost never does."

Although Stock praised Holtzman's fastball, Dick Williams had actually wanted the left-hander to rely more heavily on his array of breaking pitches. On this issue, Holtzman politely disagreed with his manager. "My fastball is my best pitch," Holtzman insisted in an interview with Dickey. "I have much better control with it than with the curve. If I get in a tight spot, 99 per cent of the time I'm going to throw my fastball." In one game alone, Holtzman had thrown fastballs on 91 out of 97 pitches, a remarkably high ratio. Williams could hardly argue with the bottom-line results.

On an unhappy front, the frustration that Sal Bando and other Oakland players had felt with pinch-runner Allan Lewis was now being shared by Charlie Finley. The Oakland owner had grown dissatisfied with Lewis since his most recent recall from the minor leagues on September 1. In one September game, Lewis missed a steal sign from third-base coach Irv Noren; on two other occasions, he succeeded in allowing himself to be picked off. Perhaps at the age of 31, Lewis had lost a crucial step, jeopardizing his only positive attribute—speed. As a result of the growing list of miscues, Finley sought another pinch-running alternative. He offered $50,000 to the Royals for a minor league prospect named Kenzie Davis, who had set a California League record by stealing 80 bases. The Royals rejected Finley's cash-only offer.

More bad news arrived on September 8, when Reggie Jackson sustained a pulled hamstring, an injury that he frequently encountered due to the muscle-bound nature of his legs. Jackson, leading the league with 112 RBIs, strained his hamstring while running hard from first to third on an extra-base hit. A similar, but more serious injury had prevented Jackson from participating in his first World Series in 1972; fortunately, the A's believed the latest occurrence would sideline him for a moderate length of seven to 10 days, allowing him to return for any post-season games.

Jesus Alou, hitting .322 since his arrival from Houston, stepped into the right field vacancy. Alou had previously filled in well for an ailing Joe Rudi in left field. "It's funny," remarked Alou to *The Sporting News* in discussing his new role as Oakland's fourth outfielder. "I was on a team like Houston, in fourth place, and I didn't play. Then I came over here to a team that is running for a pennant and I play."

Alou attributed his latest spree of hitting success to a curious tendency at the plate, an offspring of an aggressive approach at the plate that reminded observers of the free-swinging nature of contemporaries like Roberto Clemente and Manny Sanguillen. "I have always swung at bad pitches," Alou admitted to Ron Bergman.

"But now I am swinging and missing. I used to swing at bad pitches and hit them. That was hurting me because every time I hit a bad pitch, it was so bad I couldn't get good wood on it. Now I swing and miss the bad ball and that gives me a chance to come back and hit a better pitch." In a strange way, Alou's offbeat analysis made sense, but left one question unanswered. Why was he swinging and missing more often than before? Even Alou could not provide an answer to that particular mystery.

The least talented of the Alou brothers, Jesus possessed the most distinctive batting style at the plate. Jesus typified the term "nervous hitter," with his constant body twitching, Clemente-like neck rotations, and stylish bat twirling. Alou exhibited so many extraneous movements before, during, and after each one of his swings that Dick Williams could no longer bear watching him during his at-bats. Instead, Williams waited to hear the sound of bat-meeting-ball before daring to look up from his position in the dugout.

Despite the fine hitting of Alou and the presence of Vic Davalillo behind him, rumors continued to circulate about the acquisition of another outfielder. One speculated trade had the A's sending onetime Rookie of the Year candidate Angel Mangual and slumping veteran Blue Moon Odom to the Red Sox for outfielder Reggie Smith, who had requested a trade. The switch-hitting center fielder had been held back by a series of injuries, which would limit him to 115 games in 1973. Despite the physical problems, Smith was headed toward a season that would see him finish with 21 home runs and a .303 batting average; he also ran well and possessed one of the strongest outfield throwing arms in either league. So why would the Red Sox part with such a productive and talented hitter for two players who had fallen on such hard times? The Red Sox had made several bad trades in recent years, most notably the deal that had sent relief ace Sparky Lyle to the Yankees for former A's infielder Danny Cater after the 1971 season. Unfortunately for the A's, the Red Sox would not add another foolish trade to the list.

With Smith destined to remain in Boston for the balance of the season, the A's would have to seek help from within the organization. When the A's' top farm club, the Tucson Toros, saw their Pacific Coast League playoff run come to an end, Charlie Finley decided to summon reinforcements for the final weeks of the regular season. The A's recalled infielder Rich McKinney and pitcher Dave Hamilton, both of whom had spent some time in Oakland earlier in the season. When neither player reported immediately to the A's, Dick Williams castigated both of them for their tardiness. Hamilton tried to explain that their late arrival had resulted from a simple misunderstanding, but Williams had little tolerance for such excuses during a pennant race.

Another late-season recall paid his first dividend on September 11. Heralded prospect Glenn Abbott won his first major league game, an impressive five-hit, complete-game effort against the Royals. Earlier in the day, the A's did manage to make a trade with another organization when they surprisingly announced the purchase of outfielder Rico Carty from the Cubs. The onetime National League batting champion had endured a fragmented season in 1973, beginning with a failed stint as the first designated hitter in the history of the Texas Rangers' franchise. Claiming he couldn't adjust to the new DH role, Carty had hit only .232 with little power for Texas. The Cubs then acquired Carty for the waiver price, hoping that the friendly dimensions of Wrigley Field would remedy Rico's once-thundering bat. Yet, Carty hit even worse for the Cubs than he did for the Rangers, batting a punchless .214 in 22 games.

A supremely talented offensive player and arguably the best two-strike hitter of his era, Carty had enjoyed his best major league season only three years earlier. In 1970, as a member of the Atlanta Braves, Carty had led the National League with a .366 batting average and a .456 on-base percentage. He had also hit for power, accumulating career highs with 25 home runs and 101 RBIs. Then, during the offseason, Carty found his career altered by injury. A winter league collision with Matty Alou crushed his kneecap, preventing him from playing at all in 1971. Carty returned to the Braves the following summer, only to be hampered repeatedly by a pulled leg muscle.

The self-proclaimed "Beeg Boy" had also clashed with teammates throughout his career. In Atlanta, Carty had brawled with six-foot, six-inch right-hander Ron Reed in one incident and with the team's best player, Hank Aaron, in another. Carty's continuing problems with Aaron eventually influenced his trade to Texas. After his subsequent trade to Chicago, Carty sparred with another popular star player, Ron Santo, one of the Cubs' senior veterans and most prominent clubhouse leaders. Upon his arrival in Oakland, Carty pointed the finger at Santo, terming him a selfish player. Carty predicted the Cubs would never win a division title or league pennant until they ridded themselves of their longtime third baseman. Although Carty's criticism likely had little to do with it, the Cubs would trade Santo to the cross-town White Sox after the season.

Like many of Charlie Finley's acquisitions, the pickup of Carty seemed strange at the time it was made. Since the A's had acquired him after September 1, he would be ineligible for any post-season games. Furthermore, there didn't seem to be a slot for him in the lineup during the regular season either. Given his poor throwing arm, Carty posed no threat to play right field, which was already occupied by MVP candidate Reggie Jackson. So how about left field, where Joe Rudi had been slumping for much of the summer? A few weeks earlier, that scenario might have made some sense, but Rudi's bat had shown signs of a recent revival. On September 16, Rudi clubbed his first career grand slam and added a two-run double in a 9–4 win over the Rangers. Rudi's six-RBI performance was particularly impressive since he was still fighting to recover from a persistent, recurring virus.

Though listed as an outfielder, Carty's chronically fragile knees made him best suited to serve as a designated hitter, a role that he didn't like, as evidenced by his early-season flop in Texas. Deron Johnson had been a productive DH for the A's earlier in the season, but had struggled in recent weeks, his deepening ineffectiveness at the plate starting to concern Dick Williams. In an August 12th game against the Yankees, Johnson had torn a tendon in his right hand and badly jammed his thumb while sliding into third base. While Johnson tried not to use his bad hand as an excuse, the injury had robbed him of much of his bat speed, while making him vulnerable to inside fastballs and sliders. American League pitchers, quickly taking note of Johnson's injury, had wisely exploited the designated hitter's newfound vulnerability.

The A's played well in their mid-September series against Carty's former Ranger teammates, sweeping the three-game set. On September 14, in the first game of the series, Gene Tenace experienced what he told *Sports Illustrated* was "my biggest day in the majors." The hard-hitting catcher went 4-for-4 and drove in five runs in support of Catfish Hunter's 19th win, a 10-inning decision. "I looked at the scoreboard and saw that [second-place] Kansas City had lost," Tenace explained to *SI*, "and then I thought if we could win this game, we'd give Reggie Jackson another week's rest." Jackson, who had been sitting out with a hamstring pull, actually did make an appearance in the game when he pinch-hit for Dick Green.

Earlier in the month, the A's had played some of their worst baseball in another series against Texas. The ways in which the A's had lost to an inferior team particularly vexed Dick Williams, who expressed his anger at a team meeting. Williams didn't like the players' carefree behavior both during and after games with the sad-sack Rangers. After Williams' team-wide lecture, the A's captured two of three from the Royals to move six and a half games in front in the American League West.

Unlike other managers who avoided confrontations with their players, Williams believed in addressing mistakes quickly and directly. "When you make a mental error," Joe Rudi explained to the *New York Daily News*, "Dick chews you out right on the spot. You miss that cutoff man, or something like that, and when you come in from the field, you hear about it, right now. And you better not make the same mistake again." While some managers frowned on such directness out of fear of embarrassing their players, Williams' approach worked because of its consistency. "He's fair," Rudi told sportswriter Dick Young. "He'll rip into Reggie Jackson the same way he'll chew [out] a rookie. He treats everybody the same."

Two of the most pleasant individual developments of the season involved the pitching of reliever Horacio Piña and the growth of center fielder Billy North, both much-maligned offseason pickups. As a middle and long reliever, Piña continued to fool hitters with his sidearm delivery and deceptive palmball. During one stretch in September, Pina belied his frail, stringbean appearance by working in eight of Oakland's 10 games. The play of North proved even more vital. "We haven't had anybody who can go get a ball like that since Rick Monday," Dick Williams told the Associated Press. By May, North had wrested the center field position away from Angel Mangual and Billy Conigliaro. By August 17, North had moved into the leadoff spot, bumping Campy Campaneris to the second position. On September 15, North stole his 50th base of the season.

Given the aforementioned milestones, the news of September 20 came as a crushing strike to Oakland fortunes. With a runner on third and one out, North bounced a routine grounder to Twins second baseman Rod Carew. When Carew threw home to retire the lead runner, North turned his head back momentarily toward home plate as he landed awkwardly on the first-base bag. The misstep resulted in a sprained ankle. The prognosis arrived as quick and cutting to the A's; North would miss the balance of the regular season, and most likely, any playoff and World Series games.

North's impact on the A's had been considerable. He had also left an imprint on American League rivals, who had come to detest his combative, feisty, and—some would say—dirty style of play. On May 18, North had tangled with Kansas City's Doug Bird. North had also become involved in two subsequent incidents. On August 31, the Royals' Kurt Bevacqua pushed North twice while he stood a third base, in apparent retaliation for the assault on Bird. A's captain Sal Bando, standing at home plate, ran toward third base in defense of North and tackled Bevacqua. North responded well to the fisticuffs, going 6-for-14 in the three-game series with Kansas City. North said he felt special motivation for two reasons: series-long booing from the fans at Royals Stadium and racial catcalls he heard from a few select Royals partisans.

Charlie Finley's Best Trades

> Ken Holtzman from the Cubs for Rick Monday
> Billy North from the Cubs for Bob Locker
> Mike Epstein and Darold Knowles from the Senators for Frank Fernandez, Paul Lindblad, and Don Mincher
> Horacio Pina from the Rangers for Mike Epstein
> Deron Johnson from the Phillies for Jack Bastable
> Matty Alou from the Cardinals for Steve Easton and Bill Voss

In early September, the A's played the rival Angels in a series marked by cursing and trash talking between opposing players. In the September 6th game, California's Dick Lange threw a fastball directly over North's head. In this case, North had done nothing to provoke the "message" pitch; he merely had the misfortune of coming to bat after a Lange-surrendered Oakland home run. Rather than accepting the time-honored knockdown practice, North dragged a bunt between the mound and the first-base line, hoping that Lange would field the ball. Angels first baseman Mike Epstein ruined North's plan by reaching the bunt before Lange. The former Oakland slugger planted an unnecessarily firm tag on North's neck in an obvious effort to injure the pesky A's catalyst. Epstein proceeded to drop the ball, allowing North to reach first base on an error. Moments later, as Epstein prepared to hold North on the bag, the Oakland outfielder referred to the muscular first baseman as a "big goon." The remark prompted an abrupt reaction from Epstein, who was held back by an intervening Reggie Jackson. After the game, North expressed no remorse for his derogatory characterization of Epstein. "There's no one in this game who can intimidate me," North said proudly to *The Sporting News*. "There will be a time for him."

North's brash speaking manner, teamed with his on-field combativeness, had made him an unpopular player around the league. Those same qualities rated him highly in Dick Williams' mental scouting report. "North's an aggressive player," Williams told *The Sporting News* in refuting charges that his center fielder played dirty, over-the-line baseball. "He's a heck of a ballplayer. Some people say he's a hot dog, but he can play for me anytime."

North's contributions not withstanding, the A's had played uninspired, even listless ball for much of the season. Yet, their pitching and bullpen depth, buttressed by the hitting of Reggie Jackson and the relative weakness of the division, catapulted the A's to favored status in the West. On September 23, the A's officially laid rest to their divisional opponents by beating the White Sox, 10–5. An Oakland clinching—the team's third straight—had become such a yearly routine that the A's celebrated mildly after the win, quietly drinking champagne in the clubhouse.

Vida Blue won the clincher, which coincidentally represented his 20th win of the season. After a slow start, Blue's fastball had improved considerably, as had his control. Thanks also to a pair of adjustments, Blue had succeeded in making his dismal 1972 season a forgotten memory. "We've got him throwing a change-up and a hard breaking ball," pitching coach Wes Stock explained to *Sports Illustrated*. "Vida's made up his mind he wants to be a good pitcher. Eighty per cent of pitching is determination and he has all the determination in the world."

Blue's teammates had also noticed the changes in the left-hander's pitching philosophy. "In the first part of 1971, Vida was overpowering everybody," recalled Sal Bando in an interview with *SI*. "Now he is overmatching them. He found out that you can't throw the fastball for 300 innings."

In addition to recapturing some of his success from 1971, Blue had also dropped the surly demeanor that had marked much of his behavior during the latter stages of '71 and much of the '72 season. "Vida tried very hard to be an SOB," an anonymous member of the Oakland organization pointed out to *SI*, "but he's really too nice a kid to bring it off."

Yet, Blue's personality had not completely reverted back to 1971 form. "Vida's changed. The fame changed him some," acknowledged Sal Bando in an interview with Don Kowet of *Sport* Magazine. "He isn't so carefree. He's become more of a loner." Blue served as a classic example of success *not* translating into a higher degree of happiness.

With his win against the White Sox, Blue joined Ken Holtzman and Catfish Hunter in the 20-win circle; for only the 14th time in American League history, three teammates had simultaneously won 20 games. The collaboration had occurred only once before in the history of the A's' franchise. In 1931, George Earnshaw, Rube Walberg, and Hall of Famer Lefty Grove had each reached the 20-win plateau for Connie Mack's legendary Philadelphia Athletics.

Hunter, Blue, and Holtzman attacked opposing hitters with distinctively contrasting styles. Hunter relied on one key out pitch—the slider—featured by neither Blue nor Holtzman. Against left-handed hitters, Hunter augmented his repertoire with a deceiving change-up. Yet, more than anything else, Hunter succeeded because he possessed precise control of his pitches, an ability that helped ingratiate him with his catchers. Gene Tenace, who caught Hunter's pitches for parts of six seasons, says that the Oakland ace made it easy on all of the A's' receivers. "It was like a day off [behind the plate]," recalls an admiring Tenace. "[He] had tremendous control with all his pitches. You had that square box in the hitting zone; he kept it right there pretty consistently."

Hunter took special pride in pitching aggressively within the limits of the strike zone. "Know what I hate to do?" Hunter once said, thinking out loud, to Phil Elderkin of the *Christian Science Monitor*. "I hate to walk a man. It bugs me somethin' fierce, because every time you put a man on base for free it seems like he scores. I'd rather give up a hit than a walk—that's how strongly I feel about it." Not only did Hunter feel confident that he could throw any of his pitches for strikes, he *wanted* to throw them for strikes.

Hunter's control, as great as it was, only barely exceeded that of Holtzman, whose pitches featured more snap and verve than those of Catfish. Holtzman threw with the most fluid of deliveries, which made his deceptive fastball approach hitters with late explosion and movement. "What I try to do," Holtzman told Elderkin, "is set up the hitter for a pitch that I think will bother his timing." When batters began to anticipate his sneaky fastball, Holtzman countered with a large, looping overhand curveball that doubled as a change-of-speed.

Whereas Hunter and Holtzman relied on control, economy of pitches, and effective breaking balls, Blue employed a style that centered on pure power, requiring more pitches and more labor. Blue's hard-driving but seemingly effortless mechanics, which included a high kick of his powerful right leg, helped his fastball reach a pace of 94 to 95 MPH, replete with late, rising movement. Blue's recent addition of a harder breaking pitch, which featured a smaller but sharper break than his standard curveball, made him more similar in effectiveness to the scintillating pitcher of 1971 than the discounted 1972 model.

The presence of three 20-game winners on the Oakland staff vindicated the work of first-year pitching coach Wes Stock, who had replaced the amiable and popular Bill Posedel. "Bill Posedel knows more about pitching than any man I know," Catfish Hunter once told the Associated Press. Speaking anonymously, several Oakland pitchers had previously criticized Stock's relatively abrasive approach, which contrasted with the friendly, down-home style of predecessor Posedel. Yet, the comeback of Blue, the continuing improvement of Holtzman, and the sustained brilliance of Hunter had served as testimony to Stock's effectiveness.

The combined domination of Blue, Holtzman, and Hunter made the Oakland rotation the envy of baseball. In some scouts' minds, the A's had managed to surpass the excellence of Baltimore's starting rotation, which just two years earlier had featured four 20-game winners. Yes, the Orioles still had Jim Palmer, Dave McNally, and Mike Cuellar, but they had since parted with Pat Dobson, who had been traded to the Braves as part of a blockbuster deal that brought hard-hitting catcher Earl Williams to Baltimore. Based on 1973 results, one could now make a reasonable argument that the A's—and not the O's—now boasted the best group of starters in all of the major leagues.

Three 20-game winners. A third straight American League West title. A return to health of Joe Rudi and Reggie Jackson. Except for the injury to Billy North, all appeared well and calm in the Oakland kingdom. Well, not quite. In late September, the A's made news when they fired part-time scout Bill Rigney. Yet, Charlie Finley refused to call Rigney's departure a "firing."

Finley had hired Rigney, a former major league manager with the Twins, Angels, and Giants, as an administrative assistant prior to the season. Rigney's job description included a variety of duties, including broadcasting and scouting. The well-spoken Rigney served as a color announcer on radio and television for most of the season. Then, in early September, Finley removed Rigney from the booth, assigning him the more important duty of scouting the leaders in the American League East, the Orioles. Rigney joined fulltime scout Billy Herman in following the A's' likeliest opponent in the upcoming American League playoffs.

When the Orioles officially clinched the American League East, Rigney left his road assignment, figuring he didn't need to observe Baltimore's second-string lineup of backups and minor league Rochester recalls. Rigney also felt it more important to be with his wife, who had been injured in a recent fall.

Not surprisingly, Finley wanted Rigney to remain on the road stalking the Orioles. With four games to go in the regular season, Finley instructed Rigney to meet with manager Dick Williams and farm coordinator John Claiborne. Under Finley's orders, Rigney would reveal the contents of his scouting report to Williams and Claiborne, and then head home. Rigney understood Finley's directive to mean that he was being fired; Finley insisted he had not actually fired Rigney. "This was not a job on a permanent basis," Finley explained to the Associated Press during the post-season. "Because of financial conditions, we eliminated the job at the end of the season." Finley acknowledged that, with two weeks remaining in the regular season, he had ordered Rigney to scout the Orioles, but he disputed details of the broadcaster-turned-scout's departure. "He returned at the end of one week," Finley said, "and it was so close to the end of the season and since Bill had done such a fine job during the year, I told him the job was over." In Finley's mind, he had actually given Rigney a one-week paid vacation as a reward for a job well done. Clearly, Rigney felt otherwise.

Rigney's departure also left a vacancy in the broadcast booth. To replace the man that Finley called the "greatest color man that I've heard in baseball" (according to an Associated Press article), the owner hired 30-year-old Bob Waller, who had broadcast White Sox games during the 1973 season, to work the post-season games with Monte Moore. In yet another Oakland oddity, a man who had broadcast regular season games for one team would now announce playoff games for another club. After broadcasting Oakland's games in the post-season, Waller would then return to Chicago to team with former A's broadcaster Harry Caray. Only in Finley's Oakland.

Rigney could take solace in knowing that many other A's employees had lost their jobs during the season. Some had been fired; others had left on their own. The A's' playoff program depicted seven front office officials and secretaries no longer with the team. The program also contained photographs of four former Oakland players—Larry Haney, Mike Hegan, Gonzalo Marquez, and Dal Maxvill—since banished to Milwaukee, New York, Chicago (the Cubs), and Pittsburgh, respectively.

The departure of the popular and respected Rigney angered many of the players, who became even more upset when they learned they could not take their wives on the team flight to Baltimore. All of the players had expected to be able to travel with their spouses, but some were placed on stand-bye when Finley brought extra passengers on the flight. As soon as the players found out that their loved ones had lost out to a group of Finley's cronies, they were ready to put a stranglehold on the owner.

A more minor incidence of controversy occurred prior to the best-of-five playoff series against the Orioles. Former pitching coach Bill Posedel was supposed to travel with the team on its trip to Baltimore and suit up in an Oakland uniform in the dugout. When Posedel didn't make the flight, several players wondered whether Finley had interfered with the attempt at the reunion.

Controversies aside, the A's had more immediate concerns with their post-season roster of *players*. For one, their outfield had been undermined by injuries and sickness. Billy North's sprained ankle would sideline him for the entire playoff series, while Reggie Jackson's playing weight and strength and had been affected by a viral infection and a sore throat. The A's expected an ailing Jackson to play in Game One, but the injury to North left them without their center fielder and most capable leadoff batter. To compensate, Dick Williams moved Campy Campaneris back to the leadoff spot, moved Joe Rudi up to the No. 2 position, and made Sal Bando his third-place hitter. Williams also announced that Angel Mangual would assume North's position in center field.

The Oakland coaching staff might have expected that Mangual would react to the news with several leaps for joy. Earlier in the season, Mangual had stated his unhappiness as a backup and his preference for a trade. Of course, when he did play, he botched fly balls in the outfield, missed signs from the coaches, and failed to execute basic plays like the hit-and-run. Despite his frequent mental and physical mistakes, Mangual would now be the starting center fielder in the playoffs, with a chance to play a prominent role in the World Series. So how did Mangual react to being named North's replacement? He did what any Oakland player would have done: he asked to be traded. At least Mangual had the decency to say that his trade request could wait until after the season.

The collection of injuries and controversies, coupled with a general lack of respect for the Oakland ballclub, led the oddsmakers to install the Orioles as 6-to-5 favorites to eliminate the A's. "I don't believe people think of us as legitimate World Champions," Sal Bando complained to *Sports Illustrated*. "We are out to prove that we are." The prevailing sentiment of Baltimore superiority left Dick

Williams laughing. "I heard Jimmy the Greek made the Orioles 11-to-10 favorites," Williams told the *New York Times*. "That tickles me to death. Why? Because he's been wrong the last five years. And he picked Bobby Riggs, too." Riggs had predicted he would defeat Billie Jean King in the greatly hyped "Battle of the Sexes" tennis match, only to lose decidedly to the world's best female player.

With his makeshift starting lineup now in place, Dick Williams selected Vida Blue to start the first game of the American League Championship Series against the Orioles. Williams opted for his hardest-throwing left-hander, rather than staff ace Catfish Hunter, in an effort to keep Baltimore's two hot-hitting rookies, Al Bumbry and Rich Coggins, on the bench. Both left-handed hitters with intimidating speed, Bumbry and Coggins had hit .337 and .319, respectively, and had combined to steal 40 bases during the regular season. "Our job is to keep their speedsters off the bases," Williams explained to the *New York Times*. "That's one reason why I'm starting Blue." The Orioles had another blueprint in mind. Even without Bumbry and Coggins in the starting lineup, Baltimore planned to take advantage of Blue's poor pickoff move to first base. "He's got a terrible move," an anonymous Oriole informed Gannett News Service.

Williams hoped that the lack of experience of rookies like Bumbry and Coggins would hurt them later in the series, when they would encounter their first taste of the post-season. "They haven't played in a Championship Series before," Williams told the *New York Times*. "Anybody who doesn't get butterflies is crazy." The throwing of Ray Fosse also posed a hindrance to base stealers like Bumbry and Coggins. In total, Oakland catchers had thrown out nine of 16 Oriole base stealers during the course of the regular season.

In addition to considering his left-handedness, Williams selected Blue to start Game One for other reasons, too. Blue had pitched exceptionally down the stretch, making him the choice over another southpaw, Ken Holtzman. "It wouldn't surprise me if Blue was even better now than when he was having that great year in '71," observed Baltimore's Jim Palmer in an interview with *Sports Illustrated*. "He is not as tired now. He looked it [fatigued] in the '71 playoff. He had pitched an awful lot of innings."

Williams' reasoning in choosing Blue made perfect sense on several levels. Yet, Earl Weaver's right-handed platoon lineup torched the left-hander, who failed to last the first inning in Game One. Leadoff man Merv Rettenmund, replacing Coggins in right field, singled and scored on a double by former Athletic Tommy Davis. Don Baylor, subbing for Bumbry in left field, drew a walk and scored another run, helping the Orioles take an early 3–0 advantage. Baylor went on to finish the game 2-for-3 with two runs scored and an RBI. The Birds' early offensive showing proved more than enough for Palmer, who struck out 12 A's en route to an easy 6–0 win. Palmer's only real hurdle was barely avoiding Reggie Jackson's comeback smash single early in the game.

Much like their playoff series in 1971, the A's seemed to have met a superior opponent in the Orioles. Baltimore possessed advantages in the areas of pitching experience and overall depth. Over the span of two different post-seasons, the A's had now met the Orioles four times, and had lost each time. And much like the Championship Series of two years ago, Dick Williams heard the cries of second guesses from the media after the game. In the top of the first, the A's had put their first two batters on base, but left the runners stranded when the middle of the order came up empty. One reporter asked Williams why he hadn't asked his No. 3 hitter, Sal Bando, to bunt the runners over. "I'm not gonna bunt Sal Bando in the first inning for all the tea in China," responded an incredulous Williams in an interview with the *New York Times*. "Look, you people can second-guess, but I get paid to manage. Bando and [Reggie] Jackson are my two biggest RBI guys. Why would I bunt them in the first inning? If Bando bunts, then they walk Jackson."

Although very few managers would have played for the bunt in the first inning, even Baltimore players took subtle shots at Williams for his supposed strategical mistake. "I read where Dick Williams said they were going to play for runs, move the runners along," Jim Palmer told the *New York Times*. "I guess he forgot he said it."

In Game Two, Williams rested his hopes on Catfish Hunter, rather than Ken Holtzman. The decision prompted Earl Weaver to make some lineup adjustments, returning the energetic duo of Al Bumbry and Rich Coggins to the lineup. The presence of Bumbry and Coggins, however, had little impact on the game. For a change, the A's played like the Orioles, hitting four home runs against Dave McNally, while the homer-prone Hunter surrendered none. Sal Bando connected twice against McNally to lead the A's to a 6–3 win—their first ever playoff victory against the Orioles.

Bando narrowly missed a three-homer day when Bumbry leapt and stretched his glove hand over the left-field fence, bringing back a long drive. "Unbelievable," Bando told United Press International in reacting to the catch. Bando seemed just as surprised by his own performance, considering the nerves that he had felt earlier in the day. "I woke up at 7:30," Bando recalled for the *New York Times*, "and I had to get out of the hotel room. It was just nerves. I knew we had to win this game to stay alive."

Prior to the series, Jim Palmer had pointed to Campy Campaneris as Oakland's most critical offensive player. With Billy North out of the lineup, Campy had returned to the leadoff spot in the order. "I think the key to beating Oakland," Palmer had remarked to *Sports Illustrated*, "is keeping Campaneris off base." In Game Two, Campaneris reached base three times in five plate appearances, swiped a pair of bases, and scored two runs. In contrast, Baltimore tablesetters Bumbry and Coggins went a combined 2-for-9 against Hunter and Rollie Fingers. Not so coincidentally, the A's won the game handily.

Since the A's had managed a split of the two games in Baltimore, they now held the home field edge, with the third and fourth games, and if necessary, Game Five, set for the Oakland Coliseum. As the A's prepared to board their cross-country flight from Baltimore to the West Coast, a team official informed utility infielder Ted Kubiak that he might not be allowed to bring his wife aboard. Kubiak's wife had to be placed on stand-by status, awaiting the availability of an empty seat. The potential exclusion of Kubiak's wife seemed grossly unfair, considering that all other spouses were allowed to fly with the players. The players soon found out that (surprise, surprise) Charlie Finley had indirectly caused the problem. In order to accommodate over a dozen of Finley's friends—people who had no official connection to the A's—flight officials had to exclude one person. Mrs. Kubiak was probably chosen since she had decided to marry a utilityman, rather than a star like Reggie Jackson or Catfish Hunter. Fortunately, flight officials managed to include Kubiak's wife on the plane at the last minute.

Heavy rains on Sunday and Monday in the Bay Area posed a threat to Game Three, which was scheduled for Monday afternoon. Twenty minutes before gametime, American League President Joe Cronin called for a postponement, based on wet grounds and a continuing forecast of rain. Cronin's quick and early decision prompted an angry display from Finley, who argued loudly with the American League chief in the runway leading from the Oakland clubhouse to the playing field. As several media types and an embarrassed Dick Williams watched on, Finley screamed at Cronin for postponing the game so early in the day. Cronin's decision infuriated Finley on two counts: the A's had lost an almost certain sellout at the Coliseum, which was a rare event for the attendance-starved franchise, and the rainout would prove beneficial to the Orioles, who could now use Jim Palmer in Game Four on three days' rest.

"I don't think we should discuss it here in public," Cronin informed Finley. "I don't give a damn what you think," Finley fired back, according to an article in *The Sporting News*. Finley continued his mouthy diatribe, but Cronin's ruling stood. The continuing rain in Oakland throughout the day justified Cronin's initial decision; no game could have been played, either in the afternoon or evening.

A day later, the series resumed. Ken Holtzman outpitched Mike Cuellar in a game that featured a combined seven hits, three runs, and 18 strikeouts. "I never pitched a more important game or one that meant more," Holtzman would tell the *New York Times* later. With the game tied at 1–1 in the bottom of the 11th inning, Campy Campaneris led off against Cuellar. The spray-hitting Campaneris, who had reached the seats only four times during the regular season, worked the count to one-and-one before pulling a low-and-in pitch into the left field bleachers. "I look for a slider and when I see it, I hit," Campy said, simplifying the thinking behind his at-bat. "When I go up, I want to pull the ball because the third baseman is playing close to the line and there is a hole. But when I see the slider I hit it."

With the A's now up two games to one, they looked to end the series in Game Four. The A's raced out to a 4–0 lead, but Vida Blue and Rollie Fingers failed to protect the sizable margin in what had all the earmarks of a clinching game for Oakland. Fingers allowed a game-deciding solo home run to Bobby Grich in the top of the eighth, while left-hander Grant Jackson held the A's scoreless over the final two and two-thirds innings.

Rather than accept a difficult defeat gracefully and look forward to a decisive fifth game, Oakland players stewed over what might have been. "We had them by the nostrils and we let them get away from us," a disgusted Fingers said out loud in the clubhouse, according to a report in *The Sporting News*. Although Fingers was speaking to no one in particular, his next-door locker mate, Blue Moon Odom, felt Rollie was directing his comments toward Vida Blue as a way of placing blame for the defeat. "You shouldn't be talking," Odom snapped at Fingers. "If you don't give up that home run [to Grich], we don't lose the game."

Fingers yelled back at Odom, escalating the latest shouting match in the Oakland clubhouse. While the outburst might have concerned some players, others viewed the skirmish as a good sign. After all, the A's seemed to play their best when clawing at each other's throats. "We'll probably score 25 runs tomorrow," observed a wise and confident Reggie Jackson in an interview with *The Sporting News*. "You know us."

Aside from the A's' ability to play well under a veil of adversity, Jackson might have realized that Orioles manager Earl Weaver had made the curious decision to use his least experienced starter, the soft-tossing Doyle Alexander, in Game Five. Weaver's decision, which raised several eyebrows, was based on a loss of confidence in veteran left-hander Dave McNally, who had allowed two Sal Bando home runs in Game Two. Still, several writers wondered about the wisdom of switching from an experienced pitcher like McNally to a neophyte like Alexander. "To be honest," Weaver said sarcastically to the *New York Times*, "[the pitching switch] never occurred to me until about the time Bando's last shot was going over the wall."

Meanwhile, Dick Williams was concerned about the sustained ineffectiveness of one of his own players: designated hitter Deron Johnson. A productive stretch from May through July had helped Johnson become the first player in major league history to hit at least 20 home runs in a season split between the National and American leagues. (Johnson had hit one home run for the Phillies before hitting 19 for the A's.) Unfortunately for the A's, "DJ" had become an offensive nonentity in August and September. His struggles now spilled over into the post-season, where he had collected only one hit in 10 at-bats against Baltimore pitching. The extended slump apparently stemmed from a game in August, in which he had torn tendons in his right hand, causing severe pain in his thumb. Johnson talked little about the injury, until after the season. "The tendon was lying on the bone," he would explain to reporters, "and that's why it was giving me so much pain." Johnson had tried taking pain-killing shots and wrapping the thumb in sponges, but neither strategy lessened the pain.

Williams had shown patience with Johnson, but with the American League pennant on the line, he decided he could wait no longer. Williams made two adjustments in facing the junk-balling Alexander, inserting Jesus Alou as his DH replacement for Johnson, while giving the rarely-used Vic Davalillo the start in center field. Since Alexander tried to ruin batters' timing with off-speed pitches, Williams figured that he could lean on Alou and Davalillo, two of his best and most experienced breaking-ball hitters.

In the third inning, the bottom of the A's' lineup started a key rally, with some help from the Orioles' defense. Ray Fosse reached on a rare error by Brooks

Robinson, moved up to second on a sacrifice by Dick Green, and scored on a two-out single by Joe Rudi. The A's opened a more comfortable lead in the fourth inning, when Gene Tenace singled, Davalillo laced a triple, and Alou capped the rally with another single. Thanks to the July 31st acquisitions (Alou and Davalillo) and Williams' propensity to make appropriate moves at the opportune time, the A's had vaulted themselves to a 3–0 lead. The always clutch Catfish Hunter maintained the lead over the final five innings.

Hunter pitched brilliantly in perhaps his best performance under pressure to date. "You know what I like to do, really like to do?" Hunter rhetorically asked a reporter from the *Christian Science Monitor*. "I like to pitch. I'd rather be out there on the mound than anywhere. That's my business and my pleasure and man, I work at it." While other pitchers cowered under pressure circumstances, Hunter embraced them. After the series, Orioles manager Earl Weaver spoke reverently about Hunter, a man that he would have preferred pitching for *his* team in a critical fifth game situation. "He's got his doctorate in pitching," Weaver said of the leader of the Oakland pitching staff. "He's had his B.A., he went on and got his Masters, and now he's got his doctorate." Few would argue with the Weaver allegory. While the A's had exposed Doyle Alexander's youth, the Orioles had failed to break the calm of an efficient, workmanlike Hunter. "When you have a fifth game, he's the one you want pitching for you," Reggie Jackson told Leonard Koppett of the *New York Times*. "He's good *and* has the composure."

Timely, pressurized performances like the one he authored in Game Five would help earn Hunter membership in the Hall of Fame in 1987. Rollie Fingers would join Catfish in Cooperstown five years later. "Catfish, he's probably the greatest right-handed pitcher I played with," Fingers says. "When Catfish was on, I didn't even go down to the bullpen—he was that great of a pitcher. He had great control. If you had a game to win, that's who you wanted on the mound when we were playing."

In spite of a poor playoff for Vida Blue, the absence of the catalytic Billy North, and the continued helpless swinging of an injured Deron Johnson, the A's had won their second consecutive American League pennant. Of their regulars, only Campy Campaneris had produced well-rounded offensive numbers vs. the Orioles. As the A's celebrated in the clubhouse, Campaneris tried to drink simultaneously from four different champagne bottles, encouraged in Spanish by a group of Latino teammates that included Vic Davalillo and Jesus Alou. The two bench players had done *their* share by contributing some of the timeliest hits of their careers. Davalillo, a member of the Pirates' post-season teams in 1971 and '72, had filled in at first base and in center field, collecting five hits in eight at-bats. Alou had added two hits in six at-bats in the first post-season series of his career.

Even in victory, the A's failed to sidestep controversy. After the clinching victory, Reggie Jackson found himself stuck in traffic behind a pair of motorcycled police offers, who were driving under 10 miles per hour. Jackson sounded his car horn, which prompted the officers to pull him over. An angry exchange followed and a police computer check found two outstanding warrants against the Oakland star: one for a parking violation, the other for speeding. The two tickets carried a combined fine of $82. According to the police sergeant, Jackson refused to pay the fines. "I'm Reggie Jackson and I don't have to pay," the sergeant said, doing his best imitation of Jackson. Jackson spent two and a half hours in city jail before the posting of bail. It was Reggie's unique way of celebrating another American League pennant. Only in Charlie Finley's Oakland.

Chapter 17

Same Series, Different Team

Even with nearly half of the players having departed from their 1972 World Championship team—Matty Alou, Tim Cullen, Dave Duncan, Mike Epstein, Mike Hegan, George Hendrick, Joel Horlen, Bob Locker, Gonzalo Marquez, Dal Maxvill, and Don Mincher—the A's had scratched their way back to the World Series. Although oddsmakers placed the A's in the roles of slight favorites over the upstart New York Mets, Oakland faced several manpower challenges. The designated hitter would not be allowed in any World Series games, negating any dividends that a slugger like Deron Johnson might pay. Center fielder Billy North remained hobbled by a bad ankle, even though Oakland continued to list him as "questionable" for the Series. Dick Williams announced tentative plans to use Reggie Jackson in center field, while employing Jesus Alou in right field against left-handed pitching. Although Alou had hit well in the playoffs against Baltimore, the new outfield alignment represented a significant drop-off in terms of speed and defensive abilities.

In reality, North would not be able to play at all in the Series, forcing Williams to make do with his "plan B" outfield. Although his ankle remained in a cast, North hoped to travel with the team to New York for the middle three games of the Series. After Game Two, North would make his way to the Oakland Airport, only to be told that the A's had made no arrangements for him to be included on the team charter. The snub offended North, but the story would receive little attention due to another budding controversy, whose seeds were just being sown.

The issue of post-season eligibility superseded all others prior to the World Series. In the American League Championship Series, the Orioles had allowed the A's to replace two of the players on their 25-man roster. With Charlie Finley having sold backup catcher Jose Morales to the Montreal Expos on September 18 (after the September 1 deadline for freezing post-season rosters), the A's needed to petition the Orioles to employ a replacement. Baltimore gave Oakland permission to use pinch-running specialist Allan Lewis. The Orioles also agreed to allow the A's to replace an injured North with minor league infielder Manny Trillo. Thanks to the Orioles' generosity, the A's played the Championship Series with a full complement of 25 players.

While the Orioles had been gracious in making roster allowances, the A's would have to repeat the petition process with the New York Mets prior to the World

Series. The Mets agreed to permit the use of the one-dimensional Lewis, but refused to allow Trillo to play in the Series. When Finley learned of the Mets' rejection of Trillo, he actually tried to re-acquire Jose Morales from Montreal. Morales would first have to clear National League waivers. He did not, leading to speculation that the Mets themselves had claimed Morales in order to prevent the A's from using him. Even if the Mets had not, it's doubtful that the Commissioner's Office would have allowed such roster shenanigans just before the World Series. Finley's failed maneuvering, which had started with his own unwise sale of Morales after the September 1 roster-freezing deadline, left the A's with only 24 players available for their most important games of the season.

The Mets' action on Trillo, though perfectly within their rights, infuriated Finley. Charlie O. ordered the Oakland Coliseum public address announcer to make an awkward declaration prior to Game One, emphasizing that the Mets had refused to allow the A's to use Trillo in the 1973 World Series. If Finley's motivation were to simply provide Oakland fans with information, the announcement might have been defensible. But Finley had clearly tried to embarrass the Mets, who in Finley's mind, had shown audacity in refusing to play along with his roster games.

Commissioner Bowie Kuhn interpreted Finley's announcement as one inspired by sheer spite. Kuhn publicly reprimanded his favorite sparring partner among major league owners, and promised further disciplinary action after the World Series.

The eligibility issue would die down considerably after Game One, and appeared destined to become an afterthought to the Series. The late innings of Game Two would soon resurrect the roster controversy, and forever change the way that Finley would be seen by players, the fans, and the media.

Prior to Game One of the World Series, the lavish pre-game ceremonies included appearances by three celebrities. Actor Jim Nabors, a veteran of the popular *Andy Griffith Show*, performed the National Anthem. Atlanta Braves great Hank Aaron threw out the ceremonial first ball, marking one of the few times in history that an active major leaguer had performed such an honor. And Oakland's not-so-anonymous owner, Charles O. Finley, stepped out onto the field, reveling in his team's second consecutive appearance in the World Series.

Bay Area fans seemed less enthusiastic about the A's' return to the World Series. Only 46,021 fans bought tickets to Game One, far less than the capacity of the Oakland Coliseum. The atmosphere engulfing the ballpark reflected that of a spring training Cactus League game more than that of a World Series lidlifter. "When I was a kid there was excitement at the Series," Catfish Hunter explained to the *San Francisco Examiner* and *Chronicle*. "There was electricity everywhere. But there wasn't any bunting on the walls at the Coliseum. The place wasn't sold out. The crowd was acting dead. It was like an exhibition game." Hunter then delivered a message to the fans of the Bay Area. "These people don't deserve us."

Gene Tenace continued the criticism of the fans after the game. "That crowd was a joke," Tenace crowed to the *San Francisco Examiner* and *Chronicle*. "The people here just don't appreciate us and I'm tired of hearing excuses for them. They should have been standing in the aisles. If the game was played in any other city in the country, the park would be packed."

Oakland players also found fault with Charlie Finley, who had decided to allow the sale of seats in the center-field bleachers, a section normally left empty to provide the batters with a better hitting background. "The man is ridiculous," one anonymous player told the Associated Press in describing the owner's ticket policy. "Here they have all these empty seats in the upper deck and they let all those people sit in center field...There's simply no background [for hitting] this way."

The first game of the World Series pitted two left-handers, neither the ace of his respective staff. Ken Holtzman faced Jon Matlack, who owned the highest ERA of any of the Mets' starters and a sub-.500 record of 14–16. Matlack would pitch surprisingly well, except for one inning. In the bottom of the third, Matlack retired Ray Fosse and then walked Dick Green, who was thrown out stealing. With two outs and nobody on, Matlack hoped to polish off the inning by disposing of Holtzman, Oakland's ninth-place hitter. The right-handed hitting Holtzman surprised all observers by smacking a double down the left-field line. He then scored when second baseman Felix Millan allowed Campy Campaneris' simple grounder slip through his legs. Millan, normally a sound defensive player, had committed only nine errors during the regular season. Campaneris, taking advantage of Millan's fielding abnormality, stole second and came home on Joe Rudi's clutch single. The improbable two-out, two-run rally gave the A's a one-run lead heading to the ninth inning.

In the top of the ninth, Rollie Fingers faced Ed Kranepool, pinch-hitting for Don Hahn. Kranepool lined to Campaneris for the inning's first out. Fingers then walked Ron Hodges, the pinch-batter for Buddy Harrelson. When Yogi Berra called upon his third consecutive pinch-hitter, the lefty-swinging Rusty Staub, Dick Williams countered with Darold Knowles. Fingers' lack of control had clearly upset Williams, who had previously visited the mound in an effort to coax his best reliever into throwing strikes. "He wasn't concentrating," Williams said of Fingers in an interview with the *New York Daily News*. "Some guys you have to pat on the back, others you have to kick in the butt. Fingers is a *kickee*."

Knowles came on to retire the right-handed hitting Jim Beauchamp, who was batting for Staub, and then disposed of Wayne Garrett on a fly ball to short right field for the game's final outs. Thanks primarily to the surprising hitting of Ken Holtzman—and without their best reliever on the mound at game's end—the A's had taken the upper hand in the Series.

Holtzman, who had never come to bat during the regular season, took batting practice during Oakland homestands, but didn't usually fare well. "The coaches get me out easy," Holtzman said with a laugh to Red Smith of the *New York Times*. Unfortunately for the Mets, Matlack hadn't experienced similar results. "I'm not a natural hitter," Holtzman told the *San Francisco Examiner* and *Chronicle* after Game One. "I'm not even a good one." Even though Matlack had been burned by his counterpart, the Mets' left-hander didn't seem impressed. "He's a fair hitter," Matlack told Smith grudgingly.

Matlack deserved a better fate in Game One. If Felix Millan had handled Campaneris' grounder, Matlack might have pitched a shutout. The two unearned runs put New York in an early hole, forced Mets manager Yogi Berra to pinch-hit Ken Boswell for Matlack in the seventh inning, and led to an early Series appearance for ace reliever Tug McGraw. The screwballing fireman pitched two impressive shutout innings of relief, catching the attention of the A's' hitters. "I've seen good pitching for a week and haven't got a piece of the ball," lamented Dick Green to the *New York Times*. "The screwball of that last pitcher—what's his name? That's a great screwball." Rollie Fingers, who came to bat against McGraw in the eighth inning, agreed with Green's assessment of McGraw's screwball, a pitch that broke sharply away from right-handed hitters. "I couldn't have hit it with a tennis racket," Fingers admitted to sportswriter Joe Durso.

The A's had expected that the Mets would pose a threat because of their strong pitching. It came as no surprise to them because the Oakland scouting staff—comprised of Al Hollingsworth, Sherm Lollar, and Fred Goodman—had performed well in laying out accurate and informed reports about the Mets. "You can't tell an awful lot from one game," captain Sal Bando told Leonard Koppett of the *New York Times*, "but I got the impression they were just like the reports said."

In contrast to the crisp play of Game One, the Mets and A's played sloppily in the second game of the Series. A bright October sun interspersed with dark shadows created a hazy background for fielders on both teams, leading to six errors, including five by the homestanding A's. "The conditions here are very tough this time of year," Dick Williams explained to Koppett. "Luckily, we'll only have to play two more games here." Oakland players offered far less diplomatic opinions on playing at the Coliseum in mid-October. "The seeing [visibility] out there is just terrible—in the field, at bat, all over," complained Joe Rudi, usually one of the quieter A's, in an interview with Koppett "It's just a shame that World Series games have to be played under such conditions," said Sal Bando, always an outspoken critic of the Coliseum.

Fielding errors by the A's contributed to two unearned runs, which gave the Mets a 6–4 lead heading to the bottom of the ninth inning. With two outs and runners on first and second, Reggie Jackson and Gene Tenace cracked crucial RBI singles. The pair of timely hits tied the game, pushing the Mets to extra innings.

The Mets threatened to take the lead back in the top half of the 10th, when Buddy Harrelson led off with a single and moved to second on Tug McGraw's bunt. Wayne Garrett followed with a hard grounder to first, which Gene Tenace fielded nicely before throwing wildly to Rollie Fingers at first base. The error put runners on first and third with one out. Felix Millan then lofted a short fly ball to left field, where Joe Rudi made the catch. Harrelson, with above average speed as a runner, tagged and ran home, deciding to challenge the average throwing arm of Rudi. The Series' first major controversy quickly ensued.

Home-plate umpire Augie Donatelli called Harrelson out at the plate on a very close play. Willie Mays, the Mets' venerable center fielder and on-deck batter, fell to his knees, pleading with the veteran umpire to change his call. Donatelli maintained his ruling—that Ray Fosse had tagged Harrelson on the hip just before he touched the plate. Fosse, however, claimed that he had touched him on the *arm*, while Harrelson insisted that he hadn't been tagged at all. Television replays, while somewhat inconclusive at first, seemed to support Harrelson's claim that he had avoided the tag entirely.

Thanks to the questionable call, Game Two remained deadlocked until the top of the 12th. With Harrelson on third and McGraw at first, Mays bounced a two-out, run-scoring single over Rollie Fingers' outstretched arms. "I knew Fingers was going to throw me fastballs," Mays explained afterward to the *San Francisco Chronicle*. "That seems to be the only pitches any [Dick] Williams team throws me." When Cleon Jones lined a single to load the bases, Williams replaced Fingers with lefty Paul Lindblad, who would face the slugging John Milner. Milner bounded a routine grounder to second baseman, where Mike Andrews was now playing. Andrews had pinch-hit for Ted Kubiak in the eighth inning, remaining in the game to play the position the rest of the way.

Milner's ground ball had all the earmarks of the inning's final out, which would leave the A's one run down with a chance to come back in the bottom half of the inning. Yet, an uncertain Andrews stabbed clumsily at the ball, allowing it to dribble through his legs. Both McGraw and Mays scored, with Milner and Jones taking second and third, respectively. The A's now trailed by *three* runs. Jerry Grote then grounded a ball to the right side of the second base bag. Although a more difficult play than its predecessor, the grounder remained eminently playable. Andrews handled this bouncer without difficulty, but then threw wide of first baseman Gene Tenace, pulling him off the bag. Andrews' second consecutive error enabled Jones to score the Mets' fourth run of the inning. The next batter, Don Hahn, mercifully pulled a grounder to the left side of the infield, away from Andrews. Sal Bando fielded this ball without problem and threw to Tenace for the third out of the prolonged inning.

The three additional gift runs took on added significance in the bottom of the 12th, when the A's attempted to rally. Reggie Jackson tripled, Gene Tenace walked, and Jesus Alou singled to start the inning. With no one out, the A's had already managed to score one run and put runners on first and second.

If not for the three extra runs created by the infield errors, Dick Williams might have been able to utilize the mediocre-hitting Ray Fosse to sacrifice the runners over to second and third. Now, still trailing by three runs, the bunt had ceased being an option for the A's. Fosse proceeded to hit a slow ground ball to shortstop Buddy Harrelson, who tossed to Felix Millan at second base for the first out. That brought Mike Andrews, of all people, to the plate. Desperately hoping to atone for his infield butchering, Andrews worked a walk to load the bases, putting the tying run at first base. With a chance to continue a dramatic comeback, Vic Davalillo popped up to Millan and Campy Campaneris grounded to Harrelson, ending the rally—and the game.

Prior to his key RBI single in the 12th inning, much of the media had watched with anguish as Willie Mays struggled to play his position in the outfield. Several writers questioned Yogi Berra's decision to use Mays as a pinch-runner for Rusty Staub, which resulted in Don Hahn moving from center field to right field and Mays entering the game as the new center fielder. Mays failed to make two plays—when he allowed fly balls by Deron Johnson and Reggie Jackson to drop—that he would have corralled easily during his prime seasons with the A's' cross-town rivals, the Giants. "I didn't play that bad," Mays told the *San Francisco Chronicle*, disagreeing with the media's consensus that he had embarrassed himself in the field. "I'll catch the next one tomorrow."

The post-game topic of conversation soon shifted from an aging Willie Mays to an embattled Mike Andrews. After the disastrous top half of the 12th inning, Sal Bando had noticed Charlie Finley placing a call from the owner's box, located near the A's' dugout. On the other end of the line, as Bando later discovered, Oakland's team physician listened patiently to his angry employer. The impetus for Finley's call to the doctor would soon engulf the Series.

Ever the classy veteran, Andrews accepted blame for the loss and willingly described both crucial misplays. "I have no excuses," Andrews bravely told Leonard Koppett of the *New York Times* before detailing the first error. "I put my glove down for the ball and thought I had it." The second error, according to some of the A's, may have resulted from Andrews' bad back. "As I started to throw, my back started to slip and go out from underneath me." Yet, Andrews did not cite any injury in explaining why he had committed the error.

After the game, a reporter asked Dick Williams if the absence of Manny Trillo had cost the A's the game. Williams refused to use the omission of Trillo from the World Series roster as an excuse. "Let's face it," Williams told the *New York Times* bluntly, "when you get down to the 25th man, you're in trouble." Trouble indeed was just beginning, thanks to Charlie Finley.

Chapter 18

Finley vs. Andrews

Moments after the disheartening defeat, Mike Andrews received instructions to report to the team's orthopedist, Dr. Harry Walker. For a period of about five to 10 minutes, Dr. Walker examined Andrews' right shoulder. Andrews then met with Charlie Finley and Dick Williams in a private office. In a sermon that lasted approximately 40 minutes, Finley tried to persuade Andrews to sign a statement, dated October 14, 1973, and later published in *The Sporting News*, which made the following claim.

> Mike Andrews is unable to play his position because of a bicep groove tencosynotitis of the right shoulder. It is my opinion that he is disabled for the rest of the year.

Dr. Walker had signed his name to the statement. Under the words, "I agree to the above," Mike Andrews finally agreed to place his signature.

In essence, Finley had "fired" one of his players, trying to remove him from the roster in the midst of the World Series. The player "firing," a first in World Series history, was not unprecedented for Finley. During the 1967 regular season, the Kansas City A's had been struggling, a source of irritation to Finley. "Things were building to a head on one particular road trip," says Jack Aker, who was the A's' player representative that season. "One of our broadcasters was riding on the plane with us—Monte Moore. [Pitcher] Lew Krausse, who was a prankster right from the time he first came up, started ragging on Monte Moore a little bit and some other fellows came in on it. Before we know it, we had an argument on the plane. It was rowdyism, even though it was nothing that any of the stewardesses on the plane complained about. When the flight was over, they didn't complain to anyone about it, until Mr. Finley actually asked them. So, it wasn't a big deal, we didn't think.

"Then the next day, of course, we have another meeting, where Mr. Finley comes in and starts chewing everybody out. He ended up suspending Lew Krausse. At that time, Hawk Harrelson, who was outspoken, made a comment. And Mr. Finley said, 'You're gonna be gone.' Harrelson allegedly called Finley a 'menace to baseball,' a statement that Harrelson denied ever making. So we thought, well, he probably will do it, he'll probably trade him for somebody. The next day we find out he's *released* him."

Harrelson, one of the best players on the team, had been "fired," with the A's receiving nothing in return. The move surprised the baseball world, which regarded Harrelson as a quality ballplayer. Many writers wondered why Finley hadn't simply put "The Hawk" on waivers. If claimed, Finley would have received $50,000. Others felt Finley should have waited until after the season, when the trade deadline would lift, allowing him to deal Harrelson to another team. Free to sign with anyone, Harrelson ended up choosing the Boston Red Sox, more than doubling his salary with the eventual American League pennant winners.

Finley was now angry with Mike Andrews, not for anything that he had allegedly said, but for what he had done on the field. Finley contended that Andrews' shoulder injury, supposedly sustained prior to the Series, made him unavailable to play during the balance of the World Series. Finley now hoped to be able to make the case to reinstate Manny Trillo to Oakland's post-season roster. In order to fulfill his wish of adding Trillo, Finley had attempted to break the rules of eligibility, force his team physician into lying about a player's health, and publicly embarrass a respected veteran like Mike Andrews.

"The game was over and we sat for a long period of time in the bus waiting to go to the airport," says Sal Bando, recalling the scene at the Oakland Coliseum. "We did not know what was holding us up. Now we were getting cranky and complaining. It was getting ridiculous. Finally, after I'd swear it must have been an hour or so, we left. It was all during that time where Finley was meeting with the team doctor and Mike Andrews, and trying to disable him and activate Manny Trillo."

The A's reacted with disbelief when they realized that Andrews had not boarded the flight. "We found out on our way to New York," Bando says. "We were really upset because of the fact that Mike Andrews was no different in that World Series than he had been the second half of the season. He just happened to make a couple of errors." Oakland players had become accustomed to Finley's bizarre habits: his obsession with minutia, his rampant pettiness, his interference with coaches and managers. Yet, none of those annoying habits had prepared the players for the sinister act that he had committed in trying to rid himself of Andrews in mid-Series. Oakland players simmered on the flight from Oakland to New York. Finley angered them further when he ordered the stewardess to stop the showing of the flight's in-house movie, *1776*. Finley apparently didn't like the film, which he had already seen.

On the off day scheduled between games two and three of the World Series, a furious band of A's reported to Shea Stadium for a required workout. "I suggested at the workout that we wear Mike Andrews' [uniform] number on our shirts," Bando reveals. In response to the captain's words, several players taped makeshift patches featuring Andrews' No. 17 on their uniform sleeves. "Manny Trillo even wore the number of Mike Andrews," says Bando. "It wasn't anything against Manny, it was just the way it was handled with Mike [by Finley]."

Some of the A's considered taking their displeasure a step further. Reggie Jackson, who had become the A's' player representative after the trade of Mike Hegan, threatened a player boycott of the World Series. "There is a possibility of refusing to play," said Jackson, acting as the team's spokesman, in an interview with the *New York Daily News*. "There are a bunch of guys who are close to that point." Jackson also expected a grievance to be filed on Andrews' behalf with the Players' Association. If the A's' players themselves could do little to make Finley change his mind, perhaps Marvin Miller could. The head of the Players' Association pondered the question of whether Finley had done emotional harm to Andrews, thereby justifying a grievance. "Public humiliation of a player, humiliating him in the eyes of other players, aspersing his ability so as to damage his standing as a professional in the field where he earns a living—does this do him injury?" Miller asked aloud in a discussion with Red Smith of the *New York Times*. In posing the question, Miller seemed to be providing his own answer—in the affirmative.

The unified front presented by the Oakland players in the face of the treatment of Andrews provided the country with a different image of the A's. The highly publicized fights involving Vida Blue, Blue Moon Odom, and Rollie Fingers had led fans to believe that A's players didn't like each other. "People think we hate each other and that we're always fighting," Sal Bando told Red Foley of the *New York Daily News*. "That's not true. The Andrews thing proves it. We all stood behind Mike when this happened."

A report by United Press International painted Finley as the villain, at least according to the testimony of Andrews himself. Andrews told UPI that Finley had threatened to "destroy me in baseball" if he did not sign the statement that declared him injured and unfit to play. Andrews said he really didn't want to sign the agreement, but did so out of fear that Finley might follow up on his verbal threats.

Finley called a press conference that evening to respond to the verbal salvos he had been receiving. Finley reiterated his claim that Andrews' shoulder was sufficiently injured, making him unfit for World Series play. The owner added one other nugget of information, one that attempted to put Andrews in a less favorable light. Finley said that Andrews had expressed his willingness to sign Dr. Walker's statement in exchange for a guaranteed 1974 contract. "In the presence of my secretary and my farm director, John Claiborne," the Associated Press quoted Finley as saying, "Mike said he would sign that letter if I would guarantee him a contract for next year." Finley said he refused the offer. Later, Andrews denied that he had ever suggested making such a "trade"—a playing contract for the following season in exchange for his agreement to sit out the remaining games of the Series.

After Game Five, Finley would make another stunning "revelation," when he indicated that Dick Williams had played a role in the attempt to disable Andrews. "Dick thought it would be a good idea that we should have him examined by a doctor," Finley told the Associated Press on October 20. "Dick thought we had about a 10 per cent chance of getting the commissioner to O.K. it."

One day after the Finley press conference, Commissioner Bowie Kuhn met with Andrews. Then, just a few hours prior to Game Three, the commissioner rendered his ruling on the latest Finley-initiated controversy. Kuhn explained that an injured player could be replaced during the World Series, but only if he suffered a *new* injury, one deemed serious enough to create an immediate emergency requiring a new player be added to the roster. As quoted by the *New York Times*, Kuhn said that he found no proof that Andrews' pre-existing shoulder condition had "changed or worsened since the Series began, or that he had been injured in the Series." As a result, Kuhn ordered the Oakland owner to reinstate Andrews immediately, while denying Finley's request to use Manny Trillo as a substitute player on the 25-man roster.

Kuhn wasn't done. In addition to reinstating Andrews, he admonished Finley for trying to circumvent the rules while humiliating one of his players. "I might add," said Kuhn, "that the handling of this matter by the Oakland club has had the unfortunate effect of unfairly embarrassing a player who has given many years of able service to professional baseball." Although Kuhn failed to mention Finley by name, it was quite clear whom he meant in citing the "Oakland club."

Finley offered a predictable response to Kuhn's admonishment. "It is my ballclub, my money and I don't appreciate anyone telling me how to spend my money to run my business," Finley bellowed defiantly to the Associated Press. "I don't think the commissioner treated us fairly in turning down this request. He's talking about embarrassing Andrews. We're not out to embarrass Andrews. But I sure as hell was embarrassed by what he [the commissioner] did." Finley also charged Kuhn with issuing his denial letter to the media before he, as owner of the team, had received a copy of it.

Andrews attended a separate press conference in an effort to explain what had transpired between him and Finley after the second game. The veteran second baseman described an atmosphere in which a persistent, persuasive Finley had played with his emotions, making him feel guilty about the way he was hurting the team by playing with a supposedly injured shoulder. "I'm sorry I signed it," said Andrews, according to the *New York Times*, "but if I were in the same state [of mind], I'd probably do it again." Finley had tried to coerce him into signing a statement that represented, in Andrews' view, a complete fabrication. "I read a report which in my opinion was a total lie," Andrews said. "Maybe [Manny] Trillo could help the team [I thought]. I said, 'Give me the damn thing, I'll sign it.'" Andrews apologized for endorsing a dishonest statement that he knew misrepresented the facts surrounding his health. "I was embarrassed. I was beaten. For the first time in my life, I just quit," Andrews said with a tone of shame in his voice.

Throughout the episode, Dick Williams had observed the Machiavellian efforts of his owner with quiet disdain. On October 16, prior to Game Three, Williams met with his players in the clubhouse, finally ending his silence. "I'm going to deny this if it leaks out from this room," Williams said in prefacing his bombshell declaration, which was later published by *The Sporting News*, "but I'm resigning at the end of this World Series, win, lose or draw." According to some players, Williams explained that Finley's disgraceful handling of Andrews had finally pushed him to this irreversible decision, one he had been contemplating for several weeks.

Up until now, Williams had said little publicly or privately about his opinion of the Andrews mess. Williams still wasn't speaking candidly with the media about the issue, perhaps out of fear that Finley might fire him on the spot. Yet, Williams had already begun to make plans for the future. After first using a third party to let another team know of his interest in becoming their manager, he secretly telephoned officials of the New York Yankees.

One Oakland player claimed that Williams had previously told him of his desire to quit, well before the Andrews case had become an issue. Reggie Jackson said that Williams, talking to him on September 22, had informed him that he would step aside after the season. The reason? According to Reggie, Williams supposedly wanted to use Jackson as a DH while the slugger recovered from a minor hamstring pull. Finley told Williams not to use Jackson at all, apparently in an attempt to deflate his statistics and thereby reduce his negotiating power for the 1974 season. Although Finley had often tried to dictate lineup changes to his manager in the past, Williams felt he had stepped over the line of integrity with his latest demand.

Williams' resignation announcement prior to Game Three did not come as a major revelation to a veteran player like Sal Bando. "It had been floating around," Sal says, "and I think he decided he better let everyone know right then and there. It wasn't that big of a surprise. But we understood. Working for Charlie was not a normal, everyday occurrence. I mean, there were things that would happen, or he'd call Dick at the last minute. It was not baseball, and it was tough."

In the meantime, the World Series continued. The reinstated Mike Andrews, who had not made the team flight from Oakland to New York, was not available to play in Game Three, perhaps the most dramatic and well-played game of the Series. The A's won, 3–2, on Campy Campaneris' RBI single in the 11th inning. Campy's night included three hits, a stolen base, and some rare credit being sent his way. Reporters surrounded his locker after the game, putting the humble Campaneris in the spotlight usually reserved for Reggie Jackson or Catfish Hunter. Unlike his early days in the major leagues, when he hardly spoke a phrase of English, Campaneris could now answer questions posed to him by the national media. "I'm no banjo hitter," Campy told the Associated Press, "but I'm no hero, either. Many times I wish I could be a big hitter like Hank Aaron or Willie Mays, but I must be satisfied with what I've got." As Mets manager Yogi Berra put it, Campy rarely beat the opposition with a home run, "but he'll hurt you in a dozen other ways."

In the eighth inning, Campaneris had hurt the Mets by stealing a base against rifle-armed catcher Jerry Grote and scoring the game-tying run on Joe Rudi's single. Although Grote threw very well, Campaneris felt confident that he could effectively time his base-stealing jump against Tom Seaver. "I watch Seaver on television in the playoffs," Campaneris explained to the AP. "I watch him very close. Seaver is slow in his move to home plate. So I get the jump and I go." By studying pitchers on his own, as he had done since joining the Kansas City A's in the mid-1960s, Campy had once again helped his team win a game.

Unfortunately, Campaneris' moments of glory with the media were interrupted by the continuing coverage of the saga involving another Oakland middle infielder. After the 11-inning victory, Catfish Hunter claimed that the treatment of Mike Andrews had inspired the A's to play with greater intensity. "I think we busted our ass a little harder tonight," said Hunter, the starter for Game Three, in an interview with the *New York Post*. "If Finley fired everybody but nine players, we'd still go out and do our best to win." Captain Sal Bando also sounded off on the Andrews theme. "That stuff about Mike Andrews was actually good for us in the end," Bando told *Baseball Digest*. "For two whole days it made us completely forget the fact we had to face Seaver."

The win didn't completely appease Bando, however. The third baseman expressed his wishes to be traded after the Series, provided that Charlie Finley did not improve the condition of the Oakland Coliseum or the state of the team's travel arrangements. "Traveling conditions are not good and everything about the set-up at the Coliseum is not favorable," Bando complained to Red Foley of the *New York Daily News*. "For one thing, it takes too much time to get things done at the ballpark. Why do you need a written order for them to cut the grass?" Bando would later rescind his trade request.

Unlike Bando and Hunter, Reggie Jackson said that Finley's handling of Andrews had played no part in the Game Three victory. "We win in spite of him," Jackson declared in an interview with sportswriter Phil Pepe. "He's a financial empire and that's all. That's all I respect about him. It's too bad he doesn't use his money to help humanity." When a reporter asked Jackson whether Finley had ever treated him poorly for racial reasons, Jackson offered only a backhanded endorsement of his owner. "To him, all people are the same color—green."

Even though Commissioner Kuhn had reinstated Andrews to the A's' roster, at least one question remained. Would a humiliated Andrews, who had missed Game Three, rejoin the A's for the rest of the Series? Andrews telephoned Jackson from his home in Massachusetts. He wanted to know how his teammates felt about the episode and how they would react if he decided to return to the team. When Jackson told Andrews that the players supported him "100 per cent," the embattled infielder decided to book a flight to New York.

In Game Four of the Series, a 6–1 blowout for the Mets, Dick Williams sent a not-so-subtle message to Charlie Finley that the owner no longer had the final word on Andrews. In the eighth inning of a one-sided game, Williams inserted Andrews as a pinch-hitter for Horacio Piña. As Andrews strode toward home plate, the crowd of 54,817 fans at Shea Stadium treated him as one of their own, bathing him with prolonged applause as they stood from their seats. Andrews then topped an easy grounder to third baseman Wayne Garrett, who threw to first base for a routine out. As he jogged toward the Oakland dugout, the Mets' fans once again rose in support of the embattled infielder. Two standing ovations for an enemy player during the World Series. Andrews expressed appreciation for the gesture from the New York fans, not always known for their sensitive or sympathetic ways. "The ovation gave me chills, it surprised me," said an appreciative Andrews in an interview with the *New York Daily News*. "I don't think I've ever had a standing ovation in my life. To me that meant everything."

Surrounded by Met fans, Finley remained motionless in his owner's box. As Andrews ran back to the dugout, an uncomfortable Finley offered some polite applause and awkwardly waved an A's' banner. Thanks to Dick Williams' decision to use Andrews as a pinch-hitter in a lost cause of a game, the owner had received his own unsavory taste of humiliation.

Dick Green, the A's' regular second baseman, decided to have some fun with Andrews after the Game Four loss. Usually an impeccable fielder, Green had committed a fourth-inning error on a Felix Millan grounder, leading to an unearned run for the Mets. "Damn Andrews," Green said out loud in front of Murray Chass of the *New York Times*. "He fouled up that position so much I can't play it." It appeared that enough time had passed since the pratfalls of Game Two for the A's to bring back the gallows humor that often infiltrated their clubhouse.

The consensus of media opinion continued to place Andrews in a sympathetic spotlight, while targeting Finley as the proprietor of a plantation-like atmosphere in Oakland. In the November 3, 1973, issue of *The Sporting News*, Bay Area columnist Art Spander charged Finley with the following crimes:

- Ruining Vida Blue mentally during their protracted salary hassle in 1971
- Vindictively trading Mike Epstein to a last-place team as punishment for his critical assessments of the Oakland owner
- Firing scout Bill Rigney without just cause during the September stretch run
- Committing numerous acts of pettiness, such as refusing to place decorative post season bunting on the walls of the Oakland Coliseum for games One and Two of the World Series

In summary, Spander accused Finley of fostering an "atmosphere of hate" in the A's' clubhouse, with most of the anger directed toward the dictator-like owner. Spander indicated that no matter the Series' outcome, Finley had succeeded in tainting the best-case scenario of a second consecutive Oakland championship.

Finley had managed to alienate most of his players, along with the rest of the baseball world. While Finley had previously involved himself in bizarre statements and schemes, his behavior had taken a turn for the worse since suffering a heart attack in August. The irrational badgering of Dick Williams not to play Reggie Jackson, the inexplicable decision to sell Jose Morales before the playoffs, the unjust firing of Bill Rigney, the faking of attendance figures on the final day of the regular season, the cursing at Joe Cronin during the playoffs, and now, the indecent treatment of Mike Andrews had all occurred within weeks of the heart attack.

Sal Bando supports the theory that Finley's heart attack led to a major transformation in his personality. "No question," says Bando, "There was a big change in the man because I would tell you that most players—prior to the 1973 season anyhow—would consider Mr. Finley a father figure, a good friend, because he was very helpful. It seemed that with the success of the team, and with his heart attack, things started to change; he became more vindictive and more difficult to get along with."

By 1974, Finley had made enemies of almost every player on the A's' roster. "I would say that 22 of the 25 guys on our team hate him," Bando informed Marty Bell of *Sport* Magazine in July of 1974. "That holds us together." A's players often argued with each, often fought with each other. Yet, they could find common ground in their dislike of Charlie Finley.

Players like Bando saw both stages of Finley's personality, both before and after the 1973 heart attack. Other players, like the since-traded Mike Hegan, had experienced more of the kindly, family-oriented Charlie Finley during their years in Oakland. "Charlie was involved personally with so many of the players, especially his inner circle of players that he signed himself and had a close relationship with: Catfish Hunter and Dick Green and people like that. Charlie did things for them—with them—that people don't realize. He invested money for them. He would tell them, 'Give me X amount of dollars. I'll guarantee you that you won't lose anything and I'll give you everything that you make.' I can remember every time we'd go into Chicago, Dick or Catfish would stop by Charlie's office on the way to the ballpark. They'd come out smiling with a big check in their hands. Charlie did lots of things for people and players that weren't talked about and weren't discussed publicly."

Rick Monday, a member of the A's from 1966 to 1971, says he saw little evidence of direct communication between Finley and the players. "I don't really know of a great number of players that had a great deal of contact with Charlie, with the exception of Reggie Jackson," says Monday. "We all had, I think, different relationships with Charlie Finley. I think back to Arizona State University, when the draft was going to come in and being the first player selected in the draft in '65, and dealing with Charlie and the scout, Art Lilly. It was a different relationship I had; I did not look forward to the offseason because Charlie Finley was hell on wheels when it came to trying to negotiate a contract. Of course, there was no arbitration, there was no free agency, and basically you could either die, get traded, or retire. And that first option was not a really favorable one."

Still, players generally received far better treatment from Finley than did his managers. "He was a very difficult employer if you had to work one-on-one," Hegan points out. "I've talked to Alvin Dark and Dick Williams and Chuck Tanner, people like that. If you're his manager, you're on call 24 hours a day. If Charlie wakes up at six o'clock in the morning in Chicago and it's four o'clock in Oakland, and he feels like calling, he'll call. Those were the things, the eccentricities that you heard about with Charlie, but I don't think many people heard about the good things that he did for the players."

The stirrings of the Mike Andrews affair overshadowed another item of consternation to Finley—poor crowds throughout the post-season at the Oakland

Coliseum. The defending champions drew little interest from their own fans, who seemed to take the A's' success for granted. "The people here just don't appreciate us," an exasperated Gene Tenace told sportswriter Furman Bisher. The fans didn't appreciate Finley either. When the A's returned home for Game Six, a group of fans displayed a large banner that made the following declaration: "HOW COULD FINLEY HAVE A HEART ATTACK?" The banner answered its own question. "HE DOESN'T EVEN HAVE A HEART."

Another group of people showed little appreciation for Reggie Jackson, but in a much more sinister way. Although the story would not be revealed publicly until after the World Series, Jackson was playing the post-season under the protection of the FBI and a personal bodyguard named Tony Del Rio. The reason? A group calling itself "The Weathermen" had sent an ominous letter to A's broadcaster Monte Moore, who passed the note along to Dick Williams and Charlie Finley. Perhaps distracted by the death threat, Jackson had struggled during the Championship Series against the Orioles, ending up with a paltry three hits in 21 at-bats, and no extra-base hits or RBIs. In the World Series, Jackson had started out 0-for-5 before collecting four hits during the extra-inning loss in Game Two.

As he sat in his hotel room during the Series, Jackson thought about the 1960s' assassinations of Martin Luther King and John and Robert Kennedy. Even though he knew that the six-foot, five-inch, 290-pound Del Rio and a group of FBI agents were on the premises, he still wondered about his safety. "What could they do for a man standing all alone out there on the diamond?" Jackson wrote in an article that appeared in *Guideposts* Magazine. "I began to visualize a fanatic on a roof overlooking the park. He's holding a high-powered rifle; I'm in the batter's box waiting for the pitch. He lines up the cross-hairs of the telescopic sight and slowly squeezes the trigger…"

Jackson quickly realized that he could not play baseball with such thoughts running through his mind. Playing in a World Series provided sufficient pressure in and of itself, without also having to wonder about one's own livelihood. As a result, Jackson sought inspiration and comfort from a letter he had recently received from his father. Jackson had already read the letter once; he would read it again to try to put himself at ease.

On October 18, two days after Dick Williams had privately told his players of his imminent departure from the clutches of Charlie Finley, media reports circulated that he would leave the A's and might be headed to New York to manage the Yankees. Even though Williams had made it clear to interested third parties that he was extremely interested in working for the Yankees, he publicly denied the newspaper stories.

As the Mets and A's prepared for Game Five, one of New York's coaches engaged in some playful Williams-related banter with one of Oakland's pitchers. "If Williams is going to manage the Yankees," Mets bullpen coach Joe Pignatano told Darold Knowles, according to the *New York Times*, "does Finley manage the A's?" The colorful Knowles suddenly jumped up from his seat in the A's' dugout, giving Pignatano an exaggerated look of mock surprise and shock. Even in the face of the Mike Andrews story, with the team one game from elimination, and with the loss of their manager imminent, the A's had retained their sense of humor.

Chapter 19

Oh by the Way, the A's Do It Again

The Mets led the Series three games to two, but now had to go back to Oakland for Game Six, and possibly a decisive seventh game. On Friday, the A's landed at the Oakland Airport to a smallish reception of fewer than 200 fans. Most of the players walked off the plane with frowned, serious expressions on their faces, while failing to waive to the few onlookers who had bothered to attend their arrival. The results of the first five games of the Series, the distasteful handling of Mike Andrews, and the fatigue caused by a cross-country flight had left many of the Oakland players in foul moods.

Gene Tenace found two other causes of heartache—his own lack of hitting and the brilliant play of Mets shortstop Buddy Harrelson. "I've hit some good shots they took away from me," Tenace complained to George Ross of the *Oakland Tribune*. "I think they've got two shortstops out there." Harrelson's defensive play had dominated the *on-field* theme of the Series.

Mets manager Yogi Berra faced an important decision with regard to his starting rotation. He could pitch staff ace Tom Seaver on three days rest in Game Six, and use Jon Matlack, if necessary, in Game Seven. Under that scenario, Matlack would also start on three days rest. Or Berra could pitch 12-game winner George Stone in the sixth game, saving a well-rested Seaver for the possibility of a seventh game. Berra opted for a more aggressive approach, deciding to start Seaver on short rest in what he hoped would be a climactic Game Six. Of all the Mets' pitchers, none drew more respect from the A's than Seaver. "He's Mr. Baseball," Reggie Jackson told the *New York Daily News*. "They've heard about him in China. Blind people come to the park to *hear* him pitch."

The prospects of facing Seaver represented only part of the problems the A's faced in trying to square the Series at three games apiece. The sideshow created by Charlie Finley's handling of Mike Andrews had proven to be a distraction for most of the players. "I'm a man split in two," Reggie Jackson admitted to Dave Anderson of the *New York Times*. "Half of me is trying to think about Mike Andrews, the other half is trying to think about Tom Seaver." In 21 Series at-bats, Jackson had managed only five hits and two RBIs and had left eight runners in scoring position. As a result of the Andrews incident and his own struggles at the plate, Jackson seemed to be talking like a man who felt his team was on the verge of losing the World Series. "Our attitude is bad," Jackson revealed to the *Oakland Tribune*. "It just doesn't seem like a World Series." The quotes of an unnamed player reflected the feeling of discontent surrounding the A's. "I can hardly wait for Monday," the anonymous player told Ron Bergman, "when all this is over." The player was not referring to *Rick* Monday, either.

Dick Williams had other thoughts on his mind—like trying to come up with a lineup that could do some damage against the Mets' best pitcher. Williams benched his defensive-minded catcher, Ray Fosse, moved Gene Tenace behind the plate and inserted Deron Johnson at first base. Johnson had not started the first five games of the Series, in a decision that may have been sparked by Finley. "It's no secret," said one Oakland player in an interview with sportswriter Phil Pepe. "Deron is gone [after the Series]. Finley doesn't like him."

At least one New York newspaper gave the A's little hope of coming back in the Series. The headline in the October 20th edition of the *New York Daily News* read as follows:

FOR THE A'S...THERE'S NO TOMORROW
Seaver Figures to Wrap It Up Today

In the accompanying article, Jon Matlack predicted that he would not have to pitch a Game Seven. He believed that Seaver would end the Series in six. Dick Williams felt more optimistic about Oakland's chances—at least publicly. "You know the '52 Dodgers had a 3–2 lead over the Yankees," Williams told sportswriter Red Foley, referring to the Brooklyn club he had played for during his major league career. "We went back to Ebbets Field to wrap it up. Only it didn't turn out that way. We lost both games and blew the Series."

Williams could take some consolation in the knowledge that the A's would be facing a right-handed pitcher, albeit a great one in Seaver, rather than the left-handed starters who had proved so troublesome against Oakland. Even though the A's' lineup tilted heavily to the right side, Oakland had managed only 35 hits and 13 runs through the first five games. "Their lefties have been throwing the ball exactly where they wanted it," Williams told the *New York Times* in referring to starters Jerry Koosman, Jon Matlack, and George Stone, and relievers Tug McGraw and Ray Sadecki. "You can't give enough credit to [New York scout] Dee Fondy for the scouting report he gave the Mets on our hitters."

Williams' optimism over facing a right-handed pitcher proved prophetic. In the first inning, Joe Rudi singled against Seaver and scored on

Reggie Jackson's double. In the third inning, Sal Bando and Jackson teamed up, contributing a single and a run-scoring double, respectively. The A's added an insurance run in the eighth, when pinch-hitter Jesus Alou scored Jackson with a sacrifice fly. A trio of Oakland pitchers—Catfish Hunter, Darold Knowles, and Rollie Fingers—made the runs hold up in a 3–1 victory.

Rudi, Jackson, and Sal Bando all noticed a difference between Seaver's performance in Game Six and his earlier showing in the Series. "I think it's dead or something," Bando told sportswriter Red Foley bluntly in assessing Seaver's arm. "His arm must be bothering him because he threw much harder in the game at Shea." Jackson offered his own prescription, while indirectly second-guessing Berra's choice of rotation. "He needs an extra day's rest," Jackson told *Baseball Digest*. Seaver, for his part, claimed that his right shoulder felt fine.

The A's had regained the momentum of the Series, but the Mets still held the advantage on the mound. Jon Matlack, the Game Seven starter, had not allowed an earned run in 23 innings of post-season work. In contrast, Ken Holtzman had pitched badly in his first two World Series starts against New York.

Both Holtzman and Matlack kept the opposition lineups hitless through the first two innings. The game remained scoreless until the bottom of the third. With one out, Holtzman came to bat and rocked a double down the left-field line. Campy Campaneris followed with an uncharacteristic show of strength, lifting a hanging curveball over the fence in right field. Campy's first World Series home run gave the A's a 2–0 lead. Joe Rudi followed with a sharp single to center, and after Sal Bando popped out, Reggie Jackson lofted a drive deep into the right-field stands. The A's now led, 4–0. After rounding third base, Jackson trotted slowly, stopped himself one stride short of home plate, leapt in the air, and stomped both of his feet on the plate. A tight, scoreless seventh game had suddenly become an Oakland runaway.

With his signature Game Seven home run and memorable landing on home plate, Jackson began to shape the World Series reputation that would earn him the nickname "Mr. October" in later years. "If you needed a home run in the ninth inning, he usually gave it to you," says Rollie Fingers. "He was that type of player. He played great under pressure, a great pressure ballplayer in situations where the game was on the line." It was Jackson's first chance to thrive under the spotlight of the World Series, after missing the '72 Fall Classic with a ruptured hamstring, and he did not fail to take center stage.

The A's added another run against Matlack in the fifth, before the Mets posted their first run on consecutive doubles by Felix Millan and Rusty

Staub. Rollie Fingers relieved Holtzman and closed out the rally by retiring Cleon Jones and John Milner. Fingers remained in the game until the ninth, when a walk, a single, and an error by Gene Tenace at first base gave the Mets one last hope. With two outs and a left-handed hitter scheduled to bat, Dick Williams summoned Darold Knowles. The veteran reliever had now appeared in each of the seven games against the Mets, establishing a new World Series record.

With one out to go in the ninth inning, several fans hurled themselves over the railing at the Coliseum onto the playing field. A small group headed in the direction of Reggie Jackson, stationed in right field. Jackson, who had played the post-season under a death threat, decided to take no chances and ran away from the fans, who apparently thought the game was already over. They didn't realize that Tenace had bobbled pinch-hitter Ed Kranepool's apparent Series-ending ground out.

Knowles and the A's still required one more out. The Mets, having closed to within 5–2, had managed to bring the potential game-tying run to the plate. With the left-handed hitting Wayne Garrett scheduled to face the southpaw Knowles, the situation cried for Mets manager Yogi Berra to insert Willie Mays as a pinch-hitter. Mays, a right-handed hitter with power, stood a better chance of hitting a game-tying home run against Knowles than Garrett did. Mays also seemed like the appropriate sentimental choice, given that he had already announced he would retire at the end of the Series. Berra chose neither the percentages nor sentiment. He allowed Garrett to face Knowles. Garrett popped a Knowles fastball weakly to the left side of the infield.

As Campy Campaneris nestled the ball into his glove, a storm of Oakland players unleashed itself onto the field, toppling Knowles and Gene Tenace to the ground. For the second straight year on an October day, the Oakland A's celebrated their status as baseball's best team. For the first time in 12 years, a major league franchise had claimed back-to-back titles. The Yankees of 1961 and '62, the Bronx Bombers of Mickey Mantle and Roger Maris, had been the last team to repeat as World Champions.

Players, reporters, and various officials jammed their way into the A's' smallish clubhouse, where captain Sal Bando admitted that the A's had taken the Mets lightly at the start of the Series. "We beat Baltimore and figured the Series was going to be easy," Bando acknowledged in an interview with the *New York Daily News*. "But once the Mets had us one game from elimination, we woke up."

The bullpen had contributed heavily to the awakening. Rollie Fingers and Darold Knowles had combined to pitch five scoreless innings over the final two games. Except for the second and fourth games of the Series, the Oakland bullpen prospered throughout the post-season. "Our bullpen was the difference," Dick Williams told George Vass of *Baseball Digest*. "Our bullpen was deeper than the Orioles and Mets... I think our staff was better than theirs because of the bullpen."

As Charlie Finley's band played his favorite song, "Sugar in the Morning, Sugar in the Evening," Reggie Jackson answered questions from a large gathering of writers and broadcasters. Jackson pleaded with the media not to misrepresent the owner's involvement in the Series victory. "Please don't give Finley credit," Jackson told sportswriter Neal Russo. "That takes away from what the guys in this dressing room have done." After struggling in the early games of the Series, Jackson had collected four hits in eight at-bats over the final two games. He had driven in four runs, including two on his Series-cementing home run in the seventh game. Aside from theories of clutch hitting, Jackson's performance appeared aided by the playing of the final two games during the daylight hours. In night games during the Series, Jackson had managed only one hit in 12 at-bats. In contrast, his day-game performances numbered eight hits in 17 at-bats.

Once again, controversy attached itself to the winning atmosphere in the clubhouse. Although Jackson had hit well late in the Series, his lack of production in games one through five had held back the A's. *Sport* Magazine nonetheless named Jackson the Series MVP, ignoring the player whom many writers felt deserved the award: Campy Campaneris. Veteran baseball writer Dick Young chided *Sport* Magazine for making what he considered a political selection.

"In this phony, commercial world of ours," Young wrote in the *New York Daily News*, "Reggie Jackson, who had two good games, wins the MVP car instead of Bert Campaneris, who had seven good games. Do you know why?...Because Reggie Jackson is great copy, Reggie Jackson can make a fine forceful speech in New York when he gets the car." Young proceeded to describe Campy's exploits throughout the Series, including his impressive fielding and critical Game Seven home run against Jon Matlack. "He does it all, except one," Young wrote of Campaneris. "He can't speak English. This, if you're giving a car for a magazine promotion, is a terrible weakness."

An examination of the statistics certainly supported the choice of Campaneris, who had batted .353 with two RBIs to Jackson's .286 and one RBI. Campaneris, by making several fine defensive plays, had also sustained much greater impact in the field than Jackson. "Bert Campaneris has been so great for us," Dick Williams raved to Arthur Daley of the *New York Times*, "that this has to be the best World Series shortstopping since Phil Rizzuto and Pee Wee Reese were dazzling everyone in my younger days." Williams went as far as to compare Campaneris to another Hall of Fame middle infielder. "I've never seen anyone since Jackie Robinson who gets such a jump and who makes the opposition to nervous," Williams gushed in an interview with *Baseball Digest*. Even Jackson acknowledged that Campaneris, among other Oakland teammates, had built a stronger case for claiming the Series MVP award. "I thought Bert, or Joe Rudi, or Catfish should win it," Jackson told the *New York Daily News*.

Campaneris, usually one of the most modest of the A's, agreed that he deserved the award. In the dugout near the end of Game Seven, teammates Jesus Alou, Sal Bando, and Gene Tenace had told him to expect to win the car from *Sport*. "I never in my life been so disappointed," Campaneris told the *New York Times*' Dave Anderson, who disagreed with Dick Young's contention that *Sport* Magazine had chosen Jackson based on his articulation. "I think I do better job than Reggie do," Campy insisted. "I think I have seven good games."

The post-game celebration contained two other bittersweet moments. Longtime second baseman Dick Green, the glue to Oakland's right side of the infield, indicated that he would retire. "I think it's time to quit," Green told the Associated Press. "I'm happy to be going out on top." Green's announcement soon became overshadowed by another revelation. A's manager Dick Williams, speaking on national television, publicly announced his resignation, effective immediately. The news that A's players had been aware of since Game Three, which had been rumored throughout the working press, had now become official.

Reggie Jackson put his arm around his *former* manager and delivered an emotional message. "You taught me how to win," Jackson said as he kissed Williams on the cheek. "I'm sorry you're leaving." Jackson had succinctly analyzed Williams for the media over the last few days, as rumors of his move to the Yankees circulated. "He's got two rules," Jackson had said. "You hustle all the time and you don't make the same mental mistake twice." Jackson had also credited Williams for treating all players similarly. "He doesn't play favorites. But he likes you better if you are hard-nosed. If you are a candy ass, you may have trouble making his team."

Only four months earlier, Jackson had resented Williams and his coaches for being too critical. "He's the kind of guy you might like for a month and hate for a month," Jackson was now telling Maury Allen of the *New York Post*. "But he doesn't care. He just wants to win...That's what Dick has taught us."

Although Williams often bruised the egos of his players, those same players came to respect him for his toughness and listened to him for his knowledge. "Maybe not the most popular [man], but you certainly cannot argue with the results that Dick Williams got," says Rick Monday, who had played for Williams in 1971. "He had a pretty good ballclub, but he also gave them some pretty good leadership and pretty good direction." Along with three divisional titles, three pennants and two World Championships in a span of three seasons.

Williams maintained that his decision to leave the A's was not motivated by any problems with Finley. "I am leaving for personal reasons," Williams insisted to sportswriter Phil Pepe, "not out of any dissatisfaction over my relations with Finley." Williams explained that working on the West Coast while maintaining a home near Ft. Lauderdale, Florida, had created problems in maintaining a relationship with his family. Few onlookers believed Williams' graceful public sentiments. During the playoffs, Williams had confided to a friend. "I've had it up to here. I'm quitting after the season. I've had only five peaceful days all year, the five days [Finley] was in the hospital." Many players, including Catfish Hunter, sympathized with Williams. "He couldn't run the team the way he wanted," assessed Hunter in an interview with Dave Hirshey of the *New York Daily News*. "He had to check everything out first with Mr. Finley." Williams had finally decided to check *out* of Finley's neighborhood.

Both Hunter and Vida Blue decided not to attend the team's rain-soaked victory parade, which drew nearly 200,000 fewer fans than the 1972 celebration. Those players who did show up for the motorcade looked sullen and disinterested. Given the resignation of Williams and the mistreatment of Mike Andrews, the A's seemed to be in no mood to celebrate their second consecutive World Championship.

Chapter 20

No More Dick Williams to Push Around

Dick Williams said he would consider any offers from other major league teams, but he clearly had one club in mind. "Sure I'd love to be with the Yankees," Williams told sportswriter Red Foley. "Anyone who says he wouldn't is crazy." As Williams discussed his resignation during the A's' victory celebration, Charlie Finley told his manager that he wished he would return. Speaking on national television, Finley added that he would not stand in Williams' way should he *not* change his mind about returning to Oakland.

Two days later, Finley changed *his* mind regarding Williams' future. Oakland farm director John Claiborne had suggested to Finley that he exact some form of compensation in exchange for Williams' services. Any major league team wishing to hire Williams as manager would have to compensate the A's—with players and/or cash, but preferably players. When Yankee owner George Steinbrenner asked Finley for permission to contact Williams, he received a blunt response. "Absolutely not," Finley told the Associated Press. "They [the Yankees] seemed stunned and wanted to know why." Finley explained that he had recently given Williams a two-year contract extension. If the Yankees did not properly compensate the A's, "there will be court action," Finley vowed.

Finley referred to several precedents that supported his claims for compensation. In 1934, the Washington Nationals had exacted $225,000 from the Boston Red Sox in exchange for the rights to manager Joe Cronin. In 1967, the New York Mets had sent pitcher Bill Denehy and $100,000 to the Washington Senators for the right to hire Gil Hodges as manager. The compensation the Mets turned over to Washington was well worth it; in 1969, the Mets would win the first World Championship in franchise history while under the direction of Hodges.

Precedents aside, Williams felt that the most pertinent issue was Finley's failure to live up to his initial vow. In less than a week, Finley's words had changed from "won't stand in the way" to "over my dead body." Williams expressed surprise at Finley's turnabout in an interview with *The Sporting News*. "It's not like Mr. Finley to go back on his word," said Williams. "But this is an about-face." In subsequent interviews, Williams went further, stopping just short of directly calling his former boss a liar. "Charlie says one thing and does another. He's giving out a lot of false information."

Finley responded to Williams' claims by trying to clarify his initial remarks during the A's' post-game celebration. When he said he would not "stand in the way," he was referring to Williams' options in the business world, not in the baseball community. Finley said he never intended to allow Williams to walk off to another managerial job, without some sort of compensation coming his way.

Although Finley also claimed that he preferred Williams return as his manager in Oakland, reports out of Baltimore indicated otherwise. In a story written by Doug Brown that appeared in the December 8, 1973 edition of *The Sporting News*, Finley had supposedly contacted the Orioles about the availability of their manager, Earl Weaver, *during* the World Series. Finley had placed the call while Williams was still manager, several days before his publicly-expressed intention to leave the A's. According to Brown's story, Baltimore's vice-president and general manager, Frank Cashen, had refused to give Finley permission to talk to Weaver.

Baseball and contract legalities prevented the Yankees, or any other team, from negotiating with Williams. Yet, the Yankees made it clear they wanted Williams, who expressed mutual affection for wearing pinstripes. Prior to the winter meetings, the Yankees finally agreed to compensate Finley, offering starting second baseman Horace Clarke. Finley said no to Clarke, a mediocre hitter and fielder, but counter-offered by asking for one of three other players: catcher Thurman Munson, outfielder Bobby Murcer, or pitcher Mel Stottlemyre. In other words, Finley wanted one of the three best players on the New York roster, while the Yankees were offering about their 15th best player.

In stage two of negotiations, Finley met with Yankee general manager Gabe Paul at the winter meetings in Houston. Finley backed off on his request for established players like Munson, Murcer, or Stottlemyre. Instead, he asked for two of the Yankees' best minor league prospects: first baseman-outfielder Otto Velez and left-handed pitcher Scott McGregor. "Both?" exclaimed an incredulous Gabe Paul, according to Dick Young of the *New York Daily News*. "You can't have *either*."

Finley talked further with Paul, asking for either Velez or McGregor, plus a sum of cash. No sale. Finley agreed to eliminate the cash part of his request, but wanted the Yankees to include one of the following prospects—Steve Colson, Kerry Dineen, John Shupe, or Terry Whitfield—along with either McGregor or Velez. Paul's response was the same as before—no deal. The two sides had reached a stalemate, ending their meeting in Houston.

Finley's stubborn posture on ample compensation left Williams furious and frustrated. The former A's' manager told reporters that he was considering filing a lawsuit against Finley on the grounds that his former employer was running interference on his legitimate efforts to find new work. Williams also mentioned his disappointment with the American League's failure to intervene in the matter. Why didn't league president Joe Cronin step in and determine which players the Yankees should surrender to the A's in a trade for Williams?

"The problem is between New York and Oakland," claimed a neutral Cronin in an interview with *The Sporting News*. Perhaps Cronin wanted to steer away from any involvement in the case as he prepared for his own retirement from the American League office. Williams would later criticize Cronin for refusing to involve himself in the dispute, while taking a shot at the recent record of the American League chieftain. "Not letting me go to the Yankees was one of the last of many years of non-decisions by...Joe Cronin," Williams told Marty Bell of *Sport* Magazine.

Williams wanted the Yankees, the Yankees wanted him, Cronin wanted no part of the dispute, and Finley insisted that he wanted Williams to continue managing the A's. Since Williams still had a signed contract with the A's for the 1974 season, Finley reasoned, he still considered Williams his manager. In fact, he continued mailing Williams paychecks on the first and 15th day of each month through the end of the calendar year. "There is no way I'll go back to Oakland," Williams told sportswriter Dick Young adamantly. Williams later revealed that he had received the checks on a timely basis from Finley, but had neglected to cash any of them after his resignation. Williams did not want to feel beholden to Finley, at least not in any financial way.

On December 13, the Yankees, exasperated in their negotiations with Finley and with Cronin's refusal to intercede, decided to force the issue. George Steinbrenner announced that he had reached a contractual agreement with Williams to manage in the Bronx. Gabe Paul introduced Williams to the media at a Yankee Stadium press conference. Williams donned a Yankee cap and uniform jersey and smiled widely for reporters. Photographs of Williams wearing Yankee paraphernalia would become collector's items; the former A's skipper would find an immediate roadblock in his efforts to wear Yankee pinstripes during a regular season game.

A furious Finley placed an immediate protest with Joe Cronin, who was now forced to make a decision. The owner expressed his rage over his manager's refusal to honor an existing contract. Finley also informed the media of his contempt for the Yankees, who had tried to steal one of his contracted employees. "What if I tried to sign Bobby Murcer?" Finley supposed in an interview with a reporter. "Wouldn't the Yankees be furious with me for trying to sign one of their best players, one who was already under contract to New York?"

In contrast to his disagreement with Finley over the cancellation of Game Two of the recently concluded World Series, Cronin sided with the Oakland owner on the issue of control over Williams' contract. On December 20, just one week after the Yankees had signed Williams, Cronin ruled that Finley still held rights to the veteran manager. Without Finley's approval, the Yankees would not be allowed to employ Williams as their manager in 1974.

"Dick Williams was my manager yesterday, he's my manager today, and he'll be my manager tomorrow," Finley declared to the *New York Daily News*. He now refused to even negotiate the compensation issue with the hated Yankees. After several last-ditch legal efforts to secure Williams, the Yankees finally surrendered in their pursuit of the World Championship manager. On January 3, 1974, the Yankees introduced former Pittsburgh Pirates skipper Bill Virdon as their new manager. Although the Yankees publicly decided to leave their managerial door slightly ajar (just in case they could work out a compromise with Finley and obtain Williams), the organization had basically conceded defeat on the legal front. While Finley had been both technically and morally wrong in his handling of the Mike Andrews affair, he was now acting within his legal rights in maintaining possession of Williams.

Chapter 21

Great Players, No Manager

The Mike Andrews incident had represented the final insult for Dick Williams, convincing him to expedite his departure from the organization. Andrews soon followed Williams out the door, though not of his own volition. Finley placed the veteran infielder on waivers, the first step in giving him his release. Finley refused to let Andrews' exit go at that; he insulted Andrews by quoting baseball's waiver rules in an interview with *The Sporting News*. "Any team that wants him can have him for $1."

Andrews insisted that his arm and shoulder felt fine. A Boston doctor confirmed Andrews' positive feelings about the shoulder, saying that he found nothing physically wrong with the arm. Andrews did admit, however, that he had developed a mental block that affected his throws to first base. In spite of the problem, he believed he could play a capable first base while still hitting major league pitching. Andrews contacted 22 of the 24 major league teams, but none of the clubs offered him as much as a tryout.

In the aftermath of his release, and Finley's embarrassing $1 crack, Andrews received an invitation to appear on the *Dick Cavett Show*, but still no interest from any of the ballclubs. The major league career of the former Red Sox' and White Sox' second baseman had come to an end—at the age of 30. After sitting out the 1974 season completely, Andrews would play one unproductive season in the Japanese Leagues before retiring for good.

Unfortunately, much in the tradition of tragic baseball figures like Bill Buckner and Fred Merkle, most fans remembered Andrews for the one World Series incident, rather than his career accomplishments from 1966 to 1973. In 1967, Andrews had contributed to the Red Sox' "Impossible Dream" team, also managed by Dick Williams. From 1969 to 1971, Andrews reached double figures in home runs, while playing a consistently solid second base, where he efficiently turned double plays with shortstop partner Rico Petrocelli. Although Andrews was not a star, he certainly deserved better than the shabby treatment he received from Finley, and the stigma of disgrace attached to his post-season firing.

While the Williams and Andrews sagas had dominated conversation since the World Series, the Oakland players created further controversy when they met to distribute World Series shares. The players, already resentful of Allan Lewis' inclusion on the 25-man roster, cast votes on how much Series loot to give to the veteran pinch-runner. Lewis had appeared in a career-high 35 games, or well over 20 per cent of Oakland's regular season contests. Yet, the A's saw fit to give Lewis, who had failed to come to bat a single time during the regular season, a mere one-tenth of a share. At least Lewis was well-liked in the minor leagues. Fans of the Southern League's Birmingham Barons, where Lewis had played for most of the season, voted him the most popular player on the team.

Lewis did fare better than one of his teammates in earning at least some of the World Series loot. Oakland players decided to completely shut out late-season acquisition Rico Carty, who had already been denied his first opportunity at playing in the World Series. Carty's Oakland experience worsened when Charlie Finley elected not to give him a World Series ring. On December 14, Carty received another slap in the face. "I was really hurt when Finley sent me a telegram in December telling me I was released," Carty would say three years later in an interview with Russell Schneider of *The Sporting News*. "Here I was released and I had been a .300 hitter all my life." Carty was also leading the Dominican League in home runs, RBIs, and batting average at the time. As with his premature releases of Tommy Davis and Orlando Cepeda in past years, Finley would come to regret his severance of Carty. The "Beeg Mon" would make a successful comeback in 1975, emerging as one of the American League's best designated hitters. In 1978, Carty would impress Finley so much that the Oakland owner would reacquire him in a trade with the Toronto Blue Jays.

While turmoil had begun to infiltrate the A's during the 1972 championship run, it had reached its peak in 1973. One controversy after another had arisen: Reggie Jackson's complaints about the coaching staff, the resentment toward Allan Lewis, the Bill Posedel affair, the Mike Andrews escapade, ad nauseam. Somehow, the A's had sidestepped each roadblock on their way to a second straight title. Yet, at least one player felt the sideshows had been overplayed. Catcher Ray Fosse believed that the Oakland players, in combination with the out-of town media, had exaggerated the extent of the tension. "The Oakland writers are used to it," Fosse told writer Pete Swanson, "so they just laugh when something like that gets started. But [out-of-town] writers think it's dissension and fighting, so they make it into a big story.

"Sure, we had turmoil all year," Fosse acknowledged to Swanson, "but it's not really dissension. We kind of blow it up." Fosse also felt the A's actually played better in the face of trouble. "We try to stir things up," said Fosse, "because we think we're a better team when everybody's yelling at one another."

Most of the post-season news surrounding the A's continued to carry an unsavory stench, with one exception. The Baseball Writers' Association of America rewarded one of the A's—Reggie Jackson—by making him its overwhelming choice as American League Most Valuable Player. Jackson garnered all 24 first-place votes, becoming only the sixth American Leaguer to earn a unanimous selection. Jackson joined Hall of Fame first baseman Hank Greenberg, future Hall of Famers Mickey Mantle and Frank Robinson, and standouts Al Rosen and Denny McLain in sweeping the vote.

Several other A's did well in the MVP balloting. Sal Bando finished sixth in the voting, while Catfish Hunter (11th), Deron Johnson (22nd), Campy Campaneris (28th), Vida Blue (29th), and Billy North (32nd) also attracted consideration. Two former A's who had excelled in their new roles as designated hitters also picked up some votes. The Orioles' Tommy Davis finished 10th in the balloting, while 1972 bust Orlando Cepeda, now with the Red Sox, earned enough votes to place 15th. Although Deron Johnson had proved to be a wise mid-season acquisition by Finley, the Oakland owner was likely kicking himself for letting better designated hitters like Cepeda and Davis go elsewhere. Finley's net return on Cepeda and Davis? No players, no money.

Although bogged down by the Dick Williams-to-the-Yankees tug-of-war, Charlie Finley did manage to make a trade during December's winter meetings in Houston. In a bizarre move, Finley sent 28-year-old reliever Horacio Piña, one of the A's' most useful pitchers, to the Cubs for former Athletic reliever Bob Locker, who was now 35 years old.

Locker had pitched well in his one season with the Cubs, with his 18 saves, 63 appearances, and 2.55 ERA all leading the Chicago staff. So why did the Cubs trade their best reliever? When the Cubs had acquired Locker the previous winter, the sinkerballing right-hander had informed general manager John Holland that he would agree to pitch one season in the Windy City, then expect to be traded. Otherwise, Locker planned to retire after the 1973 season.

Threatened with the loss of an effective relief pitcher, the Cubs found Locker a new team, while gaining seven years in the process. Locker and Piña were pitchers of similar abilities, but the difference in their ages was substantial. So why did Finley make this trade, taking on the much older of the two pitchers? Piña had encountered some shoulder soreness during the season, but had still pitched effectively, managing a 2.76 ERA as a middle and long reliever. Piña had also responded favorably to the coaching of pitching mentor Wes Stock, who had recommended that the Mexican right-hander throw sidearm to both right-handed and left-handed hitters.

The Oakland media theorized that Finley had traded Piña merely to spite Dick Williams. In 1972, Williams had suggested the A's acquire Piña in exchange for Mike Epstein, a player that the manager had lost all respect for during the 1972 World Series. Finley quickly soured on that deal, trying to reacquire Epstein almost immediately from Texas before the Rangers later dealt him to the Angels in mid-season.

As for the other player involved in this latest deal with the Cubs, Locker had fallen into Williams' doghouse during the 1972 post-season run. By reacquiring Locker, Finley seemed to be sending a subtle message to Williams that his opinions no longer mattered in the Oakland scheme.

"How could Charlie make that trade?" an incredulous Williams asked a reporter for *The Sporting News*. "He says he wants me back as manager and then he goes and trades Piña for Locker. Piña is seven years younger and he trades him for

Locker!" Williams was right; the trade broke all the rules of logic and common sense.

Upon hearing of the deal, the flaky Locker promised not only to contribute to the Oakland bullpen but also offered to replace Williams—as manager! "I talked to Charlie about that," Locker told *The Sporting News*. "I told him I would be a player-manager. He thought I was kidding, but I was half-serious."

Nonetheless, Finley had other candidates in mind for the managerial vacancy. Third-base coach Irv Noren and Tucson manager Sherm Lollar topped the list of in-house possibilities. One Bay Area writer even mentioned the name of second baseman Dick Green, one of the most intelligent players on the team. Candidates from outside the organization included former Cincinnati manager Dave Bristol, who had led the Reds to three consecutive solid finishes in the late sixties before giving way to Sparky Anderson. Bristol then managed the Brewers with little success over two-plus seasons, losing his job 30 games into the 1972 campaign. Like Williams in 1970, Bristol had experienced a demotion from major league manager to third-base coach of the Montreal Expos, whom he had served in 1973.

While Bristol seemed like a solid manager-in-waiting, he possessed very little star appeal, lacking the glamour that Finley preferred in his managers and coaches. Finley appeared to be considering more intriguing candidates, including former Texas Rangers' skippers Ted Williams and Whitey Herzog. The other names on Finley's list all belonged to former or current major league stars who happened to be black: Satchel Paige, Frank Robinson, and Maury Wills.

The inclusion of Paige in the Oakland rumor mill seemed like the unlikeliest of all the possibilities. Although the Hall of Fame pitcher had worked one game for Finley's Kansas City A's in 1965—which at least gave him some connection to the organization—he had rarely been mentioned as a possible major league manager. Paige did not fit the managerial profile; as a player, he was a flamboyant showman who often jumped from team to team and abhorred basic conditioning regimens that included such unpleasant exercises as *running*. While Paige was a great competitor and a determined, resilient athlete who pitched well into his fifties, he seemed to lack the disciplinary skills required of managing professional athletes.

Maury Wills provided the A's with a more realistic managerial package. A star player throughout the 1960s, Wills had retired from the Los Angeles Dodgers after the 1972 season. In an example of perseverance, Wills had arrived fulltime on the major league scene at the relatively late age of 27. Within three seasons, he established himself as one of the National League's best all-around shortstops and its most prolific base stealer, setting a single-season major league record with 104 stolen bases. Given Wills' work ethic and baserunning smarts, he appeared a reasonable possibility as a big league manager.

Like Wills, Frank Robinson seemed to have managerial timbre. Few players of the 1960s rivaled Robinson in terms of toughness and intelligence. He also had some playing ability left in his soon-to-be-40-year-old body. In 1973, Robinson had slugged 30 home runs and driven in 97 runs for a bad California Angels team. But Robinson was now 38, and didn't figure to be around by the time the rebuilding

Angels fielded a quality on-field product. The Angels were willing to trade him for a prospect or two, perhaps with some cash thrown into the deal. In turn, the A's could employ Robinson as their fulltime manager, and as a part-time designated hitter, first baseman, and outfielder.

The presence of Robinson on the A's figured to appease American League MVP Reggie Jackson, who was upset by the departure of Dick Williams. Jackson had raved about Robinson's positive influence on him during the 1970–71 winter league season, when F. Robby skippered Reggie's team in Santurce, Puerto Rico. Jackson subsequently played his best extended stretch of baseball from 1971 to 1973, perhaps partly as a result of Robinson's calming, professional hand.

As speculation concerning Dick Williams' future had run rampant during the World Series, Jackson publicly recommended that Robinson stay away from the turmoil of managing the A's. "Robby has too much class to manage for Charlie Finley," Jackson told sportswriter Neal Russo. Reggie seemed to be sending his friend a less-than-subtle warning about life as an Oakland skipper. As the major leagues' first African-American field boss, Robinson would be facing ample pressure already; the looming presence of a meddling, often irrational owner like Finley might make Robinson's task nearly unbearable.

Two weeks after his World Series warning, Jackson changed his public stance on the Robinson-to-the-A's scenario. Jackson compared Robinson to Dick Williams, who had managed to survive three seasons under the oppression of Finley. "Both Frank and Dick are similar in personality and in handling people," Jackson explained to Red Foley of the *New York Daily News*. "Now I think all the class he [Robinson] has might be what he needs to manage our club. What Finley is interested in is production. He's only concerned about winning." Assuming that the A's could adequately compensate the Angels, the addition of Robinson made perfect sense for Oakland. The former Cincinnati and Baltimore star had often been mentioned as a managerial candidate; his combination of smarts, work ethic, and on-field fire made for a superior managerial resume. Robinson possessed a streak of nastiness, too, which ensured that he wouldn't be tempted to retain too congenial a relationship with his players, many of whom were still his contemporaries. As a bonus, Robinson could still hit with power. As well as Deron Johnson had produced as the Oakland designated hitter for much of the season, his home runs, RBIs, and batting average all lagged behind Robinson's basic 1973 numbers.

On another front, the hiring of Robinson as baseball's first black manager would represent a public relations coup for Finley. Stung by the fallout of the Mike Andrews and Dick Williams episodes, Finley might now regain some favor with the Oakland and national media by playing the 1970s role of Branch Rickey. "Knowing Charlie Finley, it's possible that Frank Robinson could be hired," Jackson said optimistically in an interview with Dick Edwards of *Black Sports Magazine*. "Finley wants to be first in everything and the fact that he likes the publicity wouldn't hurt either." It was inevitable that some team would hire Robinson sometime soon; why not Finley, the game's most daring, innovative, and controversial owner? Unfortunately, the plan fell through when Finley and the

Angels could not agree on compensation for the future Hall of Famer. Robinson remained in southern California and the A's remained without a manager.

More setbacks hit the A's during the winter. Finley had already maliciously and willingly rid himself of one of his second baseman when he dumped Mike Andrews after the World Series. Now Finley was losing another second baseman, one that he wanted back in 1974. Dick Green, who had mentioned retirement after Game Seven of the World Series, made it official with an announcement from his home in Rapid City, South Dakota. The 32-year-old Green, who had made retirement statements an almost annual ritual since the 1970 season, said that he fully intended to step aside this time. Finley, remaining unconvinced of Green's sincerity, elected not to accept his retirement gracefully. "I am going to Rapid City to try to talk him into changing his mind," Finley vowed to *The Sporting News*. "He is too young to give up the game."

Green had successfully returned from back surgery, managing to hit a respectable .262 with three home runs and 42 RBIs. He had lost some range defensively, but remained a deft fielder with an aptitude for positioning himself properly against hitters' tendencies. Yet, Green insisted he had made up his mind and expressed resentment toward Finley for not believing his retirement statement to be serious. Green, however, did concede that Finley might be able to persuade him to return—if he did something crazy like double his salary. "Well, I'd have to think about it," Green conceded to *The Sporting News*. "I won't say yes or no. I'm not a dummy, you know."

Some of Green's teammates put little stock in his retirement claim. When a reporter asked Catfish Hunter to comment on the loss of Green and its impact on the pitching staff, the ace right-hander replied confidently, "He'll be back." Finley himself delayed sending Green's official retirement letter to the American League office. Finley knew that if he mailed the letter, making the retirement official, and Green were to decide to return, the A's would have to wait until 60 days after Opening Day to reinstate him to the active roster. By holding on to the letter, Finley was protecting both the interest of the team and of Green.

Without Green, who would play second base for the A's? If the A's preferred a veteran, the Cardinals let it be known that their second baseman, Ted Sizemore, was available at a reasonable cost in a trade. Even if Green did decide to go through with his retirement plans, the A's didn't really need Sizemore. They already had top prospect Manny Trillo, a 23-year-old Venezuelan who had played two seasons of Triple-A ball. Oakland scouts regarded Trillo as a terrific defender, with soft, quick hands and a strong, side-arming throwing style to first base. The A's wondered how much Trillo, a slow runner with little power, would produce offensively, but seemed confident that he could hit at least .250 or .260. Given Trillo's considerable fielding ability, that would be good enough.

In mid-January, media speculation continued to focus on the A's' managerial vacancy. One line of thought centered on Dave Bristol as the man Charlie Finley would tab to replace Dick Williams. One newspaper reported that Finley had actually hired Bristol as a "head coach," who would manage the team only as a contingency against Williams returning. In other words, by giving Bristol the nebulous title of "head coach," Finley could still claim Williams to be his manager, thus preventing him from signing with another team. For his part, Finley tried to put the Bristol rumors to a quick rest. He denied that he had hired Bristol to manage, "head coach," or do anything else for the organization.

Williams put forth his own candidate for the job. "For a time I thought Dave Bristol was going to be the head coach of the A's this summer," Williams told the *New York Times*, "but now I'm leaning toward Sal Bando. He's the only guy not having salary problems with Finley. He could do the job." Several other major league managers considered Bando the smartest on-the-field player in the American League. That said, Bando quickly turned down the offer that hadn't even been made. "I was flattered that Dick thought enough of me to say what he did," Bando told Milt Richman of United Press International, "but I'm really not interested in managing now."

As an amateur player, Bando had starred at Arizona State University, where he played with his onetime Oakland teammate, Rick Monday. His collegiate coach—future A's coach and manager Bobby Winkles—had worked with him on the principle of hitting to all fields, rather than trying to pull every pitch. Winkles hoped to make the slow-footed Bando a catcher in his senior season, but the young third baseman foiled the plan by making himself eligible for the professional draft. After hitting .480 in the 1965 College World Series, the Kansas City A's made Bando their third choice in the amateur draft.

Bando showed improvement in each of his three minor league seasons, hitting for a higher average while advancing one level each summer. Kansas City scouts loved Bando's game, especially the powerful throwing arm that had made him an all-city quarterback in Warrensville Heights, Ohio. Scouts from other teams labeled Bando the best third base prospect they had seen in years.

In 1967, the A's traded journeyman infielder Ed Charles to make room for Bando, whom manager Alvin Dark considered the second coming of Brooks Robinson. At the urging of Dark, Bando altered his batting stance, adopting a deeper crouch. Bando should have retained his old approach; he hit only .192, injured himself, and received a return ticket to Triple-A Vancouver.

Bando returned to the major leagues the following season—sans the crouching stance preferred by Dark. Batting out of a straighter, more comfortable position, Bando continued to struggle. A subsequent tip from Hall of Fame batting instructor Joe DiMaggio reversed his failures at the plate. "I was getting jammed on everything," Bando explained to Ron Bergman. "Then Joe D. told me to close up my stance."

By 1969, Bando became Oakland's cleanup hitter and team captain. Even though Bando was only 25 years old, manager Hank Bauer recognized the leadership qualities and intelligence of his rugged, respected third baseman. "We didn't have a lot of veteran players when I was with Oakland," Reggie Jackson says of his first few years with the A's. "My intensity on the field was helped by playing with our captain, Sal Bando. We lived near each other in our very early years and he was very influential in my career."

"He was very friendly; off the field, he was one of the guys," says Jack Aker, a teammate of Bando's for two seasons. "On the field, you could sense that he was a leader. Even so much as when the manager would come out to talk to the pitcher, it got to where a lot of times the manager would come out and talk to Bando in front of the pitcher—which is rare. A lot of times the manager will talk to the catcher about the pitcher. Bando was so much in the ballgame and so aware; he could pick up that a pitcher might be tiring, even better than sometimes the catchers could. So he was very valuable."

Aker considered Bando a natural selection as team captain. "In the late sixties, all these fellows, like Bando, Campaneris—who was already there— Catfish came along, Reggie Jackson, Rick Monday, all of these fellows came up at almost the same time. I think everyone knew right away, as far as the veteran players, that they were gonna have some kind of team here. We didn't have a veteran who was in the right age group that could have carried on as captain when these young fellows came in. So I think [this was] partly the reason that Sal Bando was named the captain and fit in so well: he had the aptitude for it, he was a hard-nosed type of player who gave all he had every day, and expected everybody else to do [the same]. And he also was a very bright player; he made very few mistakes on the field...I think they definitely picked the right fellow."

Yet, Bando did not want to manage the A's, at least not until his playing days had ended. Bando's lack of current interest in the job seemed moot, given Charlie Finley's denial of the Bando-as-manager rumors. While Bando as player-manager was not going to occur, it was now becoming unclear whether Finley would actually be back as the A's' owner. In January, Finley raised the possibility of selling the team, assuming he could exact the right price in return.

Finley had already spent much of the winter aggravating his relationship with the Oakland fans. For some bizarre reason, Finley had decided to reduce the number of "Family Night" promotions from 12 to four. In 1973, the A's had drawn over 330,000 fans for the dozen Family Nights. That figure represented more than one-third of Oakland's total attendance for the season. Although the A's charged only half-price admission on Family Nights, they generally made up for the reduction with improved concession sales and higher parking revenues.

The owner had also decided to eliminate a 25 percent discount for purchasers of season tickets. The hefty discount had encouraged patrons to buy season tickets prior to the start of the season. By discontinuing the discount, Finley had removed all incentive to buy season tickets ahead of schedule. Fans who wanted to go to games at the Oakland Coliseum would be wiser to purchase tickets on the day of the game. In a final slap at the fans, Finley declared that he would no longer employ his popular ballgirls at home games and would discontinue the practice of ballpark fireworks.

Finley seemed so oblivious to the Oakland fans that some wondered if he had an ulterior motive for his cost-cutting maneuvers. The owner confirmed such suspicions when he announced his willingness to sell the team—for a sum of $15 million. Doctors had suggested selling the A's, as a way of reducing the stress that had led to his recent heart attack. As usual, Finley was noncommittal on the issue of whether he would definitely sell the club before the start of the new season. "Maybe I will and maybe I won't," the typically cryptic Finley offered in an interview with a reporter.

A Bay Area advertising executive expressed immediate interest in buying the franchise. John Hays (whose name had been misspelled "Hayes" in several newspaper reports) headed up a group that claimed to have the $15 million needed to complete the purchase. Hays announced that he already had a manager in mind to replace Dick Williams: recently fired scout and broadcaster Bill Rigney.

Hays might have made a tactical error by expressing his interest in Rigney, a man who had been fired by Finley only six months earlier. Perhaps Finley interpreted Hays' interest in Rigney as a slap in the face. *How dare he hire Rigney, a man I just got rid of,* Finley might have wondered aloud.

In early February, Finley made a predictable announcement. "In my opinion, the A's will not be sold," Finley wrote in a form letter to season ticket holders. When asked to expound on this pronouncement, Finley questioned Hays' ability to formulate a group with the necessary financial backing to purchase the team. Finley also seemed annoyed that Hays had publicly declared his interest in buying the club. "If he keeps on talking the way he has," Finley warned in an interview with *The Sporting News*, "I may not sell him the club for twice the amount." The words smacked of vindictiveness and pettiness, while lacking any sound business sense.

In the meantime, Finley continued to alienate many of his best players by offering them very small salary increases. Unlike his salary battles with Reggie Jackson in 1970 and Vida Blue in 1972, Finley didn't run the risk of any extended spring holdouts. The players and owners had agreed to a new system of settling contract disputes—arbitration. Under arbitration, a player would submit a salary figure, the team would counter with another figure, and an independent judge would select one of the two figures. The judge, or arbitrator, would not be permitted to select any figures in between those submitted by the player and the team. As a result, both player and team would feel motivated to submit a fairly representative figure, and not one that was substantially too high or too low.

In spite of the looming threat of arbitration, Finley had offered skimpy $5,000 raises to his four best pitchers: Catfish Hunter, Vida Blue, Ken Holtzman, and fireman Rollie Fingers. Hunter, Blue, and Holtzman had each won at least 20 games, while Fingers had established himself as arguably the American League's second-best relief pitcher after the Yankees' Sparky Lyle. Hunter expressed bewilderment over Finley's hard-line stance on new contracts. "From what I understand, the whole Oakland team may be going to an arbitrator. I don't know what Finley is thinking," a puzzled Hunter told Ron Bergman before providing an answer to his own question. "I think he's got the hots out for all of us ballplayers because we stood up for Mike Andrews."

Finley's anger with the players was creating resentment at the negotiating table, or so it seemed. A story in the *San Francisco Chronicle* quoted Holtzman as being severely critical of Finley. According to the report, Holtzman had referred to his owner by an X-rated name and had even called Marvin Miller, the head of the Players' Association, a "phony." The *Chronicle* added that Holtzman had requested a trade to the Texas Rangers, one of the A's' rivals in the American League West.

When Holtzman read the story in the *Chronicle,* he couldn't believe the words on the page. He knew he hadn't made any of the remarks attributed to him; in fact, Holtzman hadn't even spoken with a reporter from the *Chronicle* in the last few days.

The reporter hadn't misquoted Holtzman, and Holtzman wasn't lying about not having made the comments. Rather, the reporter had been victimized by a practical joke. When the writer initially had tried to interview Holtzman about his contract situation, he accidentally dialed the wrong phone number, placing a call to a rival reporter from the *San Francisco Examiner*. The *Examiner*'s reporter accepted the call, pretended he was Holtzman, and answered the questions in as controversial a way as he could muster.

The sensational story had created the impression that the normally subdued Holtzman had ripped both his boss and union leader, while asking for a trade to one of the American League's worst teams. Since the inaccurate story had been carried on the front page of the sports section, and had been subsequently picked up by a local radio station, it made for major news in the Bay Area. The *Chronicle* soon printed a retraction, explaining the fabricated nature of the original story. Meanwhile, Holtzman hoped that Charlie Finley understood the story to be a complete and utter hoax.

Unlike Holtzman and the other stars on the Oakland pitching staff, Chuck Dobson possessed virtually no leverage in seeking a new contract. After two straight years of mediocre pitching at Triple-A Tucson, the comebacking right-hander was pleased just to receive an invitation to Oakland's spring training camp. The elbow surgery that Dobson had undergone after the 1971 season had rendered him a non-roster player, with no guarantee that he would have a job with the A's, or even with their top minor league affiliate. If Dobson pitched poorly in the spring, he might be witnessing the end of his career as a professional pitcher.

In 1973, Dobson had managed a record of just 9–13 for the Tucson Toros and had been lucky to receive a brief in-season promotion to Oakland. "Last year, I was working on my high slider and hanging curve," Dobson deadpanned in an interview with *The Sporting News*. Yet, Dobson had fared much better in winter ball, impressing Oakland scouts with improved control of his slider and curveball. Dobson had also shown the ability to pitch as both a starter and reliever, an unusual trait for a pitcher with such a fragile arm. Dobson's versatility would increase his nearly minuscule chances of making the A's' Opening Day roster.

If nothing else, Dobson had caught Finley's attention with his intense desire to make a full-time return to the major league lifestyle after a nearly two-year hiatus. "When I came back [to Oakland] last year," Dobson explained to Ron Bergman,

"I noticed how great everything was—the planes, the schedule, the big league towns...And clubhouse guys that do something except just sit around and gripe after giving you a spread that consists of nothing except two pieces of bread and one slice of bologna." In Finley's mind, many of the A's were unappreciative of major league perks; Dobson, in contrast, had developed a special regard for the luxurious life of a major league team.

With spring training just a few days away, the A's had a surplus of pitching and good position players, but a dearth of other employees. No manager, no full-time public relations director, and no sidekick for No. 1 announcer Monte Moore. In mid-February, Charlie Finley filled the latter vacancy by hiring 24-year-old Jon Miller, a budding broadcaster who hailed from Walnut Creek, California, a suburb of Oakland. Miller was a broadcasting no-name, a recent college graduate who had little on-the-job experience. By the 1990s, Jon Miller would become one of baseball's most well-known announcers as the lead commentator for ESPN's Sunday Night Game of the Week.

With Miller and Moore now in place as the broadcasters, all the A's needed was an outlet to air the games. Finley had failed to sign a deal with either a television or radio station. Although most teams in the early seventies made very few of their games available over free TV, every team made sure to broadcast all, or at least most, of their games on the radio. Radio coverage served as an excellent—and inexpensive—way to promote a ballclub. Only Finley, who had put together very poor radio networks in past years, didn't seem to regard a radio contract as a very high priority. Finley even reached a new low in broadcasting history one season when he arranged for a *college* radio station to air the A's' games.

Chapter 22

The Return of the Dark Age

Newsmakers in 1974

In March, a federal grand jury indicts President Richard Nixon on charges of conspiracy to cover up White House involvement in the Watergate scandal...In the spring, President Nixon turns over transcripts of his Watergate tapes to the House Judiciary Committee...Facing impeachment in Congress, President Nixon announces his resignation on August 8. Vice President Gerald Ford succeeds Nixon as the nation's leader.

The energy crisis reaches a critical stage. Numerous service stations are closed because of a shortage of gas, while open stations sometimes feature lines that stretch for several miles...Patty Hearst, the daughter of millionaire publisher Randolph Hearst, is abducted by the Symbionese Liberation Army, which demands that $4 million in food be given to the poor as ransom...Television networks announce the cancellation of several shows that feature violence and gunfighting, and promise to carry more family-oriented programs.

Evil Knievel fails in his effort to vault the 1,600-foot divide of the Snake River Canyon...Muhammad Ali becomes the second man in boxing history to regain the world heavyweight title when he knocks out George Foreman in the second round...Nineteen-year-old Moses Malone becomes the first basketball player to advance directly from high school to the professional ranks when he signs a contract with the Utah Stars of the American Basketball Association.

The absence of a radio contract paled in comparison to the A's' largest vacancy—the managerial office. With spring training only days away, Charlie Finley had struck out in efforts to bring Frank Robinson or Dave Bristol aboard as manager. By now, Finley realized that Dick Williams had no interest in returning and would rather sit out the entire 1974 season. So, in late February, Finley placed a call to one of his many former managers—Alvin Dark. Finley asked Dark if he were willing to manage the team, but refrained from actually offering him the job. "It's a tough spot to put a man in," Dark told *Sports Illustrated*. "No matter what [the new manager] does he'll probably be wrong. The first time he loses a close game the second-guessers will have a field day." Dark, who had already been fired as manager by Finley in 1967, realized that the new manager would be subjected to endless comparisons with predecessor Williams and would be expected to win a third consecutive World Series. Dark knew that any lesser accomplishments would be considered disappointing. "So to answer your question," Dark said slyly to *Sports Illustrated*, "I'd love to."

On February 18, Finley told Dark to visit him in Oakland immediately. As soon as Dark arrived at Finley's home, the owner made him a monumental offer of a one-year contract, with bonuses for winning the division, the pennant, and the World Series. The deal lacked security, to say the least. Yet, Dark agreed to the contract, telling *Sports Illustrated* that it was "better than I've ever had in baseball."

Given the limitations of the new contract, Dark must have had some truly horrendous contracts earlier in his career. Although it was not publicly known at the time, Dark's new contract provided him with an even smaller degree of security than the usual managerial contracts. According to reports that would circulate after the 1974 season, the contract between Finley and Dark was essentially a non-guaranteed, day-to-day agreement. In other words, Finley could fire Dark at any time without having to pay off his manager for the rest of the season.

On February 20, three days before the start of spring training, Finley staged a press conference to officially introduce Dark as the 12th manager in his reign as A's owner. An impatient Finley did his best to anticipate reporters' questions, answering their queries before they had even had a chance to ask them. "Yes, he was hired by me in 1966...Yes, he was fired in 1967...Yes, I hired him again...Yes, he expects to be fired again someday."

A reporter asked Finley how much input he, as owner, would have in managing the team. "If I have any suggestions, such as putting [Ray] Fosse at shortstop and he [Dark] doesn't like it, then he'll explain to me why he doesn't," Finley ominously told *The Sporting News*. "And if I say Fosse is at shortstop, then Fosse will be at shortstop." Finley then contradicted himself later in the press conference. "Alvin had free reins then [in 1966] and he'll have free reins now." Now that Finley had made *that* clear, Dark had to sideswipe an even more difficult obstacle—trying to repair a racist image that he had developed during the 1960s.

Oakland beat writers wondered how Latinos like Campy Campaneris and Jesus Alou and African-American players like Reggie Jackson, Billy North, and Blue Moon Odom would respond to a manager who—according to some observers—held them in less regard than white players of similar talents. In particular, how would Odom relate to his new manager? In 1967, Dark had demoted Odom to the minor leagues, prompting a charge of racism from the young pitcher. Dark maintained that such criticism was unfair. "I'm a born-again Christian," Dark explained to Ron Bergman. "Being a born-again Christian, there is no color involved or race involved as far as love is concerned. Everyone will be given the fairest chance. If a player makes a mistake, I don't care as far as color is concerned. He made a mistake, that's all."

Critics of Dark had their doubts, especially those who remembered his stormy managerial tenure with the San Francisco Giants in the early 1960s. Dark had gained an especially bad reputation with the black and Latino players on the Giants, who felt that he too often pointed the finger at them after losses. The minorities on the Giants became even more infuriated when they read a series of disparaging quotes attributed to Dark in an article in *Newsday*, a newspaper in Long Island, New York.

"We have trouble because we have so many Spanish-speaking and Negro players on the team," *Newsday* writer Stan Isaacs quoted Dark as saying. "They are just not able to perform up to the white ballplayer when it comes to mental alertness." In the article, Dark went on to question the pride and intelligence of black and Latin players. Dark later claimed that Isaacs had badly misquoted him throughout the story.

In a 1974 *Sports Illustrated* article that contained excerpts of a book he had written with John Underwood, Dark tried to clarify his remarks in the Isaacs interview. Dark explained that several Giants, including Jesus Alou and Orlando Cepeda, had been guilty of "dumb baserunning" in recent games. Because Alou and Cepeda happened to be dark-skinned Latinos, Dark felt that Isaacs had inferred his comments to be racist. Dark accused Isaacs of taking some of his remarks out of their proper context and placing undue emphasis on certain negative statements that he had made.

During his days with the Giants, Dark had encountered a number of run-ins with Cepeda. Dark cited several examples of what he considered Cepeda's lack of hustle on the base paths, which had led to verbal reprimands after games. Dark described one game against the Milwaukee Braves where Cepeda was "pinch-hitting, the last out of a game on national television, and he hit a ground ball, ran about 30 feet, stopped, and walked back to the dugout." When Cepeda reached the dugout, Dark shouted at him loudly, continuing the barrage as the two men walked to the clubhouse. Although Dark admitted that he had gone too far in "showing him up in front of the other ballplayers," he made it clear that Cepeda's failure to run hard on a ground ball had prompted the reaction.

"I recall when I played for Alvin Dark," Cepeda says. "Alvin Dark segregated the team. He put [divided] the whites, the blacks, and Latins. We had to strike against that, you know, being black and being Latin." In addition to separating the players by race and color in the clubhouse, Cepeda says Dark banned the speaking of Spanish in the Giants' clubhouse, a decision that upset the Latin players, many of whom struggled with the English language. Cepeda adds that Dark habitually blamed tough Giant losses on the team's black and Latino stars, including himself, Willie Mays, and Willie McCovey. Given Cepeda and Dark's feelings for one another, Charlie Finley could be thankful that the former no longer played for the A's. Otherwise, Oakland players might have had to break up fights between Cepeda and Dark on a daily basis. Of course, they had already become accustomed to breaking up conflicts between two *teammates*, as evidenced by previous skirmishes involving Vida Blue, Blue Moon Odom, and Rollie Fingers.

Unlike the Giants of the early 1960s, the A's encountered few racial conflicts or incidents. When players did fight, they generally did so for non-racial reasons. Yet, some of the players remained dissatisfied with the lack of interaction between different ethnic groups on the club. Vida Blue had previously described the A's as a team that broke down into strict racial divisions. Pointing to the starting outfield one day, Blue illustrated his contention. Joe Rudi (a white) played left, Angel Mangual (a Latino) patrolled center, and Reggie Jackson (a black) played right. "There are three cliques on this team," Blue told *Sport* Magazine, pointing to the outfielders, "and you can see them all out there."

The cover story in the June 3, 1974, edition of *Time* Magazine supported Blue's assertion. The article, which centered on Reggie Jackson's stardom in baseball, claimed that the A's were generally "free from tangible racial tension," but surmised that "an undercurrent of division persists. Black players tend to stick together socially, as do the Latin Americans and whites. This atmosphere of tolerance minus affection is now commonplace in baseball."

Other players did not share the opinion of Blue or the *Time* Magazine feature. "We never felt that we were black or white or Latin or American," captain Sal Bando says, insisting that he witnessed no racial divisions during his days in Oakland. Bando says the common enemy found in the owner's box may have contributed to general racial harmony. "We were just one baseball team that cared for each other. I think the reason might have been the friction that Charlie [Finley] caused that had us all stick together and rely on each other. It's a negative way of getting a team concept, but in a roundabout way I think it worked."

Questions of racism aside, Alvin Dark promised to be more tactful and sensitive in relating to his players. Dark also emphasized his strong religious faith, which had come under criticism due to a well-known incident of marital infidelity. Since remarried, Dark quoted the Bible frequently and vowed that he had become a changed man—for the better. "I've reassessed my commitment to the Christian life and where I had failed in it, and my faith in Jesus Christ," Dark vowed in an interview with *Sports Illustrated*.

One day after Finley officially hired Dark to replace Dick Williams, Reggie Jackson awaited the results of his arbitration hearing, which would determine his 1974 salary. After failing to reach a contract agreement on their own, Jackson had taken Finley to arbitration, a new system designed to eliminate long player holdouts. A total of nine A's had decided to resolve their contract disputes through arbitration, more than any other major league team. While Jackson had asked for $135,000, Finley had countered with an offer of $100,000. The independent arbitrator sided with Jackson, making him the highest paid player in the history of the A's' franchise.

Another star player, third baseman Sal Bando, had already won his arbitration case. Bando would receive $100,000, rather than the $75,000 offered by Finley. Bando and Jackson now joined Catfish Hunter as the three A's making $100,000 or more in 1974. Other Oakland players did not fare as well as Bando and Jackson at the arbitration table. Left fielder Joe Rudi and utilitymen Ted Kubiak and Jack

Heidemann all lost their cases, as did first baseman-catcher Gene Tenace. The arbitrator ruled that Tenace would have to settle for $45,000, as opposed to the $52,500 that he had sought. Tenace reacted bitterly to the decision, declaring that he would only play first base for the A's, and would no longer serve as an emergency catcher behind Ray Fosse. "If they're not going to pay me to play two positions," Tenace fumed to Ron Bergman, "then I'll play only one."

Faced with an angry Tenace, an overbearing owner, and questions about his racial beliefs, Dark embarked on his second term as A's manager. During his previous tenure with the Kansas City Athletics, Dark had managed several of the organization's current stars: Bando, Dick Green, Campy Campaneris, Hunter, and Blue Moon Odom. Those players, representing one-fifth of the A's' 1974 roster, had come to know Dark as a hot-tempered, impatient man who often feuded with A's management—i.e., Charlie Finley. Those players hardly recognized the new Alvin Dark that descended on Mesa, Arizona, in spring training of 1974. Refusing to lose his temper, Dark no longer cursed or yelled at his players. When his players made mistakes, Dark talked about religion and love. Those reporters who had heard Dark profess to be a born-again Christian at his opening press conference realized that he had meant what he said. Dark had apparently undergone a deep and sincere religious conversion and intended to transfer his new lifestyle to the playing field.

Dark also received some good news with regard to player personnel. Dick Green, to no one's surprise, announced that he had changed his mind about retirement and reported to spring training in prime physical condition. Green's arrival in camp gave the A's a veteran fallback at second base in the event that young Manny Trillo struggled to hit American League pitching. Dark also learned that Tenace had reversed his pronouncement about not wanting to catch and would now be willing to go behind the plate if needed. "I'm not crazy about catching," Tenace admitted to Ron Bergman, "but maybe in the long run it can help me career-wise and financially." Dark announced plans to use Tenace as a backup catcher to Ray Fosse, and as a bullpen catcher on those days when he was not playing first base.

Tenace's change of mind came as especially good news to the A's, whose 40-man roster contained exactly one fulltime catcher, Ray Fosse. The A's had invited three other receivers, all of the non-roster variety, to spring training. The group included once-and-future Athletic Frank Fernandez and minor leaguers Tim Hosley and Buzz Nitschke, none of whom inspired much confidence in the event that Fosse experienced a season-ending injury. On the bright side, Buzz Nitschke, whose name sounded like a cross between a catcher and a linebacker, possessed perhaps the best moniker of any player in organized baseball.

Speaking of football, Vida Blue indicated that he might give up baseball after the season in favor of a career in the fledgling World Football League, a rival to the more established National Football League. The combination of unpleasant salary negotiations with Charlie Finley and the sense that he had already accomplished his baseball goals left Blue pining for a new challenge. Blue had starred at quarterback at Mansfield High School in Louisiana, throwing 35 touchdowns in his senior season. Blue's quarterbacking impressed recruiters so much that he received offers from 25 college football powers, including a major southern school, the University of Houston. The Cougars, who had just installed the new run-and-shoot offense, hoped to make Blue the first black quarterback in the history of the Southwest Conference.

Blue had signed a letter of intent to play at the university, but family tragedy interfered with the plan. In 1968, during his senior year at DeSoto High School, Blue's father died suddenly from a heart attack. Vida Blue Sr. had supported his wife and six children with his income as a factory worker. As the oldest child, Vida felt compelled to step in and assume the leadership of the household. The high school senior opted for an immediate professional baseball contract, rather than a four-year college scholarship, as a means of supporting his family.

The A's selected Blue with their first pick in the 1967 amateur draft. As he did with most of his highly recruited talents, Charlie Finley paid Blue a personal visit in an effort to secure a signed contract. Finley and Blue agreed on a salary of just over $10,000, a bonus of $40,000, and an important stipulation. At the behest of Blue's high school baseball coach, Clyde Washington, the A's agreed to pay for Blue's tuition to a four-year college. In the short-term, Blue wanted to care for his mother and siblings, but Washington hoped that Vida would return to his schooling in the future.

Blue went only 8–11 in his first minor league season, but struck out 231 batters in 152 innings. His arm strength and athleticism so impressed officials in the A's' organization that he earned a promotion to the major leagues only two years later, at the age of 19. Although Blue spent relatively little time in the minors, he gained a valuable social experience. Having grown up in the predominantly black neighborhood of Mansfield, a town of fewer than 10,000 residents, Blue had never before played with players from other racial and ethnic groups.

After Blue first arrived in the major leagues in 1969, principally on the strength of his fastball, he received help from a 32-year-old Latino pitcher named Juan Pizarro. The Puerto Rican left-hander showed Blue how to improve the control and break of his curveball while providing other fatherly advice on the art of major league pitching. "I got to be a high-class batting practice pitcher," Blue told sportswriter Wells Twombly in describing the unsophisticated pitching style he used before encountering Pizarro. "Juan showed me how to grip the ball for a curve. I really didn't have any idea."

In addition to Blue's current hints about giving up baseball, the A's faced controversies and distractions on several other fronts during the spring of '74. Reggie Jackson annoyed Charlie Finley when he signed a deal with *Puma*, agreeing to wear the company's baseball shoes in exchange for a payment of $30,000 over the next three years. Finley pointed to a pre-existing contract with *Puma's* chief rival, *Adidas*. The terms of Finley's arrangement with *Adidas* required all of the Oakland players to wear *Adidas* shoes during the regular season. Jackson refused to wear *Adidas*, saying that he would fulfill his contract with *Puma*. Finley threatened to suspend Jackson $1,000 per day. Reggie said he'd think about it.

Finley butted heads with Jackson, and the rest of the players, on another issue. Early in spring training, Finley instructed the team's traveling secretary, Jim Bank, to distribute the team's new World Series rings. The rings, supposedly a reward for the team's second consecutive World Championship, contained no diamonds, only cheap-looking synthetic emeralds. "These are trash rings," Jackson told Ron Bergman bluntly. "It's not fair, it's not right." Even quiet, reserved players like Catfish Hunter, who usually resisted controversy, sounded off on the rings. "The new rings are horsemeat," said Catfish. "This ring isn't even as good as a high school ring."

Sal Bando says the World Series rings provide another example of the personality differences exhibited by Finley after his 1973 heart attack. "To show how he changed," Bando explains, "the first World Series we won, he gave us a ring with a full carat; he gave our wives a pendant that they wore around their necks with a half a carat. He gave each player a replica of the World Series trophy that ownership receives, in appreciation for what we did. Then he comes back the next two years and we got the cheapest rings you'll ever see a World Series team have. No stones, no nothing. It was just the way he was. He went from being very generous on the one hand to being very cheap on the other."

In the spring of 1973, when Finley had rewarded his players with lavish rings in appreciation for winning the first World Championship in Oakland franchise history, he had vowed to furnish his players with even better rings the next time around. The players had fulfilled their part of the arrangement, defeating the Mets for their second consecutive World Series triumph. Finley, apparently hurt that his players had not bothered to show him any gratitude for the luxurious rings of the previous year, reneged on the promise. "Screw 'em," Finley told *New York Daily News* sportswriter Dick Young, who came out in support of the owner in the ring controversy. "The next time we win," Finley told Young, "I won't give them a thing." Finley's disdain for players he considered unappreciative and ungrateful had reached a vengeful level. He also hadn't forgotten that these were the same players who had dared to criticize him for his handling of Mike Andrews during the 1973 World Series.

With two weeks to go in spring training, Finley angered his players further by announcing an unprecedented signing in baseball history. Finley added 22-year-old Herb Washington to the roster, despite the fact that he had never played baseball above the high school level. In fact, Washington hadn't played baseball since his junior year in high school, several years earlier. So what could Washington do that so impressed Finley? Washington, a world class sprinter, had set records in the 50-yard dash, running it in five seconds flat, and the 60-yard dash, with a time of 5.8. With Allan Lewis drawing his release over the winter, Finley viewed Washington as a pinch-runner extraordinaire, someone who could win a game with his speed in the late innings.

The A's distributed a press release—written by Finley—that heralded the arrival of Washington. "Finley and Dark feel that Washington will be directly responsible for winning 10 games this year," the release declared. Dark actually had said nothing of the kind, but Finley believed such a statement, and that was seemingly all that mattered. Dark, however, did predict that he would use Washington as early as the sixth inning, depending on game situations.

The A's also announced the hiring of former major league shortstop Maury Wills, previously one of Oakland's managerial candidate, as a spring training baserunning instructor. Under a special six-day program, Wills would tutor Washington on basic baserunning skills, everything from taking a proper lead to the correct way of rounding the bases. In other words, Wills would serve as Washington's personal coach. The A's had many standout players on their roster, including Reggie Jackson, Catfish Hunter, and Vida Blue, but none of them had their own individual instructor.

Wills' instruction did benefit Washington, a novice at running the bases. The former Dodger shortstop refined Washington's sliding skills, which were coarse at best and had left him susceptible to injuring himself. Wills taught Washington the method of sliding headfirst, as a way of reducing the wear and tear to his sprinter's legs.

The signing of Washington, a football and track star at Michigan State with no college or professional baseball experience, upset most of the A's' veterans. "That's a joke," exclaimed Gene Tenace to *The Sporting News*. "This is going to cost somebody who should be in the major leagues a job." Other Oakland players tried to pleasantly kid Washington, perhaps in an effort to make him feel more comfortable in hostile surroundings. After one player compared Washington to a racehorse, second baseman Dick Green approached the ridiculed pinch-runner. "If you break a leg," Green said to Washington, according to sportswriter Bill Libby, "we'll have to shoot you." When a *Sports Illustrated* reporter asked Washington to assess how long he needed to warm up before entering a game as a pinch-runner, Catfish Hunter interjected, addressing Washington by his new nickname. " 'Hurricane,' by the time you're warmed up," Hunter chided, "the game will be over."

In addition to being upset by Washington's presence in spring training, Tenace was also angered by some of Charlie Finley's many cost-cutting features of spring training. The veteran first baseman-catcher complained loudly about a spring training bus ride from Yuma to Palm Springs, wondering why Finley hadn't sprung for the cost of a flight. "We shouldn't have to travel like this," Tenace told *The Sporting News*. "We go out and bust our rears for the owner. He should do the same for us." Several other players griped that Finley had supplied only one case of soda and soft drinks for the long bus ride, prompting Reggie Jackson to buy two more cases of refreshments with his own money. Oakland veterans later discovered that Finley had invited two minor leaguers to the major league camp in Mesa, yet had elected not to pay them big league meal money.

Finley's repeated penny-pinching maneuvers undermined Alvin Dark's efforts to create a more serene, unified, and familial atmosphere than the A's had become used to in recent years. Dark extended an olive branch to Blue Moon Odom, the same man who had accused him of racism in 1967. Dark promised the veteran right-hander the fourth spot in the starting rotation, despite his horrid pitching numbers of 1973: a 5–12 record and an ERA of 4.49. Dark's attempts at establishing a positive backdrop to preseason camp did not go unnoticed by one of the team's stars. "I feel for him," said a sympathetic Reggie Jackson, one of the few A's willing to keep an open mind about his new manager, in an interview with *Sports Illustrated*. "He's bent over backwards to create harmony, to preserve dignity. I want him to do good."

Yet, many players found the born-again Dark overbearing in his religious kindness. Others wondered if he truly lived the words that he preached. Some players laughed at his biblical quotations, his meekness, his avoidance of confrontation. They mocked his mannerisms and style of speech. They ridiculed his refusal to use obscenities. They noticed how he refused to discipline teammates who had made mistakes. They wondered aloud how a major league manager could be so lacking in fire and fury, so unwilling to use anger as a motivating force.

"Alvin, I know he was very religious," says Ted Kubiak, now a minor league manager himself, "and I think that interfered with it a little bit at times. And I think that was resented. And maybe some hypocritical stuff going on, too. I know there were a lot of questions." Oakland players had remembered Dark's alleged racism toward black and Latino players and had heard stories of his infidelity to his first wife in the 1960s.

There were also baseball-related concerns. Dark's two-and-a-half-year absence from managing had clearly damaged his knowledge of the American League. When Dark discussed other teams that the A's needed to beat during the regular season, he often referred to players since departed from those clubs. In some cases, he mentioned players who were no longer active major leaguers. Oakland's players cringed at a manager who lacked so much credibility and seemed out of touch with the game in 1974.

"You know, I'd always heard what a good manager Alvin Dark was," says Kubiak, who had first played for Dark in 1967. "To be honest with you, I didn't really see it [in 1974]…His style was so different from Dick Williams, you know, I might not have had a fair advantage of making a comparison in that one quick year. I don't think he had as much command of things as Dick did. That's the one thing that stood out."

Dark made it clear that his own managerial wishes would run second to those of his owner. For example, Dark wanted to retain pitcher Chuck Dobson in the organization, keeping him at Triple-A Tucson at the start of the season, with the possibility of being promoted to the major leagues later in the summer. Although Dobson had struggled early in spring training, Dark had seen improvement and predicted that the veteran right-hander would help the A's later in the season.

One day later, Charlie Finley released Dobson, apparently not wanting to pay him $28,500 to pitch in the minor leagues. Dark offered little objection to Finley's decision. Finley telephoned Dobson at a nearby golf course, giving him the unpleasant news as he played the 17th hole. "He told me he hated to do it, but he was having problems, like his divorce," Dobson told Ron Bergman. "I'm getting released and he's crying on *my* shoulder! Incredible!"

Dobson returned to the team's workout facilities in Mesa to gather his belongings. According to *The Sporting News*, one of his teammates offered a fairly unsympathetic farewell. "What can I tell you," said backup catcher Frank Fernandez. "Good luck on your life?" A few days later, "Broadway" Frank would receive *his* release. As for Dobson, he would remain in Mesa for a few days, eventually signing a contract with the Mexico City Leones of the Mexican League before returning to the majors with the Angels. In contrast, Fernandez would never again play in the major leagues.

Fernandez had lost out on his bid to make the team when the A's reacquired veteran catcher Larry Haney from the Cardinals. The A's had sold Haney to the Cardinals the previous September, but now felt the need for another catcher in the event that Alvin Dark chose to use Herb Washington as a pinch-runner for either Ray Fosse or Gene Tenace. In turn, the inclusion of Washington on the roster may have robbed backup outfielder Billy Conigliaro of his best chance of making the team. The A's, concerned by Conigliaro's surgically repaired knee, released the veteran. "We kept Angel Mangual instead of Billy C.," Dark explained to *The Sporting News*, "because Angel can run better, hit better, and throw better." Some of the Oakland veterans, however, pointed to Conigliaro's superior defensive abilities as the reason why he—and not Mangual—belonged on the Opening Day roster. And most of the A's felt that both Mangual and Conigliaro deserved to make the team over Washington.

The A's still needed to make three more cuts to make the 25-man limit. Finley and Dark decided to demote veteran infielder Rich McKinney, once hailed as the A's' designated hitter of the future, and right-handed pitcher Glenn Abbott, who remained a highly regarded prospect. That left one more roster decision to make. After Bob Locker surrendered a grand slam to Milwaukee's George Scott, the A's placed the veteran reliever on the 21-day disabled list. Locker had complained of recent elbow pain, similar to discomfort that had bothered him the previous spring before disappearing prior to the start of the regular season. "It only hurts when I throw hard," Locker cautioned Ron Bergman. Oh, is that all?

Team doctors told Locker not to pick up a ball until May, in the hope that he would be able to start pitching sometime during the first half of the season. The doctors' timetable proved to be overly optimistic. The right-handed reliever would spend the entire season on the disabled list, the by-product of eventual surgery to remove bone chips from his elbow. The questionable trade that had sent the healthier and younger Horacio Piña to the Cubs in exchange for Locker looked even worse.

The A's left Mesa with a dreadful spring record of 8–16, their worst since 1970, when John McNamara still managed the team. McNamara would be fired after that season. Was a similar fate awaiting Alvin Dark, who had endured a spring full of off-the-record sniping, owner-induced controversy, and annoying distractions? Dark realized that the A's needed a prosperous start to eliminate the inevitable comparisons to the successful regime of Dick Williams—and perhaps to keep his job.

Chapter 23

Gunning for the Three-Peat

The A's played the Rangers in Arlington on Opening Day. Much to their dislike, the A's faced the hard-throwing Jim Bibby, the same massive man who had no-hit them the previous summer. Bibby proved far more hittable on this occasion, giving up eight hits and six runs in four and one-third innings. Reggie Jackson collected a home run, two doubles, and a single to lead Oakland to an impressive 7–2 win.

The mood in the A's' clubhouse after the game reflected anything but a well-played Opening Day rout. In the seventh inning, with the A's leading comfortably by seven runs, Alvin Dark had made a puzzling move, removing starting left fielder Joe Rudi for pinch-runner Herb Washington. The decision angered Rudi, normally the most placid and agreeable of all the A's. "I want to play nine innings of all 162 games," Rudi told Ron Bergman in the clubhouse. "When they take you out for a pinch-runner, it makes you look like half a ballplayer."

In the second game against the Rangers, Dark made another curious move when he took Ken Holtzman out after only four and a third innings. Holtzman had surrendered eight hits, but only two runs. The next day, Dark hooked Vida Blue after he faced two batters in the fifth inning. As he walked to the dugout, Blue shouted loudly enough for Dark to hear him. "All right, Alvin Dark, it's all right the first time," Blue warned his manager, according to a report in *The Sporting News*. "But the next time you do this to me, I'm going to lay every word in the book on you."

Although Blue had directed his anger at Dark, he knew that the manager was merely following orders from a higher authority. "I knew Alvin Dark was a religious man," Blue told Ron Bergman sarcastically, "but he's worshipping the wrong god—C.O.F." Those initials belonged to one Charles Oscar Finley.

The A's scored three runs in the fifth and three more in the ninth, capping off an 8–4 win over the Rangers and removing any possibility that Blue might lose the game. Strangely, Alvin Dark used Rollie Fingers for five innings of relief, his longest stint ever in a nine-inning game. Reggie Jackson supported Fingers and Blue with one of his best games as a major leaguer, driving in seven runs with two home runs and a single. Ranger fans in the right field bleachers rewarded Jackson with a standing ovation. "I tipped my hat to them three times because it was the least I could do," Reggie explained to the Associated Press. "I appreciated them recognizing my performance." After the game, several Oakland players rewarded

Jackson with an enormous balloon shaped like a hot dog. Reggie smiled as he carried the balloon through the Dallas Airport onto the team's flight to Kansas City.

The A's won two of three from Texas in the season-opening series, but most of the conversation centered on Alvin Dark's bizarre managerial moves. In addition to removing his starters earlier than usual, Dark had raised eyebrows by employing Herb Washington as a pinch-runner in each of the games. Several writers speculated that Charlie Finley had ordered Dark to use his glorified "designated runner" as often as possible in the early stages of the season.

The extent of Finley's stranglehold on Dark became even more evident during the A's' next series. Prior to the April 10th game against the Royals, Dark explained to the media why he had decided to bench his regular designated hitter, Deron Johnson. The move seemed to make sense for two significant reasons. Johnson had struggled badly during the first series against Texas and didn't figure to break out of his slump against a tough right-hander like Kansas City's Steve Busby. As a result, Dark announced that he would use the left-handed hitting Vic Davalillo as the DH.

Moments before the game, Finley telephoned Dark in the Oakland dugout. "He asked who the DH was going to be," Dark later revealed to Ron Bergman. "I said Davalillo. He said he'd rather have Johnson." Dark made the appropriate changes on the lineup card, handed it to captain Sal Bando, and instructed him to give it to the umpires.

Dark should have stayed with his original lineup. Johnson went 0-for-4 against Busby—and then went on the 15-day disabled list. A doctor's examination determined that Johnson had suffered a pulled muscle in his right hand, the same hand that had been surgically repaired during the offseason.

On Saturday, April 13, the A's returned to the Oakland Coliseum for the first time since Game Seven of the 1973 World Series. Vida Blue pitched miserably in front of the crowd of 22,743, giving up seven runs in only one and a third innings—his worst start as a major league pitcher. Campy Campaneris and Sal Bando made fielding errors and Oakland batters struck out 10 times against complete-game winner Jim Bibby.

The A's' on-field play represented only a fraction of the embarrassment at the home opener. Much like he had done during the 1973 World Series, Charlie Finley decided not to pay for any decorative red, white, and blue bunting, leaving the stadium walls barren. There were other problems at the Coliseum, too. The Oakland grounds crew had let most of the grass grow too long, while improperly cutting the grass around the bases. "If this grass was a little higher," surmised Reggie Jackson in an interview with *Sports Illustrated*, "we could have an Easter-egg hunt." Stadium workers had also neglected to store the canvas backdrop in center field, letting it sit out all winter long. The winter cold and rain had badly faded the green-colored canvas, which now appeared the same shade of color as the bleachers. "Another year and they still haven't cleaned the tarps," Sal Bando pointed out to Bay Area sportswriter Art Spander. "Or bought new ones. They're filthy. Why couldn't someone scrub them down?" As a result of all the cost-cutting neglect, the Coliseum took on an even more drab, depressing appearance than usual.

The A's did start to play better after their home-opening fiasco, winning five of seven games. Reggie Jackson's bat carried the offense, as the reigning American League MVP totaled four home runs, 11 RBIs, and a .429 batting average during the stretch.

One of Oakland's victories occurred in particularly dramatic style, a 4–3 win over the White Sox in extra innings. With two outs and a runner on second base in the 13th inning, Gene Tenace faced White Sox relief ace Terry Forster, who had pitched five shutout innings. Tenace cracked a solid single to left, scoring journeyman John Donaldson from second base with the winning run.

Donaldson represented the latest Oakland blast-from-the-past to return to Charlie Finley's kingdom. Donaldson had played for the A's from 1967 to 1969 before being traded to the expansion Seattle Pilots. In 1970, the A's reacquired Donaldson, only to trade him away again. After a number of stops in the minor leagues, Donaldson was released most recently by the Hawaii Islanders of the Pacific Coast League, before being signed to a minor league contract by the A's.

The A's signed Donaldson merely to provide themselves with a veteran body at Triple-A Tucson and had no intention of bringing him back to the major leagues. When starting second baseman Dick Green strained his instep, the A's placed him on the 15-day disabled list and summoned Donaldson from the minor leagues. Donaldson hoped he could remain on the roster for at least 52 days, which would give him enough service time to qualify for a full four-year pension.

In the meantime, Alvin Dark's—or rather Charlie Finley's—handling of the pitching staff continued to mystify the Oakland players. Dark repeatedly lifted his starters early, but for some reason, showed little confidence in any of his relievers, except for Rollie Fingers. As a result, Fingers became ineffective due to overuse while the rest of the bullpen struggled to remain sharp because of a lack of game action. Outspoken reliever Darold Knowles tried, but apparently failed, to be diplomatic in his criticism of Dark. "I don't agree with the way—and how can I put this delicately—Alvin Dark is handling the pitchers as a whole," Knowles assessed in an interview with Ron Bergman. "He's got to realize that there are other pitchers in the bullpen besides Rollie. I'm not ripping Alvin, but he's got a quick jerk sometimes and not quick enough other times."

Dark apparently thought Knowles *was* ripping him and called for a face-to-face meeting with the veteran left-hander. The two men exchanged angry words for about 45 minutes before finally breaking up the heated conversation. Most neutral observers agreed with Knowles' take on the situation, and pointed to games like that of April 21, when the A's hosted the Angels. With the A's leading 4–3 in the eighth inning, Dark pulled Vida Blue from the game. Blue said nothing to Dark, but proceeded to grab a bat and smash it against a bat rack in the Oakland dugout. The overworked Rollie Fingers, whom Dark called upon to relieve Blue, allowed three runs while retiring only one batter. A six-run Angel explosion in the eighth gave California a 9–5 victory, while saddling Fingers with his first loss of the season.

In that same game, Angels reliever Skip Lockwood threw a fastball up and in on Reggie Jackson, knocking Oakland's cleanup hitter to the ground. Jackson, believing that Angels manager Bobby Winkles had ordered the knockdown, shouted toward the California dugout. "I'm not going to forget that," Jackson warned. Ironically, Winkles had coached Jackson during his college career at Arizona State. "We'll still be friendly," Jackson told Ron Bergman after the game, "but I'm going to bear down harder when I come to the dish against them."

Aside from the bizarre deployment of the pitching staff, the most prominent theme of the early season centered on the presence of Herb Washington on the 25-man roster. Through the team's first 16 games, Washington had stolen only one base in four attempts, missed several hit-and-run and steal signs, and showed a complete lack of baseball instincts in running the bases. In one game, with runners on first and second base, Alvin Dark sent Washington in to pinch-run at first base. Washington, perhaps not realizing that second base was already occupied, asked Dark if he wanted him to steal on the first pitch. Dark patiently told him no, while Oakland players looked on in disbelief.

Reports of Washington's salary created resentment in the clubhouse. One newspaper story claimed that Washington's salary paid him over $42,000, in addition to a bonus of $35,000. Charlie Finley denied that he was paying Washington that much, but another reporter said Washington's salary approached the $30,000 level and featured a bonus of $25,000. Either way, Herb Washington qualified as major league baseball's most overpaid player. "It's still ridiculous," an anonymous Oakland player told *The Sporting News*.

On May 3, the A's decided to release one of their players, but it wasn't Washington. Veteran outfielder Vic Davalillo, hitting only .174 through the team's first 21 games, was given his walking papers. Granted, Davalillo hadn't played well as a part-time DH and outfielder, but his off-the-field reputation for excessive drinking may have expedited his departure over Washington.

One day after the release of Davalillo, Vida Blue continued his season-long struggles, losing an 8–2 blowout to the Indians. The latest loss dropped Blue's record to 0–4, lifted his ERA to 5.18, and left Alvin Dark wondering whether he should pull his star left-hander from the starting rotation completely. Although Blue had visibly shown his anger toward Dark for early removals from games, his pitching had done nothing to support his disagreements with the manager. Blue had likely annoyed his manager further with an action that smacked of protest and disrespect. After Dark fined Blue $250 for one of his acts of insubordination, the pitcher dumped an enormous load of pocket change on the manager's desk. Blue had decided to pay the fine in pennies, nickels, dimes, and quarters.

Blue pitched much better his next time out, defeating the Orioles, 7–3. The victory gave Blue his first win of the season, while providing a much-needed psychological uplifting. "That was important for my head," Blue told *Sports Illustrated*. "After four losses, you wonder whether you're still alive."

In early May, Charlie Finley continued his reign of thriftiness by announcing that the team would no longer pay the postage for players responding to fan mail. Finley informed the players that they, regardless of their status on the team, would have to spring for the requisite number of stamps. The Finley mandate represented a policy different from the operating procedures of most other major league teams, whose owners generally paid for return letters of fan mail.

The surly atmosphere of the Oakland clubhouse, teamed with the continuing mediocrity of play on the field, left the A's in a state of near rebellion. One player even suggested that Finley should fire Alvin Dark immediately and name captain Sal Bando as player-manager. Sensing that such sentiments had placed the A's in a no-win situation under Dark, Bando called a players-only meeting. At the meeting, several players assailed Dark for allowing fundamental mistakes to go unchecked. The players, however, reached an important resolution. They agreed to cease their public criticism of the manager, perhaps realizing that such second-guessing served no useful purpose. "We just weren't playing the way we should," Gene Tenace told *The Sporting News* after the meeting. "I don't think Alvin Dark was losing those games. We were."

Bando, one of the manager's staunchest critics early in the 1974 season, says he harbored no ill feelings toward Dark as a person. Bando acknowledges that circumstances made it more difficult for Dark to succeed in his return as a major league manager. "To Alvin's credit," Bando says, "he really didn't know the team that well simply because he had been out of baseball. He was going by things he had read or remembered, and it took him awhile to see the makeup of the club. At the beginning, it was an adjustment period for him and for us. We had some disagreements, but they were strictly baseball strategy in using the strengths of our club."

Dark accepted much of the blame for the A's' middling record. The veteran manager admitted that his lack of knowledge of the team's personnel had cost the A's several wins in April and May. "I'll be honest with you," Dark told a reporter from *The Sporting News*. "I'm not doing a good job, yet. We've lost about three games we should have won...I haven't learned my pitching staff yet. I've made a few mistakes with the rest of the players, too, but no one can tell you about your pitching staff. You can talk to your players and pitching coach, but you've got to learn about the staff yourself."

In fairness to Dark, the A's had suffered a number of injuries, which had left the manager shorthanded around the infield and off the bench. Second base continued to be a nagging problem, as the A's used five different players at the troubled position through the first 30 games of the season. In the fourth game of the year, Dick Green had strained his arch while turning a nifty double play. The injury resulted in his placement on the disabled list. Ten days later, Manny Trillo joined Green on the shelf when he pulled a thigh muscle running the bases. Ted Kubiak stepped in to play second base, but a calf injury to Sal Bando forced Dark to move the veteran utilityman to third base shortly thereafter. Bando's bad leg prompted the recall of journeyman John Donaldson from Triple-A Tucson. Donaldson played second base for two games, then collided with center fielder Billy North on a short pop-up to the outfield. The A's then signed one of their former players, veteran middle infielder Dal Maxvill, who had drawn his release from the Pirates two weeks earlier. In his second game at second base, Maxie received a spike wound from the Twins' Tony Oliva. Twenty-three stitches later, Maxvill found himself on the disabled list next to Green and Trillo.

The injury to Maxvill left Alvin Dark desperate for a second baseman. The A's considered highly touted prospect Phil Garner, but the scrappy infielder had reported to spring training late and had since been moved to third base, where he suffered a back injury. Garner's status left the A's with no other choice but to promote an obscure infielder, the oddly-named Gaylen Pitts, from Tucson. Pitts would become the seventh player to man the second base position for the A's in 1974, a season that had not yet entered the month of June.

The 27-year-old Pitts had started his professional career in 1964, but had never graduated to the major league level. Ten years after first signing a major league contract, Pitts finally made his major league debut on May 12 when the A's played the rival Twins. Alvin Dark inserted Pitts as his second baseman and No. 9 hitter. Moments before the game, several veteran A's warned Pitts about playing second base, a position that had become a black hole for Oakland. They made Pitts aware that six players had tried their hand at second base prior to him and almost all had come up injured. "A few of the fellows told me not to go out and play second base," Pitts later told Ron Bergman. "They said it was jinxed." Pitts made a fielding error in his debut, but made up for it with a 1-for-4 performance at the plate and a run scored, helping the A's to a 9–2 win.

Later in the day, the A's found out that Pitts really wasn't a second baseman after all. He had played virtually his entire minor league career at shortstop, but hadn't wanted to admit to Dark his lack of experience at second base. Who could blame Pitts, considering how long he had waited for a chance to play in the major leagues? Besides, Pitts knew that he had no future with the A's at shortstop, not with Campy Campaneris around.

Two nights later, Dark flip-flopped his infield, returning Ted Kubiak to second base and sliding Pitts over to third base. In the second game of a doubleheader against the Royals, Pitts delivered a dreamlike performance, collecting three hits in four at-bats and driving in the game-winning run in the bottom of the 10th. Pitts accounted for the A's' only two runs of the game, both coming on run-scoring doubles, as Oakland prevailed 2–1 at the Coliseum.

Pitts contributed offensively in another game, but the weather wiped out his performance. An RBI double by Pitts tied the White Sox at 4–4, but heavy rains forced the umpires to stop play as the A's continued to bat in their half of the inning. When the umpires decided that play could not be resumed, the score reverted back to the last completed inning, when the White Sox led, 4–3. Under baseball's controversial rule, the umpires credited the Sox with the victory, knocking Pitts' double from the records, as if it never happened.

On May 17—or nearly a month and a half into the season—Charlie Finley finally reached an agreement with a television station to carry 20 A's games. While all other major league teams had signed television deals during the offseason, Finley had waited until over five weeks of the regular season had passed to finalize his arrangement. With about 130 games to go in the season, the A's would appear on local television an average of only once for every six to seven games.

Finley, ever the penny-pincher, added that he wanted to use members of the Oakland pitching staff to serve as color announcers on the game broadcasts. So, for example, on a night when Catfish Hunter was not scheduled to start, he would take his place in the broadcasting booth next to play-by-play man Monte Moore. Vida Blue, Ken Holtzman, and Blue Moon Odom would do the same. Under the bizarre plan, Finley would save himself the cost of hiring a full-time color commentator. Of course, Finley had no intention of paying his starting pitchers any additional money to pull double duty.

The next day, the A's lost one of their most wrenching games of the season, a 3–2 decision to the White Sox. The A's left 11 runners on base, negating a 10-strikeout performance by Vida Blue. Any loss upset Finley, but especially a loss to the White Sox, who played in his hometown of Chicago. After the game, Finley berated Dark in the manager's office for nearly 20 minutes. Although the lecture occurred behind a locked door, Finley shouted loud enough for several of the A's to hear him. "I'm playing to win," Finley screamed at Dark, according to a story that appeared in *Time* Magazine. "If you don't start playing aggressive baseball, I'll kick your bleeping ass out of here. We won two years without you and we can win again without you." If Oakland players felt no sympathy for Dark prior to the outburst, they probably did now.

The A's, coincidentally or not, rallied behind Dark after hearing Finley's demeaning dress-down. Oakland strung together four consecutive wins, capped off by a 7–4 victory over the Twins. Reggie Jackson continued his strong offensive showing, while exhibiting few effects of a badly pulled hamstring. Jackson powered a home run and a three-run double early in the game, while Joe Rudi capped off the scoring with a tie-breaking two-run double in the ninth inning. After the game, Rudi paid Jackson a compliment, one that might have been hard to dispute. " 'Super' is unbelievable," Rudi told *Sports Illustrated*, while referring to Jackson by his nickname. "He's the best player in the league." Reggie returned the favor when he termed Rudi "underrated and underpaid," a statement that likely rankled Charlie Finley, the man responsible for paying Rudi. "He's the nicest guy in baseball," Jackson told *Sports Illustrated*, "and the best left fielder in the league."

Rudi had also made himself into the most fundamentally sound player on the A's. "There are six things I look for in a ballplayer," Alvin Dark told Phil Elderkin of the *Christian Science Monitor*, "and Rudi checks out perfectly in all six." The six categories? Hitting, hitting behind the runner, bunting, running, fielding, and throwing. Although a few Oakland players hit with more power and many of them possessed faster running speed, no one hit the cutoff man, executed the hit-and-run, or ran the bases more wisely than Rudi.

On May 24, Angels right-hander Dick Lange ended Oakland's mini-streak, besting Catfish Hunter in a 4-3 decision. The tight game, the latest in a series of hard-fought matches between the A's and Angels, exemplified the growing rivalry between the California clubs. Earlier in the season, the Angels had angered the A's when Skip Lockwood floored Reggie Jackson with an inside fastball. According to a story in *Sports Illustrated*, such incidents stemmed from an initial episode that occurred in 1973. "They started it last year," said the five-foot, nine-inch Lange, the shortest pitcher in baseball, "when they referred to us as a bunch of Triple-A players." Triple-A or not, California had managed to split its first four matchups with Oakland during the 1974 regular season.

On May 31, Dick Green rejoined the active roster, having missed 43 consecutive games with an injured arch. The return of the veteran second baseman figured to restore some normalcy to the Oakland infield, where minor league refugees Gaylen Pitts and John Donaldson had been seeing too much playing time. For the first time since the opening series of the season, Dark would be able to start his regular infield: Gene Tenace at first, Green at second, Campy Campaneris at short, and Sal Bando at third. To their credit, the A's had played well without Bando in the lineup, winning seven and losing three during their captain's stint on the shelf. But the A's would need the services of Bando over the long haul if they hoped to return to the American League playoffs for a fourth consecutive season.

Chapter 24

The Fight

The A's had also fared well without Reggie Jackson, who had missed a handful of games with a bad hamstring. With Jackson in the lineup, however, Oakland's offense operated at a higher level, one of the best in the American League. In late May, Jackson's hitting streak finally ended at 15 games. Yet, Reggie's season-long average stood at .404. The A's had long since become accustomed to Jackson's mammoth home runs and pace-setting run production, but hadn't ever seen the slugger hit so consistently during his major league career.

Jackson did another kind of hitting on June 5. As the A's' players dressed in the clubhouse at Tiger Stadium, Billy North, already fully suited in his Oakland uniform, suddenly shouted a few words at Jackson, who was completely undressed. Jackson returned North's verbal volley and the two men proceeded to brawl on the clubhouse floor. Vida Blue jumped in first, attempting to break up the combatants. In the meantime, a trio of A's who were playing cards—Dick Green, Ken Holtzman, and Darold Knowles—ignored Blue's request for help in stopping the fight. Knowles, who in particular didn't care for Jackson, saw that North was winning the fight and elected not to step in.

Another player, Ray Fosse, decided to play the role of peacemaker. Assisted by Blue and other players, Fosse helped separate North and Jackson, albeit only momentarily. A few minutes later, North and Jackson tangled again, only to be broken up by Sal Bando and Gene Tenace. Unlike previous clubhouse fights involving the A's, the North-Jackson brawls contained a tinge of hatred. "I'll tell you one thing," one of the A's said anonymously in an interview with Dick Young of the *New York Daily News*. "It wasn't the regular clubhouse fight. There was no backing off. They went at it hot and heavy—twice."

The skirmishes between Jackson and North came as a surprise to some observers of the team, considering that the two men had become friends during the 1973 season. In fact, North believed that he was Jackson's *only* friend on the team. Their friendship had seemingly strengthened during the offseason, since both lived in Arizona. During spring training, they often ate breakfast together at Jackson's home and rode to the ballpark in the same car. So why the flurry of fists in the clubhouse?

Some players claimed that the fight might have resulted from an incident one month earlier. North had hit a routine ground ball to the second baseman and did not appear to run hard to first. As North jogged back to the dugout, Jackson angrily yelled at his teammate in full view of his Oakland teammates, chiding him for his failure to hustle. During the encounter, North defended himself by explaining that he had been bothered by a nagging groin pull, which prevented him from running at his usual speed and level of effort. According to an article by Murray Olderman in *Sport* Magazine, North then shouted at Jackson, "You're not No. 5," referring to manager Alvin Dark's uniform number. "I only take orders from No. 5." When Jackson stepped to the plate later in the game, several A's players complained about his obscenity-filled attempt to embarrass North.

Dark and Charlie Finley denied that the aforementioned incident had played a significant part in causing the clubhouse fight, but sportswriter Dick Young maintained otherwise. In the June 8, 1974 edition of the *New York Daily News*, Young reported that North had taken such offense to Jackson's charge of loafing that he had decided to stop talking to Reggie the next day, thus halting the friendship.

North not only gave Jackson the silent treatment, but also refused to shake his hand after each one of his next 10 home runs. North also tried to rile Jackson in retaliation for his recent criticism. In his column, Young wrote that North repeatedly uttered derogatory comments about Jackson within earshot of the slugger. One of those remarks by North triggered the fight in Detroit. "I guess Reggie couldn't take it any more," an unnamed Athletic told Young. "He [North] let go with one of his nasty cracks. Reggie, who was sitting there undressed, yelled, 'I've had enough of it,' and he charged at him."

Sal Bando claimed that the problems between the two outfielders had started much earlier than the loafing incident. "It goes back deeper than that," Bando told the *New York Daily News*. "It is a problem that doesn't exist between the base lines, but between two very strong-headed individuals."

Race relations may have played a part in creating the tensions between North and Jackson. In April, North had informed Jackson that he was spending too much time with whites and not enough time with other blacks. North told Jackson that he too often criticized black players for mistakes, while excusing his white teammates for similar errors. Jackson took offense to North's accusations. "I've made a special effort to help my own kind," Jackson told *Time* Magazine. Indeed, Jackson regularly donated thousands of dollars to African-American community groups. "But it has backfired," Reggie acknowledged. "I'm having trouble communicating with them, and that upsets me. I know they mistrust me because I spend so much time with white people. But I'll tell you something. On the field I don't respect anyone just because he's black or white. I respect him if he performs."

Having grown up in the racially mixed community of Wyncote, Pennsylvania—a suburb of Philadelphia—Jackson had always made a strong effort to integrate himself with other ethnic groups. Jackson had once roomed with Chuck Dobson, a white pitcher, dated several Caucasian women, and frequently spoke Spanish with Latino players. Jackson wanted to be liked by everyone, regardless of race. "Now ain't that some bleep?" Jackson asked rhetorically during an interview with sportswriter Phil Pepe. "Is that supposed to be bad?"

The state of his relationship with North disturbed Jackson. "This whole thing is bad," Reggie told Dick Young. "Two black guys, two teammates, It shouldn't be like this." Jackson explained that he had tried to repair his relationship with North on at least six occasions. "He was my friend," Jackson said sadly to Pepe. "He's a stubborn kid, but he's also a very intelligent kid. He's really a good person and a great ballplayer and we had a lot of good times together. I miss his friendship."

For his part, North said little, except to deny innuendo that he had initiated the fight with his former friend. "I was not the aggressor," North told Clint Roswell of the *New York Daily News*. "I am not the heavy in this situation. I was trying to defend myself." Publicly, North would say little more about the incident.

Unlike previous fights involving Oakland players, Charlie Finley reacted aggressively to the latest controversy. Finley booked a flight to Milwaukee, in order to meet the A's on the next stop of their road trip. He met with Jackson, North, and Alvin Dark in the trainer's room, and ordered his two outfielders to shake hands. According to an article by John Kuenster in *Baseball Digest*, the angry owner then addressed the team for about 20 minutes in the clubhouse. "You're World Champions," Finley screamed aloud. "Stop acting like a bunch of kids!"

As Finley scolded his players, images of a father screaming at his children came to mind. "He'd come in and have tirades," says Ted Kubiak. "He was the father of the family. He was the guy who led everything. Guys would talk back to him in meetings like kids would talk back to their parents. I always marveled at the fact that he listened. You know, he was open. He was an open guy. I just learned a lot from him, I think."

Finley hoped that Jackson and North would learn from the incident. In this case, Finley had good reason to be upset, considering that the dual fights between Jackson and North had proved costly to the A's' health. During the second go-round, Jackson fell and suffered a bruised shoulder, which prevented him from taking his usual ferocious swing. More importantly, the first fight caused a serious injury to one of the attempted peacemakers. Ray Fosse separated his cervical disk and pinched a nerve in his neck, necessitating that he be placed in traction in an Oakland hospital. As a result, the A's lost their starting catcher for what they feared would be a significant amount of time. Would the A's have to call upon the immortal Buzz Nitschke after all?

Fosse replayed the fight between North and Jackson, and his subsequent attempt at peacemaking, for the Oakland media. "I was just sitting there in my underwear," Fosse told Ron Bergman. "Billy walked in and made a few remarks to Reggie and all of a sudden they started fighting. Instinctively I jumped in and tried to break it up. Vida [Blue] was also one of the guys who tried to break it up. I was concerned about Vida because he was pitching that night."

Fosse saved Blue from injury, but not himself. During the melee, Fosse ended up on the floor with both North and Jackson. When Fosse returned to his feet, he found himself being pushed up against a locker. In the game against the Tigers later that night, Fosse felt pain in his right shoulder as he tried to make a throw to second base.

Although Finley made no public statements in assessing blame, he told Jackson that he held *him* most responsible for the altercation with North. Finley's finger-pointing bothered Jackson, who felt betrayed by the owner. The criticism would affect Jackson's play in both the field and at the plate. North noticed Jackson's failing spirit and eventually initiated a meeting with his former friend. The meeting led to a reconciliation. "It was hurting the team," North told *Sport* Magazine in describing Jackson's fragile sense of security. "Hell, the man wasn't hustling or really swinging the bat."

Conflicts such as the strained relationship between North and Jackson forced even the opposing media to cover the A's. "You know, Bill North got into fights and you covered those things," says former baseball writer Bob Fowler. "You went to interview Bill North and he told you his side, and then you went and interviewed Reggie and he told you his side." While such controversies tended to create friction with the Oakland media, Fowler says players like North and Jackson proved cooperative with the visiting beat writers, even in answering questions about fights and disagreements. "It was a very nice working atmosphere," Fowler insists. "If there was animosity, it was only directed at the local, Bay Area media. The players were more than happy to share their stories outside of the local guys."

With Ray Fosse sidelined as a result of the North-Jackson fight, Alvin Dark slid Gene Tenace from first base to catcher, moved Deron Johnson from designated hitter to first base, and installed Angel Mangual as his DH. The new lineup weakened the A's defensively and in the standings, as they lost seven of their next 10 games. Oakland's four-game lead in the West slipped to just one.

Shortly after Fosse's injury, Tenace pinched a nerve in his neck while swinging the bat awkwardly. The latest setback shelved Tenace, forcing Alvin Dark to turn to his third-string catcher, Larry Haney, with Buzz Nitschke just a phone call away.

On June 19, the A's lost their second straight game to the Red Sox, an excruciating 2–1 defeat in extra innings. In the top of the 11th inning, reliever Paul Lindblad allowed a bases-loaded sacrifice fly to backup catcher Bob Montgomery. Former Athletic Diego Segui handled the A's in the bottom of the 11th, retiring Sal Bando for the game's final out. The loss, and a managerial gaffe committed by Alvin Dark earlier in the game, left Bando in the foulest of moods.

"We had battled back, tied the game," Bando recalls, "and we led off [the 10th inning] with the eighth-place hitter getting on. Instead of putting up someone to bunt him over with the top of the order coming up, he [Dark] sent up Reggie, who was not playing that day, and Reggie ended up hitting into a double play." In actuality, Jackson pinch-hit for the sixth-place hitter, first baseman Deron Johnson, and ended up flying to center field, but Bando disagreed with Dark's strategy nonetheless.

"And then we ended up losing in extra innings," Bando says, continuing the story. "To make matters worse, I made the last out of the game. So as I came up the runway and into the clubhouse just frustrated and disgusted with losing, and making the last out, the fact that I thought we could have bunted him over in the top of the inning, I kicked a trash can and said, 'You can't manage a meat market.'"

Bando did not intend for the remark to be heard by his manager. "Alvin Dark never came into the clubhouse after the game," Bando explains. "But for some reason, he was in there that day. As I looked up, he was standing right in front of me. To make matters even worse, Glenn Dickey, the writer for the [San Francisco] *Chronicle*, happens to be in there, which was unusual. And he heard it. So the next day, headlines in the paper say: BANDO SAYS DARK CAN'T MANAGE A MEAT MARKET."

To his credit, Dark refrained from responding angrily to Bando. "Alvin and I had a conversation right after that happened," Bando says, "I went into his office. I told him where I disagreed with him. He said there was some merit to it, but I apologized for saying that. I mean, that was more temper than any substance, and he accepted my apology.

"But what was really funny about the whole thing is the next day I got a telegram from the meat packers union. They said, 'If you think managing a meat market is easy, you don't know what you're talking about.' To me, that was hilarious."

After the controversial post-game scene, the A's won three straight games and six of their next seven, leading the manager to place a positive spin on the outburst by his team captain. "It kind of relaxed the team," Dark told Ron Bergman in recalling Bando's "meat market" remark and the subsequent meeting with his third baseman. "I'll tell you, I felt better after the game than before it. I thought we'd been in a state of lethargy for about a week."

On June 24, the A's decided to make a roster change, parting company with one of the players instrumental to their regular season success in 1973. Designated hitter-first baseman Deron Johnson, hitting just .195 with seven home runs, was sold on waivers to the Brewers. Although less than a year removed from one of his most productive seasons, Johnson had been unable to find his stroke after initially injuring his thumb in August of 1973. In February, Johnson had expressed his wish to remain a member of the A's for the balance of his career. "For six years, before I came to Oakland, I was with losing clubs," Johnson told *Sport* Magazine, in referring to stints with the Phillies, Braves, Reds, and Kansas City Athletics. "I want to stay here [in Oakland] until I quit baseball." In selling Johnson's contract to the Brewers, the A's had ended that dream while removing one of their most popular players from their clubhouse. The A's had also decided to entrust the inconsistent and enigmatic Angel Mangual with the daily responsibilities of the designated hitter role.

The injury to Ray Fosse and the ineffectiveness of Deron Johnson had left the A's short at three positions: catcher, first base, and DH. The A's had initially hoped that Fosse could return to the lineup quickly, but now realized that his cervical disk injury was serious enough to mandate his placement on the disabled list. Oakland scouts recommended the acquisition of veteran catcher-outfielder Ed "Spanky" Kirkpatrick, hitting .278 in a reserve role for the Pittsburgh Pirates. The 29-year-old Kirkpatrick, a strong left-handed hitter with some power, had played for the rival Kansas City Royals from 1969 to 1973. Although a liability defensively, some in the Oakland organization viewed Kirkpatrick as a perfect fit for the A's. A Curt

Blefary play-alike, Kirkpatrick could DH against right-handed pitching while providing Gene Tenace with a capable backup behind the plate.

Charlie Finley tried to pry Kirkpatrick loose from Pittsburgh, but could not satisfy the Pirates' trade demands. Finley also telephoned Mike Epstein, recently released by the Angels. According to one report, Epstein was considering a contract with the Cubs. When the Angels had cut loose Epstein in May, they had made him available to any other major league team for the waiver price of $1. Any team claiming Epstein on waivers also would have had to pay the balance of his $60,000 salary. Now that Epstein had cleared waivers and become a free agent, the A's or Cubs could sign him for the major league minimum, leaving the Angels with the rest of the bill.

Yet, Epstein might have burned bridges leading toward Oakland with a series of scathing remarks about Finley that appeared in print during the 1973 season. At the time, Epstein explained the reasoning behind Finley's vindictive decision to exile him to the Rangers. "You either kiss Finley, or you don't play for him," Epstein said not-so-subtly in an interview with sportswriter Melvin Durslag. "Charlie Finley got rid of three us—me, Dave Duncan and George Hendrick—because we wouldn't kiss his fanny," Epstein contended. "What's more, he buried us. He sent the other two to Cleveland and me to Texas." Epstein believed that Finley had passed up the opportunity to trade him to another team, one that would have surrendered more value than relief pitcher Horacio Piña in return. "The Cubs wanted me," Epstein revealed to sportswriter Dick Young. "They offered [Joe] Pepitone and a pitcher, but instead he called up [Rangers owner] Bob Short and said, 'Take Epstein and give me anything.' So they gave him Piña."

Despite his problems with the owner, Epstein claimed that he had enjoyed playing for the A's. "I got along good with everybody but Finley," Epstein confided to Dick Young. "The night he traded me, six guys in the Oakland area, guys on the team, came over to my house and threw me a party to cheer me up. I felt awful."

After his release by the Angels, Epstein did not return to Oakland, despite the fact that he appeared to suit the A's, a team in need of a left-handed power threat. Epstein's major league career came to an abrupt end, while perennial prospect Rich McKinney earned a promotion from Triple-A. Unlike Ed Kirkpatrick, McKinney couldn't catch, and unlike Epstein, had little power, but had hit .311 against Pacific Coast League pitching.

On July 9, Ray Fosse underwent surgery to repair a ruptured disc in his neck. Fosse, who had already missed over a month of action, learned that he would be sidelined for another six to eight weeks. The prognosis meant that the A's would be without their best defensive catcher. Gene Tenace would continue to serve as the primary catcher in Fosse's absence, with backup infielder Pat Bourque taking over for Tenace at first base. Fosse's absence would weaken the A's at not one, but two positions.

The night of July 9 brought major changes to the Oakland organization. Instead of making a trade, Finley gave manager Alvin Dark permission to make an unusual in-season move—axing two of the team's coaches. Third-base coach Irv Noren and bullpen coach Vern Hoscheit, both holdovers from the Dick Williams regime, found themselves unemployed. In their place, Dark hired Bobby Hofman, one of his former coaches in Kansas City, and Bobby Winkles, the recently fired Angels manager, who had angered Reggie Jackson earlier in the season by supposedly ordering a knockdown of the Oakland slugger. Winkles would take Noren's place in the third-base coaching box, while Hofman would assume Hoscheit's duties in the bullpen.

The dual firings surprised some of the Oakland players, but not Catfish Hunter, who hurled an impressive three-hitter shutout against the Indians earlier in the evening. "If they told me that half the team had been traded—Reggie Jackson, Joe Rudi, Sal Bando, Billy North—to Mexico, I'd believe them," Hunter told *The Sporting News*. "Nothing on this club surprises me anymore."

Noren's firing represented a strengthening of Alvin Dark's power base. Noren didn't like or respect Dark and felt more loyalty to his predecessor, Dick Williams. In turn, Dark didn't trust Noren, whom he had accused of intentionally making bad decisions as the team's third-base coach. Dark had wanted to fire Noren back in May, only to be restrained by Finley, who didn't want to eat the coach's contract. Oakland players, such as pinch-runner Herb Washington, didn't agree with Dark's assessment of Noren. According to *The Sporting News*, Washington told Noren, "You're the best third-base coach I ever had." Of course, Washington hadn't had a third-base coach since *high school*, the last time that he had played baseball.

While the firing of Noren seemed inevitable, the departure of Hoscheit fell into a more unexpected category. According to one media report, Hoscheit and Dark had experienced a falling out over a relatively trivial item: the availability of baseballs for extra batting practice. When Hoscheit threatened to quit, Dark saved him the effort, firing him instead.

Hoscheit reacted bitterly to the treatment he had received from his former employer, the controversial owner. "I'm going home and retire," Hoscheit announced to *The Sporting News*. "When you meet people like this in baseball, it's time to quit. Charlie Finley is no good. He promised the coaches last year that if we did good, we'd get a raise. We won the World Series and we never got the raise. He doesn't keep his word." Hoscheit, who had been the A's' senior coach, offered no praise of Dark, either. "The manager is no good, too. He's just a horsemeat manager."

The previous week, Finley had experienced a reunion of sorts with Hoscheit and Noren's former boss, Dick Williams. On July 1, the ex-A's skipper returned to the major leagues as the manager of the Angels. That same night, Williams and the Angels hosted the A's in the beginning of a four-game series at Anaheim Stadium. The A's swept all four games, ruining Williams' debut in southern California.

In the second game of the series with the Angels, Joe Rudi, perhaps longing for a manager like Williams, revealed his own lack of respect for Alvin Dark. When Dark pulled Rudi from the game in favor of pinch-runner Herb Washington, Rudi provided the media with a sarcastic post-game nugget. "John McGraw must be turning over in his grave," Rudi told *The Sporting News*. And Williams must have been chuckling—or perhaps grimacing—in the Angels' dugout.

On July 14, Dark reached his boiling point with his players' continuing show of disrespect toward him. Upset by two instances when his starting pitchers flipped him baseballs instead of handing them off upon their removal, Dark yelled at his players in a private meeting. "When I come out to the mound," one player quoted Dark as saying, according to a story in *The Sporting News*, "I don't want to play catch out there. Just hand me the ball." Dark also delivered a message to all players who had criticized him with wisecrack remarks throughout the season. "I'm the manager of this ballclub. If you want to be the manager, phone Charlie [Finley] and ask for the job. But don't be second-guessing me."

Dark's speech, eerily reminiscent of Dick Williams' angry lecture to his players after the 1971 megaphone incident, drew a surprisingly favorable response from the majority of Oakland players. Several A's veterans had considered Dark too tolerant of fundamental mistakes and too unwilling to ride players who had failed to play smart baseball. "I thought it was good," Reggie Jackson told *The Sporting News* in offering his opinion of Dark's angry meeting with the team. "I was glad to see Alvin do it."

For the first time in 1974, Dark had made it clear that he would no longer accept public criticism and ridicule of his managerial style or strategies. Much like Williams' fire and brimstone talk in 1971, the A's seemed to carry Dark's message to the playing field, where they responded by winning four straight games.

A change in player personnel also aided the Oakland cause. In early July, the A's had sent infielder Gaylen Pitts back to Tacoma and had replaced him on the 25-man roster with a 19-year-old outfielder from Double-A Birmingham. Claudell Washington, a line-drive-hitting outfielder with speed, played a decisive role in a game against the Indians on July 8.

The A's faced Cleveland ace Gaylord Perry, who had won 15 consecutive decisions, dating back to the 1973 season. With one more win, Perry would tie the all-time American League record for most consecutive victories. Perry allowed only three runs through nine innings, but was matched by Vida Blue. In the bottom of the 10th, with the score still tied at 3–3, Perry walked pinch-hitter Pat Bourque to start the inning. Blue Moon Odom, pinch-running for Bourque since Herb Washington had already been used, moved up to second on a sacrifice bunt by rookie catcher Tim Hosley. Perry then retired Campy Campaneris for the second out. With Odom still at second, Perry faced Washington, who had tripled earlier in the game for his first major league hit. In a pressurized situation against a future Hall of Famer, Washington lined a pitch into right field for a clean single, scoring Odom with the game-winning run and halting Perry's run at the record books.

Dissatisfied with the performance of Angel Mangual, Charlie Finley had demanded Washington's recall from Double-A and ordered Alvin Dark to insert Washington into the DH role. The quick ascent of Washington through the organization had impressed Finley, the team's scouts and the coaching staff. In the early seventies, Washington had elected not to play baseball at Berkeley High

School, an expression of his dislike for extracurricular activities. Washington's self-imposed exile from scholastic baseball prevented most major league scouts from learning his identity. Jim Guinn, a part-time Oakland scout who happened to live in Berkeley, visited the school's athletic department and asked for a list of students who possessed the most athletic ability, but had not tried out for the baseball team. Informed of the 17-year-old Washington, Guinn contacted him immediately. "He's a loner," Guinn said of Washington in an interview with Bay Area sportswriter Glenn Dickey. "Someone had to encourage him." Guinn took on the role and farm director John Claiborne eventually signed Claudell to a $3,000 bonus.

On the afternoon of July 14, Washington delivered two RBIs, including a tie-snapping sacrifice fly, which helped the A's to a 7–3 win over the Yankees. Three days letter, the left-handed hitting Washington stroked two hits against southpaw Mike Cuellar, as the A's blanked the Orioles, 2–0. Washington then went 3-for-4 against Gaylord Perry, the same pitcher he had defeated earlier in the month, helping the A's to a 3–2 win over the Indians.

Washington's smooth transition from Double-A to the major leagues amazed his teammates. Many of the A's also took note of the size of Washington's bat. Although he weighed only 190 pounds, Washington swung a 42-ounce bat, a size matched by White Sox slugger Dick Allen. After a few days, Washington switched to a lighter model in an effort to quicken his bat speed during the hottest months of the season.

Even with the meteoric Washington, the A's struggled to score runs consistently. On July 19, Oakland's up-and-down offense fell victim to Indians right-hander Dick Bosman. The journeyman pitcher, who had pitched so brilliantly in stifling the A's on Opening Day of the 1971 season, threw a no-hitter in his latest outing against Oakland, missing a perfect game on his own fourth-inning error. The 30-year-old Bosman, who appeared on the verge of a trade near the June 15th deadline, became the second pitcher (along with Jim Bibby) to no-hit the A's in the last two seasons.

Two days later, Alvin Dark shuffled his lineup in a desperate attempt to inject more offensive firepower. Dark inserted Angel Mangual in left field, moved his best defensive outfielder, Joe Rudi, to first base, and benched the struggling Pat Bourque. The moves made little sense. Mangual, hitting in the .250 range with negligible power, represented only a very small improvement over Bourque. More importantly, the changes damaged the quality of Oakland's defense at two positions. The best defensive left fielder in the American League, Rudi now found himself playing an uncomfortable position at first base. Mangual, a poor defensive outfielder, often misjudged fly balls, allowing them to drop in for singles and doubles. In essence, the A's had greatly reduced their fielding ability while doing little to improve the offense. Bizarre.

At the end of July, the A's lost the services of perhaps their most important defensive player, shortstop Campy Campaneris. The starting shortstop sustained a severely sprained left ankle, which forced him into a stint on the 15-day disabled list. The injury to Campaneris meant that utility infielder Ted Kubiak would receive most of the playing time at shortstop. The A's also promoted infielder Phil Garner from Tucson, where "Scrap Iron" had been playing mostly third base. Garner would serve as a backup to both Sal Bando at third and Dick Green at second base.

On August 7, the A's ended their mystifying use of Angel Mangual in left field and Joe Rudi at first base—but only temporarily and briefly. In the two weeks since he had become the regular left fielder, Mangual had seen his batting average plummet 20 points. No, Alvin Dark and Charlie Finley didn't come to their senses; an in-game injury forced their hand. During an 8–4 win over the Rangers, Mangual pulled a hamstring muscle. As a result, Rudi returned to left field, Tenace reverted back to first base, and backup catcher Larry Haney moved in behind the plate. The injury to Mangual made the A's stronger at three defensive positions—but not for long.

Mangual returned to the lineup the next day and contributed with a hit and two runs scored. Rudi, however, proved to be the game's biggest star, as he homered, doubled, singled twice, and drove in half of Oakland's runs in a 10–2 rout of the Rangers. The outburst lifted Rudi's season average to .310, second best to Reggie Jackson among Oakland regulars, while improving his home run and RBI totals to 13 and 72, respectively. Rudi's excellence, in the face of ill-advised position switches, impressed observers of the game, who continued to call him one of the game's most underrated stars. The "underrated" label, frequently attached to Rudi, began to wear on him. "I get more ink about not getting ink than about the things I do," Rudi told The *Sporting News*. Underrated or not, Rudi had made himself into a legitimate candidate for the American League's MVP Award.

In early August, the A's wrapped up a nine-game road trip with a three-game swing in Texas. While in Arlington, Vida Blue experienced severe chest pains and paid a visit to a doctor's office. The physician suggested Blue consult a heart specialist, who decided to check the left-hander into Dallas' Baylor Hospital for a series of examinations, including a test for sickle cell anemia, a disease primarily afflicting black males. Hospital technicians then tested Blue's heart with an electrocardiogram, which revealed an irregularity.

Although the test showed an abnormality, a cardiac specialist explained that electrocardiograms performed on young black males occasionally showed irregularities even though their heart functions were actually normal. When the doctor compared Blue's most recent EKG with one that had been conducted earlier as part of a successful life insurance exam, he found that the test results matched. In other words, nothing was wrong with Blue's heart; his chest pains may have been the result of simple indigestion.

With Blue in the hospital and unable to make his scheduled start on August 7, Alvin Dark handed the gameday ball to Darold Knowles. Knowles, who had questioned Dark's use of the bullpen earlier in the season, had lost his status as Oakland's top left-handed reliever to Paul Lindblad. The underused sinkerballer responded with five effective innings against the Rangers, besting A's killer Jim Bibby in the process.

The missed start not only proved a benefit to Knowles, but to Blue himself. On August 10, a well-rested Blue surrendered only one run, scattered eight hits, and earned an impressive 5–3 win over the Boston Red Sox. The victory, which improved his record to 14–9, left Blue's catcher awestruck. "His fastball was exploding, really moving around," remarked Gene Tenace, continuing to serve as Oakland's top receiver given the absence of Ray Fosse, in an interview with *The Sporting News*. "He's throwing like he did in 1971." The A's had waited two and a half years to hear such words.

The A's lost their next game to the Red Sox, 2–1, as an aging Juan Marichal barely outpitched rookie right-hander Glenn Abbott. The lackluster defeat, which dropped the A's' record in August to a mediocre 6–6, upset Alvin Dark to the point that he made a stunning announcement the next night prior to a game against the Yankees. Dark would no longer permit the drinking of hard liquor on any team flights for the duration of the season. Players would be allowed to drink wine and beer, but the use of anything stiffer would be strictly prohibited. "I just feel that the rest of the year we all have to suffer a little, sacrifice a little to keep things going," Dark explained to *The Sporting News*. Unlike the stereotype of a hard-drinking manager, Dark was a teetotaler who abstained from all kinds of alcohol. "The hard stuff isn't too good for a ballplayer. It isn't too good for anyone."

Dark's sudden prohibition surely pleased crusaders against the evils of drink, but resulted in a sarcastic reaction from several of his players. "I think the flask is coming back in style," an anonymous player told *The Sporting News*. When Dark urged his players to abandon hard liquor and give "100 per cent of 100 per cent," another player wrote those words on a piece of tape, mockingly sticking the message to the back of his uniform. Other players offered more straightforward criticism of the Dark directive. "I think it's kind of bad," Catfish Hunter told *The Sporting News*. "I haven't seen anyone drunk on a plane, or even high."

Perhaps Dark had imposed the restriction as a delayed reaction to an incident that had cost him his job as the manager of the Kansas City A's several years earlier. On a 1967 commercial flight from Boston to Kansas City, an eyewitness had claimed to have seen rowdy behavior by several drunken players, principally pitcher Lew Krausse. After hearing about the complaint, Charlie Finley suspended Krausse and ordered a ban on the serving of alcohol on all team flights. When several players came to Krausse's defense, Dark supported his players and stood up to Finley. The owner fired Dark shortly thereafter.

On the same day that Dark announced the most recent ban on liquor, Campy Campaneris came off the disabled list. Campaneris told Dark that he didn't feel well enough to leave the disabled list, but when Finley stepped in and asked Campy to play, the manager penciled his veteran shortstop into the designated hitter's role. Campaneris went 0-for-3 as the DH, but the A's still managed a 3–2 victory over the Yankees, as Catfish Hunter ran his record to 17–9.

Four days later, Campy played his first game at shortstop since spraining his left ankle. Campaneris went 1-for-3 at the plate and played all nine innings in the field. The next game, however, Campy showed ill effects from trying to come back too quickly from the injury. In the eighth inning, Campy banged out his second hit of the game, only to come up hobbling as he reached first base. Trainer Joe Romo reacted by running from the dugout to first base, but Campaneris quickly waved him off. The Oakland players knew that their star shortstop was hurting badly, but Campy refused to leave a close, one-run game that the Tigers eventually won, 4–3.

After the game, Charlie Finley berated Romo, as if *he* were to blame for the fragile condition of Campaneris' ankle. Of course, Romo hadn't insisted that Campaneris return to the lineup a week earlier; Finley had. Perhaps Finley was upset that Romo hadn't completed his run to first base and conducted a full examination on the spot.

Campy started the next night, going 1-for-2 in a 13–3 demolition of the Tigers. After he reached on a single in the late innings, Alvin Dark had the good sense to pull him from the game, replacing him with pinch-runner Herb Washington. One question remained, however. Why did Dark start Campaneris in the first place? If Oakland's lead were only one or two games in the American League West, the decision to use an ailing Campaneris might have been more understandable. With a fairly comfortable lead of five and a half games over the second-place Royals, why were the A's risking the long-term health of their most important middle infielder and second-best base stealer? Like many of Dark's strategies, the decision seemed to lack sound reasoning.

Speaking of Dark's odd strategies, the 13–3 win over the Tigers produced another mild controversy. In the sixth inning, with the A's up 4–1 and two men out, center fielder Angel Mangual dropped a routine fly ball, allowing two unearned runs to score. Dark hooked Holtzman, replacing him with another left-hander, Darold Knowles. But why? Holtzman had pitched well and couldn't be faulted for Mangual's latest misadventure in the outfield. Furthermore, to take Holtzman out and replace him with another left-hander pitcher, instead of waiting for a right-handed batter to come to the plate, made little sense.

Dark contended that he was concerned about the condition of Holtzman's left thigh, which had been struck by a batted ball one inning earlier. The left-hander, for his part, said the leg didn't bother him and had no effect on the quality of his pitching. "I just didn't deserve to be taken out," Holtzman complained to *The Sporting News*. "I felt fine and I still had good stuff."

In the meantime, the play of the Oakland bench had become a concern to Finley and Dark. Phil Garner, called up to replace Campaneris during his stint on the disabled list, had come to bat 20 times before recording his first major league base hit. Garner, a talented prospect, seemed overmatched at the plate. Another backup, first baseman Pat Bourque, had gone 12 consecutive pinch-hit at-bats without a hit. Finally, in the Sunday rout of the Tigers, Bourque delivered an important two-run pinch-single as a substitute for light-hitting shortstop Dal Maxvill.

Bourque's late-inning heroics against Detroit failed to save his roster spot in Oakland. The next day, in a classic example of trading "my flat tire for your flat tire," Finley dealt him to the Twins for another left-handed pinch-hitter, Jim Holt. A veteran outfielder, Holt was batting in the mediocre .250 range, had not delivered a single pinch-hit, and had not managed a single home run in nearly 200 at-bats. Perhaps Finley just wanted to bring back one of his former farmhands. Holt had played in the A's' organization seven years ago, when the franchise was still located in Kansas City.

On August 24, the A's enjoyed a double dose of positive developments when Catfish Hunter earned his 19th win, allowing the Red Sox no earned runs in a route-going effort. That same day, Ray Fosse returned to active duty for the first time since undergoing surgery on his damaged cervical disk. Although Fosse did not start the game, he came in for defensive purposes after Alvin Dark used Claudell Washington as a pinch-hitter for Larry Haney.

Hunter won his 20th game his next time out, shackling the Brewers over eight innings. The 3–1 victory gave Catfish four consecutive seasons with 20 or more wins, dating back to 1971. Reggie Jackson supported Oakland's pitching stalwart with two monstrous County Stadium home runs. While Jackson's tape-measure shots drew much of the attention away from Hunter, Catfish didn't seem to mind. After the game, Hunter calmly fielded questions about reaching the 20-win circle yet again. "The thing about winning 20 is that it makes you hungry to win 20 again," a philosophical Hunter remarked to a reporter. Only four years ago, the A's had questioned whether the soft-spoken right-hander would ever amount to anything more than a 15-game winner.

Claudell Washington also contributed to Hunter's 20th victory, rapping out two hits while filling in for an injured Billy North in center field. The young, left-handed hitting outfielder continued to show a remarkable aptitude for handling major league pitching. On the day before his 20th birthday, the rookie played center field, went 5-for-5, and drove in three runs in a 10–5 thumping of the Tigers. The August 30th display so impressed Charlie Finley that he graciously rewarded Washington with a $2,000 bonus. Considering Commissioner Bowie Kuhn's dislike of bonuses, Finley decided to call the money a "retroactive pay raise." Yes, Mr. Finley still had a generous side to his complex personality.

In 1972, Washington had torn up the Class-A Midwest League, hitting .322 with 38 stolen bases and 81 RBIs. The fine season earned him a promotion to Double-A Birmingham, where he terrorized Southern League pitching over the first half of the 1974 season. In search of a left-handed hitting DH, the A's decided to promote Washington to the major leagues, bypassing the usual stop at Triple-A Tucson. The rookie sensation showed no fear of playing in the major leagues, earning him praise from Reggie Jackson. "Nothing bothers Claudell," Jackson remarked to Bay Area sportswriter Glenn Dickey. "He won't be bothered by fame. He won't be screwed up by Charlie [Finley]. He's in control of himself." Washington's calm exterior became even more impressive given his teen-aged status. "I've never seen a young player so secure," added Jackson. "He knows he's not articulate; he knows he's no financial genius, or mathematical wizard; but he knows he can play baseball."

"He's the best player for his age I've ever seen or know," Jackson told *The Sporting News*, upgrading his praise further. Although Washington had yet to show Reggie-like power at the plate, his speed and left-handed stroke reminded some in the organization of a young Jackson, circa 1967. "In two years," Sal Bando predicted in an interview with Dick Young, "he'll be a better ballplayer than Reggie." Jackson held an equally high opinion of Washington, whom he compared to both himself and Twins star Tony Oliva. "He's going to be a better player than I am," Jackson told Glenn Dickey. "He runs better than I do, and he's a better hitter at his age than I ever hoped to be."

Unfortunately, Washington would never become the superstar that Bando and Jackson had so confidently predicted. He would hit .300 or better in only one more season (1988), would fail to hit more than 17 home runs in a single season, and would never match his total of 40 stolen bases in 1975. Washington's struggles against left-handed pitching and his overly aggressive approach at the plate hindered both his ability to get on base and to produce runs. Still, Washington enjoyed a solid 17-year career as a line-drive hitter with both power and speed, and actually became a good defensive center fielder during a stint with the Yankees in the late 1980s.

In addition to Washington, the A's hoped to strike more minor league gold on September 1, when they expanded their roster by four players. They added pitcher Bill Parsons and three infielders—Manny Trillo, Phil Garner, and veteran John Donaldson—from the minors. The lefty-hitting Donaldson, who had spent time with Oakland during the early-season wave of injuries to various second baseman, needed only 24 more days of service time to qualify for his full, four-year pension. As long as Donaldson remained on the roster for the balance of the regular season, he would reach the necessary service time. In promoting Donaldson from the minor leagues, Charlie Finley had shown a considerate nature for a journeyman player who would likely contribute little to the pennant drive.

The same could not be said of Finley the following day, when the A's hosted the Angels at the Oakland Coliseum. The game was marked by Dick Williams' return to the Coliseum for the first time since his post-World Series resignation in the fall of 1973. Reggie Jackson and Joe Rudi spoiled the return for Williams by homering in support of Glenn Abbott, who earned the win with relief help from Rollie Fingers. When Fingers retired the last Angels' batter in the ninth inning, the scoreboard at the Oakland Coliseum exhibited the following not-so-subtle message, in large lettering:

GOODNIGHT, DICK

The scoreboard order had been placed by none other than Charlie Finley, who took extra pleasure in defeating a man he had considered disloyal to him. The scoreboard message, left up for several minutes, infuriated most of the Oakland players, especially Reggie Jackson. "If they ever do that again," Jackson told *The Sporting News*, "I'll walk off the field and they can fine me anything they want." Even current manager Alvin Dark bristled at the lack of class shown by his employer. A few minutes later, Jackson and Dark walked to the Angels' clubhouse to personally apologize for the embarrassing message displayed on the Coliseum scoreboard.

The A's had won all five meetings with California since Williams had been hired as the Angels' skipper. Instead of deriving simple satisfaction from the wins, Finley had felt motivated to rub a few salt pellets into the wounds of his former manager. The scoreboard directive was childish and mean-spirited, continuing the same kind of vindictive personality that Finley had exhibited since his heart attack in August of 1973. Somewhere, Mike Andrews must have felt a special degree of sympathy for Dick Williams.

Proponents of fair play had to be pleased when the Angels, after 10 straight losses to the A's, finally defeated the defending champions, grabbing a 5–2 decision at the Coliseum. The A's somehow managed to score only a pair of runs despite being the recipients of 10 walks by Angels left-hander Andy Hassler. In the field, Sal Bando committed two errors behind a mediocre performance by Vida Blue, whose record dropped to 14–14. With the win, manager Williams notched his first victory against his former club after six consecutive defeats.

In early September, the A's became concerned when relief ace Rollie Fingers endured his worst game of the season, perhaps in part due to his off-the-field problems. Fingers had separated from his wife earlier in the season, enjoyed a temporary reconciliation, and then experienced another break-up. Fingers indicated to the Oakland media that the latest separation had probably signaled the end of his marriage. On September 6, Fingers allowed four runs and nine hits in a stint of three and two-thirds innings, taking the loss in a 5-4 defeat to the Rangers. In the top of the 11th, Fingers allowed a leadoff single to Dave Nelson, who moved to second on Cesar Tovar's sacrifice bunt. With first base open and MVP candidate Jeff Burroughs scheduled to bat, an intentional walk seemed like a reasonable strategy. Dark could have instructed Fingers to pitch carefully to the hot-hitting Burroughs, who had already accumulated three hits on the night, and take his chances with a less dangerous hitter like Mike Hargrove. Instead, Dark ordered Fingers to pitch to Burroughs, who lined a run-scoring single to give the Rangers the lead. Relief pitcher Steve Foucault retired Oakland in the bottom of the 11th to saddle the A's with one of their toughest losses of the summer. For the umpteenth time in 1975, Oakland players and media engaged in widespread first and second-guessing of Dark, perhaps the most embattled first-place manager in the history of the sport.

The next day, Dark and Darold Knowles argued on the mound, as part of an ugly 8–2 loss to the Rangers. Dark had come to the mound to remove Knowles and replace him with right-hander Bill Parsons. Knowles, who didn't want to leave the game, shouted at Dark. The argument represented the second public dispute between the manager and the 32-year-old reliever. After the game, Dark apologized to Knowles in front of the other Oakland players. As much as the A's questioned many of Dark's in-game strategies and decisions, they could not criticize their manager for a failure to own up to his mistakes, something he had done on more than one occasion during the season.

The Rangers won their third straight against the A's on Sunday, as former Chicago Cubs ace Ferguson Jenkins recorded his 22nd win of the season. Jenkins struck out 10, did not allow a run until the ninth, and scattered seven hits in a 5–1 victory. With three wins in the four-game weekend series, the Rangers had given themselves some life in the American League West race, paring two games off the Oakland lead. Although less than a month of the regular season remained, the Rangers had moved to within five and a half games of the A's, who had completely lost their momentum. The two contenders would meet again in another week.

In the meantime, the A's moved on to Kansas City, where they at first feared that they might be without one of their relievers for the balance of the season. Darold Knowles, struggling with a staff-high 4.56 ERA, was diagnosed with a case of bursitis in his right hip and leg. The pain struck Knowles so severely and suddenly that he had to crawl from the floor of his hotel room to the door in order to let trainer Joe Romo into the room.

Doctors prescribed medication and rest as a way of treating his bursitis, but acknowledged the possibility that the condition might sideline Knowles for the remainder of the season—and the playoffs. If so, Knowles realized he might have made his last pitch as a member of the A's' staff. "If Alvin [Dark] is here next year," Knowles predicted to *The Sporting News*, "I very definitely will be traded. If he isn't around, I might stay."

Knowles' fears of a season-ending injury turned out to be premature. Doctors determined that Knowles had not been afflicted with bursitis, but rather a viral infection. As a result of the change in diagnosis, Knowles would be able to return to game action within a few days.

The A's lost Knowles temporarily, but gained two important victories against the Royals. Vida Blue and Catfish Hunter pitched back-to-back shutouts in a doubleheader sweep, allowing a combined six hits in the two games. Gene Tenace, Joe Rudi, and Sal Bando each homered and Campy Campaneris collected four hits to lead the A's to 3–0 and 7–0 wins over the fading Royals. In the meantime, the Rangers split a doubleheader with the Angels, falling six games back in the West. The Rangers lost the first game to none other than Chuck Dobson, who allowed only one run in pitching a complete game and earning his first win for a team other than the Kansas City or Oakland A's.

Six games separated the Rangers from the A's, as the two teams prepared to play the beginning of a three-game set on Friday the 13th. The series represented the last head-to-head meeting between the two rivals, meaning the Rangers needed to win all three games in order to have a realistic chance of catching Oakland in the season's final two weeks.

Alvin Dark and Rangers manager Billy Martin could not have planned their respective rotations any better for the start of the series. In the first game, 22-game winners Catfish Hunter and Ferguson Jenkins took the mound at Arlington Stadium. In the top of the third, the A's broke through against Jenkins with singles by Billy North and Campy Campaneris and a sac fly by Reggie Jackson. The Rangers came right back from the 1–0 deficit by scoring two runs on Lenny Randle's triple. Jenkins shut down the Oakland attack the rest of the way, preserving an imperative 3–1 win for Texas.

On Saturday night, Dark turned to the inconsistent Vida Blue as the opponent of 11-game winner Jackie Brown. The A's scored three runs against the right-hander in the first four innings to take a 3–1 lead. In the bottom of the fourth, the Rangers bounced Blue from the game with a five-run inning, capped off by Jim Sundberg's bases-loaded single. Dark understandably removed Blue and then watched his offense swing feebly against Brown, who held the A's scoreless over the last five innings. An 8–3 Texas win drew the Rangers within four games of the A's.

Dark had taken his two best shots at the Rangers by using his two premier starting pitchers. Both had failed. With Ken Holtzman unavailable after pitching a complete game on Thursday, Dark had no recourse but to give the ball to inconsistent rookie Glenn Abbott. In the meantime, the A's would have to cope with Texas right-hander Jim Bibby, who had given them so much trouble over the past two seasons.

The pair of losses left Charlie Finley in a borderline panic mode. The owner called Dark, ordering him to re-institute the rotating second-base strategy that Finley had imposed on Dick Williams during the 1972 season. Finley told Dark to start Ted Kubiak at second base, pinch-hit for him, and replace him with another second baseman, either Dal Maxvill or Dick Green. Under the plan, Dark would continue to pinch-hit for his second basemen as long as the A's needed to score runs.

The Rangers struck early against the youthful Abbott. Cesar Tovar led off with a single, advanced to second on Lenny Randle's bunt, and scored on Mike Hargrove's two-out single. As Dark pondered how long to stay with Abbott, the A's responded by scoring the tying run in the second, thanks to Billy North's two-out RBI single. In the third inning, Bibby walked Reggie Jackson and then coughed up a key two-run homer to Sal Bando. The captain's blast gave the A's a 3–1 lead.

Bando's next at-bat produced bad feelings between the two teams, whose rivalry had grown since the Rangers had replaced the more even-tempered Whitey Herzog with the highly combustible Billy Martin. In the fifth inning, Bando hit an infield grounder and ran hard to first base. As he crossed the bag, Bando landed on the foot of first baseman Mike Hargrove. Having recorded the out, Hargrove began yelling at Bando for what he considered an intentional spiking. The two men exchanged shoves and both dugouts emptied. Fortunately, most of the players concentrated on breaking up the fight between Bando and Hargrove rather than initiating their own skirmishes. Players returned to their dugouts, but the on-field display proved to all that these two teams simply didn't like each other.

With a 3–1 lead and the game of critical importance, Alvin Dark pulled Abbott with one out in the fifth. Instead of calling on long relievers Bill Parsons or Paul Lindblad, Dark summoned Rollie Fingers. The recently troubled right-hander pitched four and two-thirds brilliant innings, held the Rangers scoreless, and picked up his ninth win. A 4–1 Oakland victory pushed the A's to a comfortable five-game lead in the West, with only two weeks remaining. In much the same way that they had handled the second-place White Sox in 1972, the A's had pushed away the Rangers at the last possible moment.

Just as Charlie Finley had ordered, Dark had started Ted Kubiak at second base, only to replace him with pinch-hitter Jim Holt. Dal Maxvill then took a turn in the field before being lifted for Angel Mangual. Dick Green entered the game and remained at second for the rest of the game. With the A's leading 3–1 and then 4–1, Dark decided to keep his most experienced defensive second baseman in the field instead of taking chances with a journeyman like John Donaldson or rookies like Phil Garner and Manny Trillo.

The A's' players didn't like the reincarnation of the Ferris wheel at second base, but they realized the importance of salvaging one game against the Rangers. Perhaps too relaxed after the critical win against the Rangers, the A's dropped three of their next four. Yet, the Rangers also lost three of four, failing to capitalize on Oakland's subpar play.

On September 26, Oakland's fortunes rose. The A's edged the Twins, 2–1, while the Rangers conceded both ends of a doubleheader to the White Sox. The day's results clinched the A's at least a tie in the American League West divisional race. Ever the big-game pitcher, Catfish Hunter walked no one and allowed a mere seven hits in notching his career-high 25th win of the season. Yet, Hunter's pre-game gesture ranked as even more impressive than his latest clutch pitching performance.

When he arrived at the Oakland Coliseum, Hunter presented a greeting card to backup infielder John Donaldson, who would officially complete his fourth year of service time upon the finish of the game that evening. The card, signed by the Hunter family, read as follows: "From the four of us for your fourth." Donaldson, now eligible for a full baseball pension, thanked Hunter for the card. "That shows what kind of class Hunter has," Donaldson told *The Sporting News*. The exchange between Donaldson and Hunter, which exemplified some of the camaraderie felt between Oakland players, received very little attention outside of the Bay Area. It seemed that the national media preferred to concentrate their reporting on dissension and conflict in the Oakland clubhouse.

The next day, the A's lost to Chicago, but ended up clinching their fourth consecutive division title when the Rangers fell to the Royals. Judging by the tepid celebration in the Oakland clubhouse, an uninformed observer would have had a difficult time recognizing that the A's had actually won the American League West. For the first time in four seasons, the A's had lost the game they played on the day of the clinching. The team had also played listless baseball for most of September, winning one, losing one, winning two, losing two. Players like Billy North criticized the A's for their repeated failures at playing fundamental baseball. Opposing scouts offered a similar critique of the defending World Champions. Yet, Alvin Dark insisted that Oakland's problems resided in the area of run production, not any poor execution of fundamentals.

Although the A's would not play another important game until the playoffs, they could not escape another bit of controversy in playing out the regular season schedule. Dark pulled 19-game winner Ken Holtzman from his final start, preferring to rest him before the Championship Series. As a result, Dark denied Holtzman his last chance at winning 20 games. The move did not sit well with Holtzman, who did his best to control his anger. "I plan to retire, anyhow," Holtzman told *Sports Illustrated* with resignation. Fortunately for the A's, a frustrated Holtzman did not mean what he said.

On September 30, two days before the end of the regular season, Charlie Finley exacted revenge on a local media that he felt had been unfairly critical of him and his team. The A's informed Bay Area beat writers that they would not be allowed on the team's charter flights during the post-season. Finley also announced that the A's would no longer make flight or hotel reservations for the writers. Under baseball's standard operating procedure, teams usually booked accommodations for local newspapers, which would then be billed later on for airline and hotel expenses. The A's, at the behest of Finley, had decided to abandon that courtesy.

Chapter 25

A Rematch with the Birds

On October 2, the A's played their final game of the regular season. Even though the outcome of the game meant nothing to the playoff-bound A's, Alvin Dark still had one decision to make with regard to his post-season lineup. Who would start at catcher against the Baltimore Orioles in the American League Championship Series: Ray Fosse, a .196 batter during an injury-interrupted season, or Gene Tenace, a better hitter but the lesser of the two defensively?

Fosse had not displayed his usual mobility since returning from an injured cervical disk. While the lineup in the regular season finale contained backups like Jesus Alou, Angel Mangual, Jim Holt, and Dal Maxvill, Dark decided to start Fosse at catcher. Although Fosse went 0-for-3, he looked fluid behind the plate and threw out two potential base stealers, Morris Nettles and Denny Doyle. Fosse's performance convinced Dark to name him as the starting catcher for the playoffs, and potentially, the World Series.

For the third time in four years, the A's prepared to meet the Orioles in the American League playoffs. In 1971, the Orioles had swept the A's in three games. In 1973, the A's had rallied from an early one-game deficit to post a dramatic series victory, three games to two.

On paper, the 1974 Orioles featured many of the same players that they had used the previous season. Yet, the O's had won only 91 games, six fewer than in 1973. Injuries limited staff ace Jim Palmer to 26 games and a 7–12 record. Speedsters Al Bumbry and Rich Coggins suffered under the weight of sophomore slumps after batting .300 as rookies. Bumbry fell off to .233 and Coggins to .243. Furthermore, veteran infield mainstays Boog Powell and Brooks Robinson combined to drive in only 104 runs, hardly the kind of run production expected from a team's first and third basemen.

While those numbers looked unimpressive, the Orioles entered the post-season riding the momentum of recent fine play. Baltimore won 28 of its final 34 games, including nine straight to complete the regular season. The Orioles carried that caliber of play into the first game of the Championship Series. The Birds pecked at 25-game winner Catfish Hunter, scoring single runs in the first and fourth innings, before exploding for four runs in the fifth. Home runs by Brooks Robinson and Bobby Grich knocked Hunter from the game after four and two-thirds innings. The Cy Young candidate, who had pitched so well in September, surrendered a total of three home runs and six runs, while ending up on the short side of a 6–3 loss. Twenty-two-game-winner Mike Cuellar pitched eight solid innings to give the Orioles yet another Game One victory—their third straight against the A's.

Rather than rely on the maddeningly inconsistent Vida Blue in the second game, Alvin Dark decided to use Ken Holtzman as his starter against Dave McNally. The two left-handers matched scoreless innings through the first three frames before the A's capitalized on an error by the usually impeccable Oriole infield. Grich dropped a foul pop-up off the bat of Sal Bando, giving the A's' third baseman another swing against McNally. Two pitches later, Bando deposited a McNally pitch into the left field bleachers, giving the A's a 1–0 lead.

The A's tacked on another run in the sixth, which gave an effective Holtzman a larger margin for error. In the eighth inning, light-hitting Ray Fosse, who had hit only four home runs during the season, smacked a three-run blast against reliever Grant Jackson. With Holtzman in command, the A's finished off the Orioles, 5–0.

Vida Blue and Jim Palmer mirrored the brilliance of Holtzman in a classic third game pitching matchup. Both pitchers had underachieved during the regular season; in addition, Blue had never won a game in the playoffs. In Game Three, Palmer and Blue offered vintage performances. Palmer allowed four hits and Blue permitted only a pair of safeties. The game produced only one extra-base hit, a fourth-inning home run by Sal Bando. Sal's blast accounted for the only scoring of the game, a 1–0 Oakland victory. And for the first time in his career, Blue claimed a victory in the post-season.

One of Blue's teammates called it his finest pitching performance, better even than any of his games in 1971. "Vida pitched the best game of his career because this was a pressure game," captain Sal Bando told the *New York Daily News*, "the third game of the playoffs tied at 1–1." The complete game left Alvin Dark amazed at Blue's ability to sustain velocity from start to finish. "He threw as hard for nine innings as anyone can possibly throw," Dark told the *Daily News*. Except for a half-dozen curveballs, Blue threw only fastballs to the Oriole hitters.

As Blue tried to downplay the significance of his first playoff triumph, Gene Tenace tried to contain himself from strangling Alvin Dark. In the seventh inning, Tenace had drawn a one-out walk, only to be lifted for pinch-runner Herb Washington. Tenace marched into the dugout and fired his helmet into the ground. The helmet bounced and rolled—next to Dark's feet. "I wasn't trying to hit him," Tenace told the Associated Press, defending his intent with the helmet. A disgusted Dark picked up the helmet and hurled it onto the dirt in front of the A's' dugout.

Nonetheless, Tenace was upset by his removal from the game. "I don't think you take one of your best defensive players out," Tenace told United Press International, in referring to the A's' one-run lead at the time of his removal. When a reporter asked him if he thought Dark had unilaterally made the decision to insert Washington as a pinch-runner, Tenace pointed the finger at the owner. "It's definitely coming from Charlie," said Tenace. "He's the one who introduced the designated runner."

A Rematch with the Birds

Thus far, the playoffs had matched the pattern of the 1973 series—a Baltimore win in the first game followed by consecutive victories for the A's. In 1973, the Orioles had come back to win Game Four, pounding Vida Blue and Rollie Fingers in the late innings. Alvin Dark hoped for a different scenario this time around, especially with his best starting pitcher on the mound.

Catfish Hunter met Mike Cuellar for the second time in the series. Unlike the first game, Hunter proved effective in the early innings, as he kept the Orioles scoreless over the first five frames. "He's the kind of pitcher that hitters are anxious to hit off," Alvin Dark told sportswriter Phil Pepe. Dark likened Hunter to Hall of Famer Robin Roberts and two other pitchers from an earlier era. "Howie Pollet was like that, and Preacher Roe. You think about how easy they are to hit off, but you never hit them." Unfortunately for Hunter, the A's' batters couldn't hit Cuellar either; the screwballing left-hander no-hit them over the first four and two-thirds innings. Then, without warning, Cuellar mysteriously walked four consecutive batters, including the patient Gene Tenace, whose base on balls forced in the first run of the game. The quartet of walks gave Cuellar, usually a control specialist, a total of nine for the game. Earl Weaver yanked the man known as "Crazy Horse," despite the fact that he had not yet allowed the A's a base hit.

Left-hander Ross Grimsley retired Claudell Washington to end the threat, but the A's struck again in the seventh, when Sal Bando walked and Reggie Jackson plated him with a double. Incredibly, Jackson's blow represented Oakland's first—and only—hit of the afternoon. The A's, with a two-run lead, needed only nine more outs to return to a third World Series. Hunter pitched a scoreless seventh, but allowed the first batter of the eighth inning to reach safely. Alvin Dark, who had utilized the quick hook all season long, signaled to his bullpen, where Rollie Fingers had concluded his warm-ups. With a man on first and no one out, Fingers set the Orioles aside in the eighth inning.

The A's maintained their 2–0 advantage heading to the bottom of the ninth. When Fingers retired the leadoff man, right fielder Rich Coggins, the pennant seemed inevitable. Fingers then committed a cardinal baseball sin. With the middle of the order coming up—Bobby Grich, Tommy Davis, and Boog Powell—Fingers walked Paul Blair. Grich followed with a single, pushing Blair to second. Davis, the former Athletic and arguably the American League's best designated hitter, hit a slow grounder that the Oakland infield turned into a force play at second. With Blair at third and pinch-runner Enos Cabell at first base, Fingers needed one more out to clinch the pennant. Powell, reduced to platoon status at the age of 33, stepped in against Fingers. The lefty-hitting slugger, 0-for-7 in the playoffs, rocked a two-out single, scoring Blair with the Orioles' first run.

With the tying run now at second in the form of a pinch-running Jim Palmer (the Orioles had no equivalent of Herb Washington), the power-hitting Don Baylor strode to the plate. The young left fielder, 4-for-14 in the series, wiggled his bat as he awaited the first delivery from Fingers. Baylor, pulling a major surprise, dropped his bat into bunting position, but couldn't reach a slider that broke low and away from the plate. Baylor then fouled off three pitches, including a very hittable fastball, eventually working the count to 2-and-2. During the sequence, Fingers had mixed his fastball and slider, trying to keep both pitches away from Baylor. What would Fingers throw now? Baylor might have expected Fingers to throw his trademark slider, his most effective pitch against right-handed hitters, toward the outer half of the plate. Instead, Fingers released a fastball, a pitch that he allowed to gravitate toward the middle of the plate. Baylor swung hard, but *through* the fastball. Fingers' mistake pitch aside, the A's had managed to win their third straight Championship Series. In the process, they had succeeded the Orioles of 1969–71 as the winners of three consecutive American League pennants.

But how exactly did the A's manage to win another Championship Series, considering the persistent struggles of their most important hitters? Gene Tenace went hitless in 11 at-bats, Billy North garnered only one hit in 16 at-bats, Joe Rudi went 2-for-13, Reggie Jackson collected two hits in 12 at-bats, and Campy Campaneris (by now the primary post-season leadoff man) managed only three hits in 17 tries. Once again, the A's had won their most important games of the season with their two constants—pitching and defense, defense and pitching, in whatever order you preferred. Aside from two meaningless errors committed by Dick Green in the 1–0 win in Game Three, the A's had played flawlessly in the field. Oakland's front-line pitching had been equally responsible for the three playoff wins. Although only five different pitchers made appearances in the four games, three of them did not allow any runs—Vida Blue, Ken Holtzman, and reliever Blue Moon Odom. The other two—Catfish Hunter and Rollie Fingers—had teamed up to win the clincher.

Even Alvin Dark had contributed to the Oakland cause. He had allowed Holtzman and Blue to pitch complete games, and had wisely concentrated the bulk of Oakland's innings on the shoulders of his best pitchers. Dark had also been sparing in his use of Herb Washington, employing the pinch-running specialist in only two of the playoff games, both Oakland wins. For one of the few times all season, several A's publicly applauded the work done by Dark. "I just wanted to win for Alvin Dark," said Hunter, the winner of the clinching fourth game, to the Associated Press. "Alvin has received a lot of bad publicity and he's done a hell of a job." Earlier in the season, Catfish and many of his teammates had second-guessed Dark's managerial decisions—especially his quick hooks of starting pitchers—a practice that Hunter now regretted. "Sure I got on him," Hunter admitted to the AP. "Sal [Bando] got on him, and it's bad to get on the manager. Everyone was against him, myself included. But he proved himself by winning. Believe me, it's tough to take over a championship team and win again."

In retrospect, Bando says Dark struggled in his handling of the club over the first 50 to 60 games of the season, primarily due to his unfamiliarity with his players. From mid-season on through the post-season, Dark's managing improved considerably. "Once a third of the season was over," Bando says, "Alvin had a firm handle of the club and what guys can do." Still, Dark had more work to do in 1974. He knew that his owner wanted nothing less than another World Championship.

Chapter 26

The Freeway Series

A second consecutive Championship Series defeat of the Orioles landed the A's in the World Series against the surprising Los Angeles Dodgers. In the National League playoffs, the Dodgers had handled the Pittsburgh Pirates fairly easily, winning in four games. Los Angeles' pitching, led by starters Don Sutton and Andy Messersmith, had pinned down a Pirate offense that featured a succession of hard hitters—Manny Sanguillen, Willie Stargell, Richie Zisk, and Richie Hebner.

Given the ease with which the Dodgers' pitching had retired the best of the Pirate hitters, the matchup against a weak Oakland offense did not bode well for the A's. Certainly, Alvin Dark could count on his own pitching core of Catfish Hunter, Vida Blue, Ken Holtzman, and Rollie Fingers to perform well, but the manager had to wonder whether the A's would be able to score *any* runs against Dodger Blue. The oddsmakers must have harbored similar concerns, making the Dodgers the favorites against the two-time defending champions. Oakland's 90-win regular season and four-game playoff win over the Orioles had left much of the betting public unimpressed.

The A's had other concerns, as well. Rumors suddenly sprang up that Charlie Finley planned to move the franchise to New Orleans after the World Series, win or lose. Robert Nahas, the president of the Oakland Alameda County Coliseum, Inc., told reporters that the rumors had no merit. Nahas pointed to a document that contained incontrovertible proof—the A's' lease with the Coliseum extended for another 13 seasons, through the year 1987.

Aside from the unsubstantiated discussion of a franchise move, three very real controversies struck the A's—before the World Series had even begun. The most minor of the events involved former Oakland infielder Mike Andrews. Still stung by Charlie Finley's shabby treatment of him one year earlier, Andrews filed a $2.5 million libel lawsuit against the owner, claiming Finley had slandered him by trying to remove him from the A's' roster during the 1973 World Series. The suit contended that Finley had caused the former major league second baseman "severe mental anguish and emotional distress."

More trouble arose after the A's worked out at Dodger Stadium prior to Game One. Blue Moon Odom approached Rollie Fingers in the clubhouse and made mention of Fingers' recent marital problems. "Rollie has been having trouble with his wife and a lot of guys on the team have been ribbing him about it," an anonymous teammate explained to sportswriter Phil Pepe. "Real personal stuff. I guess he got fed up. About three weeks ago, he made an announcement. He'd had it with the cracks. No more. Cut it out, or he'll whip some butts." Fingers' teammates had abided by Fingers' decree, until Odom decided to test the waters. In response, Fingers threw his right fist at Odom, sending the pitcher sprawling into a shopping cart that doubled as a bat rack. Odom retaliated by ramming his head into Fingers' chest, pushing him backward into a locker. Fingers banged the back of his head against a metal hook contained inside the locker and suffered a large cut to his scalp, which required five stitches. "It didn't affect my pitching," recalled Fingers in an interview with a reporter, "but I was burned up because I couldn't wash my hair for four days." Odom emerged from the scuffle a bit more damaged than Fingers. Odom twisted his ankle, jeopardizing his availability for the start of the Series.

Fingers and Odom, good friends before the exchange of fists, quickly shook hands in an effort to put the fight behind him. Both players tried to minimize the severity of the fight and the injuries. According to the *New York Daily News*, Odom called the fight a "little thing, nothing to get excited about it," while Fingers described the incident as a "friendly scuffle." In an effort to keep the clubhouse atmosphere light, Billy North hurried over to Odom's locker and entertained the pitcher with a few seconds of shadow boxing.

Alvin Dark did not hold such a humorous opinion of the latest fight involving Oakland players. "These players have been together so long—many of them all the way through the minors—that they may know each other too well," Dark explained to *Sports Illustrated*. "There is more needling among players on this team than on any I know of. Sometimes the needling can get too serious."

The largest pre-Series controversy, however, involved staff ace Catfish Hunter. On October 11, the day before the start of the Series, the *Chicago Sun-Times* reported that Hunter and his lawyer, Jerry Kapstein, had charged Charlie Finley with a breach of contract. According to the report, Hunter's two-year contract, which he had signed prior to the 1974 season, stipulated that Finley pay a $50,000 installment to the Jefferson Standard Life Insurance Company of Greensboro, North Carolina. Hunter claimed that Finley had refused to make the deferred payment, which amounted to half of the pitcher's $100,000 salary. The *Chicago Sun-Times* reported that Hunter had threatened to declare himself a free agent after the Series if Finley did not make the payment immediately.

Finley telephoned the *Sun-Times'* chief rival, the *Chicago Tribune*, in an effort to refute the story. "It's not even worth commenting on," Finley told the *Tribune*. "But you can be assured that we do not owe any player any money." Hunter, for his part, refused public comment on the story, saying that he didn't want to detract from the team's goal of trying to win the World Series.

On October 12, the *Chicago Sun-Times* followed up on its original story by conducting an exclusive interview with American League president Lee MacPhail. In the follow-up, MacPhail explained that Charlie Finley had tried to make the $50,000 payment to Hunter on October 4, the day before the start of the playoffs, only to have the pitcher reject the offer. MacPhail believed that Finley's recent offer of restitution weakened Hunter's case for free agency. "The fact that Mr. Finley did offer Hunter a check for the disputed $50,000 puts an entirely different light on the situation," commented MacPhail. "I seriously doubt that Hunter will win his free agency."

Others disagreed with MacPhail's assessment. Dick Moss, a lawyer for the Players' Association, said that Finley's last-minute offer did not make up for his initial failures to make payment. Moss told reporters that Hunter's lawyers, back in mid-September, had informed Finley in writing of defaulted payment. Moss then quoted from the standard player's contract. "The Player may terminate this contract upon written notice to the Club, if the Club shall default in the payments to the Player provided for... and if the Club shall fail to remedy such a default within 10 days after the receipt by the Club of written notice of such default." In other words, Finley had failed to pay the deferred money within 10 days of receiving the letter from Hunter's camp; therefore, Hunter could declare himself a free agent.

Marvin Miller, the head of the Players' Association, informed Hunter that he could file for free agency beginning on September 26, 10 days after Finley had received written notice. With the A's still trying to fend off the Rangers for the Western Division title, Hunter did not want to file for free agency—at least not during the regular season. That same day, Hunter won his 25th game of the season. On October 4, Moss sent Finley a telegram, informing him that Hunter's contract would expire the day after the A's' season came to an end, be it after the playoffs or the World Series. Moss' telegram made it seem fairly certain that Hunter intended to become a free agent.

Most of Catfish's teammates—and ex-teammates for that matter—couldn't blame the pitcher for wanting to leave a team owned by Finley. The embattled owner was now facing charges that he ran the organization like a pre-Civil War plantation. In an interview with Bay Area columnist Wells Twombly, Vida Blue accused Finley of racism, a claim that he had previously made in 1972. "He treats his black players like niggers," Blue said bluntly. Cleveland Indians catcher Dave Duncan, a former Athletic who had often sparred with Finley, tried to offer Blue some twisted consolation. "Don't feel bad," Duncan advised Vida, according to an article by Twombly. "He treats his non-black players like niggers, too." Racist or not, Finley's reputation had reached rock-bottom in the baseball world.

The resolution of the Hunter affair would have to wait until after the final games of the season had been played. In the meantime, one Oakland player did his best to downplay the generally turbulent image of the A's. "We're really one big, happy family," maintained Gene Tenace in an interview with the *New York Times*. "And we have the average family's trouble and flair-ups." Tenace said that fights between players did not signify dislike for each other. "We may fuss and fight but we don't wind up hating each other. No cliques, nothing like that. Sal Bando is sort of the leader of the team...If somebody needs some advice, they'll probably go to Sal."

Another player discredited the severity of the pre-Series fight between Rollie Fingers and Blue Moon Odom. "The fight yesterday was very mild," backup infielder Dal Maxvill claimed to the *New York Times*. Maxvill disputed the notion that the two pitchers had tried to punch each other. "No punches thrown, just some shoving. Rollie fell over a basket on the floor and cut his head against the front of a locker." A reporter then asked Maxvill if any other fights had taken place during the early hours of the morning. "There have been no fights yet," Maxvill replied wryly to the *New York Daily News* as the clock read 11:00 A.M. "But, of course, it's still early." The visiting clubhouse attendant at Dodger Stadium, a man named Jim Muhe, approached a few of the A's near the batting cage. "You guys haven't been here half an hour and I already believe everything I've heard about you. I've been around this clubhouse for 15 years and thought I'd seen everything, but in 10 minutes you showed me I hadn't." Welcome to the world of Charlie Finley and the Swingin' A's.

The A's had more tangible concerns than that of their traveling soap opera. Injuries topped the list of worries for Alvin Dark. The fight between Fingers and Odom had left the latter on crutches as he entered the clubhouse prior to Game One. Alvin Dark announced that Odom would spend most of the first game in the clubhouse icing the foot. "He'll be my last resort if I need a right-handed pitcher," Dark explained to the *New York Daily News*.

The status of the A's' most feared power hitter ranked as an even greater concern. The A's listed Reggie Jackson, bothered by a pulled hamstring throughout the Championship Series, as questionable for the first game of the World Series. Unlike the playoffs, when the A's used Jackson as a DH, Reggie would have to be able to run well enough to play the outfield. The reason? For the second straight fall, World Series rules prohibited the use of a designated hitter. Although Jackson categorized himself as only 85 percent healthy, he insisted he would play right field in Game One.

On the afternoon of October 12, the A's and Dodgers took to the field at Dodger Stadium. The pitching matchup featured Ken Holtzman, who had not allowed a run in his one playoff start, and Dodgers ace Andy Messersmith. The top of Alvin Dark's lineup, which included a last-second change, read as follows: "Campaneris, SS; North, CF; Bando, 3B; Jackson, RF." Jackson's hamstring felt well enough for him to take his accustomed place in the cleanup spot.

After Wayne Newton performed the National Anthem as a late replacement for the ailing Sammy Davis, Jr., the A's and Dodgers made history by commencing the first all-California World Series. The recently dormant A's' offense reached Messersmith in the second inning, when Jackson led off with an opposite-field home run, his 30th of the season. In the fifth, Holtzman started another rally with a one-out double, advanced to third on a wild pitch by Messersmith, and scored on a daring play called by Alvin Dark. With two strikes on Campy Campaneris, Holtzman broke from third. Needing to put the ball in play, Campy bunted the ball precisely toward the mound, allowing the slow-footed pitcher to score on the suicide squeeze. If Campaneris had fouled the ball off, he would have been called out on strikes and Holtzman would have been forced back to third base. If Campy had missed the pitch entirely, the Dodgers likely would have tagged Holtzman out for an inning-ending double play.

Oakland's defense, nearly impenetrable in the playoffs, made two critical errors in the bottom of the fifth. Campaneris fumbled a one-out grounder by Davey Lopes. When Bill Buckner followed with a hit-and-run single to right field, Jackson dropped the ball, allowing Lopes to score all the way from first base. Holtzman then walked Jimmy Wynn, moving Buckner into scoring position. Even though the A's still lead, 2–1, an impatient Alvin Dark called upon Rollie Fingers to face the right-handed duo of Steve Garvey and Joe Ferguson, the Dodgers' fourth and fifth-place hitters. Fingers struck out Garvey and hit Ferguson with a pitch, but escaped further trouble by retiring Ron Cey, another right-handed hitter, on a fly ball to Joe Rudi in left field.

In the eighth inning, the A's attempted to add to their one-run advantage. Campaneris lined a leadoff single against a tiring Messersmith. After a sacrifice bunt by Billy North, Sal Bando bounded a chopper to the left side of the infield. Ron Cey fielded the ball cleanly, hurried his throw, and fired wildly past Steve Garvey. The error allowed Campy to score, while pushing Bando to third base. Reggie Jackson then lofted a fly ball to medium right-center field. Jimmy Wynn, the Dodgers' center fielder, glided over to make the catch, only to be cut off suddenly by right fielder Joe Ferguson, who possessed a much stronger throwing arm than Wynn. Ferguson caught the ball on the run and fired to the plate—on the fly. The perfect throw struck down Bando to complete a dramatic double play. "That was the best throw I've ever seen," Wynn told *Sports Illustrated*. He was now glad that Ferguson had charged in front of him to make the catch.

The A's took their 3–1 lead to the bottom of the ninth. Fingers retired the first two batters, Davey Lopes and Bill Buckner, with ease. Wynn, the Dodgers' leading long-ball hitter with 32 during the regular season, kept the LA cause alive with a home run to left-center field, just beyond the extended reaches of North and Rudi. Fingers then surrendered a line single to Steve Garvey. Having pitched four and a third innings of pressurized relief, a tiring Fingers gave the ball to Alvin Dark, who had made his way to the mound. Who would the manager call upon to face Ferguson, a dangerous right-handed power hitter? Glenn Abbott, an unproven young right-hander making his first trip to the World Series? Not a chance. Dark instead selected the team's latest center of the storm, potential free agent Catfish Hunter, who had pitched only three days earlier in the clincher against Baltimore. "The Cat" promptly struck out Ferguson, preserving a dramatic Game One victory on the road. "It was the perfect time to bring the Catfish in," Dark told *Sports Illustrated*, patting himself on the back. "He isn't scheduled to pitch until Tuesday [Game Three]." That would give him two full days of rest before his first start.

The A's had become accustomed to watching Hunter pitch brilliantly in the playoffs—as a starter. Now Hunter had entered a game under much different circumstances and pitched effectively as a stand-in for a fatigued Fingers. Hunter had also set aside any thoughts of his potential free agency. "When I put this uniform on," Hunter told sportswriter Phil Pepe, "I'm 100 percent. I don't go out to lose, I go out to win. I don't care if it's a cow pasture game." Other A's pitchers attested to his high level of effort. "I've never seen a man pitch with more determination," Darold Knowles told Dave Anderson of the *New York Times*. "He's a deadly professional."

With Hunter slated to start the third game, the A's chose Vida Blue to pitch Game Two against Don Sutton, the Dodgers' best starter over the second half of the season and the playoffs. The curveballing right-hander, overshadowed by Andy Messersmith for much of the season, hadn't lost a game in two months. The Dodgers quickly supported Sutton by scoring a run in the second on Steve Yeager's RBI single. In the sixth inning, Steve Garvey reached on an infield single and scored on Joe Ferguson's long home run to the center-field bleachers.

Sutton continued to hold the three-run lead until the eighth, when the A's loaded the bases with one out. Billy North, the fastest man on the A's, figured to score at least one run by simply hitting the ball on the ground. After all, the chances of turning a double play against North ranked low on the list of probabilities. North hit a ball on the ground all right, but in the wrong place. Dodger shortstop Bill Russell fielded North's grounder up the middle, stepped on the second-base bag for one out, and then threw to first. But Russell's hurried throw sank too quickly, short-hopping Steve Garvey. With a sweeping scoop of his glove hand, the sure-handed Garvey fielded the hop cleanly, completing the double play. "The key play of the game," assessed Sal Bando in an interview with *Sports Illustrated*. "If he didn't catch the ball, we have two runs and a man on second."

Sutton ran into another jam in the ninth when he hit Bando with an errant pitch. Reggie Jackson followed with a checked-swing grounder, good for a two-base hit, down the left-field line. With the tying run coming to the plate, Dodgers skipper Walter Alston called upon his best relief pitcher, Mike Marshall, to face Joe Rudi. The A's' left fielder roped a single to center, scoring both Jackson and Bando.

Marshall recorded the inning's first out by striking out Gene Tenace. Rudi, still standing on first base, suddenly noticed the presence of Herb Washington on the diamond. Much like he had done on Opening Day, Alvin Dark had decided to use his designated pinch-runner for his starting left fielder. This time, the strategy made some sense. Down 3-2 with one out and a runner on first base, the speed of Washington gave the A's a better chance of putting the tying run in scoring position via the stolen base.

The presence of Marshall on the mound, Washington pinch-running at first base, and Steve Garvey holding him on provided an intriguing triumvirate of Michigan State alumni. Both Washington and Garvey had graduated from Michigan State, while Marshall had worked there as a professor. Thinking aggressively, Washington took a big lead off first base. Marshall, a well-conditioned athlete with a quick spin move to first base, stepped off the rubber repeatedly, and then threw to first base. Washington dove back ahead of Steve Garvey's tag—safely but barely. Marshall then tried another pickoff, twirling his body around quickly and firing to Garvey. Washington hesitated for a moment, his legs frozen, before turning back to first base. Garvey slapped the tag on Washington, who dove headfirst into the bag. First base umpire Doug Harvey made a decisive call—OUT!

The pickoff of Washington eliminated the A's' most realistic hopes of tying the game. When Marshall struck out pinch-hitter Angel Mangual, the national media began the inevitable process of placing goat horns squarely on the head of Washington. "It was a perfect set-up," Steve Garvey told *Sports Illustrated*, explaining the pickoff of Washington. "Marshall stepped off the rubber three times and we froze Herb. The throw was on the money." During spring training, Charlie Finley had boasted that Washington would prove directly responsible for at least 10 victories. In this case, he had at least indirectly contributed to a World Series loss.

As the A's waited for their plane at the Los Angeles Airport, Reggie Jackson approached Washington. "You'll bounce back," the superstar told the pinch-runner, according to sportswriter Phil Pepe. "You made a mistake. You'll have to learn from it." Alvin Dark came by next, patted Washington on the shoulder, and offered him similar words of encouragement.

With an off day scheduled between the second and third games, the A's flew upstate for the continuation of the Series in Oakland. Oakland players originally thought they had the option of attending a Monday workout at the Oakland Coliseum, but during the flight, Charlie Finley unilaterally decided to make the practice mandatory. "What do we have to work out for?" an irked Sal Bando asked the *New York Daily News*. "We've played 190 games already. The day off would do us more good than the workout."

An optional workout might have also saved a 52-year-old sportswriter named Murray Olderman from the wrath of Reggie Jackson. During the Monday afternoon session, Vida Blue informed Jackson of Olderman's arrival on the Coliseum premises. Jackson left the batting cage and unfurled a vicious verbal attack on Olderman, shouting at him for about 10 minutes while the writer's 16-year-old son watched on. "You better not get around me," Jackson said in a threatening tone, according to the *San Francisco Chronicle*. "I want to embarrass you. You made me look like a bleep."

Both Jackson and Blue had been angered by Olderman's feature article about Reggie, which appeared in the October edition of *Sport* Magazine. Blue accused Olderman of quoting him in the article without ever speaking to him. Olderman later admitted that he had used second-hand quotes from Blue that had been given to him by other writers.

The cover of the October *Sport* showed Reggie wearing a military helmet and holster under a headline that read, "Reggie Jackson: Blood and Guts of the Fighting A's." Jackson had consented to the unusual pose and had allowed Olderman into his home, but didn't agree with some of the San Francisco writer's conclusions about his personality and lifestyle. In the article, Olderman alternately praised and criticized Jackson, describing him as "utterly charming or maddeningly harsh." Olderman lauded Jackson for being "glib and charming and witty and spirited," but pointed out that "he can be sullen and evasive and quarrelsome." Olderman also portrayed Jackson as hypocritical, given that both a Holy Bible and a gun lay atop the television set in the right fielder's home.

The Commissioner's Office soon learned of Jackson's angry public display toward Olderman. Moments before Game Three of the Series, Major League Baseball's director of public relations, Joe Reichler, approached Jackson as he threw warm-up tosses to Jesus Alou. The aide to the commissioner questioned Jackson about his threat to keep Olderman out of the Oakland clubhouse. "The commissioner doesn't want anything like this ever to happen again," Reichler warned Jackson, according to United Press International. "If it does, there's going to be a serious problem, a very serious problem, and I think you know what I mean by that." In other words, Commissioner Bowie Kuhn might fine or even suspend Jackson for a similar outburst. Jackson nodded at Reichler, promising that he would avoid such confrontations in the future.

While many reporters applauded the Commissioner's Office for adopting a get-tough stance on media relations, one of the nation's most influential sports writers expressed a contrasting opinion. After the Series, *New York Times* writer Red Smith chided baseball officials for their reprimands of both Jackson and Dodger relief pitcher Mike Marshall, a man notorious for belligerent treatment of writers and broadcasters. "Murray Olderman is a nice guy," Smith wrote in the October 20th edition of the *New York Times*, "but if Jackson doesn't like what he writes, he's entitled to tell him so. And there is nothing in the rules of baseball or Mike Marshall's contract that forbids him to be as bumptious a boor as he likes." Smith's rather unexpected support of Marshall and Jackson struck some as rather strange, but really should have come as no surprise, considering the legendary writer's history of criticizing management and supporting players. Perhaps Smith might have taken a different stance had Jackson verbally accosted him in front of *his* son.

With Jackson still in the lineup, the A's and Dodgers had to wait an extra 15 minutes to start Game Three due to national television coverage of President Gerald Ford's address to the nation in Kansas City. Prior to the game, the unflappable Catfish Hunter discussed the issue of nervousness with several members of the media. "A lot of guys get nervous before big games," Hunter acknowledged to a reporter. "I've never been that way. I'm pitching, I just concentrate on the batter. If he hits me, the world doesn't come to an end. If I get him out, I'm still not in the Hall of Fame."

Dodger manager Walter Alston might have had reason for nervousness in making his pitching selection for Game Three. Alston matched Hunter with former A's left-hander Al Downing, the choice over Doug Rau. While neither left-hander had been particularly successful in 1974, the aging Downing had won a mere five games during the season.

Alston's decision to pitch Downing prompted Oakland reporters to question Alvin Dark about possible lineup changes. After the A's had faced two right-handed starters in the first two games of the Series, would Dark now use a more heavily right-handed lineup in Game Three? Dark acknowledged that he was considering several changes, such as flip-flopping Campy Campaneris, the post-season leadoff man, and Billy North, the second-place hitter. Another possibility involved dropping North or Campaneris to the No. 6 position while moving Joe Rudi to the second spot. "Will you check it with Finley?" a writer for the *New York Times* asked Dark about the new lineup combinations. "I talk over all possible changes with the general manager," Dark said diplomatically. "Every general manager is entitled to that respect." Of course, anyone remembering the Deron Johnson-Vic Davalillo switch during the first week of the regular season already knew the answer to the writer's question.

The game itself took on a sideshow quality when the Oakland Coliseum's public address announcer informed the fans that Charlie Finley planned to ask President Ford and former President Nixon to throw out the ceremonial first pitches before the next two games in Oakland. With a telephone by his side in the owner's box, Finley made a grand showing of dialing the appropriate phone numbers. Both political leaders declined the offers, claiming that previous engagements prevented them from traveling to the Bay Area. Rather than make an announcement over the stadium's public address, Finley informed the media of the rejected invitations through a speaker in the press box. That way, Finley avoided the embarrassment of telling the Oakland fans that he had struck out—twice.

In and around the various announcements, Al Downing struggled badly in the third and fourth innings. Billy North, batting out of the leadoff spot for the first time in the Series, singled and moved all the way to third on a hit-and-run groundout by Campy Campaneris. After a walk to Sal Bando, Reggie Jackson topped a high bouncer in front of the plate. Catcher Joe Ferguson, the right fielder in the first two games of the Series, bobbled the ball, allowing North to score and Jackson to reach first base safely. Joe Rudi drove in the A's' second run with a ground single up the middle, past the dive of second baseman Davey Lopes. In the fourth, Downing walked the light-hitting Dick Green to start the inning. With Green at second and two outs, Campaneris supplied a clutch, two-out single to center field. The official scorer charged Ferguson with his second error of the game when Jimmy Wynn's throw from center field caromed past him, allowing Campy to move up to third base. "The ball never should have been thrown," Ferguson surmised in an interview with the *New York Times*. "We had no chance at home plate. If the pitcher feels there is a chance, he should be backing up the plate. He was standing on the mound." No matter the fault defensively, Campy's hit gave the A's a 3–0 lead and knocked an ineffective Downing from the box.

Hunter pitched brilliantly until the eighth, when Lopes drove a pitch to deep center field. For a moment, Lopes seemed destined for a double or triple, only to have North make a terrific backhanded catch. Momentarily spared by his defense, Hunter surrendered a line-drive home run to Bill Buckner, the Dodgers' talented young left fielder. "There were a couple of people up here from North Carolina [Hunter's home state] that wanted me to give up a home run," Hunter joked later with the *San Francisco Chronicle*. "They'd never seen one before."

The fans also saw the last of Hunter, as Alvin Dark called upon Rollie Fingers. The A's' relief ace allowed a quick single to his first batter, Jimmy Wynn. Fingers then faced Steve Garvey, who represented the tying run. Garvey ripped a Fingers pitch to the right side of the infield. For a moment, the Dodgers seemed destined to enjoy a first-and-third, one-out situation. They would have, if not for the presence of Oakland's terrific second baseman. Dick Green dove for the Garvey liner, grabbed it on the fly, and fired to Gene Tenace at first base for an inning-ending double play.

In the bottom of the eighth inning, the A's encountered their latest mini-controversy. Tenace singled, only to be lifted for pinch-runner Herb Washington. Tenace, never happy to be removed for a pinch-runner, mouthed a few words toward Washington. The former Olympian, distracted by a cascade of boos from the Coliseum rafters, couldn't hear what Tenace said, but believed the veteran catcher-first baseman was mad at him. After the game, Tenace explained that he had merely offered Washington a few words of encouragement and nothing more. Still, Tenace *was* upset that Alvin Dark had yanked him from a close game.

In the ninth inning, Fingers allowed a leadoff home run to Willie Crawford, the Dodgers' right fielder. With the Oakland lead down to one run, Joe Ferguson hit a hard-hit grounder to the left side, which Campy Campaneris failed to handle. Fingers then toughened, striking out Ron Cey. Bill Russell followed by grounding to the right side, where Dick Green scooped up the ball quickly, starting a 4-6-3 double play. Thanks in large part to the defensive play of Green, the A's had won the game, 5–2, and taken the lead in the Series, two games to one.

Green's game-ending double play represented the third twin-killing of the night for Oakland. The deft fielding second baseman tied a World Series record by taking part in all three double plays. When asked about the double plays, Green expressed surprise at matching the record, then fired several shots at the condition of Oakland's home field. "When you take into account how bad the infield is in the Oakland Coliseum," Green told the *San Francisco Chronicle,* "making three double plays in any game, let alone a World Series, is something. We've complained about our infield for years and sometimes I wonder why we keep bothering. No one is going to do anything about it." Other Oakland players agreed with Green's rating of the Coliseum playing field. Even Joe Rudi, perhaps the most reserved of the A's, had ripped the quality of the Oakland sod earlier in the season. "The field is just awful," Rudi complained to *The Sporting News.* "I think the Oakland Coliseum field is the worst in the American League." Still, it hadn't derailed the American League's best defensive second baseman.

Another clutch pitching exhibition by Catfish Hunter had lifted the A's to a one-game lead over the Dodgers. One reporter asked him if his contract dispute with Charlie Finley had managed to distract him on the mound. "No," Hunter replied to the *San Francisco Chronicle*, "and I won't think about it until our season is over. Our team fights in hotels and fights in the clubhouse, we get that off our shoulders and go out and play baseball."

Even the continuing malaise of the Oakland offense had not prevented the A's from assuming a two-games-to-one lead in the Series. "We're not getting runs the way we did the first three months of the season," Alvin Dark moaned to the *New York Times*. "This team's not been hitting since the middle of the summer."

The Dodgers didn't seem impressed with the A's' offense—or other parts of their game. Several Dodger players noted the generally unimpressive way in which Oakland had won Game Three, expressing disbelief that the A's had somehow managed to take the lead in the Series. On two occasions, Dodger hitters had laced line drives, only to have them caught by Dick Green, who then doubled off LA's Jimmy Wynn each time. "The A's are getting away with murder," fumed Dodger catcher Joe Ferguson in an interview with the *New York Times*. "They haven't beaten us yet. We gave them the game and hit three or four line shots that they caught. They are definitely a team of opportunity."

Bill Buckner, in revealing his frustration over the Series' turn of events, insulted the general caliber of the A's' ballclub. "We definitely have a better team," Buckner snorted to the *San Francisco Chronicle*. "The A's have only a couple of players who could play on our club," said Buckner, who mentioned Reggie Jackson, Sal Bando, Joe Rudi, and most members of the Oakland pitching staff as the only ones worthy of consideration for the Dodger roster. "Other than that, I think if we played them 162 games, we'd beat them a hundred times." The newspaper clipping from the *Chronicle*, which contained Buckner's quotes, soon reached the hands of Charlie Finley.

Prior to Game Four, Finley called a team meeting to inform the players of Buckner's disparaging statements. As he held up the clipping, Finley exhorted his players to prove Buckner wrong. Surprisingly, some of the A's did not appreciate Finley's attempt at motivation. "I don't need no pre-game dump," Reggie Jackson informed *Sports Illustrated*, "to rev me up."

In Game Four, Alvin Dark made news by omitting Gene Tenace from his starting lineup. Tenace's name appeared in the original lineup, but after a meeting with Finley, Dark unveiled a revised batting order. Several reporters overheard Finley talking to his manager. "Last night you had your way," Finley bellowed (according to *The Sporting News*), referring to the Game Three lineup changes that Dark had instituted. "Tonight I have mine."

Dark didn't want to keep Tenace on the bench, but still had to explain the decision to the media as if he agreed with it. Dark told reporters that he wanted to make room for another left-handed hitter, Claudell Washington, against the right-handed Andy Messersmith. Tenace, having just completed batting practice, received official word of the change from third-base coach Bobby Winkles.

The last-minute alteration did not sit well with Tenace, the MVP of the 1972 World Series. "Finley is trying to bury me," Tenace complained to *The Sporting News*. "He treats me as just another number. I want to be treated like a man." Other players sympathized with Tenace's plight. "Personally," Sal Bando told *The Sporting News*, "I think he should have been in there." Tenace also criticized Dark for his failure to resist Finley's lineup changes. "I have no respect for Dark, for not backing me up," Tenace complained to the *San Francisco Chronicle*. "I don't see how a man can let himself be dominated that way." Tenace added that he wanted to play for another team in 1975. "I'd like to be traded. I could continue to play for the A's, but I don't want to." Yet, Tenace didn't believe that Finley would accommodate him. "I think he would get a big kick out of seeing me rot on the bench," seethed Tenace in an interview with United Press International. "He's that kind of a man."

Ken Holtzman, of all people, made up for the absence of Tenace's right-handed power hitter. Holtzman once again showed surprising value at the plate when he pounded a home run to left field against Messersmith. A giddy Holtzman almost didn't complete his rout around the base paths. "I was light-headed going around," Holtzman told the *New York Times*, in discussing his lack of familiarity with hitting home runs and running the bases. "I remember tripping going over first base. I forgot where it was." The home run, Holtzman's second extra-base hit of the Series, gave the A's a 1–0 lead. The Dodgers vaulted right back in the top of the fourth, however, scoring a pair of runs on Bill Russell's two-out triple.

The Dodgers held their 2–1 advantage until the bottom of the sixth. Billy North drew a leadoff walk and moved to second on an errant pickoff throw by Messersmith. Sal Bando blooped a single in front of Joe Ferguson in right field, scoring North with the tying run. Walks to Reggie Jackson and Claudell Washington, sandwiched around a sacrifice bunt by Joe Rudi, loaded the bases for the A's.

The intentional walk to Washington made sense for the Dodgers, considering that the next scheduled batter, Ray Fosse, had picked up only one hit in 11 World Series at-bats. Alvin Dark decided to take a chance on his weak bench, sending the lefty-hitting Jim Holt to the plate to face Messersmith. The numbers did not look favorable. Holt, a .143 hitter for the A's after being acquired in a trade with the Twins, had failed to deliver a single hit in 24 pinch-hit at-bats.

Dodger manager Walter Alston might have considered a move to the bullpen, but a switch to a left-handed pitcher would have allowed Dark to employ Jesus Alou, a much better hitter than Holt. Alston left Messersmith in the game and watched Holt break out of his pinch-hitting slump with a line single to right field. The unlikely hit scored Bando and Jackson, while advancing Washington to third. Dick Green's ground ball force out pushed across the A's' fourth run of the inning, cementing a 5–2 lead. In the ninth inning, with Ron Cey on first and one man out, Green contributed again when he made a diving stop of a Von Joshua grounder near the second-base bag. Green corralled the ball, tossing to Campy Campaneris to start another game-ending 4-6-3 double play. "The last play might have been the best one of the Series," claimed Alston in an interview with the *New York Times*. "That double play was one of the best I've ever seen."

The A's were fortunate, however, considering Green's poor positioning on the play. "Our book on Joshua says he hits them up the middle," Green admitted to the *Times* after the game. "I was out of position when he hit it and had to hurry for it." Rollie Fingers, who had noticed Green playing too far toward first base, considered motioning him closer to second base. "I noticed that Dick was seven or eight steps out of position," Fingers told the *Times*. "I almost motioned him to move over, but didn't." In spite of the judgment errors by Green and Fingers, the A's had pulled off a highwire double play.

Even after the win, Charlie Finley took his turn in the continual game of verbal-thrashing enjoyed so much by the A's. Gene Tenace's pre-game complaints over his omission from the lineup and his insinuations about Dark and Finley did not sit well with the owner. "When I took this club," Finley preached to sportswriter Dick Young, "I told my players they could grow their hair down to their belly-buttons if they wanted and wear whatever clothes they wanted, but that I am the owner of the ballclub, and Mr. Dark is the manager of the ballclub, and if they don't like the way we run it, they can pack their bags and get the hell out, right now!" Ah yes, It was Finley at his diplomatic best.

The A's had more immediate concerns than the latest feud between Finley and his players. In order to win the Series in a taut five games, the A's would have to beat Don Sutton, the Dodgers' most effective starting pitcher. Campy Campaneris started Game Five by leading off the bottom of the first inning with a single, but was erased on Billy North's force-out grounder. North promptly stole second, and when Steve Yeager's throw caromed into the outfield, the Oakland center fielder popped up from the bag and raced to third. Sal Bando then plated North with a sacrifice fly to left field, giving the A's the early 1–0 lead.

In the second inning, the A's added to their margin. Ray Fosse, with only one hit in the World Series, lined a Sutton fastball into the left-field bleachers. With Vida Blue pitching well and shutting out the Dodgers over the first five innings, Game Five seemed well in hand.

The Dodgers attempted to build a comeback in the sixth inning. Tom Paciorek pinch-hit for Sutton, who had settled down to shut down the A's over the last three innings. The backup outfielder lined a double into left-center field, splitting the placement of Claudell Washington and Billy North. Blue walked Davey Lopes, putting the tying runs on base with no one out. Rather than play for the big inning, Walter Alston instructed Bill Buckner to lay down a sacrifice bunt. With runners now on second and third, Jimmy Wynn flied out to left field, scoring Paciorek. Steve Garvey followed with a two-out ground single between Sal Bando and Campy Campaneris, bringing home Lopes with the tying run.

Mike Marshall came on in place of Sutton and pitched a scoreless sixth inning. After the Dodgers failed to score in the top of the seventh, several fans at the Oakland Coliseum spent their seventh-inning stretch tossing debris onto the field. With objects like Frisbees, apples, beer cans, and whiskey bottles falling all around him, Dodger left fielder Bill Buckner complained to umpire Doug Harvey. The umpires decided to halt play until the fans had ceased the round of garbage-tossing, allowing the grounds crew to clear the outfield. The unruly behavior resulted in a delay of six minutes before the A's could come to bat.

Rather than use the unexpected down time to throw warm-up pitches, Marshall elected to join the umpires and players in conversation. Marshall then threw his first pitch to Joe Rudi, the A's' leadoff batter in the seventh. Usually a strong opposite-field hitter, Rudi turned on Marshall's pitch quickly, launching it into the left-field stands. The first-pitch home run gave the A's a 3–2 lead. Having noticed the Dodgers' strategy of trying to jam him with fastballs throughout the Series, Rudi anticipated a similar pitch from Marshall. "I hit an inside fastball, belt-high," Rudi told the Associated Press. "Believe it or not, I was looking for it." Rudi found an additional clue in Marshall's decision *not* to throw warm-up tosses. "When they had the mess in the outfield and he didn't take any warm-ups," Rudi explained to the *San Francisco Chronicle*, "I thought he might try to sneak one by me." Marshall's strategy backfired, leading several writers to question his decision to forego warm-up tosses during the unusually long delay. After the game, the media asked Marshall if he regretted his decision not to warm up. "I only answer questions I'm interested in," Marshall responded rudely to the *San Francisco Chronicle*. One interrogator followed up by asking Marshall what kind of pitch he threw to Rudi. "When I don't answer a question," Marshall said after pausing for a moment, "it means I don't hear it." Lovely.

As the A's took the field in the top of the eighth inning, Alvin Dark made several defensive changes. The unhappy backup, Gene Tenace, moved in to play first base, with Joe Rudi retreating to his more accustomed position in left field. Those moves strengthened the A's defensively at two positions. Dark also solidified his mound options by summoning Rollie Fingers to relieve Blue Moon Odom, who had succeeded starter Vida Blue. Vida was hoping for his first win in World Series play.

Bill Buckner led off against Fingers with a line single to right-center field, which Billy North misplayed badly. The ball rolled to the wall, allowing Buckner to run to second. As North and Reggie Jackson scurried to retrieve the ball near the wall, Buckner rounded the bag at second and continued running to third. Jackson, the owner of a much stronger throwing arm than North, picked up the ball and fired to Dick Green, who made an on-line relay throw to Sal Bando at third. Bando, the recipient of the perfect throw, dramatically applied the tag to a sliding Buckner for the first out of the inning. Instead of having the tying run at second with no one out, Buckner's base-running gaffe had demoralized the Dodger offense. Fingers then retired Steve Garvey and Joe Ferguson on routine fly balls to finish off the inning.

"I saw them still chasing the ball and figured I had a good chance of going to third," Buckner told the *San Francisco Chronicle*, attempting to defend his overly aggressive baserunning. "It took two perfect throws to get me." Perfect throws aside, Buckner had committed a costly fundamental error in allowing himself to be retired at third base as the inning's first out.

The baserunning mistake brought the A's within one inning of their third straight World Series victory. Ron Cey, Bill Russell, and Steve Yeager, the sixth, seventh, and eighth-place hitters, represented the last three scheduled Dodger threats against Fingers in the ninth. Cey launched a fly ball deep to right field, pushing Reggie Jackson to the warning track. The 1973 Most Valuable Player backtracked and reached up for the ball to record the first out. The lefty-swinging Willie Crawford, batting for Russell, lofted a high pop-up behind second base. Dick Green, the A's' best defensive player throughout the five games of the Series, called off Campy Campaneris and made the catch. Two outs. Walter Alston then called upon backup outfielder Von Joshua, 0-for-3 in the Series, to pinch-hit for Yeager. The left-handed hitter reached for the Fingers delivery, tapping it softly back to the mound. Fingers snared the one-bouncer, crow-hopped two steps toward first base, and fired to Gene Tenace. Three outs—World Series over.

With that historic third out, the A's joined baseball's most famous franchise, the New York Yankees, as the only teams to claim at least three consecutive World Championships. The Yankees had first turned the trick by winning four in a row (1936 to 1939) and then bettered the mark by winning five straight championships (1949 to 1953). Other storied teams like the St. Louis Cardinals, Brooklyn Dodgers, New York Giants and Oakland's predecessor, the Philadelphia Athletics, had all enjoyed success over a long stretch of years, but none had won back-to-back-to-back World Series titles.

Red and green fireworks, set off at the moment that Rollie Fingers recorded the final out, filled the sky above the Oakland Coliseum. Hundreds of fans, mostly younger ones in their teens and twenties, streamed onto the field in a search for souvenirs. Forced to dodge the oncoming admirers, A's players raced to the dugout, which provided safe access to the victorious clubhouse celebration.

Oakland players and staff engaged in a frenetic but brief post-game party that lasted fewer than 40 minutes. Relief pitcher Darold Knowles, a forgotten man in the '74 World Series after appearing in every Series game the year before, climbed atop his locker and poured wine and champagne on any teammates within reach. Reggie Jackson, more heavily involved in the latest World Series triumph, good-naturedly poured champagne over the head of Commissioner Bowie Kuhn, whose office had warned the A's' right fielder about his behavior toward the media just a few days earlier. Kuhn did not object to Reggie's latest show of emotion. Jackson also sprayed a combination of champagne and shaving cream on broadcaster Joe Garagiola, who had hosted the World Series pre-game shows for NBC-TV. "We wait for the door to open," Jackson explained to a reporter from *Sports Illustrated*, "and when it does, we go through."

Still, questions remained. Who would *Sport* Magazine choose as its World Series MVP? In 1973, the magazine had made the controversial selection of Jackson over Campy Campaneris, whom many sports writers had favored. Some of the attending media promoted Dick Green as the 1974 choice, based on his spectacular fielding in each of the five Series games. Green's fielding had contributed directly to three of the four A's' victories. He had taken part in six double plays, tying a record for the most twin killings in a five-game World Series. Green's defensive work highlighted Oakland's defensive superiority over the Dodgers. "Fielding was the main difference between the teams," acknowledged Dodger manager Walter Alston in an interview with Stanley Frank of *Sport* Magazine. Yet, sportswriters more concerned with offensive numbers could not help but notice Green's paltry hitting. Green did not manage a single hit during 13 World Series at-bats. No Series MVP, outside of pitchers, had ever gone hitless for an entire Fall Classic.

Not surprisingly, *Sport* Magazine settled on a more conventional MVP selection: relief pitcher Rollie Fingers. The Oakland fireman saved two games, won one, and held Dodger hitters to only two runs over nine and a third innings. Still, *Sport* did give Green heavy consideration. The A's second baseman finished a close second in the voting. Furthermore, the New York Baseball Writers named Green the winner of their World Series MVP award—the Babe Ruth Award. The New York scribes had never before given their award to a player who had endured a hitless Series. Green's defensive play had been *that* good.

As a younger player, Green had been influenced by another World Series hero—New York Yankee second baseman Bobby Richardson. When Green first entered the American League in 1963, he considered Richardson the circuit's best defensive second baseman. Green sought advice from Richardson and patterned his style of play after the Yankee veteran.

Throughout much of his career, Green had played second base with a workmanlike grit that left him overlooked among writers and fans. "Dick Green was what we called a 'two-outs-in-the-ninth-inning' player," says Jack Aker. "He was a guy that we wanted the ball hit to with two outs in the ninth inning when we were trying to hold the lead. He was not flashy, but any ball—routine balls that were hit to him—we always counted on being gobbled up."

In the World Series, Green played the position with a more discernible flair that nearly matched his stylish clothing. "The best dresser on the team," Reggie Jackson once told sportswriter Joe Gergen. And perhaps the best defensive player on the team. Green's Richardson-like fielding in the World Series left such an impression that *Sport* Magazine writer Stanley Frank included him in an updated version of the famed baseball poem, "Tinker to Evers to Chance."

> Enshrined in baseball's myth and romance
> Is Chicago's Tinker to
> Evers to Chance
> But that DP combo was never the menace
> Of the A's' Campaneris to Green to Tenace

While many of the A's happily shouted obscenities during the clubhouse celebration, manager Alvin Dark, not given to verbal profanity, provided a religious backdrop to the proceedings. "A lot of people won't understand this," Dark told the *San Francisco Chronicle* in his first post-game interview, "but glory be to god." One reporter followed up Dark's declaration with a more secular line of questioning. Would Alvin return to manage the A's in 1975? Dark replied by thanking Charlie Finley for allowing him to return to baseball and said that he would discuss his future with the owner at a later date.

Finley spent much of his time in the clubhouse directing players to a podium, where they would be interviewed by NBC on live television. A reporter asked

Finley if he intended to bring Dark back for another season, given the friction that existed between him, the players, and of course, the owner. "I will have to sit down and talk about next year with him," Finley answered the *San Francisco Chronicle* in his usually cryptic, side-stepping way. "He did a real good job. He's a fine gentleman. We were very happy to have him."

As the celebration continued, the media questioned the future status of other Oakland personnel in the room. Several reporters surrounded Gene Tenace, who only four days earlier had asked to be traded. "There's no reason for me to leave this club," Tenace told the *San Francisco Chronicle*, changing course on his previous desire. Regardless of his own wants, did Tenace *expect* to be traded? "No, I don't think they'll trade me. Claudell Washington is a hell of a ballplayer and he's got to play in the outfield, so Joe Rudi's got to play first base and you keep Fosse at catcher." Under that scenario, Tenace would be left without a position, or at best, as a platoon player. "If that happens," Tenace continued, "they're going to platoon me. [Then] I've got to ask them to trade me." The interview with Tenace left reporters thoroughly confused. In other words, Tenace wanted to stay and didn't think he would be traded, but he felt the A's would probably platoon him, and if they did, then he would prefer to be traded.

Few championship teams had so many lingering questions hanging over their immediate future. Would Tenace return? Would Dark resign, be fired, or be brought back for another season of torture under Charlie Finley? And what about Catfish Hunter? Would the staff ace, as had been reported prior to the Series, pursue free agency as a result of a contractual mistake by the owner?

Finley and Dark answered one of the questions quickly. One day after the World Series victory, Finley publicly announced his desire to have Dark return. Rather than accept the one-year deal immediately, Dark contemplated the offer for one night. Dark then agreed to return. The new contract contained an increase in pay, and offered Dark a bit more security than his 1974 deal. Under terms of the old contract, Finley could have fired Dark at any time and would not have been liable to pay his manager for the rest of the season. Now, if Dark were to be fired, he would receive his severance pay for the balance of the year.

The new contract still seemed like a small reward for leading a team to its third consecutive title. Although Dark had made many mistakes during the regular season, he had managed the playoffs and World Series with conviction, precision, and the proper extent of aggressiveness. Dark had also led the A's to the title with a weaker bench and a thinner bullpen than either of the championship teams managed by Dick Williams.

In rewarding Dark with a new contract, Finley couldn't resist taking another shot at Williams. The owner pointed out that the A's had beaten the Orioles in four games and the Dodgers in five, while Williams' teams had required the full five games to win the Championship Series and the full seven games to claim the World Series in each of the previous two seasons. Only someone like Finley would nit-pick about the number of games it took his team to win the championship.

The status of Gene Tenace remained in doubt, especially after Finley continued his nearly annual offseason tradition of making trades with the Cubs. On October 23, less than a week after winning the World Series, Finley sent three players—second baseman Manny Trillo and extraneous relievers Darold Knowles and Bob Locker—to Chicago for longtime Cubs star Billy Williams. "We feel he will be the finest designated hitter in the American League," Finley boasted to *The Sporting News*. "He hits with authority and consistency." While many Cub followers mourned the loss of one of their longtime stalwarts, Oakland fans and players reacted with favor to the trade. "This is not just some *guy* you pick up," Reggie Jackson told Ron Fimrite of *Sports Illustrated*. "This is a Hall of Famer."

As a 10-and-5 player (at least 10 years in the majors and at least five with his current team), Williams had the right to reject any trade attempt by the Cubs. Chicago management had provided Williams with a list of six teams, five of which the onetime batting champion rejected. Williams agreed to report to Oakland for two reasons: the A's gave him a stronger chance of playing in the post-season than the Cubs, and Charlie Finley agreed to give him a two-year contract worth $300,000. The rebuilding Cubs had indicated that they would only offer a one-year deal.

In acquiring Williams, the A's surrendered considerable talent. Although Locker had missed the entire season after elbow surgery and Knowles had pitched poorly for Alvin Dark, the willingness to include Trillo represented a greater risk. Trillo had struggled in brief trials as a major league hitter, but his soft hands and limitless range made him the heir apparent to Dick Green at second base. What would the A's do if Green went ahead with his latest retirement threat and left the game for good? The A's had already waived journeyman John Donaldson, now that he had qualified for a pension with four years of service, and would soon part ways with Dal Maxvill, whose large salary made him too expensive for Finley's shrinking budgetary tastes.

The addition of Williams filled a major need for the A's—a left-handed hitter with some power who could protect Reggie Jackson in a batting order top-heavy with right-handed hitters. A skilled line-drive hitter, the 1972 National League batting champion possessed a lifetime batting average of .296. Although Williams had slumped in 1974, his .280 average and 16 home runs indicated he had ample productivity remaining in his slowing bat.

Aside from his sweet left-handed swing, Finley also liked Williams' reputation as an easygoing, likable person. "He's not a pop-off," Finley told Ron Bergman proudly while using one of his pet phrases. "I've been watching him six and a half years and he's a team player." One of the current A's had already attested to Williams' strong influence. As a young player with the Cubs, Billy North had found Williams a willing helper. "Williams taught me how to play baseball," North told the *Chicago Tribune*. "He's the best hitter there is. More important than that, he's a great human being. Pro isn't the word. He's a man—at his job and at living…Billy Williams is the man who's been more help to me than anybody."

After praising Williams' quiet, professional nature, Charlie Finley delivered a not-so-subtle message to his outspoken players—principally Gene Tenace—who had complained about playing time in the past. "There seems to be players who think they can manage this club better than Alvin Dark," Finley exclaimed to *The Sporting News*, perhaps forgetting that he himself felt he could manage better than Dark. "Those who think they're smart enough should come to me, put in an application, and relate to me the reasons they should be managing." Finley continued his caustic diatribe against the team's most vocal complainers. "What this team needs is more talent and less pop-offs," sounded Finley, who promised to make additional trades before the start of the 1975 season.

The trade for Williams also created a glut of first baseman, left fielders, and designated hitters. With Williams penciled in as the DH, Dark would have to play Claudell Washington regularly in the field. Left field seemed like a possible destination, necessitating a move of Joe Rudi to first base. Since the A's preferred the defensively superior Ray Fosse at catcher, the Williams deal left Tenace without a regular position, at least on the surface. The Oakland media circulated rumors that the A's would soon trade Tenace, perhaps in a deal for a second baseman.

The proposed shifting of Rudi to first base made no sense. Rudi, who had just won his first Gold Glove award, ranked as the American League's best defensive left fielder. "It took me eight years to win a Gold Glove as an outfielder," Rudi said half-sarcastically in an interview with *Sports Illustrated*, subtly expressing his displeasure with the possible position change. "Now they move me to a new position." Preferences aside, why would the A's weaken two positions by relegating Rudi to first base? A better solution would have seen the A's move Washington, a tall man who had not yet become a good outfielder, to the infield. Yet, neither Finley nor Dark publicly considered that option.

Finley and Dark seemed too willing to tinker with *Rudi*, who had just completed his finest season. Rudi finished second to the Rangers' Jeff Burroughs in the American League's MVP vote, just ahead of more publicized teammates Sal Bando and Reggie Jackson, who placed third and fourth, respectively. Rudi earned five and a half first-place votes, while Burroughs picked up 10 first-place tallies. Several Oakland players wondered aloud how Burroughs, who had tailed off badly in September for the second-place Rangers, could win the award over a member of the first-place A's. While Rudi conceded that Burroughs had enjoyed the better statistical season, Bando suggested that the writers vote for two separate awards—Most Valuable Player and Most *Outstanding* Player. Under such a system, the writers could have recognized Burroughs for compiling the best set of statistics while also rewarding a player like Rudi, Bando, or Jackson for contributing most within the context of helping a team win the pennant.

In the meantime, Charlie Finley had promised to make more trades. On the same day that the A's added Billy Williams, Finley reacquired left-handed hitting first baseman Pat Bourque from the Twins. The interest in Bourque, a mediocre hitter, was mystifying enough. The talent that Finley sent to Minnesota to recover Bourque made the deal almost appalling from Oakland's perspective. Finley packaged two minor league prospects, outfielder Dan Ford and pitcher Dennis Myers, in the deal for Bourque. Ford, perhaps the best outfield prospect in the A's' system, would become a fine player for the Twins and Angels during an 11-year career. The dispatching of Ford would rank as one of Finley's worst trades as Oakland's general manager.

Chapter 27

The Kingdom Begins to Crumble

Making trades made Finley happy; a decision by the Major League Baseball Players' Association had not. On October 17, only moments after the A's had defeated the Dodgers in the World Series, the Association had filed the first of two grievances on behalf of Catfish Hunter. The first grievance cited the American and National leagues, and Commissioner Bowie Kuhn, for failing to recognize Hunter's free agency. The following day, the Association filed a grievance specifically against Finley, claiming the owner had violated Hunter's contract by not making the appropriate insurance payment of $50,000 during the 1974 season.

Finley called his continuing disagreement with Hunter a mere technicality, but the pitcher and his agent suspected that they had caught the owner making a critical mistake. In the spring of 1974, Hunter had negotiated a two-year contract with Finley. Under terms of the deal, Hunter would earn $100,000 per season, but would receive only $50,000 as up-front salary. In order to minimize his tax burden, Hunter's contract called for Finley to pay the remaining $50,000 into a life insurance fund. As deferred money, the $50,000 would not be subject to immediate taxation. Hunter would receive the deferred money once his playing career had come to an end.

Although Finley had agreed to the contract, he repeatedly balked at making the payment to the insurance company. Finley wouldn't specify why, but the reason was clear to any accountant. If he made the payment, he wouldn't be able to deduct the $50,000 as a business expense, thus hurting him at tax time. The payment might cost Finley $20,000–25,000 in taxes.

On November 19, Finley and the Players' Association made their cases to independent arbitrator Peter Seitz. As the neutral member of the arbitration panel, Seitz would cast the decisive vote on Hunter's contract status in December after studying the contrasting arguments over a period of a few weeks. Even if Seitz awarded him free agency, Hunter had initially indicated that he wanted to return to Oakland under a long-term contract. Hunter said he preferred playing for a team in a city where he had become comfortable. The pitcher later altered his stance. "If I become a free agent," Hunter told *The Sporting News*, sounding a warning to his owner, "I know I won't play for the A's. I don't think Finley appreciates what I've done for the A's."

The two sides waited for Seitz's decision, which would be announced publicly on December 13. That day, Seitz unveiled his bombshell ruling to Finley and Marvin Miller, the head of the Players' Association. Seitz instructed Finley to pay Hunter the $50,000 in question, at a rate of six per cent interest. In addition, Seitz announced that Hunter would become a free agent—immediately. For the first time in major league history, a player had become a full-fledged free agent without having been released by his previous team.

Seitz's decision shocked Finley, most of the other major league owners, and American League president Lee MacPhail, while vindicating Hunter, his agent, and the Players' Association. "I think it was fair and just, and I knew we told the truth," a satisfied Hunter told the Associated Press. "I had the feeling all the time it was going to come out this way." The ruling made him free to negotiate with any of the 24 major league teams, including the A's, with no compensation due Oakland should he sign with another club. Under the Seitz decision, Finley would not be allowed to match any offers made to Hunter. The independent arbitrator had done the unprecedented—making a player a free agent, with no strings attached. When a reporter asked him what he might now say to Finley, the pitcher responded with a smile, "I would say, 'Many thanks.'"

Based upon Hunter's earlier remarks and the acrimonious negotiating style of Finley, Oakland players figured they had lost one of their most respected teammates, the team's best starting pitcher, and the man who had just been named the winner of the American League's Cy Young Award. Although Catfish publicly refused to rule out the A's, his friends knew he had little interest in returning to Oakland, not with the opportunity to sign with large-market clubs in New York or Chicago, or free-spending teams in San Diego or Montreal, both of whom craved a marquee talent like Hunter.

The potential loss of Hunter did not please his Oakland teammates, on a variety of levels. First and foremost, Hunter was one of the club's most popular personalities. "He was a great guy, well-liked by his teammates," says Blue Moon Odom in recalling his pitching contemporary. "If you had anything wrong to say about Catfish, then something was wrong with *you*. One of the best guys I ever came in contact with."

The A's' catchers, who loved Hunter's easygoing nature and his willingness to defer to their knowledge in calling games, wanted no part of losing him to another team. "When I went over to Oakland in '73," Ray Fosse revealed to sportswriter Sid Bordman, "Catfish Hunter never shook me off. I asked him why and he told me, 'It's your job to know the hitters.'" Jim Pagliaroni, who caught Hunter in 1968 and '69, supports Fosse's contention. "He had four great pitches," says Pagliaroni, "but he never shook off his catcher. And I went out [to the mound] one time and asked him, 'Don't you have any thoughts of your own [on pitch selection]?' And he said, 'I figure you know what you're doing back there. I have trust in you.' That just blew me away." Like Pagliaroni and Fosse, catchers like Dave Duncan, Larry Haney, and Gene Tenace also appreciated the authority that a respected pitcher like Hunter bestowed on them.

Other Oakland players sounded off on the impending departure of their pitching leader. "With Catfish, we were World Champions," Reggie Jackson declared to *Sport* Magazine. "Without him, we have to struggle to win the division." Jackson had previously suggested that he himself might have to be traded to another team for a pitcher, someone comparable to Hunter. "If they traded Hank Aaron, Willie Mays, and Babe Ruth, they can trade Reggie Jackson," the Oakland right fielder had told the *San Jose Mercury News* only hours before Hunter's arbitration decision. "I expect to be traded in three weeks."

Baseball writers quickly circulated a series of trade rumors. The A's reportedly asked the Phillies for half of their starting infield—Mike Schmidt and Dave Cash—in exchange for Jackson. The Phillies rejected the proposal. The Dodgers discussed the possibility of trading star first baseman Steve Garvey and utilityman Lee Lacy, or Lacy in tandem with star pitcher Don Sutton. Another rumor indicated the Indians might offer starting pitcher Gaylord Perry and second baseman Jack Brohamer. The most frequently mentioned rumors involved the Orioles. Charlie Finley supposedly asked for infielder Bobby Grich and one of two players, either outfielder Don Baylor or pitcher Ross Grimsley.

Yet, Finley was not ready to give up Jackson, or give up the notion of keeping Hunter. Finley announced that he would file a lawsuit against any team attempting to sign Hunter. He sought a temporary injunction to prevent Hunter from being courted by other teams, but a Superior Court judge in Alameda County turned down his request. Finley then announced that he would appeal the arbitration panel's decision on the grounds that it had exceeded its authority in making Hunter a free agent.

Commissioner Bowie Kuhn, in a rare occurrence, actually found himself in agreement with Finley. Kuhn advised the 23 other major league teams to refrain from negotiations with Hunter. The commissioner's directive angered Marvin Miller and Hunter's team of four country lawyers, headed up by 68-year-old J. Carlton Cherry.

A few days later, Kuhn reversed field and gave all teams permission to negotiate with Hunter. Within three hours of the commissioner's change of policy, 12 teams contacted Cherry's office in Ahoskie, North Carolina, in pursuit of Hunter, the game's first true free agent. As Christmas passed and New Year's Eve approached, practically every major league team had called to make an opening offer. Both New York teams made it clear they wanted Catfish, while teams in smaller markets warned the small-town Hunter about the perils of playing in a large city. Several teams tried to use their own players and coaches—those who were friends of Catfish— to persuade Hunter to sign with them. The Brewers told Mike Hegan, a former Athletic, to meet with Hunter in an effort to lure him to the land of bratwurst. The Indians sent star pitcher Gaylord Perry, Hunter's frequent hunting companion during the offseason. The Padres dispatched a party of two—manager John McNamara and "executive" coach Bill Posedel, both former Oakland employees— to meet with their one-time pitching hand. In total, 48 baseball representatives descended on the small tobacco-farming burgh of Ahoskie, which had suddenly become the center of the baseball universe.

Hunter said he would consider proposals from any major league team. "I'll take the best offer," Hunter told Gerald Eskenazi of the *New York Times*. Catfish wanted the total package, taking into account such factors as salary, endorsement and investment possibilities, the stability of ownership, and the quality of the team. Hunter eventually narrowed his choices to eight teams, a group that surprisingly included the A's. Why? Hunter's lawyers had heard that Charlie Finley might sell the team. In that case, Hunter might be interested in a return to Oakland.

Despite recent rumors of a sale of the A's to a group headed up by former Giants manager Herman Franks, Finley was not about to sell the franchise. Hunter thus eliminated the A's from all consideration and reduced his list of potential teams to a final five: the Braves, Indians, Padres, Royals, and Yankees.

On New Year's Eve, the New York Yankees concluded the largest bidding war in baseball history. Needing a starter to replace the soon-to-be retired Mel Stottlemyre, the Yankees signed Hunter to an unprecedented five-year contract worth a record $3.75 million, including a $1 million signing bonus. The decision surprised some, given Hunter's previous comments about New York. In 1971, Hunter had expressed trepidation about leaving his hotel room during Oakland's stays in New York City. "New York still scares me to death," Catfish had told Pat Jordan of *Sport* Magazine.

Three years later, a more mature Hunter had changed his mind. Even though teams like the Padres had made better financial offers, the endorsement opportunities of New York and Hunter's relationship with Yankee director of scouting Clyde Kluttz, the man who had originally signed him for the Kansas City A's in 1964, had swung him in the direction of the Bronx. "He never lied to me," Hunter said of Kluttz in an interview with *Sport* Magazine. "He's my friend. That's why I signed with the A's, and that's why I signed with the Yankees." Kluttz convinced Catfish that New York was not only livable, but would provide him with the recognition that he could never receive in San Diego. Former A's teammates Curt Blefary and Mike Hegan also suggested he could live in suburban areas around New York, such as northern New Jersey, with its benefit of no state income tax. The Yankees thus won out over 21 other major league teams, each of which had placed bids on the Cy Young Award winner. Other than the A's, only the San Francisco Giants had refused to make Hunter an offer.

Although Hunter had developed close relationships with several of his Oakland teammates and had come to like the Bay Area community, he expressed relief over his escape from Charlie Finley's clutches. Catfish had grown uncomfortable playing for a man who too often treated his players like possessions. In 1965, Finley had instructed Hunter to pose for an embarrassing publicity photo by sitting in the lap of venerable pitcher Satchel Paige, whom the A's had signed in an attention-getting stunt. Finley's subsequent badgering of Hunter to repay a $150,000 loan sooner than anticipated had also bothered him. "I'd felt like I just got out of prison,"

Hunter told *Sport* Magazine of his feelings upon departing the A's, "even if I did regret how the other players might feel about my leaving the club."

The needless loss of Hunter resulted in the retirement of another player. Thirty-three-year-old Dick Green called it quits—again—saying that he did not want to return to a team that couldn't return to the World Series. "I'm just not coming back," Green declared to Bay Area sportswriter Glenn Dickey. "Catfish is the best pitcher in baseball and we won't win without him." Although Green had retired each of the past three offseasons only to return in spring training, the veteran second baseman said he fully meant to retire this time around.

The retirement of Green left the A's with only 31 players on their 40-man roster. Coupled with the recent trade of Manny Trillo to the Cubs and the release of Dal Maxvill, Green's departure also left the A's without a natural, everyday second baseman. Alvin Dark had only two options remaining: utility infielder Ted Kubiak and converted third baseman Phil Garner, who had hit .330 as a minor league player in 1974. Each player had his limitations. Kubiak had never hit well enough to merit regular playing time, while Garner lacked the range desired of a middle infielder. Garner had also been playing winter ball at third base—not at second base.

On January 18, more changes came to the A's. Charlie Finley announced the hiring of White Sox broadcaster Bob Waller, who had worked with Harry Caray in Chicago over the past two seasons. Waller had angered White Sox manager Chuck Tanner with his frequent criticisms of the team's performance. The 15th announcer employed by Finley since 1961, Waller would replace Jon Miller and team with Oakland fixture Monte Moore in the broadcast booth. Although the 23-year-old Miller had teamed well with Moore, he was apparently not favored by KPIX-TV, the A's' flagship station in San Francisco.

The configuration of the broadcast booth ranked far behind the largest concern facing the A's in 1975: how would the A's compensate for the annual 20 to 25 wins of the departed Catfish Hunter? "I've got to hit 10 more home runs this year," Reggie Jackson told a reporter, laying out the necessary formula of success, post-Catfish. "Sal Bando will have to drive in 25 more runs. Vida Blue will have to win six more games. Billy North will have to steal 25 more bases. The 'Catfish' is gone, and everybody is going to have to do something to make up for those 25 games he won last year." The A's also needed more efficiency from veteran starter Blue Moon Odom, who had continued the inconsistent pattern of his career by winning only one game and posting an ERA of 3.83 in 1974.

Given the lack of proven commodities after Blue and Ken Holtzman in their starting rotation, the A's extended spring training invitations to two aging starters. Charlie Finley telephoned former Athletic Lew Krausse, who had been released by the Braves over the winter. Finley also contacted a well-known Bay Area star, the former ace of the rival Giants. Finley hoped that another big name—that of future Hall of Famer Juan Marichal—could take Hunter's place in the rotation.

The 37-year-old Marichal had given up nearly five runs per nine innings for the Red Sox in 1974, but had won five of six decisions. As a one-time star in the Bay Area and a six-time 20-game winner, Finley believed that Marichal would serve as a drawing card for the A's. Furthermore, the signing of Marichal figured to deflect some of the criticism that Finley had been leveled with since his needless contract snafu with Hunter.

Finley felt so confident that he would be able to sign Marichal that he ordered his public relations staff to include the pitcher's biography in the team's organization book. Marichal's entry in the book became a curiosity when the Dominican right-hander rejected the offseason overtures from Finley. The high-kicking right-hander decided to sign with another California team—the Dodgers—the same team the A's had defeated in the 1974 World Series.

Chapter 28

The Perils of Arbitration

Newsmakers in 1975

One of the longest running wars of the 20th century comes to an end when South Vietnam falls to North Vietnam...Terrorists bomb the historic Fraunces Tavern in New York City...Prominent labor leader Jimmy Hoffa mysteriously disappears, fueling years of speculation over his fate.

President Gerald Ford, who succeeded the impeached Richard Nixon, survives a pair of assassination attempts... For the first time ever, women are permitted to enter American service academies...Patty Hearst is found, after first being taken hostage by the Symbionese Liberation Army and then working with the organization as an accomplice.

"One Flew Over The Cuckoo's Nest," starring Jack Nicholson, wins the Academy Award for Best Picture...International soccer star Pele signs a three-year, $7 million contract with the New York Cosmos of the North American Soccer League...Frank Robinson becomes the first black manager in major league history.

Perhaps Juan Marichal had decided to avoid Finley at all costs after watching the majority of Oakland's veteran players take their contracts to arbitration. Finley low-balled his top stars, Sal Bando, Joe Rudi, Reggie Jackson, and Ken Holtzman, so severely that each player decided to take his chances in front of an arbitrator. The owner simply refused to budge from his initial offers, which in some cases, represented pay cuts for his best players.

Bando's arbitration case became especially nasty. Finley publicly demeaned his third baseman's abilities on every level, from his inability to hit for a high average to his supposedly diminishing fielding skills. In an effort to avoid further insults and an outright confrontation, Bando tried to withdraw his case from the arbitrator and reach a new contract through peaceful means. "Everything he does," Bando told Dick Young of the *New York Daily News*, "there must be a battle and I'm sick of it. I think most of our men are sick of it. You get to a point where hassling every day isn't amusing anymore. I want out."

Yet, Finley would not allow Bando to withdraw his case from arbitration "unless I agree that he can. And the only way I will agree is if he signs the contract I have offered him," Finley informed the Associated Press. Finley proceeded to call Bando ungrateful and unappreciative before launching a final insult. "If he wishes to become the village idiot," said Finley, "let him be my guest."

In the past, Finley had reserved such vicious name-calling for only his worst enemies in baseball, namely Commissioner Bowie Kuhn. While some observers of the A's laughed off Finley's "village idiot" remark, Bando admits that it did sting him. "It hurts to a degree," says Bando, "because no one wants to be talked about like that. But I also considered the source and the circumstances." Bando realized that Finley could become particularly nasty at negotiation time, sometimes saying things that he didn't necessarily believe in a desperate attempt to save money. "Charlie was like that," says Sal. "He did not set a good example."

Insults aside, the arbitrator ruled in Finley's favor—a salary of $100,000 instead of the $125,000 that Bando sought. Finley gloated over his victory against his team captain. "I'm extremely happy about it," Finley exulted to reporters. After all, he had just saved himself $25,000.

Finley also defeated Ken Holtzman, who had been insulted by the owner's refusal to offer him a raise, at the arbitration table. Two weeks later, the veteran left-hander hinted that he might not stay with the A's throughout the entire 1975 season. "If a business opportunity I have works out right and everything is conducive to leaving at mid-season," Holtzman warned in an interview with the Associated Press, "I'd quit then." Holtzman then fired another shot in the direction of his owner. "I'd like to let him go out and find another 19-game winner."

Unlike Bando and Holtzman, Ted Kubiak came to understand Finley's way of doing business during negotiating sessions and arbitration hearings. "He was difficult, and I had my troubles with him in arbitration," says Kubiak, who had lost his arbitration case with Finley in 1974. "He'd say I didn't belong in the big leagues and that he saved my career. You know, you want to choke the guy. And then it comes out after—and this is a true story—after the arbitration, he hands me a watch and he has a gift for my wife and he says, 'Don't worry about it. It's just business. Don't believe anything I said.' You learn what the guy's tactics were."

Now that the arbitration season had ended, it was time to begin on-field preparations for a defense of the latest World Championship. As the A's began spring training in Mesa, Alvin Dark examined his *alleged* 40-man roster. In reality, the list contained far fewer names. "We're supposed to have 40 men on our roster, right?" the disgruntled Sal Bando asked sportswriter Dick Young. "We have 31—and that includes Herb Washington, a pinch-runner who isn't worth a damn; Catfish Hunter, who is gone; and Dick Green, who is retiring. That gives us 28 men to start out with. So we ask ourselves, is our owner trying to win?" Looking at the bright side of the situation, Dark and Finley would have to make only three cuts to reach the 25-man limit.

Dark announced several adjustments to his lineup, in an effort to compensate for the roster's dwindling number of players and improve the team's depreciating offense. Dark told Gene Tenace, his regular first baseman in 1974, to concentrate on catching. The switch relegated Ray Fosse, a sub-.200 hitter in 1974, to second-string status. Dark moved Joe Rudi to first base, clearing the way for Claudell Washington to play left field. Dark also delivered a surprising message to Reggie Jackson, telling his regular right fielder to work out at first base in spring training. Jackson had never before played the position—either in the majors or minors. Furthermore, Reggie's two greatest defensive attributes, his speed and throwing arm, would be wasted by playing the infield corner.

Rudi, however, felt that switching Jackson to first base on a fulltime basis made sense. "Why don't they move Reggie?" asked Rudi in an interview with United Press International, emphasizing his displeasure with his own move to the infield. "He has bad legs. He gets hurt all the time. It would be much less demanding on him at first base." Rudi then suggested an even more logical possibility. "Or they could move Claudell," Rudi said, hoping that Finley and Dark might pick up the hint. "Why can't they make him a first baseman?"

Dark—or shall we say Finley—might have made Rudi his original selection to play first base based on the thinking that Rudi would complain less about it than Jackson or Washington. Given Rudi's gentlemanly, laid-back demeanor, his outspoken criticism of the move surprised some writers. Yet, it did little to sway Finley, the architect of the lineup restructuring. "Rudi's a good left fielder," Finley countered to *The Sporting News*, "but Washington's speed will enable him to reach balls that Rudi couldn't reach." Perhaps Finley hadn't consulted with the voters of the Gold Glove Award. "I don't care how much Rudi pops off," Finley added venomously. "He can pop off every hour on the hour if that makes him happy." Finley would soon realize the error of his changes. With Rudi at first base and Washington in left field, the A's would prove to be a far inferior defensive team in 1975.

Dark also decided to give Phil Garner plenty of work at second base. Having failed in their bid to convince Dick Green to return, the A's announced that they had given their 1974 World Series star his unconditional release. Charlie Finley also brought back Dal Maxvill—as a coach, not as a player—for the specific purpose of working with Garner on his transition from third to second. Garner had not played second base in five years, when he was still playing college baseball for the University of Tennessee.

In the meantime, the offseason loss of Catfish Hunter spurred on a desperate search for pitching throughout the spring. The A's had hoped that Lew Krausse would provide a boost to the team's pitching depth, but the one-time bonus baby pitched poorly in his early spring outings. In his first game, Krausse surrendered two home runs to a collegiate lineup, that of Arizona State, the alma mater of Reggie Jackson and Sal Bando. In his second appearance, Krausse allowed a three-run homer to Cubs catcher George Mitterwald. Krausse's early struggles doomed him to a return to Triple-A.

The departure of Hunter continued to be felt in the later stages of the spring, culminating in a flurry of trades and signings during the final week of the exhibition season. The A's latched onto veteran starter Roger Nelson, a one-time standout with the Reds who had been cut loose by the White Sox earlier in the spring. Finley also purchased two veteran relievers and familiar names, Horacio Piña from the Angels and Skip Lockwood from the Yankees. Both had previously spent time in the A's' organization, Piña in 1973 and Lockwood when the franchise was still playing in Kansas City. Finley earmarked both hurlers for Triple-A Tucson, with the idea that they would be able to help the A's later in the season. As vested veterans, Lockwood and Piña had the option of rejecting minor league assignments, which they both did. As a result, both pitchers became free agents, with Piña opting to return to the Mexican League. Finley also tried to add veteran left-hander Claude Osteen, who had been cast off by the Cardinals. One day after Alvin Dark remarked that the A's "were almost sure" of signing Osteen, the former Dodger stalwart signed a contract with the White Sox.

The final week of bargain basement hunting continued when the A's signed veteran infielder Billy Grabarkewitz, another former Cub. Grabarkewitz, a classic one-year wonder, had hit .289 with 17 home runs and 84 RBIs for the Dodgers in 1970. Since then, Grabarkewitz had batted no higher than .226 for a full season while putting in time with the Dodgers, Angels, Phillies, and Cubs. Only a respectable .288 average in a late-season tenure with the Phillies in 1973 broke up a string of futile batting efforts for Grabarkewitz. No longer an everyday player, the A's hoped that Grabarkewitz could fill in at third base and shortstop while providing Phil Garner with an experienced fallback at second base.

On March 28, the A's continued to make shadowy pickups when they announced the acquisition of minor league outfielder Don Hopkins from the Montreal Expos. Hopkins, who had never played higher than Class-A ball, had batted .301 with 49 stolen bases for Kinston of the Carolina League in 1974. Listed as a non-prospect by most scouts, Hopkins had never hit a home run in five seasons of minor league ball. Did anyone say Allan Lewis?

Unbelievably, the A's announced that they would use Hopkins as a pinch-runner, much like their pre-existing pinch-runner, Herb Washington. Not satisfied with one pinch-running specialist, Charlie Finley felt he needed to have two-of-a-kind. "You're kidding," a disbelieving Sal Bando told *The Sporting News*. "Two pinch-runners? My only question is who are we going to hit when we pinch-run for the other guys."

Jesus Alou was no longer available to pinch-hit. Finley decided to release Alou to make room for Hopkins, even though the youngest of the Alou brothers was in the midst of a terrific spring. "Maybe I'm overrating myself," Alou mused aloud to *The Sporting News*. "I think this team needs a guy who does the type of job I can do." In 1974, Alou had batted a respectable .268 in 220 at-bats and had led all Oakland reserves with seven pinch-hits. Alou could now ask Tommy Davis how it felt to be released while enjoying one of his best springs at the plate.

The A's also released another bench player, first baseman Pat Bourque, after he refused to accept a demotion to the minor league camp. In 1974, Bourque had picked up seven pinch-hits while splitting time between the A's and Twins. Charlie

Finley now had nothing to show for the senseless offseason deal in which he had given up heralded prospect Dan Ford.

On the final day of spring training, Finley made another trade with—you guessed it—the Cubs. He acquired relief pitcher Jim Todd, whom the Cubs had deemed expendable, in exchange for a player to be named later, which would turn out to be minor league outfielder John "Champ" Summers. At first, the A's told Todd that he would start the season on the major league roster, only to have Finley change his mind and send him to Tucson. When Alvin Dark scheduled Todd to pitch in an intra-squad game, the right-hander initially refused. Pitching coach Wes Stock advised Todd to pitch in the game, warning him that Finley might not take too kindly to such a refusal. "Finley is the kind of guy you can get off on the wrong side of," Todd told Ron Fimrite of *Sports Illustrated*. Already aware of his new owner's penchant for vindictiveness, Todd made the wise decision to pitch, giving up only one hit in an eye-opening three-inning relief stint.

The payment for Todd—Champ Summers—figured to spend another season at Triple-A before officially becoming the player to be named and then being sent to the Cubs. The minor league veteran, who had come to bat only 24 times for the A's in 1974, appeared trapped in a logjam behind Claudell Washington, Billy North, Reggie Jackson, and Joe Rudi. The trade to Chicago would liberate him from his dead-end status in Oakland, giving him a chance to play a more prominent role with the Cubs. Shortly after his arrival in the Windy City, Summers would take aim on what he described as a harmful atmosphere in the Oakland dugout and clubhouse. "The last time I struck out for Oakland," Summers told Roy Blount, Jr., of *Sports Illustrated*, "I felt like my world had dropped from under me. I came back to the bench and maybe somebody said something, but most of them looked away." Summers said that his newfound Cubs teammates offered more support and camaraderie to struggling players, creating a more pleasant atmosphere for all players on the team.

Finley's new-look A's finished the spring with a record of 7–11, despite a tidy .294 team batting average. The Oakland lineup had shown the ability to produce runs, but the departures of Catfish Hunter and Dick Green had weakened both the pitching and defense. When asked about the A's, Angels manager Dick Williams offered a surprising evaluation of the potential impact of the two key player losses. "I don't think losing Hunter is fatal," Williams predicted to *The Sporting News*, while expressing a minority opinion. "I think Green being gone will hurt you more than the loss of Hunter in the long run...I think he [Green] should have been the Most Valuable Player of the World Series, even though he didn't get a hit." Williams remembered the two spectacular double plays that Green had started, along with the other fine fielding plays he had made against the Dodgers in the Series.

And what did the national media think of Oakland's chances in the post-Catfish era? A pre-season survey of baseball writers indicated that the A's would win their fifth consecutive Western Division title, but would lose in the playoffs. Who would the A's fall victim to? Some writers suggested the Yankees, who had added both

Hunter and former Giants' star Bobby Bonds to their roster during the winter. Rangers manager Billy Martin, a man once recruited by Charlie Finley to be Oakland's manager, thought even less of the A's chances than the national writers. "I thought *we* should be the team to beat even *before* Oakland lost Catfish," Martin told Ron Fimrite, while boasting about a Rangers team that had surprised many by finishing second in the American League West in 1974. "Now I definitely think we should be favored."

Favorites or not, even the A's themselves realized that they would face a more difficult task in trying to repeat as Western Division champions. "We have a funny type of ballclub," Alvin Dark told *Sports Illustrated*. "We really only played for three and a half months last year. When we got ahead by nine games, we played about .500 ball in August and September. This year it will take a little more a little longer."

Chapter 29

Still Good, But Not Great

As the season began, Charlie Finley tried to create extra incentive for his charges to win a fifth consecutive division title, a fourth straight pennant, and a fourth consecutive world title. Finley offered to give all of his players diamond rings in the shape of four-leaf clovers— provided they were the only ones left standing come the final game of the World Series.

On April 8, the A's opened up the regular season at home against the White Sox. Three players not on the Opening Day roster in 1974 started for the A's: Billy Williams at DH, Claudell Washington in left field, and Phil Garner at second base. Vida Blue, who had not started on Opening Day since 1971, took the ball in place of the departed Catfish Hunter. The list of reserves and relief pitchers included four players—infielder Billy Grabarkewitz, outfielders Jim Holt and Don Hopkins, and pitcher Mike Norris—not with the team at the beginning of the 1974 season.

The new blood played a large role in the first game against the White Sox. In the second inning, Williams doubled in his first-ever American League at-bat. Garner followed with a two-run single, giving Oakland the early jump against knuckleballer Wilbur Wood. Blue, whom Alvin Dark predicted would win 25 games, pitched seven strong innings, followed by Rollie Fingers, who saved the 3–2 victory.

Gene Tenace hit a grand slam in the next game, but the A's lost when the bullpen combination of Blue Moon Odom, Paul Lindblad, and Fingers allowed four runs in the eighth and ninth innings. The following day, Mike Norris made his major league debut and stifled the White Sox with a three-hit shutout. Norris, a third-year pro who had never pitched above the Double-A level, displayed good control and a live, darting fastball. Reggie Jackson supported the rookie by connecting on a three-run homer, his first hit of the new season, helping the A's to a comfortable 9–0 win.

Quoting the Bible, Alvin Dark compared Norris to the biblical figure Jeremiah. "Call unto me and I will answer thee, and show thee great and mighty things, which thee knowest not," Dark told *Sports Illustrated*, while referring to Jeremiah 33:3. "Norris just might be the prophet sent down to save us," added Dark.

The new-look A's compiled a pair of four-game winning streaks, helping them to a record of 12–8 in April. The record looked even more impressive considering the team's newfound defensive problems and an injury suffered by Campy Campaneris, who had strained his back on Opening Day. The muscle strain sidelined Campy for seven of the A's' early season games.

With Campy out, the A's utilized Ted Kubiak at shortstop. Although sure-handed, Kubiak lacked the range and quickness of Campaneris in the field. In left field, Claudell Washington appeared uncertain, often letting looping line drives and short fly balls fall in front of him. As one teammate described Washington in *The Sporting News*, he "treats fly balls as if they were bombs." Behind the plate, Gene Tenace struggled to throw out opposing runners, gunning down only one of the first 10 players to attempt stolen bases. At first base, Joe Rudi played adequately, but nowhere near the Gold Glove level he had achieved in the outfield.

The A's also lost their most impressive young pitcher during the first month. Mike Norris had pitched brilliantly in his first two starts, allowing no earned runs and only four hits in 16 innings. In his third start, Norris faced only one batter before asking to leave because of pain in his right elbow. Although initial X-rays showed no abnormalities, doctors eventually found calcium deposits on the elbow. "If he can't pitch in two weeks," Alvin Dark told Jim Kaplan of *Sports Illustrated*, "God will provide." God would have to provide another pitcher entirely. On April 29, Norris underwent surgery, ending his rookie campaign.

The season-ending injury to Norris forced the A's to dip into their farm system for pitching help. Finley and Dark called upon reliever Jim Todd, the last-second pickup in spring training. The Cubs had given up on Todd because they felt he did not throw hard enough to succeed against major league hitters. Attempting to prove the Cubs wrong, Todd notched saves in his first two appearances for the A's, before igniting a bench-clearing rhubarb in a game against the Angels. Bruce Bochte, who had homered and doubled earlier in the game, came to the plate against Todd in the sixth inning. Todd sailed a fastball up and in against the left-hitting Bochte, nicking him in the side of the helmet. Angels manager Dick Williams promptly led a surge of Angels from the dugout onto the field. Oakland and California players exchanged punches in two groups along the first-base line. In one pile, Williams found himself double-teamed by Todd and backup outfielder Angel Mangual, who had not enjoyed playing for Williams in Oakland. "Everybody who work me over," Mangual told *The Sporting News*, "I get 'em sooner or later."

After the umpires broke up the array of brawls, Williams stood at home plate and yelled at Todd, challenging him to continue the fight. When Todd refused to leave his station on the mound, Williams called him gutless. Dark then stepped from the Oakland dugout, walked toward Williams, and tried to calm his managing counterpart. After the game, Finley blasted Williams for putting on a "bush show."

One day after the brawl with the Angels, the A's continued to add to their collection of pinch-runners. Finley sent minor league pitcher Howell "Buddy" Copeland to the Cubs (the Cubs again!) for switch-hitting infielder-outfielder Matt "The Scat" Alexander, considered a non-prospect by most scouts. Cut from the mold of Allan Lewis and Don Hopkins, the 28-year-old Alexander had shown little ability to hit or field well, but possessed an abundance of footspeed. In order to make room for Alexander, the A's demoted another former Cub, Billy Grabarkewitz, to the minor leagues. Grabarkewitz had batted only twice in six games. Thus, Grabarkewitz joined the likes of long-gone A's Orlando Cepeda and Art Shamsky in "Club Zero"—veteran players who failed to register a single hit during their all-too-brief careers in Oakland.

The addition of Alexander to the roster now gave the A's *three* players who specialized in pinch-running. "The Scat" joined Hopkins and Herb Washington on the Oakland relay team. The team's beat writers, and Washington himself, wondered how long the A's could continue to carry such a large contingent of runners. The current overload left Alvin Dark short of capable pinch-hitters and defensive replacements.

The A's used their supply of swiftness to open up May with a dramatic 4–3 win in 12 innings. Oakland's speedburners blitzed the White Sox' catchers and pitchers, stealing four bases over the final five innings. "We beat you with the long ball, on defense, with speed, every way," said Billy North, who ended the game with an RBI single in the 12th, in an interview with *Sports Illustrated*.

The A's certainly had plenty of speed on their 25-man roster, but not enough good hitters on the bench. One of the specialized pinch-runners would have to go. Since Matt Alexander had just arrived on the scene, he seemed safe. That left Don Hopkins and Herb Washington vulnerable to either a minor league demotion or outright unemployment. On May 5, the A's made their decision; they requested waivers on Washington for the purpose of giving him his unconditional release.

Charlie Finley's great experiment with "Hurricane Herb" had come to an end, an indirect result of the offseason departure by Catfish Hunter. Without Hunter, the A's faced added pressure to score more runs to support a thinner pitching staff. With a need to score more often, Alvin Dark needed to use pinch-hitters more frequently, making a non-hitter like Washington an unaffordable luxury. Alexander and Hopkins could at least play a position in the field and swing a bat. Washington could do neither.

A few of the A's expressed sympathy for Washington, citing his amiable personality and high level of intelligence. Others took a less sensitive approach. "I'd feel sorry for him if he were a player," Sal Bando bluntly told *The Sporting News*. "He got a bonus and a salary and a full World Series share, didn't he?" Washington did not appreciate such sentiments. He fired back at his critics among the players and the media, especially those who had questioned his credentials to serve a major league team. "The toughest adjustment was putting up with egocentric players," Washington told *The Sporting News* without naming names, "and a ton of bull*bleep* from front-runners on the team, front-runners in the media, and front-runners among the fans…Some of the players are nice guys. Some are jerks, too." Bando was most likely at the top of Washington's list.

At first, the A's contemplated replacing Washington on the roster with veteran pitcher Roger Nelson, whom they had signed off the waiver-wire scrap heap during spring training. Charlie Finley changed his mind, however, instead promoting backup catcher Charlie Sands from Triple-A. Like many of the Oakland players, Sands owned a World Series ring, having contributed as the third-string catcher to the Pittsburgh Pirates' World Championship effort in 1971. Having grown dissatisfied with the hitting of backup first baseman-outfielder Jim Holt, Finley hoped that Sands might provide a better left-handed threat off the bench. Yet, as soon as Sands arrived in Oakland, Holt proceeded to smack two consecutive, game-winning pinch-hits.

On May 10, the A's enjoyed a reunion with Catfish Hunter for the first time since their former ace had discarded Finley's prison stripes in favor of the pinstripes preferred by the Yankees. During pre-game warm-ups at the Oakland Coliseum, one A's fan taunted and booed Hunter for his supposed lack of loyalty in leaving the A's. Catfish responded calmly, instructing the fan to boo Finley instead.

Hunter showed little anxiety in pitching before his former hometown fans. With his typically precise pitch-making, Hunter mastered the Oakland lineup, winning 3–0. "It's just like a trade," Sal Bando observed wryly in an interview with Ron Fimrite of *Sports Illustrated*. "Except we didn't get anything in return." Bando's dagger was clearly thrown in the direction of Finley.

On the positive side, the loss of Hunter had not affected attendance at the Oakland Coliseum, where larger crowds had shown up to watch the A's than during the championship season of 1974. Yet, Charlie Finley remained unsatisfied. In an interview with the *San Francisco Examiner*, Finley predicted that the Bay Area could not support two major league franchises over the long haul. Finley's warning spurred on another set of rumors about the A's relocating to greener pastures in any one of three cities: New Orleans, Seattle, or Toronto.

Oakland's poor economy and the location of the Coliseum both worked against the A's in their quest to maximize attendance. "We might be better off having the stadium in the suburbs," Sal Bando suggested to *Sports Illustrated*. "Baseball makes its money from the average-income people. There aren't enough of those in Oakland." Even Oakland players, many of whom ranked in the above-average income bracket, stayed away from the downtown area, preferring instead to live in the suburban regions.

In mid-May, the A's assembled their first five-game winning streak of the season. Billy Williams, who had scuffled in his transition to the American League and to the unfamiliar role of designated hitter, hit three home runs during the stretch. Vida Blue improved to 8–1 by pitching back-to-back wins over the Yankees, one in the Bronx and one in Oakland.

Although the state of the A's pitching had ranked as the biggest concern in spring training, the eight-man staff succeeded in catapulting the team to the best record in the American League through games of May 15. In addition to Blue's work anchoring the rotation, Ken Holtzman pitched brilliantly over his first nine starts, while Dave Hamilton and Glenn Abbott added solid contributions. In the bullpen, Jim Todd pitched so effectively that he temporarily took over the fireman role that had belonged to Rollie Fingers exclusively since mid-1971. Although Todd didn't throw hard, his sinking fastball—dubbed the "super sinker" by Alvin Dark—featured plenty of movement. Several opponents claimed that the movement on Todd's pitches was not created by natural forces, but rather by *illegal* ones. "It's a known fact he throws a greaseball," charged Tiger manager Ralph Houk in an interview with *The Sporting News*. Both Todd and Dark denied the accusation.

Only one member of the pitching staff had struggled through the first month and a half of the season. Blue Moon Odom, making five appearances, had given up 16 hits and nine walks in only nine innings. Dark didn't want to pitch Odom at all, but had been forced by a higher authority—namely, Charles Oscar Finley. "There were times when he ordered Dark to pitch John Odom when Odom shouldn't have been pitching," captain Sal Bando told the *Boston Herald* after the season. "Odom would lose and it hurt us." Odom's ERA reached such a bloated rate—11 runs per nine innings—that the A's finally asked him to accept a demotion to Triple-A, but the veteran right-hander refused the assignment. Nonetheless, Odom's career in Oakland seemed to be coming to an end. One sign of his possible departure occurred when the A's signed veteran reliever Orlando Peña, recently cut by the Angels, and assigned him to Tucson. Peña and Roger Nelson gave the A's two experienced options at Triple-A should they decide to trade or release Odom.

Although the A's had played well over the first six weeks, their small lead over division rivals Kansas City and Texas left Charlie Finley concerned. Oakland's pitching had overachieved in the absence of Catfish Hunter, but Finley wanted more help for the mound. On May 16, as the A's prepared to start a series in New York, Finley sent popular utility infielder Ted Kubiak to the Padres in a straight-up swap for right-hander Sonny Siebert. The 38-year-old Siebert had won three of five decisions for San Diego, but also owned an ERA over 4.00. The A's then replaced Kubiak with middle infielder Teddy Martinez, acquired in a trade with the Cardinals for minor league pitchers Mike Barlow and Steve Staniland.

With much the same flourish that he had exhibited during the whirlwind 1972 season, Finley continued his flurry of trades two days later. On May 20, the A's finally parted ways with longtime veteran Blue Moon Odom, sending the injury-prone pitcher and $15,000 in cash to the Cleveland Indians for two veteran starters. The deal netted the A's Jim Perry—the brother of Gaylord Perry—and former Washington Senators' ace Dick Bosman, who had frequently enjoyed success pitching against Oakland.

When Odom heard about the trade, he beamed about the prospects of playing Cleveland. "I always wanted to pitch for a black manager," Odom said of playing for Frank Robinson in an interview with *Sport* Magazine. As soon as Odom arrived in Cleveland, he would alter his gleeful stance and make a strange request of Indians management. Figuring that he would lose about $8,000 in potential playoff and World Series money, Blue Moon asked the Indians to raise his salary by that figure. Not surprisingly, the Indians refused to give the struggling Odom any more money. Odom pouted, infuriating Frank Robinson. General manager Phil Seghi soon sent Odom packing to the Atlanta Braves.

The trade of Odom to Cleveland ended a run of service for one of the most senior A's, one who had played with the franchise during the Kansas City years. Contrary to popular belief, Odom had not been dubbed "Blue Moon" by Charlie Finley at the start of his professional career, but had actually been given the moniker much earlier in his life. "Back in fifth grade in football practice," Odom says, "a guy named Joe Mars started calling me 'Moonhead.' I really didn't like that. [He said] 'I'm calling you that because your face is round. We can't call you 'Yellow Moon' [because of] your complexion. So we're gonna call you 'Blue Moon.' "

The nickname referred not only to the roundness of Odom's face, but also to his frequently somber expression as a youth. Unfortunately, sadness would follow Odom in his post-playing days. Unlike most of his Oakland teammates, Odom would encounter a series of struggles after his retirement: financial debt, drug use, severe depression, psychiatric treatment, and a jail term for threatening to kill his wife with a gun. In 1985, police arrested Odom for selling a gram of cocaine to a fellow employee at the Xerox Corporation. Odom refuted the charge of dealing drugs, but did not deny using cocaine. A jury later convicted him on two counts of selling cocaine. No longer the colorfully brash pitcher known as "Blue Moon," John Odom spent 55 days in a county jail.

Having struck rock-bottom, Odom rectified many of his personal problems in later years. Fully retired, he began to spend much of his time playing in benefit golf tournaments, as part of the effort to raise money for the Major League Baseball Players Alumni Association. Odom also grew to appreciate his nickname, which gave him a strong identity in retirement. "I used to hate that name," Odom says, "but now I love it. I'm known all over the world as Blue Moon now."

In trading away the 12-year veteran of the A's, Charlie Finley had settled on Bosman and *Jim* Perry in exchange for the longtime A's' right-hander, but only after making a run at acquiring *Gaylord* Perry. Gaylord's name had been mentioned in trade rumors because of his strained relationship with Indians manager Frank Robinson. Finley called Phil Seghi to find out how serious he was about trading Gaylord. Seghi asked Finley what he would be willing to offer. Finley suggested Blue Moon Odom. Seghi countered by asking for another pitcher named Blue—Vida Blue—and Reggie Jackson, as well. *That* request ended that set of trade talks—quickly.

Of the three players in the deal that did take place, Jim Perry was the most well-known. After winning 17 games for Cleveland in 1974, the veteran right-hander had suddenly lost six of seven decisions to start the 1975 season and seen his ERA rise above 6.00. Perry had pitched the bulk of his career with the Twins from 1963 to 1972, and had won 44 games during the team's division-winning seasons of 1969 and '70. "A great, great seven-inning pitcher," says former Minnesota writer Bob Fowler. "You know, in that era we had a pretty good bullpen with Ron Perranoski and Stan Williams. But he was a battler; he was a tough, tough guy. Boy, he took the ball against anybody, never flinched."

Fowler says the Twins tended not to score many runs for Perry. "It seemed to me Jim Perry was always in 2–1 games," Fowler recalls. "I mean, he and Bert Blyleven. It was unbelievable. Where someone else would go out and with [Harmon] Killebrew and [Tony] Oliva, we'd score 28 runs or something. But with Jim Perry, it was always 2–1. Just a tough competitor."

Throughout much of his career, Jim Perry had been overshadowed by his younger brother, a future Hall of Famer. "[He was] very much like his brother, Gaylord," Fowler says. "They came from the same stock. But not as notorious as Gaylord." Unlike Gaylord, Jim did not throw a spitball or a greaseball. The older Perry relied on a more standard repertoire of pitches, along with his inherent toughness, in his efforts to retire opposing batters.

The series of deals cost the A's a couple of prospects and some cash, but greatly changed the current structure of the pitching staff—for the better. In addition to workhorses Vida Blue and Ken Holtzman, the A's could call upon three accomplished veteran starters in Perry, Bosman, and Siebert. The trades balanced the rotation, giving Oakland three right-handers to go with the two incumbent left-handers. The arrivals also took pressure off youngsters Dave Hamilton and Glenn Abbott. The A's sent Abbott back to the minor leagues for more seasoning, while Dark dispatched Hamilton to the bullpen, giving Oakland another left-handed pitching option in the late innings.

Neither Perry nor Bosman had pitched well in Cleveland, but mitigating circumstances might have contributed to their subpar performances. The Indians had the worst record in the American League and could not support either pitcher with a good offense, capable defense, or reliable relief pitching. A few Cleveland writers also speculated that Perry's pitching had been affected by the angry relationship between his brother, Gaylord, and Indians manager Frank Robinson. The two had failed to get along since Robinson's arrival as a player in Cleveland late in the 1974 season, when Perry discovered that Robinson made more money than him. The Indians' subsequent hiring of Robinson as their manager had created an awkward and uncomfortable situation for both men.

In the meantime, the A's hobbled through their worst stretch of the season, as they lost four straight games, including a three-game set in Boston. The A's played miserably during the series at Fenway Park, losing the first game, 10–5, in Blue Moon Odom's final appearance in an Oakland uniform. The Red Sox rocked Vida Blue and Ken Holtzman in the next two games, winning 7–0 and 7–3. The Boston series also provided the setting for a nasty confrontation between Sal Bando and Reggie Jackson.

Earlier in the season, Jackson had made a major baserunning error, when he broke late from first on an apparent bloop single to the outfield by Joe Rudi. Jackson was forced out at second, negating what should have been a base hit for Rudi. In continuing his season-long troubles on the base paths, Jackson made another baserunning mistake against Boston. The latest error in judgment prompted a dugout lecture from Bando, never shy to castigate teammates for poor play. Jackson, offended that Bando had criticized him within earshot of other players, shouted back at the captain. Several A's interceded, separating the two stars.

Alvin Dark, who claimed he heard racial remarks during the latest incident, called a clubhouse meeting after the game. Dark urged his players to refrain from allowing any of their disagreements to escalate into racial catcalling. Dark's speech smacked with irony, considering the accusations of racism that Orlando Cepeda and other players had leveled at him during his days in San Francisco.

In spite of the biting argument between Bando and Jackson, the two stars generally liked and respected one another. "We had a very close-knit family with Catfish, Joe Rudi, and Sal Bando," Jackson says with fondness. "My intensity on the field was helped by playing with our captain, Sal Bando. We lived near each other in our very early years and he was very influential in my career."

Although reporters tended to portray the A's as a team filled with friction, some of the Oakland players claim the media exaggerated the tone and significance of their clubhouse and dugout arguments. In fact, many former A's recall their teams of the early seventies as a tightly grouped familial unit. "Despite what you read about, fights and all that," Bando explains, "those were all disagreements—there wasn't cliques in terms of people going in different directions. Guys on our club all would socialize together and do things together."

Bando says he enjoyed the company of most of the A's, but became particularly friendly with three of his teammates. "Gene Tenace was my roommate for all those years and Joe Rudi—the three of us, were very close. And then Ray Fosse I got very close to. We were all friends…They were team players, giving guys. They were considerate; they were very moral people who were very close to their families. We were all family-oriented and we all lived out in the same area of Oakland together."

Like most families, the A's fought amongst themselves, yet still felt a special bond toward one another. "The thing that I remember with those guys is just the day-to-day camaraderie, and the good times, and the laughter," says Ted Kubiak. "They were all just a great bunch of guys. You know, Dick Green and Reggie, of course. It was a lot of fun on the bus trips. Rollie Fingers would go nuts and Bando would get on him, and then they'd get on each other. We just had a real good time."

Following the three losses to Boston, the A's moved on to Cleveland for a four-game series. Sonny Siebert, a one-time member of the Cleveland organization, made his Oakland debut against the Indians. Siebert threw hard in shutting out the Indians on one hit over five innings, winning a 3–0 decision over Gaylord Perry. Two days later, Jim Perry lasted only two innings in losing to his former teammates, 6–0. In the second game of the doubleheader, Dick Bosman concluded the triumvirate of pitching debuts with six and two-thirds innings of three-run baseball. Bosman, with relief assistance from the surprising Jim Todd, helped the A's to a 6–3 win, their third in four games against the Indians.

Bosman's victory initiated a five-game winning streak, helping the A's finish with a 16–10 record during the month of May, while improving their overall record to 28–18. Bosman added another win during the streak, beating the Indians for the second time in a week. As the A's headed to June, they held a slim one-game lead over the Royals and a three-game edge over the Twins.

Of the new pitchers, only Jim Perry showed any signs of his pre-Oakland difficulties. Perry had lasted fewer than five innings in his first two starts against Cleveland and Milwaukee, respectively, leading to speculation that the A's might try to demote him to Tucson. The 39-year-old right-hander refused the minor league assignment and took his turn against the light-hitting Orioles on June 10. Perry walked Al Bumbry to start the game before retiring the next 17 batters in succession. In the sixth inning, Bumbry became the first Oriole to pick up a hit—a harmless two-out single. Perry allowed no other hits and only one more walk to polish off a complete-game shutout. Gene Tenace and Claudell Washington touched Ross Grimsley for home runs, supporting Perry's first win as a member of the A's.

Perry's one-hitter was the A's' second during the month. Two days earlier, Ken Holtzman had narrowly missed a no-hitter against the Tigers when Billy North misplayed a catchable fly ball. With two outs and two strikes on Tom Veryzer in the ninth inning, the Tiger shortstop lifted a high fly toward deep left-center field. North broke late for the ball, which the wind dropped onto the warning track untouched. Since North had failed to come close to putting his glove on the ball, the official scorer properly ruled Veryzer's drive a double. Holtzman followed up the unsuccessful bid at his third career no-hitter by striking out Ron LeFlore to end the game.

Although Holtzman refused to blame the center fielder for his failure to preserve the no-hitter, several Oakland players claimed that North had broken in at first before retreating toward the deeper regions of left-center field on Veryzer's drive. To his credit, North pointed the finger at himself. After he retrieved Veryzer's double and fired the ball back to the infield, he threw his glove several feet into the air. "I wanted that no-hitter," an angry North told the Associated Press. "I blame myself."

Standout pitching kept the A's atop the Western Division, compensating for a lineup that had not fulfilled expectations. Three of the team's most important hitters—Sal Bando, Reggie Jackson, and Billy Williams—found themselves hitting below .240. The nagging futility prompted Jackson to come up with an unflattering nickname, referring to himself, Bando, and Williams as a "wealthy ghetto" during an interview with *Sports Illustrated*.

On June 15, just before the annual trading deadline, Charlie Finley continued his recent trend of adding veteran, thirtysomething pitchers to his staff. Finley acquired right-hander Stan Bahnsen from the White Sox for the hefty price of left-hander Dave Hamilton and infield prospect Chester "Chet" Lemon. Unlike the deal that netted Oakland Dick Bosman and Jim Perry from Cleveland, the latest trade seemed heavily tilted against the A's. Bahnsen, with an ERA over 6.00, had fallen victim to Chuck Tanner's ill-advised three-man rotation, which had placed too much of a burden on his right arm. Most scouts considered Lemon, a talented hitter with power and speed, the best prospect in the Oakland system. They also liked Hamilton, who was three years younger than Bahnsen, and possessed the versatility to start or relieve. Finley himself would later regret the deal. In the spring of 1976, Finley would repeatedly call White Sox general manager Roland Hemond, hoping to reacquire Lemon. The trade reminded some observers of another Finley transaction—the offseason deal that had sent outfield prospect Danny Ford to the Twins for mediocre first baseman Pat Bourque.

A week later, two of the A's most prominent players became involved in a disturbing off-the-field incident—through no fault of their own. As the A's hosted the Royals in a four-game weekend series, Reggie Jackson and Vida Blue received threats on their lives in the form of a terrifying letter. The author of the letter claimed he would kill Jackson and Blue sometime during the series with the Royals. Charlie Finley informed both players that they could sit out the series if they wished. Blue and Jackson decided to play. Blue pitched well over a stint of eight and two-thirds innings, earning a no-decision. Jackson performed even better throughout the series, rapping out six hits in 18 at-bats, collecting a home run and four RBIs. For the second time in the last three years, Jackson had decided to play under the specter of a death threat. Jackson had not only *played*, but he had played *spectacularly*.

Spearheaded by their in-season pitching additions, the A's enjoyed their most successful month of the season in June. The team compiled winning streaks of four games, five games, and eight games on their way to claiming 20 of 29 contests during the month. Dick Bosman and Jim Todd each won three games, while Sonny Siebert and Jim Perry added a victory apiece. In other words, five pitchers not on the staff at the beginning of the season had accounted for 40 per cent of Oakland's victories in June.

The bullpen continued to buttress the starters, while the offense showed improvement, as well. Paul Lindblad extended his streak of scoreless pitching to 22 and one-third innings and stretched his perfect won-loss record to 6–0. And in one three-game series against the Twins, Campy Campaneris scored eight runs, Claudell Washington swiped a half-dozen bases, and Reggie Jackson smashed three home runs.

By the end of June, the A's' record stood at 48–27, giving them a seven-and-a-half-game lead in the West. At the same juncture in 1974, Oakland's lead had consisted of only three and a half games. Somehow, without Catfish Hunter, with phenom Mike Norris sidelined for the season, and with half the pitching staff acquired since Opening Day, the A's had managed to improve their club from their 1974 standing. Alvin Dark deserved some of the credit for the team's upward mobility. Dark had decided to use only Vida Blue and Ken Holtzman in a regular rotation on three to four days' rest, in an effort to maximize the number of starts they could make. Depending on off days and rainouts, Dark would then turn to his second-line starters: Dick Bosman, Sonny Siebert and, if necessary, Jim Perry.

Superior relief pitching and increased run production had played major roles over the first three months of the season. The bullpen, bolstered by the threesome of Rollie Fingers, Jim Todd, and Paul Lindblad, had earned saves or wins in 40 of the 48 victories. Lindblad had not lost a single game despite being used frequently. "As the only left-handed reliever we have," Todd explained to Ron Bergman, "Lindblad has a real burden. He always *has* to get a guy out." Lindblad's ability to warm up quickly and pitch in the cold, damp air of Oakland made him an especially tempting option for Dark. In the meantime, Todd's presence relieved the workload of Fingers, who had pitched too many long relief stints in 1974. "Todd has been the key," Fingers told Ron Fimrite of *Sports Illustrated*. "He's given Paul and me a big break." Now used more selectively and for shorter outings, Fingers' fastball appeared quicker and his slider more explosive. "He's the best I've ever seen," Todd told *The Sporting News* in praising Fingers. "With men on base...I've never seen anybody get out of jams better than he does."

The offense, helped by the acquisition of Billy Williams and the graduation of Claudell Washington and Phil Garner to regular duty, had produced the second-highest run total in the American League—behind only the Red Sox, who played in a ballpark much more favorable for hitters. Through games of July 1, Washington led the A's in batting average (.306) and in stolen bases (31), while Williams and Garner had improved the offensive production at DH and second base, respectively. Garner had also supplied surprisingly solid defensive play in the middle infield, prompting Alvin Dark to make the following remark to *The Sporting News*: "He's as good at making the double play as anyone in the league."

The play of Washington, however, had stood out above all others in the A's' lineup. His speed and line-drive hitting justified Alvin Dark's decision to use him as the No. 3 hitter in the Oakland order and earned him selection to the American League All-Star team. Only his fielding remained a concern, although even that had improved since his early-season follies in left field. Washington's season seemed to be playing itself out in dream-like fashion until the fateful occurrence of July 11.

As Washington woke up from his sleep in his apartment, he felt dizzy and decided to go back to bed. Washington awoke a second time and proceeded to black out. As he fell to his bed, he sustained a small cut on his head. When Washington regained consciousness, he decided to call a local hospital and have himself checked out. Although doctors could not pinpoint an exact reason for the fainting spells, a scan of his brain showed no significant abnormalities. "They don't know what caused them," a mystified Washington told *Sports Illustrated*. Doctors nonetheless cleared Washington, who had first experienced fainting spells at the age of 16, to return to the lineup. "I guess I'm just going to pass out every now and then," Washington conceded to Bay Area sportswriter Glenn Dickey.

After struggling to hit .250 earlier in the season, Reggie Jackson continued his midsummer assault on American League pitching. On July 25, Jackson beat the White Sox with a game-ending two-run homer in the bottom of the 13th inning. Earlier in the game, Jackson singled, doubled, stole a base, and also threw out a runner. "I guess I did it all," Jackson bragged candidly to *Sports Illustrated*. Close observers of the A's noted that Jackson had played much of the season with more desire, intensity, and intelligence than at any point in his career—including his MVP year of 1973.

Jackson's power surge, teamed with the sustained hitting and speed of Claudell Washington, had made up for the season-long slump of Sal Bando. With his average hovering near the unaccustomed .200 mark, the captain resorted to superstitious remedies. Bando removed the mustache he had worn since 1972, when the A's became known as the "Mustache Gang." Now clean-shaven, Bando went 1-for-10 over his next three games. The mustache would have to return.

In early August, the A's discovered an outside source of motivation when they learned of some intriguing comments made by Cincinnati Reds star Johnny Bench. The All-Star catcher predicted that his team would win the National League pennant and would easily handle the three-time defending World Champions in the World Series. Bench added that only two A's—Reggie Jackson and Joe Rudi—would be able to crack the roster of the "Big Red Machine."

"Is that so?" said Rollie Fingers, one of several A's to react angrily to Bench's statements, in an interview with *The Sporting News*. "Why, Johnny Bench couldn't carry the catching gear over here." Fingers further demeaned Bench's ability to handle a pitching staff. "I'd hate to pitch to him," Rollie said to *Sports Illustrated*. "He can't think behind the plate. All he knows is he has five fingers on his hand, but he doesn't know which ones to put down."

Other players responded with more diplomatic disbelief to Bench's vitriol. "Bench says the only A's who could make the Reds are Reggie and Joe?" third-string catcher Larry Haney asked incredulously during an interview with *The Sporting News*. "Our whole pitching staff could make that team." One could also have made a strong argument for Billy North and Claudell Washington beating out either Cesar Geronimo or Ken Griffey in the Reds' starting outfield. In addition, players like Gene Tenace, Campy Campaneris, and Sal Bando might not have supplanted Cincinnati regulars Tony Perez, Dave Concepcion, and Pete Rose, but would certainly have made the Reds' 25-man roster as reserve or part-time players.

While the A's on-field talent was still formidable, their front office was not, in large part because of Finley's cheapness. On August 4, Finley's undermanned front office became even smaller when John Claiborne, the team's director of minor league operations, announced his resignation. Finley shed no tears over Claiborne's departure, saying the A's didn't require a minor league director because of their recent decision to join the major leagues' central scouting bureau. "We just didn't need him anymore," Finley told *The Sporting News*, sounding like Ebenezer Scrooge to Claiborne's Bob Cratchett. "I told him at the start of the season to go ahead and look for another job. He will not be replaced." Finley would soon change his mind, replacing Claiborne with Syd Thrift, a well-respected executive formerly with the Pirates and Royals.

Developments over the past year had hastened the 36-year-old Claiborne's departure. Once Finley had eliminated all but two full-time scouts, Claiborne had asked for permission to travel more often in order to evaluate prospects firsthand. Finley, not wanting to spend money on travel expenses, told Claiborne to stay in his office. Claiborne had also become increasingly frustrated by Finley's refusal to consult him on trades involving minor league prospects. Finley had dealt Dan Ford to the Twins for Pat Bourque without seeking the advice of Claiborne. Finley had included Chet Lemon in the package for Stan Bahnsen—also against the wishes of Claiborne. "Prospects are a dime a dozen," scoffed Finley in an interview with *Sports Illustrated*. As a result of Finley's unwillingness to listen to Claiborne, the

Oakland farm system was almost devoid of legitimate prospects at the upper minor league levels.

In spite of the front office turmoil, Oakland continued to play well against American League competition. The A's won 18 of 29 games in July, giving them four consecutive months of winning baseball. Ken Holtzman paced the pitching staff, winning five of six decisions during the month. Vida Blue added three victories, including two against the rival White Sox. The continuing excellence of the pitching staff helped the A's build up a season-high 11-game lead over the second-place Royals.

After reaching peak efficiency in June and July, troubles arose in August. The A's started the month by playing their closest pursuers, the Royals, who took two of three from Oakland. The A's lost three of five to the Rangers before splitting a four-game set with the Red Sox. The 11-game lead soon shrank to five and a half games. As a result, Royals manager Whitey Herzog hinted at the fallibility of the A's, while taking a subtle poke at Charlie Finley and Alvin Dark. "It's a great team," Herzog told *Sports Illustrated* in prefacing his criticism. "But eight of their guys have played 105 games, and another has played 99. They've got to be tired...Charlie Finley keeps making out the lineups and Alvin Dark keeps playing them. Dark knows they need a rest, but what can he do? And when something does happen, they haven't got any bench."

Something *did* happen. Joe Rudi tore ligaments in the base of his left thumb while trying to check his swing. The hand injury would sideline him for most of August and September. The pitching staff also received a blow when Jim Perry continued to pitch poorly, forcing the A's to give him his unconditional release on August 13. Aside from his one-hit and three-hit efforts against the Orioles, Perry had been hit hard almost every time he took to the mound as one of Dark's starters.

The release of Perry ended the right-hander's 17-year major league career. He retired from the game with impressive numbers: 215 wins, 174 losses, and a respectable ERA of 3.45. Perry also left behind a trail of respect, both for his pitching and his character. "Just a quality guy," says Bob Fowler, who knew Perry best as a member of the Twins. "He was also the Minnesota team's player rep. He was a pretty intelligent guy. He didn't have a law degree, but he was pretty politically-minded by nature. A pretty savvy guy."

On the same day that the A's released Perry, they announced the purchase of former American League stolen base king Tommy Harper from the Angels. With Rudi facing extended time on the sidelines and with the farm system lacking in first base prospects, the A's hoped that the aging Harper would be able to play the infield corner in the interim. Harper made his Oakland debut on August 13, in the second game of a three-game home series against the Yankees. Harper, playing first base and batting eighth in the order, went 0-for-3 against Catfish Hunter, who defeated his former mates for the third consecutive time.

Former All-Stars Acquired By Charlie Finley (1970–76)

Felipe Alou
Matty Alou
Mike Andrews
Rico Carty
Orlando Cepeda
Nate Colbert
Vic Davalillo
Tommy Davis
Al Downing
Ron Fairly
Ray Fosse
Billy Grabarkewitz
Mudcat Grant
Tommy Harper
Mike Hegan
Darold Knowles
Willie McCovey
Denny McLain
Don Mincher
Jim Perry
Sonny Siebert
Billy Williams

The loss of Rudi left the A's vulnerable to left-handed pitching, especially given the season-long struggles of Sal Bando. After a nasty arbitration hearing with Charlie Finley, Bando had reported to spring training at just over 200 pounds, significantly trimmer than at any point during his major league career. The lost weight had failed to counteract the pressure Bando felt after hearing Finley denigrate him during the arbitration proceeding. "Maybe I'm not hitting because I'm trying too hard to make Finley eat his words," Bando conceded to a reporter. By August 17, Bando's season average had fallen to .199, the lowest it had ever been at such a late juncture in a season.

On August 18 and 19, the A's reached a low point as a team when they dropped two straight to the Tigers, a rebuilding club that had compiled the worst record in the American League. The dual losses decreased the divisional lead over Kansas City to five and a half games.

The A's bounced back the next day, as Sonny Siebert salvaged the last game of the Tiger series with a 2–1 win. Even in victory, the A's found another reason to squabble. As Campy Campaneris led off third base, Reggie Jackson prepared to face a two-strike pitch. Campaneris danced off the bag, feigning a steal of home plate. Distracted by the fake, Jackson swung at and missed the next pitch, completing the strikeout. As Jackson walked back to the dugout, he mouthed a few angry words in the direction of Campaneris. "I don't know what he's talking about," said an incredulous Campaneris, who often tried to distract opposing pitchers by making quick dashes down the third-base line. "I'm just doing my job."

The lack of recent clutch hitting by Jackson underscored the A's' recent offensive problems, especially the lack of production from the middle of the order. The injury to Rudi, the continuing slump of Bando, and the difficult American League transition experienced by Billy Williams all continued to contribute to the difficulties in scoring runs.

Heading into their August 30th tilt with the Red Sox, the A's had lost four of their last five games. The A's, who had scored only 10 runs combined during the four losses, found themselves trailing in yet another game. Red Sox slugger Jim Rice, not blessed with great running speed, attempted to steal second base. The throw by Gene Tenace appeared to beat Rice to the bag, but second-base umpire Rich Garcia ruled the Red Sox left fielder safe. Sal Bando and Alvin Dark argued the call fiercely with Garcia, who ejected the Oakland manager. As he walked back to the dugout, Dark loosened the third-base bag from its mooring, carried it over to the third base stands, and heaved it into one of the box seats. A's players laughed loudly at Dark's comic demonstration.

The A's ended up winning the game in 10 innings, 7-6, on an RBI single by Bando, who credited Dark for spurring on the comeback. "We came to life after he did that," Bando told Ron Fimrite of *Sports Illustrated* in assessing the importance of Dark's temper tantrum. "It was like a pep talk at half-time."

In spite of the win, Charlie Finley went to work trying to acquire a veteran hitter for the stretch drive, as he had done in 1972 with Matty Alou, and in 1973 with Rico Carty, Jesus Alou, and Vic Davalillo. Finley set his sights on three players of varying talents: the Rangers' Jim Fregosi, former Athletic Deron Johnson (now with the White Sox), and the Twins' Tony Oliva.

The 33-year-old Fregosi, a one-time front-line shortstop with the Angels, seemed the least appealing of the three players on Finley's list. No longer capable of playing the middle infield on an everyday basis, Fregosi had served the Rangers as a part-time first baseman and DH. Through games of August 21, Fregosi was hitting .269 with only four home runs, numbers that were simply inadequate for a DH-first baseman, even a part-time one. Besides, if he couldn't play regularly for an also-ran like Texas, how could anyone expect him to significantly help a pennant-contending team in Oakland?

Deron Johnson had made the A's regret their decision to dump him on Milwaukee the previous summer. Although no longer with the Brewers, Johnson had enjoyed a rebirth as the regular DH with the White Sox. In his first 119 games, Johnson had totaled 15 home runs and 62 RBIs and had made a strong case for himself as the American League's Comeback Player of the Year. If the A's decided to reacquire the 36-year-old slugger, they could move Billy Williams to first base for the injured Joe Rudi and utilize Johnson as their designated hitter.

Oliva remained the most attractive possibility, however. Given Minnesota's embarrassing standing in the American League West—30 games back of the

A's—the Twins had decided to make Oliva available in trade talks. Although bothered by increasingly painful knees, Oliva had managed to hit .285 with 13 home runs and 51 RBIs through the Twins' first 126 games. Unlike Fregosi and Johnson, Oliva was a left-handed hitter capable of hitting for both average and power, an ideal man to protect Reggie Jackson in Oakland's fragile batting order.

On paper, Oliva seemed like an ideal fit for the A's, but at least one observer expressed his doubts. "Tony at that time was a DH," recalls former Twins beat writer Bob Fowler. "Tony was at the end of his career. Tony, we always said, could hit from a rocking chair, and in essence, did. [But] I mean, he couldn't run. He had seven knee operations on one knee, I believe it was his right. And two on the other. He was a cripple, you know, trying to play baseball.

"So yes, they [the A's] would have liked to have had him as a DH. But really, when you look at that Oakland team...they had good speed. And really, Tony as a DH might have hurt them in the long run because he would have clogged up the bases. He was a one-base-at-a-time guy, and probably hindsight being what it is, Charlie Finley might have liked to have had the name and the recognition. Yet, for that team and its speed and being able to go first to third, Tony might not have been the right guy."

In the past, Finley had been able to complete trades for accomplished hitters and pitchers by giving up cash, prospects, or a combination of the two commodities. In this case, the Twins wanted players, not cash, from Finley. As much as Finley wanted Oliva, he had virtually nothing to trade to Minnesota. The rebuilding Twins needed prospects, younger players capable of replacing aging stars like Oliva and the since-traded Harmon Killebrew. Finley had foolishly surrendered one prospect, Chet Lemon, to Chicago for Stan Bahnsen and had traded another prospect, Dan Ford, to the Twins in the ill-fated Pat Bourque deal. Come to think of it, the A's probably could have used Ford himself. In 103 games with the Twins, Ford had batted .261 with 13 home runs and 51 RBIs, highly respectable numbers for a rookie who had completed a fast ascension to the major leagues. As a result of Finley's excessive tinkering, the A's no longer had Ford and they weren't going to get Oliva. The A's would have to make do with an aging Tommy Harper and perennial disappointment Rich McKinney sharing first base.

As the A's wrapped up August with a record of 15–16, their first losing month of the season, Finley did manage to swing a deal for an established player—albeit one with less potential for impact than either Oliva or Deron Johnson. On August 31, just before the deadline for freezing post-season rosters, Finley acquired versatile infielder-outfielder Cesar "Pepi" Tovar from the Rangers for a player to be named later.

Tovar, a veteran of 11 seasons with the Twins, Phillies, and Rangers, was best known for playing all nine positions in a major league game. Coincidentally, Tovar matched a record that was originally set by the A's' Campy Campaneris on September 8, 1965. In his first minor league season, Campaneris had actually pitched ambidextrously in a late-season game for Daytona Beach of the Florida State League. He later played left field, center field, and third base in the minor leagues. Remembering his unusual pitching stint and his versatility, Charlie Finley decided to use Campaneris in a promotional stunt. With the A's hopelessly out of contention in 1965 and the season winding down, Finley announced the staging of "Campy Campaneris Night" as a way of drawing more fans to the ballpark. Under the promotion, Campy would start the game against the Angels at his accustomed shortstop position, then rotate around the infield and outfield before winding up at pitcher and catcher.

Campaneris played the seven infield and outfield positions without incident. In the eighth inning, Campaneris took to the mound. Throwing right-handed, Campaneris faced Angels outfielder Jose Cardenal, who happened to be his second cousin. Campy retired Cardenal on a pop-up before allowing two walks, a hit, and a run in a one-inning stint. Then in the ninth, Campaneris experienced additional adventures when he went behind the plate. Ed Kirkpatrick, a burly catcher for the Angels, singled to lead off the inning. A sluggish runner, Kirkpatrick promptly stole second base against the inexperienced Campaneris. Later in the inning, with runners on second and third, the Angels attempted a double steal, with Kirkpatrick breaking from third base. Campaneris fired to second baseman Dick Green, who immediately returned the throw to home plate.

Green's throw beat Kirkpatrick by several feet. As Campaneris held the ball and prepared to apply the tag, Kirkpatrick rammed into him. The slightly built Campaneris fell to the ground, bounced up quickly, and challenged Kirkpatrick to a fight. Cardenal, the next scheduled batter, separated Kirkpatrick and his cousin, but the collision left Campy with pain in his shoulder. As the trainer carted Campaneris off the field, Charlie Finley fretted that his grand promotion had blown up in his face. Fortunately for the A's, X-rays on the shoulder proved negative. Finley would not have to invoke the $1 million insurance policy that he had taken out on Campaneris' health.

The nine-position stunt irritated most of the veteran A's. "It ended up costing us the ballgame," recalls Jack Aker. "It was a close ballgame. He pitched in the eighth inning, gave up a run. He played catcher in the ninth inning and dropped a sure out, the sure third out." The A's eventually lost the game in extra innings. "The players were pretty much upset," says Aker. "Even though it was a great feat for Campaneris, that's not what we were out there for; we were out there to try to win the ballgame. We felt like we more or less gave a game away just so Mr. Finley could have a stunt."

Three years after the Campaneris promotion—at the urging of Twins owner Calvin Griffith—Cesar Tovar also played an inning apiece at each position, including catcher and pitcher. "Griffith thought it was a good idea," says Bob Fowler, the Twins' beat writer at the time. "It was a late September game as I recall it. The first position he played, he was the starting pitcher, and he got them out. And then the second inning, he caught. And it was absolutely hysterical, because he came out in the catcher's garb with his chest protector—the bottom of his chest protector almost dangled on the ground. He looked like a Little Leaguer. The place was just howling with delight at the sight of Cesar coming out of the Twins' first base dugout in the catching garb—it was just hysterical."

While Campaneris played primarily as a shortstop during his major league career, Tovar was a more legitimately versatile player. Tovar played second base, third base, and the outfield regularly throughout his career, and also saw some time at shortstop. "He played all those positions during games that were significant games," Fowler points out. "I mean he was not a stiff that you just threw at third base because Harmon [Killebrew] was hurt or something. I mean, he could play all those positions."

Now 35 years of age in 1975, Tovar didn't figure to bring much of a hitting dimension to the A's. In 102 games with the Rangers, Tovar had batted a mediocre .258 while drawing only 27 walks. Yet, Tovar could still run, having stolen 16 bases, and still displayed versatility, having played the outfield, third base, and second base for the Rangers. Tovar also brought an affable personality to the Oakland clubhouse, along with a charitable, caring nature. "He was very articulate," Fowler says, "very good to talk to. I remember another thing, too, about Cesar Tovar; he used to confiscate his equipment at the end of the season. He was a packrat. You'd see his locker at the end of the year and he'd have 80 bats and 30 gloves and 50 dozen balls. He used to ship them to Caracas under the guise that he needed them for his winter workouts." In actuality, Tovar had more philanthropic intentions. "Well," Fowler says, "he would take the equipment and give it to the kids in Caracas to play ball with."

In order to make room for Tovar on the 25-man roster, the A's finally parted company with Angel Mangual, their once-promising center fielder of the future. After an impressive debut season in 1971, Mangual had regressed in almost every phase of the game. Somehow Mangual had lasted nearly five seasons in Oakland despite a continuing stream of fielding errors and an inability to produce at the plate. Once dubbed a "miniature Roberto Clemente," Mangual had fallen into the baseball oblivion known as "irrevocable waivers." Yet, Mangual felt no antagonism toward Charlie Finley. "I never had any problems with Mr. Finley," Mangual revealed to *The Sporting News*. "And I would like to play for him all my life." Mangual's major league career, however, had come to an end.

Fortunately for the A's, the Royals had failed to take full advantage of Oakland's August swoon. The Royals won 16 of 28 games during the month, but a pair of three-game losing streaks in late August prevented Kansas City from denting Oakland's lead. As the two teams headed into September, the Royals found themselves seven and a half games back in the West.

The Royals needed to pile together a long winning streak to pose a threat to the A's. After losing to the White Sox in the first game of a doubleheader on September 1, the Royals did just that. Kansas City strung together eight straight victories, sweeping consecutive four-game sets against the White Sox and Angels. The Royals' streak lopped two and a half games off the standings, placing them within five lengths of first place. Playing their best baseball of the summer, the Royals prepared to travel to the Oakland Coliseum, where they would meet the A's in a most pertinent three-game series.

The A's had won three straight games of their own, but would have to play the Royals without two injured regulars: first baseman Joe Rudi and shortstop Campy Campaneris, who had been out of action since pulling his groin while running out a bunt attempt on August 26. In facing Royals 12-game winner Dennis Leonard, who had won seven straight decisions, Alvin Dark prepared a makeshift lineup that featured Tommy Harper at first base and Teddy Martinez at shortstop. Martinez had played well defensively in Campaneris' absence, making only one error in the field. Yet, his sub-.200 batting average and lack of speed had done little to help a slumping offense.

The Royals enjoyed a profitable start to the series when promising third baseman George Brett clipped Ken Holtzman with a solo home run in the top of the first, but the A's took the lead in the bottom of the third on Sal Bando's two-run shot. In the sixth inning, the A's assembled a five-run rally, highlighted by Gene Tenace's two-run homer. Claudell Washington added a solo blast in the eighth, his first long ball since June, to complete an easy 8–2 victory.

With their lead now up to six games, the A's started the inconsistent Glenn Abbott in the second game. Abbott and Royals lefty Paul Splittorff pitched creditably, each allowing a solo home run before giving way to their respective bullpens. The game remained tied at 1–1 through the regulation nine innings, and continued to be deadlocked for four more innings. Rollie Fingers pitched exceptionally well in relief, throwing six innings of pressurized, shutout ball.

In the bottom of the 14th, Royals reliever Marty Pattin retired Tommy Harper and Gaylen Pitts for the first two outs. Campy Campaneris, who had entered the game as a defensive replacement in the ninth inning, then grounded a ball to the left side of the infield. Freddie Patek, who had homered for the Royals' lone run earlier in the game, allowed the grounder to go under his glove and through his legs, enabling a limping Campaneris to reach first base. Noticing that he was still bothered by the groin pull, Alvin Dark ordered Campy *not* to steal second base. Campaneris, noticing that Pattin was paying little attention to him, decided to ignore the manager's directive and headed for second. Campy stole second easily and then scored on Billy North's dribbling single to the outfield. The A's' most important victory of the season, a 2–1 decision in 14 innings, had improved their lead to seven games while crushing the collective morale of the young Royals.

Campaneris' daring steal of second base captured much of the post-game attention, but it didn't completely overshadow the brilliant relief work of Fingers. "He's been doing this for four year," observed Paul Lindblad, Fingers' bullpen mate since 1973, in an interview with *The Sporting News*. "He's the greatest. The scouts in the National League all say he's the best. He's better than Mike Marshall, he's better than Clay Carroll. He's better than all of them."

The extra-inning win lessened the importance of the next game, but the A's held little back in pounding the Royals, 9–1. Phil Garner went 4-for-4, Billy North added three hits, Sal Bando clubbed a three-run homer, and Gene Tenace knocked out a two-run blast to support Vida Blue's 19th win. Blue pitched a complete game despite walking six Royals, effectively resting a bullpen that had pitched eight innings the previous night.

The three-game sweep of the Royals ended the pennant race. The A's now led by eight games with only three weeks remaining. The schedule looked favorable, as well, with sub-.500 teams like the Twins, Rangers, White Sox, and Angels representing their opponents in 15 of their final 18 games. The A's would play the Royals only once more—a three-game set in Kansas City on September 19, 20, and 21.

With the A's' magic number for clinching a tie now reduced to one, Kansas City's Steve Busby outpitched Glenn Abbott in the first game of the series, winning a 5–4 decision. The next day, the A's clinched at least a share of the Western Division title by clubbing the Royals, 16–4. Billy Williams, whose power production had risen over the second half, hit his 23rd home run in support of Vida Blue's 20th win.

The Royals rallied to win the third game, but the victory mattered little in the standings. On September 24, after three consecutive losses, the A's prepared to play the White Sox. In spite of the losses, the A's still held a five-game lead over the Royals, while their magic number for clinching the division outright remained at one.

Blue, with a record of 20–11, faced White Sox rookie Jesse Jefferson in an overwhelming mismatch. The A's torched Jefferson for eight runs over the first four innings, before scraping relievers Rich Hinton and Pete Vuckovich for five more runs. Reggie Jackson slammed two home runs, his 33rd and 34th of the season. Claudell Washington drove in four runs and Sal Bando added three hits and three RBIs. Playing one of their best all-around games of the season, the A's won, 13–2, to clinch their fifth consecutive Western Division crown.

Unlike their tepid clubhouse celebrations of 1973 and '74, the A's rejoiced their latest divisional championship more enthusiastically. Some of the newer A's, who had never before played in the post-season, felt special satisfaction in the Oakland clubhouse. Billy Williams, a 15-year veteran of runner-up teams in Chicago, drank from one of the 48 bottles of champagne supplied by Charlie Finley. "Beautiful," Williams shouted, according to *The Sporting News*. "Absolutely magnificent. Ain't no feeling like this. Never knew champagne tasted so good. Fifteen years to pour champagne."

Another newcomer to the A's had almost played as long as Williams without reaching the post-season. "Thirteen years," said Tommy Harper, who had played on also-ran teams in Cincinnati, Cleveland, Seattle, Milwaukee, Boston, and California before finding solace in the Bay Area. "I knew I'd get to the right place if I kept moving around," Harper told *The Sporting News*.

Harper had been more than a passive bystander during the A's' stretch run. As part of the Oakland bench, which had been so important to the team's championships of 1972 and '73, Harper had quietly replaced the injured Joe Rudi at first base. In 34 games with the A's, Harper hit .319 and stole seven bases. During his most productive stretch, Harper collected 14 hits in 34 at-bats.

Other reserves contributed, as well. Backup shortstop Teddy Martinez made only two errors while filling in for Campy Campaneris. Martinez' deftness in turning the double play drew approval from second base partner Phil Garner. In 20 starts at shortstop during Campaneris' absence, the A's won 14 games.

The versatility of Oakland's bench moved Charlie Finley to call the 1975 A's "the best ballclub we've had in the 15 years I've owned it. We've got two players, Tommy Harper and Ted Martinez, who can play six positions; another player, Cesar Tovar, who can play five positions; some who can play four; and a number who can play three," Finley told *The Sporting News*. One could forgive Finley for his overly exuberant assessment of the '75 A's in the afterglow of the division clinching. He had obviously forgotten that the A's no longer had a pitcher named Catfish Hunter. No matter how well the A's had played during the regular season, the loss of a 25-game winner would likely have an impact—eventually.

Although the September 24th game against the White Sox represented the last meaningful contest with regard to the pennant race, the A's added an historical footnote four days later. In the season finale against the Angels, Alvin Dark planned to give Vida Blue a five-inning tune-up before using him in the second game of the playoffs. Blue pitched five innings—five no-hit innings. Sticking to his original plan, Dark removed Blue after the fifth. Glenn Abbott worked a hitless inning, as did Paul Lindblad. Dark then called on Rollie Fingers, who pitched two more scoreless—and hitless—innings to complete a 5–0 victory. For the first time in baseball history, *four* pitchers had combined to throw a no-hitter in a regular season game lasting at least nine innings.

In the past, Finley had paid bonuses to any of his pitchers who had thrown no-hitters. In 1968, Finley had rewarded Catfish Hunter with a $5,000 bonus for pitching a perfect game against the Twins. The price of a mere no-hitter was a bit less—$1,500. When a reporter asked Finley if he would still pay the $1,500 bonus, even though it had taken four pitchers to complete the no-hitter, the owner cursed angrily and repeatedly. Rollie Fingers, the last of the four no-hit pitchers, offered a possible solution. "I think we all ought to share $1,500," Fingers told *The Sporting News*. "Vida should get five-ninths, Abbott and Lindblad one-ninth each, and I should get two-ninths."

Chapter 30

A Flop at Fenway

As well as the A's had played during a surprising regular season, the post-season matchup did not bode well. The Eastern Division champion Boston Red Sox featured an intimidating lineup, one headlined by Rookie of the Year and Most Valuable Player Award favorite Fred Lynn and fellow rookie slugger Jim Rice. Thanks to their powerful offense, the Red Sox had claimed the East with 95 wins. Although the A's had forged a slightly better record than the Red Sox, they would have to play the first two games of the series at Fenway Park, a difficult stadium for road teams—and for left-handed pitchers.

During the A's' final regular season visit to Fenway in August, Alvin Dark had used three right-handed pitchers as his starters—Stan Bahnsen, Glenn Abbott, and Sonny Siebert. None of the three had pitched particularly well, but the A's still won two of the three games. Would Dark repeat the trend of using right-handers at Fenway in the playoffs? After all, he no longer had the luxury of calling upon Catfish Hunter, one of the top five right-handed pitchers in the league.

Some members of the media speculated that Dark might use one of his right-handed *relievers*, either Jim Todd or Rollie Fingers, as a starter in Game Two. Such a strategy seemed dubious. Fingers hadn't started a game since 1973, when he had made two starts for Dick Williams, and hadn't been a full-time starter since early in 1971. Todd had started six games for the Cubs in 1974, but with little success.

Ignoring the argument of left-handers vs. right-handers, Dark decided to use his two best starters—Vida Blue and Ken Holtzman—in the first two games of the series. Although both happened to throw left-handed, Dark felt they gave him stronger chances of winning than lesser right-handers like Dick Bosman and Stan Bahnsen or relievers like Todd and Fingers. Dark did surprise the media when he announced that Holtzman would pitch Game One, followed by Blue in the second game. Blue, a 22-game winner, had pitched appreciably better than Holtzman during the regular season. But Dark considered Blue's poor record in the post-season. In previous playoff and World Series appearances, Blue had won just once while losing five times.

In spite of the problems created by dispatching left-handers upon Fenway Park, the oddsmakers still made the A's slight favorites, based on their fine regular season showing and their status as defending World Champions. Their previous experience in the playoffs also heavily outweighed that of the Red Sox, a relatively young team. Only a handful of Red Sox—Carl Yastrzemski, Rico Petrocelli, Bernie Carbo, Dick McAuliffe, and former Athletic Deron Johnson (since acquired from the White Sox)—had ever participated in the post-season.

"The balls aren't the same balls, the bats aren't the same length, it's further between the bases," Reggie Jackson told Ron Fimrite of *Sports Illustrated* in describing playoff baseball. In other words, pitching in the playoffs was better, hitting was tougher, and every defensive play took on added importance. A greater sense of tension enveloped each player. Playoff baseball was just different.

The A's also received a pair of breaks with regard to injuries. Although Joe Rudi, who had missed six weeks in August and September with strained tendons in thumb, had re-injured his hand in the final regular season game, he deemed the second injury as far less serious. Rudi, the team's premier defensive outfielder and best situational hitter, would be available to take part in the playoffs. The A's also discovered that rookie outfielder Jim Rice would be unable to play for the Red Sox due to a broken arm. The young right-handed slugger had led the Red Sox in home runs during the regular season, while finishing second to Fred Lynn in batting average and RBIs. In addition, the first-game pitching matchup favored the A's slightly. Holtzman, 18–14 with a 3.15 ERA, would face fellow 18-game winner Luis Tiant, whose ERA had topped off at a fairly high 4.02.

In the bottom of the first, Holtzman retired Juan Beniquez and Denny Doyle before allowing a single to Carl Yastrzemski, one of the few players still left from the Red Sox' "Impossible Dream" season of 1967. Holtzman then induced a sharp grounder from cleanup man Carlton Fisk, who bounded the ball to the left side of the infield. Sal Bando backed up on the ball slightly, allowing it to take an extra hop and skip past him for an error. Yastrzemski rounded the bag hard at second and headed for third, waived on by third-base coach Don Zimmer. The defensively erratic Claudell Washington retrieved the ball in left field and overthrew the cutoff man, the throw bounding off Bando's glove. The second error of the inning allowed Yastrzemski to score while enabling Fisk to move up to second. Fred Lynn followed with a ground ball to second baseman Phil Garner, who misplayed the ball so badly that it reached the outfield. Fisk scored the inning's second run on the third error. Three errors, two plays, and two unearned runs.

The game remained 2–0 until the bottom of the seventh, when Billy North dropped an easy fly ball for another error and Washington misplayed Fred Lynn's high drive to left field. Thinking that the ball would bounce high off the "Green Monster," Washington retreated several steps toward the infield in order to play the carom. The ball dropped near the base of the wall, however, indicating that Washington could have made the catch had he stayed back. The Red Sox ended up scoring five runs off the combination of Holtzman and relievers Jim Todd, Paul Lindblad, Glenn Abbott, and Dick Bosman, cementing a 7–1 victory in Game One.

Dating back to their 1971 playoff appearance against the Orioles, the A's had never played so poorly in a playoff or World Series game. In making four errors, the A's had set a new Championship Series record. They had also failed to make up for their defensive escapades with nonexistent hitting and shaky relief pitching, all of which had badly stained the first game of the playoffs. "The second game is the key one," a calm and philosophical Alvin Dark told *The Sporting News*. After all, Dark had seen his team lose the first game of the 1974 playoffs before rebounding to win the series. "We just need a split here," Dark said of the two games in Boston. Although the A's had lost the first games of previous Championship Series—in 1971, '73, and '74—they had never played as sloppily as they did in losing the first game to the Red Sox. Major improvement would be needed to salvage a split at Fenway.

Faced with a sudden post-season crisis, Alvin Dark made several lineup changes for Game Two. Dark removed Claudell Washington from left field and installed him as the DH, where he could do no damage with his glove. Joe Rudi, more experienced in playing the "Green Monster" at Fenway, replaced Washington in left. Dark inserted Ray Fosse as his catcher, moved Gene Tenace to first base, and benched his regular DH, Billy Williams, who had gone hitless in the first game.

The A's responded well in the early stages of Game Two. Reggie Jackson reached Red Sox starter Reggie Cleveland for a two-run homer in the first inning. The A's added a single run in the fourth to make it a 3–0 game. Vida Blue, cruising with three scoreless innings, seemed primed to hold the advantage and give the A's the tying game in the series.

The blueprint fell apart. In the bottom of the fourth, Carl Yastrzemski drew the Red Sox close with a two-run homer. Carlton Fisk followed with a ringing double and moved to third on Fred Lynn's clean single. With the right-hand hitting Rico Petrocelli coming to the plate, Alvin Dark suddenly yanked Blue, replacing him with right-hander Jim Todd. The sinkerballer induced a double-play grounder by Petrocelli, but Fisk scored the tying run on the play.

In the top of the sixth, the A's tried to retake the lead, only to be held back by Boston's outfield defense. Carl Yastrzemski, playing a masterful left field throughout the series, corralled a Sal Bando drive off the "The Wall" perfectly. Yastrzemski returned the ball to the infield quickly enough to hold Bando, a runner with average speed, to a single. Later in the inning, Joe Rudi swatted a drive to right-center field that seemed capable of scoring a run from first. Fred Lynn raced to the gap, cutting off the drive on his backhand side. Rudi reached second with a double, but Lynn's quickness in retrieving the ball and returning it to the infield prevented the runner from scoring. With runners on second and third and two out, left-handed reliever Rogelio "Roger" Moret retired Claudell Washington to end the threat.

Prior to the short-circuited rally by the A's' offense, Jim Todd had pitched just one inning before Alvin Dark made a desperation move—summoning Rollie Fingers in the *fifth* inning. Fingers pitched a scoreless frame before running into trouble in the bottom of the sixth. The Oakland fireman gave up a double to Yastrzemski, who reached the left field wall with his opposite-field drive, and a run-scoring single to Carlton Fisk. The Red Sox now led for the first time, 4–3. In the seventh, Rico Petrocelli homered off a Fenway Park light tower, giving the Red Sox a two-run cushion. Lynn completed the scoring with a bloop RBI-single in the eighth. The A's' offense failed to score over the final five innings, completely shut down by relievers Moret and Dick Drago. As the A's completed an exasperating 6–3 loss, Red Sox fans taunted Charlie Finley by chanting, "Good-bye Charlie, Good-bye Charlie, we hate to see you go." Finley stood up from his seat near the third base dugout, raised his arms to the fans, and smiled uncomfortably.

The Red Sox had suddenly moved within one game of their first trip to the World Series since 1967. As Reggie Jackson told *Sports Illustrated* in assessing the Red Sox, "Now they know they can slay the giant." The A's could no longer draw comfort from past Championship Series. In the brief history of the playoffs, no team had come back from a two-games-to-none deficit to advance to the World Series.

On the brink of playoff embarrassment, Finley ordered Alvin Dark to make more changes for Game Three. Finley demanded that Campy Campaneris bat leadoff in favor of the hitless Billy North (no hits in seven at-bats), who would now bat eighth. In context, this would turn out to be a relatively small adjustment; Finley had even bigger changes in mind.

After a day off for travel, the A's returned to the West Coast. The worst-case scenario had fully developed. In games one and two, Alvin Dark had burned Blue and Holtzman, his best starters, and had still lost twice. That left Dark with his best right-handed starter, Dick Bosman, to start Game Three. Bosman had won 11 of 15 decisions since joining the A's in the mid-season trade with the Indians.

Charlie Finley, however, lacked the confidence to pitch Bosman in the third game. At the behest of Finley, Dark informed Ken Holtzman that *he* would start the game against veteran right-hander Rick Wise on only *two* days' rest. Holtzman, who had pitched over six innings in the first game, had not made a start during the regular season on anything less than a three-day interval.

Dark's—or rather Finley's—decision to use Holtzman left the manager and the owner vulnerable to an array of second-guessing. In the first place, why hadn't Dark started Bosman, his best right-handed starter, during one of the games at Fenway Park? Furthermore, with Bosman having pitched only one-third of an inning in Boston, how could Finley resist using him n Oakland? Didn't a relatively rested Bosman stand a better chance of pitching well than a tired Holtzman on only two days' rest? And why wasn't Catfish Hunter here? The last second guess, no fault of Dark's, was reserved solely for Charlie Finley.

Holtzman pitched well over the first three innings, keeping the Red Sox off the scoreboard to maintain a scoreless tie. In the fourth inning, another costly fielding mistake by Claudell Washington led directly to an unearned Red Sox run when Rico Petrocelli followed with an RBI single. In the fifth, the Red Sox broke the game open when Rick Burleson started the inning with a double, and Denny Doyle, Carl Yastrzemski, and Carlton Fisk each lashed singles. The three-run rally pushed Holtzman from the game while giving the Red Sox a 4–0 lead.

In the sixth, the A's threatened to make a run at Red Sox starter Rick Wise. The A's scored one run before watching the rally stall. Red Sox shortstop Rick Burleson went deep into the hole to plug up Sal Bando's potential infield single, which would have loaded the bases with one out. With two runners on and two out, Wise faced

Reggie Jackson, representing the potential tying run. Jackson struck out, ending Oakland's best chance at making the game a close one.

The A's tried to mount another comeback in the eighth inning. With a run already in, runners on first and third, and one man out, Jackson stepped to the plate to face a tiring Wise. Jackson went with an outside pitch, lining it into the left-center field gap. Carl Yastrzemski, the defensive star of the series, gave chase while knowing he had no chance to make a catch. "All I thought of was to cut the ball off," Yaz explained to *The Sporting News*. "I didn't think I had a chance, but I just dove as far as I could and all of a sudden, the ball was in the webbing of my glove." Yastrzemski leapt to his feet and threw to second base, holding Jackson at first. Although Yaz had not caught the ball on the fly, he had managed to cut it off before it bounded to the outfield wall. If the ball had eluded Yaz, the A's would have scored two runs and Jackson might have ended up at third with a triple. Reality dictated otherwise. Thanks to another miraculous play by an aging but still skilled outfielder, only one run had scored, the runner from first had stopped at third, and Jackson had settled for a long single.

The A's now trailed, 5–3. Red Sox manager Darrell Johnson called on his best reliever, Dick Drago, to replace Wise. Drago threw one pitch to Joe Rudi, who promptly bounced into an inning-ending double play. Although the A's still had one more inning to bat, their season had effectively come to an end. Gene Tenace drew a one-out walk in the ninth before Drago retired Billy North and pinch-hitter Jim Holt to finish the game and the series. With a 5–3 win, the Red Sox had finally ended Oakland's dynastic string of post-season victories.

Often criticized for acting like spoiled children in victory, as evidenced by their many post-game fights and arguments, the A's showed a different side to their character in losing. Several A's—Reggie Jackson, Sal Bando, Joe Rudi, and Rollie Fingers included—all walked over to the Boston clubhouse to offer their congratulations to the new American League champions. Oakland's stars spent several minutes in the Red Sox' clubhouse, discussing the series and Boston's newfound status as a World Series participant.

In the aftermath of their first post-season loss since 1971, many players and writers sounded off on a common refrain: *It might have been different if Catfish Hunter were still around.* The A's could have used Hunter to pitch Game One at Fenway Park, while reserving Vida Blue or Ken Holtzman to pitch Game Three on full rest, rather than the paltry two days that Charlie Finley's panic had created. Veteran sportswriter Steve Jacobson, working for *New York Newsday,* asked Sal Bando if the loss of Hunter was the biggest blunder by a franchise in baseball history. After a short pause interrupted by laughter, Bando responded. "If it wasn't the biggest," Bando told Jacobson, "I haven't heard of any bigger." Without specifically naming the culprit, Bando had fired another indirect shot at the tempestuous owner.

Chapter 31

The Last Hurrah

Criticism of Finley's bungling of the Catfish Hunter affair soon gave way to discussion of the A's' future—and the ways for the team to improve. Given the failures of the Oakland left-handers at Fenway Park, the A's desperately needed another high-quality right-handed pitcher to balance the rotation. "We've got to get someone like Don Sutton who'll go out there and pitch," Sal Bando told *The Sporting News*. "You can't get a Catfish Hunter in a trade, but you can go out and get someone who can win you 15 games." In 1964, Charlie Finley had come close to signing Sutton out of the amateur ranks, but bemoaned the youngster's lack of a colorful nickname along the lines of "Blue Moon" or "Catfish," or a memorable surname like "Fingers." Finley insisted that Sutton adopt a nickname as part of any agreement with the A's, but Sutton refused the bizarre demand, ending the negotiations. By now a vested veteran in 1975, but still lacking a suitable nickname, Sutton would have nicely filled out a top of the rotation that already contained Vida Blue, Ken Holtzman, and Dick Bosman.

While Bosman had pitched well for the A's, another mid-season pitching acquisition had not fared as well. Although Sonny Siebert hadn't pitched terribly in an Oakland uniform, he had shown little durability, averaging fewer than five innings per start. Siebert's availability had also been affected by a series of groin injuries and continuing problems with his sinuses. Siebert's fragility convinced Charlie Finley to cut him loose.

The A's' pitching problems figured to get worse if Ken Holtzman followed through on his hints at retirement. Unlike most of his teammates, Holtzman's boyhood had not included dreams of becoming a major league player. "I didn't want to be a professional athlete," Holtzman admitted to Larry Elderkin of the *Christian Science Monitor*. "I thought maybe I'd like to be a lawyer, or something like that." The owner of a masters' degree in business administration, Holtzman told reporters of his interest in entering private business in the metropolitan areas of either Chicago or St. Louis. Over the last two years, Holtzman had speculated that his playing career might not last much beyond the 1975 season.

Holtzman was beginning to tire of the constant travel, which kept him away from his family for long stretches during the season. "I figure I'll pitch maybe two, three more years," Holtzman had said in a 1973 interview with Bay Area sportswriter Glenn Dickey. "I'll have my 10-year pension then. I've never thought I'd be the kind of guy who would pitch 17 years. When the thrill is gone, when it's a chore to suit up, that's when I'll quit." Holtzman had indicated that winning a World Series was his chief goal; since he had achieved that, he regarded all else as "anticlimactic." If Holtzman did retire, the A's would have little to chance to repeat as divisional champs, much less even *think* of making it back to the World Series.

Aside from pitching, Charlie Finley craved another big hitter for the middle of the Oakland order. An examination of the playoff statistics revealed a lineup filled with unproductive players. The group included Gene Tenace and Billy Williams, the two key components behind Reggie Jackson, who had combined to go hitless in the three games against Boston. Finley had tried, and failed, to acquire Tony Oliva in August; now he set his sights on Brewers first baseman George "Boomer" Scott, who had led the American League in RBIs, but had been accused of selfishness by his Brewer teammates. Who would the A's trade to Milwaukee for a star like Scott? The Brewers needed a center fielder, so perhaps a package headed up by Billy North would suffice. North, who had been hampered by calcium deposits and bone spurs in his foot during the season, figured to be 100 per cent by 1976. If the A's acquired Scott, they could play him at first base, return Joe Rudi to left field, and slide Claudell Washington over to center. Still, such a scenario represented uncertainty for the A's, given Washington's inconsistencies in the outfield.

Finley created more uncertainty on October 17, when he announced that Alvin Dark would not return to manage the team. Finley refused to call the move a "firing," but the short statement issued to the press made it clear that Dark's contract would not be renewed. The decision may have been spurred by an article in the October 2nd edition of the *Hayward* (California) *Daily Review*. A story in the *Review* appeared under the following headline:

ALVIN DARK SAYS THAT UNLESS HE CHANGES HIS WAYS, FINLEY'S GOING TO HELL

Dark claimed that the reporter had taken his comments out of context. When asked about the article, Finley reacted nonchalantly, saying that Dark's words had not bothered him. Finley did not attribute the "firing" of Dark to the newspaper article, but rather to the manager's heavy involvement with the church. "I believe that Dark's outside activities interfered with managing the club," Finley told *The Sporting News*, making a statement that was sure to infuriate Christian leaders.

Once again, Finley had failed to consult his players, many of whom felt Dark had done a better job of managing in 1975 than he had during the World Championship season. Even Sal Bando, at one time Dark's staunchest critic on the A's, had become a convert. "He should have been named Manager of the Year," Bando told the Associated Press, only a year and a half after claiming that Dark couldn't manage a meat market. "Alvin made a few mistakes his first year and admitted them. This past season he had the smarts and got the most out of the team." Dark had taken a team with only two above-average starting pitchers—Vida Blue and Ken Holtzman—to its fifth consecutive appearance in the post-season.

Rumors immediately centered on one man as the successor to Dark. The name of Gene Mauch, most recently the manager of the Expos and the man at the helm when the Phillies experienced their late-season collapse in 1964, came up again and again. Finley found Mauch appealing for two reasons: he liked that Mauch was a big name among managers and also preferred a disciplinarian who stressed fundamental play, one of the weaknesses during the Dark regime.

If Dark had remained as manager, he was prepared to make certain changes. Dark wanted to move Joe Rudi back to left field—against Finley's wishes—and preferred to trade Billy Williams, who had finished the season with a career-low .244 average. Dark also wanted to keep Ray Fosse, who had been rumored as the player to be named later in the trade that had netted the A's Cesar Tovar from the Rangers.

With Dark out of the picture, Finley set his sights on making his own changes. He hoped the Rangers would take Fosse off his hands, rather than take the cash option needed to complete the deal. Texas settled for money, but Finley still managed to unload Fosse, selling him to the Indians, his original major league team. In the meantime, Finley sought several star players in potential trades. Gaylord Perry headed up Finley's list of potential pitching help. Now with Texas, Perry had run afoul of manager Frank Robinson in Cleveland. The Red Sox' Rick Wise loomed as another target of Finley. The owner also desired two high-impact offensive players: the previously mentioned George Scott and Dodgers outfielder Jimmy Wynn.

Finley offered the Brewers Reggie Jackson in a one-for-one deal that would bring Scott to the Bay Area. In exchange for Wynn, the A's talked about giving up a package that would include Billy North and Paul Lindblad, who was also rumored to be part of a package for Perry. In another potential deal, Finley suggested Sal Bando as possible compensation to the Red Sox for Wise, the man who had beaten the A's in the final game of the Championship Series. Unfortunately, the A's no longer had any high-level minor league prospects that could be used to pad any blockbuster trades. Perhaps they could put together a trade for one of the players in the Scott-Wynn-Perry category, but probably not two of them, and certainly not all three.

One of the potential trades quickly fell through. Wynn ended up being traded, but to Atlanta, not Oakland, in a blockbuster six-player deal. The Brewers considered offers for Scott, but decided to hold on to the burly first baseman. The Rangers adopted a similar stance with Perry. The best Charlie Finley could do was to send career minor league outfielder Charlie Chant to the Cardinals for speedy infielder Larry Lintz, who became the A's' latest pinch-runner extraordinaire. Finley also parted ways with four veterans by cutting infielders Tommy Harper, Dal Maxvill, and Billy Grabarkewitz, and pitcher Sonny Siebert. For some reason, Finley didn't announce the departures of Harper and Siebert until February, nearly three months after the fact. The releases of Siebert, Maxvill, and Grabarkewitz came as no great shock, but the decision to waive Harper smacked of Finley's typical cheapness. The veteran first baseman-outfielder had hit well and run well during his 34-game stint in Oakland, but made too much money for Finley's liking. The owner didn't like paying utility players, even productive ones, at premium rates.

While Finley failed to add any big-name players to his stable during the offseason, he did find a marquee manager. The attempt to secure Gene Mauch fell through, however. Mauch apparently wanted the job, but wanted to bring in his own pitching coach. Finley insisted that his new manager retain holdover pitching coach Wes Stock, Finley's favorite on the staff. After considering one of his coaches, Bobby Winkles, and former Royals manager Jack McKeon, Finley settled on Chuck Tanner, who had been fired by the White Sox only one day earlier.

"He'll be the best manager I've ever had," Finley told *The Sporting News* in his typically understated way. Tanner, perhaps the most optimistic and upbeat manager in either league, used a strange choice of words in describing his reaction to the Oakland appointment. "I'm feeling outstandingly exotic, or whatever the word is," Tanner said breathlessly, while wearing an absurd 10-gallon hat bearing the A's' logo.

Tanner had forged a reputation as an enthusiastic players' manager, a man who publicly defended and stressed the strengths of his players, even in the face of extreme criticism. During his tenure in Chicago, Tanner had accomplished what other managers had failed to do repeatedly—finding a way to extract the most from the talented, but moody Dick Allen. In 1972, under the guidance of Tanner, Allen had reached the upper limits of his extraordinary skills by batting .308 with 37 homers and 113 RBIs and winning the American League MVP Award.

In contrast to his handling of Allen, Tanner's use of the White Sox' pitching staff had drawn criticism from the Chicago media. In 1972, Tanner and his pitching coach, Johnny Sain, had made the controversial decision to use a three-man rotation, often pitching knuckleballing left-hander Wilbur Wood and right-handers Stan Bahnsen and Tom Bradley on only two days' rest. In the short term, the unusual rotation had paid dividends. Wood won 24 games, Bahnsen established a career-high with 21, and Bradley tied his best with 15 victories. The heavy workload may have taken its toll, however, on both Bahnsen and Bradley. In 1972, Bahnsen made 41 starts while Bradley started 40 games. Within two years, both right-handers saw their ERAs rise above 4.00 and their won-loss records dip below the .500 level. Both careers were near the end.

In Chicago, Tanner had dealt with several controversies, including the day-to-day presence of Dick Allen and the interference of general manager Stu Holcomb. Such problems figured to seem minuscule in comparison to the soap opera style of the A's, where players fought and argued with regularity and the owner did his best to make life unbearable for his manager of the day. Nonetheless, Tanner anticipated little difficulty in managing a team filled with loud, volatile personalities. "There are a lot of good kids who go to bed at 8:00 P.M. every night, are no trouble at all, are great to be around, and hit .180," Tanner explained to *The Sporting News*. "Give me the outspoken good player."

Now that his managerial choice had been finalized, Charlie Finley started to confront rumors of an impending move of the franchise to Seattle. Finley denied the speculation, instead proposing a plan that would improve the condition of his financially-ailing club. At the owners' meetings in January, Finley championed one of his favorite causes—interleague play. "Think of the rivalries," Finley exclaimed to *The Sporting News*. "There would be the A's and the Giants, the Yanks and Mets, the White Sox and Cubs, the Dodgers and the Angels." Finley believed that interleague play, specifically a number of regular season series against San Francisco, would increase attendance at the Oakland Coliseum while cutting down on travel costs.

As usual, the other major league owners initially resisted Finley's attempt at change. Former sportswriter Bob Fowler says Finley's idea of interleague play might have gained more immediate acceptance if he had tried a gentler, more logical approach. "I think if he had not been such a character, if he had not been such a square-peg, round-hole kind of guy, he could have certainly gotten the people to do it. If he could have presented his ideas with charts and graphs to show how they could have made even more money than they were making, all of those things would have been rubber-stamped." Twenty-one years after Finley's proposal—and just months after his death from heart disease—the major leagues would institute a plan of interleague play similar to the one he had suggested.

One week after discussing interleague play, Finley officially introduced Chuck Tanner to the Oakland media at a press conference, where the owner wholeheartedly refuted all rumors of the A's being moved to Seattle, or any other North American location. A few days later, Finley quietly announced through a press release that the A's would raise ticket prices for their top two levels of seats by 50 cents apiece. By not mentioning the ticket increase at the press conference, Finley hoped to minimize the negative feedback leveled at him by the Oakland writers.

Finley faced bigger problems than mere criticism of his ticket price hike. Many of his best players, including seven represented by powerful agent Jerry Kapstein, remained unsigned as spring training neared. Two of Kapstein's clients, Campy Campaneris and Ken Holtzman, wanted multi-year contracts. Finley explained that, as a matter of policy, he had no intention of handing out contracts for more than one season. Finley failed to mention that he had previously signed Campaneris, Billy Williams, and Catfish Hunter to two-year deals.

Finley did not have to worry about any of the players taking him to the arbitration table, since arbitration had been suspended while major league players and owners continued to negotiate a new collective bargaining agreement. Still, Finley ran the risk of losing the players outright after the season. A recent landmark decision by independent arbitrator Peter Seitz had made two veteran pitchers, Andy Messersmith and Dave McNally, free agents. With the old collective bargaining agreement having expired, the possibility existed that a new agreement would result in all unsigned players becoming free agents at the end of the 1976 season. Even without a new agreement, all players who played out the option year of their contracts might also become free agents. By refusing to sign players beyond the upcoming season, Finley seemed to be playing with contractual fire.

In a related development, the unsigned Reggie Jackson told Finley that he preferred to sign a multi-year contract and remain in Oakland. Rumors persisted that Finley might trade Jackson to the Orioles for an unnamed outfielder and pitcher Mike Torrez, who would fill the team's need for a quality right-handed starter. Although the A's held 20-year-old right-hander Mike Norris in high regard, the youngster had missed most of the 1975 season after surgery to remove bone chips from his pitching elbow. No one knew for sure if Norris would be able to return, given his history of arm trouble. Without a healthy Norris, the A's badly required a front-line starter who threw from the right side. In order to acquire such a player, the A's would have to at least consider the possibility of trading a player the caliber of Reggie Jackson.

Jackson remained unsigned, as did fellow outfielder Billy North, starting infielders Joe Rudi, Campy Campaneris, and Sal Bando, first-string catcher Gene Tenace, and Oakland's three best pitchers—Vida Blue, Ken Holtzman, and Rollie Fingers. Now that arbitration had been temporarily removed as an option, Finley mailed each of the players automatically renewed contracts—at the maximum 20 percent pay cut. The pay decreased angered most of the players, whom the media began referring to as the "Oakland Nine." The nine players did have one recourse. They could play out their options and declare themselves free agents after the 1976 season. In other words, Finley ran the risk of losing arguably his nine best players without any compensation in return.

Finley's salary tactics, which featured demeaning insults, telephone hang-ups, and unreturned calls, proved especially frustrating to Ken Holtzman. "All he would have to do," stipulated Holtzman in an interview with the *New York Times*, "is negotiate with me in good faith, in a civil tone of voice and I probably would sign. I like the Oakland area. I like the guys on the ballclub. I don't want to leave." Holtzman recalled how Finley had cut his salary by 10 percent after acquiring him from the Cubs prior to the 1972 season. Holtzman also remembered an incident in the fall of 1972, right after the A's had won their first World Series. As a large gathering of fans welcomed the players back to Oakland, Finley had scolded Holtzman, embarrassing him in front of his father-in-law. "Charlie just doesn't know how to treat people," said Holtzman, expressing the sentiments of many of his teammates.

Holtzman's life had become more miserable after assuming the role of Oakland's player representative from a beleaguered Reggie Jackson. Over the past 10 years, A's player reps had been subjected to more abuse from Finley than any other players. "I honestly believe it cost me my job with the A's," says Jack Aker, who served as Oakland's player representative for two seasons before being left unprotected in the 1969 expansion draft. "I think it cost me what should have been better years in '67 and '68 because I had so many problems with Mr. Finley. It was almost constant. Almost every day there was a problem of some sort." Finley frowned upon the idea of a Players' Association and warned many of the A's not to attend union meetings. Given his resentment of the Association, Finley harassed Aker—often over petty and trivial matters. "The real problem that I had with Mr. Finley was the little things," recalls Aker. "Maybe a player or two on the club did not autograph all the balls in the clubhouse before the game. I would be called into his office immediately the next day as soon as I got to the ballpark. It was little things like this; it was a constant thing." Finley also kept count of the number of bats used by the players and charged them each time they tossed baseballs into the stands.

Ken Holtzman and the rest of the unsigned—and unhappy—players reported to spring training on time. The A's also invited a few new players to camp, including veteran third baseman Ken McMullen. The former Senator, Angel, and Dodger infielder had been released by Los Angeles during the winter. The A's planned to look at McMullen as a pinch-hitter and utility infielder, and as possible insurance should they decide to trade Sal Bando for a pitcher.

On April 2, as spring training narrowed to its last few days, the A's announced that they had made a trade. The deal did not involve Sal Bando, which had been rumored. No, this trade would be even bigger—much bigger. Oakland's most recognizable player, perhaps the man most synonymous with their successful seasons of 1971 through 1975, was now gone. Charlie Finley had traded the unsigned Reggie Jackson, along with the unsigned Ken Holtzman, and minor league hurler Bill Van Bommel to the Baltimore Orioles for right-hander Mike Torrez, outfielder Don Baylor, and pitcher Paul Mitchell.

Although a trade involving Jackson and the Orioles had been rumored for months, the official announcement of the deal still shocked a group of disbelieving Oakland players and writers. Jackson, the A's' best left-handed power hitter and most recognizable player, had been with the club since 1967, when the team still played in Kansas City. Holtzman, their second-best starter after Vida Blue in 1975, had been critical to the success of the 1972, '73, and '74 championship teams.

The comments of Joe Rudi epitomized the feelings of many of the A's regarding the blockbuster trade. "I don't think the guys we got from Baltimore are as good as Kenny or Reggie," Rudi explained succinctly to *The Sporting News*. "Torrez isn't as good a pitcher as Kenny. And Baylor is no Reggie Jackson."

Charlie Finley disagreed strongly with Rudi's assessment, calling the trade the *best* he'd ever made. Finley added that he would have made the trade even if both Jackson and Holtzman had already signed long-term contracts. "This trade was made because I feel this deal will lead us to another World Championship," Finley told the Associated Press in prefacing another bombshell proclamation. "I feel that Baylor is the equal of Reggie Jackson." In 1975, Jackson had totaled 36 home runs, 104 RBIs, 17 stolen bases, a .332 on-base percentage, and a .511 slugging percentage. Baylor had accumulated a better on-base percentage and stolen more bases, but his .489 slugging percentage, 25 home runs, and 76 RBIs hadn't come close to matching Jackson's power numbers. In addition, Baylor couldn't throw—the result of a severe shoulder injury—which meant that he could play only left field and first base.

Still, Finley liked the potential of Baylor, who at 26 was three years younger than Jackson. "I don't mean this out of [dis]respect to Jackson," Finley told the AP. "I think Baylor is outstanding and will be even more outstanding in the next few years." Baylor remained unsigned, however, raising the possibility that he too could leave the A's after the season.

In surrendering three unsigned players, Finley had acquired two players—Torrez and Mitchell—who had already signed contracts and could not become free agents after the season. Finley pointed to Torrez' 20-win season in 1975, but claimed that the inclusion of Mitchell was the key to the deal. In 1975, Mitchell had won 10 of 11 decisions for Rochester, the Orioles' top minor league affiliate, and was considered one of the best pitching prospects in the game. Mitchell, as well as Torrez, figured to be a part of Oakland's revamped starting rotation.

One week later, Finley changed his mind concerning the rationale behind the trade. In an interview with Roger Williams of the *San Francisco Examiner*, Finley admitted that Jackson's lofty contract demands had bothered him. Finley had asked Jackson's agent to lower his asking price. When Jackson refused, Finley felt he had no other choice but to trade his superstar. Otherwise, the A's might have lost Jackson—and received nothing in return—at season's end.

Aside from shaking the emotional structure of the team, the six-player trade resulted in several lineup changes. Chuck Tanner returned Joe Rudi to left field and moved Claudell Washington to right field, his natural position in the minor leagues. Baylor would become the regular first baseman and occasional DH, filling in for Billy Williams from time to time. Tanner also announced that Torrez would become his Opening Day pitcher, fitting into the assignment that he had originally given to Holtzman. Vida Blue would pitch the second game, followed by Stan Bahnsen, one of Tanner's best pitchers during their days with the White Sox. The surprising decision to use Bahnsen as the third starter left Dick Bosman wondering about his role with the team in 1976.

Tanner also prepared to reunite with another one of his former White Sox pitchers when the A's acquired right-hander Tom Bradley from the Giants in a trade. Although the A's ticketed Bradley to start the season at Triple-A Tucson, Tanner hoped to see Bradley in Oakland before much of the regular season had elapsed.

Perhaps distracted by those rumors, the A's struggled in spring training. Oakland won just four of 14 exhibition games, the team's worst showing ever in the Cactus League. The A's fared better once the regular season began, winning their first three games, before dropping three straight to the rival Rangers. The pattern of .500 baseball continued over the first month of the season. Oakland finished April with a record of nine wins and eight losses.

Attendance at the Oakland Coliseum, always a problem for the A's, only worsened in the absence of Reggie Jackson. No longer featuring one of the American League's marquee power hitters, the A's resorted to a different brand of baseball. Chuck Tanner instructed his fastest baserunners—Billy North, Campy Campaneris, Claudell Washington, and Don Baylor—to attempt stolen bases at every opportunity. The strategy generally paid off, helping the A's to steal nearly two bases per game. Yet, the aggressive style of offense also brought a downside. In one game, with the A's trailing by three runs, Gene Tenace tried to steal second base. Tenace strained ligaments in his left knee, an injury that would sideline him until July.

The heralded Paul Mitchell, facing pressure to justify the controversial trade with the Orioles, did not pitch well in his Oakland debut. Opposing hitters also banged Mitchell badly in his second start. Tanner replaced Mitchell with Mike Norris, who had pitched well in several early-season relief stints.

April's mediocre level of play soon gave way to an atrocious month of May. The A's started the month by losing five of their first seven games. On May 17, the A's began perhaps their worst stretch of play since becoming division winners in 1971. A 5–4 loss to the Twins signaled the beginning of an eight-game losing streak. Jim Todd lost two straight games in extra innings. Starting pitchers lost six consecutive decisions. Don Baylor, the new cleanup man in the aftermath of the Reggie Jackson trade, struggled to raise his batting average above .200. At least Baylor had an excuse, having suffered a slight fracture in his left wrist. The injury, coupled with the cool early-season weather in the Bay Area, robbed Baylor of his usual power stroke. The newfangled lineup also had to make do without Billy Williams, sidelined by back spasms. Even when healthy, Williams hadn't hit well. Like Baylor, his batting average rested uncomfortably under .200. Several writers suggested that Williams would retire after the season.

With Gene Tenace injured and Sal Bando also wallowing under .200, the once-powerful Oakland lineup had taken on the look of an also-ran. Other than Vida Blue and Mike Torrez, the pitching had done little to compensate for the offensive shortcomings. Except for a 10-strikeout game against the Angels, Paul Mitchell continued to experience major league shellings at a regular clip. Mike Norris pitched inconsistently in his return from the bullpen. Rollie Fingers fared so poorly that Chuck Tanner relegated him to the inglorious role of long relief. The A's of the early seventies seemed light years away.

On June 15, just hours before the annual trading deadline, the A's took an even larger step away from their glory years. With the A's getting set to host the Red Sox at the Oakland Coliseum, Charlie Finley announced the sales of two of his star players. With little prior warning, Finley sent Joe Rudi and Rollie Fingers to the Red Sox, one of the contending teams in the American League East. In exchange, the A's received a record $1 million apiece for their starting left fielder and best relief pitcher. Fingers and Rudi switched dugouts before the game and put on their new Red Sox uniforms, but did not play that night. After announcing the blockbuster sales, Finley told the Associated Press: "The night's not over." It certainly wasn't. Finley followed up the sales of Rudi and Fingers moments later when he sent another star—Vida Blue—to the Yankees for $1.5 million.

In one fell swoop, the A's had stripped themselves of three of their most important players. So why did Finley suddenly decide to dispatch his best starter, his top reliever, and his best defensive outfielder? Given that Blue, Fingers, and

Rudi represented nearly half of Oakland's impending free agent class, Finley considered the threesome unsignable beyond 1976. Finley also needed to negotiate contracts with Sal Bando, Campy Campaneris, Gene Tenace, and Don Baylor, four other players eligible for post-season free agency. Realizing that he had little chance (or perhaps desire) to sign Blue, Fingers, and Rudi to long-term contracts, Finley decided to acquire *something* in return. Otherwise, the players would be able to leave as free agents without compensation, ala Catfish Hunter.

"It was a difficult decision," Finley admitted to the Associated Press, "but I made every effort to sign them. "I'm sorry to see Rollie and Joe go. They are two fine athletes and two fine gentlemen. I'm very disappointed over having to do what I did." Earlier in the day, Finley had actually signed Blue to a new four-year contract, before surprising the left-hander with the news that he had been sold to New York. Finley had signed Blue to the contract only as a pre-condition of his sale to the Yankees.

So why didn't Finley trade the players in question, receiving some form of player compensation, other than cash, in return? Finley claimed that prior to selling the players he had tried to make a trade with the Red Sox. He had discussed the possibility of acquiring players like Fred Lynn, Rick Burleson, Rick Wise, and Cecil Cooper in exchange for Rudi and Fingers, but had been unable to come to an agreement. Finley had also approached the Brewers about a trade of Rudi for left-handed hitting catcher Darrell Porter. When Finley refused to allow the Brewers to negotiate a long-term contract with Rudi, Milwaukee turned down the deal. As a result, Finley settled for record cash compensation in return for Rudi and Fingers.

Finley's actions quickly caught the attention of Commissioner Bowie Kuhn. Disturbed and angered by Finley's firesales, Kuhn came down with a shockingly unprecedented ruling. On June 18, three days after Finley had made his transactions with the Red Sox and Yankees, Kuhn announced that all three sales were null and void. Kuhn ordered Blue, Fingers, and Rudi, who had yet to debut with their new teams, to return to the A's. The commissioner condemned the transactions, in which the A's had received only cash, and no players in return. "Shorn of much of its finest talent in exchange for cash," Kuhn proclaimed to the Associated Press, "the Oakland club, which has been a divisional champion for the last five years, has little chance to compete effectively in its division. I would be remiss...if I did not act now...to prevent a development so harmful to baseball as this." Citing one of his powers as commissioner under Article One, Section Four of the major league agreement, Kuhn declared that the player sales would not be allowed because they violated "the best interests of baseball." Those words would become a common refrain for Kuhn until the end of his reign as commissioner in 1984.

Finley responded to Kuhn's surprising decision by filing a $10 million lawsuit against the commissioner, claiming restraint of trade. Finley ordered manager Chuck Tanner not to use any of the three players in a game for the A's until the issue was settled in court. So, for the time being, Tanner was forced to make do with a 22-man roster, instead of the usual 25 players. Finley's attorney, Neil

Papiano, explained the rationale behind the owner's decision. "If Charlie uses any of the players," Papiano detailed to the Associated Press, "then, in essence, he is ratifying the commissioner's position." Papiano added that the three players shouldn't even be allowed into the Oakland clubhouse. Why? "The A's have been known to hurt themselves in the lockerroom," said a half-joking Papiano, referring to the numerous fights that had taken place before and after games during the 1970s.

American League President Lee MacPhail questioned the wisdom of Finley's refusal to use the three players. "What bothers me is that they are not being played," MacPhail told the Associated Press. We can't let it go beyond another day or two. It is not fair to the players. They cannot be allowed to remain in limbo too long." The absence of Rudi, Fingers, and Blue was not only hurting the A's as a team, but was harming the bargaining power of each individual player. Each day missed translated into fewer chances for Rudi, Blue, and Fingers to add to their usually impressive statistical totals.

Finley found allies in other camps. Yankee manager Billy Martin, angered by the ruling that had denied him the services of Blue, sarcastically compared Kuhn to the game's first commissioner. "What he's trying to be is another Judge [Kenesaw Mountain] Landis," Martin told the *New York Daily News*. Marvin Miller, the head of the Players' Association, also criticized Kuhn, telling the *Daily News* that he had "single-handedly plunged baseball into the biggest mess it has ever seen...It's raised the potential for litigation which would last for years. He is asserting a right to end all club owners' rights with respects to all transactions. Whenever there's a trade made, he can decide that one team did not get enough value and can veto the deal."

Fingers, Blue, and Rudi remained in limbo, unable to suit up for the A's because of Finley's edict, while similarly prevented from joining their new teams in Boston and New York because of Kuhn's ruling. Fingers remembers his disappointment over Kuhn's decision to negate his sale to the Red Sox. "At the time, Charlie Finley knew that all three of us were playing out our options. We were gonna go to another ballclub. And all he was trying to do was to try to get some cash for us. I was happy to be going to Boston. I was going to a contending ballclub. They had some great players there—a good pitching staff. I loved pitching in Fenway Park. I was looking forward to going to Boston."

The forced inactivity frustrated all three players. "We were getting pretty disgusted with the whole thing," says Fingers, who remained powerless to change the situation. On June 24, nine days after the transactions had first been announced, Kuhn ordered Finley to "remove any restraints" against using the three players. Kuhn told Finley to allow Tanner to play Fingers, Rudi, and Blue. Once again, the stubborn Finley refused to allow the players to suit up.

On June 27, the entire roster of A's players decided to take the matter into its own hands. As Fingers says, "It got to the point where we had a team meeting in the clubhouse [that day],and we told Chuck Tanner that guys weren't gonna play. [The] Minnesota [Twins] had come to town, and we were *not* gonna play the ballgame; we were gonna forfeit the ballgame to Minnesota if we were not activated."

Captain Sal Bando took a poll of Oakland players, who voted 21–0 in favor of striking, with two abstentions. Fingers vividly recalls the scene in the A's' clubhouse just minutes before the scheduled first pitch against the Twins. "Everybody was in the clubhouse in their regular clothes, about 15 minutes before the game. Chuck Tanner called up Charlie Finley and said, 'The boys aren't gonna play unless you do something about it.' Chuck Tanner [then] came out of his office and started reading the lineup." Tanner announced the following names: North, Campaneris, Baylor, Bando, Tenace, *Rudi*... "As soon as he said Rudi's name, the boys put their uniforms on," Fingers says. Finley had finally given in to the players' threat of a boycott, allowing Rudi to return to the starting lineup and Blue and Fingers to resume their roles on the pitching staff. The A's, perhaps motivated by the return of their three lost teammates, defeated the Twins, 5–3.

Although the players were relieved that they had been reinstated, the resolution to the scenario proved less than ideal. "I still had to play out the year in Oakland," Fingers points out, while recalling that the A's had played mediocre ball during the absence of the three stars. "The hardest part was sitting around for almost two weeks and not playing. I didn't pitch for two weeks because Charlie Finley felt as though he were right, and Joe Rudi didn't hit for two weeks, and Vida Blue missed about five starts in two weeks." The A's went just 6–5 during the absence of the three players. The inactivity also had a prolonged effect on two of the players. Rudi struggled to regain his batting stroke and Blue did not win his next game until July 6, more than three weeks after Finley had initially tried to sell off the three stars.

Off the field, Finley's $10 million suit against the Commissioner's Office would prove futile. In 1977, U.S. District Judge Frank McGarr came down with a ruling in favor of Bowie Kuhn. McGarr cited a pre-existing agreement between the major league owners and the commissioner. Under that agreement, owners had promised never to challenge a commissioner's decision in the courts. In 1978, Finley would file an appeal. The Supreme Court refused to even hear the case, quietly bringing to an end a two-year saga that had begun so loudly with three blockbuster sales—sales that would never come to be.

Bolstered by the returns of three important players, the A's played their best ball of the season in July, winning 17 of 28 games. Sal Bando, who had hit two home runs on the day that Rudi, Fingers, and Blue rejoined the playing ranks, banged seven home runs during a seven-game stretch. The A's also received another boost in manpower. On July 23, Gene Tenace returned to catching for the first time since straining his knee on a stolen base attempt. With Tenace unavailable to play behind the plate, the A's had struggled to find adequate catching. On two occasions, the A's had botched rundown plays when their catchers had failed to cover home plate. The mental errors had contributed directly to two losses.

Unfortunately, the A's bridged July and August by losing six straight games, including five to the Twins. "When you're a fan, you can laugh at this, but when you're an owner, all you can do is cry," Charlie Finley told *The Sporting News*, reacting to the sudden reversal of fortune. "The way they played against Minnesota, losing all five games, was a disgrace. I can't believe it happened." Yet, Finley still believed the A's would catch the first-place Royals. "Kansas City is looking over their shoulders," claimed Finley. "In my opinion, they're going to choke."

In the meantime, Chuck Tanner tried to fight off controversy in the clubhouse. Utilityman Cesar Tovar, on the disabled list since May 31, complained to Marvin Miller of the Players' Association that the A's had refused to activate him, even though he was now healthy enough to play. Tovar claimed that his broken right wrist had healed sufficiently. Such a quick recovery from a major injury typified Tovar, who took pride in playing hurt and returning quickly from injuries. Throughout his career, Tovar had willingly allowed himself to be hit by pitches as a way of reaching first base. "He got hit a lot," says former Twins beat writer Bob Fowler. "He was a very strong guy. He was muscle-bound, very low body fat, if you will. And loved to get hit. He was sort of *wild* that way."

Fowler compares Tovar to former National League infielder Ron Hunt, another master at getting hit by pitches. "He'd show the bruise," Fowler says in describing Tovar's typical routine after being hit. "It was a proud thing with him to get hit and not flinch. He never—no matter even if Nolan Ryan drilled him—he refused to flinch. He'd run to first base [as if to say], 'You can't intimidate me. You can't hurt me.' "

Knowing that he was no longer hurt, Tovar bristled at the A's' decision to keep him disabled. After speaking to Marvin Miller, the A's finally relented and activated the veteran utilityman. In order to make room for Tovar on the 25-man roster, Tanner decided to option pinch-runner Larry Lintz to Tucson. Lintz did not take the news well, engaging Tanner in a shouting match over the demotion.

Another unhappy player, reliever Jim Todd, had a more legitimate reason for complaint. During a 24-game stretch, Todd did not pitch—not even once. Todd suggested that his status as Oakland's player representative (replacing the traded Ken Holtzman) had prompted Charlie Finley to mandate he not be used in any games. Todd asked Tanner for a meeting, but the manager insisted that Finley had played no part in his recent absence from games.

Shortly after Finley's diatribe, in which he had referred to Oakland's play as a "disgrace," the A's assembled a season-high nine-game winning streak to move within seven games of the first-place Royals. The win streak actually prolonged Sal Bando's career in Oakland. Unbelievably, in light of the recent cancellation of player sales by the commissioner, Finley had agreed to make another sale by selling Bando to the Yankees. The Yankees didn't want Bando to play third base—they already had the defensively nimble Graig Nettles to fill that role—but sought a right-handed hitting DH to balance their lineup. When the A's pulled back into the pennant race, Finley canceled the sale of Bando to the Bronx.

The A's stayed within striking distance of the Royals throughout August. On the next to last day of the month, Finley decided to import a veteran bat capable of filling the DH role and providing some power off the bench. Revisiting a transaction he had tried to make a few years earlier, Finley purchased future Hall of Famer

Willie McCovey from the Padres. "The reason for getting McCovey was for getting us to the playoffs," Finley explained point-blank to *The Sporting News*.

Given McCovey's experience and Oakland's need for a left-handed bat, the deal made perfect sense. Two days later, Finley tried to make another transaction, one that made no sense at all. With the A's only seven games back and Sal Bando sharing the league lead in home runs, Finley once again attempted to sell his captain and third baseman—this time to the Rangers. Finley made a verbal commitment on a trade with Texas, contingent on the Rangers' ability to sign Bando to a long-term contract. Bando asked for four years and $600,000. The Rangers said no, killing the deal. The same day, Finley's attorney, Neil Papiano, told reporters that Finley planned to file an injunction in an effort to have Rollie Fingers and Joe Rudi sent to the Red Sox and Vida Blue dispatched to the Yankees. After previously indicating that he felt his team could still make the playoffs, and even after acquiring some pennant-contending help in McCovey, Finley was now acting as if the post-season meant nothing to him.

Although McCovey had batted only .203 for the Padres, he slid quickly into Oakland's designated hitter role, replacing another slumping veteran, Billy Williams, who hinted that he would retire after the season. Williams remained on Oakland's 25-man roster for the moment, but the versatile Cesar Tovar did not. In order to make room for McCovey, the A's released Tovar. Finley likely hadn't forgotten Tovar's complaint to the Players' Association about the A's' refusal to reinstate him from the disabled list earlier in the season.

With 24 games remaining, the A's moved within five games of the first-place Royals. Six head-to-head matchups with Kansas City gave the A's hope that they could catch the Royals before the end of the regular season. On September 14, Finley once again reverted to his playoff-hopeful mode, acquiring veteran first baseman-outfielder Ron Fairly from the Cardinals. Chuck Tanner planned to use "The Mule" as a left-handed pinch-hitter in the late innings, but would soon expand the role of the former Dodger and Expo.

On September 20, the eve of a showdown series between the two leaders in the American League West, the A's trailed the Royals by six games. With the A's no longer having a Catfish Hunter or Ken Holtzman to use in the biggest game of the season, Chuck Tanner fell back on eight-game winner Stan Bahnsen. Hoping to win all three games in order to have a realistic chance of catching the Royals, the A's dropped the first matchup, 3–1. Doug Bird outpitched Bahnsen with six innings of one-run baseball and won for the first time since August 22.

The A's rallied to win the next two games, but still found themselves five games out in the West. After splitting a two-game series with the White Sox and creeping within four and a half games, the A's hosted the Royals in what amounted to a last-gasp series at the Oakland Coliseum. If the A's could sweep all three games, they would still harbor hopes of a sixth consecutive division title.

In the first game, Ron Fairly homered for the third time in the two weeks since being acquired and Sal Bando added his 26th home run, giving the A's an 8–3 win. After Bando homered to lead off the sixth, Dennis Leonard hit Don Baylor with a pitch, precipitating a dugout-clearing brawl and Baylor's ejection. During the melee, Claudell Washington flattened Leonard with a fist to the pitcher's head.

The A's drew within two and a half games when Mike Torrez outdueled Marty Pattin, 1–0, in the second game of the series. Torrez allowed only two hits and retired the final 14 batters he faced. The victory left the A's confident that they could sweep the series, since the Royals would pitch left-hander Larry Gura, one of the least-used hurlers on the Kansas City staff, in the final game.

The A's placed their hopes with disappointing rookie Paul Mitchell. Once considered the key to the Reggie Jackson trade, Mitchell lasted only two innings, having surrendered three runs and six hits. In the meantime, the soft-tossing Gura mastered Oakland's hitters, keeping them off balance with his mix of curveballs and change-ups. Gura shut down the middle of the Oakland order—Joe Rudi, Gene Tenace, Sal Bando, and Don Baylor—pitched a four-hitter, and won a 4–0 shutout decision.

The loss virtually eliminated the A's from playoff contention. The Royals needed just one more victory or A's loss to officially clinch the division title. Two nights later, the Royals fell to the Twins, 4–3, then waited out the results of the game later that evening between the A's and Angels. Thanks to the pitching of Vida Blue and Frank Tanana, the two teams played scoreless baseball over the first 11 innings at the Oakland Coliseum. In the top of the 12th inning, Angels center fielder Rusty Torres, formerly a failed prospect with the Yankees and Indians and batting a mere .206 on the season, cracked a solo home run against Blue. Two singles, sandwiched around an error by Billy North in center field, gave the Angels a 2–0 lead. Journeyman reliever Dick Drago, the same man who had been on the mound when the Red Sox defeated the A's in the '75 playoffs, came on to retire Oakland in the bottom of the inning, ending the game.

For the first time since 1970, the final year of John McNamara's reign, the A's had failed to make the playoffs. Observers and fans of the A's considered what might have been. If only Blue, Joe Rudi, and Rollie Fingers hadn't been forced into exile for a crucial two-week stretch in the middle of the season, the A's might have matched—or outlasted—the Royals for the Western Division title.

After playing out the final two meaningless games of the season, the A's held a small champagne party in the clubhouse of the Oakland Coliseum. Even though the A's had no pennant to celebrate, they had found another occasion to commemorate: the impending freedom of several of the team's stars. The A's' seven free agents-in-waiting purchased 36 bottles of champagne for the players, coaches, and manager Chuck Tanner. "This is to celebrate the liberation of the Oakland Seven," said Billy North, one of the few A's under contract for the following season, in an interview with *The Sporting News*. "I feel sorry for anyone who has to play for this club next year," said Rollie Fingers, who had already announced that he would not return to Oakland. In addition to Fingers, players like Gene Tenace, Campy Campaneris, Sal Bando, Joe Rudi, and Don Baylor couldn't wait to escape from Charlie Finley's prison.

Even a relative newcomer like Willie McCovey seemed anxious to play elsewhere. The future Hall of Famer had refused to start the final game of the season in protest of his lack of playing time down the stretch. Like the others, "Stretch" would soon be saying goodbye to the Bay Area—and to Mr. Finley.

Chapter 32

A Baseball Dynasty

Except for center fielder Billy North, whom he had re-signed to a two-year contract, Charlie Finley allowed almost everyone of his top players to leave while still in the prime of their playing careers. "No telling how many championships we could have won," Sal Bando said several years later in an interview with Sid Bordman of the *Kansas City Star*. "We had everything on the field—speed, pitching, defense, and power. But no management. Some of the things Charlie did were good. But he did more destroying. He destroyed the A's."

As one of the multitude of Oakland free agents, Bando signed a contract with the Milwaukee Brewers. Rollie Fingers and Gene Tenace moved down the coast to the San Diego Padres. Don Baylor and Joe Rudi also moved south—to the California Angels. Campy Campaneris became the starting shortstop for the Texas Rangers. And Willie McCovey returned to his original major league team, the rival San Francisco Giants. "Charlie Finley is going to wind up with nothing," Rudi said in a 1977 interview with sportswriter Ross Newhan. "It's like the good man says, 'You reap what you sow.' And Charlie has sowed only garbage for a lot of years."

Finley's inability and unwillingness to sign any of his free agents sowed a lineup filled with over-the-hill stars and mediocre prospects for 1977. In response to the avalanche of free agent losses, Finley tried to fill in some of the team's growing holes. He traded manager Chuck Tanner—in much the way that the Cleveland Indians and Detroit Tigers had once traded skippers Joe Gordon for Jimmy Dykes—to the Pittsburgh Pirates for 33-year-old catcher Manny Sanguillen, who would succeed the tandem of Gene Tenace and Larry Haney behind the plate. At first base, 35-year-old Dick Allen would replace the combination of Tenace and Tommy Harper for a total of 50 games before opting to retire. After designated hitter Billy Williams decided to retire following the 1976 season, the A's signed veteran slugger Earl Williams (no relation to Billy), at one time a budding star with the Atlanta Braves. With Rollie Fingers now gone, Finley made a trade for 37-year-old reliever Dave Giusti, the relief ace of the Pirates' 1971 World Championship team. The A's tried to fill other gaps with untested minor leaguers like infielder Rob Picciolo, third baseman-outfielder Jim Tyrone, outfielder Mitchell Page, and pitcher Rick Langford. Of the four, only Page and Langford would enjoy success in the major leagues—and mild success at that.

The new mix proved disastrous. The 1977 A's placed last in the American League West, 38 and a half games back of the first-place Kansas City Royals. To make matters worse, the A's finished one-half game off the pace of the newly born Seattle Mariners, one of baseball's two expansion teams. The dynasty, which had reached its peak only three seasons earlier, had given way to a full-fledged on-field embarrassment.

As much as the A's' dynasty accomplished from 1971 to 1975, Sal Bando felt the team could have performed even better had Charlie Finley handled his players differently. "I've seen how people respond to fair treatment," Bando said in a 1985 interview with Sid Bordman. "I know I would have been a better player treated fairly. Reggie [Jackson] was a very good player, but he would have been better. Campy [Campaneris] was such a sensitive person. As good as he was, he could have been better."

Although Campaneris, Bando, Rudi, Jackson, Gene Tenace, Catfish Hunter, Ken Holtzman, and Rollie Fingers had all turned 30 or older by 1977, the A's likely would have contended for the American League West title for at least two more seasons—assuming that Finley had retained most or all of his free agents and had not made the disastrous trade involving Jackson and Holtzman. The Royals, a good young team in the midst of winning three straight division titles, would have certainly posed a challenge, but the A's would have remained the favorites in the West. In the East, the New York Yankees would not have gained the services of Jackson, Hunter, and Holtzman, and likely would not have won the American League pennant in 1977 and '78. It's all supposition, of course, but it's not unreasonable to suggest that if the A's had retained Hunter all along, they might have accomplished more than a division title and a runner-up finish in 1975 and '76, respectively. And without the implementation and effects of collectively-bargained free agency, which cost the team the remainder of its nucleus of stars, the A's could have won two more pennants and World Championships in 1977 and '78.

By 1979, age had caught up with several of Oakland's former stars. Catfish Hunter struggled to a 2–9 mark with the Yankees and retired after the season. Ken Holtzman pitched poorly in 33 games with the Chicago Cubs and also called it quits. Sal Bando slumped to a nine-home run, 43-RBI season in Milwaukee. Joe Rudi batted only .242 with 61 RBIs for the Angels. Rollie Fingers fell off to 13 saves and a 4.50 ERA in San Diego. Campy Campaneris split the season between Texas and California, batting .230 with a paltry 13 stolen bases. Of the former A's-turned-free-agents, only Gene Tenace and Reggie Jackson enjoyed productive seasons in 1979.

Of the slumping players, only Fingers would bounce back in 1980, remaining an effective reliever for four more seasons. Jackson remained a legitimate star, batting a career-high .300 in 1980 while leading the American League with 41 home runs. The other Oakland ex-patriots, however, ceased being regular players or left the game entirely. For those speculating about continuing Oakland supremacy into the 1980s, the argument had largely become irrelevant.

Still, the A's accomplished more during the 1970s than any other major league team at that time. As the team's owner and general manager beginning in the 1960s, Charlie Finley realized that he was a relative novice at baseball. He listened intently to his scouts—people like Joe Bowman, Dan Carnevale, Tom Giordano, Clyde Kluttz, Art Lilly, Don Pries, Jack Sanford, and others—who told him which amateur players to pursue as free agents and which ones to draft. As a result, the A's developed future stars like Bando, Vida Blue, Campaneris, Fingers, Hunter, Jackson, Blue Moon Odom, and Tenace. In later years, a more confident and penurious Finley pushed out many of his veteran scouts and tended to ignore the advice of those he still employed. Yet, he still managed to exhibit a deft hand in making trades and signing bargain basement role players. "I have to give the guy a lot of credit," says Ted Kubiak. "I mean, he put some teams together. For someone who came into baseball that didn't know anything, he really developed and did a lot of talking, did a lot of phone calling."

In 1971, Finley made perhaps his best trade, sending an underachieving Rick Monday to the Cubs for the enigmatic Ken Holtzman, who would win 77 games over four seasons in Oakland. Finley also engineered the five-player deal that brought a young left-handed power hitter (Mike Epstein) and an important left-handed reliever (Darold Knowles) to the Bay Area. Without Epstein, the A's might not have won the American League West—and therefore might not have even qualified for the 1972 World Series. In 1973, the A's might not have won the World Championship without Knowles, who pitched in all seven games of the Series against the New York Mets.

After the 1972 season, Finley acquired a much-needed center fielder in Billy North for an aging middle reliever in Bob Locker. In his first four years with the A's, North played a solid center field, stole 212 bases, and become both a capable leadoff man and No. 2 hitter. Finley also swung unheralded deals for key role players like Matty Alou, Deron Johnson, and Horacio Pina, who would fill important holes in the outfield, at designated hitter, and in middle relief during the 1972 and '73 seasons.

The A's of 1972, '73, and '74 tend to be grouped into one single unit. The core of the team—Tenace, Green, Campaneris, Bando, Rudi, Jackson, Hunter, Blue, Holtzman, and Fingers—played on all three championship teams. Yet, the secondary players on each of those teams were different, and each team faced unique obstacles in winning the World Series. So which one of the three teams was the best?

"I might have to say the first year," Ted Kubiak says in selecting the 1972 team, "only because we were not picked to win [the Series]. We were facing the 'Big Red Machine' there that time, the beginnings of it anyway. We were the long-haired kids coming in there being the underdogs. It was a very tough Series." The 1972 A's also overcame serious obstacles in defeating the heavily-favored Reds. Oakland played all seven games of the World Series without its marquee position player, Reggie Jackson, and without its best left-handed reliever, Darold Knowles. "I personally thought that the Mets and the Dodgers were not that good a club that we played [as compared with the Reds]," Kubiak continues, "and I think everybody might say that—I don't know. We came back home from New York down three games to two, knowing that we had to win. It was up in the air, but I just really had the feeling we were gonna come back and win. And the Dodgers didn't show us anything; I don't think they showed us much at all. We didn't think they were that good defensively."

Sal Bando casts his vote for the team that defeated the Mets in the middle of the championship run. "We became more of a stable club in '73, an experienced club in '73," claims Bando, who says the '72 team suffered from having so many player transactions and personnel changes. "I thought the '73 team, when healthy, was the best, simply because I thought we had more depth in the bullpen in '73. I thought we were a complete team; there wasn't anything we did not have. We had speed; we had power; we had defense; we had pitching. We had great depth in the bullpen; we had [Darold] Knowles and [Paul] Lindblad as left-handers, we had [Rollie] Fingers and [Horacio] Piña. I thought Horacio was kind of the difference."

In 1973, the side-arming Pina pitched 88 innings as the primary right-handed long reliever. Pina's 2.76 ERA ranked second among all A's relievers, and his effectiveness allowed Dick Williams to cut down Fingers' heavy workload during the season.

Prior to the Yankees of 1996–2001 (who bore a striking on-field resemblance to the A's in terms of strong pitching, generally good-but-not-great offenses, and an uncanny ability to win close post-season games), should we classify the A's of the early 1970s as the last true dynasty in major league baseball? First, we need to attach a definition to the word *dynasty*. According to the *American Heritage College Dictionary,* a dynasty is a "succession of rulers from the same family or line," or a "family or group that maintains power for several generations." Obviously, neither definition applies specifically to a *sports* dynasty, a subjective term that has been created by sportswriters and broadcasters in an attempt to describe teams that have won a number of championships and thereby place those teams in proper historical context. Yet, if we apply the first definition from *American Heritage* and substitute the word *champions* for *rulers*, and replace the word *family* with *organization,* we may have come close to establishing an appropriate definition of a sports dynasty: "a succession of *champions* from the same *organization.*"

If we use this newly created definition, the key word becomes *succession*. A succession can also be thought of as a *sequence*. One of the definitions of the word *sequence* involves the playing of card games, where a sequence occurs with at least "*three* or more playing cards in consecutive order." So we might say that *three* becomes the magic number—in terms of three consecutive World Championships.

In between the A's of 1971–75 and the Yankees of 1996–2000, only three teams won as many as three consecutive divisional crowns—the Yankees, Toronto Blue Jays, and Braves—but no club won more than two straight World Championships. The Reds, Yankees, and Blue Jays each defended their titles once before succumbing in the third season.

Since the mid-seventies, several teams have been categorized as "dynasties." In the 1990s, a few broadcasters and writers have argued that the Braves deserve the dynasty distinction. From 1991 to 2001, the Braves won 10 out of a possible 11 divisional titles, four National League pennants, and one World Series. The Braves captured National League flags in 1991 and '92, but lost to an inferior Philadelphia Phillies team in 1993 before recovering to win three more league titles. Most importantly, the Braves won only one World Series (1991) during the 11-year span, while losing one Series in four straight games (1999) and losing another Series to an inferior opponent (1996). Given any definition, one World Championship in a span of over a decade hardly qualifies a team for dynasty status.

The Blue Jays won three straight American League East crowns, two pennants, and two World Series during their three-year reign from 1991 to 1993. Yet, a third-place, sub-.500 finish in the strike year of 1994 signaled the end of the Jays' success, as the team failed to finish higher than second for the balance of the decade. The Jays' accomplishments, while noteworthy, fall short of the demands of our dynasty requirements.

The Yankees experienced a strikingly similar run to the Blue Jays in the late 1970s. After winning the American League pennant in 1976, the Yankees lost to the Reds in an embarrassing and one-sided four-game sweep. Bolstered by the addition of free agent right fielder Reggie Jackson, the Yankees won two more pennants in '77 and '78 and elevated themselves to the level of World Champions. In 1979, the Yankees fell well short of the post-season, finishing in fourth place, 13 and a half games out in the American League East. So from 1976 to '78, the trophy count for the "Bronx Zoo" Yankees stood as follows: three divisional titles, two American League pennants, and two World Series crowns. The numbers are impressive enough to put the Yankees close to dynasty contention. Close, but just a bit short of our requirement of three consecutive World Championships.

Still, we might be able to permit some leeway in the discussion of what constitutes a dynasty. In returning to our original definition of a dynasty, the word *succession* implies a *sequence of three* that is continuous and uninterrupted. But what about a team that wins only *two* consecutive World Championships? If such a team could accomplish something *additional*, such as reigning supreme over its division or league for a longer stretch of seasons—without interruption—then perhaps we should categorize this team as a dynasty, at least under the less rigid interpretation. Under this new interpretation, we might be tempted to classify the 1970s Yankees as a dynasty—if only they had won a fourth straight division in 1979 after their back-to-back World Series titles. We might consider doing the same with the Blue Jays of the 1990s—if they had managed to tack on a fourth consecutive division title after their two World Championship seasons. Two World Series crowns, bookended by *four* division titles, would likely have been enough to place the Yankees or the Blue Jays at the dynasty level. Yet, without a fourth division win, just as without a third World Series championship, the Yankees and Jays fall just short.

Some baseball historians have classified the Cincinnati Reds of 1970, '72, '75, and '76 as a dynasty. Yet, the Reds lost the World Series in 1972 (to the A's, no less), and did not even qualify for the playoffs in 1971, '73, or '74. How then can the Reds of the 1970s be described as a true dynasty, when they did not *continuously* win World Championships, and did not *continuously* win division titles or pennants for a span of at least three seasons?

The Reds of 1975 and '76 represent two of the most dominant teams in major league history. The "Big Red Machine" featured one of the most fearsome offensive lineups ever, comparable to the 1927 and 1961 Yankees and the 1930 Philadelphia A's. Yet, two straight World Championships, even ones as impressive as the Reds of '75 and '76, hardly constitute a *succession or sequence*. Therefore, if we continue to enforce our original definition and line of reasoning, winning back-to-back World Series by itself (no matter how dominantly a team might have performed) does not qualify one as a dynasty. And with no surrounding divisional titles or pennants, the Reds fail to qualify on the less rigid count, as well. The Reds of 1974 did not even make the playoffs, finishing four games back of the Dodgers in the National League West. In 1977, the Reds once again fell short of the post-season, finished second to the Dodgers, a full 10 games back.

In contrast to the Reds of the seventies, the A's won three straight World Series and American League pennants, piggybacked by five consecutive divisional crowns. This succession of winning pennants and World Championships—much longer than that of the Reds, the 1970s Yankees, and the 1990s Blue Jays and Braves—coupled with continuous divisional supremacy, smacks of a true dynasty. After all, the A's won consistently over a period of *five* uninterrupted seasons, while also managing to outlast all other major league teams for *three* uninterrupted seasons.

Yet, when historians refer to dynasties of the 1970s, they inevitably mention the Reds first, followed by only a fleeting mention of the A's. Why? The answer can be found in the *way* the Reds won in 1975 and '76. The Reds won 108 games in 1975, a full 20 games over the second-place Dodgers, before outlasting the Boston Red Sox in arguably the most compelling World Series ever. The following summer, the Reds won 102 games, 10 lengths in front of Los Angeles. The "Machine" then annihilated a very good Yankees team in the Fall Classic, four games to none.

In contrast, the A's of 1972–74 never won more than 94 games in the regular season and never staked claim to a divisional title by more than six games. (In some ways, the A's were like the Yankees of 1996–2001, who similarly didn't dominate the American League during that span of regular season performances, except for their 114-win runaway in 1998.) In the World Series, the A's failed to sweep a National League opponent, twice winning in seven games and once in five games. Yet, the A's won when they *had* to. For example, Oakland snared two deciding fifth games in the American League Championship Series and two seventh games in the World Series. In fact, the A's never lost a decisive fifth game of a playoff series, or a Game Seven in the World Series, during the 1970s.

A few years ago, Rollie Fingers provided an explanation for the A's' ability to win such "elimination" games. "At the end of the season, we'd be really hungry for World Series checks because Charlie Finley didn't pay us much," Fingers said. "A lot of us there got a taste of it early in our careers, so we wanted to get there again and again and again."

Even if supporters of Cincinnati were to concede that the Reds were not a true dynasty, they might argue that the "Big Red Machine" teams of 1975 and '76 were better and more dominating teams than the A's. The two teams did not meet head-to-head—well, not exactly. In 1972, the A's, playing without the injured Reggie Jackson and Darold Knowles, defeated a Reds team that was similar to the clubs of 1975 and '76. Of the eight regulars on the 1972 Reds, six played for the championship teams of 1975–76—Tony Perez, Joe Morgan, Dave Concepcion, Pete Rose, Cesar Geronimo, and Johnny Bench. Only two regulars were inherently different: Ken Griffey Sr. succeeded Bobby Tolan in the outfield, and George Foster essentially replaced third baseman Denis Menke, with Rose moving from left field to third base to accommodate Foster's bat in the lineup. On the pitching staff, the top three starters—Gary Nolan, Don Gullett, and Jack Billingham—remained the same, as did two of the key relievers—Pedro Borbon and Clay Carroll. Therefore, the A's of 1972, playing without two of their most instrumental players, defeated a team that could be regarded as the direct predecessor to the Reds of 1975 and '76.

Yet, *on paper,* the Reds of the mid-seventies were clearly better than Cincinnati's 1972 team, thanks to the addition of Foster's right-handed bat and a deeper bullpen that featured newcomers Rawly Eastwick and Will McEnaney. So, how would the A's of the early 1970s have fared against those Reds of the mid-seventies? As a means of comparison, let's assemble composite lineups of the A's of 1972–74 and the Reds of 1975–76.

Position:	A's player	Reds player
Catcher	Gene Tenace	*Johnny Bench*
First Base	Mike Epstein	*Tony Perez*
Second Base	Dick Green	*Joe Morgan*
Shortstop	Campy Campaneris	*Dave Concepcion*
Third Base	Sal Bando	*Pete Rose*
Left Field	Joe Rudi	*George Foster*
Center field	*Billy North*	Cesar Geronimo
Right Field	*Reggie Jackson*	Ken Griffey Sr.

The head-to-head analysis of the lineups heavily favors the Reds. Cincinnati rates advantages at catcher, all of the infield positions, and left field. The A's come out ahead at only two positions, center field and right field. While such an analysis is fun to create and provides an entertaining conversation piece, it really does little to tell us which is the better team. Baseball is not a game where position players match up, like they would in basketball or football. First basemen do not "lock heads," second basemen don't guard each other, and outfielders don't set picks on one another.

Baseball's matchups involve *pitchers* vs. *hitters*, and vice-versa. It is here where the A's gain an advantage. Oakland's superior starting pitching poses a problem—even for Cincinnati's stacked Hall of Fame lineup. In short series, teams with strong pitching tend to handcuff teams filled with power hitters. While Gary Nolan, Don Gullett, Jack Billingham, and Fredie Norman all rank as competent starters for Cincinnati, they would be hard-pressed to crack the front of Oakland's rotation of Catfish Hunter, Vida Blue, and Ken Holtzman. In the bullpen, relievers like Pedro Borbon, Clay Carroll, and Rawly Eastwick would probably rate no higher than second-best among the Oakland relievers, behind Rollie Fingers.

An examination of the benches also tilts in the direction of Oakland. A reserve core of Dave Duncan, Mike Hegan, Don Mincher, Ted Kubiak, Deron Johnson, Vic Davalillo, and Matty and Jesus Alou gives the A's speed, excellent defensive backups at catcher, first base, and the middle infield, four solid singles-hitting pinch-hitters, and two legitimate power hitters. The Reds' bench—consisting of Bill Plummer, Dan Driessen, Bob Bailey, Darrel Chaney, Ed Armbrister, Terry Crowley, and Merv Rettenmund—was good, but not nearly as powerful or as deep as the Oakland contingent.

So which teams were better, the A's of the early seventies or the Reds of the middle seventies? They never played each other in real games, only in virtual reality, so we'll never know for sure. And even if they did play head-to-head in a World Series, the end result wouldn't necessarily prove that one team was essentially better—only that one team had performed more effectively in a short series.

More to the point, a tangible examination of each team's actual accomplishments proves that the A's did achieve more over a longer period of time. The A's had more collective success than the Reds, when factoring in both regular season consistency and post-season efficiency. When one adds up the results, Cincinnati's two divisional crowns, two league pennants, and two World Championships in two years are not as impressive as Oakland's five divisional crowns, three league pennants, and three World Series victories over five years. The bottom line is this: two seasons do not make a dynasty; five seasons do.

Rollie Fingers offers little hesitation when asked about the best ballclubs that he played on during his Hall of Fame career. "Those years, we were the best team I've ever seen," Fingers says of the A's of 1972 to '74. "We had a solid bench, pitching, hitting, speed, everything."

"I can't explain that club," says Ted Kubiak. "It was just a unique club, as far as what they could do. It was almost like Dick [Williams] would send them out there and that was it. I mean he used to sit in the dugout and watch them play. Geez, pitchers getting guys out easy; players were always in the right position defensively."

In spite of off-the-field disagreements and never-ending controversies, the A's played to maximum efficiency once the games began. "When you were on the field," says Kubiak, "I mean, it was like one big gigantic unit. And the thing that amazed me was how well they played the game. You talk all the time about not making mistakes and hitting cut-off men and being able to pitch guys in a certain way. I mean, that club was just unbelievable."

Appendices

Appendix A

1971 Oakland A's (Regular Season Statistics)

Players

Regulars	Gam.	AB	R	H	HR	RBI	BA	OBP	SLG	SB
Duncan, Dave (c)	103	363	39	92	15	40	.253	.309	.419	1
Davis, Tommy (1b)	79	219	26	71	3	42	.324	.368	.411	7
Green, Dick (2b)	144	475	58	116	12	49	.244	.321	.354	1
Campaneris, Campy (ss)	134	569	80	143	5	47	.251	.290	.323	34
Bando, Sal (3b)	153	538	75	146	24	94	.271	.380	.452	3
Rudi, Joe (lf)	127	513	62	137	10	52	.267	.306	.386	3
Monday, Rick (cf)	116	355	53	87	18	56	.245	.337	.439	6
Jackson, Reggie (rf)	150	567	87	157	32	80	.277	.355	.508	16

Catchers	Gam.	AB	R	H	HR	RBI	BA	OBP	SLG	SB
Blefary, Curt	50	101	15	22	5	12	.218	.325	.386	0
Fernandez, Frank (2 stints)	4	9	1	1	0	1	.111	.200	.222?	0
Tenace, Gene	65	179	26	49	7	25	.274	.381	.430	2

Infielders	Gam.	AB	R	H	HR	RBI	BA	OBP	SLG	SB
Anderson, Dwain	16	37	3	10	0	3	.270	.372	.378	0
Brown, Larry	70	189	14	37	1	9	.196	.228	.233	1
Clark, Ron	2	1	0	0	0	0	.000	.500	.000	0
Epstein, Mike	104	329	43	77	18	51	.234	.368	.438	0
Garrett, Adrian	14	21	1	3	1	2	.143	.308	.286	0
Hegan, Mike	65	55	5	13	0	3	.236	.300	.291	1
LaRussa, Tony	23	8	3	0	0	0	.000	.000	.000	0
Mincher, Don	28	92	9	22	2	8	.239	.375	.391	1
Webster, Ramon	7	5	0	0	0	0	.000	.000	.000	0

Outfielders	Gam.	AB	R	H	HR	RBI	BA	OBP	SLG	SB
Alou, Felipe	2	8	0	2	0	0	.250	.250	.375	0
Hendrick, George	42	114	8	27	0	8	.237	.256	.289	0
Hovley, Steve	24	27	3	3	0	3	.111	.314	.185	2
Mangual, Angel	94	287	32	82	4	30	.286	.326	.362	1

Pitchers										
Hunter, Catfish	38	103	14	36	1	12	.350	.362	.408	1

Pitchers

Starters	Gam.	ERA	W	L	S	GS	CG	IP	H	BB	SO
*Blue, Vida	39	1.82	24	8	0	39	24	312.0	209	88	301
Hunter, Catfish	37	2.96	21	11	0	37	16	273.2	225	80	181
Segui, Diego	26	3.14	10	8	0	21	5	146.1	122	63	81
Dobson, Chuck	30	3.81	15	5	0	30	7	189.0	185	71	100
Odom, Blue Moon	25	4.29	10	12	0	25	3	140.2	147	71	69

Relievers	Gam.	ERA	W	L	S	GS	CG	IP	H	BB	SO
*Gardner, Rob	4	2.35	0	0	0	1	0	7.2	8	3	5
*Roland, Jim	31	3.18	1	3	1	0	0	45.1	34	19	30
*Knowles, D.	43	3.59	5	2	7	0	0	52.2	40	16	40
*Lindblad, Paul	8	3.94	1	0	0	0	0	16.0	18	2	4
Grant Mudcat	15	1.98	1	0	3	0	0	27.1	25	6	13
Locker, Bob	47	2.86	7	2	6	0	0	72.1	68	19	46
Fingers, Rollie	48	2.99	4	6	17	8	2	129.1	94	30	98
Klimkowski, R.	26	3.38	2	2	2	0	0	45.1	37	23	25
Patterson, D.	4	7.94	0	0	0	0	0	5.2	5	4	2
Panther, Jim	4	11.12	0	1	0	0	0	5.2	10	5	4
Lachemann, M.	1	54.00	0	0	0	0	0	.1	2	1	0

Appendix B

1972 Oakland A's (Regular Season Statistics)

Players

Regulars	Gam.	AB	R	H	HR	RBI	BA	OBP	SLG	SB
Duncan, Dave (c)	121	403	39	88	19	59	.218	.287	.392	0
Epstein, Mike (1b)	138	455	63	123	26	70	.270	.378	.490	0
Cullen, Tim (2b)	72	142	10	37	0	15	.261	.286	.331	0
Campaneris, Campy (ss)	149	625	85	150	8	32	.240	.279	.325	52
Bando, Sal (3b)	152	535	64	126	15	77	.236	.342	.368	3
Rudi, Joe (lf)	147	593	94	181	19	75	.305	.348	.486	3
Mangual, Angel (cf)	91	272	19	67	5	32	.246	.286	.364	0
Jackson, Reggie (rf)	135	499	72	132	25	75	.265	.352	.473	9

Catchers	Gam.	AB	R	H	HR	RBI	BA	OBP	SLG	SB
Blefary, Curt	8	11	1	5	0	1	.455	.455	.636	0
Haney, Larry	5	4	0	0	0	0	.000	.000	.000	0
Tenace, Gene	82	227	22	51	5	32	.225	.307	.339	0

Infielders	Gam.	AB	R	H	HR	RBI	BA	OBP	SLG	SB
Anderson, Dwain	3	7	2	0	0	0	.000	.125	.000	0
Brown, Larry	47	142	11	26	0	4	.183	.252	.197	0
Cepeda, Orlando	3	3	0	0	0	0	.000	.000	.000	0
Clark, Ron	14	15	1	4	0	1	.267	.353	.400	0
Garrett, Adrian	14	11	0	0	0	0	.000	.083	.000	0
Green, Dick	26	42	1	12	0	3	.286	.348	.357	0
Hegan, Mike	98	79	13	26	1	5	.329	.384	.430	1
Kubiak, Ted	51	94	14	17	0	8	.181	.252	.245	0
Marquez, Gonzalo	23	21	2	8	0	4	.381	.480	.381	1
Martinez, Marty	22	40	3	5	0	1	.125	.186	.125	0
Maxvill, Dal	27	36	2	9	0	1	.250	.270	.278	0
McNulty, Bill	4	10	0	1	0	0	.100	.250	.100	0
Mincher, Don	47	54	2	8	0	5	.148	.281	.167	0

Outfielders	Gam.	AB	R	H	HR	RBI	BA	OBP	SLG	SB
Alou, Matty	32	121	11	34	1	16	.281	.346	.347	2
Alyea, Brant	20	31	3	6	1	2	.194	.265	.323	0
Brooks, Bobby	15	39	4	7	0	5	.179	.319	.179	0
Brown, Ollie	20	54	5	13	1	4	.241	.317	.315	1
Hendrick, George	58	121	10	22	4	15	.182	.208	.306	3
Shamsky, Art	8	7	0	0	0	0	.000	.125	.000	0
Voss, Bill	40	97	10	22	1	5	.227	.299	.330	0

Pinch-Runners	Gam.	AB	R	H	HR	RBI	BA	OBP	SLG	SB
Lewis, Allan	24	10	5	2	0	2	.200	.200	.300	8

Pitchers

Starters	Gam.	ERA	W	L	S	GS	CG	IP	H	BB	SO
Hunter, Catfish	38	2.04	21	7	0	37	16	295.1	200	70	191
Odom, Blue Moon	31	2.50	15	6	0	30	4	194.1	164	87	86
*Holtzman, Ken	39	2.51	19	11	0	37	16	265.1	232	52	134
*Blue, Vida	25	2.80	6	10	0	23	5	151.0	117	48	111
*Hamilton, Dave	25	2.93	6	6	0	14	1	101.1	94	31	55
McLain, Denny	5	6.04	1	2	0	5	0	22.1	32	8	8

Relievers	Gam.	ERA	W	L	S	GS	CG	IP	H	BB	SO
*Kilkenny, M.	1	0.00	0	0	0	0	0	1.0	0	0	0
*Knowles, D.	54	1.37	5	1	11	0	0	65.2	49	37	36
*Roland, Jim	2	3.86	0	0	0	0	0	2.1	5	0	0
*Shaw, Don	3	16.88	0	1	0	0	0	5.1	12	2	4
Waslewski, G.	8	2.04	0	3	0	0	0	17.2	12	8	8
Fingers, Rollie	65	2.51	11	9	21	0	0	111.1	85	32	113
Locker, Bob	56	2.65	6	1	10	0	0	78.0	69	16	47
Horlen, Joel	32	3.00	3	4	1	6	0	84.0	74	20	58
Segui, Diego	7	3.57	0	1	0	3	0	22.2	25	7	11

Appendix C

1973 Oakland A's (Regular Season Statistics)

Players

Regulars	Gam.	AB	R	H	HR	RBI	BA	OBP	SLG	SB
Fosse, Ray (c)	143	492	37	126	7	52	.256	.293	.354	2
Tenace, Gene (1b)	160	510	83	132	24	84	.259	.391	.443	2
Green, Dick (2b)	133	332	33	87	3	42	.262	.310	.340	0
Campaneris, Campy (ss)	151	601	89	150	4	46	.250	.311	.318	34
Bando, Sal (3b)	162	592	97	170	29	98	.287	.378	.498	4
Rudi, Joe (lf)	120	437	53	118	12	66	.270	.320	.414	0
North, Billy (cf)	146	554	98	158	5	34	.285	.376	.348	53
Jackson, Reggie (rf)	151	539	99	158	32	117	.293	.387	.531	22
Johnson, Deron (dh)	131	464	61	114	19	81	.246	.332	.407	0

Catchers	Gam.	AB	R	H	HR	RBI	BA	OBP	SLG	SB
Haney, Larry	2	2	0	1	0	0	.500	.500	.500	0
Hosley, Tim	13	14	3	3	0	2	.214	.313	.214	0
Morales, Jose	6	14	0	4	0	1	.286	.333	.357	0

Infielders	Gam.	AB	R	H	HR	RBI	BA	OBP	SLG	SB
Andrews, Mike	18	21	1	4	0	0	.190	.292	.238	0
Bourque, Pat	23	42	8	8	2	9	.190	.404	.476	0
Garner, Phil	9	5	0	0	0	0	.000	.000	.000	0
Hegan, Mike	75	71	8	13	1	5	.183	.237	.254	0
Kubiak, Ted	106	182	15	40	3	17	.220	.268	.313	1
Marquez, Gonzalo	23	25	1	6	0	2	.240	.240	.280	0
Maxvill, Dal	29	19	0	4	0	1	.211	.250	.211	0
McKinney, Rich	48	65	9	16	1	7	.246	.319	.338	0
Trillo, Manny	17	12	0	3	0	3	.250	.250	.417	0

Outfielders	Gam.	AB	R	H	HR	RBI	BA	OBP	SLG	SB
Alou, Jesus	36	108	10	33	1	11	.306	.318	.361	0
Carty, Rico	7	8	1	2	1	1	.250	.400	.750	0
Conigliaro, Billy	48	110	5	22	0	14	.200	.261	.255	1
Davalillo, Vic	38	64	5	12	0	4	.188	.224	.203	0
Johnstone, Jay	23	28	1	3	0	3	.107	.167	.143	0
Mangual, Angel	74	192	20	43	3	13	.224	.259	.302	1

Pinch-Runners	Gam.	AB	R	H	HR	RBI	BA	OBP	SLG	SB
Lewis, Allan	35	0	16	0	0	0	—	—	—	7

Pitchers

Starters	Gam.	ERA	W	L	S	GS	CG	IP	H	BB	SO
*Holtzman, Ken	40	2.97	21	13	0	40	16	297.1	275	66	157
*Blue, Vida	37	3.28	20	9	0	37	13	263.2	214	105	158
Hunter, Catfish	36	3.34	21	5	0	36	11	256.1	222	69	124
*Hamilton, Dave	16	4.39	6	4	0	11	1	69.2	74	24	34
Odom, Blue Moon	30	4.49	5	12	0	24	3	150.1	153	67	83

Relievers	Gam.	ERA	W	L	S	GS	CG	IP	H	BB	SO
*Knowles, D.	52	3.09	6	8	9	5	1	99.0	87	49	46
*Lindblad, Paul	36	3.69	1	5	2	3	0	78.0	89	28	33
*Gardner, Rob	3	4.91	0	0	0	0	0	7.1	10	4	2
Fingers, Rollie	62	1.92	7	8	22	2	0	126.2	107	39	110
Pina, Horacio	47	2.76	6	3	8	0	0	88.0	58	34	41
Abbott, Glenn	5	3.86	1	0	0	3	1	18.2	16	7	6
Dobson, Chuck	1	7.71	0	1	0	1	0	2.1	6	2	3

Appendix D

1974 Oakland A's (Regular Season Statistics)

Players

Regulars	Gam.	AB	R	H	HR	RBI	BA	OBP	SLG	SB
Tenace, Gene (c)	158	484	71	102	26	73	.211	.370	.411	2
Rudi, Joe (1b)	158	593	73	174	22	99	.293	.337	.484	2
Green, Dick (2b)	100	287	20	61	2	22	.213	.269	.275	2
Campaneris, Campy (ss)	134	527	77	153	2	41	.290	.348	.366	34
Bando, Sal (3b)	146	498	84	121	22	103	.243	.360	.426	2
Washington, Claudell (lf)	73	221	16	63	0	19	.285	.328	.376	6
North, Billy (cf)	149	543	79	141	4	33	.260	.348	.337	**54**
Jackson, Reggie (rf)	148	506	90	146	29	93	.289	.396	.514	25
Mangual, Angel (dh)	115	365	37	85	9	43	.233	.267	.367	3

Catchers	Gam.	AB	R	H	HR	RBI	BA	OBP	SLG	SB
Fosse, Ray	69	204	20	40	4	23	.196	.244	.324	1
Haney, Larry	76	121	12	20	2	3	.165	.185	.248	1
Hosley, Tim	11	7	3	2	0	1	.286	.375	.286	

Infielders	Gam.	AB	R	H	HR	RBI	BA	OBP	SLG	SB
Bourque, Pat	73	96	6	22	1	16	.229	.333	.302	0
Donaldson, John	10	15	1	2	0	0	.133	.133	.133	0
Garner, Phil	30	28	4	5	0	1	.179	.207	.214	1
Holt, Jim	30	42	1	6	0	0	.143	.182	.143	0
Johnson, Deron	50	174	16	34	7	23	.195	.243	.345	1
Kubiak, Ted	99	220	22	46	0	18	.209	.269	.223	1
Maxvill, Dal	60	52	3	10	0	2	.192	.300	.192	0
McKinney, Rich	5	7	0	1	0	0	.143	.143	.143	0
Pitts, Gaylen	18	41	4	10	0	3	.244	.326	.317	0
Trillo, Manny	21	33	3	5	0	2	.152	.222	.152	0

Outfielders

	Gam.	AB	R	H	HR	RBI	BA	OBP	SLG	SB
Alou, Jesus	96	220	13	59	2	15	.268	.291	.332	0
Davalillo, Vic	17	23	0	4	0	1	.174	.240	.174	0
Summers, Champ	20	24	2	3	0	3	.125	.160	.167	0

Pinch-Runners

	Gam.	AB	R	H	HR	RBI	BA	OBP	SLG	SB
Washington, Herb	92	0	29	0	0	0	---	---	---	29

Pitchers

Starters

	Gam.	ERA	W	L	S	GS	CG	IP	H	BB	SO
Hunter, Catfish	41	2.49	25	12	0	41	23	318.1	268	46	143
Abbott, Glenn	19	3.00	5	7	0	17	3	96.0	89	34	38
*Holtzman, Ken	39	3.07	19	17	0	38	9	255.1	273	51	117
*Hamilton, Dave	29	3.15	7	4	0	18	1	117.0	104	48	69
*Blue, Vida	40	3.25	17	15	0	40	12	282.1	246	98	174

Relievers

	Gam.	ERA	W	L	S	GS	CG	IP	H	BB	SO
*Lindblad, Paul	45	2.06	4	4	6	2	0	100.2	85	30	46
*Knowles, D.	45	4.22	3	3	3	1	0	53.1	61	35	18
Parsons, Bill	4	0.00	0	0	0	0	0	2.0	1	3	2
Fingers, Rollie	76	2.65	9	5	18	0	0	119.0	104	29	95
Hooten, Leon	6	3.24	0	0	0	0	0	8.1	6	4	1
Odom, Blue Moon	34	3.81	1	5	1	5	1	87.1	85	52	52

Appendix E

1975 Oakland A's (Regular Season Statistics)

Players

Regulars	Gam.	AB	R	H	HR	RBI	BA	OBP	SLG	SB
Tenace, Gene (c)	158	498	83	127	29	87	.255	.398	.464	7
Rudi, Joe (1b)	126	468	66	130	21	75	.278	.339	.494	2
Garner, Phil (2b)	160	488	46	120	6	54	.246	.296	.346	4
Campaneris, Campy (ss)	137	509	69	135	4	46	.265	.339	.330	24
Bando, Sal (3b)	160	562	64	129	15	78	.230	.338	.356	7
Washington, Claudell (lf)	148	590	86	182	10	77	.308	.349	.424	40
North, Billy (cf)	140	524	74	143	1	43	.273	.374	.330	30
Jackson, Reggie (rf)	157	593	91	150	36	104	.253	.332	.511	17
Williams, Billy (dh)	155	520	68	127	23	81	.244	.343	.419	0

Catchers	Gam.	AB	R	H	HR	RBI	BA	OBP	SLG	SB
Fosse, Ray	82	136	14	19	0	12	.140	.193	.191	0
Haney, Larry	47	26	3	5	1	2	.192	.222	.308	0
Sands, Charlie	3	2	0	1	0	0	.500	.667	.500	0

Infielders	Gam.	AB	R	H	HR	RBI	BA	OBP	SLG	SB
Grabarkewitz, Billy	6	2	0	0	0	0	.000	.000	.000	0
Harper, Tommy	34	69	11	22	2	7	.319	.373	.464	7
Holt, Jim	102	123	7	27	2	16	.220	.294	.293	0
Kubiak, Ted	20	28	2	7	0	4	.250	.300	.286	0
Martinez, Ted	87	86	1	15	0	3	.172	.200	.172	1
Maxvill, Dal	20	10	1	2	0	0	.200	.200	.200	0
McKinney, Rich	8	7	0	1	0	2	.143	.250	.143	0
Pitts Gaylen	10	3	1	1	0	1	.333	.333	.667	0
Sandt, Tommy	1	0	0	0	0	0	—	—	—	0
Tovar, Cesar	19	26	5	6	0	3	.231	.310	.269	4
Walling, Denny	6	8	0	1	0	2	.125	.125	.250	0

416

Outfielders	Gam.	AB	R	H	HR	RBI	BA	OBP	SLG	SB
Alexander, Matt	63	10	16	1	0	0	.100	.182	.100	17
Chant, Charlie	5	5	1	0	0	0	.000	.000	.000	0
Hopkins, Don	82	6	25	1	0	0	.167	.375	.167	21
Mangual, Angel	62	109	13	24	1	6	.220	.241	.275	0

Pinch-Runners	Gam.	AB	R	H	HR	RBI	BA	OBP	SLG	SB
Washington, Herb	13	0	4	0	0	0	---	---	---	2

Pitchers

Starters	Gam.	ERA	W	L	S	GS	CG	IP	H	BB	SO
*Blue, Vida	39	3.01	22	11	1	38	13	278.0	243	99	189
*Holtzman, Ken	39	3.14	18	14	0	38	13	266.1	217	108	122
Bahnsen, Stan	21	3.24	6	7	0	16	2	100.0	88	37	49
Bosman, Dick	22	3.52	11	4	0	21	2	122.2	112	24	42
Siebert, Sonny	17	3.69	4	4	0	13	0	61.0	60	31	44
Abbott, Glenn	30	4.25	5	5	0	15	3	114.1	109	50	51
Perry, Jim	15	4.66	3	4	0	11	2	67.2	61	26	33

Relievers	Gam.	ERA	W	L	S	GS	CG	IP	H	BB	SO
*Lindblad, Paul	68	2.72	9	1	7	0	0	122.1	105	43	58
*Hamilton, Dave	11	4.04	1	2	0	4	0	35.2	42	18	20
Norris, Mike	4	0.00	1	0	0	3	1	16.2	6	8	5
Todd, Jim	58	2.29	8	3	12	0	0	122.0	104	33	50
Fingers, Rollie	75	2.98	10	6	24	0	0	126.2	95	33	115
Mitchell, Craig	1	12.27	0	1	0	1	0	3.2	6	2	2
Odom, Blue Moon	7	12.27	0	2	0	2	0	11.0	19	11	4

Index

Aaron, Hank "The Hammer," 47, 64, 105, 124, 226, 240, 249, 343
Abbott, Glenn, 201, 215, 225, 288, 307, 310, 313, 325, 356, 359, 371–73, 375–76
Adair, Jerry, 118, 133, 210–11
Adcock, Joe, 49
Agnew, Spiro, 193
Aikens, Willie Mays, 104
Aker, Jack "Chief," 34, 37, 87–88, 99, 109, 111, 126, 195, 245, 274, 336, 369, 386–87
Alexander, Doyle, 236–37
Alexander, Matt, "The Scat" and "Sonny," 354–55
Ali, Muhammad, 11, 279
Allen, Dick or Richie "Wampum," 55, 85, 117–18, 168, 201, 205, 305, 384, 397
Allen, Maury, 260
Allison, Bob, 7, 28, 53
Alou, Felipe "Pancake," 17–18, 20–21, 36, 64, 76, 119–20, 178–79, 216, 366
Alou, Jesus "Jay," 179, 215–16, 220, 222, 224–25, 236–37, 239, 243, 257, 260, 280–81, 317, 328, 332, 350, 366–67, 404
Alou, Matty, 119, 122–24, 128, 136, 143, 155–56, 158, 167–68, 175–76, 178–79, 183, 185, 196, 203, 215–16, 226, 228, 239, 366–67, 399, 404
Alston, Walter, 326, 328, 332, 335
Alyea, Brant "Bruno," 90, 97, 177–78
Amoros, Sandy, 148
Anderson, Dave, 255, 260, 326
Anderson, Dwain "D," 17, 97, 123, 179
Anderson, Sparky, 143–44, 147, 149–50, 152–57, 159–60, 166–67, 172, 194, 270

Andrews, Mike, 24, 215–16, 219, 243–51, 254–55, 261, 266–68, 271–272, 275, 285, 311, 321, 366
Andy Griffith Show, 240
Anthony, Merle, 222
Aparicio, Luis, 24, 220
Appling, Luke, 1, 5, 195
Armbrister, Ed, 404

Bahnsen, Stan, 118–19, 361, 364, 368, 375, 384, 388, 394
Bailey, Bob "Beetle," 404
Baker, Dusty, 119
Ballew, Bill, 107
Ball Four, 12
Bando, Sal, 4–7, 9, 17, 19–20, 24, 35, 37, 45, 47–49, 55, 57–58, 60–61, 64–67, 69–71, 75–76, 83–84, 86, 91, 99, 101, 104, 106–08, 110, 114–18, 120, 122–23, 127–28, 135, 143, 146, 149, 152, 155, 159, 162, 167–69, 171–74, 187, 194, 198, 201–02, 204–05, 207–08, 224, 228-29, 232, 234, 236, 242–44, 246–47, 249–52, 257–60, 269, 273–74, 282, 285, 290, 293, 296–301, 303, 306, 310–13, 318–20, 323–27, 329, 331–34, 339, 345, 347–50, 355–57, 359–61, 363–64, 366–67, 371–72, 376–79, 381–83, 386–87, 389–90, 392–95, 397–400, 403
Banks, Ernie "Mr. Cub," 186
Barlow, Mike, 357
Barnum and Bailey, 88
Bastable, Jack, 198–99, 228
Bauer, Hank, 1, 3, 5, 158, 273
Baylor, Don "Groove," 233, 319–20, 343, 387–90, 392, 394–95, 397

Beauchamp, Jim, 241
Beckert, Glenn "Bruno," 90
Belanger, Mark "The Blade," 66–67
Bell, Marty, 252, 265
Bench, Johnny "Hands," 47, 75, 141, 144, 154, 158, 160–62, 168, 170, 173, 189, 364, 403
Beniquez, Juan "TiTi," 376
Bennett, Gene, 145
Bergman, Ron, 1, 2, 4, 7–9, 11–12, 16–17, 20, 25–26, 32, 36–37, 44–45, 48, 50, 52, 54, 64, 81, 86, 93, 107–08, 117, 120–21, 124, 182, 184–85, 189, 199–200, 216, 224, 256, 273–76, 280, 283, 285, 287–92, 294, 299, 301, 338, 362
Bernstein, Carl, 193
Berra, Yogi, 52, 241–42, 244, 249, 255, 257–58
Berry, Ken, 18
Bevacqua, "Dirty" Kurt, 228
Bibby, Jim, 215, 289–90, 305–06, 313
Bickel, Dr. William, 12–13
Billingham, Jack, 153, 159, 165–66, 403–04
Billings, Dick, 192
Bird, Doug, 200, 228, 394
Bisher, Furman, 253
Blair, Paul "Motormouth," 7, 66, 319
Blefary, Curt "Clank," "Buff," 36, 42, 55, 66, 69, 83–84, 90, 95, 97–98, 104, 113, 123, 151, 179, 216, 301–02, 344
Blount, Roy, 31, 351
Blue, Vida, 6, 12, 16–21, 25–26, 31–33, 36–40, 42–44, 47–51, 54–58, 60–61, 64–71, 73, 75, 79–85, 89–94, 103–04, 107–10, 112, 115–16, 118, 128–29, 132, 135, 137–39, 145, 150, 155, 162, 171–73, 179–180, 185, 188, 190, 192, 201–04, 210, 212, 220–21, 229–30, 233, 235–37, 247, 251, 269, 275, 281–84, 286, 289–92, 295, 297, 299, 306–07, 311–13, 318–21, 323, 326–27, 333–34, 345, 353, 356, 358–59, 362, 365, 372–73, 375, 377, 379, 381, 383, 388–89, 391–92, 394, 399, 404
Blue, Vida, Sr., 284
Blyleven, Bert "Flying Dutchman," 194, 214, 358
Bochte, Bruce, 354
Bonds, Bobby "Bo Bo Junior," 352

Borbon, Pedro "El Brujo," 155–56, 166, 403–04
Bordagaray, Stanley "Frenchy," 85
Bordman, Sid, 342, 397–98
Bosman, Dick, 19–20, 186, 305, 357, 359–62, 375–76, 378, 381, 388
Boswell, Dave, 136
Boswell, Ken, 242
Bourque, Pat, 178, 223, 302, 304–05, 308, 339–40, 350, 362, 364, 368
Bouton, Jim "Bulldog," 12, 217
Bowman, Joe, 399
Bradley, Tom "Fry," 126, 384, 388
Bragan, Bobby, 4, 199
Brando, Marlon, 79
Brett, George, 371
Brewer, Jim, 136
Brezhnev, Leonid, 79
Brinkman, Eddie, 19, 102
Bristol, Dave, 33, 270, 272–73, 279
Broberg, Pete, 191–92
Brock, Lou, 119
Brohamer, Jack "Hammer," 343
Brooks, Bobby "The Hammer," 89–91, 97, 99
Brown, Doug, 264
Brown, Gates, 135–36
Brown, Jackie, 313
Brown, Joe, 52
Brown, Larry, 14, 25, 35, 47, 99, 101, 109, 122–23, 174, 179, 182
Brown, "Downtown" Ollie, 97–98, 104, 107, 186
Brubaker, Mary, 63
Buckner, Billy, 267, 325, 329, 331, 333–34
Bumbry, Al "Bumble Bee," 233–34, 317, 361
Burleson, Rick "The Rooster," 378, 390
Burrell, Stanley, 63
Burroughs, Jeff, 58, 215, 311, 339
Busby, Steve, 290, 372

Cabell, Enos "Big E," 319
Campanella, Roy, 171
Campaneris, Bert "Campy," 6, 17, 19, 21, 25, 35, 37, 47, 49, 54–55, 61–62, 69, 91, 99, 103, 108, 114–15, 117, 119, 122, 132–37, 141–46, 152–53, 155, 159, 162, 166–67, 169, 173–74, 189, 193–96, 199,

202–04, 209, 219–20, 227, 232, 234, 237, 241–43, 249–50, 257–60, 269, 274, 280, 283, 290, 294, 296, 304–08, 312, 320, 324–25, 329–30, 332–33, 335–36, 353–54, 362, 364, 366–71, 373, 378, 385–86, 388, 390, 392, 395, 397–99, 403
Caray, Harry, 10, 117, 231, 345
Carbo, Bernie, 376
Cardenal, Jose "Junior," 196, 369
Cardenas, Leo "Chico," 18
Carew, Rod, 34, 75, 227
Carey, Max "Scoops," 195,
Carlton, Steve "Lefty," 47, 124, 150, 162, 180
Carnevale, Dan, 399
Carroll, Clay "Hawk," "Sheriff," 153, 156–57, 160–61, 167, 371, 403–04
Carson, Johnny, 185
Carty, Rico "The Beeg Mon," 124, 178, 216, 225–27, 268, 366–67
Cash, Dave, 90, 343
Cash, Norm, 32, 48, 75, 131, 136
Cashen, Frank, 264
Cater, Danny, 109, 225
Causey, Wayne, 54, 194
Cavarretta, Phil, 102
Cavett, Dick, 58
Cedeno, Cesar, 119
Cepeda, Orlando "The Baby Bull," "Cha Cha," 105–07, 109–10, 112–15, 128, 179–84, 187, 216–17, 220, 268–69, 281, 355, 360, 366
Cey, Ron "The Penguin," 325, 330, 332, 334
Chance, Frank, 336
Chaney, Darrel "Norton," 149, 168, 404
Chant, Charlie, 203, 383
Chapin, Dwight, 142, 151
Charles, Ed, 273
Charlie O. (the mule), 49, 68
Chass, Murray, 18, 21, 64, 66, 68, 89, 165, 251
Cherry, J. Carlton, 343
Chylak, Nestor, 133–34
Ciensczyk, Frank, 84
Claflin, Larry, 157
Claiborne, John, 231, 247, 263, 305, 364
Clark, Ron, 123
Clarke, Horace "Hoss," 264

Clemente, Roberto "The Great One," 8, 47, 98, 124, 186, 224, 370
Cleveland, Reggie "Grover," 377
Coggins, Rich, 233–34, 317, 319
Colavito, Rocky, 55
Colbert, Nate "June," 366
Colborn, Jim, 114
Coleman, Joe, 131, 135, 175
Colson, Steve, 264
Concepcion, Dave, 144–45, 155, 159, 162, 166, 168, 364, 403
Conigliaro, Billy "Billy C," 55, 104, 185–87, 193–94, 199–200, 214, 222, 227, 288
Conigliaro, Tony "Tony C," 18, 186, 222–23
Cooper, Cecil, 390
Copeland, Howell "Buddy," 354
Corwin, Tom, 120
Cosell, Howard, 82
Cottrol, Bob, 89
Cox, Billy, 171
Cratchett, Bob, 364
Crawford, Willie, 330, 334
Cronin, Joe, 134, 183, 200, 235, 251, 263–65
Crowley, Terry, 404
Cuellar, Mike "Crazy Horse," 28, 67, 68, 70, 230, 235, 305, 318–19
Cullen, Tim "The Worm," 109, 123, 127, 135, 174, 179, 187, 239

Daley, Arthur, 31, 96, 105, 141, 185, 259
Dark, Alvin, 1, 5, 15, 252, 273, 279–83, 285–96, 298–315, 317–22, 324–34, 336–39, 345, 348–57, 359–60, 362–63, 365, 367, 371, 373, 375, 377–78, 382–83
Davalillo, Vic, 215–16, 222, 225, 236–37, 243, 290, 292, 329, 366–67, 404
Davis, Kenzie, 224
Davis, Jr., Sammy, 324
Davis, Tommy, 9–10, 18, 22, 27–28, 31, 38–39, 45, 54, 56, 61, 64–65, 67–68, 73, 76, 83, 89, 119, 178, 216–17, 233, 268–69, 319, 350, 366
Del Rio, Tony, 253
Denehy, Bill "Big D," 263
Devine, Bing, 119
Dick Cavett Show, 267
Dickey, Glenn, 8, 49–50, 74, 108, 188, 205, 224, 301, 305, 309–10, 345, 363, 381

DiMaggio, Joe "The Yankee Clipper," 8, 37, 59, 88, 147–148, 273
Dineen, Kerry, 264
Dobson, Chuck, 12–13, 16, 20, 33–34, 42–43, 48–49, 60–61, 64, 68, 70–71, 73, 75, 77, 81, 90, 94–95, 102, 194, 276–77, 287–88, 298, 312
Dobson, Pat, 114, 230
Donaldson, John, 17, 35, 178, 291, 293, 296, 310, 314, 338
Donatelli, Augie, 242
Downing, Al "Giggi," 328–29, 366
Doyle, Denny, 317, 376, 378
Drago, Dick "Dynamic Dick," 116, 378–79, 395
Driessen, Dan, 404
Drysdale, Don "Big D," 156
Duncan, Dave, 1–3, 17–18, 25–26, 32, 37, 42, 45, 50–52, 57–58, 60–61, 66–68, 76, 86, 88, 90–91, 93, 100, 102, 108, 114, 116, 119–20, 122, 128, 141, 145, 159, 165–66, 168–69, 172, 174, 181, 188–91, 196, 205, 212, 239, 302, 323, 342, 404
Dunning, Steve "Stunning," 119–20
Durocher, Leo "The Lip," 74–75, 108, 187
Durslag, Melvin, 302
Durso, Joe, 18, 32, 55, 69, 144, 219, 242
Dusan, Gene, 122
Dykes, Jimmy, 397

Earnshaw, George, 229
Easton, Steve, 119, 228
Eastwick, Rawly, 403–04
Edwards, Dick, 271
Edwards, Doc, 54
Ehrlichman, John, 193
Elderkin, Phil, 181, 230, 295, 381
Eldridge, Larry, 51
Ellis, Dock, 47–48
Elson, Bob, 39
Engel, Bob, 160–161, 165
Epstein, Mike "Super Jew," 26–27, 33–34, 40–42, 45, 61, 64, 68, 71, 73, 77, 83, 90–91, 103, 105–07, 109, 113–15, 117–118, 126, 128, 132–33, 137, 143, 151–52, 155–56, 163, 165, 169, 179–81, 183, 187, 189, 191–92, 196, 198, 201, 216, 228, 239, 251, 269, 302, 399, 403
Ervin, Jr., Sam, 193

Eskenazi, Gerald, 112, 344
Etchebarren, Andy, 66
Evers, Johnny, 336

Fairly, Ron "The Mule," 366, 394
Falls, Joe, 101
Feeney, Chub, 183
Ferguson, Joe, 325–26, 329–32, 334
Fernandez, "Broadway" Frank, 18, 26, 42, 52, 54, 57, 177–78, 228, 283, 288
Fimrite, Ron, 61, 64, 143, 338, 351–52, 363, 367, 376
Finegold, Dr. Joseph, 13
Fingers, Rollie, 12, 15–16, 20, 34–35, 44, 49, 53, 61, 69, 71, 85–86, 91, 94–95, 98–99, 101–02, 106, 108, 111, 115, 120, 127, 129, 132, 135, 144–45, 149, 154, 157, 159, 167–70, 173, 180, 190, 196, 210, 212, 234–37, 241–43, 247, 256–58, 275, 281, 289, 291–92, 310–11, 313, 319–25, 330, 332–36, 353, 356, 360, 362–64, 371, 373, 375, 377, 379, 386, 389–92, 394–95, 397–400, 403–04
Finley, Charlie, 1–11, 14–15, 20, 23, 25, 27, 33, 37–41, 43–45, 49–56, 59, 63, 68, 71, 73, 75, 77, 79–93, 95, 97–101, 103–10, 113, 117–23, 125–28, 131–32, 134, 136–39, 141, 152–53, 157–58, 161–62, 170–77, 179–84, 186, 188–89, 190–92, 196–201, 204, 206–11, 213–17, 219–20, 223–26, 228, 231–32, 235, 238–41, 244–53, 255–56, 259, 261, 263–77, 279–93, 295, 298–300, 302–04, 306–11, 313–15, 318, 321–24, 327, 329–33, 336–58, 361–62, 364–70, 372–73, 378–79, 381–99, 403
Finley, Luke, 170
Finley, Martin, 170
Finley, Shirley, 139, 162
Fisk, Carlton "Pudge," 114, 220, 376–77
Flood, Curt, 19
Foley, Red, 247, 250, 256–57, 263, 271
Fondy, Dee, 256
Ford, "Disco" Dan, 340, 351, 362, 364, 368
Ford, President Gerald, 279, 328–29, 347
Ford, Whitey, 19, 34, 126
Foreman, George, 279
Forster, Terry, 291

Index

Fosse, Ray "The Mule," 189–91, 193–94, 201, 204, 210, 212, 221, 224, 233, 236, 241, 243, 256, 268, 280, 283, 288, 297, 299–302, 307, 309, 317–18, 332–33, 337, 339, 342, 349, 360, 366, 377, 383
Foster, George "The Destroyer," 75, 167, 403
Foucault, Steve, 311
Fowler, Bob, 6, 19, 26, 53, 76, 87–88, 110, 115, 118, 128, 194, 300, 358–59, 365, 368–70, 385, 393
Fox, Howard, 136
Frank, Stanley, 335–36
Franks, Herman, 344
Frazier, Joe, 11
Freehan, Bill, 32, 114, 131, 135, 137, 142, 203
Fregosi, Jim, 367–68
Fryman, Woodie, 131–32, 137
Furillo, Carl, 171

Garagiola, Joe, 335
Garcia, Rich, 367
Gardner, Rob, 20, 35–36, 178–79, 192, 197, 203–04
Garner, Phil "Scrap Iron," 294, 306, 308, 310, 314, 345, 349–50, 353, 363, 371, 373, 376
Garr, Ralph "The Road Runner," "Flip," 119

Garrett, Adrian, 57
Garrett, Wayne, 241–42, 250, 258
Garvey, Steve "Mr. Clean," 325–27, 330, 333–34, 343
Gehrig, Lou "Iron Horse," 158, 170
Gergen, Joe, 75, 336
Geronimo, Cesar "Chief," 144, 148, 151, 153, 159, 168, 364, 403
Gerst, Bob, 79–83, 89
Gibson, Bob "Hoot," 58, 80, 150
Gionfriddo, Al, 148
Giordano, Tom, 399
Giusti, Dave, 397
Goodman, Fred, 242
Gordon, Joe, 1, 120–21, 397
Gosger, Jim, 48
Grabarkewitz, Billy, 350, 353–55, 366, 383
Grammas, Alex, 167

Grant, Jim "Mudcat," 9, 12, 16, 44, 52–55, 60–61, 68, 71, 76–77, 178, 216, 366
Grateful Dead, 102
Greek, Jimmy the, 233
Green, Dick, 10, 14, 17, 21, 24–25, 35, 57, 61, 66–67, 69, 75, 91, 95, 98–99, 108–09, 119, 122–23, 127, 135, 146, 153, 155–56, 161, 167, 169, 174, 187, 194–95, 197, 199–200, 210, 217, 220, 227, 237, 241–42, 251–52, 259, 270, 272, 283, 286, 291, 293–94, 296–97, 306, 313–14, 320, 329–36, 338, 345, 348–49, 351, 360, 369, 399, 403
Greenberg, Hank, 268
Grich, Bobby "Lizard," 235–36, 317–19, 343
Griffey, Ken, Sr., 364, 403
Griffith, Calvin, 136, 369
Grimsley, Ross "Crazy Eyes," 146, 159, 319, 343, 361
Grimsley, Will, 202
Gross, Milton, 38
Grote, Jerry, 243, 249
Grove, Lefty, 125, 229
Guinn, Jim, 305
Gullett, Don, 154–55, 403–04
Gura, Larry "Stoney," 395

Haggerty, Mike, 39, 63
Hague, Joe, 167
Hahn, Don, 241, 243–44
Hairston, Johnny, 9
Hall, Dick "Turkey Neck," 28
Hall, Tom "The Blade," 157, 168
Haller, Bill, 160
Hamilton, Dave, 102–03, 131, 135–36, 159, 162, 177–79, 192, 194, 201, 203, 214, 225, 356, 359, 361
Hamilton, Jack "Hairbreadth Harry," 222
Haney, Larry, 90, 123, 127, 178–79, 232, 288, 300, 306, 309, 342, 364, 397
Hano, Arnold, 27, 64
Hargrove, Mike "The Human Rain Delay," 311, 313
Harper, Tommy, 220, 365–66, 368, 371–73, 383–84, 397

Harrah, Toby, 19
Harrelson, Buddy, 241–43, 255
Harrelson, Ken "Hawk," 34, 102, 216, 245–46
Harris, Luman, 105, 182
Harris, Vic, 112
Hart, Jim Ray, 203–04
Hartnett, Gabby, 195
Harvey, Doug, 327, 333
Hassler, Andy, 311
Hays, John, 275
Hearst, Patty, 279, 347
Hearst, Randolph, 279
Hebner, Richie "The Gravedigger," 321
Hegan, Jim, 94, 217
Hegan, Mike, 40–42, 56, 64, 70–71, 73, 76, 85–86, 90, 93–94, 97–98, 101, 132–34, 137, 148–52, 155–56, 158, 169, 172, 179–81, 187, 198, 204, 215–18, 223, 232, 239, 247, 252, 343–44, 366, 404
Heidemann, Jack, 189, 282–83
Hemond, Roland, 361
Hemphill, Paul, 59
Hendrick, "Silent" George, 47, 76, 90, 99, 137–38, 142, 153, 155, 186–91, 200, 239, 302
Hendricks, Elrod, 69
Herman, Billy, 231
Hertzel, Bob, 134, 145
Herzog, Whitey, 270, 313, 365
Hiller, John, 131
Hinton, Rich, 372
Hirshberg, Al, 4, 118, 139, 151, 154
Hirshey, Dave, 261
Hisle, Larry, 51
Hodges, Gil, 171, 263
Hodges, Ron, 241
Hoffa, Jimmy, 347
Hofman, Bobby, 303
Holcomb, Stu, 215, 384
Holland, John, 74, 269
Hollingsworth, Al, 63, 160, 168, 171, 242
Holt, Jim, 308–09, 314, 317, 332, 353, 356, 379
Holtzman, Ken, 73–76, 84, 90–92, 94–95, 98–99, 102, 106–08, 114, 116, 122, 127–28, 143–44, 150, 154–55, 167, 173, 179, 185, 190, 194, 197, 203, 220, 222–24, 228–30, 233–35, 241, 257, 275–76, 289, 295, 297, 308, 313–15, 318, 320–21, 324, 332, 345, 347–48, 356, 359, 361–62, 365, 371, 375–76, 378–79, 381–83, 385–87, 393–94, 398–99, 404
Hoover, J. Edgar, 79
Hopkins, Don "Hoppy," 350, 353–55
Horlen, Joel "Joe," 90, 94, 98, 103, 110, 128–29, 135, 169, 182, 239
Horton, Willie "Boozie," 82, 131, 133, 204
Hoscheit, Vern "Bud," 114, 211, 303
Hosley, Tim "Hose," 283, 304
Houk, Ralph, 357
Hovley, Steve, 18, 21
Howard, Elston, 186
Howard, Frank "Hondo," "The Capitol Punisher," 20, 62
Howsam, Bob, 141, 160
Hunt, Ron, 393
Hunter, Jim "Catfish," 6–7, 9, 12, 16, 18, 20, 23, 33, 36–37, 43–44, 49, 51, 57–61, 64, 67–68, 70, 73, 75, 85–86, 94, 99, 102, 108, 114, 116, 118, 125–26, 128, 132, 135, 143, 146, 149–51, 153, 158–59, 161, 166–67, 173, 185, 190, 194, 200, 204, 213–14, 220–21, 227, 229–30, 233–35, 237, 240, 249–50, 252, 257, 260–61, 269, 272, 274–75, 282–83, 285–86, 295–96, 303, 307, 309, 312, 314, 317, 319–20, 322–23, 325–26, 328–30, 337, 341–46, 348–49, 351–53, 355–57, 360, 362, 365, 373, 375, 378–79, 381, 385, 390, 394, 398–99, 404

Isaacs, Stan, 281
Izenberg, Jerry, 19

Jackman, Phil, 69
Jackson, Grant "Buck," 28, 235, 318
Jackson, Reggie "Buck," "Super," 2, 5–9, 14–15, 17–18, 21, 24, 26, 28, 36–40, 45, 47–49, 51, 54, 58, 61, 67, 69, 76, 79, 85–86, 88, 91, 97–101, 103–04, 107–08, 110–12, 114–16, 119, 121–22, 127–28, 137–39, 141–43, 154, 163–65, 167–70, 173–74, 178, 185, 187–88, 192, 198, 200, 204–06, 210–11, 216–17, 221–22, 224, 226–29, 231–39, 242–44, 246, 249–53, 255–60, 268, 271, 273–75, 280, 282,

Index

284–87, 289–92, 295–300, 303–04, 306, 309–10, 312, 319–20, 324–29, 331, 334–35, 338–39, 343, 345, 347, 349, 351, 353, 358–64, 366–68, 372, 376–79, 383, 386–89, 395, 398–99, 401, 403
Jacobson, Steve, 379
Jauss, William, 13
Javier, Julian "The Phantom," 149, 155, 167
Jefferson, Jesse, 372
Jenkins, Ferguson, 80, 311–12
John, Tommy, 33
Johnson, Alex, 18
Johnson, Arnold, 3
Johnson, Bob, 216
Johnson, Darrell, 379
Johnson, Dave "Rook," 25, 66, 90
Johnson, Deron "DJ," 198–99, 201, 203–04, 207, 216, 222, 226–28, 236–37, 239, 244, 256, 269, 271, 290, 300–01, 329, 367–68, 376, 399, 404
Johnstone, Jay "Moon Man," 197, 214–15, 217
Jonathan Livingston Seagull, 95
Jones, Bobby, 79
Jones, Cleon, 243, 257
Jones, Stan, 45
Jordan, Pat, 33, 59–60, 125, 344
Josephson, Duane, 95
Joshua, Von, 332, 335

Kaat, Jim "Kitty Cat," 6, 18, 195
Kaline, Al, 8, 32, 48, 131–32, 135
Kapstein, Jerry, 322, 385
Kelly, Pat, 19
Kekich, Mike, 112
Kennedy, Bob, 1, 5, 37, 147
Kennedy, Robert F., 253
Kilkenny, Mike "Killer," 97
Killebrew, Harmon "Killer," 6, 18, 28, 32, 34, 53, 168, 358, 368, 370
King, Billie Jean, 193, 233
King, Martin Luther, 253
Kirkpatrick, Ed "Spanky," 116, 301–02, 369
Klimkowski, Ron "Klem," 20, 64
Kline, Steve, 55
Kluttz, Clyde, 6, 125, 344, 399
Knievel, Evil, 279
Knowles, Darold, 26–27, 42, 45, 61, 69, 76, 86, 91, 94, 97, 108, 111, 120, 127, 129, 131, 137, 170, 173, 175, 179, 212, 216, 220, 228, 241, 253, 257–58, 291, 297, 306–08, 311–12, 326, 335, 338, 366, 399–400, 403
Kokor, Steve, 44
Koppett, Leonard, 40, 237, 242, 244
Koufax, Sandy, 31, 32, 47, 58, 74
Koosman, Jerry, 256
Kovner, Fred, 16
Kowet, Don, 229
Kranepool, Ed, 241, 258
Krausse, Lew, 194, 245, 307, 345, 349
Kubek, Tony, 197
Kubiak, Ted "Smooth," 14, 18, 112–114, 118, 123, 127, 135, 138–39, 158–59, 171, 178–79, 187, 194, 208, 210, 234–35, 243, 282, 287, 293–94, 299, 306, 313–14, 345, 348, 354, 357, 360, 399–400, 404
Kuenster, John, 299
Kuhn, Bowie, 12–13, 15, 81, 83, 92–93, 104, 134, 141, 146, 152–53, 160–61, 170, 183, 191, 214, 240, 247–48, 250, 309, 328, 335, 341, 343, 348, 390–91

Lacy, Lee, 343
LaGrow, Lerrin, 132-34, 136, 202
Landis, Kenesaw Mountain, 391
Lange, Dick, 228, 296
Langford, Rick, 397
LaRoche, Dave, 127
LaRussa, Tony, 14, 17–18, 35, 76, 112
Lau, Charlie, 3, 10, 37, 100
Lawson, Earl, 160
Lawson, Steve, 113
Lee, Bill "Spaceman," 220
LeFlore, Ron, 361
Leggett, William, 25, 85
Lemon, Chester "Chet," 361, 364, 368
Lemonds, Dave, 118
Leonard, Dennis, 371, 394–95
Lewis, Allan "The Panamanian Express," 126–27, 142, 151, 155, 157, 160, 167, 194, 206–08, 224, 239, 267–68, 285, 350, 354
Libby, Bill, 14, 286
Lilly, Art, 252, 399
Lindblad, Paul "Bladder," "Bug," 16, 20, 23, 26–27, 177, 178–79, 228, 243, 300, 306,

313, 353, 362–63, 371, 373, 376, 383, 400
Lindsey, Joe, 122
Lintz, Larry, 383, 393
Locker, Bob, 16, 20, 22, 44, 61, 85–86, 94–95, 98–99, 110, 114, 120, 127, 129, 135, 177–78, 180, 187, 216, 228, 239, 269–70, 288, 338, 399
Lockwood, Skip, 292, 296, 350
Lolich, Mickey, 61, 65, 131–32, 135
Lollar, Sherm, 63, 171, 242, 270
Lombardi, Vince, 4
Lopat, Eddie, 1
Lopes, Davey, 325, 329, 333
Lyle, Sparky "The Count," 112, 196, 225, 275
Lynn, Fred, 375–77, 390

Mack, Connie, 229
MacPhail, Lee, 322–23, 342, 391
Malone, Moses, 279
Maloney, Jim, 31
Mangual, Angel "Little Clemente," 18, 44, 47, 53–54, 67, 69, 74, 89, 95, 99, 119, 133, 157, 162, 165–66, 177, 185–87, 194, 199–200, 206, 214, 225, 227, 232, 282, 288, 300–01, 304–06, 308, 314, 317, 327, 354, 370
Manson, Charles, 11
Mantle, Mickey, 111, 258, 268
Marichal, Juan "The Dominican Dandy," 307, 345–47
Maris, Roger, 8, 258
Marquez, Gonzalo "Mandrake the Magician," 132, 135, 138, 155, 157–58, 184, 187, 199, 206, 215, 223, 232, 239
Mars, Joe, 358
Marshall, Mike, 326–28, 333–34, 371
Martin, Billy, 3, 131–34, 136–37, 194, 202, 312–13, 352, 391
Martin, Jerry, 104
Martinez, Marty, 97, 112–114, 122–123, 179
Martinez, Teddy, 357, 371, 373
Matlack, Jon, 241, 255–57, 259
Mauch, Gene, 4, 383–84
Maxvill, Dal, 122–23, 127–28, 135, 138, 156, 175, 178, 187, 193, 215–16, 232, 239, 294, 313–14, 317, 324, 338, 345, 349, 383
May, Lee "The Big Bopper," 75
May, Rudy "Dude," 200
Mays, Willie "The Say Hey Kid," 8, 32, 148, 242–44, 249, 258, 281, 343
McAndrew, Jim, 150
McAuliffe, Dick "Muggs," 131, 135–36, 376
McCovey, Willie "Stretch," 168, 217, 281, 366, 394, 396–97
McDaniel, Lindy, 94
McDowell, "Sudden" Sam, 33–34
McEnaney, Will, 403
McGaha, Mel, 1
McGarr, Frank, 392
McGlothlin, Jim "Red," 158
McGraw, John, 303
McGraw, Tug, 242–43, 256
McGregor, Scott, 264
McGuff, Joe, 195
McKeon, Jack, 384
McKinney, Rich, 178, 185, 207, 214–15, 225, 288, 302, 368
McLain, Denny, 19, 32, 42, 57–58, 81–82, 85, 90–92, 94–96, 102, 104–07, 110, 174, 183, 268, 366
McLain, Kristen, 107
McLain, Sharon, 96
McMullen, Ken, 387
McNally, Dave, 66–67, 70, 230, 234, 236, 318, 385
McNamara, John, 1–3, 5–7, 10, 16, 18, 23, 25–26, 75, 137, 288, 343
McNulty, Bill 57, 177
McRae, Hal, 75, 149, 161, 166
Mehl, Ernie, 120–21
Meir, Golda, 107
Melton, Bill, 182
Menke, Denis, 144, 146–49, 151, 153–55, 159, 166–68, 204, 403
Merkle, Fred, 267
Merullo, Lenny, 41
Messersmith, Andy "Bluto," 18, 321, 324–25, 331–32, 385
Millan, Felix "The Cat," 241–42, 251, 257
Miller, Jon, 277, 345
Miller, Marvin, 188, 247, 276, 323, 343, 391, 393

Index

Milner, John "The Hammer," 243, 258
Mincher, Don, 1, 5–6, 17, 26–29, 34–35, 42, 76, 112–16, 121–23, 128, 156–57, 169, 172–75, 177, 179, 183–84, 208, 216, 228, 239, 366, 404
Mitchell, Paul, 387–89, 395
Mitterwald, George, 91, 349
The Mod Squad, 86
Monday, Rick, 2, 5–7, 17, 18, 35, 42–43, 47, 51, 61, 69–74, 76, 84, 88–89, 99, 200, 227–28, 252, 256, 261, 273–74
Montgomery, Bob, 300
Moore, Monte, 10, 39, 63, 120, 132, 208–09, 231, 245, 253, 277, 295, 345
Morales, Jose, 213–14, 239–40, 251
Moret, Rogelio "Roger," 377–78
Morgan, Joe, 73, 153–55, 157–60, 162–63, 166–67, 403
Morrison, Jim, 11
Motton, Curt, 66–67, 69
Mrs. Fields Cookies, 55
Muhe, Jim, 324
Mullen, John, 47
Muncie, Bill, 53
Munson, Thurman "Squatty Body," 189, 264
Munzel, Edgar, 209–10
Murcer, Bobby, 36, 75, 264–65
Murphy, Tom, 18
Myers, Dennis, 340

Nabors, Jim, 240
Nahas, Robert, 321
Napp, Larry, 109
Nash, "Jumbo" Jim, 194
Nelson, Dave, 311
Nelson, Roger "Spider," 350, 355, 357
Nettles, Graig "Puff," 202, 393
Nettles, Morris, 317
Newcombe, Don, 58, 171
Newhan, Ross, 397
Newton, Wayne, 324
Niarhos, Gus, 52
Nicholson, Jack, 347
Nicklaus, Jack, 79
Nightingale, Dave, 48, 136, 157
Nitschke, Buzz, 283, 299–300

Nixon, President Richard, 11, 19, 56, 79, 92, 193, 329
Nolan, Gary, 143–44, 153, 403–04
Noren, Irv, 58, 133, 159–60, 210–11, 224, 270, 302–03
Norman, Fredie, 404
Norris, Mike, 353–54, 362, 386, 389
North, Bill, 177–79, 185, 187, 193, 196, 199–200, 204, 209–10, 217, 219–20, 222–23, 227–29, 232, 234, 237, 239, 269, 280, 294, 297–300, 303, 309, 312–14, 320, 322, 324–26, 329, 332–34, 338, 345, 351, 355, 361, 364, 371, 376, 378–79, 382–83, 386, 388, 392, 395, 397, 403
Northrup, Jim, 136

Odom, John "Blue Moon," 6, 12–13, 34, 43–45, 54, 61, 64, 68, 73, 75, 77–78, 81, 84–85, 90, 95, 99, 102, 108–09, 111, 114, 126–27, 129, 132, 135, 137–38, 153–54, 159–60, 165–66, 173, 185, 194, 196, 198, 203, 220, 225, 236, 247, 280–81, 283, 286, 295, 304, 320–24, 334, 345, 353, 357–59, 381, 399
Odom, Perrie, 77
Olderman, Murray, 210, 298, 327–28
Oliva, Tony, 6–7, 34, 48, 75, 124, 294, 310, 358, 367–68, 382
Oliver, Al "Scoop," 51, 168
Orta, Jorge, 126
Osteen, Claude "Gomer," 350

Paciorek, Tom "Wimpy," 333
Page, Mitchell, 397
Pagliaroni, Jim, 59, 342
Paige, Satchel, 270, 344
Palmer, Jim, 66, 68–70, 135, 230, 233–35, 317–19
Panther, Jim "Pink," 20, 81
Papiano, Neil, 391, 394
Parker, Wes, 149
Parsons, Bill, 310–11, 313
Patek, Fred "The Flea," "Moochie," 371
Patterson, Daryl, 35
Pattin, Marty, 371, 395
Paul, Gabe, 264–65
Pele, 347
Pena, Orlando, 196, 357

Pepe, Phil, 22, 89, 101, 139, 150, 190, 207, 250, 256, 261, 298–99, 322, 325, 327
Pepitone, Joe, 302
Perez, Tony "Doggie," 75, 144, 146–47, 149, 153–54, 158–59, 166, 168, 173, 364, 403
Perranoski, Ron, 358
Perry, Gaylord, 73, 80, 190–91, 304–05, 343, 357–60, 383
Perry, Jim, 6–7, 18, 80, 200, 357–62, 365–66
Petrocelli, Rico, 215, 267, 376–78
Phillips, Harold "Lefty," 15
Phoebus, Tom "Feeby," 7
Picciolo, Rob, 397
Pierce, Ton, 194
Piersall, Jimmy, 120
Pignatano, Joe, 253
Pina, Horacio "Ichabod Crane," 180, 197–98, 227–28, 250, 269, 288, 302, 350, 399–400
Piniella, Lou, 200
Pitts, Gaylen, 294, 296, 304, 371
Pitzer, Daniel, 19
Pizarro, Juan, 216, 284
Plaschke, Bill, 158, 163
Plummer, Bill, 404
Pollet, Howie, 319
Popham, Art, 63
Porter, Darrell, 390
Posedel, Bill "The Chief," 35, 42, 59, 71, 139, 142, 230, 232, 268, 343
Powell, Boog, 66–68, 75, 317, 319
Pries, Don, 6, 36, 399

Randle, Lenny, 312–13
Randolph, Willie, 202
Rau, Doug, 328
Reed, Ron, 226
Reese, Pee Wee, 171, 259
Reese, Rich, 59
Reichler, Joe, 328
Rettenmund, Merv, 233, 404
Rice, Jim, 367, 375–76
Richards, Paul, 4
Richardson, Bobby, 336
Richman, Milt, 273
Rickey, Branch, 4, 271
Riggs, Bobby, 193, 233

Rigney, Bill, 231–32, 251
Ringling Brothers, 88
Ripken, Jr., Cal, 115
Rizzuto, Phil "The Scooter," 194, 259
Roberts, Dave, 150
Roberts, Robin, 319
Robinson, Brooks "The Vacuum Cleaner," "The Head," 66, 69, 236, 273, 317
Robinson, Frank "The Judge," 14, 24, 32, 64, 66, 69, 205, 268, 270–72, 279, 347, 357–59, 383
Robinson, Jackie, 146, 171, 260
Rodriguez, Aurelio "Chi-Chi," 132
Rodriguez, Ellie, 114
Roe, Preacher, 319
Roland, Jim, 16, 20, 97
Romo, Joe, 308, 312
Rose, Pete "Charlie Hustle," 141, 143, 145, 150, 153–55, 158–61, 167, 171, 190, 364, 403
Rosen, Al, 268
Ross, George, 255
Roswell, Clint, 299
Roundtree, Richard, 83
Rudi, Joe "Gentleman Joe," "Cow," 6, 18, 21, 35–37, 49, 51, 58, 61, 68, 76, 91, 95, 99–101, 108–09, 114, 117, 120, 128, 133, 138, 142–44, 146–52, 166, 168, 187, 189–90, 196, 204–06, 214, 217, 220, 222, 224, 226–27, 231–32, 241–42, 249, 256–57, 260, 282, 289, 295, 303–06, 310, 312, 320, 325–26, 329–34, 337, 339, 347, 349, 351, 354, 359–60, 364–67, 371, 376–77, 379, 382–83, 386–88, 390–92, 394–95, 397–98, 403
Rumill, Ed, 12
Rush, Red, 39
Russell, Bill, 326, 330, 332, 334
Russo, Neal, 259, 271
Ruth, Babe "The Bambino," 158, 170, 210, 336, 343
Ryan, Nolan "The Ryan Express," 47, 109–10, 217, 393

Sadecki, Ray, 256
Sain, Johnny, 384
Sanders, Reggie "Doctor Strangeglove," 97
Sands, Charlie, 355–56
Sanford, Jack, 399

Index

Sanguillen, Manny, 90, 189, 224, 321, 397
Santo, Ron, 226
Schang, Wally, 85
Schmidt, Mike, 343
Schneider, Russell, 34, 268
Schraff, Jim, 87
Schwarz, Glenn, 180
Scott, George "The Boomer," 100, 288, 382–83
Scrooge, Ebenezer, 364
Seaver, Tom "Tom Terrific," "The Franchise," 47, 80, 150, 249, 255–57
Secretariat, 193
Seelbach, Chuck, 132, 135
Seghi, Phil, 357–58
Segui, Diego "Siggy," 12, 16, 20–21, 54, 61, 68–71, 94, 103, 119, 179, 195, 300
Seitz, Peter, 341–42, 385
Serpico, Frank, 79
Shaft, 83
Shamsky, Art, 104, 107, 109–10, 112–13, 119, 216, 355
Shantz, Bobby, 50
Shaw, Don, 97, 99, 127, 131
Shore, Ray, 98, 146, 150, 155
Short, Bob, 19, 26–27, 81, 302
Shupe, John, 264
Siebert, Sonny, 357, 359–60, 362, 366, 375, 381, 383
Sims, Duke, 133
Singer, Bill "The Singer Throwing Machine," 223
Simmons, Ted "Simba," 119
Sivyer, Debbie, 55
Sizemore, Ted, 272
Skinner, Samuel J., 143
Skowron, Moose, 28
Slaton, Jim, 221
Slayback, Bill, 133
Smith, Curt, 209
Smith, Mayo, 63, 66
Smith, Red, 80, 82, 150, 152, 241, 247, 328
Smith, Reggie, 225
Snider, Duke, 158, 171
Soar, Hank, 67
Soderholm, Eric "The Viking," 91
Southworth, Billy, 154
Spander, Art, 251, 290
Splittorff, Paul, 371

Stanhouse, Don "Stan the Man Unusual," "Full Pack," 81
Staniland, Steve, 357
Stanley, Mickey, 131
Stargell, Willie "Pops," 7, 168, 321
Staub, Rusty "Le Grand Orange," 241, 244, 257
Steadman, John, 120-21
Steinbrenner, George, 76, 263, 265
Steiner, Mel, 144, 154
Stennett, Rennie, 90
Stevens, Bob, 147
Stevens, Sandy, 53
Stock, Wes, 198, 211, 224, 229–30, 269, 384
Stone, George, 255–56
Stottlemyre, Mel, 77, 264, 344
Stouffer, Vern, 33
Stroud, Ed "The Creeper," 109
Suarez, Ken, 49
Suker, Dr. Jacob, 13
Sullivan, Haywood, 1
Summers, John "Champ," 351
Sundberg, Jim, 313
Sutton, Don, 326, 333, 343, 381
Swallow, Ray, 8
Swanson, Pete, 268
Swoboda, Ron "Rocky," 148

Talbot, Fred, 216
Tanana, Frank, 395
Tanner, Chuck, 252, 345, 361, 384–85, 388–95, 397
Tate, Sharon, 11
Taylor, Tony, 138
Tenace, Gene "Steamboat," 18, 23, 26, 32, 42, 51–52, 68, 73, 76, 84, 90–91, 93, 102–03, 111–12, 120, 123, 127, 132, 135–37, 143–46, 152, 154–59, 161–63, 165–67, 169, 172–74, 178–81, 185, 187–89, 191, 193–94, 198, 201, 217, 227, 230, 237, 240, 242–43, 253, 255–60, 283, 286, 288, 291, 293, 296–300, 302, 306–07, 312, 317–20, 326, 330–39, 342, 349, 354, 360–61, 364, 367, 371, 377, 379, 382, 386, 389–90, 392, 395, 397–99, 403
Thrift, Syd, 364
Tiant, Luis "El Tiante," 214, 376
Timmerman, Tom, 68, 131, 133
Tinker, Joe, 336

Todd, Jim, 351, 354, 356–57, 360, 362–63, 375–77, 389, 393
Tolan, Bobby, 141, 154–55, 158–59, 162, 166–67, 403
Torre, Joe, 47, 119, 168
Torres, Rusty, 395
Torrez, Mike, 386–87, 389, 395
Tovar, Cesar "Pepi," 311, 313, 368–70, 373, 383, 393–94
Trillo, Manny, 239–40, 244, 246, 248, 272, 283, 293–94, 310, 314, 338, 345
Trimble, Joe, 171
Twombly, Wells, 21, 31, 39, 42, 284, 323
Tyrone, Jim, 397

Uhlaender, Ted, 144–45
Underwood, John, 281

Valentine, Bobby, 200–01
Van Bommel, Bill, 387
Vare, Robert, 51
Vass, George, 142, 259
Velez, Otto, 264
Verigan, Bill, 83
Veryzer, Tom, 361
Vietnam, 193, 347
Virdon, Bill, 265
Voss, Bill, 119, 228
Vuckovich, Pete, 372

Walberg, Rube, 229
Walker, Dr. Harry, 180–81, 184, 214, 245, 247
Waller, Bob, 231, 345
Walsh, Dick, 15
Washington, Claudell, 304–05, 309–10, 319, 331–33, 337, 339, 349, 351, 353–54, 361–64, 371, 376–78, 382, 388, 395
Washington, Clyde, 284
Washington, Herb "Hurricane," 285–86, 288, 290, 292, 303–04, 308, 318–20, 326–27, 330, 348, 350, 355
Watt, Eddie, 67
Weaver, Earl "The Earl of Baltimore," 28, 48, 66–67, 71, 114–15, 190, 233–34, 236–37, 264, 319
Wertz, Vic, 148
Whitfield, Terry, 264

Wilhelm, Hoyt, 35
Williams, Billy, 13, 119, 213, 338–39, 353, 356, 361, 363, 366–67, 372, 382–83, 385, 388–89, 394, 397
Williams, Dick, 1, 3–13, 15–16, 18, 20–28, 31–32, 35, 37–38, 41, 44–45, 47–48, 51–52, 54–55, 57–58, 60–61, 63–69, 71–75, 77, 82, 84–86, 89–97, 99–100, 103–09, 112–15, 117–23, 126–28, 131–32, 135–37, 139, 141–57, 159–60, 162, 165–73, 175, 177–80, 184, 186, 189–90, 192, 196–201, 203–08, 210–15, 217, 219–27, 229, 231–37, 239, 241–45, 247–53, 256–61, 263–67, 269–273, 275, 279–80, 282, 287–88, 303–04, 310–11, 313, 337, 351, 354, 375, 400, 404
Williams, Earl "Heavy," 230, 397
Williams, Roger, 388
Williams, Stan, 358
Williams, Ted "The Splendid Splinter" 15, 27, 42, 81, 124, 270
Wills, Maury, 270, 286
Wilson, Don, 47
Wilson, Hack, 22
Wilson, Willie, 104
Winkles, Bobby, 273, 292, 303, 331, 384
Wise, Rick, 150, 378–79, 383, 390
Wood, Wilbur, 118, 126–27, 196, 353, 384
Wooden, John, 79, 193
Woods, Jim, 120, 209, 217
Woodward, Bob, 193
Wright, Clyde "Skeeter," 18, 114
Wynn, Jimmy "The Toy Cannon," 325, 329–31, 333, 383

Yastrzemski, Carl "Irish," 7, 42, 75, 208, 376–79
Yawkey, Tom, 4
Yeager, Steve, 326, 333–35
York, Jim, 21
Young, Dick, 19, 47, 48, 80, 134, 139, 151, 166, 186, 227, 259–60, 264–65, 285, 297–99, 302, 310, 333, 347–48

Zimmer, Don "Popeye," 376
Zisk, Richie, 321
Zuk, Bob, 8